Comparative
Regional Systems

Pergamon Policy Studies on International Politics

Related Journals*

 PERGAMON POLICY STUDIES ON INTERNATIONAL POLITICS

Comparative Regional Systems

West and East Europe, North America, The Middle East, and Developing Countries

Edited by
Werner J. Feld
Gavin Boyd

Pergamon Press
NEW YORK • OXFORD • TORONTO • SYDNEY • FRANKFURT • PARIS

Pergamon Press Offices:

U.S.A.	Pergamon Press Inc., Maxwell House, Fairview Park, Elmsford, New York 10523, U.S.A.
U.K.	Pergamon Press Ltd., Headington Hill Hall, Oxford OX3 0BW, England
CANADA	Pergamon of Canada, Ltd. Suite 104, 150 Consumers Road, Willowdale, Ontario M2J 1P9, Canada
AUSTRALIA	Pergamon Press (Aust.) Pty. Ltd., P.O. Box 544, Potts Point, NSW 2011, Australia
FRANCE	Pergamon Press SARL, 24 rue des Ecoles, 75240 Paris, Cedex 05, France
FEDERAL REPUBLIC OF GERMANY	Pergamon Press GmbH, Hammerweg 6, Postfach 1305, 6242 Kronberg/Schönberg, Federal Republic of Germany

Copyright © 1980 Pergamon Press Inc.

Library of Congress Cataloging in Publication Data
Main entry under title:

Comparative regional systems.

(Pergamon policy studies)
Bibliography: p.
Includes index.
1. Regionalism (International organization)—
Addresses, essays, lectures. 2. International relations
—Addresses, essays, lectures. I. Feld, Werner J.
II. Boyd, Gavin.
JX1979.C574 1980   341.24   79-26147
ISBN 0-08-023358-9
ISBN 0-08-023357-0 pbk.

Printed in the United States of America

Contents

Preface and
Acknowledgments

This volume has been designed to assist students, professionals, and the interested public in their efforts to comprehend the patterned and unpatterned forms of international activity through which states relate to the most important entities in world politics – their neighbors. Much of the cooperative and conflictual behavior in international politics occurs within regional contexts, hence the importance of understanding the sources and forms of this behavior, and the issues which contribute to it as well as those which it produces.

For comprehensive examination of the various regional systems it has been necessary to invite contributions from numerous distinguished area specialists and generalists. All have written with much sensitivity, insight, and dedication, seeking to build on vast accumulations of knowledge in order to provide full and integrated learning experiences. We are grateful to these authors, and we trust that contact with their minds through this volume will encourage readers to follow the development of their more specialized studies.

The preparation of this work was given much encouragement by Richard C. Rowson, President of Pergamon Press, who saw a need for comparative studies of politics above the national level and below the global level. Richard's encouragement gave confidence and was a stimulus to achievement.

Each of us is indebted to many colleagues who have aided the development of our thinking on regional systems, and Gavin Boyd is grateful to members of the Political Science Department at the University of New Orleans, whose hospitality he enjoyed while working on the volume during the summers of 1978 and 1979.

I
Perspectives

1 The Comparative Study of International Regions

Werner J. Feld
Gavin Boyd

References to international regions are common in the everyday language of politics. Such references identify geographic clusters of states, such as those in "Western Europe" or the "Middle East." Persons who use these terms normally imply that the states in the group are in several respects interdependent, mainly because of their geographic relatedness; that this relatedness is a source of cultural and other affinities between those states; that consciousness of area identity can motivate some or all of those states to deal collectively with "outside" powers; and that policies toward any state in the group should take account of the likely reactions of its neighbors.

This volume is intended to be a comparative analysis of international regions. As in the comparative study of nation states, we confront the problem of identifying the variables with the highest degrees of explanatory power that will help us to understand differences and similarities between the various international regions. At this level of analysis the problem is very difficult because there is less agreement among scholars regarding the essential attributes of a region. Regional organizations may cover only part of what is clearly recognizable as the regional territory. Moreover, with the regions, however defined, nonstate actors play important roles, although nation states are the dominant actors, and the complex interactions between the nation states, as well as between these and the nonstate actors, may not be institutionalized.

To cope with the basic problems of regional analysis we have listed clusters of variables that form linked patterns within each international region, and at the end of the list we have focused on the developmental issues that appear to be posed in the various regions of world politics. At the beginning of these lines of inquiry we list the configuration of the region, which is built up by mapping the basic attributes of the states in the area and their major patterns of relations. This configuration is then expanded at several levels of analysis:

1. Political sociology, including national patterns of societal beliefs and values, and of cohesion and cleavages, as well as socialization processes;
2. Political cultures, in their cognitive, affective, behavioral, and evaluative aspects;
3. Political psychology, including especially elite beliefs, values, operational codes, and political skills;
4. Authority structures and influence patterns, covering in particular relationships between governments, political parties, and interest groups;
5. Interdependencies, within and outside the region, affecting policies across the issue areas;
6. Regional institutions, including their evolution, legitimacy, levels of development, and their outputs;
7. Regional foreign policy behavior, with special attention to inputs, processes, operating styles, and outputs;
8. Regional cooperation and conflict, resulting from the interaction of foreign policy behaviors; and
9. Developmental issues, including order, growth, and institutional expansion.

These areas of inquiry have been taken up by the contributors to this volume, although with differing degrees of emphasis. Each of the regional studies is comparative, across the nine analytical approaches.

REGIONAL CONFIGURATIONS

One of the difficult problems in determining the configuration of a region is the delineation of its boundaries. Bruce Russett, in a seminal study, has addressed this question, using a vast amount of empirical data and elaborate quantitative techniques.(1) His criteria for the identification of regions are social and cultural homogeneity, political attitudes on external issues as manifested in the voting of governments in the United Nations, political interdependence as indicated by participation in intergovernmental networks, economic interdependence as evidenced by intraregional trade in relation to national income, and geographic proximity. All these variables are significant, but differences in the weights attached to them can lead to widely diverging results. There are problems of perception and judgment in the use of aggregate data, and one of Russett's critics has suggested that his regions have as little substance as "the emperor's new clothes."(2)

In this volume we identify regions with emphasis on geography, utilizing the insights of area specialists who are sensitive to factors such as consciousness of regional identity, felt cultural and other affinities, and perceived interdependencies. The regions are Western Europe, Eastern Europe and the USSR, North America, East Asia, South Asia, the Middle East, Latin America, and Africa. The first three are globally central regions, whose members, collectively, and in some cases individually, dominate the processes of global and transregional politics.

All the factors that make up the configuration of a region determine its prospects for development as an international system and for the evolution of collective decision-making mechanisms through which common interests can be managed. The most important features of a regional configuration are its relative degrees of balance and complementarity, and the extent to which its states are oriented toward integrative behavior. A relatively balanced distribution of economic capabilities makes for genuine equality in relationships, beyond what might be guaranteed in formal commitments, while extreme inequalities cause weaker states to fear that they will be disadvantaged in any schemes for regional cooperation. The economic power of states, of course, includes the capabilities of transnational enterprises based in their territories, whose apolitical pursuit of gain can cause apprehensions in weaker political economies. In virtually every regional system, there are considerable imbalances in the distribution of economic power, and there is little prospect of these being moderated; indeed, if some form of market integration has begun, the imbalances will tend to increase. Complementarity in economic capabilities tends to develop between industrialized democracies on the basis of multiple market-oriented specializations, depending on whether government policies are relatively liberal or neomercantilist. Levels of economic complementarity between developing countries tend to be low; and, although they can be raised advantageously by planning for regional growth and diversification, the necessary collective will is usually lacking.

In terms of balance and other characteristics of developmental significance, the regional configurations studied in this volume can be ranked in rough order, although with some difficulties. Relatively high degrees of balance and complementarity are evident in Western Europe, where there are several core members and a gradation of economic power levels, and where firm unanimity rules protect the interests of small members. To a considerable extent, the differences in economic power levels can be offset by issue-based coalitions, especially because there is no compact between the three major members – West Germany, France, and Britain – for joint domination of the system. Regional policy orientations in the West European system are constructive, but integrative only with qualifications.

Africa can be ranked next in terms of balance, but not complementarity. Several states – including Nigeria, Egypt, and Algeria – have capabilities for central roles in this system, but there are greater disparities in economic power between them and the numerous small African states than there are in the European Community, and levels of interdependence in this Third World system are low. There is more complementarity, although with much greater economic disparities, in East Asia where there are two large core members, one an economic superpower. Orientations towards regional cooperation in this grouping are relatively weak; but, in the Japan-ASEAN cluster, in which the main regional economic exchanges occur, they are stronger than any in any subregion of the African grouping.

Marked contrasts in economic power levels, degrees of complementarity, and the extent of constructive orientation are evident in North America, Latin America, and South Asia. In each of these regions, there is a very strong core member, but in Latin America and South Asia, this member's orientation towards regional cooperation has been low and it has preferred to deal bilaterally with small neighbors. Brazil, the core member of the Latin American system, however, has been somewhat more positive than India in its attitude toward regional development. In the North American case, the great disparity between the political economies of Canada and the United States imposes limits, from the Canadian point of view, on the possibilities for close collaboration.

Finally, there is the Middle East configuration, distinguished by autarkic and antagonistic policy orientations that severely limit the prospects for cooperation. Here there are less marked disparities in economic power, but there is little complementarity, and attitudes towards neighbors tend to be more distrustful and conflictual than in other Third World regions. Strains in relations between members of this region, moreover, tend to be severe because of the presence of Israel, a state that lacks acceptance in the area, and also because of the competitive involvement of the two superpowers.

Superpower involvement is prominent in the East Asian, South Asian, African, and Latin American systems. Only in Latin America, however, has the United States striven to promote regional cooperation, and its efforts in this regard during the 1960s were continued only halfheartedly during the 1970s. Soviet penetration of the Third World regions, which is political and military rather than economic, aims at the cultivation of potentially affinitive and dependent states in order to gain advantages over the United States in what is seen as a contest for global domination. East Asia is the most critical area of superpower competition outside Europe, and its affairs are dominated by interactions between its two core members — Japan and China — with the United States and the Soviet Union.

Within its own regional system, comprising the Northern East European states and Mongolia, the USSR imposes a strongly hierarchical pattern of relations. This tends to exert increasing pressures on the subordinate states, as their leaderships seek to cope with Soviet integrative policies, under the auspices of the Council for Mutual Economic Assistance (CMEA), while endeavoring to strengthen their legitimacy and improve their performance through cautious liberalization measures.

Thus, the various regions have configurations with diverse prospects for evolution as subglobal international systems. In Western Europe, the relative levels of political development attained by the member states and their significant, although uneven, advances in collective decision making are enabling them to move towards more and more comprehensive management of their interdependencies and their relations with the outside world. Of the regions in the Third World, Latin America has a significant mix of capabilities for integrative ventures, but is affected by a lack of political will. In other Third World groupings, regional cooperation, although urgently needed for accelerated modernization, is difficult to achieve, not only because of the lack of a common political will but also because of the weak capabilities of the political economies in these areas. The situations in these regions and in Latin America raise questions about the possibilities for external leadership and support in schemes for regional cooperation. The support of the United States was a major factor in the initial stages of the integrative endeavor in Western Europe after World War II, and during the 1960s the United States was eager to promote regional cooperation in Latin America; although there were no enduring results in that Third World involvement, a significant capability for constructive participation in regional collaboration was demonstrated.

POLITICAL SOCIOLOGY AND POLITICAL CULTURES

The characteristics of national polities are shaped in multiple patterns of causation by societal factors, political cultures, authority and influence patterns, policy processes, and performance levels. Societal groups may operate with much spontaneity and vigor, expressing diverse forms of rationality, under weak or strong authority structures, at high or low levels of institutional development. Elites may provide leadership, exercise power with threats of coercion, or represent interests and bargain on their behalf. The authority structure may be functional, eliciting societal cooperation, aggregating demands, and managing the political economy; or it may lack legitimacy, be prone to pluralistic stagnation, and fail to provide coherent administration. Several basic types of states can thus be identified, using criteria of significance for their actual or potential involvement in regional systems.

A national society may be relatively advanced, homogeneous, and open, or backward, fragmented, and relatively closed. Most of the national societies in the Third World are deeply divided, vertically and laterally, by linguistic, ethnic, cultural, religious, and class or caste cleavages. A common result is pervasive minority consciousness, with alienation from and distrust of the national polity. Cooperation within and between national elites may thus be difficult, while ruling groups, which themselves may be divided by social cleavages, may be absorbed in the intractable problems of enlisting support from the diverse segments of society and, thus, exposed to highly parochial forms of socialization. Most societies in the advanced states, however, tend to have relatively homogeneous cultures, and are open to interchanges and cooperation with foreign societies. These advanced open social systems have significant capacities for spontaneous self-organization, and for the development and support of political institutions on a national scale. In each, however, there are critical relationships between the various forms and degrees of nationalism, and the kinds and levels of individualism, which in turn are related to the relative mix of consummatory and instrumental values.

Political cultures, based in or imposed on national societies, give orientation to political behavior and, through policy processes, to the shaping of statecraft. Relatively advanced political cultures are necessary for the support of wide-ranging regional cooperation. The development of such cooperation tends to be hindered by the divisions and parochialism of Third World political cultures, but many advanced political cultures tend to set upper limits to integrative policy behavior in regional contexts, as has been evidenced in the European Community. Relatively strong nationalist qualities persist in the political cultures of industrialized democracies, despite the growth of their interdependencies with each other and, in part, because some are more effective than others in managing such interdependencies. In addition to their nationalist qualities, moreover, the political cultures of industrialized democracies are oriented towards policymaking on a basis of interest group pluralism which, because of deficiencies in the aggregating structures, can cause stagnation, disjointedness, and sectoral bias in the political process, while excluding holistic national and regional considerations.

Political cultures are embedded in general cultures and reflect interplays between their value orientations and elite political behavior. Geography and social distances influence the evolution of general cultures, political cultures, and elite behavior, thereby affecting senses of national and regional identity. Most of the literature and art forms which shape general cultures are directed at national audiences, the symbolic uses of politics to build consensus are distinctly national and subnational, and elites in power exhibit senses of responsibility to their own nations and to friendly neighbors. With long social distances, societal interaction becomes infrequent, and evolving general cultures, having little influence on each other, become quite dissimilar. Advanced cultures do tend to interpenetrate, but on the whole tend to remain geographically bounded.

Affinities between national political cultures to a large extent determine possibilities for understanding, trust, and cooperation between neighboring countries. Such affinities result from interpenetration, particularly of the general cultures, and its degrees tend to be greater if these cultures are relatively advanced. Incentives to undertake regional cooperation, of course, tend to be greater for groups of advanced states, but responsiveness to these incentives is strongly influenced by cultural affinities and social distances, as is illustrated in the European Community's relations with Japan.

General cultures differ basically in their value orientations, which are reflected in the political cultures, subject to the effects of elite behavior. Most Third World general cultures have intense affective dimensions which give strongly personal qualities to political relationships, thus making for high degrees of parochialism while hindering institutional development. Political relationships based on felt obligations to broad community and national values tend to be made more feasible within the general cultures of industrialized democracies because their affective qualities are less intense, while their cognitive and motivational aspects give rise to more active concerns with general community and national interests. These concerns, however, derive mainly from consummatory values which are tending to be displaced by instrumental values in the advanced open states, and the principal effect is sectoral bias in their policies, at the expense of general and national as well as regional interests, as high decision makers choose between public policy options on a basis of comparative political advantage.

POLITICAL PSYCHOLOGY AND AUTHORITY PATTERNS

Elite political psychologies tend to be highly potent determinants of regional policy behavior. In general, such elites may be conceptually complex or simplistic, trustful or suspicious, and collaborative or authoritarian. In most developing states, primary elites are authoritarian, inclined to cognitive simplicity, little disposed to self-critical rationality, and strongly affected by primordial and personal attachments. In the exercise of power they tend to be arbitrary, ideosyncratic, inconstant, and intensely preoccupied with problems of support mobilization through unstable clientelist networks. The parochial and short-range perspectives of individuals in these networks tend to preclude leadership recognition of and concern with holistic national and regional issues. The secondary elites, subjected to inhibiting forms of political discipline in weakly institutionalized structures, contribute little to the development of regional policies. Leadership attitudes toward the common dependency relationships with industrialized democracies frequently entail disinterest in regional questions, especially because economic and military resources acquired from those democracies can help the consolidation of domestic political power and assist modernization. In industrialized democracies, however, primary elite psychologies are strongly conditioned by relatively high levels of formal and informal accountability and the critical judgment of independent opinion leaders, as well as by the generally constructive but competitive and often questioning attitudes of leaderships in neighboring states. The representative, consultative, and administrative structures through which these leaderships function, however, leave open many opportunities for political rather than comprehensively rational decision making. Chapter 2, written by Daniel Druckman, examines the problems of political psychology in a regional context.

National authority structures and influence relationships differ in ways which enable primary elites to achieve varying levels of performance in the management of their political economies, and of relations with neighboring states. Differing levels of effectiveness in public policy cause some states to benefit more than others in regional schemes for trade liberalization, and, of course, are associated with contrasts in bargaining capabilities that affect regional interaction. Of the industrialized democracies, some are highly coherent and vigorous national actors because of the degrees of hierarchy in their government structures and the strength of supporting influence patterns, while in others political power is fragmented with dysfunctional results. The highly coherent international actors benefit substantially from trade liberalization schemes and market integration arrangements, but do not have incentives to undertake extensive policy integration with neighbors, as this may entail losses of autonomy. The more polyarchic and less coherent industrialized democracies tend to be ambivalent towards trade liberalization schemes, especially because of domestic protectionist pressures, and have difficulties in responding to the challenges of the more integrated and more purposeful advanced political economies. In Western Europe, the major contrasts between West Germany, France, and Britain, in terms executive strength and achievements in public policy, are associated with diverging attitudes towards market integration, policy coordination, and the possibilities for structural integration within the European Community. Among the developing states there are greater diversities in authority structures and domestic influence relationships, with varying consequences for levels of performance; and all these contrasts are associated with highly unstable institutions and patronage networks. Regional cooperation is, thus, more difficult for developing states and is affected by greater uncertainties.

REGIONAL FOREIGN POLICY BEHAVIOR

Foreign policy behavior in regional contexts is influenced by short and medium social distances and, often, by affinities and interdependencies with neighbors, as well as by the size and relative economic and military power of those neighbors. Perceptions of social distances, of course, are affected by felt regional identities and by cultural and other similarities that facilitate communication, understanding, and cooperation. Rivalries, antipathies, and antagonisms can be felt across short social distances, and, thus, may motivate quests for links with distant states, but growing interdependencies associated with economic development can gradually moderate hostile feelings between neighbors. Such a process can be aided, of course, if there are some advances in political development that facilitate the growth of more constructive foreign policy orientations. The main forms of regional foreign policy activity are the projection of national power, bargaining in relation to converging or conflicting interests, cooperation and conflict, and the use of communications to provide information and define the meanings of regional and extraregional situations. The various mixtures of behavior increase or decrease understanding and trust while affecting the orientation of receiving states and their neighbors. In the West European system the general effect is to raise levels of interdependence while tightening the linkages between each state's domestic and regional policies.

Projections of military power by relatively large states influence patterns of relations in Third World regions, depending on the policy orientations of those states, the strength of regional organizations, and the degrees of solidarity between the smaller states. In East Asia, the projection of Chinese power influences the behavior of the small Southeast Asian states, and is not significantly offset by their mutual ties, which are weak, or by any major regional organizations, but the effects of this power projection are moderated by the restraints on Chinese policy that derive from the Sino-United States relationship. In Latin American politics the projection of Brazilian power is strong, but its effects are moderated by the conditioning of several decades of efforts to promote regional cooperation, by various ties between the smaller states, by the leadership efforts of medium sized states, and by the influence of the United States as a basically constructive intrusive power.

In Western Europe projections of military power are directed at the Soviet military complex and have little influence in the regional pattern of relations. Much of the interactions in this pattern comprise forms of integrative and competitive bargaining, in which all members of the European Community participate, and which are conducted under significant normative restraints, based on widely accepted notions of equity. The competitive element, however, is strong and causes extensive use of linkages as states seek to maximize the utility of their leverage by tying cooperative moves on one issue with demands for concessions on another. The manipulation of linkages is a prominent feature of the protracted bargaining over matters of policy coordination within the European Community. There are many discontinuities in this pattern, and these are due basically to numerous crossnational differences between decision makers with reference to perceptions of functional requirements, political interests and bias, and capabilities, as well as for the will to engage in cooperative measures in the general community interest.

Bargaining in Third World regions is more restricted, less frequent, and deals with less substantive issues. Incentives to cooperate are weak. Broadly inclusive participation in the interaction is made difficult by suspicions and antagonisms, and the immediate gains to be expected from cooperation are small. High levels of political motivation, thus, are necessary for vigorous and sustained regional collaboration, but such motivation is often precluded by the narrow value orientations of Third World leaderships. The influence of regional institutions on the behavior of states in these groupings is generally weak and so, also, are the restraints of shared norms and values. Finally, the attitudes of each administration towards the others tends to be strongly influenced by uncertainties about their stability, as well as by deeply rooted fears, suspicions, and antipathies deriving from past rivalries and conflicts.

Regional foreign policy behavior stimulates and is also affected by the emergence of transregional relations and systems. Such systems are interactive patterns extending across the boundaries of regional systems, and are usually based on lower levels of cohesion than is evident in advanced regional systems. If there are major asymmetries in a transregional system, the disadvantaged states within a given region will have motivations to collaborate for collective bargaining to ensure more equitable negotiated allocations of values on their own behalf. The oil producing states (OPEC) make up the core of a transregional system, while individually they are members of regional systems. If primary commodity cartels emerge, they will also become central elements in transregional systems. Donald Lampert explores the patterns of transregional relations in detail in chapter 13.

Finally, regional foreign policy behavior is influenced by interactions with the global system. The principal actors in that system are large advanced states with interests extending well outside their immediate environments, and with capabilities for the management of statecraft across long social distances. Regional foreign policy actions may be responses to global political or economic initiatives and changes, but cause changes in the global system. Chapter 14, authored by Werner J. Feld, presents an overview of the interaction patterns between regional organizations and the global system.

INTERDEPENDENCIES, COOPERATION, AND CONFLICT

Regional patterns of interaction can be judged according to their outputs. In the relatively advanced West European system there is a fairly comprehensive collective management of common interests through policy coordination, relating mainly to the regulation of an integrated market. The member states participate equally in this management, although under the influence of numerous bargaining asymmetries that involve transnational enterprises as well as other member governments. Contrasting with this relatively developed pattern of interchanges are the occasional, restricted, and much less substantial interactions of Third World regions, which produce few benefits for the participants and do little to strengthen their motivations for further cooperation.

Regional interactive processes are shaped by crossnational compatibilities and incompatibilities between foreign policy inputs, as well as by differences in bargaining capabilities. The incentives to interact, in most regions, are economic and are strongest within groups of advanced states.

The economic foreign policy processes of industrialized democracies are highly diffuse and pluralistic, and there are marked variations in the coherence and effectiveness of their inputs. Such inputs are aggregated and ordered under strong direction by the political elites in West Germany and Japan, but not very coherently in the United States. While societal influences on foreign economic policy have diverging and conflicting as well as unifying effects in any industrialized democracy, these inputs exhibit varying degrees of compatibility and incompatibility between such democracies. In general, the industrial, commercial, banking, and other interests that make foreign policy demands seek prosperity that will be shared with neighbors, but their specific objectives are matters of sectoral and/or national advantage, and beggar-thy-neighbor policies are sometimes pursued. Various interest groups are tending to enter into closer collaboration with their governments as these administrations attempt more active management of their foreign economic relations, in order to meet domestic expectations for overall performance in public policy under pressures generated by forms of national competition in trade, investment, and monetary affairs. Governmental inputs into foreign economic policy tend to be moderately compatible between advanced open states because of widely shared perceptions of common interest, attributable to the socializing influence of frequent contacts between officials of these states at international conferences and through intergovernmental consultations. At the highest decision-making level, the personality characteristics of executives in the industrialized democracies also tend to be compatible across national boundaries, mainly because of processes of international socialization; but, of course, these executives differ in their relationships with domestic political forces. Some are subjected to strong interest group demands, sometimes with negative implications for regional cooperation, while others are better placed to provide leadership, and can work with greater freedom to express integrative or nationalist purposes in their regional policies.

The management of foreign economic relations by developing states is generally elitist and rather autocratic. Government officials mostly provide discreet inputs in very subordinate ways; there is little articulation of societal aspirations, and indigenous business groups generally limit their concerns to protectionist requests that are advanced through clientelist networks. Crossnationally, the most significant compatibilities and incompatibilities are those between leadership personality characteristics; in the Third World, generally, these are little affected by international socialization and cultural interpenetration, but are influenced very much by the internal requirements of solidarity building, and by primordial and personal attachments and antipathies that relate to neighboring states.

Regional economic cooperation is most developed in Western Europe, whose states are virtually all members or aspiring members of the European Community. In this cluster of states there are strong feelings of regional identity, based on geography and cultural affinities, and there is extensive productive interaction for the management of interdependencies. In the Third World, the Latin American societies evidence strong consciousness of regional identity, and their leaderships have made significant (although only partially successful) efforts to promote cooperation within their grouping. There is a somewhat weaker sense of regional identity in Africa, where levels of economic and political development are lower while, in the Middle East, consciousness of area identity is quite pervasive but gives rise to little cooperation. In East Asia, feelings of regional identity are weaker but there is more subregional cooperation than in the Middle East, although less than in Latin America. Harold K. Jacobson and Dusan Sidjanski survey regional economic cooperation arrangements throughout the world in chapter 3.

REGIONAL DEVELOPMENT

As an international polity, a regional system can develop. Cohesion and solidarity between national societies may increase, their governments may become more oriented towards integrative activity, the processes of collective decision making may become more institutionalized and draw greater support, and the cooperation resulting may become more substantial, producing greater benefits for the region as a whole. These possibilities have been illustrated in the recent history of the European Community, and some potential for regional development has been evidenced in the various Latin American schemes for integration.

International political development is analogous to national political development. There are problems of identity, legitimacy, integration, participation, institution building, leadership, and performance. The problems of identity, legitimacy, and integration concern the evolution of a political culture that will support collective decision making. Resolving these problems necessitates overcoming suspicions and antagonisms between states, and building up confidence in regional institutions and the goodwill of other members in the grouping. In a region of industrialized democracies, such cohesion and integration at the societal level tends to be hindered by competitiveness in foreign economic policies which causes uneven distribution of the benefits of trade liberalization. In Third World regions, the development of cohesion and support for common institutions is difficult because of the divisive effects of cultural, ethnic, and religious differences, the strength of historic antipathies, the small communication flows, the low levels of trade, and the degrees to which each national leadership tends to be immersed in its own domestic support problems.

Problems of participation in regional and subregional decision making are also more difficult to resolve in the Third World because there is usually a weak consensus about the norms to be followed, and because smaller states tend to fear that any formal rules will be ignored by larger states when opportune. Smaller states, thus, hesitate to participate in cooperative ventures, while larger states are often inclined to deal bilaterally with their smaller neighbors rather than submit to the restraints of multilateral decision making.

In a region of industrialized democracies, there are likely to be participation problems with different dimensions. Each state's need for effective involvement in the collective decision processes will be substantial, but the terms or conditions on which such participation is feasible will vary greatly, because this is a matter of involvement in bargaining over multiple linked and unlinked issues, and differentials in bargaining assets undermine the formal equality associated with decisional rules in high-level regional meetings.

The building of regional institutions to accommodate the articulation of demands and the bargaining by national administrations, and to shape and implement regional policies, is a requirement that can be met on a federal or confederal basis and through the gradual development of structures to continue initial ventures in cooperation or the making of fairly decisive national commitments to substantial integrative measures on the basis of a strong common political will. Confederal structures require less collective resolve, because the attachments of government leaders to concepts of national sovereignty are understandably strong. But confederal decision making tends to be inadequate for the management of the interdependencies of a group of industrialized democracies and, as these continue to grow larger and more diverse, the need for more directed interaction also grows. A strong case is then presented for transition to federal-type structures.

A political strategy for regional institution building is likely to be more successful when interest groups recognize the potential advantages of wider policy coordination. The utility of such a strategy will depend primarily on the regional mix of elite political psychologies influenced, of course, by accumulated experiences of interaction.

Leadership is necessary for the development of a regional system; that is, for the promotion of forms of societal integration, the spread of a sense of regional identity, and the growth of elite and mass support for regional institutions. Regional leadership is difficult to provide, however, because primary elites tend to be deeply socialized by their own political interests. The greater the diversity of cultures, moreover, and the higher the levels of antipathies and distrust, the more difficult it is for leadership to function transnationally. The establishment of the European Community was an achievement of transnationally collective leadership in unusually favorable circumstances, under the stimulus of unifying external challenges. But in the recent history of the European Community, leadership in the interests of growth has been provided only in small degrees, and regional cohesion has been negatively affected by the phase of strong French national assertiveness under de Gaulle.

A regional system's provision of benefits for its members, through collective decision making across the issue areas, depends mainly on its leadership and institutional development, and on the participation of members in its affairs, as well as on its degrees of societal integration and cohesion. The main hindrance to performance in a region of advanced open states is national competitiveness in the management of foreign economic policy, and this difficulty is likely to persist if the collective decision process is confederal. Yet it cannot be denied that the development of federal-type regional institutions may well give rise to grave difficulties including, especially, stagnation at the policy level because of unmanageable pluralism, and the circumvention and obstruction of federal authority by national governments.

A regional system, it goes without saying, can experience political decay as well as political development. This was evidenced in the European Community during the 1960s when support for the common institutions and for advancement toward wider policy coordination and institutional integration was set back by French policy. In Latin American regional and subregional ventures, shared national commitments to integration that were initially strong have weakened seriously over the past decade and a half; the praetorian regimes which became established in the 1970s have exhibited less positive attitudes towards regional cooperation than the relatively democratic governments which they replaced. Gavin Boyd, in chapter 12, examines the problem of political change in regional systems.

THEORY

The study of regional systems has developed mainly through analysis of the politics of economic and political integration in the European Community and of the modest Latin American attempts at subregional cooperation. In these, and to some extent in other regional contexts, interdependencies are measured by trade, investment flows, and the production of transnational enterprises. Crossnational attitudinal changes indicate levels of societal integration. The most significant decision processes, those within the European Community, are examined to determine how executives and bureaucrats make choices holistically or with sectoral bias, and with tendencies towards disjointed incrementalism or fragmented issue linkage.

The principal findings are that trade liberalization and the removal of barriers to investment flows within a group of industrialized democracies stimulate transnational economic exchanges, raising levels of interdependence but also challenging member governments to become either more cooperative or more competitive in their management of foreign economic relations. Some states benefit substantially from the market integration, while others are disadvantaged because of differing levels of achievement in economic administration and differing capabilities for, and orientations toward, neomercantilist or liberal economic statecraft. The increasing competitiveness in external economic policies, in conjunction with rising interdependencies, tends to compound the difficulties of collective decision making and, thus, of performance in the regional system. This invalidates the predictions of neofunctional theorists that regional cooperative ventures would be satisfactory experiences that would motivate expansion of the areas of collaboration and the setting up of appropriate institutions. It is questionable whether neofunctional theory retains validity as an explanation of the widening collaboration that can develop in the early stages of regional trade liberalization, but its value as an aid in understanding more advanced forms of regional collaboration between industrialized democracies and as a predictor of future trends has become particularly doubtful. The increasing competitiveness which accompanies the growth of complex interdependencies was not envisaged, nor were foreseen the increasing domestic pressures for higher economic performance on each national administration, pressures that materially affect the political interests of those administrations. There is a general tendency to respond to these pressures by shifts in the direction of neomercantilism, within the restraints imposed by complex interdependencies, but both the development of this tendency and the restrained observance of liberal economic principles as the normative basis for integration are influenced by the varying inclinations of national administrations toward disjointed incrementalism, with sectoral bias. Hence, if there is continued policy coordination because of the need to manage interdependencies, this is likely to be a slow, fitful, disconnected, and undirected process, the effects of which on societal attitudes will tend to have negative implications for structural integration. It is always possible, however, that these will be overcome by vigorous transnational leadership for transfers of authority to new central institutions.

The Latin American experience is one of failures of political will in regional integration ventures. The military regimes established in most of this region's states are strongly nationalistic and seek economic strength mainly by attracting direct investment from industrialized democracies and by expanding exports to those democracies. Relations between these military regimes are affected by distrust, antipathies, and rivalries, and by apprehensions that any gains from trade liberalization will be unequal and virtually impossible to redistribute. The Latin American economic system is almost stagnant because of all these problems. Yet there are numerous bureaucrats, academics, intellectual leaders, and political and military figures, particularly in the Andean Group, who recognize the potential benefits of economic integration schemes.

In theorizing about regional systems, one must be sensitive to the diversity and the potency of domestic foreign policy inputs in two important respects. Large numbers of these inputs, in diffuse reciprocal causation, tend to orient executives towards _political_ rather than rational decision making, both in the prismatic contexts of developing states and in the open systems of the industrialized democracies. Further, many of these inputs tend to perpetuate primary and secondary elite attitudes towards the perceived attributes of neighboring states that are based on historical memories and that have affective dimensions that are highly resistant to change. The development of regional systems theory, then, must draw heavily on research in comparative foreign policies. The main object is to understand regional integrative behavior by states. This will be the principal concern of the final chapter, by Charles A. Duffy and Werner J. Feld.

NOTES

(1) Bruce M. Russett, International Regions and the International System: A Study in Political Ecology (Chicago: Rand McNally, 1967).

(2) Oran R. Young, "Professor Russett: Industrious Tailor to a Naked Emperor," World Politics 21, no. 3 (April 1969): 486-511.

2 Social-Psychological Factors in Regional Politics
Daniel Druckman

A number of psychologists have sought applications for their concepts in political settings, just as some political scientists have attempted to use psychological concepts and methods in their analyses. The resulting products, documented in several collections and monographs, have served to define and shape a discipline concerned with the social-psychological aspects of political processes, most notably those germane to international relations.(1) The progress made to date has formed the basis for a long agenda of research topics. Some of these topics are located at the interdisciplinary juncture where the study of relationships among nations merges with the social psychology of interaction among persons and groups. One focus, in particular, that could benefit from such an understanding is regional politics. Whether the regional actors are conceived of in terms of nations or their representatives, developments in both of these disciplines are relevant. This chapter addresses the impact of social-psychological factors on regional politics.

The importance of the psychological aspects of regional politics has been magnified by recent developments. For example, the Camp David Middle East Summit highlights the role played by individuals in transforming relationships between regional actors. The content and quality of their interactions could be seen as contributing to the destiny of the region. Carter's persuasive ability and his tactical use of the deadline forced Begin and Sadat to resolve the remaining issues that prevented agreement.(2) Journalistic and biographical accounts provide glimpses of other major interpersonal transactions. Some of these could be regarded as turning points that set in motion processes that changed the traditional relationships between nations. Examples include the Kissinger era of shuttle diplomacy in the Middle East; the Castro-Nixon exchanges during the Eisenhower years; Valasco's domination of Peru and its relations with Chile, Bolivia, and Ecuador; and Soviet-United States interactions toward the end of World War II as the two countries attempted to deal with conflicting interests over Poland.(3) The processes involved in these interactions are not unlike those observed in such less-exalted settings as the small-group laboratory. In each of these theatres social-psychological factors affect the course of relations.

The literature abounds with anecdotal and illustrative evidence that supports the assumption of relevance. Having made this assumption, one must probe further for a finer articulation of the way in which social-psychological factors operate in the area of regional politics. Such probes involve confronting issues that relate to the development of a framework for analysis. Stated in succinct form, the issues are as follows: What is the nexus between social-psychological and political processes in regional systems? In what kinds of settings are these connections drawn most vividly? Who are the actors in these settings? and Which social-psychological processes impinge on the course of regional politics? These questions are intended to be provocative. They should serve to provide a focus for a framework designed to contribute to an understanding of the problem. Each is discussed in turn.

The nexus between psychological and political processes is drawn by treating the former as variables embedded within political contexts. The contexts are construed in terms of the patterns of relationship among two or more regional actors. Referred to elsewhere as a "context-relevant approach," this conceptualization precludes the dilemma of attempting to link distinct levels of analysis.(4) It assumes that contextual and psychological factors interact, the one influencing the other in a reciprocal manner. Such an assumption underscores the contention that regional politics is understood best by an interweaving of structural and psychological considerations.(5) Interpersonal transactions affect and reflect the patterned relationships among the nations being represented.

The nature of the relationship between nations is defined in terms of patterns of interaction. Such patterns are not viewed as static, as background within which psychological processes operate. In contrast to this "realist" conception of international relations, these patterns are fluid, changing as conditions and interests are redefined. Relationships change as regional actors alter their objectives or strategic courses. However, at any point in time a relationship can be depicted in terms of a particular pattern. Whether the pattern is construed along a continuum, to wit, the extent of interdependence, or construed as part of a typology, it is important to delineate the alternatives.

For the most part, the literature on regionalism has not recognized distinctions among patterns of interaction. Formal definitions of regional subsystems imply that there is a characteristic type of process for interstate transactions within a region. This is usually some form of exchange, for mutual benefit, between cooperating neighbors. For example, Thompson's necessary and sufficient conditions for a regional subsystem include the following:

1. The actors' pattern of relations or interactions exhibits a particular degree of regularity and intensity to the extent that a change at one point in the subsystem affects other points.

2. The actors are generally proximate.

3. Internal and external observers and actors recognize the subsystem as a distinctive area or "theatre of operation."

4. The subsystem logically consists of at least two and quite probably more actors.(6)

Overlapping these conditions are Russett's criteria for a region which, in addition to economic and social homogeneity, proximity, and interaction frequency, include interdependence, loyalty, and an "areal unit defined by an ad hoc problem" or an "administrative convenience."(7) Cooperative exchanges or interdependencies are also highlighted in definitions based on systems theory(8) and those based on anthropological materials.(9) The common elements in all of these definitions are summarized by Campbell's criteria for defining an entity – similarity, proximity, pregnance, and common fate (i.e., interdependence).(10)

However, the high degree of cohesion implied by the above definitions may exist among only a small subset of regional systems. Intraregional cooperation is evident in such areas as the European Community, the Nordic Council countries, and the North American axis from Canada to Mexico. It is less evident in most of the other major regions of the world. In these areas regional politics takes other forms, as is recognized by Guetzkow's distinction (applied by Yalem to regional systems) between isolation and collaboration in interstate relations.(11) Differentiating more precisely, this distinction can be extended to take account of such variants on the theme as conflict, dominated, penetrated, and transforming systems. Each of these forms can be illustrated. Conflict regions include such areas as Somalia/Ethiopia and Uganda/Kenya in Africa, the Korean peninsula, Vietnam and Laos, India and Pakistan, and, perhaps, Greece and Turkey due to rivalries in Cyprus. The most obvious examples of dominated regions are Eastern Europe and the African colonies under Western European rule. Penetrated regions consist of the U.S. and Soviet spheres of influence in Central America and parts of Africa. Among the relatively isolated nations within regions are the People's Republic of China (PRC), Spain, and Cambodia. Cuba and Albania are also isolated due largely to alliances maintained with foreign nations hostile to their regional neighbors. Regions undergoing transformation include the Middle East, the southern horn of Africa, and the lower Andean nations of South America.

Relational concepts are another means for drawing a nexus between political and psychological processes. Each of the patterned relationships among regional actors can be shown to have a counterpart in interpersonal relations. The forms stated above can be divided into those whose underlying mechanisms are influence processes (conflict, dominated, penetrated) and those where exchange is the essential concept (cooperative, transformed). Much of the social-psychological literature is organized around these two themes.(12) Similarly, international relations (IR) scholars are becoming increasingly cognizant of the importance of influence and exchange processes in their analyses. Nowhere is this more evident than in the burgeoning literature on complex interdependence.(13) Emphasized in both the psychological and IR literatures are relational dynamics. Whether construed as growth toward (or decline of) cohesion and integration or as movement from conflict to collaboration (or the reverse), the basic mechanisms are similar. Relational patterns are created or transformed as the result of influence attempts and exchange transactions. The ongoing interactions turn on these social-psychological processes, as does much of the analysis that follows.

The intersection between political and psychological analysis is found in settings where official, quasi-official, or less formal cross-national interactions occur. Face-to-face interactions provide the analyst with materials germane to the topic addressed in this chapter. Interactions like these occur during activities as diverse as intergovernmental negotiations, multilateral conferences, problem-solving workshops, and cultural exchanges. Characterized as being embedded within a broader political environment, each of these settings contains processes that reflect and affect the course of regional politics. These are the more immediate conditions which, following Pentland, can be exploited to encourage the "social learning" needed for changes in internation relationships. Anticipating the focus of this essay, Pentland notes that:

> The interactions of elites in intergovernmental negotiations, economic transactions and less formal contacts, as well as the social and spatial mobility of the general public as evidenced in tourism and the migration of labour across borders, are often assumed to increase the general "sense of community" of those involved. These phenomena, besides being researchable, are also susceptible to influence (for or against integration) by governments and other interested parties. The same is true of personal and mass communications, integration being enhanced to the extent that capabilities for communication and transaction increase to accommodate increased loads.(14)

While the mechanisms responsible for these effects are not clearly understood, the problem is defined as follows: How do these types of extended interactions influence a "sense of community" among regional actors? So defined, this problem makes pivotal a social-psychological analysis of regional politics.

Relevance is one criterion for choosing the settings selected for analysis. Another is accessibility to the analyst. The ongoing interactions can be observed as these unfold, thus providing data that have implications for such processes as psychological constraints on decision making. Indeed, examples of in situ analyses have multiplied in recent years, as is attested to by the developing literature on intergovernmental negotiations (e.g., the Benelux Economic Union, Trieste, the Scandinavian Economic Market, SALT, MBFR, Military Base-Rights), conference diplomacy (e.g., Conference of the Committee on Disarmament, Law of the Seas, UNCTAD, and such regional conferences as OAS, OPEC, and SELA), and exchange programs.(15) A third advantage is primarily methodological. Conferences and negotiations can be reduced in scale for experimentation. Experimental simulation can be used in testing causal hypotheses adduced from observations made in situ or in problem-solving workshops.(16) The heuristic benefits that are derived from such manipulation are evidenced in several recent applications. Much of the discussion that follows draws on this literature and, in so doing, shows how the technology of experimentation augments interpretive analyses that are based on field materials.

The third question addressed above concerns the actors whose interactions have consequences for regional politics. Gamson's distinction between authorities and potential partisans is useful.(17) Authorities are decision makers who can be construed as either "targets of influence" or "agents of control." Potential partisans are actors who attempt to influence decisions and are viewed as either "agents of influence" or "targets of control." These roles are interchangeable, cutting across the elite/mass distinction. Elites and non-elites alternate between the roles, depending on the issue domain. The relationship between these types of actors, viewed as either "agents" or "targets," provides insights into the operation of power in a political system. And those insights contribute to an understanding of the dynamics of intraregional politics.

Implications for regional politics derive from the way in which the authority-partisan relationship impinges on intersocietal interactions. A first cut on this linkage can be described as a two-step process. Partisans attempt to influence authorities' decisions by promoting certain perspectives. To the extent that authorities are receptive to these influence attempts, the perspectives will be channeled into positions taken in intergovernmental forums. This process highlights the relevance of social-psychological mechanisms. Such mechanisms underlie the way in which partisan perspectives are formed, and the impact of these perspectives on decisions. Construed in this manner, decisions are outcomes that emerge from an extended process of learning and communication. The learning of perspectives takes place in such settings as problem-solving workshops and intercultural exchanges. Communication between authorities and partisans occurs directly and indirectly in institutionalized and informal transactions. Learning and communication are at the core of a social-psychological analysis.

Two problems, then, for a psychological analysis of regional politics are: How are new perspectives learned? and How are values and interests communicated within and between societies? These questions concern mechanisms, channels, and actors. Learning involves changes in perceptions, stereotypes, identifications, and beliefs. Communication includes persuasion, debate, and exchange – the use of language to cajole, wheedle, and influence another's perspectives. Their place in the domain of regional politics is defined by the settings and actors that serve to link intra- and intersocietal transactions. These transactions, depicted in figure 2.1, are affected by psychological factors in a manner not unlike that in which a formal communication channel is affected by intrusions. They weave through the elements of the model shown in the figure both as facilitating or inhibiting influences and as mechanisms that underlie the political processes.

The model is recursive, highlighting the pivotal role of intersocietal (intraregional) relationships. These relationships influence perspectives and bargaining which, in turn, affect the relationships in the next iteration. That iteration consists of a process described as follows. Shaped by various socialization experiences (e.g., exchange programs), perspectives impinge on a bargaining process; they affect bargaining positions as these are mediated by an intrasocietal communication process involving policy-influences ("partisans") and policymakers ("authorities"); bargaining outcomes then affect intersocietal relationships, reinforcing or changing them, and the relationships' feedback on the perspectives and on bargaining processes to complete the cycle. Though not treated in this essay, external factors (events occurring outside of the regional subsystem), over which regional actors have little control, also have an impact on existing intraregional relations. Each of the other model components is treated in an attempt to make evident the dynamic interplay between structural and psychological factors in regional politics.

The model places psychological processes in the context of regional politics. Following Pentland(18) and disavowing presumptions of "psychological determinism," it is asserted that political attitudes and behaviors are pervasive in the creation of a "community of action" that is so essential for regional integration or identification. Attitudes and behaviors are central in problems of how partisans' perspectives are acquired and changed; of how these perspectives are communicated between policy-influencers and policymakers; of the impact these perspectives have on intersocietal negotiations; and of the way in which negotiation outcomes or decisions affect intersocietal relationships. Whether the patterned relationship between states is cooperative, conflictual, or in the process of being transformed depends in large part on these perspectives, communications, and negotiation outcomes. And social-psychological factors determine the form that these processes take. The remainder of this essay focuses on those psychological mechanisms that impinge on the course of regional politics.

The discussion is organized into five parts. First, the formation, content, and accuracy of views about other nations in the region are

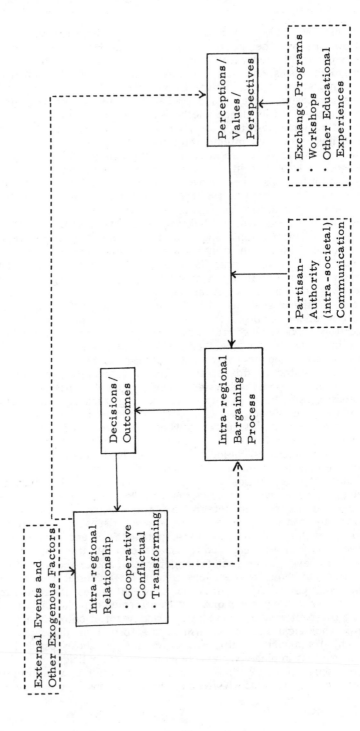

Fig. 2.1. Processes and influences on regional politics: a social-psychological model.

considered. Second, the conditions and experiences that contribute to changes in views about others are discussed, followed by a brief section on processes of intrasocietal communication between partisans and authorities. Next the negotiation processes by which societies communicate and adjust their values and interests are elucidated, including implications of negotiation outcomes for relationships among the regional actors. Finally, an attempt is made to integrate the previous discussion toward a social-psychological theory of regional politics.

Perceptions, Images, and Views

For Deutsch, Jervis, Bauer, White, and others, perceptions are intervening variables in the relationship between nations. They are part of the process of communicating across national boundaries, a process that shapes the orientations and policies of one nation toward another. According to Deutsch, the essence of "political community" lies in the ability of people to communicate, which requires that they understand the same language and perceive the world in similar ways.(19) Accurate perceptions are essential for effective communication. Communication is impeded when images are stereotypes – oversimplications or generalizations based on inadequate evidence.

A wide range of factors has been hypothesized or shown to affect the content and accuracy of perceptions. The factors pertain, for the most part, to societal characteristics and intersocietal patterns of interaction. While reflecting these factors, perceptions can also be seen to affect them. Such a cyclical conception places perceptions in the dual role of intervening and independent variables. As intervening variables, perceptions mediate between the intersocietal relationship (cooperative, conflictual) and the communication process; as independent variables they determine, to some extent, the nature of relational and communication patterns. Viewed in either of these ways, perceptions are an important element in regional politics. For this reason it is appropriate to examine the factors that shape the form and determine the accuracy of these images.

Just as experimental psychology reveals that perceptions are neither templates of reality nor projections of inner feelings, the material of international relations suggests that they are neither isomorphic to, nor projections of, a structured pattern of interaction. Rather they are imperfect images whose content develops from both inter- and intrasocietal experiences. Regions are one type of context for these experiences.

Regions as structured fields for perceptions

Regions vary in the extent to which they provide structured fields for intergroup perception. The more integrated the nations within the region, the more perceptions will be biased by the structural context of interactions; the more autonomous the regional actors, the more perceptions will reflect ingroup needs, motives, and interests. According to LeVine and Campbell, "With fewer (more) opportunities for mutual observation, the groups are more (less) ambiguous stimuli for each other, and this allows more (less) autistic perception, that is, the development of images that are detached from (attached to) the actual attributes of the outgroups."(20)

Opportunities for interaction, visibility, and salience are some of the variables suggested by this proposition. The content and accuracy of perceptions may be predictable on the basis of a number of aspects of the intersocietal relationship, including proximity, frequency of contact, type and institutionalization of the relationship, and dimensions of difference (e.g., customs, appearance, culture) between the nations. They may also be predicted from those intranational experiences that give rise to motives, desires, guilts, fears, and frustrations.

Frequent contact between members of different societies is likely to enhance the accuracy of mutual perceptions. Thus, those members who have more regular interaction with "foreigners" than with some groups in their own nation will probably have more accurate perceptions of the other nation's members. These include individuals who live close to borders, elites, and cosmopolitans whose identification is less national or more international. Spatial proximity and opportunities for travel are two conditions that promote accuracy by facilitating contact and interaction. Another is the extent to which the interaction is patterned or institutionalized. Such interactions enhance accuracy by providing a structured field for perceptions. Indeed, more accurate (less-biased) perceptions have been shown to characterize roles that interact in these structured settings.(21) One such role is that of the Foreign Minister, although this finding may also characterize other types of government officials who participate in international conferences. These representatives have also been shown to have similar perceptions.(22)

It seems plausible to assume that familiarity produces accuracy. Equally plausible is the contention that members with similar experiences will agree on their choice of adjectives to describe the foreign culture. Their images should reflect what they see more than they should reflect projections of relatively unique experiences. However, several studies suggest that this may be only partially correct. There is more likely to be agreement on evaluative than on descriptive content. In their crosscultural study of stereotypy, Druckman and his associates found a higher level of agreement among nationals of each of the three cultures in depicting familiar (and friendly) nations than unfamiliar (and unfriendly) nations on the evaluative traits (e.g., naive-shrewd, snobbish-modest, dependable-not dependable). Considerably more agreement was obtained on the evaluative traits than on descriptive traits (e.g., tall-short, undemocratic-democratic, sparsely or densely populated).(23) Obtained also by Lambert and Klineberg,(24) this finding describes the tourist who exclaims upon returning from a trip that "everything was wonderful, just wonderful" while revealing his (her) detailed knowledge about the country, its customs, and institutions.   There are many adjectives that can be used to describe a familiar country and its people, though only a few evaluational words are likely to be highly salient. Put in another way, regional neighbors are likely to evoke more complex imagery while at the same time being evaluated on fewer dimensions than are more distant, less familiar nations – within or outside of the region.

Learning theory and the content of perceptions

Accuracy is also related to the content of perceptions. It is defined in terms of the correspondence between image and group characteristics. More accurate images are those that reflect observed group characteristics. However, the "characteristics" are not simply those behaviors that are displayed on a regular basis. Rather, they are part of a complex stimulus field from which an observer chooses elements for description. Which elements are chosen may be predictable, in part, from the framework provided by learning theory.

The learning-theory approach takes into account both the " 'true' nature of the group described, and 'projected' preoccupations of the describing group."(25) In the terms of the theory, the former is referred to as "stimulus intensity," the latter as "drive" and "incentive motivation." One variable that determines the relative importance of these components is familiarity. As familiarity with members of a foreign culture increases, it is more likely that salient group characteristics will be included in one's imagery. Less familiarity will, on the other hand, increase the projective content of perceptions. Cutting across this distinction, however, is the nature of the relationship between the societies. Whether the relationship is friendly or hostile is likely to bias perceptions for both familiar and unfamiliar cohorts. For the former, it impinges on the choice and interpretation of observed characteristics; for the latter, it provides a definition for a vague stimulus field, i.e., it determines, in part, which motivational tendency will be projected onto the "outgroup." This process is illustrated by Merton.(26)

Merton's examples highlight the relationship between the content of stereotypes and the hostility or friendliness felt toward an outgroup. Evaluations produce labels that serve to justify these feelings. A flexible emotional language describes the same behavior as either "stingy" or "thrifty," "clannish" or "proud," "shrewd" or "tricky," "dogmatic" or "principled," "irrelevant" or "insightful," and so on. Viewed this way, the cognitive process consists of superimposing a "good-bad" matrix on the adjectives used by one group to depict another. Selves and friends are "generous," "brave," and "progressive," while disliked groups are "stingy," "aggressive," and "immoral." Recurrent themes illustrate another component of learning theory – habit strength.

Traits that reappear in descriptions of other groups are not unlike habits. Though defined by learning theory as "response strength," habit has also been used to depict perceptual rigidity.(27) Strength of association applies to both familiarity with making a particular response to a well-defined stimulus and the preservation or inertia of a stereotype. Both are established through reinforcement, repetition, and socialization practices. The stronger the association between a stimulus (outgroup) and a response (stereotype), the more resistant it is to change. Experimental studies make apparent the variables that contribute to a hardening of perceptions. Foremost among these is stress. The conditions that increase stress make it more likely that an individual will rely on habitual images and stereotypes. Increased stress has been found to produce an increased "primitivation" of perceptual organization, difficulty in shifting to new solutions to a problem or to respond to a changed situation, and a reduced ability to perform well in problem-solving tasks.(28) Important implications derive from extrapolating these findings to the arena of international politics, where flexibility or persistence of images play a central role in the analysis of policy decisions.

Emphasized in the literature on international politics is the idea that images tend to linger despite changed conditions.(29) Failure to adapt to an unfolding situation is often cited as being a cause of policy crises, as well as having disturbing psychological effects on the policymaker.(30) Jervis notes that images may serve as a framework from which attributions of the other's intentions are derived.(31) According to Lockhart, "the image...exerts considerable influence over perception by producing habitual patterns of selective attention, interpretation, and retention."(32) Statesmen also cling to images that reflect existing patterns of intersocietal interaction. A danger here is that images and "actual" interaction patterns could become mutually reinforcing, resulting in hardened perspectives about the other's intentions. When this occurs, efforts designed to alter perceptions, or to assuage dysfunctional side effects, are unlikely to produce desired results. Such efforts are discussed in the next section. They are considered part of the learning process as this relates to the context of regional politics.

Changing Perceptions and Views About Others

Regional politics unfold in a dynamic environment where actors must anticipate and adjust to changed relationships. Adjustments are made along perceptual, cognitive, and behavioral dimensions. Concentrating on such multidimensional adjustments, however, exposes ambiguities. Most troublesome, perhaps, are the complex and multidirectional links among these dimensions. As is noted in the literature on regional integration, it is possible that cognitive-perceptual adjustments follow sequentially from "prior experiences of an institutional or behavioral character....(or), on the other hand, it seems reasonable to suppose that the cycle works in such a way that institutional-behavioral adjustments come about as a result of prior cognitive adjustments."(33) The analytical implications of this ambiguity turn on the uncertain chain of effects produced by changes in one dimension. This dilemma prompts a more basic technical question: "How can perceptions be changed?"

Causal problems are recognized also by the cyclical model discussed above. Such a conception posits an intertwining of perceptions and realities. It renders problematic any attempts that are made to separate the two ostensible purposes for changing perceptions: to adjust perceptions to changing realities, or to change perceptions in order to have an impact on or to affect realities. The adjustment process may produce unintended effects; the impact strategy may result in undesirable adjustments. Recognizing the dangers of misguided attempts to change perceptions, Kelman notes that:

> (I)t is important to keep in mind that there are dangers not only in perceiving changes that have actually not occurred, but also in failing to perceive changes that have in fact occurred. . . .(T)he relationship between perceptions and reality is more complex than is often assumed, for perceptions not only represent realities, but often create them by way of self-fulfilling prophecies.(34)

And, difficult as it seems to affect perceptions, these side effects may result from mere attempts to do so.(35) These implications are raised once again below in conjunction with technical considerations. Indeed, they are at the core of the problem of designing environments or arranging conditions conducive to change.

Perceptual change occurs as a result of certain learning experiences. Based on assumptions concerning the structure and content of these experiences, attempts have been made to create conditions for change. Foremost among these efforts are international exchange programs and problem-solving workshops. While each of the several variants on these themes is designed to provide individuals with insights into cultural differences and perceptions, they differ on a number of dimensions. These differences are highlighted in the discussion that follows. Emphasized particularly are the programs or workshops that are conducted in the context of regional subsystems.

Perhaps a critical difference between these experiences is their purpose. The institutional or personal motivation for initiating these ventures is linked to the nature of the relationship among the participating countries. Exchange programs are purported to facilitate the implementing of a nation's foreign policy.(36) They are one of several channels of contact between governments whose relationship can be depicted as one of complex interdependence.(37) Often instituted as the result of a negotiated Treaty of Friendship and Cooperation,(38) these programs are designed to reinforce the on-going (or newly-established) relationship. Workshops, on the other hand, are meant to facilitate communication between conflicting societies. They are often viewed as inputs into a more complex resolution process. By promoting trust and open communication, these experiences could provide the preconditions for agreements that might ultimately lead to a transformed intersocietal relationship. Whether defined by official or private auspices, these purposes determine the structure and potential impact of the experiences.

International exchange programs

Understandably, exchange programs have not had substantial effects on attitudes. Since the programs are usually instituted in a climate of intersocietal cooperation, participants are likely to develop contacts that reinforce existing positive attitudes. Conversely, if the programs were instituted between conflicting nations, participants would probably not promote relationships conducive to change. How, then, can exchange programs be expected to have an effective impact on perceptions and attitudes? Some clues are provided by the few studies completed to date. Among the factors identified are: (a) the relative status of the host and visiting nations, (b) the specific goals of the exchange, (c) cultural differences, and (d) those idiosyncratic variables that affect one's adjustment to the new environment.

Each of these factors makes apparent the importance of the nature of interpersonal contacts. Contact per se with members of another culture does not create predictable effects on attitudes.(39) Contact can provoke areas of sensitivity or offer the promise of a pleasant and rewarding relationship. While the former effect will cause visitors to minimize contact, the latter could lead to deep friendships between the visitor and his host. Morris found a high relationship between the perceived national status accorded his country and the depth of contact with Americans. Those students who perceived that Americans accorded their nation a high status were more likely to develop deep friendships than were those who perceived that their hosts accorded their nation a low status.(40) Moreover, Mishler notes that "the experience of national status deprivation...will not only affect the visitor's general attitudes toward the host country, but will reduce the possibilities of positive experiences during the sojourn by limiting the nature of his personal contacts."(41) Equal status contacts are especially important for exchangees whose purpose is to study in the foreign culture. Such contacts provide benefits for students who, according to Merritt, "experience an impact on their perspectives by the host country significantly different from that experienced by students and others who go abroad but not to study."(42) Lengthy stays in the host country and a conducive home environment would seem to insure that the new perspectives will be transmitted to a student's compatriots. This problem will be considered in the next section.

Another type of sensitivity for exchangees is cultural differences. Such differences between the host and the home country of the visitor may be either less or more of a problem in the case of regional exchanges. On the one hand, nations within the same region are likely to differ less than do those situated in different areas. On the other hand, to the extent that the regions are structured fields for intergroup perceptions, small intraregional differences are likely to be noticed. Whether these differences will be a source of sensitivity depends, in part, on personality factors and on the relationship between the exchangee and his own nation.(43) Some visitors will exaggerate the differences in order to rationalize negative attitudes, or to displace aggressions, resulting from frustrations or fears acquired in the home environment. These tendencies will impede interaction. Other visitors will make genuine efforts to seek out and maintain contacts, relishing the opportunity to explore their differences. This distinction may be similar to that made by Kelman and Bailyn between perceptual levelers and sharpeners. Their data suggest that "levelers" may experience their visit in different ways than "sharpeners."(44)

Regions pose other problems for exchange programs. Historical relationships of conflict, domination, or penetration characterize most regions of the world. These, together with histories of warfare and intense rivalries, fuel resentments that are difficult to overcome. Moreover, these feelings may linger despite ongoing efforts to transform relationships.(45) Under such conditions, then, it would seem unrealistic to expect perceptual changes to result from an exchange experience, or for that experience to have a long-term impact on attitudes. Recognizing this problem, several investigators have proposed workshops or encounters that are deemed effective in dealing with intense feelings and rigid perceptions.

Problem-solving workshops

Like exchange programs, workshops are intended to enhance cross-cultural understanding. Broadened perspectives, increased sensitivity, and changed perceptions or attitudes are goals of both approaches. Here, however, the similarities end. The approaches differ in concept, technique, and role in the process of regional politics. Of the two, the problem-solving workshop is the more ambitious enterprise.

Viewed by some as an integrative device, workshops draw on developments in several areas. Literature on conflict resolution and theories of intergroup relations, group process, and regional politics contribute ideas that are used by workshop designers. If these are combined creatively, the resulting synthesis could produce desired perceptual changes. More often, however, the application is eclectic, due largely to an emphasis on the exploratory aspects of the approach. Designers have valued the enterprise more for its heuristic potential than for its hypothesis-testing features, and the usual results have been fleeting perceptual changes and unpredictable effects.(46)

The exploratory motif stems from the fact that the technique itself is still evolving. It does not consist of a set of established and tightly-defined procedures. Rather, as Kelman notes, it is "open to change, extension, and recombination."(47) This is true of each of the several variants of the general approach.(48) Referred to also as "pilot workshops," these efforts are characteristically lacking in structure and third-party control over the sequence of events. While serving heuristic purposes, this format poses problems for the analyst. It makes difficult any attempt to assign causes to the observed effects.

The workshop task is a melange of techniques which include role-reversal, sensitivity training, brainstorming, simulation, and various forms of third-party feedback that are designed to encourage an analytical orientation to the problems. Add to these techniques considerations of choice and method for recruiting; participants, location, types of third-party involvement, timing of interventions, the balance between structured and unstructured activity, inter alia, and the result is a complex package of factors that create an atmosphere within which participants interact.(49) It is this atmosphere that accounts for the observed effects of the workshop experience.

Variations in emphasis, however, create somewhat different atmospheres. The two major variants on the theme are the Doob and Burton approaches. Doob and his colleagues focused on group process, while Burton pioneered the analytical approach to international problem-solving.(50) The former directs attention to affect in an attempt to enhance trust; the latter encourages theoretical discussion in order to achieve a better articulation of the issues.(51) Whether each approach has actually produced these effects is controversial.(52) Equally controversial, but perhaps more important, are the implications of the distinction for theories of perceptual change.

The Doob and Burton approaches reflect fundamental differences about the role of motivation and cognition in conflict situations. Social psychologists are divided over the relative importance of these processes. Some, like Merton, point to a flexible emotional language that can be used to justify feelings – changed feelings will be followed by corresponding changes in descriptions.(53) Others follow Hammond in claiming that cognitive processes in themselves can cause conflict: reconciliation depends on cognitive change; motivational factors are less important.(54) Attempts to arbitrate the contrasting positions indicate that both processes are important, their relative importance being a function of a variety of conditions as are elucidated by Druckman and his associates.(55) Both are components of perception. Perceptual change depends on changes in both types of factors. Recognizing this, Cohen and his colleagues juxtaposed elements of the Doob and Burton approaches in their Middle East pilot workshop.(56) Although they took a step in the right direction, even these designers could not produce the desired changes. As in the earlier efforts, insufficient attention was given to the mechanics of the interaction process.

Dazzled by their lofty goals, workshop designers have given little thought to the precise conditions needed to bring about changes in perceptions. These are suggested by the results of experiments, most notably those carried out in the consistency-theory tradition.(57) Central to this tradition is the proposition that affect and cognition will be adjusted to coincide with changes in behavior – more so if the behavioral change is regarded as having been made voluntarily. Numerous experiments provide examples of procedures that can be used to bring about such changes. One example is to furnish the participant with more extreme arguments that support his stated position. Typically he will moderate his stated position, become more positively disposed toward the object, and justify the new position in terms of greater understanding.(58) However, argumentation is only one method for producing desired effects. A broad empirical literature provides a variety of clues that can be exploited by workshop designers. Particularly relevant is the recent work on intercultural learning and communication.(59)

Although the approach is "more effectively designed to produce changes in participants than to feed such changes into the policy process,"(60) the latter is clearly a goal of all workshop designers. Common features of all workshops are that they enhance the chances that new information and ideas will be fed into the policy process, to wit, that they are catalysts for change. Barriers to this end have been a lack of communication channels, a hostile environment, a failure to develop influence strategies, and solutions that go beyond what decision makers are prepared to consider. There is little wonder, then, that the workshop approach to policy change has been ineffectual.(61) Short of such impact, however, the techniques may be useful. Shown to aid participants in identifying negotiable issues and in distinguishing these from nonnegotiable problems the workshop experience can contribute to the prenegotiation process by preparing the ground for negotiation.(62) Transfer is, of course, facilitated to the extent that the participants have access to negotiators or are themselves involved in formal negotiations. These problems are considered in the sections to follow.

Communicating Views and Perspectives: Partisans and Authorities

Two problems of transfer are highlighted by exchange programs and workshop experiences. One of these is a problem of retention; the other is a problem of communication. "Communication" depends for its effects on retention of the changed perceptions and perspectives. "Retention" is largely a function of the extent to which the transfer environment is conducive to change. Faced with compatriots who have not changed, returning participants must cope with the discrepancy between the learning situation and the transfer setting. Such a discrepancy fosters "unlearning," as this is explained by the principle of retroactive inhibition. This principle asserts that retention is a function of activities occurring subsequent to the original learning; with decreasing similarity, retention never reaches the level attained with maximum similarity. The principle can be used to predict either decay (negative transfer) or sustenance (positive transfer) depending on the extent of similarity between the settings of interest.(63)

Assuming some degree of retention, the next problem to be considered is that of communication and persuasion. This, too, is primarily a problem of social psychology. Characteristics of the source and the recipient of the communication, as well as the nature of that interaction, render an influence attempt either effective or ineffective. Particularly germane is the interaction (discussed above) between partisans and authorities. Perspectives are shaped by the outcomes of these interactions, and these become part of the ongoing intrasocietal dialogue. Integrating new perspectives into that dialogue is a dynamic process that has implications for regional politics.

Partisans and authorities are prototypes for actors who play a central role in the influence process as it operates in most societies.(64) Authorities are decision makers who also manipulate priorities. Guided by their perspectives, they are receptive to influence attempts in varying degrees. Partisans are the influence agents who attempt to manipulate access to and affect the perceptions of authorities. Guided also by their perspectives and interests, they must take initiatives similar to the way aspirants for positions do when they attempt to influence selectors.(65) Perspectives depend for their viability on the intersection between partisan initiatives and authority receptiveness. Just which perspectives are likely to prevail depends, in part, on variables defined by that interaction process.

One set of variables are those that impinge on authorities' receptivity to influence. Types of influence sectors, skills within those sectors, and the diversity of viewpoints to which authorities will respond are predictable on the basis of such characteristics as affiliations, world views, network structures, and accountability. Cosmopolitan authorities respond primarily to technical specialists, while locals rely for advice on generalists. Intramural authorities (centralized, well-defined, and small) prefer bargaining or interpersonal skills, while their extramural counterparts (diverse, amorphous, large) respond to influence agents who demonstrate oratorical skills. And more accountable decision makers are likely to be receptive to more diverse views than are those who are less accountable to constituents.(66) To the extent that these variables determine the nature of receptivity they also make evident the kinds of perspectives that authorities will adopt.

Another set of variables are those that affect the initiatives taken by partisans to influence authorities' perceptions. Types of initiatives, access, and postures may be predictable from features of the social system in which their activities are embedded. Established systems emphasize career socialization, credential acquisition, and adaptation to changing role requirements. "Influentials" are those who have advanced in the system, as is illustrated in Putnam's study of senior civil servants in Western Europe.(67) Initiatives consist, for the most part, of acquiring the desired skills, either technical or political. Flexible systems provide more latitude and opportunities for influencing authorities' perceptions.   Affiliations and charm are more important than background and credentials. By providing a greater variety of channels for influence, flexible systems make possible the transition from partisan to authority or to appointment to valuable consultative roles.(68) Such opportunities increase the probability that new perspectives will be adopted – a precondition for changed intraregional relationships.(69)

But, changed perspectives may not result in changed behavior. While effectively influencing the way policymakers view a situation, partisans may not alter the way they act. The link between perceptions and behavior must be firmly established if a change in the former is to lead to a change in the latter. Preliminary analyses suggest that this may not be the case. Walker compared references to regional role conceptions to role behavior. Conceptions were assessed by a content analysis of foreign policy speeches while behavior was defined by an events analysis of policy-related actions. He found no relationship between the frequency of references to regional role conceptions and the frequency of regional role behaviors.(70) One implication of this finding is that there is no link. Another is that the link is undirectional; changing the behavior of policymakers may affect their perceptions of the situation but not vice versa (see previous section). Walker's correlation may be attenuated by having selected situations where role behavior did not precede role conceptions. If this is so, more attention should be paid to behavior; i.e., rather than altering perspectives per se, influencers should perhaps concentrate on altering policy-relevant behaviors.

The influence process discussed above has implications for the broader context of regional politics. Relevance is established by the way perspectives impinge on intersocietal relationships. This process is depicted in figure 2.1. It can be summarized as follows.

Perspectives include descriptions and evaluations of other nations. They are shaped by socialization experiences, changed by such intercultural programs as workshops and exchanges, and communicated through an intrasocietal dialogue between partisans and authorities. Translated into actions, the perspectives affect intersocietal processes. They may determine a willingness to negotiate, affect negotiating behavior, or be the subject of the negotiation. Emerging from these activities is a redefinition or reinforcement of existing relationships – an outcome that feeds back on the domestic perspectives.

Operating at this intersection between domestic and international politics are social-psychological processes. Those related to acquiring, changing, and communicating perspectives have been discussed up to this point. The remaining sections highlight the factors that impact on those intersocietal processes having implications for existing relationships.

Negotiating Values and Interests

Just as regions provide structured fields for perceptions, they serve as contexts for intergovernmental negotiations. The interplay between regional politics and negotiations is another example of the nexus between political and social-psychological processes. Construed also as context and process, these linkages are emphasized in several recent treatments of regional negotiations. Commenting on regional integration in the Commonwealth Caribbean, Axline notes that:

> (A) series of appropriate integrative measures can be identified which define different stages of the integration process, each of which provides a focus for negotiations among member countries. These negotiations, in turn, provide the basis for analyzing the politics of regional integration.(71)

The key issues in the integration process are those on which the principal actors take positions during the negotiation. Recognizing that negotiations are intertwined with regional politics, Axline highlights reciprocal effects.

Reciprocal effects of context and process are also noted by Strauss. In keeping with the approach of this essay, he concludes that "(T)he foregoing were, then, the principal conditions for the general strategy, range of tactics, and interactions so characteristic of the negotiating context. . .(known as) the 'Negotiations for Benelux.' "(72) Characteristic forms of these negotiations are predictable from specific contextual properties just as "these negotiations, at least in their cumulative impact, have profoundly influenced the overall relationships among the respective nations."(73) Whether analyzing the negotiations leading to an economic union of the Benelux countries, the bargaining structure of NATO, or the antagonistic cases of U.S.-Soviet bargaining over the Balkans, or the ethnic negotiations in Kenya, he sought linkages between relationships in the regional system and negotiating patterns. Compelling as his conclusions seem, however, he did not explore the impact of context and process on intervening perspectives or values. Nor did he probe the microprocesses of negotiations, a level at which social-psychological influences are magnified.

Focusing on negotiation entails a shift in our level of analysis from the individual to the dyad or small group of representatives. Coordination is the primary objective of negotiation, in contrast to attitude or perceptual change – the goals of most workshops, exchange programs, or other educational experiences. Both are, however, psychological processes that require social learning.

Successful coordination is a central problem for negotiators. It depends on an accurate assessment of the other's intentions, strategies, and interests. That it is rarely achieved is not surprising. Shared goals, accurate perceptions of the other's utilities for various outcomes, and an agreed-upon rate of exchange for concessions are only some of the conditions that must be met in order for the parties to synchronize their moves toward an agreement.(74) And one set of variables that impinge on these conditions, interfering with or facilitating coordination, are those defined by regional politics.

Three variables are highlighted in this analysis: value or ideological differences, relative power, and the type of relationship among the regional actors. Distinctions raised by these variables are similar or contrasting value orientations, more industrially-advanced versus less-developed states, and cooperative, conflictual, or transforming regional systems. If these variables are considered analytically, their effects can be understood in terms of the statistical concept of components of variance, or in terms of interacting factors in different regional systems. Both analytical strategies are used here in considering the relative importance of these variables as they interact in each of the three regional environments.

Cooperative systems

The context provided by cooperative regional systems creates a characteristic pattern for negotiations among the member states. The primary regional concerns are those related to trade and development. Operating within a shared framework of values, the members concentrate their efforts on integration – promoting plans for region-wide benefits and equitable distributions of these benefits. When they do this, different interests are articulated, asymmetries become evident, and conceptual problems are defined. Each of these poses a problem for coordinating in negotiations. And as lingering problems they threaten to undermine the foundations for political integration – a shared goal of the regional actors.

Coordination of strategies is made difficult by contrasting preferences for the outcome of negotiations whose purpose is to provide a plan for regional integration. Such conflicts of interest have been shown to be related to power asymmetries. Disparities in the overall strength of the regional actors partly determine their choice of negotiating strategy. Identified originally by Haskel, these strategies are referred to as expansive versus distributive.(75) Primary interest in expanding the joint gains – a "strategy of the strong" – clashes with an interest in an equitable distribution of gains – a "strategy of the weak."

Shown to interfere with negotiations in such diverse areas as the Nordic community, the UDEAC regional system in central Africa, and the CARICOM system in the Commonwealth Caribbean region, this strategic distinction seems to have considerable explanatory power.(76) Negotiating difficulties produced by this strategic asymmetry include synchronization problems, most notably where the actors are alternatively "hard" and "soft" on different issues.(77) Results obtained in several laboratory studies indicated that differences in the relative importance of the issues under consideration hindered negotiations. The greater the difference in the priority-ordering of the issues, the greater the hostility, fewer concessions, less reciprocation in decision making, and fewer agreements.(78) Resolution of these coordination problems led to reduced hostility and more concessions in the laboratory, just as they led to a linked expansive-distributive policy outcome in the "real world."(79)

The technical issues of integration also give rise to conflicts. Rooted primarily in cognitive processes, these conflicts interfere with a coordination of understanding. How to calculate and apportion prospective joint gains from investment schemes, whether to use uniform or variable tax rates as a substitute for the customs duty, and the "phased freeing of trade" versus the "integration of production" solutions to a free trade area are examples of cognitive conflicts that occur within homogeneous coalitions of regional actors, to wit, strong or weak states.(80) That such disputes are difficult to resolve has been demonstrated in experiments designed by Hammond and his colleagues. Nor are they any easier to resolve than conflicts of interest. Understanding of another's cognitive structure often requires the help of sophisticated technical aids as illustrated by Hammond and Brehmer.(81) And such disputes are further complicated by conceptual problems, so often observed in military base-rights negotiations,(82) that turn on the distinction between national independence and the interdependence required by integration schemes. Too often, resolutions are achieved through mutual compromise rather than by cognitive change. Little wonder, then, that few integration plans survive the test of time.

Conflictual systems

The context provided by conflictual regional systems also creates a characteristic pattern for negotiations. Like discussions between co-operating neighbors, negotiations between adversaries are influenced primarily by considerations of power rather than values. Unlike co-operative negotiations, however, power is a precondition and resource; values, when introduced, are an irritant, causing the talks to break down. Referred to by Strauss as "antagonistic negotiations,"(83) these talks are often protracted, difficult, increasingly antagonistic, marked by mutual distrust, and seen to contain elements of false rather than genuine bargaining. Jockeying for a competitive advantage, actors are manipulative, coercive, and persuasive within a wider political, economic, and geographic arena. Acting strategically, negotiators are cognizant of the link between a shifting balance of power among their nations and the shifting balance that obtains within the negotiations.

Not merely a determinant of bargaining strategies, relative power is a stake in the deliberations; decisions to continue negotiating turn on assessments of the current balance of power. Nowhere is this more evident than in arms control negotiations. An urge for symmetry makes "States hypersensitive to newly-perceived inadequacies (which they) tend to correct by leveling up to parity in a variety of force categories."(84) Whereas force improvements are made routinely under the guise of bargaining chips, the prospect of limitations on forces may destabilize those regions contiguous to the area under consideration; i.e., there are fears of force-redeployment into areas that have been relatively stable. Construed by some as "side effects,"(85) such adjustments make evident the observation that regional actors use these negotiations to accomplish goals that transcend the particular issues defined for bargaining.

While focusing on narrowly-defined interests, negotiations between adversaries are intended to serve broader purposes. Introducing these into the negotiation framework, however, could cause problems. Repeated experiments have shown that when the link between broader values and position differences (referred to as "conflicting interests") is made explicit, the conflict is more difficult to resolve than when the values remain implicit.(86) As described in propositional form by Druckman and Zechmeister, the dynamics of this process reveal that through time and repeated encounters the groups become further polarized, serving, in turn, to exacerbate the intensity of future conflicts.(87) Such spirals(88) can be avoided by limiting the scope of the issues to be discussed in negotiation. Referred to by Fisher as "fractionating the issues" or by Deutsch as "issue control," the procedure has been shown to be effective. Bargainers have less difficulty in achieving a mutually beneficial solution.(89) But what is achieved may be only minor adjustments that serve to sustain the system in which hostility and value differences are maintained.(90) By confronting their values, regional actors take a step toward transforming the system from conflictual interaction patterns to those which are cooperative.

Transforming systems

The interplay between context and process is most evident in regions that are undergoing transformation. In these systems, negotiations are a vehicle for change. They provide opportunities for regional actors to confront differences in underlying values. Value debate is part of a process in which conflict spirals give way to cycles of reciprocity or exchange. Value convergence is a necessary, though perhaps not sufficient, condition for moving the system from the former state to the latter. Whether convergence actually occurs depends, in part, on moves taken during the course of negotiations.

Reflecting the evolutionary pattern of regional politics in transforming systems, negotiations proceed in stages. Coordination of perspectives or values precedes the exchange of concessions that produce an agreement. Zartman's distinction between formula and detail captures the dynamics of this process.(91) The formula is a framework from which details can be deduced. It is the conceptual solution that must occur before positions on issues can be represented in a bargaining space. Referred to also as "referent principles," it is a cognitive structure for the agreement, providing the terms by which the situation is jointly defined and according to which the specifics for implementation are framed.(92) Implied here is a psychological process that leads to a convergence of understanding. Such outcomes are turning points that move the deliberations to the next stage.

A formula is a concept that resolves divergent perceptions of a problem or situation. It is the idea that provides a just solution to the Middle East dilemma of territorial expansion versus defensive necessity, of Israeli concern with sovereign security as against P.L.O. concern with sovereign repatriation, or the difference between Panama's emphasis on sovereignty and the U.S. insistence on defense. Being relevant to the problem, a formula may focus on global issues, such as an overall rapprochement between Italy and Yugoslavia rather than a division of Trieste; or on specific issues, such as a cease-fire in Cyprus or a freezing of the stalemate in place in Vietnam.(93) It can emerge as a result of shifting conceptions, as when the idea of nuclear parity in SALT became one of foreclosing coercion rather than permitting deterrence; it can be arrived at inductively, as was the case in the Kissinger shuttle diplomacy effort; or it can be the result of sudden insight helped by deadline pressures, as is suggested by accounts of the Camp David Middle East summit. In each case the formula appeared to address the heart of the controversy. How to find it, however, is less apparent.

Attempts have been made to prescribe procedures from personal experience,(94) as well as to derive them from experimental evidence. Common elements of these approaches are debate and a problem-solving orientation. Effectively executed, debates can produce "a mutual appreciation and adjustment of the perceptions and preferences of several or all of the parties concerned."(95) A technique for conducting such a debate, referred to as exploring the "Region of Validity," consists of three phases: restating accurately the other person's position, exploring areas of agreement in the other's stand, and inducing assumptions of similarity.(96) While the empirical evidence on effectiveness is not encouraging, the experimentation has suggested some of the conditions that might affect its impact. Laboratory results indicate that negotiators must be skillful role-reversers, their positions should not be incompatible, they should not be highly committed to their initial positions, and their negotiating orientation should be individualistic rather than competitive.(97) Results of analyses on real-world negotiation data add the requirements that information-needs be critical in the short run, that there be little familiarity with positions, that the procedures be used in a nonevaluative context, and that negotiators not be restricted by fears that they are giving advantages to their opponents.(98) Taken seriously, these conditions could lead to a resolution of value differences, a negotiation outcome that would impact propitiously on the broader relationship among the regional actors.

Nowhere is the link between micro- and macrolevel processes more evident than in the study of intraregional negotiations. Concepts used to depict processes at one level can be translated for analysis at the other. Such robustness renders the laboratory a heuristic device. Laboratory findings enhance understanding of processes in more complex settings; they also suggest procedures for dealing with problems that arise in those settings. The laboratory work, discussed above, alerts us to cognitive conflicts that impede negotiating coordination in cooperative regional systems. Strategies that limit the size of issues can make negotiation possible in conflictual regional systems. And, techniques that enable regional actors to debate their differences in values could make negotiation an effective vehicle for change in systems where existing relationships are at issue. The variables shown to affect these processes in laboratory negotiations are, conceivably, the prescriptions for breaking a deadlock or resolving a technical problem in regional conferences. Effectively executed, these prescriptions can lead to outcomes that have implications for the regional system.

Negotiation outcomes and the regional system

The relationship between negotiation outcomes and system processes turns on the distinction between behaviors and structures. Behaviors refer to the flow of communications exchanged between regional actors, including those that take place in negotiations. Structures are the network of formal relationships among the nations, most notably as these reflect power rankings. Intertwined as they are in the dynamics of regional politics, though not in the extreme sense of having no autonomy, behaviors and structures affect each other in a reciprocal manner.(99) While differences between them in rate of change suggest asymmetric effects,(100) impacts in both directions reveal the importance of social-psychological factors in regional politics. Both types of effects are considered here briefly.

Structures have a regularizing effect on behaviors. The distribution of power and alignments provides a framework for international transactions. Tendencies for lessened conflict between minor nations within blocs and toward increased conflict between superpowers within their sphere of influence are examples of structurally-conditioned effects.(101) Opening moves in bargaining can be seen to establish a framework of expectations that condition subsequent play as described by Rubin and Brown.(102) And, more generally, relationships between rank and interaction obtained in small-group research suggest that structures set the tone for the patterns of behavior that unfold.(103) Such predictable behavior, in turn, reinforces or perpetuates the structures that obtain. They may even further rigidify these structures, as Sharp illustrates in her analysis of the effects of the MBFR process on superpower arms control regimes.(104)

Given these structural effects, how then can negotiation outcomes alter the existing relations among regional actors? One way in which this can occur is through the behavior of representatives. By their negotiating efforts, diplomats can achieve a comprehensive formula that paves the way to a changed relationship. The Trieste affair was notable in this sense. According to Campbell, "the negotiation. . .paved the way to a normal and very good relationship between Italy and Yugoslavia."(105) More insidious, perhaps, are the effects of informal interactions among representatives. They can "consciously create rank incongruences, break down isomorphisms, make interpersonal relations less rank-dependent, etc., in short try to avoid the pitfalls of perfect equilibrium and consonance that may lead to strong identification and feelings of behaving correctly, but also to strong rigidity."(106) Extending the process further, resulting outcomes can create domestic bureaucracies that serve to institutionalize the new relationship.(107) Such domestic structural changes affect perspectives on both sides of the border. Partisans on one side become domestic constituents with a stake in preserving the changes; those on the other side are provided with evidence that meaningful changes, conducive to a stable peace, have, in fact, occurred.

Clearly, then, social-psychological processes are part of the dynamics of regional politics. Not only are these factors central in learning and communication, they also play a role in the creation of structures. The interplay between structures and behaviors is another way of addressing the nexus between political and social-psychological processes. Such a nexus is established not by analogy or isomorphism but by linkages, a theme suggested by the model in figure 2.1 and carried forward in the concluding discussion to follow.

CONCLUSIONS

That social-psychological factors play an important role in regional politics was recognized early by Deutsch and reinforced more recently by Pentland, Haas, and others.(108) Representing this viewpoint in regional studies, Rosenthal concludes that the most important link between conceptual models and the evidence found in case studies is "the capacity of individuals and small groups to influence decisions (a feature which until recently) has been virtually ignored by students of regional integration."(109) The trend toward reconceptualizing integration has highlighted psychological considerations, both as underlying mechanisms and as factors interwoven with structural variables in the analysis of relational dynamics. Nowhere is this trend more evident than in the recent work on interdependence.

Often construed as "mutually-contingent behavior," interdependence is seen as creating a new type of international politics and bargaining.(110) This new reality is one in which the structures of politics and the psychological aspects of bargaining (and related interactions) affect one another in a reciprocal manner. The "psychological aspects" are processes which produce outcomes that have consequences for intersocietal relations. They are the expectation/evaluation/adjustment cycles observed in bargaining experiments, as well as the tactics used to influence an opponent.(111) Furthermore, they are the perceptions that develop into perspectives, the sentiments and identifications that produce cohesion, and the cognitive processes that provide conceptualizations of schemes for new regional structures. Perspectives, affinities, and concepts are the "stuff" from which regional structures emerge or are dissolved. They develop through ongoing intra- and intersocietal dialogues, much as these are discussed above and summarized below.

Four general conclusions serve to summarize the preceding analysis and to point the way to further research.

Regions are structured fields for perceptions. The accuracy and content of perceptions are affected by such variables as proximity, frequency of contact, type and institutionalization of the intersocietal relationship, and dimensions of difference between the societies. Conditions that facilitate contact and interaction enhance accuracy. As familiarity with members of a foreign culture increases, it is more likely that salient group characteristics will be included in perceptions. Less familiarity is likely to increase the projective content of perceptions. However, which characteristics are included is a function of the nature of the relationship as well as the extent to which certain "traits" have been repeatedly associated with that group. Institutionalized relationships provide a structure either for selecting among diverse observations or for deciding which motivational tendency will determine the content of perceptions. When these images become persistent characterizations or hardened perspectives, they may create problems. Most notable perhaps is the often-observed tendency of "committed" policymakers to fail to adapt to changed conditions.

Regional dynamics are intertwined with perceptual dynamics. Changed circumstances require changed perceptions, but the circumstances themselves may be affected by perceptions. Perceptions are affected by the nature of interpersonal contact experiences. Contacts that offer the promise of pleasant and rewarding relationships can lead to perceptual change. Such contacts depend on (a) the status accorded the visitor, (b) the specific goals of the interaction, (c) the extent of cultural differences, and (d) idiosyncratic variables. Counterpoised against the facilitating effects of these variables, however, are socialization histories and institutionalized relationships that impede change. These background factors are difficult to overcome, as evidenced in the results of exchange programs or the more intense experiences provided by workshops. What is required is a more systematic approach to perceptual change, one that is based on an understanding of the interaction among affective, cognitive, and behavioral dimensions. Contributing to such understanding is experimentation designed to evaluate alternative argumentation strategies, confrontation tactics, or contrived environments. Certain techniques have already proven to be effective in applied settings.

The impact of new perspectives on regional politics depends on the extent to which these views are retained and communicated. Communication consists of influence attempts which are part of an ongoing intra- and intersocietal dialogue. While influence must be exerted in several directions by multiple actors, an essential intrasocietal communication process is that involving partisans and authorities. Retention of new perspectives turns on the receptivity of authorities to partisans' initiatives. Variables defined by that interaction process determine which perspectives will be adopted. Receptivity is affected by such variables as affiliations, world views, and accountability. Types of initiatives taken by partisans are related to characteristics of the social system. Whether acquiring certain skills or nurturing contacts is the appropriate prerequisite for influence would seem to depend on whether the system is established or flexible.

Regions are contexts for intergovernmental negotiations. Negotiating patterns are related to various types of regional systems. Focusing on integration schemes, negotiators in cooperative systems work toward coordinating different strategies and conceptions. Striving for a competitive advantage, negotiators in conflictual systems work toward the resolution of small issues that will alter the balance of power ever so slightly in their favor. Aspiring to a convergence of values, negotiators in transforming systems aim their efforts in the direction of a framework agreement that will address the essence of their differences. Just how to achieve these goals is an empirical issue that has received attention: techniques for resolving cognitive conflicts, fractionating the definition of issues, and role-reversing are examples. Though difficult to implement in situ, the techniques could be reinterpreted as broad prescriptions for negotiators. Ultimately their use could impact on regional structures by leading to an acceptable comprehensive formula, by altering routinized diplomatic behavior, or by creating domestic bureaucracies with a stake in preserving the new agreement.

Finally, the following research projects are among those suggested by each of the conclusions.

(1) Cross-sectional comparisons. The content and accuracy of perceptions, assessed by interviews, could be compared for different types of regions. The regions would vary in terms of proximity of neighboring nations, frequency of intersocietal contacts, nature of relationships, and extent of cultural differences. Descriptive and evaluative dimensions of perceptions can be assessed for each of several types of roles.

(2) Longitudinal comparisons. Examine perceptions and attitudes at different points of time for regions undergoing changes in relationships or contact experiences. By charting trends in perceptions over time, the impact of specific events can be noted. Perceptions would be assessed by interviews or in simulations of regional dynamics.

(3) Identify cohorts of partisans and authorities. Effectiveness of attempts to influence prevailing societal perspectives can be compared for different types of nations within regions. The nations would vary in terms of type of social system, as well as in authorities' affiliations, orientations, and constraints on their behavior.

(4) Case studies of negotiating behavior. Negotiating patterns could be compared for regions characterized by cooperative, conflictual, or transforming relationships. Focusing on transforming regional systems, alternative techniques for producing a convergence of values could be evaluated, as well as the extent to which relationship changes coincide with changes in diplomatic behavior, negotiating process, and outcomes.

These projects would be of value to both psychologists and political scientists. On the one hand, psychological processes would be probed in complex real-world environments; on the other hand, structural explanations of political processes would be challenged by the need to take into account psychological factors. Both disciplines would benefit from a methodological strategy that combines experimentation with probes made in situ.

NOTES

(1) For example, see Herbert C. Kelman, ed., International Behavior: A Social-Psychological Analysis (New York: Holt, Rinehart and Winston, 1965); Joseph H. de Rivera, The Psychological Dimension of Foreign Policy (Columbus, Ohio: Charles E. Merrill, 1968); Jerome D. Frank, Sanity and Survival: Psychological Aspects of War and Peace (New York: Vintage, 1968); Amitai Etzioni, "Social-Psychological Aspects of International Relations," in The Handbook of Social Psychology edited by Gardner Lindsay and Elliot Aronson (Reading, Mass.: Addison-

Wesley, 1968); Robert Jervis, Perception and Misperception in International Politics (Princeton: Princeton University Press, 1976); and Margaret G. Hermann, ed., A Psychological Examination of Political Leaders (New York: The Free Press, 1977).

(2) "Carter Has Moved Into Center of Arab-Israeli Chessboard," Washington Post, September 24, 1978, p. A19.

(3) The Poland example is discussed in de Rivera, Psychological Dimension of Foreign Policy, pp. 363 ff.

(4) This approach is discussed at length in Daniel Druckman, "The Person, Role, and Situation in International Negotiations," in Hermann, A Psychological Examination of Political Leaders; and in Robert Mahoney and Daniel Druckman, "Simulation, Experimentation, and Context: Dimensions of Design and Inference," Simulation and Games, 6 (September 1975): 235-70.

(5) See Etzioni, "Social-Psychological Aspects of International Relations," p. 582.

(6) William R. Thompson, "The Regional Subsystem: A Conceptual Explication and a Propositional Inventory," International Studies Quarterly 17 (March 1973): 89-117.

(7) Bruce M. Russett, "International Regions and the International System," in Regional Politics and World Order edited by Richard A. Falk and Saul H. Mendlovitz (San Francisco: W.H. Freeman, 1973), see pp. 183-87.

(8) James G. Miller, "The Nature of Living Systems," Behavioral Science, 21 (September 1976): esp. 402-05.

(9) Robert A. LeVine and Donald T. Campbell, Ethnocentrism (New York: Wiley, 1972), Chap. 7.

(10) Donald T. Campbell, "Common Fate, Similarity, and Other Indices of the Status of Aggregates of Persons as Social Entities," Behavioral Science, 3 (January 1958): 14-25. Cooperative exchanges are suggested by the pregnance and common fate criteria. Pregnance is good continuation or good form: "Elements forming a part of spatial organization or pattern. . .tend to be perceived as part of the same unit" (LeVine and Campbell, Ethnocentrism, p. 105). Common fate is defined as "elements that move together in the same direction, and otherwise in successive temporal observations. . .are more likely to be perceived as parts of the same organization" (LeVine and Campbell, Ethnocentrism, p. 105). When applied to regions, these gestalt principles suggest degrees of interdependence among regional actors — pregnance and common fate are symptoms of highly interdependent regions.

(11) Harold Guetzkow, "Isolation and Collaboration: A Partial Theory of Inter-Nation Relations," Journal of Conflict Resolution 1 (March 1957): 48-68. A regional application is presented in Ronald Yalem, "Theories of Regionalism," in Regional Politics and World Order edited by Richard A. Falk and Saul H. Mendlovitz (San Francisco: W.H. Freeman, 1973), pp. 218-31.

(12) For example, see Theodore M. Newcomb, "Individual and Group," American Behavioral Scientist 21 (May/June 1978): 631-50.

(13) An excellent recent statement of this perspective is provided by Robert O. Keohane and Joseph S. Nye, Power and Interdependence: World Politics in Transition (Boston: Little, Brown, 1977).

(14) Charles Pentland, International Theory and European Integration (New York: The Free Press, 1973), pp. 50-51.

(15) For a systematic treatment of the effects of exchange programs see Richard L. Merritt, "Effects of International Student Exchange," in Communication in International Politics, edited by Richard L. Merritt (Urbana: University of Illinois Press, 1972), pp. 65-94.

(16) This is a two-way street. Hypotheses generated from field studies can be tested in the laboratory and vice versa. This interplay is illustrated by P. Terrence Hopmann and Charles Walcott, "The Impact of External Stresses and Tensions on Negotiations," in Negotiations: Social-Psychological Perspectives edited by Daniel Druckman (Beverly Hills: Sage, 1977), pp. 301-23. Another example of field to laboratory analysis is Daniel Druckman, Richard Rozelle, and Kathleen Zechmeister, "Conflict of Interest and Value Dissensus," in Druckman, Negotiations, pp. 105-31. Another example of laboratory to field analysis is P. Terrence Hopmann and Teresa C. Smith, "An Application of a Richardson Process Model: Soviet-American Interactions in the Test Ban Negotiations 1962-1963," Journal of Conflict Resolution 21 (December 1977): 701-26. A looser application of laboratory-derived hypotheses can be found in John W. Burton, Conflict and Communication: The Use of Controlled Communication in International Relations (London: Macmillan, 1969).

(17) William A. Gamson, Power and Discontent (Homewood, Illinois: The Dorsey Press, 1968), esp. chap. 2.

(18) Pentland, International Theory and European Integration, pp. 48-51.

(19) Karl W. Deutsch, Nationalism and Social Communication: An Inquiry into the Foundations of Nationality (New York: Wiley, 1953), Chaps. 4 and 8. See also Karl W. Deutsch, The Nerves of Government (New York: The Free Press, 1963).

(20) LeVine and Campbell, Ethnocentrism, p. 160.

(21) Daniel Druckman, "Ethnocentrism in the Inter-Nation Simulation," Journal of Conflict Resolution 12 (March 1968): 45-68.

(22) George Modelski, "The World's Foreign Ministers: A Political Elite," Journal of Conflict Resolution 14 (June 1970): 135-75.

(23) Daniel Druckman, Faizunisa Ali, and J. Susana Bagur, "Determinants of Stereotypy in Three Cultures," International Journal of Psychology 9 (December 1974): 293-302.

(24) Wallace E. Lambert and Otto Klineberg, Children's Views of Foreign Peoples (New York: Appleton-Century-Crofts, 1967), esp. chap. 9.

(25) LeVine and Campbell, Ethnocentrism, p. 163.

(26) Robert K. Merton, Social Theory and Social Structure (Glencoe, Illinois: The Free Press, 1957), chap. 9.

(27) Donald T. Campbell, "Social Attitudes and Other Acquired Behavioral Dispositions," in Psychology: A Study of a Science edited by Sigmund Koch (New York: McGraw-Hill, 1963), pp. 94-172.

(28) Each of these effects of stress was demonstrated in laboratory experiments. Reviews of these studies can be found in Hopmann and Walcott, "The Impact of External Stresses," pp. 301-23, and in Daniel Druckman, Human Factors in International Negotiations: Social-Psychological Aspects of International Conflict (Beverly Hills, Calif.: Sage, 1973), pp. 55-60.

(29) The argument that perceptual rigidity hinders strategic flexibility is made by E.C. Hargrove, "Presidential Personality and Revisionist Views of the Presidency," American Journal of Political Science 17 (June 1973): 819-35; and by Charles Lockhart, "Flexibility and Commitment in International Conflicts," International Studies Quarterly 22 (December 1978): 545-68.

(30) For example, see chapters II and III in Report to the Commission on the Organization of the Government for the Conduct of Foreign Policy, vol. 2, Appendix D, by Alexander George (Washington, D.C.: Government Printing Office, 1975).

(31) Jervis, Perception and Misperception in International Politics, 1976.

(32) Lockhart, "Flexibility and Commitment," p. 555.

(33) Ernst B. Haas, The Obsolescence of Regional Integration Theory (Berkeley: University of California Press, 1975), pp. 33-34.

(34) Herbert C. Kelman, "Israelis and Palestinians: Psychological Pre-requisites for Peace," International Security 3 (Summer 1978): 176-77.

(35) See G.H. Boehringer, V. Zeroulis, J. Bayley, and K. Boehringer, "Stirling: The Destructive Application of Group Techniques to a Con-flict," Journal of Conflict Resolution 18 (June 1974): 257-75.

(36) The place of exchange programs in the context of foreign policy is discussed by Merritt, "Effects of International Student Exchange," pp. 65-94.

(37) See Keohane and Nye, Power and Interdependence, 1977.

(38) For an example of a recent treaty that included provisions for exchanges of scientific and technical personnel, see Supplementary Agreement Number 3 of Treaty of Friendship and Cooperation with Spain, submitted by Secretary of State Henry A. Kissinger to the President of the United States (Washington, D.C.: Government Printing Office, 1976).

(39) Experimental results on the effects of contact are reviewed by Louis W. Stern, Richard P. Bagozzi, and Ruby Roy Dholakia, "Media-tional Mechanisms in Interorganizational Conflict," in Druckman, ed., Negotiations, see pp. 370-73.

(40) R.T. Morris, The Two-Way Mirror: National Status in Foreign Students' Adjustment (Minneapolis: University of Minnesota Press, 1960).

(41) Anita L. Mishler, "Personal Contact in International Exchanges," in Kelman (ed.) International Behavior, pp. 553-54.

(42) Merritt, "Effects of International Student Exchange," pp. 69-70. However, equal-status contacts may not produce favorable attitudes when the valence of the experience is negative. Salter and Teger found that equal status between visitors and hosts did not affect attitudes as much as did the valence of the experience. If the contact was under unpleasant circumstances, the possible benefit of genuine intimate contact was overruled (see Charles A. Salter and Allan I. Teger, "Change in Attitudes Toward Other Nations as a Function of the Type of International Conflict," Sociometry 38 (June 1975): 213-222).

(43) See Mishler, "Personal Contact in International Exchanges," pp. 556-57.

(44) Herbert C. Kelman and Lotte Bailyn, "Effects of Cross-Cultural Experience on National Images: A Study of Scandinavian Students in America," Journal of Conflict Resolution 6 (December 1962): 319-34.

(45) Exchange programs may work best in regions where relationships are in the process of changing. This may be the case for three reasons: a) a "honeymoon period" provides an atmosphere conducive to change; b) rivalries and hostilities are less intense, and c) lacking a history of cooperation renders the experience one that will not merely reinforce existing positive attitudes. Given the changed atmosphere in the Middle East, Kelman's list of psychological prerequisites for achieving peace in that region are timely. See Kelman, "Israelis and Palestinians," especially pp. 176-85.

(46) Note especially the results of the Stirling workshop reported in three articles of the Journal of Conflict Resolution 18 (June 1974): Leonard W. Doob and William J. Foltz, "The Impact of a Workshop Upon Grass Roots Leaders in Belfast," pp. 237-56; G.H. Boehringer et al., "Stirling," p. 257-75; and Daniel I. Avery et al., "Rationale, Research, and Role Relations in the Stirling Workshop," pp. 276-84.

(47) Herbert C. Kelman, "The Problem-Solving Workshop in Conflict Resolution," in Merritt, Communication in International Politics, p. 175.

(48) For example, Burton, Conflict and Communication; Resolving Conflicts in Africa: The Fermeda Workshop edited by Leonard W. Doob (New Haven: Yale, 1970); and Stephen P. Cohen et al., "Evolving Intergroup Techniques for Conflict Resolution," Journal of Social Issues 33 (Winter 1977): 165-89.

(49) On problems of recruiting participants, see Leonard W. Doob, "A Cyprus Workshop: An Exercise in Intervention Methodology," Journal of Social Psychology 94 (December 1974): 161-78; on the importance of location, see Kelman, "The Problem-Solving Workshop in Conflict Resolution"; for two types of third-party intervention, compare Burton, Conflict and Communication, to Doob, Resolving Conflicts in Africa; on problems of timing, see Daniel Druckman and Thomas Bonoma, "A Conflict Resolution Workshop for Health Service-Delivery Professionals: Design and Appraisal," International Journal of Group Tensions 7 (March 1977): 1-28; and for a treatment of the structured/unstructured activity issue, see Cohen et al., "Evolving Intergroup Techniques."

(50) Doob, Resolving Conflicts in Africa; Burton, Conflict and Communication.

(51) Other dimensions of difference exist between the approaches. These are treated at length in the comparison made by Kelman in "The Problem-Solving Workshop."

(52) Ibid., and Boehringer et al., "Stirling."

(53) Merton, Social Theory.

(54) Kenneth R. Hammond, "New Directions in Research on Conflict Resolution," Journal of Social Issues 21 (Winter 1965): 44-66.

(55) See Druckman et al., "Conflict of Interest and Value Dissensus."

(56) Cohen et al., "Evolving Intergroup Techniques."

(57) For a recent review of these experiments see Phillip G. Zimbardo, Ebbe B. Ebbeson, and Christina Maslach, Influencing Attitudes and Changing Behaviors (Reading, Mass.: Addison Wesley, 1977).

(58) This is demonstrated in an applied setting by Jacobo A. Varela, Psychological Solutions to Social Problems: An Introduction to Social Technology (New York: Academic Press, 1971).

(59) For a review of the empirical literature, see Daniel Druckman, "The Influence of the Situation in Inter-Party Conflict," Journal of Conflict Resolution 15 (December 1971): 523-54. For a survey of the recent work on intercultural communication, see Molefi K. Asante, Eileen Newmark, and Cecil A. Blake, eds., Handbook of Intercultural Communication (Beverly Hills: Sage, 1979).

(60) Kelman, "The Problem-Solving Workshop," p. 177.

(61) Ibid., Doob and Foltz, "The Impact of a Workshop."

(62) Druckman and Bonoma, "A Conflict Resolution Workshop."

(63) The empirical relationship may be curvilinear. Citing early studies on retention of memorized material, Hilgard concluded that "(w)ith maximum similarity, the interpolated activity provides positive transfer, hence increases the efficiency of recall. Maximum interference with recall is predicted to fall at some intermediate value of similarity." Ernest R. Hilgard, Theories of Learning (New York: Appleton-Century-Crofts, 1956), pp. 344-45.

(64) Gamson, Power and Discontent.

(65) The aspirant-selector interaction is described in Robert D. Putnam, The Comparative Study of Political Elites (Englewood Cliffs, N.J.: Prentice-Hall, 1976), see chapter 3 on elite recruitment.

(66) The cosmopolitan/local distinction is made by Merton, Social Theory and Social Structure, chap. 10; the distinction between intramural and extramural selectors is made by Putnam, The Comparative

Study of Political Elites, chap. 3, and the effects of accountability to constituents were obtained in an experiment reported by James A. Breaugh and Richard J. Klimoski, "The Choice of a Group Spokesman in Bargaining: Member or Outsider," Organizational Behavior and Human Performance 19 (1977): 325-36.

(67) Robert D. Putnam, "The Political Attitudes of Senior Civil Servants in Britain, Germany, and Italy," in The Mandarins of Western Europe edited by Mattei Dogan (New York: Halsted Press, 1975), pp. 87-127.

(68) The established/flexible distinction also has implications for problem-solving workshops. Ideal types of participants may differ in the two types of systems. The less permeable established political systems would seem to require as participants those who are closer to the locus of decision making. This requirement may be relaxed in more flexible systems; those further removed from the decision making process have a greater chance of influencing the prevailing perspectives.

(69) Emphasized by the above conceptualization is the idea that change is contingent on influencing central decision makers. However, direct communication is only one of the methods for influencing them. Effectiveness would seem to depend on efforts exerted in several directions by multiple actors. Implied here is a "more total view of the international political process and its ramifications" (Kelman, "The Problem-Solving Workshop," p. 201).

(70) Stephen G. Walker, "The Congruence Between Foreign Policy Rhetoric and Behavior: Insights From Role Theory and Exchange Theory." Paper presented at the Annual Meeting of the International Society of Political Psychology, Washington, D.C., May 26, 1979. Low correlations between attitudes and behaviors are also found in the social-psychological literature. For a review of these studies and an appreciation for the complexity of the issue, see Allan W. Wicker, "Attitudes Versus Actions: The Relationship of Verbal and Overt Behavioral Responses to Attitude Objects," Journal of Social Issues 25 (Autumn 1969): 41-78.

(71) W. Andrew Axline, "Integration and Development in the Commonwealth Caribbean: The Politics of Regional Negotiations," International Organization 32 (Autumn 1978): 953-73.

(72) Anselm Strauss, Negotiations: Varieties, Contexts, Processes, and Social Order (San Francisco: Jossey-Bass, 1978), pp. 161-62.

(73) Ibid., p. 172.

(74) An extended discussion of the problem of coordination in international negotiations can be found in Druckman, "The Person, Role, and Situation in International Negotiations," pp. 422-27.

(75) Barbara G. Haskel, "Disparities, Strategies, and Opportunity Costs: The Example of Scandinavian Economic Market Negotiations," International Studies Quarterly 18 (March 1974): 3-30.

(76) For the Scandinavian negotiations, see Ibid.; for UDEAC, see Lynn K. Mytelka, "Fiscal Politics and Regional Redistribution: Bargaining Strategies in Asymmetrical Integration Systems," Journal of Conflict Resolution 19 (March 1975): 138-60; for CARICOM, see Axline, "Integration and Development in the Commonwealth Caribbean."

(77) The "hard" versus "soft" distinction was introduced in P. Terrence Hopmann, "Bargaining in Arms Control Negotiations: The Seabeds Denuclearization Treaty," International Organization 28 (Summer 1974): 313-43.

(78) These findings were obtained in three experiments: G. Matthew Bonham, "Simulating International Disarmament Negotiations," Journal of Conflict Resolution 15 (September 1971): 299-315; Daniel Druckman, "Position Change in Cognitive Conflict As a Function of the Cue-Criterion Relationship and the Initial Conflict," Psychonomic Science 20 (1970): 91-93; and David A. Summers, "Conflict, Compromise, and Belief Change in a Decision Making Task," Journal of Conflict Resolution 12 (June 1968): 215-21.

(79) See W. Andrew Axline, Caribbean Integration: The Politics of Regionalism (New York: Nichols, 1979), p. 128.

(80) For a discussion of gains from investment schemes, see Haskel, "Disparities, Strategies, and Opportunity Costs"; the uniform versus variable tax rate issue is presented by Mytelka, "Fiscal Politics and Regional Redistribution"; and the free trade area proposed solutions are discussed by Axline, Caribbean Integration.

(81) The cognitive conflict experiments are reviewed in Berndt Brehmer and Kenneth R. Hammond, "Cognitive Factors in Interpersonal Conflict," in Druckman, Negotiations, pp. 79-103. Special attention is given to technical aids in Kenneth R. Hammond and Berndt Brehmer, "Quasi-Rationality and Distrust: Implications for International Conflict," in Human Judgment and Social Interaction edited by Leon Rappoport and David A. Summers (New York: Holt, Rinehart, and Winston, 1973), pp. 338-91.

(82) See, for example, Brian H. Tracy, "Bargaining as Trial and Error: The Case of the Spanish Base Negotiations 1963-1970," in The Negotiation Process: Theories and Applications edited by I. William Zartman (Beverly Hills: Sage, 1978), pp. 193-224.

(83) Strauss, Negotiations, chapter 13.

(84) Jane M. O. Sharp, "MBFR as Arms Control," Arms Control Today 6 (April 1976): 1.

(85) Fred Charles Ikle, How Nations Negotiate (New York: Harper & Row, 1964), chapter 4.

(86) Experimental evidence is presented in Kathleen Zechmeister and Daniel Druckman, "Determinants of Resolving a Conflict of Interest: A Simulation of Political Decision-Making," Journal of Conflict Resolution, 17 (March 1973): pp. 63-88; and in Druckman et al., "Conflict of Interest and Value Dissensus."

(87) Daniel Druckman and Kathleen Zechmeister, "Conflict of Interest and Value Dissensus: Propositions in the Sociology of Conflict," Human Relations 26 (August 1973): 449-66.

(88) Spiraling effects can be seen in negotiations between alliances. Increased cohesion by one bloc has been observed as resulting from increased accusations made by the other. (See Ole R. Holsti, P. Terrence Hopmann, and John D. Sullivan, Unity and Disintegration in International Alliances: Comparative Studies (New York: Wiley, 1973). Through time the blocs become increasingly polarized as the process unfolds recursively.

(89) The concept of "fractionation" was introduced in Roger Fisher, "Fractionating Conflict," in International Conflict and Behavioral Science edited by Roger Fisher (New York: Basic Books, 1964). The effectiveness of controlling the size of issues in bargaining is demonstrated by Morton Deutsch, Donnah Canavan, and Jeffrey Rubin, "The Effects of Size of Conflict and Sex of Experimenter Upon Interpersonal Bargaining," Journal of Experimental Social Psychology 7 (July 1971): 258-67.

(90) This argument is made in Daniel Druckman, Human Factors in International Negotiations, pp. 17-19; and in Sharp, "MBFR as Arms Control."

(91) I. William Zartman, "Negotiations: Theory and Reality," Journal of International Affairs 9 (January 1975): 69-77.

(92) I. William Zartman and Maureen R. Berman, "The Practical Negotiator," (New York: Academy for Educational Development, 1978), p. 75 (mimeo.).

(93) The Trieste example is discussed in John C. Campbell, Successful Negotiations: Trieste 1954 (Princeton, N.J.: Princeton University Press, 1976). The Cyprus and Vietnam examples are discussed in Zartman and Berman, "The Practical Negotiator."

(94) One set of prescriptions is: (1) Keep flexible and comprehensive; (2) remember that the problem, not the opponent, is the "enemy" to be overcome; (3) do not be deterred by unfriendly behavior; (4) keep talking; and (5) think of detailed applications while thinking of broader formulas (Zartman and Berman, "The Practical Negotiator," pp. 121-24). Although ultimately both sides should adhere to these suggestions, unilateral adoption is not precluded. One side's behavior may serve as a model for the other.

(95) Karl Deutsch, The Analysis of International Relations (Englewood Cliffs, N.J.: Prentice-Hall, 1968), p. 131.

(96) Anatol Rapoport, Strategy and Conscience (New York: Harper and Row, 1964).

(97) These conditions illustrate the types of variables investigated in laboratory settings. They are, however, only a small sample. Others include accountability to constituents, agendas, concession rates, pre-negotiation experience, salient solutions, size of issues, stresses, and third parties. Since most of the findings would seem to have implications for negotiations in general rather than for regional negotiations in particular, only fleeting attention has been paid to them in this section. For recent reviews of results, the interested reader is referred to Druckman, Negotiations, and to Druckman, "The Person, Role, and Situation in International Negotiations."

(98) Timothy D. King, "Role Reversal and Problem Solving in International Negotiations: The Partial Nuclear Test Ban Case" (Ph.D. Dissertation, University of Minnesota, 1978).

(99) Keohane and Nye, Power and Interdependence.

(100) The direction of causation emphasized in the literature has been from structures to behaviors. This emphasis may be due in part to an assumption that structures are relatively invariant while behaviors (or events) are episodic. See Daniel Druckman and Robert Mahoney, "Processes and Consequences of International Negotiations," Journal of Social Issues 33 (Winter 1977): especially pp. 79-83.

(101) Erich Weede, "World Order in the Fifties and Sixties: Dependence, Deterrence, and Limited Peace," Papers, Peace Science Society (International), 24 (1975): 49-80.

(102) Jeffrey Z. Rubin and Bert R. Brown, The Social Psychology of Bargaining and Negotiation (New York: Academic Press, 1975), pp. 262-69.

(103) See Johan Galtung, "Small Group Theory and the Theory of International Relations: A Study in Isomorphism," in New Approaches to

International Relations edited by Mortan A. Kaplan (New York: St. Martin's Press, 1968), pp. 270-302.

(104) Sharp, "MBFR as Arms Control."

(105) Campbell, Successful Negotiation, p. 157.

(106) Galtung, "Small Group Theory," p. 293.

(107) A discussion of how this has worked in the area of arms control can be found in Abram Chayes, "An Inquiry into the Workings of Arms Control Agreements," Harvard Law Review 85 (1972): 905-69.

(108) Deutsch, Nationalism and Social Communication, Pentland, International Theory and European Integration; Haas, The Obsolescence of Regional Integration Theory.

(109) Glenda G. Rosenthal, The Men Behind the Decisions (Lexington, Mass.: Lexington Books, 1975), p. 134.

(110) Keohane and Nye, Power and Interdependence. See also the reviews by Kal J. Holsti, "A New International Politics? Diplomacy in Complex Interdependence," International Organization, 32 (Spring 1978): 513-30; and by Henry R. Nau, "From Integration to Interdependence: Gains, Losses, and Continuing Gaps," International Organization 33 (Winter 1979): pp. 119-47.

(111) These processes are explicated in the context of international relations by Glenn H. Snyder and Paul Diesing, Conflict Among Nations: Bargaining, Decision-Making, and System Structure in International Crises (Princeton: Princeton University Press, 1977), chapter 4. See also Daniel Druckman, "Boundary Role Conflict: Negotiation as Dual Responsiveness," Journal of Conflict Resolution 21 (December 1977): 639-62.

3 Regional Patterns of Economic Cooperation*

Harold K. Jacobson
Dusan Sidjanski

FACTORS IN REGIONAL ECONOMIC COOPERATION

Regional economic cooperation has become a salient feature of world politics in the latter half of the twentieth century. Numerous agreements for regional economic cooperation have been signed and ratified. International institutions have been established to oversee the implementation of these agreements. In some instances, intraregional trade among the states adhering to an agreement has increased sharply and significantly, and there have been numerous other important achievements of regional economic cooperation as well. This chapter explores the reasons for the present prominence of regional economic cooperation, analyzes the systems that exist and what they have accomplished, and probes the significance of regional patterns of economic cooperation for the global political system and its future.

A simple explanation for the contemporary prominence of regional economic cooperation would be that productive processes have outgrown most, and perhaps all, nation states; most, if not all, nation states are too small to be effective economic units in the contemporary period. Several arguments could be marshaled to support this explanation. Hardly any states have within their own borders all of the resources needed for modern production. Few contemporary nation states contain sufficient population to constitute markets that would allow manufacturers to take full advantage of opportunities for economies of scale. Some modern technology is so expensive as to be beyond the means of most nation states or of firms operating in single nation states. Transnational corporations (TNCs) have become so large and their operations so extensive that single nation states are incapable

*This chapter is an outgrowth of a research project that has been supported by a grant from the Ford Foundation. We gratefully acknowledge this assistance.

of monitoring them and guiding or controlling their behavior. Environmental pollution resulting from production processes frequently cannot be confined within the borders of a single nation state. Even this brief list of arguments constitutes a compelling case for regional economic cooperation.

It would, however, be incorrect to explain contemporary patterns of regional economic cooperation just in economic terms. A desire to be able to deal more effectively with purely economic issues has hardly ever been the sole motive in the creation and successful operation of a regional economic cooperation system, and sometimes it has not even been the most important motive. Nor would pure economic rationality explain the membership of all contemporary economic cooperation systems, some of which contain states that are not even geographically contiguous. Factors other than economic issues are also crucially important to explain the contemporary patterns of regional economic cooperation. Tradition and the desire for greater power, influence, and security have all played vital roles, as will become apparent when we examine particular systems.

Doctrines Concerning Economic Cooperation

Before dealing with the various individual systems for regional economic cooperation, though, we need to consider certain general economic issues that are involved in regional cooperation.

From the eighteenth century, when the processes of industrialization began to gain momentum, until now nation states have provided the organizing framework for economic development. Nation states have made specialization in production and exchange possible by minting money and by creating legal systems that would structure and enforce contractual relationships. In principle, there is no reason why there could not be as much specialization and trade among nation states as there has been within nation states. Indeed, liberal economists have always argued that production and, thus, welfare would be maximized if there were free trade that would allow maximum specialization among states. In practice, however, barriers to international trade have been ubiquitous. States have enacted tariffs which increase the price of imports to consumers and, presumably, thereby decrease the demand for them. Such tariffs may have been enacted merely to gain revenue to support the operations of government, but they also can have the purpose of limiting imports and, thereby, protecting domestic industry. More recently, states have also enacted quantitative restrictions which precisely limit imports. Some states have established monopolies for foreign trade, and the bureaucratic organizations controlling these monopolies determine how much of which products shall be imported and from which states and, also, what to export and to which states. Controlling foreign exchange can have virtually the same consequences. There are also numerous other national regulations relating, for example, to health matters and licensing requirements that constitute barriers to trade whether or not they were intended to have this effect.

Regional economic cooperation has many meanings in the contemporary period, but common to virtually all of them is the mutual granting by members of regional systems of preferential treatment with respect to limitations on trade. Classical liberal economic doctrine has defined different types of regional economic cooperation.(1) In a free trade area, tariffs and other barriers to trade are eliminated among the states participating in the system. In a customs union, in addition to eliminating barriers to internal trade, the member states adopt a uniform tariff for trade with third parties. A common market is a customs union in which there is a free flow of factors of production; labor and capital can move from one state participating in the system to another without restriction. An economic union includes the features of a common market and, in addition, the economic policies of the member states are harmonized. Complete economic integration would add full unification of economic institutions and policies, including the adoption of a common monetary system. These terms can be useful reference points, even though actual agreements for regional economic cooperation seldom conform exactly to such ideal types. Often elements of one type are mixed with those of others, and the terms are frequently used indiscriminately.

From the perspective of classical liberal economic doctrine, regional economic cooperation must always be a second best solution, global free trade is the proper formula for maximizing welfare. But the choice that national and international leaders and officials have faced has not been between global free trade and regional economic cooperation, but rather what steps should and could be taken to lessen the many obstacles to trade that nations have erected.

Economic analysis has demonstrated that, even from the free trade perspective, regional economic cooperation can have beneficial effects. In his classic study, Jacob Viner pointed out that, if the consequences of a customs union is to shift production from a higher cost domestic source within one member state of the union to a lower cost source in another member state, new trade will have been created by the establishment of such a union.(2) If, on the other hand, production is shifted from a lower cost source outside the union to a higher cost source within the union, trade will have been diverted. From the perspective of free trade, then, the test of the merits of a particular customs union is whether or not, on balance, its trade creation effects are greater than its trade diversion effects. Beyond these, what are termed static effects of customs unions, there can also be dynamic effects. Eliminating obstacles to trade among the members of a customs union will create a larger market that should stimulate investment. Firms that previously were in a privileged position in national markets could be faced with competition from firms in other member states, and this competition should promote efficiency. If the static and dynamic effects of a customs union contribute to accelerated economic growth in the member states of a customs union, this could lead to increased trade between the members of the union and other states, and, thus, could contribute to increased global welfare. In terms of classical liberal economic doctrine, whether the creation of a particular customs union should be favored or opposed can only be determined after an analysis of the projected consequences of a particular agreement; a general answer is impossible. Nor is it possible to define in the abstract natural domains for regional economic cooperation.

Beyond the justification for regional economic cooperation in classical doctrine, two other doctrines have been developed. The first of these is, in some respects, a variant on the classical argument. The classical argument was developed in the context of market economies, and it is particularly applicable to such economies where the market forces of supply and demand as expressed in prices determine what should be produced and how it should be distributed. The argument rests heavily on the doctrine of comparative advantage, the notion that welfare will be maximized by states specializing in the production of those items in which they are most efficient, or which they can produce at the least cost.

To be applied to states with planned economies, the classical, liberal position about customs unions requires some modification. In planned economies, planners rather than the market determine what should be produced and how it should be distributed. They also set prices. When a group of market economies eliminates obstacles to trade, shifts in production will occur as a result of market forces. Trade among planned economies, on the other hand, can only be based on national planners providing for such trade in their national plans. Between 1917 and 1945, when the USSR was the only state to have a centrally planned economy, planning was done on an overwhelmingly national basis; and in the years immediately following World War II, this tradition was continued in the USSR and was extended to the states in Eastern Europe that had newly established communist regimes. Communist planners conceived international trade almost exclusively as a device for obtaining goods, materials, and services that could not be obtained domestically. An important reason for communist planners not according much importance to international trade in these years was the assumption in communist doctrine of enduring hostility between communist and capitalist states. Therefore, it would be unwise to be dependent on a presumed enemy. In addition, for a communist country to give much importance to trade with capitalist economies where market forces determined the quantity of goods to be produced and at what price would introduce uncertainties that could enormously complicate planners' tasks.

After World War II, however, a new situation emerged. There were several communist countries, each with a centrally planned economy, and international trade among them need involve neither the ideologically objectionable consequence of becoming dependent upon presumed foes nor the technical difficulty of incorporating uncontrolled elements into national economic plans. Soon there was discussion in the communist world of an international socialist division of labor, and principles were elaborated to guide specialization among communist states.(3) Like the doctrine of comparative advantage, these principles maintain that there should be specialization in production among communist countries according to efficiency. Countries should specialize in the production of those goods for which they are most efficient. However, the principles limit specialization by mandating that each country should have a "balanced economy" and that historical differences in levels of economic development among individual countries should be eliminated. Since the principles contain no guidelines for the harmonization of these objectives with that of promoting efficiency, and since calculating relative efficiency in the absence of prices determined by market forces is difficult, when central planners attempt to arrange international trade among countries with centrally planned economies, the process can involve at least as much bargaining as the application of rational analytical techniques.

There are, consequently, important differences between the practice of regional economic cooperation among states with centrally planned economies and that among market economies, as well as in the rationales guiding such cooperation. The governments of countries with market economies need only alter barriers to trade; private entrepreneurs guided by the interacton of supply and demand as reflected in prices will, then, determine the location and level of production. When communist countries cooperate, these matters must be settled by bargaining and agreement among central planners.

The other new doctrine that has been developed to justify regional economic cooperation applies particularly to less developed countries (LDCs). In terms of classical liberal economic theory, the case for regional economic cooperation among LDCs is unconventional, for it involves essentially competitive rather than complementary economies. The traditional argument assumed that the states involved in regional economic cooperation would already conduct substantial trade among themselves, and eliminating obstacles to this trade would permit economies of scale by enlarging the size of the market and promote greater efficiency by increasing competition and facilitating specialization. Less developed states, however, usually exported the same primary products to and imported finished goods from industrialized countries with very little trade among themselves. To maintain that their economies should be merged required a different rationale from that contained in classical liberal economic doctrine. Raul Prebisch, in his capacity first as Executive Secretary of the United Nations Economic Commission for Latin America (ECLA) and then as Secretary-General of the United Nations Conference on Trade and Development (UNCTAD) played a major role in formulating and propagating this new rationale.(4)

The case that he and others developed rested on the assumption that industrialization was vital to significant economic development. Starting from this premise, they argued that developing countries should produce domestically substitutes for manufactured goods that they previously imported, and that the scope for a strategy of achieving industrialization by import substitution could be substantially increased

if markets of a sufficiently large size were available. Regional economic cooperation would be a way of creating larger markets. Prebisch and
the others further maintained that, as they developed, the newly
created industries would require protection against competition from
firms in the industrialized countries. Regional economic cooperation
could provide this protection.

Prebisch and other advocates with similar views also favored LDCs
pursuing export-oriented industrialization strategies; that is, strategies
that involved promoting the production of industrial goods for export to
the developed countries. Import substitution could be a prelude to
export promotion. The doctrine that they propounded argued that
through industrialization the LDCs could, in addition to raising their
levels of per capita gross national product (GNP), diversify their
exports and reduce their dependency on the export of one or a few basic
products to one or a limited number of developed countries for earning
foreign exchange.

Thus, while regional economic cooperation among already industrialized countries has as one of its objectives eliminating inefficient
producers, regional economic cooperation among LDCs seeks to protect
newly-established and uncompetitive producers until they become more
efficient. While the classical liberal economic doctrine concerning
regional economic cooperation stresses eliminating barriers to trade
among participating countries, the doctrine that Prebisch advanced also
stresses erecting barriers against trade with nonparticipating countries.
This doctrine further maintains that LDCs should use regional economic
cooperation as a means of increasing their bargaining power vis-a-vis
already industrialized countries.

Given the importance attached to the development of new industry,
the weakness of market mechanism in LDCs, and the tendency of
undirected new investment there to concentrate in the already more
developed areas among them, the doctrine postulates that a considerable measure of central direction will be required at both the state and
interstate levels to direct investment so as to insure an equitable
distribution. Thus, the doctrine has elements in common with that
created to guide regional economic cooperation among states with
centrally planned economies.

These, then, are the basic economic doctrines that guide contemporary regional economic cooperation. They have had an important
influence on international affairs in the second half of the twentieth
century. Before examining the extent of regional economic cooperation
in the contemporary world and its achievements, however, we need to
review aspects of the development of the world economy, especially in
the period between the two world wars.

The Protectionism of the 1930s and the Post-World
War II Commitment to Free Trade

Since the beginning of industrialization in the eighteenth century, the level of obstacles to international trade has fluctuated. During the nineteenth century, Britain, the pioneer industrializing state and the premier economic power, attempted to lead the world in the direction of free trade. It began reducing its tariffs in the 1820s and finally adopted a policy of free trade in 1846 with the repeal of the corn laws. The Cobden-Chevalier Treaty between Britain and France in 1860 constituted a major advance toward free trade among the economically most important states of the time. The free trade movement, however, was not universal. The United States adopted protective tariffs virtually at the outset of its independence, and maintained them throughout the nineteenth century; and Germany adopted a protective tariff in 1879. Throughout the nineteenth century, trade within colonial empires was privileged. Trade between the metropole and its colonies was not subject to the same obstacles that a metropolitan country might enforce against other countries; and, in certain instances, this was also true of trade among a country's colonies. The most important instance of regional economic cooperation was the Zolverein, starting in 1819, which united an increasing number of German states in a customs union that endured until German unification was completed in 1871. The level of the Zolverein's external tariffs, though, was modest. Despite the exclusivist policies of colonial empires and the protectionist policies of the United States and Imperial Germany, during the nineteenth century, there was a general sense of movement toward an open world market under British leadership. International trade grew substantially.

World War I fundamentally dislocated the global economy and interrupted its growth. The governments of the major belligerent states assumed control of large portions of their foreign trade so that it could be integrated into their war production efforts and so as to deny the benefits of trade to enemy states. When the revolution established the communist regime in Russia in 1917, state control of foreign trade became a permanent feature there. Attempts were made throughout the 1920s to reestablish an open world market, but they ultimately proved futile. In 1930, after the stock market crash, the United States adopted the Smoot-Hawley Tariff, which raised already high American tariffs even higher, doubling them in some instances. Other countries retaliated. Economic difficulties spread throughout the world. In 1931, Britain was forced to abandon the gold standard; the following year it adopted its first protective tariff since the repeal of the corn acts. A few months later, Britain and other commonwealth states adopted the system of commonwealth preferences, whereby their trade with one another would be subject to lower duties than would apply to trade with other countries.

The principal advocate for free trade abandoned the quest and turned instead to trade within the protected area of its commonwealth and empire. Other metropolitan countries followed a similar policy.

After Hitler came to power, German trade was increasingly directed toward the smaller states in Southeastern Europe and toward Latin America. International trade increasingly came to be conducted within economic groups rather than on a global basis, and the volume of trade declined instead of growing as it did in the nineteenth century. During the late 1920s, the average annual value of world exports was $32 billion; in the late 1930s it was only $23 billion.(5) Patterns of trade shifted dramatically. Between 1929 and 1938, Britain's imports from Europe fell by 16 percent while its imports from Oceania (principally Australia and New Zealand) increased by 53 percent.(6) During this same period, France's imports from Europe fell by 21 percent while its imports from Africa rose by 75 percent. Belgium and the Netherlands similarly redirected their trade toward their colonies.

World War II disrupted the global economy still further. Then, however, as the planning for the peace settlement and postwar period proceeded, the United States assumed the role that Britain had played in the nineteenth century of being the leading advocate of free trade. The United States GNP had become the largest in the world as early as the last third of the nineteenth century, and by the turn of the century it was twice as large as that of Great Britain. The United States' move away from protectionism began with the passage of the Trade Agreements Act of 1934. This act permitted the President to reduce tariffs by as much as 50 percent in return for reciprocal cuts by other countries. These cuts in the U.S. tariff would be generalized to virtually all other countries. Generalizing the tariff cuts was seen as an instrument for working toward freer trade. Successive renewals of the act extended this authority. The Department of State, the President, and the majority in Congress had concluded that United States' products could compete favorably on world markets and that U.S. producers and the United States broadly would benefit from freer trade. Many Americans were particularly anxious to obtain greater access for trade to the colonial territories of the European countries. Although the United States had had this concern since the earliest days of its sovereignty, the strength of the desire had fluctuated.

By 1938, the United States had negotiated reciprocal trade agreements with 18 countries,(7) and in November of that year it negotiated an agreement with Great Britain. In August 1941, President Franklin D. Roosevelt and Prime Minister Winston Churchill issued a joint declaration, the Atlantic Charter, that outlined the common principles that the two leaders declared would govern their states' policies toward future world order. The fourth of these principles pledged access "on equal terms, to the trade and raw materials of the world. . . ."(8) When the United States provided Great Britain with supplies that were essential for its war effort under the lend-lease program, Article VII of the agreement signed in 1942 that governed the arrangements committed the two countries to take "agreed action" after the war directed "to the elimination of all forms of discriminatory treatment in international commerce, and to the reduction of tariffs and other trade barriers. . . ."(9)

In 1946 the United States proposed to the Preparatory Committee of the United Nations Economic and Social Council (ECOSOC) that a tariff negotiation be held. The proposal sought to take advantage of the renewal of Congress in 1945 of the Trade Agreements Act. The United States hoped that tariff reduction negotiations could take place simultaneously and that the agreed reductions could be extended to all countries participating in the negotiations and could be embodied in one treaty. Conferences and negotiations ensued, and in 1947 the General Agreement on Tariffs and Trade (GATT) was signed. The Agreement provides a legal framework for multilateral negotiations to reduce obstacles to trade. The United States and other countries envisaged that a broad-membership international governmental organization (IGO) would be created that would have among its functions the administration of the agreement, but it has proved impossible to establish such an IGO. Instead, over the years a rudimentary institutional structure has been created on the basis of the agreement. This institutional structure and the agreement, together commonly referred to by the acronym GATT, have provided the regime that has governed the preponderance of international trade since World War II. Twenty-three states signed the agreement in 1947; as of 1979 there were 84 contracting parties. All of the world's most important trading states, the United States, Canada, France, Italy, the Federal Republic of Germany, the United Kingdom, and Japan, have been members since the mid-1950s. Those that were among the victorious powers in World War II were among GATT's founders, and those that had been defeated joined subsequently. The most important countries with communist governments, the USSR and the People's Republic of China, have never been members. From its creation GATT's membership has regularly accounted for more than 60 percent of the value of world trade, and this proportion has grown to include more than 70 percent in the 1970s.

The most fundamental principle of GATT is nondiscrimination. The contracting parties to the agreement commit themselves to extend most-favored-nation treatment to each other; that is, contracting parties must extend to each other the most favorable tariff rates given to any country. The agreement was a broad commitment to work toward free trade. Nevertheless, in Article I, paragraph 2, the agreement expressly permitted existing preferential trading arrangements, like the system of commonwealth preferences; and Article XXIV permitted the creation of free trade areas and customs unions under certain conditions. The most general condition is that the new tariff level should not be higher or more restrictive than the general incidence of the tariffs that existed prior to the formation of the new arrangement.

Regional economic cooperation in the period since World War II, thus, took place in a context shaped by particularly strong memories of the harmful consequences of the protectionism of the 1930s and by a newly-created legal and institutional regime that committed the major trading states to lowering obstacles to trade on a nondiscriminatory basis. The GATT has been strongly backed by the state with the most powerful economy in the world, the United States. United States economic power was particularly strong during the formative years of the regime. In 1950, GNP of the United States accounted for more than a third of the world total. Even by 1975 it was almost a quarter, so U.S. policy has continued to be a major factor in the world economy.

REGIONAL ECONOMIC COOPERATION AMONG DEVELOPED STATES WITH MARKET ECONOMIES

An analysis of regional economic cooperation in the period since World War II may appropriately begin with an examination of cooperation among developed states with market economies. States in this category were the first to launch far-reaching regional schemes. The accomplishments of these schemes are more extensive in several respects than those of cooperative ventures involving states in other categories, and some of these schemes have been used as models for those that have been adopted in other geographic regions.

OEEC and OECD

The first steps toward regional economic cooperation were taken in connection with efforts for postwar reconstruction.(10) When in June 1947, in his commencement address at Harvard University, Secretary of State George C. Marshall offered extensive U.S. economic assistance for the reconstruction of Europe, he made the offer conditional upon the European states reaching agreement among themselves on their requirements and on the actions that they would take. Fear of communist advances in Europe if economic conditions were not rapidly improved spurred the United States to action. The offer of assistance was made conditional because the United States government was convinced that cooperation among the European states was essential to their recovery. It was convinced that adequate economic progress could not be achieved if the European states pursued the same nationalistic economic policies that they had followed in the 1930s.

Eighteen European countries responded by creating in April 1948 the Organization for European Economic Cooperation (OEEC).(11) OEEC formulated a joint program for reconstruction and allocated American assistance among the European recipients. In addition, it inaugurated a program to promote trade. This involved the adoption of a Code of Liberalization that committed member states to progressively eliminate quantitative restrictions on imports and the creation of a clearing system for payments for trade among the organization's members. OEEC's activities facilitated a rapid increase in intra-European trade which between 1948 and 1958 grew twice as fast as total world trade. This trade spurt made a vital contribution to European recovery.

In 1960 it was agreed that OEEC should be transformed into the Organization for Economic Cooperation and Development (OECD), and that as part of the transformation Canada and the United States should become full members. OECD has continued its predecessor's trade liberalization functions, and has added others. Eventually, Japan, Australia, and New Zealand also joined OECD so that the organization's 24 members include the developed states with market economies in Western Europe, North America, East Asia, and Oceania.(12) The level of a state's economy and the nature of its economic system have become the principal criteria for membership in the organization. Only partly in jest, the OECD is sometimes referred to as the "rich countries' club." Although its member countries accounted for only 20 percent of world population in the 1970s, they accounted for 60 percent of world production, 70 percent of world trade, and 90 percent of the development aid given to poorer countries. What binds OECD's members together is the extensive economic ties that they have with one another and the fact that they face common economic problems; at their level of development, for some purposes at least, economic regionalism has come to be defined in functional rather than geographical terms. We will return to OECD, but first it is essential to consider the economic cooperation schemes that have been developed among subsets of OECD's members.

The European Communities

The European Communities are by far the most important of these. In 1950 French Foreign Minister Robert Schuman responding to different demands expressed by European leaders and through the European movement proposed that France and the Federal Republic of Germany should place their coal and steel production under a common authority and that this scheme would be open to participation by other countries. Four other countries – Belgium, Italy, Luxembourg, and the Netherlands – joined France and Germany, and in 1952 the European Coal and Steel Community (ECSC) came into being. The ECSC treaty committed the six states to create a common market for coal and steel and it provided for the establishment of institutions with supranational powers to manage this process. The institutions were supranational because under specified conditions the High Authority, an autonomous body of the community, and the Council of Ministers could take decisions that would be binding on individuals and firms in the six states without the governments of those states having to take implementing action, as is normally the case with international governmental organizations.

Given the geographical distribution of natural resources, creating a common market for coal and steel among the six countries – particularly between France and West Germany – was a logical step to take. This rationale, however, had existed ever since coal and steel became important ingredients in production, and, although the six countries were geographically contiguous, plausible economic arguments could have been advanced to support more or less inclusive groupings. The creation of ECSC cannot be explained in economic terms alone, nor were economic motives the most important ones propelling the national leaders who prepared the treaty. The most important motivation was a concern for security, a desire to prevent the recurrence of conflict between France and Germany and, more broadly, in Western Europe. When Robert Schuman proposed the common market for coal and steel he said, "The solidarity in production thus established will make it plain that any war between France and Germany becomes not merely unthinkable, but materially impossible."(13) The controls that the victorious powers had maintained on steel production in West Germany could not be maintained indefinitely, and France feared that West Germany's steel production would soon exceed its own. France proposed to give up unilateral authority over its own steel production in return for establishing supranational control over West Germany's. French leaders also believed that integrating West Germany into a Western European supranational organization would be a way of lessening the probability of the United States and the Soviet Union becoming embroiled in a potentially disastrous controversy over the future of West and East Germany.(14) Leaders in West Germany also wanted to preclude Franco-German conflict. In addition, they saw membership in the ECSC as a way for West Germany to gain legitimacy in the global political system.

Under the pressure of deepening Cold War tensions that were stimulated by the war in Korea, in 1952 the six member countries of ECSC signed the European Defense Community (EDC), which would have merged their military forces. When, after considerable delay, the French National Assembly in effect rejected the EDC treaty by deciding not to consider it, Western European leaders who were deeply committed to the process of achieving integration began a search for other means to promote their goals. They agreed to press the six states to create a nuclear energy community and a broad economic common market. Action in these two areas could be seen as extensions of the ECSC. Nuclear power, like coal, is a source of energy; and a persuasive argument could be made that all sources of energy should be treated alike. Efforts to merge the six countries' coal and steel industries soon encountered obstacles caused by national differences in other areas, economic policies, transport and social security systems for instance. To merge coal and steel fully and successfully one would have to lessen and eliminate these other differences.

This sequence of events is important because it illustrates the continuing blending of security and economic motives in the process of Western European economic integration. The leaders of the movement have had as their objective the creation of a federation that would include France and West Germany. Decisions about how to proceed represented tactical judgments, not abstract commitments to some foreordained concept of economic regionalism. The steps that they proposed after the defeat of EDC had an economic logic and would bring economic benefits, but their pressure for action was motivated by more than this.

Prodded by the integrationists, in 1957 the six countries agreed to create the European Atomic Energy Community (EAEC or Euratom) and the European Economic Community (EEC), and the two new treaties came into effect January 1, 1958. The former committed the six countries to common, joint, and cooperative action for the development of the peaceful uses of nuclear energy and to the creation of a common market for nuclear materials in which there would be no obstacles to trade among the six countries and there would be a common tariff for trade with nonmember states. The commitment in the EEC treaty was much broader. It involved the creation of a general customs union for manufactured goods; customs duties and quantitative restrictions on trade among the six countries were to be eliminated according to a fixed time schedule that also provided for the creation of a common external tariff (CET) on trade with nonmember states. The treaty involved a commitment to take measures to insure the free movement of labor and capital within the six countries. Further, the six states agreed in the treaty to create a common market for agricultural products and to adopt a common agricultural policy (CAP). They agreed to develop a common transport policy and a common antitrust policy. The treaty also contained provisions concerning monetary and social policy and economic relations with the member countries' colonies and former colonies.

In 1967, the separate institutions created by the ECSC, Euratom, and EEC treaties were merged. Since then, common institutions have managed the affairs of the three communities. The Commission is the keystone to the structure.(15) In a conventional international governmental organization it would be termed the executive head, but its authority is much greater than one would find in a typical IGO. A collective body, the Comission consists of individuals appointed by agreement among the member states for fixed terms. In certain instances, its decisions are legally binding, but more often the Commission initiates proposals that are then considered and adopted by the Council of Ministers. The Commission had a staff in the 1970s that numbered about 8,000. The Council of Ministers is comprised, as the title implies, of ministers from the member states; which minister will sit depends upon the subject being considered. The Council generally has final authority, but it can alter a proposal of the Commission only by a unanimous decision. When decisions are taken by a qualified majority, voting is weighted roughly in accordance with the population of the member states. Despite the qualified majority that is required the voting rules preclude taking a decision that is opposed by all of the smaller states or by more than one of the larger states. There is an Assembly which has the power to give its formal opinion on actions of the Commission and Council, to force the collective resignation of the Commission, and to reject the entire budget. It also has more general budgetary power in limited areas. Since 1979 the Assembly has been comprised of representatives chosen by direct election. This has given the communities a new political dimension. Finally, there is a Court of Justice to which community institutions, states, and individuals have access. Starting in 1973 the heads of government of the member states of the European communities have met regularly to give overall political direction to the integration process. The President of the Commission has attended these sessions. In the late 1970s, the European summit regularly met three times a year.

The European Communities have made substantial progress, and that of the economic community is particularly impressive. All tariffs and quota restrictions on intracommunity trade in nonagricultural items were eliminated by July 1, 1968, and the Common External Tariff went into effect on the same date. To insure that the stimulus to competition provided by the creation of the customs union would not be lost because of collusive arrangements among firms, community agencies have implemented a vigorous antitrust policy. Substantial progress has been made toward allowing workers to move freely among the member states in search of employment, and some restrictions on the movement of capital have been eliminated. The CAP was put into effect for most commodities by mid-1966 and was completely in effect by mid-1968. The system involves common support prices for basic agricultural commodities. Threshold prices are set for imports from non-community sources. Their level is designed to insure that the price of imported commodities will be at or above the target price set for the support of the particular commodity. Variable levies are charged on imports. These are designed to make up the difference between world prices and threshold prices. Effective protection on some products can range from 50 to 100 percent. Trade and other economic relationships between the members of the community and most of their former colonies have been governed by special conventions. Community policies have gradually superseded national policies with respect to all external commercial matters, and all members of the European Communities except the United Kingdom participate in a common monetary system which began in 1979.

The United States has generally favored steps toward economic and political integration in Western Europe even though they have involved discrimination against U.S. exports since intra-community exports have received more favorable treatment than those from outside the community. The United States felt that its security interests would be best served by Western European integration. American officials wanted to prevent a recurrence of Franco-German conflict and thought that a unified Western Europe would help to counterbalance possible Soviet expansionism.

Furthermore, the United States believed that the process of European integration would stimulate the economies of the member states and, thereby, increase the demand for U.S. products. Through negotiations in GATT during the so-called Kennedy Round, the United States successfully sought to influence the level of the EEC's Common External Tariff on nonagriculture goods and to insure that it would be lower than the previously existing individual tariffs.(16) The objective was to minimize the trade diverting effects of the creation of the European Common Market. The United States has also sought, but with less success, to minimize the limits on its agricultural exports to the members of the EEC that have been imposed as a consequence of the CAP.

EFTA

The United Kingdom was invited to participate in the negotiations that led to the creation of the European Coal and Steel Community and later in those that led to the creation of Euratom and the EEC, but on both occasions it refused. The UK did not want to abandon the commonwealth preference system nor what it perceived as its special economic relationship with the United States. UK agricultural policies differed from the CAP and resulted in considerably lower food prices. There has been broad unwillingness in the UK to embrace the integrationist goals that have been the motive force for the support by many on the continent for the European Communities. At the time of the ECSC negotiations, the socialists were in power in the UK, and they were reluctant to become deeply involved with the six continental countries where centrist parties ruled. There was also some skepticism in the UK that the ambitious plans for European integration would prove feasible.

On the other hand, the UK's trade with the six countries involved in the European Communities was substantial. In 1951, when the ECSC treaty was under negotiation, exports to the six countries accounted for 10 percent of the UK's total; by 1957, when the Euratom and EEC treaties were being negotiated, this proportion had jumped to 14 percent. To avoid the discrimination against its exports that the Common External Tariff would involve, the UK explored the possibility of creating a free trade area for all of the members of OEEC, but this failed because it was unacceptable to France. The UK then turned to the creation of an alternative regional trading group, and in 1959, the UK, Austria, Denmark, Norway, Portugal, Sweden, and Switzerland signed an agreement creating the European Free Trade Association (EFTA), which came into effect the following year. The EFTA convention provides for free trade in industrial goods among the member states. There is no common external tariff. Finland negotiated an agreement of association with EFTA in 1961, and Iceland became a full member in 1970.

To some extent, EFTA fulfilled the UK's objectives. Between 1958 and 1962 the UK's exports to its partners in EFTA increased by 45 percent, and by 1962 they accounted for 12 percent of the UK's total exports. However, during the same period, the UK's exports to the six member states of the EEC increased by 73 percent, and in 1962 they accounted for 19 percent of the UK's total exports. As the 1960s developed, it became increasingly clear that the UK's economy was more closely linked with those of the members of the EEC than with those of its partners in EFTA. Moreover, the GNPs of the member states of the European Communities were growing at a considerably faster rate than that of the UK, which increased the attraction for the UK of joining the Communities.

The Enlargement and Extension of the European Communities

In 1961, the government of the United Kingdom decided to apply for membership in the European Communities, and negotiations ensued; but British entry was ultimately blocked in January 1963 by a French veto. In 1967, the government of the United Kingdom made a second attempt to join the European Communities, but its application again met the same fate. The situation did not change until after the resignation from the French presidency of Charles de Gaulle in 1969. Later that year, the heads of government of the six member states of the Communities agreed in principle to their enlargement. Negotiations with Denmark, Ireland, Norway, and the United Kingdom began June 30, 1970. They were concluded January 22, 1972. The Treaty of Accession provided that they would become members of the European Communities January 1, 1973; and Denmark, Ireland, and the United Kingdom did join the communities then. Denmark and the UK withdrew from EFTA just before they joined the European Communities; the UK's joining EEC also meant that it had to abandon its system of commonwealth preferences. Norway did not join the European Communities because the proposal to join failed to gain a majority in a special referendum that was held on the issue. Norwegian voters rejected membership, despite the fact that more than half of Norway's exports went to the member states of the Communities. A referendum on joining the Communities was also held in Denmark. Danish voters approved membership. A smaller proportion of Denmark's exports went to the member states of the Communities than of Norway's. The explanation of the pattern of voting in each country is complex; it is only necessary for present purposes to underscore that prospective economic advantage was obviously not the sole determining factor.

After Denmark, Ireland, and the United Kingdom joined the European Communities in 1973, the remaining members of EFTA – Austria, Iceland, Norway, Portugal, Sweden, and Switzerland – and the EFTA associated state – Finland – negotiated free trade agreements with the European Communities. These agreements provided for the progressive establishment of free trade in industrial products between the members of EFTA and EEC. A free trade area in industrial products between EFTA and EEC was established July 1, 1977. Most of Western Europe had become a free trade area.

In 1979, the European Communities negotiated an agreement with Greece under the terms of which Greece would become a member of the Communities on January 1, 1981. Negotiations were also underway between the Communities and Portugal and Spain, looking toward their ultimate full membership. Although expanding the European Communities to include Greece, Portugal, and Spain raised complex economic issues, the governments of the nine members of the Communities were strongly motivated to take this action. They hoped that membership in the Communities would strengthen and preserve the relatively new and fragile democratic institutions in the three countries. Again, economic rationality was not the foremost consideration in deciding the dimensions of regional economic cooperation. Noneconomic factors have been crucial in determining which states might be included in the European Communities and also in determining which states could not be included. Even though strong arguments could be made for their joining, the formal and legal neutrality of Austria, Sweden, and Switzerland makes it difficult for these countries to contemplate membership because of the integrationist goals associated with the Communities' institutions. Similarly, Finland's proximity to the Soviet Union has barred it even from full membership in EFTA.

Beyond the free trade agreements that the European Economic Community has negotiated with the members of EFTA, under the rubric of its Mediterranean policy it has also negotiated preferential trading agreements with several countries that border the Mediterranean Sea. The most extensive of these is with Turkey. Other agreements are with Cyprus and Malta, Algeria, Morocco and Tunisia, Israel, and Egypt, Jordan, and Syria. In addition 57 African, Caribbean, and Pacific (ACP) countries, (all former colonies of the community's member states), are associated with the EEC under the terms of an agreement that is periodically renegotiated. The current definition of the nature of the association was defined in the agreement negotiated in Lome in 1975 and in the revision of this agreement which was negotiated in 1979. This agreement, which replaced the previous Youande agreement, gives the ACP countries free access for many of their projects to the EEC markets and it contains arrangements for stabilizing the export earnings of the ACP countries. Under previous agreements, the ACP countries were required to accord products from EEC countries preferential access to their markets, but this requirement was dropped when the Lome agreement was negotiated in 1975.

The 1976 population of the nine members of the European Communities totaled 258,656,000. This is larger than the population of the USSR or the United States, and is exceeded only by that of the People's Republic of China and India. If the populations of Greece, Portugal and Spain were added, as they eventually will be, the total population would be 313,365,000. The member states of the European Communities, by themselves, are an enormous economic unit. With the states that are linked to the Communities through preferential trading arrangements – member states of EFTA, the Mediterranean countries, and the ACP countries that adhere to the Lome agreement – it is a truly formidable trading block.

Despite its strong support for the creation of the European Communities and its favorable attitude toward the expansion in the committees' membership, particularly the UK's entry, successive United States administrations have frequently worried about the consequences of the communities' development and policies for U.S. economic interests. As has already been mentioned, the United States sought through negotiations in GATT during the Kennedy round to insure that EEC's Common External Tariff would be lower than the individual tariffs that it replaced. Later in the Tokyo Round of GATT negotiations, 1975-1979, the CET was reduced still further, as was the U.S. tariff. The United

States has also used GATT and other international fora to seek to lessen the protective character of EEC's Common Agricultural Policy.

A North American Common Market?

Some in the United States have argued that the best way to counter what they believed were the pernicious effects of the EEC's regional trading bloc would be for the U.S. to create its own regional trading bloc. Of course, the United States and the Canadian economies have always been closely linked. In 1965 the two countries signed an agreement committing themselves to eliminate all obstacles to trade between them in automobile products. This agreement took effect provisionally immediately on being signed, and it was given definitive effect the following year. It created a free trade area in automobile products between the two countries. Some have suggested going farther to create a general customs union or a common market including at least the United States and Canada and possibly Mexico and other countries. Through the 1970s, no action was taken on these suggestions, but they continued to have a certain appeal and their attractiveness probably increased as the economic difficulties that the industrialized countries encountered continued. These difficulties also stimulated Australia and New Zealand to consider going beyond their free trade agreement of 1965 to even possibly full economic union.

Regionalism and Interdependence Among OECD Members

Sparked by the legal and institutional framework of the European Communities, there has been a tendency toward an increased regionalization of trade among the industrialized countries of the North Atlantic area. Table 3.1 shows intraregional exports as a percentage of total exports for three groupings of states – the original members of the European Communities, EFTA, and Canada and the United States. The growth in the relative importance of intra-Community trade was most dramatic in the case of EEC, but it also occurred in the other two areas as well. After Denmark, Ireland, and the United Kingdom joined the EEC, intra-Community exports came to constitute an even larger portion of the group's total exports, more than 50 percent in 1977.(17) On the other hand, intra-EFTA exports fell back to just over 17 percent of the group's total exports in 1977. The United Kingdom as a major market and producer was an important factor in giving EFTA whatever coherence it had as a regional trading group; without the United Kingdom, EFTA appeared to be primarily a group of countries that for one reason or another could not join the European Communities. Indeed, more than 46 percent of EFTA's total exports went to the EEC in 1977.

Even the European Economic Community, with its relatively high proportion of internal trade, however, cannot operate as a self-

Table 3.1. Intraregional Exports as a Percentage
of Total Exports

Regional Grouping	YEAR			
	1938	1948	1958	1968
EEC[a]	27.5	26.2	30.1	45.0
EFTA[b]	18.3	17.4	17.7	23.8
Canada and the USA	19.0	22.0	27.2	35.2

Source for data: United Nations Secretariat, Department of Economic and Social Affairs, Statistical Office, Statistical Yearbook, 1963 (New York: UN, 1964), and, 1969 (1970)

[a]Belgium, Federal Republic of Germany, France, Italy, the Netherlands, and Luxembourg.

[b]Austria, Denmark, Finland, Iceland, Norway, Portugal, Sweden, Switzerland, and the United Kingdom.

contained economic unit. The members of the EEC are dependent upon trade with less developed countries to obtain essential raw materials; and their economic relationships with the United States, Japan, Australia, and New Zealand are extremely important to them. In the 1970s, just as the United States, Canada, and Japan found that there were several important economic issues (for instance concerning energy, unemployment and inflation) that they could not solve alone, the member states found that the European Communities also proved to be too restrictive a framework for them to be able to tackle these issues successfully.(18) Instead, solutions had to be sought within more inclusive frameworks such as the OECD and the annual summit meetings of the heads of government of the seven economically most important countries – Canada, the Federal Republic of Germany, France, Italy, Japan, the United States and the United Kingdom.

The Western economic summits have attempted to define broad orientations for the economic policies of the advanced industrial states with market economies. The OECD has provided a framework for more specific cooperative activities. OECD's supreme organ is the Council, on which each of the organization's 24 member states are represented, and which operates according to the principle of unanimity. OECD's objectives are to promote economic growth in its member states and to strengthen aid from these countries to less developed countries. The organization has interpreted this mandate broadly to include such issues as science and educational policies and environmental problems. OECD organizes and publishes studies and research, it facilitates the exchange of information among its member states, and it attempts to shape member states' policies through the adoption of normative pronounce-ments. Its activities have mitigated the tensions that have arisen as a consequence of the creation by some of its members of regional trading groups, and they have made a contribution to the creation and con-tinued functioning of the relatively liberal trading system that has been so important a feature of the global economy since World War II.

Economic cooperation among the industrialized states with market economies can be viewed as occurring within an overall framework established with OECD. Although 19 of the 24 members of OECD are in Western Europe, given the inclusion of Canada, the United States, Japan, Australia and New Zealand, and the noninclusion of such European states as the German Democratic Republic, Czechoslovakia, and Poland, it is clear that type of economic system and level of economic development are more important criteria for membership than geography. Among the member states of OECD there are various smaller groupings: the European Communities, the European Free Trade Association, and the limited and loose connection between the United States and Canada and between Australia and New Zealand. Geography plays some role but not a predominant one in defining each of these groupings. It is especially important to recall how important other factors have been in the historical evolution of the European Communities, the grouping that has moved farthest toward achieving economic integration. In the current enlargement of the Communities, Greece, which is physically separated from the nine present members, has been the first of the three candidate states to be accorded membership. These smaller economic groupings within OECD are important as the growth in intraregional trade demonstrated, but their prominence should not obscure the broader interdependence among the OECD members. In the 1970s, almost 70 percent of the exports of OECD's members went to other OECD states. This propor-tion of internal trade is even higher than that of the European Communities. Interestingly, in 1938 the 24 states that constitute OECD also sent about 70 percent of their exports to one another. The interdependence among these states has an enduring quality.

REGIONAL ECONOMIC COOPERATION AMONG STATES WITH CENTRALLY PLANNED ECONOMIES

Comecon

The origins of regional economic cooperation among states with cen-trally planned economies date from the same period and events that set in motion cooperation among developed states with market economies. The USSR and other Eastern European states had been among the principal recipients of the relief and reconstruction assistance provided through the United Nations Relief and Rehabilitation Administration (UNRRA) during its existence from November 9, 1943 through June 30, 1947. Like the states of Western Europe, these countries had continued to have serious reconstruction problems after UNRRA ended its opera-tions. When the Western European states began in the summer of 1947 to develop their response to Secretary of State Marshall's offer of assistance for the reconstruction of Europe, the Soviet Union made it clear that it would not participate in any joint planning of reconstruction or in any joint allocation procedure. The USSR did not want its economy or those of the states of Eastern Europe with newly-established communist regimes linked tightly with the economies of the capitalist states of the West. By 1948, the destination of more than 44 percent of the exports of the USSR and the other communist states of Eastern Europe was within the region. In 1938, only 10 percent of the exports of these states had their destination within the region.(19) The Communist Information Bureau (Cominform), linking communist parties throughout the world, was formed in 1947; and in January 1949, after OEEC had been created, the Soviet Union and Bulgaria, Czechoslovakia, Hungary, and Romania established the Council for Mutual Economic Assistance (Comecon). Since then, Comecon has been the principal institutional setting for economic cooperation among states with centrally planned economies.

Geography and type of economic system have clearly been important in determining Comecon's membership. But they have not been the only factors. Had it not been for the quarrel between Yugoslavia and the USSR, which resulted in Yugoslavia's expulsion from the Cominform in June 1948, Yugoslavia would have been a logical candidate for membership. As it was, Yugoslavia began to participate in the activities of Comecon only in 1964. An agreement was signed then that permitted Yugoslavia to participate in those activities that were of special concern to it. It gave Yugoslavia a relationship with Comecon similar to the special status that it enjoys with OECD. Albania joined Comecon later in 1949, but ceased participating in the organization in 1961. The German Democratic Republic became a member in 1950. The People's Republic of China started sending observers to Comecon in 1956, but stopped this practice in late 1961. Mongolia became a member in 1962, Cuba in 1972, and Vietnam in 1978. From this history it is apparent that the nature of a state's relationship with the USSR is a crucial determinant of whether or not it will join Comecon or participate in the organization's activities. The Council for Mutual Economic Assistance is an organization of some but not all states with centrally planned economies. The core of the membership is in Eastern Europe, but it also includes states in Asia and the Caribbean.

During the first years of its existence, Comecon conducted few activities. Indeed, its Charter was not even published until 1960. It began to undertake active programs in the late 1950s, and these programs and the organization's structure were further strengthened in the early nineteen-sixties. The decision to develop Comecon in the late 1950s was clearly linked to the evolution in the relationships between the Soviet Union and the smaller communist states in Eastern Europe toward more traditional interstate patterns. It was also an element in the strategy that was crafted to deal with the economic issues that contributed to the Hungarian revolt in 1956. Then, too, it was only by the mid-1950s that the newly-founded communist regimes in Eastern

Europe completed their first planning cycle reorienting their economies in the new directions that they had chosen; economic cooperation among communist state became more feasible after this initial phase had been completed. In addition, steps to strengthen Comecon have often closely followed progress toward economic integration in Western Europe. The initial activation of Comecon occurred simultaneously with the preparation of the Euratom and EEC treaties. Khrushchev submitted an ambitious program for strengthening Comecon just after the United Kingdom announced its first bid to join the EEC.

In institutional structure, Comecon is a conventional IGO. The supreme organ is the Council, on which all members are represented. Unanimity is required for decisions to be taken. An Executive Committee, which is also comprised of representatives of all member states, meets between sessions of the Council and oversees the implementation of its decisions. Comecon has a secretariat in Moscow, which is headed by the Secretary to the Council. This individual has always been a national of the Soviet Union. Much of the detailed work of Comecon is done in some 20 standing commissions which are comprised of experts who deal with the coordination of production plans in relatively narrow branches of economic activity. There is also, as a subordinate body of the Executive Committee, a Bureau on Generalized Problems of Economic Plans. None of these institutions has supranational powers. On the other hand, since the Council is often comprised of heads of governments, and the membership of the Executive Committee is at the level of deputy head of government, and since production is organized in the member countries on the basis of government plans, if these bodies are able to reach unanimous agreement, it is likely that their decisions will be implemented.

Comecon works through specialization agreements and joint projects. The first procedure is intended to permit larger production runs by reducing duplication, and it results in bilateral and multilateral agreements for the delivery of goods. In the first stage of a joint project, there is a pooling of capital, construction equipment, and qualified personnel. Once the project is underway, the output is shared among the participating countries according to their contribution of capital and services. The most notable joint projects are the Druzhba oil pipeline, which transports oil from the Soviet Union to Hungary, the German Democratic Republic, Poland, and Czechoslovakia; the integrated power grid linking the power systems of the European member countries; and the railway freight-car pool, a common pool drawn upon by member countries. The International Bank for Economic Cooperation (IBEC) clears payments among Comecon's members. Since their currencies are inconvertible, having the IBEC perform clearing functions allows the states merely to be concerned with their overall balance of Comecon trade, rather than having to balance all accounts bilaterally.

There can be no question that Comecon is an important focal point for the trade of its member states. In 1977, the destination of more than 55 percent of the exports of its European members (Bulgaria, Czechoslovakia, German Democratic Republic, Hungary, Poland, Romania, and the USSR) was within Comecon.(20) This percentage exceeds that of any other contemporary regional economic grouping, even the EEC. The extent to which the exports of the various members of Comecon are concentrated within the region varies. Bulgaria's proportion of 77 percent is the highest, while Romania's of 41 percent is the lowest. Although the data are scanty, it appears that the exports of the non-European members of Comecon (Cuba, Mongolia, and Vietnam) are also heavily concentrated toward other members of the organization. About 65 percent of Cuba's exports go to Comecon members.

The size of the USSR's economy dwarfs those of the other members of Comecon. The USSR's GNP is more than seven times greater than that of Poland which has the next largest, and more than 28 times that of Hungary which has the smallest GNP of Comecon's European members. The GNPs of the non-European members are even smaller than that of Hungary. Given the overwhelming size of the USSR's economy, not surprisingly it is the dominant trading partner with Comecon. All of the other members of the organization, except Romania, export more to the Soviet Union than they do to their other partners combined. Czechoslovakia, the German Democratic Republic, and Poland, however, all have higher per capita GNP's than the Soviet Union, and much of the intra-Comecon trade is the exchange of Soviet raw materials for manufactured goods from other countries.

Comecon and Interdependence

How important the Council for Mutual Economic Assistance will prove to be in the future is somewhat moot. Prior to World War II, most of the trade of the Comecon's members was with other countries. The Eastern European states traded predominantly with Western Europe, mainly supplying raw materials in return for manufactured goods. Industrialization was the prime objective of the post-World War II economic plans of the Soviet Union and the Eastern European states with communist regimes. This implied changing the prewar orientation of their economies. In the more than three decades since the conclusion of World War II, great progress has been made toward achieving the objective of industrialization.

By the late 1970s, however, many of Comecon's members had begun to encounter serious economic problems. Like all countries throughout the world, they were beginning to face resource shortages. Several members were encountering difficulties in sustaining rapid rates of economic growth and, particularly, in maintaining the pace of technological development. Comecon member countries characteristically trade less than states with market economies of comparable size and levels of economic development.(21)

In the 1970s, several Comecon member states sought to improve the performance of their economies through foreign trade, particularly with countries with market economies. East-West trade increased substantially. Some of the smaller Eastern European countries moved to join the institutions that were crucial to the global capitalist trading system. In the late 1970s, Cuba, Czechoslovakia, Hungary, Poland, and Romania were members of GATT; and Romania was a member of the International Monetary Fund. Although intra-Comecon exports as a proportion of the members' total exports were still high in the 1970s, they were lower than they had been in the preceding decade. As the 1970s came to a close, the crucial issues concerning regional economic cooperation were the extent to which and how rapidly the Comecon countries would move to expand still further their economic ties with countries with market economies.

REGIONAL ECONOMIC COOPERATION AMONG LESS DEVELOPED COUNTRIES

Schemes for regional economic cooperation among the less developed states in the southern hemisphere began to come into being about a decade after the launching of those involving centrally planned economies and developed states with market economies. Many of the schemes have had antecedents in earlier periods. Efforts to promote cooperation among the Central American states date to the nineteenth century, and several of the regional cooperation schemes in Africa and the Caribbean tie together states that shared a common colonial rule. This past history has shaped and facilitated cooperation schemes, but it has not in any way insured their success.

Latin America and the Caribbean

The contemporary movement toward economic cooperation among developing countries started in Latin America. Raul Prebisch formulated and began to propogate arguments about the gains that LDCs could achieve from regional economic cooperation when he was Executive Secretary of ECLA from 1948 through 1962. This was the period during which the economic cooperation schemes among the developed states with market economies and with centrally planned economies were launched. It was a period when these two groups of states rapidly increased their trade and achieved substantial economic growth. The economies of the LDCs grew too, but not as rapidly as Prebisch and others would have liked; and although their exports expanded steadily, they fell from 25 percent of world exports in 1938 and 30 percent in 1948 to 21 percent in 1962.(22) Prebisch saw regional economic cooperation among LDCs as a way of arresting and reversing this decline.

The first regional economic cooperation institution to be established for Latin America was the Inter-American Development Bank (IDB), created in 1959. The Organization of American States (OAS) played a role in the conception of IDB. Membership was originally limited to states that were members of OAS, but a specific exception was made at an early date for Canada, and the general requirement was dropped in 1976.(23) Over the years the IDB has established an identity independent of OAS. Its headquarters is in Washington, D.C., and the United States has been the largest single contributor to the bank's funds. The IDB makes loans backed by its ordinary resources that have interest rates close to the rate on the commercial market. In addition, through the Fund for Special Operations, it makes long-term loans at low interest rates that may be partially or wholly repaid in the currency of the country where the project being financed is carried out.

IDB has a broad mandate to promote the economic development of its less developed members individually and collectively. Within this mandate it has actively sought to promote economic cooperation among American states generally. In 1964 it created the Institute for Latin American Integration (which is known by the acronym INTAL after the Institute's title in Spanish, Instituto para la integracion de America Latin) in Buenos Aires which has conducted an active program of research, training, advisory services and publications.   The IDB has frequently provided direct assistance for integration schemes. In addition, IDB loans for national projects in such areas as the development of transportation facilities have often had as their ultimate purpose facilitating economic cooperation among American states. Lack of adequate facilities for inter-American communication was identified at an early stage as one of the most significant obstacles to inter-American economic cooperation. National projects can contribute to overcoming this obstacle if they are conceived as components of a regionwide grid.

There is one other regional organization that includes a large number of states located throughout Latin America and the Caribbean, the Latin American Economic System (known as SELA, the acronym of its name in Spanish, Sistema Economica Latinoamericano). Created in 1975, SELA's broad aim is to promote cooperation to achieve the self-sustaining and independent development of the region. It is empowered to take a number of specific steps including creating Latin American multinational enterprises. The Latin American Economic System has 26 members.(24) As of 1979, SELA had established a number of action committees in various sectors of economic activity and was moving toward the establishment of a Latin American Multinational Fertilizer Marketing Enterprise and a Multinational Enterprise for Handicraft Promotion and Marketing. SELA also acted as a caucus to coordinate the policies of its member states in negotiations with the EEC and in various UN bodies.

In addition to these two regionwide schemes, there are also four important economic cooperative efforts involving smaller numbers of states. These are: the Latin American Free Trade Association (LAFTA); the Central American Common Market (CACM); the Caribbean Community (CARICOM); and the Andean Group.

The Montevideo Treaty creating LAFTA was signed in 1960 in the wake of the establishment of the EEC and EFTA, and the treaty came into effect the following year. The original signatories of the treaty were: Argentina, Brazil, Chile, Mexico, Paraguay, Peru, and Uruguay. Colombia and Ecuador acceded to the treaty in 1961, Venezuela in 1966, and Bolivia in 1967. Although Mexico is physically separated from the other members of LAFTA, its level of economic development is similar to that of several of them. Between 1955 and 1961, trade among the states that eventually constituted LAFTA declined by almost 40 percent. It was hoped that LAFTA would contribute to reversing this trend. Although the treaty commits the members to establishing on a reciprocal basis a free trade area within a period of 12 years from its entry into force, the depth and extent of this commitment has been weakened. The treaty itself permits member states to restrict, in a nondiscriminatory way, trade in agricultural products. Then, at the first conference of the contracting parties, an interpretation was adopted that limited the commitment to trade in manufactured consumer goods and capital goods. The treaty encourages the member states to negotiate industrial complementarity agreements which allow particular sets of states to reduce tariffs in narrow economic sectors more rapidly than would be possible otherwise, in the hope of facilitating Latin American multinational enterprises.

Progress in LAFTA has been somewhat disappointing. The system of reciprocally negotiating tariff negotiations on a product by product basis has proved cumbersome, and once the items that were included in the traditional intraregional trade were covered, negotiations have made little headway. More than 11,000 concessions have been granted, but the largest share of these were granted prior to 1965. The member states have been very reluctant to remove tariff protection from newly-established manufacturing enterprises. Some twenty industrial complementarity agreements have been signed, primarily among the most highly industrialized countries. Intraregional exports which were only 8 percent of the total exports of LAFTA's member states in 1960,(25) had risen to 13 percent in 1977.(26) However, in 1977, 29 percent of LAFTA's exports went to the United States and 23 percent to the nine members of the EEC. LAFTA is still only a minor factor in the trade of its member countries.

The General Treaty on Central American Economic Integration creating the Central American Common Market (CACM) was signed by Guatemala, El Salvador, Honduras, and Nicaragua in December 1960, and Costa Rica acceded to the treaty in July 1962. Efforts to unite the Central American states have a long history. From the time that they gained independence until 1838, the Central American states constituted a single political unit, the Federal Republic of Central America. Since the disintegration of the Federal Republic there have been several attempts to link the five states. All of them have small populations (only Guatemala has more than five million inhabitants) and relatively small territories. The states form a compact geographic unit, and a strong case can be made for the advantages of economic cooperation among them. The General Treaty committed the states to eliminate tariffs on intraregional trade on all but a limited number of goods and to establish a common external tariff. It provided for the establishment of the Central American Bank for Economic Integration. It also endorsed a Regime for Central American Industries, designed to promote new investment. Industries that qualified for this regime would enjoy privileged status within the five states, including free trade, special consideration with respect to the reduction of the import duties on imported raw materials, and preference in official imports.

By mid-1966, almost all of the tariffs on items in intra-CACM trade had been eliminated and uniform customs duties had been established for about four-fifths of the items imported from extra-CACM sources. By May 1969, the common external tariff protected 97.5 percent of the tariff items. Intraregional exports jumped from 8 percent of the member states' total exports in 1960, to 27 percent in 1970. Equally important, the structure of intraregional trade changed substantially. In 1960, foodstuffs and live animals were the largest single category of intraregional exports, accounting for almost half of the total. In 1970, manufactures were the largest category, accounting for more than a third of the total. On the other hand, the regime for integration industries yielded few results. Only Guatemala and Nicaragua established integration industries. Nonetheless, the early years of the Central American Common Market brought promising progress.

But there were also problems. Some member states argued that the benefits of a common market were not shared equally. Some governments attributed balance of payments difficulties that they encountered to the progress made toward trade liberalization. These arguments became intertwined with disagreements stemming from factors unrelated to CACM. Tensions mounted, and in 1969 violence erupted between El Salvador and Honduras. Since the so-called "soccer war," the Central American Common Market has been in a continual crisis. Honduras and El Salvador no longer trade with one another, and some of the community institutions have ceased to function. The level of intracommunity exports as a proportion of the member states' total exports has declined. During the late 1970s, the governments of Nicaragua and other Central American countries were preoccupied with internal conflicts.

Despite CACM's success in increasing intraregional exports, in the 1970s more than a third of the member states' exports went to the United States and more than a fifth to the nine members of the EEC. The economies were still strongly oriented toward the industrialized states of the northern hemisphere.

The Caribbean Community came into being in 1973. The members of the community are: Antigua, the Bahamas, Barbados, Belize, Dominica, Grenada, Guyana, Jamaica, Montserrat, St. Kitts-Nevis, Anguilla, St. Lucia, St. Vincent, and Trinidad and Tobago. The total population of the members of CARICOM in the late 1970s was less than five million. Six of the members are independent, seven (Antigua, Belize, Montserrat, St. Kitts and Nevis, St. Lucia, and St. Vincent) remain under the sovereignty of the United Kingdom. Belize is in Central America and Guyana is in South America. The other members are islands among which independent states (i.e., Cuba, Haiti, and the Dominican Republic) and non-independent territories (i.e., Puerto Rico, the Virgin Islands, Guadeloupe, Martinique, and the Netherlands Antilles) are interspersed. All of the members of CARICOM experienced British colonial rule; this is their common tie. In 1958, before any of the territories attained independence, they were united by colonial fiat in the West Indies Federation. However, the federation was dissolved in 1962 when Jamaica and Trinidad and Tobago achieved independence and decided to withdraw because they felt that its objectives were too restricted and that membership was not to their advantage. In 1965 Antigua, Barbados, and Guyana signed an agreement for the establishment of the Caribbean Free Trade Association (CARIFTA). Between then and 1971, this agreement was modified and eventually won the adhesion of all of the present members of CARICOM except the Bahamas. CARICOM is, then, an extension of CARIFTA. Although the Bahamas is a member of CARICOM, it does not adhere to the common market that is a major aspect of the organization's cooperative economic activities.

The common market annex to the CARICOM agreement commits signatories to the liberalization of trade on products originating in the region (except for those included on a reserve list) and to the establishment of a common external tariff. Special provisions are made for the less developed member countries (i.e., all members other than Barbados, Guyana, Jamaica, and Trinidad and Tobago). They need not eliminate tariffs on intraregional trade local products as rapidly, and they are also given a longer period to adjust to the common external tariff. The CARICOM treaty provided for the creation of the Caribbean Development Bank and the Caribbean Investment Corporation. The CARICOM treaty also commits the member states to functional cooperation with respect to such matters as the development of common shipping and air transport services, scientific and technological research, health and educational services, and social insurance.

Despite some early successes, progress in CARICOM has been disappointing. When the treaty was signed in 1973, intraregional exports constituted more than 10 percent of the member states' total exports.(27) They have not reached that level since. Obstacles have been imposed to trade, and functional cooperation schemes have been frustrated. Sharp divergencies in orientation toward economic policies have developed among the larger member states with Jamaica moving to the left and Trinidad and Tobago continuing a market-oriented course. The member states have continued to rely heavily on trade with the industrialized countries; about 75 percent of their exports go to the United States and the European Communities.

The final important regional economic cooperation scheme in Latin America is the Andean Group. The Treaty of Cartegena was signed by Bolivia, Chile, Colombia, Ecuador and Peru on May 26, 1969, and Venezuela adhered to the Treaty in 1973. All six states are also members of the Latin American Free Trade Association. Frustrated by LAFTA's slow pace, they hoped that more rapid progress could be made in a smaller grouping. They also hoped that by linking their economies they could counter the economic dominance in LAFTA of Argentina, Brazil, and Mexico, particularly that of Brazil. The provisions of the Treaty of Cartegena are the most far-reaching of those of any of the regional economic cooperation schemes in Latin America and the Caribbean.

The Andean Group is the only one of these schemes to have a community organ analagous to the Commission of the European Communities.(28) The Junta (or Board) of the Andean Group is composed of three individuals chosen by the member states for three year terms. The Board heads the permanent secretariat and has the responsibility of formulating proposals for consideration and decision by the Commission, an intergovernmental body comprised of one representative from each member state. In several areas, the Commission can only act on the basis of a proposal formulated by the Board, and even when the Commission may act on its own, the Board may submit a proposal. The Board is charged with representing the overall interests of the community as opposed to the separate interests of the individual member states.

The Cartagena Agreement contains provisions for the creation of a customs union, and progress has been made in the elimination of obstacles to intraregional trade and the establishment of a common external tariff. Trade within the Andean region, however, has never been very extensive. At the time of the treaty signing, intraregional exports accounted for less than 3 percent of the members' total exports, and though this proportion has increased with the creation of the customs union, as of the late 1970s, it had not attained the level of 10 percent.

The Andean Group's more significant accomplishments have been in other areas. The group has adopted industrial development programs for such sectors as metalworking, petrochemicals, and the automotive industry. It has also adopted a common code for foreign investment that contains relatively stringent provisions concerning the proportion of national participation required, the amount of profits that may be remitted, and the extent to which technology must be transferred. This regulation is widely regarded as one of the Andean Group's most important achievements. It was also the cause of Chile's withdrawal from the group in 1976. After Augusto Pinochet came to power in 1973, he began to reverse the policies of his predecessor. As part of his drive to attract foreign investment, he requested that provisions of the group's foreign investment code be softened. When this suggestion was refused by the other members of the group, Chile withdrew.

The members of the Andean Group, like the member states of the other regional economic cooperation schemes that we have been considering, export more to the United States and the members of the European Communities than to any other state or group of states.

Africa

Africa is similar to Latin America and the Caribbean, in that it contains a large number of states with relatively small populations. Both areas offer many possibilities for regional economic cooperation. There are important differences between the two areas, though, that have significant consequences for attempts at cooperation. The predominant number of African states gained their independence in the 1960s. While some states in the Caribbean area became independent only recently, most of the states in Latin America and the Caribbean achieved this status early in the nineteenth century. As a consequence, national political institutions are less firmly rooted in Africa which can both facilitate and hinder regional economic cooperation. There may be fewer powerful groups who would attempt to block regional cooperation to protect their personal interests. On the other hand, there are no well-developed national bureaucracies to implement joint decisions. A second important difference is that the level of economic development is lower in Africa. The average GNP per capita in 1976 in South America was $1,230, in Central America it was $1,000, but in Africa it was only $420.(29) The limited purchasing power in African states restricts opportunities for intraregional trade.

The members of the African Development Bank include virtually all of the states in the area except Rhodesia/Zimbabwe and South Africa. Although the treaty creating the bank was signed in 1963 and went into effect the following year, the bank did not begin operations until 1966. Its mandate is to contribute to the individual and joint economic and social development of its members. Through the projects that it has financed it has sought to increase the complementarity of the economies of its member states and to stimulate expanded trade among them. The bank's resources are relatively modest. Its ordinary capital is less than $1 billion, in comparison with the Inter-American Development Bank's almost $6 billion. Since membership in the bank is limited to independent African states, the major donor countries have been reluctant to provide large sums of money to an organization in which they would have no voice. Difficulty in raising money was among the reason's for the African Development Bank's slow start.

There have been four important attempts to create customs unions in Africa: the East African Community (EAC); the Central African Customs and Economic Union (which is known by the acronym for its name in French, Union Douaniere et Economique de l'Afrique Centrale, UDEAC); the West African Economic Community (Communaute economique de l'Afrique Ouest, CEAO); and the Community of West African States (ECOWAS). The first three represent attempts to maintain links that were created in the colonial era. The last is an ambitious attempt to override divisions left from the colonial era and join anglophone and francophone states.

Under British colonial rule, Kenya, Uganda, and Tanganyika (now Tanzania) were united in a customs union. The three territories also had a common tax collection service and operated joint rail, air, port, and postal and telecommunication services. There was also monetary co-operation. When the three territories became independent in the early 1960s, their leaders made many rhetorical commitments to maintaining this unity. In 1967, the presidents of the three countries signed a treaty creating the East African Community.

The treaty created an elaborate institutional structure headed by the East African Authority (which consisted of the presidents of the three countries), which was responsible for the general direction of the community. Three East African Community ministers, one from each country, resident at community headquarters in Arusha, Tanzania, were responsible for the supervision of the day-to-day functioning of the community. There were various ministerial councils to provide policy guidance in functional fields. A secretariat headed by a secretary-general performed the essential administrative functions. In addition, there was an East African Legislative Assembly and several judicial bodies. East African Airways, East African Harbors, East African Posts and Telecommunications were established as autonomous corporations and were required to operate on a commercial basis.

Despite this elaborate institutional structure, EAC soon foundered, and in 1977 it completely collapsed. The process of disintegration had begun even before the community was established. In 1966, the three countries established their own central banks and abandoned the joint East African monetary board. In 1970, restrictions on the exchange of currencies were imposed. Kenya consistently exported more to its partner states than it had imported from them. To counter this tendency and because of payments difficulties, obstacles to trade were imposed. Kenya and Tanzania adopted very different approaches to managing their economies. Kenya chose to rely on a market approach while Tanzania opted for extensive planning and governmental control. When Idi Amin came to power in Uganda (1971), the community was put in a state of crisis that lasted until the final collapse in 1977. Because President Julius Nyerere of Tanzania refused to meet with Amin, the East African Authority could not be convened. Expedients were found so that essential community business could be conducted, but in 1977 an impasse was reached on budgetary issues causing the collapse.

In 1965, intracommunity exports were 20 percent of the three countries' total exports.(30) This proportion declined steadily there-after; by 1977 they were only 11 percent. Like the members of the other regional economic cooperation schemes, Kenya, Tanzania, and Uganda export more to the United States and the nine members of the EEC than to any other single source. The concentration of their exports on these two markets, however, has been smaller than in the other cases. Given the extent to which the East African Community disintegrated during the 1970s, its collapse will probably have little impact on the trading patterns of the former member states.

The Central African Customs and Economic Union and the West African Economic Community bring together respectively most of the states that formerly were administered as French Equatorial Africa and French West Africa. The UDEAC treaty was signed in

1964, and it was revised and strengthened a decade later. UDEAC replaced the Equatorial Customs Union which was created in 1959 just before independence was granted to the states of French Equatorial Africa. Cameroon, the Central African Republic, Congo (Brazzaville), and Gabon are members of UDEAC. Chad was a member until 1968 when it withdrew. Difficulties concerning the distribution of benefits between the land-locked and coastal states were among the reasons for its withdrawal.

A customs union is the central feature of UDEAC. Since the three coastal states have a greater opportunity to collect customs duties than land-locked Central Africa, the three have established a solidarity fund from which an annual lump sum payment is made to Central Africa. There is a "single tax" regime for industrial products that are manufactured in one member state for sale within the region. The state where the product is manufactured collects the tax and distributes the proceeds to its partner states in proportion to sales. UDEAC has also taken steps after the revision of the treaty in 1974 in the direction of industrial programming.

Intraregional exports as a proportion of the member states' total exports have increased from a level of less than three percent at the time that the treaty was signed to a level of eight or nine percent.(31) UDEAC's exports are heavily oriented toward the European Economic Community, and particularly toward France.

This is even more the case with respect to the West African Economic Community. The CEAO came into effect in 1974. As in the case of UDEAC, the new treaty replaced a rudimentary customs union that dates to 1959. The members of CEAO are: Ivory Coast, Mali, Mauritania, Niger, Senegal, and Upper Volta. The CEAO treaty provides for the free movement of goods that originate in the area and have not undergone industrial processing, a preference scheme for industrial products that originate in the region, and a common external tariff. These features are to be imposed gradually over a 12-year period. The treaty also provides for other types of economic cooperation through joint industrial programming, the formation of multinational corporations, and the conduct of joint projects. Intra-CEAO exports have never been even 10 percent of the member states' total exports, and since the signing of the treaty, they have been less than 5 percent.

The Economic Community of West African States was formed in 1975. It is an ambitious attempt to join together nine states that were former French colonies (Benin, Guinea, Ivory Coast, Mali, Mauritania, Niger, Senegal, Togo, and Upper Volta), four that were British colonies (Gambia, Ghana, Nigeria, and Sierra Leone), two that were Portuguese (Cape Verde and Guinea-Bissau), and one state that escaped colonial rule (Liberia). The treaty aspires to create a full common market, but at this stage too little has been accomplished to estimate how successful the attempt will be.

Asia

The average per capita GNP in Asia in 1976 (excluding Japan and the Middle East) was $290, making it the poorest area of the world. The large populations and territories of several Asian states diminish the need for regional economic cooperation. Nevertheless, there has been some regional economic cooperation within the area.

The Asian Development Bank was established in 1966. As of the late 1970s, it had 42 members: 28 from the region, and 14 from outside the region.(32) With ordinary capital resources of almost $10 billion, its resources were greater than those of the other regional development banks. Japan is the largest contributor. The headquarters are in Manila, the Philippines.

Beyond the Asian Development Bank, there are two regional economic cooperation schemes that merit attention: the Regional Cooperation for Development (RCD) and the Association of South East Asian Nations (ASEAN). RCD was created among Iran, Pakistan, and Turkey in 1964. The declaration on which RCD is based included a commitment in principle to freer trade among the three states, and some trade liberalization has occurred. In addition, RCD sponsors other cooperative activities. The member states have been able to establish joint-purpose enterprises in which the equity is shared or there is a commitment to purchase the enterprise's products. Intraregional trade, however, accounts for only a miniscule portion of the three countries' exports.

ASEAN was established in 1967 by Indonesia, Malaysia, the Philippines, Singapore, and Thailand. ASEAN operates with a minimal institutional structure. Each member country has a national secretariat, headed by a Secretary-General. An ASEAN Secretary-General was not appointed until 1976. ASEAN has eleven permanent committees that prepare recommendations for projects in specific sectors, for example air transport and meteorology. There is also a Committee of ASEAN Central Banks and Monetary Authorities and the Special Coordinating Committee of ASEAN (SCCAN). SCCAN is responsible for the joint negotiations with the EEC. Intraregional trade within ASEAN has actually declined relative to the member countries' total exports, though it has increased in absolute terms. The organization's most significant accomplishments are in coordinating the policies of the members in negotiations with the EEC, Japan, and the United States, the destination of most of their exports.

Other Third World Organizations

This important accomplishment of the ASEAN countries provides an appropriate conclusion for this brief survey of regional economic cooperation among less developed countries. It underscores what has been obvious in each case: the most important trading partners of the member states of the cooperation efforts are not the other members of the economic communities to which they belong, but instead are the industrialized states of the northern hemisphere – particularly the United States, the European Economic Community, and Japan. For this reason, the countries that belong to the regional economic cooperation schemes among LDCs have devoted at least as much attention, and probably more, to IGOs in which they can collectively confront the industrialized states of the northern hemisphere with their economic situation, present proposals for bettering their condition, and attempt to negotiate agreements for joint action. The organizations that figure most prominently in this strategy are the United Nations itself and the United Nations Conference for Trade and Development (UNCTAD). In negotiations in such bodies, the LDCs seek to achieve a unified position through the caucus that is known as the Group of 77. This caucus originated at the first session of UNCTAD in 1964, and its name is derived from the fact that at that time it brought together 77 LDCs. Now the caucus includes more than 100 states. For many purposes, the LDCs of the southern hemisphere as they are joined in the Group of 77 must be considered a regional grouping. In the UN and UNCTAD, the Group of 77 has constantly sought to improve the trading position of the LDCs vis-a-vis the industrialized states of the northern hemisphere. They have gained a generalized system of preferences whereby specific manufactured goods that they export to the developed countries receive preferential tariff treatment. They have also attempted to gain programs to stabilize at a high level the prices that they receive for the commodities that they export, but they have been less successful in this endeavor.

The some 50 African, Caribbean, and Pacific states that are associated with the EEC through the Lome Agreement have pursued similar strategies in that setting. Through the Lome Agreement they have gained a system for stabilizing their earnings from their commodity exports.

Finally, LDCs that export commodities have banded together in the hope they could improve their earnings through acting as a cartel. The members of the Organization of Petroleum Exporting Countries (OPEC) have pursued this strategy with spectacular success. OPEC has had more profound consequences for its members, and for the world economy, than any of the other international organizations that have been formed to unite southern hemisphere countries. As in the case of the OECD, functionally defined ties are more important with respect to OPEC than geographic propinquity. The 13 members of OPEC are located on three continents.(33) What unites them is their common interest in achieving the highest possible price for the petroleum that they export.

REGIONAL ECONOMIC COOPERATION AND INTERDEPENDENCE IN THE CONTEMPORARY WORLD ECONOMY

The mere length of the list of regional economic cooperation efforts that have been launched since World War II ought to leave no doubt about their prominence in contemporary world politics. Regional economic cooperation clearly has become a salient feature that must be considered in analyses of the contemporary global political system. Having made this point, though, various caveats are also in order.

First, some regional cooperation schemes have clearly been more important than others. There can be no doubt about the preeminence of the European Communities. Whether or not the Communities eventually lead to a federal government among their member states, their consequences, both for their member states and for the rest of the world, have already been profound. The European Economic Community is now the largest single trading unit in the world economy. The member states of the EEC are no longer free to act individually in international economic relationships such as tariff-cutting negotiations, but must act jointly. The Council of Mutual Economic Assistance (Comecon) ranks next in importance because of the extensive trade among its members. No other economic cooperation efforts have been as significant as EEC and Comecon.

A second point that needs to be made is that geography and economic logic only partially explain the membership in the regional economic cooperation schemes that have been created. To point out the prominence of regional efforts is not to argue that geography has been the determining force in the world economy. Membership in contemporary economic cooperation schemes inevitably has been determined by factors other than geographic propinquity and economic logic. To underscore the point one need only ask why Switzerland is not a member of the EEC, why Yugoslavia is not a full member of Comecon, why Panama and Belize are not members of CACM, why Gambia is not a member of CEAO, why Equatorial Guinea is not a member of UDEAC, and why Brunei is not a member of ASEAN? The answer in each case would be found in the historical relationships between the particular country and the members of the regional cooperation agreement. The broad point is that human choices can ignore or override geographic and economic logic, and frequently they do.

Finally, the prominence of regional economic cooperation in contemporary world politics must be seen in the perspective of growing global interdependence. The issue is most apparent with respect to less developed states. Although trade with their geographic neighbors can be important to them, trade with northern hemisphere states is far more important. For the LDCs, regional economic cooperation can only be an element in a broader economic strategy, and it is unlikely to be the most important element. Even the member states of the European Communities and the Council for Mutual Economic Assistance cannot solve all of their economic problems in isolation; instead they must trade and cooperate with nonmembers as well.

At the same time that the several regional cooperation schemes have been launched, great progress has also been made in the direction of creating an open world economy. Obstacles to trade have been reduced substantially since the end of World War II. As a consequence, international trade has increased phenomenally, and production processes have been internationalized.

It is true that protectionist pressures increased in the 1970s in the developed states with market economies, and these countries moved to establish quantitative controls in various sectors through voluntary agreements.(34) Some analysts have expressed fears that these might be a prelude to a reinstitution of the nationalistic economic policies of the 1930s. Their arguments, however, ignore the general open trading systems that constitute the broad context within which these restrictive agreements have been established and the continuing increase in levels of international trade. The quantitative restrictions established on international trade in the last two decades are more properly viewed as efforts to manage the structural transformations involved in the growth of manufacturing capacity in the countries of the southern hemisphere. The fact that the governments of developed states with market economies are not willing to allow this process to occur without their intervention, to minimize the domestic social costs of transformation, does not negate the argument that interdependence is increasing. Even the countries with centrally planned economies which completely control foreign trade are becoming more interdependent.

These trends toward the internationalization of production process and interdependence have simple explanations. People throughout the world desire to improve their material conditions. They judge the performance of their governments in terms of the economic progress that is made. Modern technology offers unparalleled opportunities for better material welfare, but deploying this technology is often impossible without cooperation among states. These pressures explain growing interdependence and why states and regions are driven to cooperate with others. Because of these pressures, regional economic cooperation is unlikely to become an alternative to global interdependence. Rather, it will continue to be part of a strategy for dealing with interdependence, an important instrument to affect how the gains of interdependence will be distributed.

NOTES

(1) For broad reviews of the economic issues involved in regional economic cooperation see: Bela Balassa, The Theory of Economic Integration (Homewood, Ill.: Richard D. Irwin, 1961); and Sydney S. Dell, Trade Blocs and Common Markets (New York: Knopf, 1963).

(2) Jacob Viner, The Customs Union Issue (Washington, D.C.: Anderson Kramer Associates, 1961), p. 43.

(3) The Council of Mutual Economic Assistance adopted an official elaboration of these principles in 1964. Extracts from the text of this decision, which was entitled "Basic Principles of International Socialist Division of Labour," are reprinted as Appendix VI in Michael Kaser, Comecon: Integration Problems of the Planned Economies (London: Oxford University Press, 1967), pp. 249-54. Kaser's study remains one of the best analyses of CMEA.

(4) For a convenient summary of his view on this and other issues relating to the position of less developed states in the world economy see: United Nations, Towards a New Trade Policy for Development: Report by the Secretary-General of the United Nations Conference on Trade and Development (New York: UN, 1964, Sales No. 64.II.B.4).

(5) P. Lamartine Yates, Forty Years of Foreign Trade (London: Allen and Unwin, 1959), p. 28.

(6) These calculations are based on data found in League of Nations, Economic Intelligence Service, Review of World Trade, 1938 (Geneva: League of Nations, 1939), p. 32.

(7) Belgium, Brazil, Canada, Colombia, Costa Rica, Czechoslovakia, Cuba, Ecuador, El Salvador, France, Finland, Guatemala, Haiti, Honduras, Netherlands, Nicaragua, Sweden, and Switzerland.

(8) The Atlantic Charter, as reprinted in Ruhl J. Bartlett, ed., The Record of American Diplomacy (New York: Knopf, 1948), pp. 623-25, on p. 624.

(9) "Lend-Lease: Report of President Roosevelt to Congress, June 11, 1942. House Document No. 779," as reprinted in Ibid., pp. 643-47, on p. 647.

(10) For a good historical survey of the development after World War II of economic regionalism in Western Europe see: Richard Mayne, The Recovery of Europe (Garden City, N.Y.: Anchor/Doubleday, Rev. ed., 1973).

(11) Austria, Belgium, Denmark, Federal Republic of Germany, France, Greece, Iceland, Ireland, Italy, Luxembourg, Netherlands, Norway, Portugal, Spain, Sweden, Switzerland, Turkey, and the United Kingdom.

(12) The 24 members of OECD are: Australia, Austria, Belgium, Canada, Denmark, Finland, France, Federal Republic of Germany, Greece, Iceland, Ireland, Italy, Japan, Luxembourg, Netherlands, New Zealand, Norway, Portugal, Spain, Sweden, Switzerland, Turkey, United Kingdom, and the United States. Yugoslavia is an associate member.

(13) The text of his speech may be found in Royal Institute of International Affairs, Document on International Affairs, 1949-1951, selected and edited by Margaret Carlyle (London: Oxford University Press, 1953), pp. 315-17, on p. 316.

(14) See Jean Monnet, Memoirs (Garden City, N.Y.: Doubleday, 1978), pp. 290 ff.

(15) For a discussion of the functioning of the institutions of the European Communities see: Roy Pryce, The Politics of the European Community (London: Butterworths, 1973).

(16) See Ernest H. Preeg, Traders and Diplomats: An Analysis of the Kennedy Round of Negotiations Under the General Agreement on Tariffs and Trade (Washington: Brookings, 1970), pp. 220-23.

(17) United Nations Secretariat, Department of Economics and Social Affairs, Statistical Office, Yearbook of International Trade Statistics (New York: UN, 1978), vol. I, p. 30.

(18) For a trenchant analysis of the European Communities attempts and the failures of these attempts see Ernst B. Haas, The Obsolescence of Regional Integration Theory (Berkeley: University of California, Berkeley, Institute of International Studies, 1975).

(19) United Nations Secretariat, Department of Economic and Social Affairs, Statistical Office, Statistical Yearbook, 1961 (New York: UN, 1962), p. 420.

(20) United Nations Secretariat, Department of Economic and Social Affairs, Statistical Office, Yearbook of International Trade Statistics, 1977 (New York: UN, 1978), vol. 1, p. 30.

(21) See Frederic L. Pryor, The Communist Foreign Trade System (Cambridge, Mass.: MIT Press, 1963).

(22) United Nations Secretariat, Department of Economic and Social Affairs, Statistical Office, Statistical Yearbook, 1963 (New York: UN, 1964), p. 451.

(23) As of 1976 the members of IDB were: Argentina, Barbados, Bolivia, Brazil, Canada, Chile, Colombia, Costa Rica, Dominican Republic, Ecuador, El Salvador, Guatemala, Haiti, Honduras, Jamaica, Mexico, Nicaragua, Panama, Paraguay, Peru, Trinidad and Tobago, United States of America, Uruguay, and Venezuela.

(24) Argentina, Barbados, Bolivia, Brazil, Colombia, Costa Rica, Cuba, Chile, Dominican Republic, Ecuador, El Salvador, Grenada, Guatemala, Guyana, Haiti, Honduras, Jamaica, Mexico, Nicaragua, Panama, Paraguay, Peru, Surinam, Trinidad and Tobago, Uruguay, and Venezuela.

(25) UN Document TD/B/609 (Vol. II), "Economic Cooperation and Integration among Developing Countries," May 20, 1976, Annex V.

(26) UN Secretariat, Department of Economic and Social Affairs, Statistical Office, Yearbook of International Trade Statistics, 1977 (New York: UN, 1978), vol. I, p. 30.

(27) UN Document TD/B/609.

(28) For a description and analysis of the institutions of regional cooperation efforts among LDCs see UNCTAD, Current Problems of Economic Integration: The Role of Institutions in Regional Integration among Developing Countries (by Dusan Sidjanski) (New York: UN, 1974, Sales No. E.73.II.D.10.).

(29) International Bank for Reconstruction and Development, World Bank Atlas, 1978 (Washington, D.C.: IBRD, 1978).

(30) UN Document Td/B/609.

(31) Ibid.

(32) Afghanistan, Australia, Bangladesh, British Solomon Islands, Burma, Cook, Fiji, Gilbert and Elice Islands, Hong Kong, Indonesia, Japan, Korea, Laos, Malaysia, Nepal, New Zealand, Pakistan, Papua New Guinea, Philippines, Republic of China (Taiwan), Republic of Korea, Republic of Vietnam, Singapore, Sri Lanka, Thailand, Tonga, and Western Somoa; and Austria, Belgium, Canada, Denmark, Finland, France, Federal Republic of Germany, Italy, Netherlands, Norway, Sweden, Switzerland, United Kingdom, and United States of America.

(33) The members of OPEC are: Algeria, Gabon, Libya, Nigeria, Ecuador, Venezuela, United Arab Emirates, Indonesia, Iran, Iraq, Kuwait, Qatar, Saudi Arabia.

(34) See Susan Strange, "The Management of Surplus Capacity: Or How Does Theory Stand up to Protectionism 1970s Style?", International Organization, 33, no. 3 (Summer 1979): 303-34.

II

Globally Central Regional Systems

4 Western Europe

Werner J. Feld

In the minds of people all over the world, Western Europe is almost synonymous with the European Community (EC). This term is convenient shorthand for three communities: the European Coal and Steel Community (ECSC) established in 1952; the European Economic Community (EEC, better known as the Common Market) set up in 1958; and the European Atomic Energy Community (Euratom) created in the same year.

The increasing identification of Western Europe with the European Community has a sound basis. Since the enlargement of the EC in 1973, when Great Britain, Ireland, and Denmark joined the original members – France, Germany, Italy, and the Benelux countries – Greece signed an accession treaty in 1979 and Spain and Portugal are likely to follow in the early 1980s. As a consequence, outside the Community we will find only three Nordic states (Norway, Finland, and traditionally neutral Sweden), the other neutrals (Austria and Switzerland), and three Mediterranean states (Turkey, Cyprus, and Malta). All these countries are located along the periphery of the West European region; their combined populations constitute only 23 percent of the region; and in terms of Gross National Product (GNP), their share is less than 15 percent of total GNP of the region (see Table 4.1). Most of these countries are linked to the EC by bilateral trade agreements reducing or completely eliminating most tariff barriers between the Community members and West European nonmembers. Hence, the whole region is moving rapidly toward becoming an enormous, unified trade bloc.

In terms of political and economic power, considerable differences exist among West European countries. At the upper level of power are France, the Federal Republic of Germany, the United Kingdom, and Italy. These countries are the most influential on the regional and global levels. In the lowest level of power category fall Luxembourg, Cyprus, Malta, and Iceland. All other states in the region can be pegged within this middle-level power spectrum; their specific influence de-

Table 4.1. Profiles of West European Countries – 1977

Country	Area 1,000 sq. km	Agricultural Area 1,000 sq. km	Tillage 1,000 sq. km	Population thousands	Inhabitants per sq. km	Crude Birth Rates	Unemployment Rate as % of total labor force	Total Civilian Employment (thousands)	Agriculture, Forestry and Fishing %	Industry %	Other %	Gross National Product at current prices and exchange rates billion US$	GNP per capita at current prices and exchange rates US $	Gross Domestic Expenditure on R & D in natural sciences and engineering; % of GNP	Consumer Prices % increase 1978 (Dec. 77-Dec. 78)	Consumer Prices: average annual increase 1973-1978 % per year	Total Official Reserves million SDR, Dec. 31, 1978	Exports (goods only) total exports as percentage of GNP at current prices	Infant Mortality (deaths in first year per 1,000 live births)	Per Capita Energy Consumption total primary energy requirements in tons of oil equivalent	Telephones per 1,000 inhabitants	Television Sets per 1,000 inhabitants
Austria	83.9	37.7	16.3	7,520	90	11.4	1.6	2,988	11.8	40.6	47.6	57.9	6,380	1.2	3.7	6.9	4,611	20.4	16.8	3.30	304	247
Belgium	30.5	15.2	8.1	9,830	322	12.4	6.3	3,711	3.3	37.9	58.8	96.4	8,060	1.2	3.9	9.2	4,535	45.7	15.3	4.53	300	255
Denmark	43.1	29.3	26.5	5,089	118	12.2	6.1	2,414	9.1	30.4	60.5	54.6	9,040	1.1	7.1	11.0	2,471	21.9	8.7	3.91	494	308
Finland	337.0	27.2	25.5	4,740	14	13.9	5.0	2,101	12.9	34.8	52.3	32.2	7,170	1.0	5.9	13.8	972	16.7	12.0	4.98	409	306
France	549.1	322.3	190.9	53,084	97	14.0	4.9	20,962	9.6	37.7	52.7	466.7	8,830	1.8	9.7	10.7	10,692	10.4	11.4	3.36	293	268
Germany	248.6	132.3	80.1	61,400	247	9.5	4.0	24,511	6.8	45.3	47.9	634.4	8,800	2.1	2.4	4.8	41,353	22.8	15.5	4.25	344	306
Greece	132.0	88.2	39.0	9,268	70	15.5	1.1	3,167	28.4	30.3	41.3	31.5	2,830	—	11.5	15.5	914	10.4	20.3	1.54	238	126
Iceland	103.0	22.8	—	221	2	18.0	0.5	98	14.2	37.9	47.9	2.0	8,680	0.9	46.9	39.8	23	26.7	9.6	5.88	411	234
Ireland	70.3	48.5	12.5	3,180	45	21.4	9.4	1,022	23.1	30.3	46.6	12.0	2,940	0.8	7.9	15.3	2,064	46.8	15.7	2.38	150	192
Italy	301.2	175.3	123.2	56,446	187	13.4	7.1	19,847	15.9	38.6	45.5	236.0	3,470	0.9	11.9	17.0	11,380	23.0	17.7	2.46	271	213
Luxembourg	2.6	1.3	0.6	355	137	11.4	0.4	147	5.9	45.1	49.0	3.3	7,700	—	3.4	7.9	—	45.7	10.6	10.64	442	257
Netherlands	40.8	20.8	8.5	13,853	340	12.5	0.9	4,555	6.3	33.2	60.5	128.9	7,680	1.9	3.9	7.8	5,822	41.1	9.5	4.58	391	255
Norway	324.2	9.0	8.0	4,043	12	12.5	0.9	1,824	9.0	32.3	58.7	40.0	8,800	1.2	8.1	9.5	2,209	21.1	10.5	4.90	366	259
Portugal	92.1	41.3	36.6	9,773	106	18.6	6.3	3,781	20.7	33.1	34.4	17.8	1,670	0.2	23.3	19.8	1,507	12.4	38.9	0.93	119	65
Spain	504.8	275.8	206.6	36,672	73	18.0	6.8	12,462	20.5	37.4	41.9	141.1	3,150	0.3	16.5	18.8	7,963	8.8	15.6	1.85	239	184
Sweden	450.0	37.2	30.0	8,255	18	11.6	1.8	4,099	6.1	34.3	59.6	85.9	9,480	1.8	7.4	10.3	3,376	24.4	8.0	6.09	689	352
Switzerland	41.3	20.0	3.8	6,327	153	11.5	0.4	2,817	8.5	42.7	48.8	84.6	9,580	2.2	0.7	4.1	16,550	28.9	9.8	3.87	634	273
Turkey	780.6	538.3	277.0	42,135	54	32.3	9.5	14,151	55.8	13.6	30.6	50.8	1,130	—	37.7	24.5	761	3.7	—	0.76	28	12
United Kingdom	244.0	185.7	69.8	55,919	229	11.7	5.5	24,450	2.7	40.0	57.3	307.1	4,370	2.1	8.4	16.1	13,100	23.5	14.1	3.78	394	320

Source: Adapted from The OECD Observer, no. 97, March 1979 pp. 19-26.

98

pends on particular situations such as geographic location (as in the case of Turkey) or control over needed raw materials such as crude oil or natural gas (as in the case of Norway and the Netherlands).

All regions are affected by influential external forces, and Western Europe is no exception. The most prominent external actors for this region are the United States and the Soviet Union whose actual and potential intrusive activities must be taken into consideration by national and regional decision makers at all times. The United States participates significantly in West European affairs through strategic, political, and economic links which it has with most of the members. The position of the Soviet Union as a potential adversary of Western Europe, coupled with its extraordinary military might, creates relationships which affect many political and economic concerns in Western Europe. If we follow Cantori and Spiegel's definition of an intrusive system as politically significant participation of external powers in the international relations of a regional system,(1) we must consider OPEC and its member countries as intrusive systems in Western Europe. The impact which their oil embargo and the increase of oil prices has had, especially on the Community countries, is evidence of significant involvement in the regional system. Changing technology in the production of energy, however, may alter the situation in the future and it is conceivable that in the next century the Arab oil producing countries may lose their roles as intrusive powers.

SOCIETAL AFFINITIES AND DIVERSITIES
WITHIN WESTERN EUROPE

Economic and Political Patterns

Seymour Lipset has asserted that "the more well-to-do a nation, the greater the chances it will sustain democracy."(2) He argues that high levels of industrialization, urbanization, wealth, and education correlate with democracy. Clearly, these conditions are present in many countries of Western Europe, although there are strong regional variations, especially in the United Kingdom (i.e., the less developed areas of Wales and Scotland) and Italy (where the Mezzogiorno continues to lag economically far behind the north). Ireland, the economically weakest member of the EC, has little industrialization compared with its Community partners, and a large percentage of its population (23.1 percent) is employed in agricultural pursuits. Indeed, the further a country is located from the center of Western Europe, the greater the share of its population engaged in farming (see Table 4.1). Greece's farm population is 28.4 percent of its working force, that of Portugal 32.5 percent, and the Turkish farmers are 55.8 percent.

Greece and Spain have upgraded their economic systems appreciably during the last few years, and Portugal is making slow, though steady, progress. Continuing troublesome conditions in Turkey and Cyprus are apt to affect their economies adversely. Inflation rates remain high in most countries. Other economic data are found in Table 4.1.

All West European states have basically capitalist economic systems tempered in varying degrees by social welfare programs, planning, restraints on monopolies, and state ownership of selected enterprises. Comprehensive social services exist in all countries and have become part of their political cultures. Planning is on a large scale in France and Denmark, but held to a minimum in Germany. Antitrust regulations vary from country to country, with the antitrust provisions of the EEC and ECSC treaties constituting a backup system.(3) State ownership of whole industries or particular enterprises is most widespread in the United Kingdom, Italy, and France.

Europeans are proud to cite their common cultural heritage, but historically conditioned factors have produced certain differences in their political cultures. Britain used to present the picture of a broadly homogeneous society, but this may be changing. Germany's Prussian, Imperial, Weimar, and Nazi histories provide inputs into her political culture which could be divisive, but her current political system accords well with those of her EC partners. Italy is rent by political cleavages partially caused by the recent history of national unification and the period of fascism. The Netherlands also contains a diversity of historically-conditioned political allegiances, but has developed an overall consensus suited to the other political cultures of Western Europe's core. Similar cleavages are present in France, where Gaullism has significantly influenced the traditional political culture. On the other hand, the Scandinavian countries have relatively homogeneous political cultures, despite many conflicts in their histories.

Greece returned to a democratic system in 1974 after having been ruled by a military dictatorship since 1967. This shift was the consequence of events in Cyprus. During the summer of 1974, the Greek military regime of "The Colonels" was the guiding spirit of the overthrow of the government of Archbishop Makarios whose term as president had been extended twice by parliament and who had received an overwhelming popular vote in February 1973. The overthrow of President Makarios and the substitution by a regime closely related to the Greek military prompted an invasion of Cyprus by the Turkish armed forces. This led to the resignation of the Greek military regime and the scheduling of popular elections. The elections resulted in the installation of a democratically-oriented government under the leadership of Premier Caramanlis, a post which he has continued to hold.

Spain has been moving steadily toward democracy since the death of General Francisco Franco in 1975 when the 500-year-old monarchy was restored with the proclamation of Juan Carlos de Borbon as King of Spain. In 1977 the first free elections were held in 41 years. Eighty percent of eligible voters turned out for the elections. A center-right coalition government was installed as a result of the elections and has remained in power since that time.

While Portugal's right-wing authoritarian regime was somewhat weakened in 1968 following Prime Minister Salazar's permanent physical incapacity, and was less oppressive than the Spanish type, liberalization measures introduced under Salazar's successor, Dr. Marcello

Caetano, were only modest. In 1969, two opposition groups were permitted to run candidates in the elections for the national assembly, but many restrictions upon voting continued. Further progress toward liberalizatin of the political system was opposed by the ruling military group under President Tomas. In April 1974, General Antonio de Spinola overthrew the existing regime and promised the Portuguese people a new democratic system. In turn, de Spinola was ousted by a group of younger officers whose political orientation was clearly Leftist, and Vasco Goncalves was appointed Premier. Popular elections and the liquidation of Portugal's colonies in Africa were promised. At the same time, the younger officers formed the Armed Forces Movement which became the power base for a strong shift toward a communist-oriented political system. While the vista of free elections initially created considerable euphoria among the Portuguese people, it became clear very soon that the new rulers were primarily interested in promoting the Communist Party of Portugal. All parties right of the middle-ground Popular Democrats were prohibited. Nevertheless, elections were held on April 25, 1975, that were conducted in a free and orderly fashion excluding, however, the parties whose activities had been prohibited. In these elections, the Socialist Party polled the largest number of votes (approximately 37 percent) followed by the Popular Democrats (26 percent), with the Communists and allied splinter groups only receiving 17 percent of the votes.(4) However, despite the voice of the people as expressed in this election, the Armed Forces Movement did not want to give up power and it took another year to enact a democratic constitution. Finally, in June 1976, a new president was elected by popular vote and the Socialist Party formed the first democratic government in more than 50 years.

Linguistic Diversity

Western Europe's linguistic diversity is considerable. Generally, language boundaries run along national frontiers, but there are major exceptions. Belgium is divided into Flemish- and French-speaking parts; and in Luxembourg, French and German are spoken plus a dialect mixture of the two. The Belgian linguistic struggle has created some internal political problems, but has scarcely affected relations among the nine EC members. There are a number of linguistic minorities whose political importance is small as far as interstate relations are concerned – the Scottish and Welsh nationalists in Britain, the German-speaking Italians in South Tyrol, the French-speaking Italians in the Valley of Aosta, and the Bretons in Brittany, France.

Linguistically, the diversity of the peripheral countries is even greater than that in the center of Western Europe. Culturally and historically, several broad groupings can be distinguished: the Scandinavian countries; Iberia; the East Mediterranean states, i.e., Greece, Turkey, and Cyprus; and perhaps Austria and Switzerland.

The linguistic diversity in the West European region is being reduced somewhat by a growth of multilingualism among the youth and by Europe-wide television programs (Eurovision),(5) which stimulate the acquisition of multilingual skills. These TV programs may also help to overcome prejudices and unfavorable stereotype perceptions which individuals in some countries have of other members and their citizens – perceptions deriving from differences in tradition and culture as well as long-standing habits and customs.

Religious Diversity

The distribution of major religious denominations in Western Europe has the potential of stimulating divergent trends among the countries of the region. There are several patterns of religious belief: mainly Roman Catholic countries which include Italy, France, Belgium, Spain, Portugal, and Ireland; those with approximate Catholic and Protestant parity, i.e. Germany, the Netherlands, and Luxembourg; and the largely Protestant countries of Great Britain, Denmark, and the Nordic states. Greece is made up of mainly Greek Orthodox; and Turkey is mostly Islam.

The Catholic church has been politically powerful, especially in Italy, Spain, and Ireland; but its defeat in the new Italian divorce law may foreshadow a weakening of its position. Relations between the church and the powerful communist party, formerly arch enemies, however, have somewhat improved. In France, the influence of the Catholic church has never been as significant as in Italy and Ireland, and political issues have never been drawn along clear-cut Catholic-secular lines.

In Germany, the political influence of both the Catholic and Protestant churches has been on the wane during the last decade or two. In the Netherlands, where political dominance by the religious parties was traditional, there have been signs of a fundamental realignment of the party system which may diminish considerably the influence of both churches.

In Great Britain, where politics were rooted in religion during the nineteenth century, the ties between religion and party have largely disappeared, although for many middle class voters, religious values support their political loyalties.(6) In Denmark the church plays no significant role in politics.

Despite the different religious patterns found in most West European countries, one cannot conclude that they disturb interstate relations in any way. On the contrary, the transnational connections of the two major churches (Catholic and Protestant) may strengthen other processes promoting affinity among the nine countries.

The Greek Orthodox Church as such does not have a particularly strong influence in the politics within Greece, but the church's religious dogma and nationalism have often been considered interchangeable.(7) In Malta, the removal by the Catholic church of the ban on voting for the Labour Party contributed, in part, to the success of that party in 1971 and to the appointment of Dom Mintoff as Prime Minister.

Orientations and Mutual Trust

The orientations of the people in the central West European states toward each other are friendly and fundamentally cooperative. Membership in the EC signifies the existence of common economic interests which support these orientations. But there are conflicting national interests which are pressed in competition with those of other EC members. Orientations toward peripheral members are also friendly, but cooperative tendencies are more ambiguous. While preferential economic agreements of various kinds have been concluded by the EC with all peripheral countries and cooperation has, thereby, been stimulated, these tendencies are affected by differences in the political systems of some of the countries and by divergent perceptions of interests.

Toward the outside states, people and governments of Western Europe generally display a collaborative spirit in consonance with their economic and strategic interests. A major concern is the promotion of international trade, especially with industrially advanced countries. Trade expansion in the Third World may be coupled subtly with an extension of political influence. The defense partnership with the United States remains a significant orientation, arousing criticism from time to time because of perceived American high-handedness. Peaceful economic and cultural intercourse with the Soviet East European bloc continues to have a high priority. Concern with deliveries of petroleum products from the Middle East, however, has led to selfish pursuits of national interests, seriously weakening regional solidarity.

The orientations of the peripheral countries and their people may be affected by special concerns such as a perceived community of interests of the Scandinavian countries; problems of neutrality in Sweden, Switzerland, and Austria; the Greek-Turkish competition in Cyprus; and the civil war in Ireland. The orientations of the Maltese toward some West European countries were probably also affected adversely by the rejection of some of Prime Minister Mintoff's demands on the NATO countries and especially Britain. These unfavorable orientations, however, are probably offset to some extent by favorable attitudes stemming from the large-scale employment of citizens of many of these countries in the EC member states.

Toward outside states, the orientations of the peripheral countries and their people are generally open and friendly, but depend in individual cases on economic, political, and strategic interests and basic ideologies. Regarding the United States, the orientations are also strongly conditioned by American economic and natinal security policies. For example, disenchantment with the latter type of policies has affected the views of Norway and Sweden. Greece and Turkey, who used to be very favorably inclined toward American economic and security policies, have had a change of heart as a result of the dispute over Cyprus. Greece resented the apparent favoritism of the Nixon administration toward Turkey and demanded a reduction of American bases on its soil. At the same time, the Greek government quit the military structure of NATO. Turkey was offended by congressional action halting military and economic aid until the Turks were willing to compromise on Cyprus; it seems that this action may well have had a permanent adverse effect upon Turkish feelings toward the United States, although the embargo on U.S. arms shipment to Turkey has been lifted. Portugal's orientations toward the United States improved materially after the revolutionary turmoil during 1972 and 1975. In Spain, the United States national security policies continue to evoke favorable reactions.

Similar considerations apply to orientations toward the Soviet Union. Soviet policy aiming at detente and closer economic and cultural cooperation between Western and East Europe evokes warm reactions in Scandinavian countries and, perhaps, also in Greece and Turkey. In Spain, this situation is somewhat ambiguous. Austria and Finland are dependent to a large degree on Soviet economic goodwill and cooperation and, therefore, their orientations reflect this factor.

The foregoing orientations of West European governments and people are based mainly on utilitarian considerations, although traditions and long-accepted stereotypes may play their part. When it comes to mutual trust, affective and social-psychological factors tend to assume a predominant role.

In 1976, an EC Commission-sponsored biennial public opinion survey in the Community countries (Euro-Barometre) asked which nationals of the EC member states (and of a few selected outside countries) the respondents "trusted very much, fairly much, not very much, or not at all." The responses are most interesting, if not astounding. Perhaps the most intriguing pattern of responses pertains to trust in the Italians: 51.4 percent of the Italians distrust themselves, while only 43.5 percent gave a positive answer. Who does trust the Italians most? The British (33.9 percent), clearly not an enviable record. Averaging of the responses shows that of the four big countries in Western Europe, Great Britain is trusted most (59.3 percent), followed by Germany (52.6 percent), and France (52.2 percent), and Italy least (32.6 percent).

As for who trusts whom, the British are trusted most by the Irish (74.6 percent) and the Dutch (60.2 percent); surprisingly, the Germans are trusted most by the Dutch (65.1 percent), the Luxembourgers (62.9 percent), and the Belgians (60.6 percent); and the French are trusted most by the Belgians (68.1 percent) and the Germans (55.6 percent). Of the smaller EC countries, the Dutch are the most trusted (60.2 percent), and their greatest admirers are the Germans (73 percent).

One of the most surprising findings of the survey is the strong trust in the Americans. Sixty-seven percent of all respondents in the Common Market countries trusted them either very much or fairly much. The Germans clearly feel closest to the Americans with 74.6 percent expressing themselves in favor. The percentage for the British is 63.2, followed by the Irish with 62.3 percent, and the Dutch with 61.7 percent. On the other hand, the Soviet Union is trusted least (19.7 percent); in the forefront are the Germans and the Irish (15.4 percent) expressing themselves this way, followed by the U.K. with 17.3 percent. The People's Republic of China also evokes mainly distrust by the people in the Common Market (48 percent). Finally, it is noteworthy that trust for the Swiss people among the Common Market countries is higher in most instances than for other members of the EC (60.5 percent). Both the Germans and the French express their greatest trust with 86.9 percent and 78.3 percent respectively. (See Table 4.2 for additional data.)

Finally, a significant finding has been unearthed by the public opinion polls of the European Community Commission during the last few years regarding the patterns of understanding between the Community countries. Twenty-eight percent of all respondents asked in the Fall of 1978 indicated that this understanding has progressed over the last year. Twelve percent said that it had lost ground, and 38 percent believed that it has stayed the same. It is noteworthy that the number of those who "don't know" has increased from 15 to 22 percent.(8) The important aspect of this question to our discussion is that this survey gives us some insight into basic attitudes toward the climate of cooperation that exists within the Community countries, attitudes that not only reflect traditions and stereotypes, but are also influenced by the psychological and social mood of the moment.

AFFINITIES OF THE POLITICAL SYSTEMS

The contemporary political systems of the West European countries display high degrees of fundamental similarity. Constitutionally, all are parliamentary democracies with representative institutions, freely contested elections, generally unrestricted party formation, and competitive party systems. The commonality of these characteristics is not affected by the differences in electoral arrangements, which range from single member constituencies with one-run plurality in Great Britain to nearly pure proportional representation in the Netherlands. It is strengthened by the similarity of major party groupings across most countries; the three main categories are the confessional-conservative, lay-liberal, and socialist parties. Underlying all political systems, at least in principle, is the recognition of a "legitimate opposition,"(9) an essential feature for free political choice, and also the vehicle of peaceful government succession.

Of course, the maturity of parliamentary constitutional practice varies from country to country. Portugal and Spain have moved only recently from decades of dictatorship to parliamentary democracy, and Greece is also a recent returnee to this system of government. In troubled Cyprus, the Turks ceased to participate in the proceedings of the House of Representatives, and in 1975 a Turkish-Cypriot state was created within a federal republic. This new state is also based on the principles of parliamentary democracy.

Table 4.2. Who Trusts Whom?

Trust In	Trust By									
	France	Belgium	Netherlands	W. Germany	Italy	Luxembourg	Denmark	Ireland	U.K.	Row Total
British	42.1	58.4	60.2	55.2	36.5	33.2	55.5	74.6	84.9	59.3
Dutch	58.1	61.7	86.5	73.0	38.2	53.0	51.2	48.2	63.9	50.2
French	89.4	68.1	57.4	55.6	39.9	53.3	34.7	44.9	43.1	52.6
Germans	59.1	60.6	65.1	94.9	52.3	62.9	58.2	54.3	55.7	52.2
Italians	36.2	32.6	36.7	27.0	43.5	25.8	25.7	35.6	33.9	32.6
Swiss	78.3	60.1	68.5	86.9	49.0	61.5	43.5	40.7	62.1	60.5
Russians	27.3	18.6	18.4	15.4	28.5	7.3	18.1	15.4	17.3	19.7
Americans	51.0	46.9	61.7	74.6	57.2	51.6	42.3	62.3	63.2	67.2

Source: Euro-Barometre, no. 10 (1979), pp. 74-78.

The party labels in Western Europe may not always clearly indicate to which of the three categories a particular party belongs. For example, in Turkey, the Justice Party is conservative and the Republican People's Party leans to the left. In the Netherlands, the Democrats "66" constitute the radical left. Moreover, in Malta there is no liberal party, and in a number of countries some parties are outside the three categories.   Obviously, this is the case with the communist parties, which have considerable strength in Italy and France, but cannot be ignored either in Portugal and Spain. A rather new party in Germany has been formed by the environmentalists, calling itself the "Green List," with no attachment to the traditional party groupings.

Western Europe's political systems generally espouse the doctrine of constitutionalism, which seeks to assure effective government by the majority with a guarantee of rights for the minority and individuals. They follow the "pluralistic" concept which views democratic society as comprising groups that articulate and pursue their interests through parties and other organizations, competitive and cooperative. According to S.M. Lipset, "the chances for stable democracy are enhanced to the extent that groups and individuals have a number of cross-cutting, politically relevant affiliations. To the degree that a significant proportion of the population is pulled among conflicting forces, its members have an interest in reducing the intensity of political conflict."(10) To curb the potential for intensive conflict as a result of the presence of powerful contentious groups, all states are committed to a measure of governmental intervention to assure freedom, equality, and property rights of their citizens. With a political culture stressing the value of social conscience, their interventions aim at creating "positive" freedom for the self development of the individual, as defined by Thomas H. Green,(11) although in the southern tier of states the attainment of this objective remains largely elusive.

Levels of legitimacy are high in most polities. In the eyes of a substantial number of people in all but the southern peripheral countries, the performance of governmental institutions has been reasonably effective and the treatment of citizens by the institutions has been relatively close to their expectations. The degree of support for governmental authority has been more consistently high in Great Britain, the Netherlands, and Denmark – more than in Germany and France where governmental structures have undergone significant changes. Future degrees of legitimacy will depend on a number of factors, among which popular expectations in Western Europe will be very important. If the expectations are disappointed over an extended period, alienation will set in, the level of legitimacy will fall, and the stability of the democratic structures will be endangered.(12)

The substantial voting strength of the communist parties in France and Italy registers protest against the prevailing "establishment" despite temporary support by the Italian CP of the Christian Democratic minority government. On the other hand, this voting strength does not always reflect commitment to Marxist-Leninist philosophy. In Italy, a neo-fascist movement is also active; it may be nothing more than a strong reaction to the economic turmoil and labor unrest during the early 1970s, but it could be an expression of serious disenchantment with democracy, especially as practiced in that country.

Eurocommunism

During the last decade, we have witnessed the emergence of a somewhat curious political phenomenon in Western Europe: Eurocommunism. What are the major features of this movement? It was the Italian Communist Party (PCI) that, under the leadership of Enrico Berlinguer, developed the concepts of Eurocommunism. They are: 1) respect for democratic methods including majority rule and acceptance of, and compliance with, the results of periodic free elections; 2) basic recognition of the need for a free market economy and no insistence on complete nationalization of private enterprise, but extensive state planning is considered necessary; 3) strong support for the European Community and the direct elections to the European Parliament, but the Community must be "democratized"; and 4) continued membership in NATO. These concepts are quite similar to those of the socialists in Western Europe, and they have now been accepted also by the French Communist Party (PCF). Its leader, Georges Marchais, much more the typical communist party secretary general than the elegant and sophisticated Berlinguer, made the switch from the traditional Marxist-Leninist ideology only very recently. Indeed, Marchais admitted that the PCF had changed, but whether this change will persist is doubtful since Marchais broke with the "Common Program" of the socialist-communist coalition in the 1978 general elections in France.

In Spain, the communist party was legalized only in the Spring of 1977. But its chief, Santiago Carillo, has quickly become a staunch supporter of Eurocommunism and expressed himself strongly in favor of a "democratic, parliamentary, multi-party socialism."(13)

Various statements of the leaderships of the communist parties in Italy, France, and Spain stress their commitment to the new ideas. The economic specialist of the PCI, Giorgio Napolitano, declared that in Italy no further nationalizations of industry were envisaged, and that the state in its planning would have to create the conditions to induce private investments in sectors considered essential for Italy's economic welfare. Special incentives for such investments would be offered, including favorable credits.(14) All three parties have sharply criticized the despotic conditions in the Soviet Union and deplored the violation of human rights of dissidents in that and other East European countries. They have condemned the 1968 invasion of Czechoslovakia by Soviet armed forces and proclaimed the principle of their independence from the Soviet Union, but they have not made a clear break with the sister party in the USSR. No real schism exists between Moscow and the Eurocommunists and, of course, there is no empirical evidence whether Eurocommunism can become a viable ideology of its own or will remain nothing more than a variation of European socialism. In the meantime,

Eurocommunism may have deleterious effects upon the loyalty of the satellite regimes of Eastern Europe to the Soviet Union. Their leaders are likely to sympathize in the bottom of their hearts with the tendencies toward autonomy shown by the communist parties of Italy, Spain, and France and wish for a similar status for themselves with an accompanying relaxation of Soviet domination.

While it is always possible that Eurocommunism represents a departure from the Soviet brand of communism, at present this remains an untested assumption. The important question is not how the Eurocommunists behave when they are outside the government working to participate in its control, but what actions they will take when they are in power or favorably positioned to exercise power. When the latter happens, the old undemocratic, staunchly pro-Soviet face may reemerge. This is a true dilemma for the present leaders and people, especially of Italy and France.

The future of Eurocommunism is likely to depend on the outcome of a soul-searching internal debate that started in the PCI in 1979, and on the attitudes of the West European socialist parties toward their competitions to the left. The main lines of the intra-PCI struggle will be drawn between the hard-line left wing of the party, which never fully accepted Berlinguer's gradualness, and members of the right wing who have counselled even more moderation. The PCI losses in the general elections of 1979 – from 34.4 to 30.4 percent of the popular vote(15) – form the background for this debate, which may send important signals to other communist parties in Western Europe.

The attitudes of the West European socialist parties have always been more or less negative toward the communists. However, when the French Socialist Party formed its Common Program with the PCF, it gave Eurocommunism a lift and a measure of respectability. Most other socialist parties have usually remained aloof from, if not hostile toward, any common action with the communists. This has been the case especially with the German Social-Democratic Party and the British Labour Party. In this connection, it is interesting to note that, traditionally, the socialist parties are strong and the communist parties weak in those countries where a single or a dominant trade union organization has been in existence for several decades. Examples for such a situation are Germany, Great Britain, Austria, and the Scandinavian countries. On the other hand, where the trade union movement is fragmented, the strongest union is normally closely affiliated with the communist party. The result, then, is likely to be a weak socialist party as is the case in Italy now and has been until fairly recently in France.

INTEREST GROUPS

The hallmark of a pluralistic society is a plethora of interest groups. Western Europe is no exception. However, the number and distribution of interest groups varies from country to country; their number is greater and the kinds of interests pursued more extensive in the mature democracies of the central and northern parts of the region than in southern peripheral states. But the differences may gradually disappear as the economic levels of the latter improve and the practices of democratic pluralism become more familiar.

All over Western Europe, interest group representatives have become more effective since World War II. The targets of interest groups may be the executive with its many civil servants, parliamentarians, and party officials. In some cases, interest groups may use parties as a transmission belt for the pursuit of their interests; in other cases, they may compete with the parties for the ear of administrators or even parliamentary deputies. This depends on which governmental unit is able to accommodate the interests best and produce appropriate public policy action, and this, again, depends on the structure of governmental decision making and the prevailing norms and attitudes within a particular polity.

In Western Europe, the most important interest groups are found in the industrial and commercial sectors, the farm population, the churches, and the professions. The significance of these groups is a function of the type of economy a country has and the traditions of influences. Around these main categories of interest representation cluster a host of other special interests, most defending the socio-economic position of their members, and some advancing a particular cause, for example protecting the environment which has become a transnational enterprise in Western Europe.

In a number of countries including France, Italy, and the Benelux states, the constitutions have set up Economic and Social Councils in which various interests have formal representation. The power of these councils is fairly limited; they are mostly advisory, but in the Netherlands the Council has the power to make certain regulations binding for industry.(16)

In Germany, the constitution (Basic Law) guarantees the right "to form associations and societies" (Art. 9). As of May 1979, nearly 1,000 interest groups had offices in Bonn. Among them are the offices of influential umbrella groups which are the top level national organizations in industry and commerce – for example the Federation of German Industry (BDI) – and of organized labor – primarily the German Trades Union Federation (DGB), and the German Association of Farmers. In the economic sphere, these leadership groups tend to balance each other's power, although this power is, at times, reinforced by top level or lower group officials also being elected to Germany's federal parliament. A number of union officials also are members of the Bundestag.

An additional dimension of interest group authority in Germany flows from the federal nature of the governmental system. The governments of the individual states fulfill the roles of interest groups inasmuch as they seek to promote the particular socioeconomic interests of their area with respect to the expenditures of the federal government.

In France, General de Gaulle attempted, during his presidency under the Fifth Republic, to curb the extensive influence which both interest groups and political parties exercised during the Third and Fourth Republics on the governance of France. As a consequence, interest group attention switched to the executive. But this tactic did not produce the desired influence on public policy, although increasing numbers of councils, committees, and commissions were set up in which government officials were to consult group representatives on specific policy issues.(17) Indeed, the fundamental divergence of interests pursued by the groups has made it easy, at times, to rule by division. On the other hand, in contemporary France, the influence of the Assembly has risen again to some degree and, therefore, the relations of interest groups with parliamentary groupings and parties have again been strengthened, although it should be noted that these contacts were never entirely abandoned even under de Gaulle.

What the examples of Germany and France show is the basic similarity in interest group activity in the two countries. The major difference is the degree of centralization of effort and this, in turn, is a function of the constitutional system with a federal type of government inducing greater decentralization. Another important factor is political culture and tradition. For example, in Italy, society is highly segmented and the Christian Democrats have occupied a hegemonist role since World War II, factors which have given their particular imprint on interest group activity.(18) In Sweden a homogeneous political culture has resulted in a consensus about the roles of the state, party, and interest representation that has led to maximum integration of the latter with public life.(19)

Ideologically, groups representing industry and commercial interests have usually been mainly conservative or liberal but, regardless of the label, have sought to promote market economies. On the other hand, many labor unions in Western Europe are not only seeking to improve the economic and social welfare of the worker vis-a-vis his employer, but want to transform society in general into a socialistic system. This is especially the case with left-wing union federations in France and Italy, while organized labor in Germany and the Netherlands gives lip service to socialist ideals without exerting much vigor in translating these ideals into reality. Unions in other West European countries may fall between the two positions described.

Interest group activity is likely to proliferate and become more effective in those West European countries where parliamentary viability is declining and the majority of decisions, in effect, is being taken in committees with the plenum having only a confirmatory role. In such circumstances a double transfer of power may be taking place: from parliament to the executive, and from the executive to the top-level bureaucracy where the necessary expertise lies especially in economic, financial, and technical matters. The result is enhanced influence of interest groups on many issues through effective lobbying in committees, many of which in Western Europe frequently meet behind closed doors, and through extensive and often intimate contacts between group leaders and functionaries on the one hand and bureaucrats on the other.

While, so far, our attention has been primarily focused on national interest groups, the creation of the European Communities has prompted the establishment of an increasing number of transnational groups covering the entire EC area. In addition, a few groups encompass the whole West European region. Understandably, most of the more than 500 EC-related interest groups are concerned with industry and commerce (about two thirds) and with agriculture (about one third), but union federations also have a few European umbrella organizations in Brussels.

How effective are the European-level interest group confederations, (located mostly in Brussels) in obtaining favorable results when presenting the demands of their constituent national groups directly to the Community institutions? The answer depends, to some extent, on the degree of cohesion and level of administrative capability of these organizations. The most prominent agricultural umbrella confederation, COPA (Comite des Organisations Professionelles agricoles de la C.E.E.), leads all other organizations in efficiency. UNICE (Union des Industries de la Communite Europeene) and other industrial and commercial umbrella organizations are less effective; and the labor organizations such as ECFTUC (European Confederation of Free Trade Unions in the Community) and others have had much less influence than their agricultural and industrial counterparts, despite repeated reorganizations on the European level.(20)

There seems to be general agreement that the objectives of national economic interest groups tend to become diluted in all umbrella organizations, including COPA and UNICE, because the structuring of a united front requires the reconciliation of conflicting economic interests. This, in turn, requires bargains and compromises and seems to confirm Lindberg's observation with regard to these organizations that "Common positions are reached when interests coincide, but otherwise decision making is of the lowest common denominator type, with final agreement rarely exceeding what the least cooperative participant is willing to grant."(21)

REGIONAL INSTITUTIONS

Regional organizations abound in Western Europe and provide many links among the countries of the region in the economic, security, and political spheres. As suggested in the introduction to this chapter, the European Communities and especially the EEC have become a major focus of activity not only for the member states, but also for the remainder of the region. Some of the member countries also belong to two intergovernmental organizations (IGOs) within the territorial confines of the Community. Belgium, the Netherlands, and Luxembourg founded in 1944 the Benelux Union, an IGO with economic objectives which continues to operate at present but has lost much of its significance. The other IGO is the Western European Union which has limited military and political purposes and to which the original Six and Great Britain belong.

An IGO of interest today mainly for non-EC members is the European Free Trade Association (EFTA). But all EFTA members are also affiliated with the EC through free trade agreements. These countries are Austria, Finland, Iceland, Norway, Portugal, Sweden and Switzerland. Moreover, the Scandinavian EFTA countries are also members of the Nordic Council. One regional IGO to which all West European states belong is the Council of Europe, concerned primarily with political matters.

Extraregional IGOs, in which most West European countries hold membership, are the Organization for Economic Cooperation and Development (OECD), to which also the United States, Canada, and Japan belong, as well as NATO. Beyond these two IGOs, all countries are members of the United Nations and many of its specialized agencies. Since the Nine, on many matters dealt with by the United Nations, often have common or converging interests, organizational contacts are frequent, strengthening collaborative dispositions.

Without doubt, the European Community institutional framework plays the most important role among regional IGOs. Because of the various arrangements made with non-EC countries in Western Europe, the institutional decision making of the European Community also affects, to varying degrees, these countries as well. Another institutional structure likely to have a significant impact on most of the West European region is that of the NATO organization, but its scope is, of course, limited mostly to the national security-political sphere. Other IGOs whose institutions may have an influence, albeit minor, on policymaking for all countries are the Council of Europe and the OECD.

The European Community decision making system has many intriguing aspects. It involves processes of multilevel interaction and interpenetration among the Community institutions, national governments, administrations, and legislatures, subnational legislators and officials, and interest groups, a relationship much more intensive and extensive than that usually prevailing between traditional IGOs and national authorities or professional groups. The goals pursued by national economic groups in the member countries, the domestic politics within each member state, and the interstate politics within the Community have complex effects on the making of specific EC policies.(22) Especially as far as external issues are concerned, the general foreign policy goals pursued by the member states and the pressures exerted by third countries both on the national and Community level may also materially affect the collective outcome.

According to the ingenious arrangement devised by the framers of the EC treaties, it is the Commission that is to act as the driving motor of the decision making apparatus. It is the initiator of proposals upon which the Council of Ministers is called to act. A third organ, the Committee of Permanent Representatives (CPR), has the duty of preparing the sessions and decisions of the Council, which usually meets only a few days each month, and of carrying out any tasks assigned to it by the Council. In addition, the staff of the CPR is frequently consulted informally by the Commission before it submits a formal proposal to the Council. In order to accomplish these missions, the CPR, composed of the ambassadors from the nine member states and their staffs (totaling about 300 civil servants), has established a number of working groups, subcommittees, and special ad hoc committees patterned after the administrative structure of the Commission.(23)

The Community machinery for decision making must be seen in broad political terms. During the last 15 years, the Council of Ministers representing the national governments gained power over the Commission as it became clear that the process of political integration and the establishment of a European government would not make the expected progress and, in fact, began to falter. As a consequence, the CPR has also gained a measure of influence which was not foreseen when the Communities were established. The continuing strength of the national governments induces the Commission, which was to be completely independent from these governments, to seek advice and reassurance regarding the proposals it makes to the Council. Hence, no matter how anxious the Commission may be to advance various facets of political integration, it has to face up to the political reality that any success is dependent on the goodwill of the national governments.

The frequently conflicting interests reflected by the demands made on and supports given to the regional system have resulted in continuing struggles between proponents and opponents on many issues. To be successful in realizing any economic, social, or political demands requires the use of all the political strategies and tactics known to pluralistic, competitive societies. Pressures are brought to bear by governmental and nongovernmental actors on specific targets in the national and European political systems, and shifting coalitions among actors on subnational, national, and European levels are commonplace. Among the nongovernmental actors are the national and regional interest groups discussed in the preceding section. Despite the growing regionalization of interest groups, it would be an error to assume that the European-level organizations have become either the chief or the most effective carriers of interest group demands. Rather, the national interest groups remain the kingpins for lobbying efforts, and the major thrust of all economic interest groups continues to be at the level of national governments.

The multiplicity of levels through which Community decisions must pass results in a very slow resolution of major issues and frequently produces great ambiguities. National interests continue to dominate the scene and the crystallization and support of Community interests emerge only slowly. Some of the institutions in the European Community structure, such as the European Parliament and the Economic and Social Council, represent primarily a forum for debate, but have no significant decisional power. The European Parliament (EP) has been utilized as a partner for the Commission to advance the latter's objective, but it has been a partnership that has rarely produced resounding victories. Because of a lack of a persistently viable pipeline with the national parliaments of the Nine, European Parliamentarians have only occasionally been able to exert influence upon their own national governments through their home legislatures.

In June 1979, the members of the EP were for the first time elected directly by the people in the nine member states instead of indirectly by their national parliaments, and supporters of a united Europe hoped that this election would strengthen the legitimacy of the parliament and lead to the acquisition of new powers and competences. However, the voter turnout for the elections was disappointing with only six out of ten registered voters going to the ballot boxes. In Belgium, Luxembourg, and Italy where voting is compulsory, the electoral participation was 92, 85.6, and 85.9 percent respectively, while at the lower end of the spectrum were the United Kingdom with 31.3 percent and Denmark with 47.1 percent. In the Netherlands, a surprisingly low 58 percent of the registered voters entered the voting booths. France and Germany were somewhat above 60 percent.(24) Although the fact of direct elections may raise the moral authority of the EP, its political effectiveness may not have been enhanced. In the political culture of Europe, a 60 percent voter turnout is hardly "representative." Some of the deputies elected – the Gaullists and the Labour Party representatives – in fact, want to make sure that the Parliament's powers remain negligible. How strong the desire of other deputies is to upgrade the Parliament's effective authority and how much their political clout at home is to obtain national support for this effort is far from clear, and a healthy dose of skepticism is warranted.

In the meantime, it is noteworthy that while the socialists form the largest single group of deputies (111), they occupy only slightly more than 25 percent of total seats. A coalition of Christian Democrats and Conservatives with a combined figure of 170 deputies may well form the leadership group in the EP. For a distribution of seats in the Parliament see Table 4.3.

It is important to emphasize that while the different party groupings are composed of mixed nationalities, agreement within the individual groupings regarding goals and methods is often difficult to reach. This became especially evident during the campaign for the 1979 elections. For example, among the socialists there were considerable disparities in positions springing mainly from their differing national party platforms. For the German SPD, the right of codetermination of workers in enterprises where they are employed has always been an outstanding achievement, but codetermination has been frowned upon by the Italian socialists. Opinions regarding the extent of nationalization of private enterprises vary among the socialist parties and so do the views with respect to the degree of instituting a planned economy. All these differences play a role in conceptualizing a unified Europe, although there is basic agreement that the strong orientation toward free enterprise and the lack of accountability of the EC institutions toward the people living in the member states must be changed to reflect basic social democratic tenets. Similar, but less serious, problems in defining

Table 4.3. Breakdown of Seats in the European Parliament by
Party Groups and Nationalities, 1979.

Parties

(Figure in parentheses indicates former distribution)

Socialist Group	111	(66)
European People Party Group	107	(53)
Liberals and Democratic Group	40	(23)
Conservative Group	63	(18)
Communist Group	44	(18)
EPD Group	23	(17)
Various nonattached	22	(3)

Member States

Belgium	10 CD, 7 Socialists, 4 Liberals, 2 FDR, 1 Volksunie
Denmark	3 Social Democrats, 3 Liberals, 2 Conservatives, 1 Centre Democrat, 1 Progress Party, 1 People's Socialist Party, 5 anti-EEC movement
Germany	42 CDU/CSU, 35 SPD, 4 FDP
France	25 Mrs. Veil List, 22 PS, 19 PCF, 15 Chiracquians
Ireland	7 Fianna Fail, 6 Fine Gael, 1 Socialist
Italy	30 CD, 24 Communists, 13 Socialists and Social Democrats, 2 Republicans, 3 Liberals, 4 MSI, 3 Radicals, 2 Extreme Left
Netherlands	10 CD, 9 Socialists, 4 Liberals, 2 Democracy 66
U.K.	60 Conservatives, 17 Labour, 1 Scottish Nationalists, 2 Unionists, 1 Catholic (Northern Ireland)
Luxembourg	3 Social Christians, 2 Liberals, 1 Socialist

Source: Agence Europe Bulletin, June 11/12, 1979.

objectives were also encountered by the Christian Democrats, whose new name in the EP is the European People's Party, and by the Liberals, renamed the European Liberal Party.

Perhaps the most effective of the major Community institutions is the Court of Justice. Over the years, the Court has contributed significantly to the progress of economic, social, and perhaps political integration through its vigorous development of Community law. Its decisions have a truly supranational nature: they are directly binding on individuals, business enterprises, and governments in the Community member states, without the necessity of additional independent affirmative action by the national authorities. One of the most significant jurisdictional assignments made to the Community court is the responsibility for treaty interpretations. The extensive jurisprudence of the court in this area has led to the gradual acceptance of the supremacy of Community law over conflicting national law. Controversies between Community institutions and member governments about treaty violations have also led to repeated court intervention. In all cases, the decisions of the court have eventually been obeyed.

Finally, an "institution" not created by the EC Treaties and clearly operating outside the Community framework has had a growing impact on the activities of the Community system. It is the regularly convened summit conference of the heads of state and chiefs of government of the member states, now known as the European Council. Initiated in 1969, these summit conferences now meet four times a year and have become the primary source of Community and indeed West European initiatives. Some of these initiatives announced with great fanfare are mainly programmatic and are not always fully implemented. Indeed, years may pass before the initiatives are translated into reality. Examples are the direct elections to the EP launched at the summit meeting in The Hague in 1969 and the economic and monetary union announced at the same meeting. As we have seen, direct elections to the EP did take place in 1979, but the European Monetary System inaugurated in 1979 is only a partial beginning to a complete economic and monetary union. The results of this endeavor should reach beyond the boundaries of the community.

The NATO institution mainly responsible for processing national security demands is the Council and its subordinate committees. Since unanimity is required in taking decision within the Council, the method of accommodating, modifying, or rejecting demands by individual or several member governments is to seek consensus through various compromises. Although the common defense of Western Europe by its nature has high priority for all countries in the region, it does not have the pervasive impact and the shared interest which economic matters have.

The institutions of the other regional IGOs, such as the Council of Europe, OECD, or WEU, affect to varying degrees the policies of member states by their recommendations, but they have not the saliency and effect of EC or NATO decisions. Indeed, the effects of the EC decision making process, in which, as we have stressed, the voice of national governments of the member states normally is more influential than that of the Community institutions, often touch nonmembers as well. Reasons are the Community's preferential trade relationship with the EFTA countries; the preferential trade arrangements with Spain, Cyprus, and Malta; and the association with Turkey.

Decision making in the Western European region is, thus, both multilateral and bilateral. In fact, there is a complex interplay between both types of decision making, and final outcomes are usually the result of intensive bargaining on all decision levels. In this bargaining, diplomatic pressures by foreign service officials of member governments play a major role.(25) However, interactions between bureaucratic and elected political elites are also significant and nongovernmental actors are utilized wherever possible to influence decision making centers within their own countries as well as in other countries of the region through their transnational connections.

Legitimacy

What is the level of legitimacy the regional institutions have gained so far? If we define legitimacy as confidence in and support of institutions by the people in terms of viewing them as the proper entities to make authoritative decisions, we have a number of public opinion surveys to measure the legitimacy of the EC institutions. In this connection, S.M. Lipset's view is relevant according to which legitimacy of an institution is closely related to its effectiveness.(26) This view, which has become widely accepted and directly incorporated into Easton's notions of specific and diffuse support,(27) suggests that legitimacy and effectiveness are very much two sides to the same coin. That is, rather than one preceding the other, the existence of one presumes the existence (or rapid appearance) of the other. This allows for some asymmetry in the working of either dimension – rather like a coin with one side larger than the other for a temporary period.

The importance of these considerations lies in the fact that Community institutions can only assume legitimacy for those political functions where they are seen as effective. This does not mean that being effective will inevitably bring about legitimacy. What we do mean is that perceived effectiveness is necessary – though not entirely sufficient – for legitimacy. If we could measure the areas of activity where European institutions are seen as being relatively more effective than national institutions, then we could gain at least an idea of where the notion of integration fits into a larger context of political consciousness at the mass level.(28)

The 1973 and 1976 Euro-Barometres included a battery of items directly addressing the issue of effectiveness. Those interviewed were questioned about several areas of government activity: "For each of the problems I am going to mention, would you say they would be better dealt with by a European Government or by a (Respondent's country) government?" The problems included pollution of the environment, military defense, scientific research, aid to underdeveloped countries, investments by foreign firms and their control, supervision of advertising, drug addiction, economic growth, relations with the Americans or Russians, poverty and unemployment, housing, rising prices, and problems of subnational regionalism. Some questions asked in the 1973 survey were repeated in 1976, others were new. The results are summarized by country and the entire Community in Table 4.4.

There is considerable difference of opinion on the areas in which a European government might be more effective than national governments – some problems are much more "European" than specifically national. Moreover, some problems elicit European responses in one country and national responses in others. But without getting bogged down in details, it seems that the general pattern is one of relegating impersonal problems to Europe, while more specific, personal problems are reserved to the nation states. Hence, military matters, negotiations with the superpowers, foreign aid, international negotiations, research, control of multinational corporations, economic growth, and the fight against drugs are more likely to be assigned to the Community institutions, while the "bread and butter" issues such as prices, poverty, foreign investment, pollution, and regional problems are perceived mostly as being best handled by the national governments. But it is important to note that much of the rationale behind the growth of the movement for European unification was premised exactly on dealing with these issues. In a sense, mass publics seem to allow a wide degree of latitude and discretion to the Community in dealing with United Nations kinds of concerns. It appears to be viewed as a supranational diplomatic service important for remote and long-range issues that do not disturb the day-to-day life of Europe. But for "bread and butter" issues, solutions within the familiar national context are more appealing.

Perhaps the most interesting information which can be gleaned from Table 4.4 and which does not speak well for the legitimacy of the Community institutions is the decline in the public's perception from 1973 to 1976 that issues might be handled more efficiently by the Community institutions than by the national governments. In every case, with the exception of investment, the support for assigning functions to these institutions has decreased. Insofar as public opinion conditions political developments, it seems reasonably certain that growth areas for Community functions exist, but that across all of the member states they will be restricted to symbolic or to remote concerns. Daily life remains the respnsibility of the nation states, and as long as nation states continue to assist citizens in meeting the exigencies of daily life, there is no likelihood that they will turn to an alternative organ to continue work already done satisfactorily. Indeed, the distinct public opinion shift toward giving functions to the nation states suggests that only when the national governments fail do publics look toward a vague and undefined "Europe" for help. The idea of Europe implies solving problems with one's neighbors. However, the Community may not be the only alternative in such an event. If

Table 4.4. Problems Better Solved By a "European Government" (responses in percent of total)

1973/1976 Issue	France a	France b	Belgium a	Belgium b	Holland a	Holland b	Germany a	Germany b	Italy a	Italy b	Luxembourg a	Luxembourg b	Denmark a	Denmark b	Ireland a	Ireland b	Great Britain a	Great Britain b	EC TOTAL a	EC TOTAL b	1976 Issue (if different)
Environment	63	55	56	45	76	57	65	59	65	57	72	39	57	34	37	29	41	35	59	46	Fighting Pollution
Military	61	49	67	50	76	59	81	56	67	40	87	25	47	33	39	27	47	43	62	44	Strengthening Defense
Investment	48	53	40	56	28	54	40	56	56	45	43	49	24	46	34	36	31	40	39	48	Checking MNCs
Negotiations	78	58	87	58	83	62	75	55	83	52	92	42	70	41	75	47	61	52	77	53	Defending European Interests
Prices	57	53	49	56	52	57	63	52	58	49	69	54	38	37	33	39	31	44	49	49	Fighting Rising Prices
Poverty	56	28	44	37	56	43	55	30	52	38	73	36	47	21	27	30	33	22	48	31	Reducing Inequality
Drugs	81		71		70		64		75		86		53		33		47		64		
Growth	64		62		65		52		64		72		48		43		39		55		
Foreign Aid	83		81		78		83		85		91		59		73		71		78		
Research	85		80		77		75		81		91		82		74		59		77		
Housing	13		17		15		18		24		22		6		13		10		15		
Regional Self-Rule	12		21		25		13		14		25		7		19		10		15		
Unemployment	37		43		45		43		43		38		33		33		28		38		

a = 1973 Survey
b = 1976 Survey

Source: Euro-Barometres, no.s 2 and 5.

problems can be solved in cooperation with neighbors from the point of view of Breton, Fleming, Scotsman, or Valdotian, a return to regional and ethnic roots could be an even more likely alternative than the Community, although such an option could be eventually an indirect road to broader European unification.(29)

To summarize, then, public opinion support and perceived effectiveness of Community institutions suggests a relatively low level of legitimacy which is also reflected in the glacial progress of political integration, if any at all, that has occurred during the last decade. In this connection, it is significant to point again to the elections to the European Parliament with voter turnout of only slightly more than 60 percent. This contrasts to an average favorable attitude of 70 percent for the election of the EP recorded by respondents in the fall of 1978, which in itself is a decline of two points from the apex a year earlier.(30) This is a clear indication that the level of legitimacy reached by the EP leaves much to be desired.

On the other hand, the willingness of much of the general public to turn over the solution of international and security problems to the Community institutions augurs well for the legitimacy of NATO. Indeed, the political consultation mechanism of NATO has been increasingly used for evolving a common stand on difficult international issues by most of the West European countries. We will return to this matter later in this chapter.

INTERDEPENDENCIES

Interdependencies arise from the interface of needs and capabilities of governments and their people across national boundaries. They may also stem from transnational contacts of individuals and socialization processes that might ensue. Interdependencies are manifested by border-crossing flows of people, civilian and military goods and services, capital, and information in response to varying needs in one or more countries in accordance with the capabilities of others.

The best indicator of regional interdependence is trade because it encompasses shipments from one country to another of everything from raw materials to manufactured consumer goods according to a division of labor generally based on comparative advantages. In Western Europe, interregional trade has been expanding impressively since World War II. A significant factor was the establishment of the Common Market. There was a more than eight-fold rise in trade among the original Six from 1958 to 1972, while trade between the Community and third countries only increased three times. This trend has continued until now. It is interesting to note that during the first 14 years of the Community, trade between the three new EC members and the original six grew faster than that with other nonmember countries. In 1972 the European Community was the principal trading area for its nine members, as an average 51.8 percent of EC exports went to Community countries and 52 percent of the imports came from the Community area. But the importance of the Community to individual countries showed considerable variations. It ranged from Belgium-Luxembourg (exports 74 percent, imports 71.3 percent) and Ireland (exports 77 percent, imports 69.1 percent), to Denmark (exports 42.7 percent, imports 46.0 percent) and Great Britain (exports 30.2 percent and imports 31.6 percent).(31)

Trade among the original EFTA members grew beginning with EFTA's establishment in 1960, but trade of some of these countries with the Community expanded even faster.(32) The enlargement of the Community and the free trade agreements with the EFTA residual countries have, of course, enforced this trend and, thus, interdependence throughout the region is likely to be strengthened during the 1980s when Greece, Spain, and Portugal become full members of the EC and tariff barriers are gradually dismantled. Even up to now, the trade of Greece and Spain has tended to favor the EC, while Portugal's trade was more oriented toward non-EC members.

Overall, West European countries trade chiefly with one another. Of all exports of Western Europe in 1978, 65.1 percent went to the region and 62.7 percent of all imports came from Western Europe.(33)

Agricultural Trade

In the agricultural sector, a high degree of complementarity exists between the EC countries. The strongest emphasis on intensive agriculture appears to be in France, Ireland, and Denmark; as for output, France and Italy are the largest per capita producers of wheat and other crops, whereas Denmark and Ireland are at the top in livestock products.(34) The Common Agricultural Policy (CAP) of the Community seeks to balance farm output among the member states in such a way as to reach maximum self-sufficiency without disturbing too much the traditional pattern of agricultural production and exchange, but has not quite succeeded because of the considerable currency fluctuations which began in 1969 and upset the traditional patterns.

The CAP, which is an extremely complex and complicated policy permeated by the domestic politics of the member states, has implications which reach far beyond the Community. This policy instituted a scheme of variable levies for a large number of products that was to replace the conventional machinery of commercial policy such as customs duties and quotas. The levies are tied to an interlocking system of domestic target prices for certain commodities, threshold prices for bringing the prices of an imported product to the level of the target price and, thereby, determining the size of the levy, and sluice gate prices which serve as minimum prices for imports of certain products (pork, eggs, and poultry) and, thus, set the upper limit of the levy.(35) In principle, the levies are designed to cover the gap between world prices and those fixed for the internal market. Thus, the internal price has become a factor regulating not only the internal market, but also the Community's international trade. The CAP, therefore, contains elements of a common commercial policy, but this external farm policy tends strongly toward protectionism because the import levies do not lend themselves to reduction in the same manner as do tariffs and, in addition, Common Market preferences are built into part of the CAP.

In the Spring of 1973, pressures built up within the Community to modify the CAP because of the effects of high food prices on inflation in Europe. The British, especially, wanted to substitute deficiency payments to individual farmers (subsidies) for the high guaranteed prices for farm commodities which continued to rise year after year.(36) These pressures were fueled by the growth of enormous surpluses of some commodities, including butter. When the EC Commission approved the sale of 200,000 metric tons of butter from its 400,000 ton stockpile to the Soviet Union at 20 percent of normal Community prices, and with a loss of $362 million to be borne by the EC Agricultural Guidance and Guarantee Fund (i.e., the taxpayers), a loud chorus of criticism arose.(37)

In addition to the large and costly surplus problem generated by the CAP, the adjustment mechanism for the currency fluctuations necessary to assure at least a semblance of a common agricultural market has caused production and marketing dislocations and added cost. It introduced so-called Compensatory Monetary Amounts (CMAs) which would either be paid or collected on agricultural shipments from one member country to another, depending on whether the currencies of the countries involved had devaluated or upvalued. The initiation of the European Monetary System in 1979, hopefully bringing a measure of stabilization to the EC exchange markets, may lead to an eventual dismantlement of the CMAs.

Border Crossing Investments

Adding to the interdependence caused by the growth of intraregional trade is the increasing pace of transnational business collaboration between individual firms. National enterprises in different countries take advantage of economies of scale by manufacturing various parts of a product in particular plants located in one or the other country, sharing research and development facilities, and engaging in joint marketing ventures across the EC and beyond.(38) Similar activities by subsidiaries of multinational corporations (MNCs) located in various West European countries likewise strengthen economic interdependence (see Table 4.5). A large number of these corporations have their headquarters in West European countries, especially in the United Kingdom, Germany, and the Netherlands. These companies have created many links in other West European countries through border-crossing investments. With respect to this table, we should note that a link does not indicate the number of subsidiaries but merely that one or more subsidiaries have been established by a parent company in another European country. If we add United States MNCs to the total list, we find that 15,832 such links have been established throughout Western Europe.

Table 4.5. Number of Parent Companies for Each Western European Country Having Subsidiaries and Associates in a Given Foreign Country (Data as of 1970).

COUNTRY OF SUBSIDIARY OR ASSOCIATE	Austria	Belgium	Denmark	France	Germany	Italy	Luxembourg	Netherlands	Norway	Portugal	Spain	Sweden	Switzerland	United Kingdom	TOTAL
Austria	—	4	4	43	297	10	3	19	1	—	—	27	83	54	545
Belgium	2	—	9	136	138	25	3	141	4	1	2	39	87	233	820
Denmark	2	3	—	10	39	3	2	16	24	—	—	104	18	80	301
France	3	101	24	—	387	58	7	90	9	1	4	55	158	340	1237
Germany (FR)	27	31	58	153	—	39	17	136	21	2	3	111	260	337	1195
Italy	11	28	13	136	183	—	5	44	3	—	—	38	137	158	756
Luxembourg	1	31	6	20	39	18	—	6	1	—	—	2	14	39	177
Netherlands	2	42	19	58	191	10	6	—	10	—	2	60	73	247	720
Norway	1	3	24	14	16	2	1	7	—	—	—	104	14	46	232
Portugal	—	14	2	24	24	6	—	18	1	—	4	19	19	65	196
Spain	2	28	4	138	148	24	2	33	2	—	—	26	47	134	588
Sweden	2	5	46	15	63	5	2	20	44	—	—	—	32	107	341
Switzerland	11	24	11	116	291	36	5	43	13	—	1	57	—	183	791
United Kingdom	5	29	39	118	179	14	3	83	22	—	3	91	99	—	685
Total	69	343	259	981	1995	250	56	656	155	4	19	733	1041	2023	8584

Source: Adopted from Yearbook of International Organization (13th Edition, 1970-71).

Intraregional Communications Flows

As pointed out earlier, interdependencies can also be created through a variety of personal contacts, including mail and electronic means. Although statistics on personal communications (mail, telephone, telegraph) are difficult to find, it is reasonable to assume that in keeping with the very high level of trade among the EC countries the flow of mail as well as telephone and telegraph traffic must be correspondingly large. In most countries, direct long distance dialing is available and people have little hesitation to use it.

With respect to mass media, we have already noted Eurovision through which Europe-oriented programs are telecast simultaneously in several countries. Regular television programs can be seen in two or more countries if the station's antenna is close to the borders. Many radio stations can be heard over most of Western Europe with the French and Germans filling the air waves more than any other nationality. Prominent newspapers published in the larger countries are sold by newsstands in all major cities.

Exchange of people and transnational travel are brought about by a number of causes. Increasingly, young men and women enroll in universities in countries other than their own.(39) A number of universities and educational institutes of a particularly "European" character have opened their doors and offer special facilities for European intellectual intercourse. Examples are The College of Europe in Bruges, Belgium; INSEAD (The European Institute for Business Administration) in Fontainbleau, France; and recently the European University at Florence, Italy. A very large number of academic conferences dealing with a great variety of subjects are organized every year in different countries that bring together individuals of many nationalities and serve as an excellent means of elite communication. Similar meetings are also held by national and international nongovernmental organizations (NGOs) pursuing transnational objectives in every field of human endeavor, or by European umbrella NGOs.(40)

Perhaps the greatest inducement to elite travel is found in the institutional structure of the Community. Innumerable meetings of Commission committees and working groups bring a large number of high- and middle-ranking national civil servants of the EC countries to Brussels many times a year. Additional meetings of working groups may be organized by the Secretariat of the Council of Ministers of the Community or by the Permanent Representatives of the member states accredited to the EC. Sessions of the European Parliament necessitate many trips to Strasbourg by legislators elected to this body; the average time spent by these individuals away from their national capitals has been estimated at 45-70 days.

Of course, the trips to Brussels do not exhaust crossnational travel and contacts by political and administrative elites of the EC countries. Direct communication and contacts among these elites and their counterparts in nonmember states are frequent and include formal and informal diplomatic transactions involving the heads of state and chiefs of government and other high officials.

Finally, tourism has developed on a large scale. Millions of tourists swarm each year all over Western Europe. Tourist buses from every part of Western Europe bearing tourists from all walks of life are a familiar sight. Tourists travel in packaged tours by chartered train or plane and journey to every area of the continent. As for the effect of this voluminous travel, a caveat is in order. The assumption that transnational travel broadens the horizons and destroys national prejudices is often not correct. In many instances, prejudicial stereotypes of the people and customs in foreign countries are, in fact, reinforced by what travelers see, frequently superficially, during their trips.

Although tourism covers all of Western Europe and especially its southern tier, the volume of other communications flows as discussed above is much lower in these areas than in the central and northern parts of the region.

Security Interdependence

The fact that the vast majority of the West European countries are members of NATO has created an interdependent security community of major significance. Table 4.6 shows the defense expenditures of the European NATO members in net and per capita figures as well as in percentages of government spending and GNP, indexes of NATO defense expenditures between 1970 and 1975, and the size of national armed forces of which a substantial portion is earmarked for NATO purposes.

The indexes suggest increasing expenditures by European NATO members for the Alliance and, thereby, greater engagement and a higher degree of interdependence. During the last decade, more cooperation among the so-called Eurogroup in NATO has been witnessed involving, in some cases, the joint production of aircraft and weapons.

The Eurogroup, formed in 1968, is open to all European members of NATO; at present the participants are Belgium, Denmark, Germany, Greece, Italy, Luxembourg, the Netherlands, Norway, Portugal, Turkey, and the United Kingdom. They hope to ensure a stronger and more cohesive European contribution to the common defense and, thereby, strengthen the security of the people of Western Europe. This is being done by the coordination of defense efforts and making the best use of the available resources.

Apart from collaboration in the procurement of defense equipment, groups have been established in such fields as cooperative training, logistics, medical matters, and long-range planning. Efforts in the equipment field aim at the introduction of battle tanks and other armored vehicles, antiaircraft guided missile systems, combat and transport planes and helicopters, and ships and submarines.(41)

Eurogroup ministers meet regularly to discuss the potential for further progress in the above fields, review defense achievements, and make plans for the future. All these activities clearly tend to strengthen further the interdependencies created by the formation of NATO and

Table 4.6. Defense Profile of European NATO Members

1976 (1975)

A

Country	$ million	$ Per head	% Government spending	% of GNP (1975)	Armed forces (in thousands)			% of men 18-45
					Army	Navy	Air	
Belgium	2,013	204	10.2	2.7	64.0	4.4	19.9	4.7
Britain	10,734	190	11.0	4.9	177.6	76.2	90.2	3.3
Denmark	861	168	7.4	2.2	21.8	5.8	7.1	3.4
France	12,857	241	20.6	3.9	338.5	70.0	104.4	4.9
Germany*	15,220	242	23.5	3.7	345.0	39.0	111.0	3.9
Greece	1,249	138	26.0	6.9	160.0	17.5	22.0	11.6
Italy	3,821	68	8.6	2.6	240.0	42.0	70.0	3.2
Luxembourg	23	68	2.9	1.1	0.6	—	—	0.4
Netherlands	2,825	205	9.8	3.6	75.0	18.2	19.0	4.0
Norway	902	223	7.6	3.1	20.0	9.0	10.0	5.2
Portugal	748	85	n.a.	6.0	36.0	13.8	10.0	3.8
Turkey	2,800	70	29.4	9.0	375.0	40.0	45.0	5.7

*Incl. aid to West Berlin.

Table 4.6. (Continued)

B

INDEXES OF NATO DEFENSE EXPENDITURE,
CURRENT AND CONSTANT PRICES**
(in local currency, 1970=100)

Country	% Growth (1970-75)
Belgium	13.2
	4.5
Britain	15.7
	2.4
Denmark	13.2
	3.6
France	11.6
	2.5
Germany	11.0
	4.6
Greece	25.3
	11.5
Italy	13.6
	2.1
Luxembourg	13.6
	5.9
Netherlands	12.8
	3.9
Norway	10.6
	2.0
Portugal	16.2
	1.0
Turkey	39.3
	21.1

**Average annual compound growth rates over period shown.

Source: Adapted from the International Institute for Strategic Studies
(London), The Military Balance, 1976-77.

its successful operation over the past thirty years. Present and future joint production of equipment and a definite agreed division of labor regarding the production of particular weapons and other materiel by individual countries for common use will further intensify the web of interdependence.

REGIONAL FOREIGN POLICY BEHAVIOR

Three fora exist in Western Europe for the formulation of regional foreign policies:

1. The Community institutions, especially the Commission, to which the EC Treaties have assigned selected external policy competencies.
2. An intergovernmental foreign policy coordination mechanism utilized by the foreign ministries of the EC member states and operated by what is called the Political Committee. This process is also known as "political cooperation."
3. Political consultation in NATO in which most European NATO members participate and which deals primarily with security-political matters.

The EEC treaty stipulates the formulation of common commercial policies toward third countries, and offers to the nine member governments the unusual foreign policy instrument of "association." This instrument has been successfully employed on many occasions to affiliate third countries, and made it possible to forge strong links with developing countries in Africa, the Caribbean, and the Western Pacific. The formulation and, to a lesser degree, the implementation of specific EC policies is entrusted to a substantial number of civil servants of the European Community. Most of the "Eurocrats" are assigned to Directorate-General (DG) I of the EC Commission, but they cannot act with full autonomy. The member governments keep close tabs on European Community activities in external affairs through 1) directives by the EC Council of Ministers, representing mainly national interests; 2) liaison committees(42) composed of national officials; and 3) the Committee of Permanent Representatives (CPR). As pointed out earlier, this unit has become very influential in all EC decision making processes.

In the foreign policy coordinating mechanism of the European Community member governments, the EC officials of DG I play only a very limited role. Coordination is carried out through periodic meetings of the foreign ministers of the Nine. The spadework for these meetings is handled by the political directors of the foreign ministries of the member states who, with their staffs, constitute the Political Committee. This body convenes at least four times a year, but in recent years it has met much more often.

The major task of the foreign ministers at their periodic sessions is consideration of important foreign policy questions. The member governments can suggest for consideration any issue pertaining to general foreign policy problems or to such matters as monetary affairs, energy, and security. Whenever the work of the foreign ministers or of the Political Committee impinges on the competences and activities of the European Community, the Commission is requested to submit its own position on the matter under consideration and is invited to send a representative. During the discussion in the Political Committee regarding the preparatory Conference on European Security and Cooperation (Helsinki), it was felt that the conference was likely to deal with problems affecting the activities and competences of the European Community in the international trade field. Therefore, a European Community representative was invited and Franco Malfatti, then president of the Commission, participated in some of the sessions. The foreign policy coordination activities of the Political Committee are supplemented by periodic sessions of staff members in the embassies of the Nine, located in different capitals of the world. Such meetings had already taken place prior to the creation of this committee when EC affairs affecting third countries needed to be discussed and coordinated, but their scope has now been expanded.(43)

In NATO, political consultation had always taken place from the earliest days of the Alliance, but it was given a new impetus when the Report of Three Foreign Ministers on Non-Military Co-operation within the Alliance was adopted in 1956. This report called for consultation on all matters of interest to the Alliance during the formative stage of government decision making. Consultation has considerably developed over the years. The highest authority in the Alliance, which provides the forum for such consultation, is the North Atlantic Council, meeting twice a year at ministerial level and at least once a week at the level of the permanent representatives. Consultation also takes place through the Political and other committees and in working groups. In recent times, political consultations have been taking place on a variety of subjects, ranging from issues involving the Alliance directly to those international political questions which touch on the interests of each of the allies separately. In the latter respect, the members of the Alliance regularly exchange information and views on developments in the Middle East, East Asia, the Mediterranean, and other areas.

Substantive Issues

The control over tariffs and the CAP exercised by the Community institutions in concert with the member governments has given the EC system a powerful influence over shape of international trade. The Community accounts for about 22 percent of world trade (not considering trade within the Nine) and, thereby, is the largest trading unit. Thus, it is not surprising that its voice in trade negotiations is weighty. Its power is further strengthened by the free trade areas established with most EFTA countries and the preferential agreements concluded with nearly all countries rimming the Mediterranean. Hence, in the multilateral trade negotiations (MTN-The Tokyo Round) concluded in 1979 in Geneva, the Community was able to attain many of its objectives, sometimes perhaps at the expense of other countries, including the United States.(44)

The economic importance of the Community-Mediterranean relationship is illustrated by the fact that, apart from Libyan oil deliveries, 36.5 percent of the exports of all Mediterranean countries go to the EC while 37.6 percent of their total imports come from the Community.(45) Nevertheless, the United States opposed the Community's Mediterranean policy because of concern about the adverse effects on American exports of citrus fruits and other goods to the area, although the amounts involved are relatively small. As a matter of principle, the United States has proclaimed again and again that the preferential agreements are violations of GATT, which only permits fullfledged customs unions and free trade areas to be exempted from the most-favored-nation clause. The Community has admitted a possible violation but continues to claim its special responsibility for the countries of the area.

A powerful tool for this expansion of the Community's economic and political influence, from which all of Western Europe is likely to benefit, is its association policy. Initiated when the EEC came into force with special tariff preferences granted to most of the Six's former colonies in Africa, the association was expanded in 1975 through the Convention of Lome to over 50 countries in Africa south of the Sahara, the Caribbean, and the Western Pacific. This convention not only provides duty-free access of goods produced in the Lome affiliated countries to the EC member states, but also established a $4 billion European Development Fund for financial assistance and the so-called Stabex system of providing some measure of price stability for certain export commodities of the affiliated countries. Indeed, the Stabex system is at least a partial fulfillment of a long-held aspiration of all developing countries: establishment of a mechanism to counter the wide fluctuations of primary commodities. However, this system covers only exports to the Community members, not to third countries.

Another feature of the Lome Convention and the Mediterranean agreements of the Community is a strong emphasis on industrial and technological cooperation. This is supplemented by institutionalized and, at times, purposely expanded contacts between parliamentarians and civil servants from the EC member states and the Lome affiliates. The consequence is the development of close relationships between the Community and the affiliated states which may have long-term implications for the distribution of international power and influences. The main beneficiary of this close relationship is likely to be the Community business world, but the institutionalized cooperation with the Lome affiliates and Mediterranean countries might also be helpful for the pursuit of EC member states' foreign policies in various international fora and particularly the United Nations. Indeed, it may offer decided advantages to the EC economies when badly needed raw materials available in the Lome countries should fall into short supply on the world markets.

The renewal of the Lome Convention which expires in 1980 is now being negotiated. Although the affiliated countries have been satisfied with some aspects of the convention, their demands for added financial benefits and expansion of the Stabex system were considered excessive by the EC negotiators and compromises were eventually reached.(46)

Energy Problems

A matter of greatest concern to all of Western Europe is, of course, the supply of crude oil and natural gas. Several strategies have been pursued to assure adequacy of supply, especially from OPEC, an "intrusive" power, and these strategies have been utilizing both the political cooperative approach and the EC external policy system. The first method was used primarily for the North-South Dialogue and specifically for the Ministerial Conference on International Economic Cooperation (CIEC) which had several meetings from 1975 to 1978. Delegates from 27 countries participated, of which 19 were Third World countries. The CIEC negotiations failed, primarily because the Third World was mainly interested in the stabilization of indexing of raw material prices, general development problems, and such financial support as debt moratoriums or cancellations. Many of these issues already had a powerful forum for discussion in UNCTAD. Indeed, some of the issues debated and bargained over at UNCTAD IV (Nairobi, April-May 1977) were also topics at the CIEC meeting in Paris a month later. As a consequence, the North-South Dialogue moved to the United Nations, undoubtedly the proper place for these negotiations. We should note that intergovernmental foreign policy coordination on economic matters in the various UN fora among the EC countries and indirectly through OECD channels (also among other West European countries) has been remarkably successful, although from time to time on a specific issue full agreement may not have been reached.

The second strategy, the so-called Euro-Arab Dialogue, is procedurally a combination of the EC external relations system and intergovernmental foreign policy coordination. Its basic purpose is the creation of relationships and mechanisms to enhance the security of crude oil supplies.

The areas of cooperation with which the dialogue deals include industrialization, basic infrastructure, agriculture and rural development, financial cooperation, trade, science, technology, culture, labor, and social questions. Several working groups study these areas of cooperation, identify worthwhile projects, and make proposals for action to a general committee. Concrete progress in these areas has been very limited, despite a number of joint meetings.(47) Nevertheless, the Euro-Arab Dialogue has strengthened the network of relations between the EC countries and the Arabs, but how much it has actually enhanced the security of oil supplies is difficult to say. It may be prudent to be skeptical of any plan that would hope to sway the oil producers to a decisively more favorable attitude toward Western Europe in times of crisis.

Supplementing the Dialogue is the generally hostile attitude of the Nine as a collectivity toward Israel's objectives in the Middle East. During a Dialogue meeting held at Tunis in February 1977, the Europeans felt constrained to reiterate concerns expressed earlier over the continued Israeli occupations of Arab territories since 1967, and to restate that a solution of the Middle East conflict will be possible only "if the legitimate rights of the Palestinian people to give effective expression to its national identity is translated into fact."(48) The Nine also opposed any move by Israel to alter unilaterally the status of Jerusalem. According to the final communique, the Arabs expressed their appreciation for this attitude. Later meetings of the General Committee have been more relaxed, but the position of the Nine was expressed again, perhaps more forcefully, to a much wider public during the meeting of the European Council in London at the end of June 1977. A "Declaration on the Middle East" issued at that time reemphasized the need for Israel to end the territorial occupation maintained since 1967 and requested that Israel be ready to recognize the legitimate rights of the Palestinian people and their need for a "homeland."(49) Although, not surprisingly, this declaration aroused a very negative reaction in Israel and a vigorous diplomatic protest, it simply confirmed and continued a policy line drawn by the nine member states, individually and as a group, which began with the Copenhagen summit in December 1973. The deep official sympathies for Israel held by most EC governments were abandoned as a result of the oil debacle and powerful pressures from the Arab oil producers. National interests, perhaps even survival, were the motivating forces for this change in policy. Even the successful conclusion of the peace treaty between Egypt and Israel received little applause by the nine despite efforts in the Political Committee to come up with a more enthusiastic coordinated response.(50)

Strategic-Political Issues

In the strategic-political area, political cooperation among the Nine through the foreign policy coordinating mechanism and the consultation mechanism has produced important results. The main examples are the Conference on Security and Cooperation in Europe (CSCE) concluded in 1975 and the negotiations on the Mutual and Balanced Force Reductions (MBFR). The coordinating and consultative machinery was active in the preparatory and negotiating phases of CSCE and in the post-CSCE phase, and an exchange of information has continued to take place on the implementation of the final act by all signatories at Helsinki. In addition, all the allies consulted among themselves in preparing their positions for the Belgrade review meetings convened in 1977. In addition, the United States government, through the NATO Council, consulted its allies in detail during the rounds of talks with the Soviet Union on Strategic Arms Limitation (SALT). It should be noted that the United States generally accepted the common position on CSCE worked out in the Political Committee of the Nine and later confirmed through the NATO consultation machinery.

The foreign policies discussed in preceding pages which were either the result of special EC external competences or of coordination in the Political Committee or through NATO consultation should not leave the reader with the impression that Europe now "speaks with one voice" in all international matters. Many issues are brought to the Political Committee where coordination does not prove to be feasible. In fact, the number of foreign policy issues where cooperation among the Nine is successful is relatively small(51) and mainly in the economic field. Divergent national interests prevail; a prime example has been the oil and energy crisis in the fall of 1973 when the Netherlands was singled out by Arab oil producers as an "unfriendly" country and was cut off from all oil supplies. Despite the professed solidarity of the Community countries, the Dutch were not extended mutual help and had to threaten the shutoff of North Sea gas flowing from the Netherlands to its Community neighbors in order to obtain some assistance. At the same time, France, following her recent friendly and accommodating policies toward the Arab countries, was hoping to come unscathed out of the energy crisis. She was the first of the Community countries to make a barter deal with several Arab oil producing countries, negotiating a 20-year supply of oil against the delivery of weapons and other French high technology items. Whether the recent effort of the Nine to limit oil consumption from 1975 to 1985 to the 1978 level will be more successful remains to be seen.(52)

Up to this point, we have focused on various issue areas in West Europe's foreign policy behavior. We will now proceed to an examination of the region's relations with the two superpowers, both of them so-called intrusive systems.

EC RELATIONS WITH INTRUSIVE SYSTEMS

Relations with the United States

The United States has many links with and interests in Western Europe. American security involvement in Western Europe began when Communist insurgents attempted to take over Greece during 1946/1947. With Great Britain unable to provide financial and military support, the United States came to the rescue, and this intervention became the basis for President Truman's containment policy. Soon afterward, NATO came into being and, within it, increased United States participation in the defense of Western Europe.

Intense United States economic involvement started with the initiation of Marshall Plan aid and the establishment of the Organization of

European Economic Cooperation (OEEC, later the OECD) on the insistence of the United States to support Marshall Plan activities through the liberalization of trade and interstate payments. Trade between the United States and the EC from 1958 to 1977 increased dramatically: U.S. exports rose from $2.8 billion to $26.4 billion while U.S. imports expanded from $1.7 billion to $22.4 billion. Exports to all of Western Europe in 1977 amounted to $33.4 billion (28 percent of total U.S. exports) while imports into the United States from these countries in the same year totaled $27.5 billion (18.6 percent of total).(53)

Regardless of the remarkable increase of U.S. exports to the Community, the United States has persistently attacked the CAP as a form of discrimination against United States' shipments of agricultural commodities. The United States government has argued that in view of its high efficiency, American agriculture could offer its products at considerably lower costs than European farmers. Therefore, increased American farm exports would benefit European consumers, and it was considered arbitrary to exclude American farm products from the Community markets.

In recent years, however, the agricultural situation has changed drastically. World prices have risen enormously and many farm commodities are in short supply. Instead of promoting the export of certain farm products, such as soybeans and cotton seeds, the United States has sought to limit shipments to Europe, at least on a temporary basis. Not surprisingly, this has aroused shock and anger in the EC after the United States had been preaching free trade for so many years. Fortunately, the U.S. restrictions were lifted quickly as more and more cries for European self-sufficiency in these products were heard, especially in France.(54) Meanwhile, in spite of U.S. concerns, agricultural exports have shown a general upward trend during the 1970s although they had declined from 1966 to 1969.(55)

We have already mentioned that the United States government has objected to the preferential treatment given the imports to the Community from the Mediterranean countries. With respect to the EC association policy, a primary bone of contention had been the granting of "reverse preferences." This means that the affiliated country is granted not only reduction or elimination of tariffs for goods shipped to the Community, but that it offers certain tariff preferences for the import of Community products. The United States and other non-member states considered reverse preferences by the associated countries to Community exports of manufactured goods as discriminatory against third country manufacturers. The Lome Convention dispensed with the need for reciprocal preferences. It gives the associated countries the option to grant special trade concessions to the EC countries, but also allows them to make the preferences available to third countries. Thus, this source of friction between the United States and the EC has been eliminated.

As we have mentioned earlier, the next Lome Convention is in the process of negotiation and will be concluded, despite present disagreements. Thus, the next decade may witness increased commercial and financial intercourse between the Community countries and the CPA affiliates at the expense of export and investment activities by the American business community, resulting in lowered United States influence in Africa. While the United States government appears to be quite relaxed about the potential rise of Community influence in the Lome territories, the Mediterranean, and perhaps in the Third World generally, pressures by American business interests may give rise to different attitudes among American foreign policymakers. The quest for critical raw materials in Africa and other Third World countries needed to keep domestic industries running smoothly may spur competitive action and perhaps preemption of such materials, for which the Community could be in a better supply position than the United States. Although there is a clear economic imperative for economic cooperation between the United States and the Community, the perceived priority for national solutions to remedy adverse economic and political situations may prevent the formation of rational cooperation policies and, thereby, constitute a major challenge to United States foreign policy.

A few comments need to be made about the transnational investment patterns between Western Europe and the United States. Although direct investments by American firms in Europe continued to expand during the last few years, the increases have become smaller. Nevertheless, the total American investment in Europe at the end of 1977 amounted to $60.6 billion.(56) Among the major reasons for the slowdown in these investments were West European policies making dismissals of workers very expensive and plant closings almost impossible even if, through price controls on certain items, profits are cut to zero. Other reasons are more rapid escalation of production costs in Western Europe than in the United States, and volatile foreign exchange markets. These factors have also induced some American MNCs to sell their subsidiaries in Western Europe. However, despite this recent trend, Western Europe retains the lion's share of American direct investment abroad with over 37 percent of total investment.

The reverse flow of investments shows a different trend. Direct investments by European firms in the United States have accelerated during the last few years at an increasing pace. Their total has risen from $6.1 billion in 1965 to $28.9 billion in 1978 and continues to increase. Investors located in the United Kingdom, West Germany, Switzerland, the Netherlands, and France accounted for the bulk of the new investments.(57)

The increasing economic and political power of the Community and the benefits of this power enjoyed by Western Europe in general have created some apprehensions in the minds of many Americans that Western Europe might become as much a competitor as it is an ally. On the other hand, Henry Kissinger's initiative in April 1973 for redefining and reinvigorating the Atlantic partnership was received with little enthusiasm by most of the European countries who did not want to perpetuate the image of Europe being the junior partner of the United

States. Although some Americans still fret about paying twice as much in taxes for the common defense as do their European counterparts, the greater efforts promised by all members of the Alliance to enhance NATO's military capabilities are likely to reduce transatlantic frictions. And the transatlantic summit meetings which are now being held twice a year may help in defining common problems and implementing common solutions which would allay many of the mutual suspicions that might continue to linger on.

EC-Soviet Relations

The intrusive relationship of the Soviet Union with Western Europe is responsible for many economic and political concerns of the region. In turn, the foreign policies of Western Europe, economic as well as strategic-political, have a significant impact on the USSR. In this connection, it should be noted that EC preferences not granted to the Soviet Union can be overcome by manipulation of prices of goods to be exported to the Community since, under the Soviet system, prices can be altered arbitrarily without regard to cost factors. However, few imports from the Soviet Union are manufactured goods normally sensitive to tariff preferences; rather, most items are raw materials needed in the EC countries and are subject to low or no duties at all.

The Soviet Union is a substantial trading partner of Western Europe as a whole. In 1978, imports from the Soviet Union amounted to $11.7 billion and exports to the USSR were $10.0 billion.(58) In this trade, the Soviet Union is guided by its economic and political interests as reflected especially in the objectives manifested during the CSCE negotiations. These are the acquisition of advanced western technology and long-term credits, and, overarching these goals, the pursuit of general detente. If, in the attainment of these goals, Europeans are reassured that their perceptions of a Soviet military threat are groundless, all the better because it might lead to demands that American military forces be withdrawn from Europe. However, the prospects for such a development are very dim as the policies evolved in the coordinating mechanism of the Nine and within NATO discussed earlier demonstrate. Indeed, the shadow of the Soviet Union's occupation of Czechoslovakia in 1968 and the enormous Soviet buildup in tanks and intermediate range missiles hangs heavy over Western Europe.

REGIONAL INTEGRATIVE DEVELOPMENT:
PAST AND FUTURE

When the European Community treaties were negotiated in the 1950s, they were seen by their authors and some of the general public as first steps that could lead eventually to the political unification of Western Europe. These treaties established central institutions endowed with authority to wield certain government-like powers over the people in the Community countries and to issue regulations that had the force of law and were applicable directly to the populace without national legislation. Integration theorists (especially the neofunctionalists), envisaged that the creation of the unified market among the original Six, activating pressures for economic integration, appropriate decisions by the central institutions, and an enthusiastic and technically skillful European Community civil service, would set in motion a process of political integration which would expand incrementally the Community's functions and authority until a European government would emerge.(59)

Initially, this theory seemed to be confirmed by events. The expansive logic of neofunctionalism appeared to operate as predicted. There was spillover from one economic sector to another, from one policy area to another; and central authority expanded when specified goals could not be achieved with the means available and required reaching out into related sectors, additional policy areas, and the development of new institutional capabilities.(60)

General de Gaulle's first veto of Britain's entry into the Community in January 1963, however, put brakes on this process. The General's reassertion of France's independence and grandeur and his renewed glorification of the national interest at the expense of the Community interest set the stage for rekindling the fires of nationalism in other EC countries. The political integration process stagnated, especially when France boycotted Community institutions during the second half of 1965, a crisis that had its roots in French opposition to any expansion of the Community institutions' authority, and in fear of losing national prerogatives.(61)

The loss of momentum in political integration continued after de Gaulle's departure, but economic integration progressed well; and, during the summit meeting of the heads of state and chiefs of government of the Six in January 1969, it finally was decided to enlarge the Community. During this meeting the creation of an economic and monetary union was proclaimed as a major goal to be attained by the end of the 1970s. This objective exceeded the goals defined in the Community treaties and was seen by many as an essential step toward the political unification of Western Europe.

When we examine the progress made toward economic and monetary union and political integration among the EC countries, however, we see frustration and slowdowns.(62) While the rhetoric of governmental leaders and political parties in support of political integration flows freely, actual progress has not matched the many and repeated declarations that political union needs to be accomplished.(63)

During the 1970s, many initiatives were undertaken by the EC Commission to introduce incrementally an economic and monetary union, but until 1978 these proposals remained largely dead letters.(64) Then at the European Council meeting in Bremen in July of that year, France and Germany proposed to stabilize the exchange rates of the member states by introducing a European Monetary System (EMS) in 1979, culminating perhaps later in a European Monetary Fund of from

$30 to $50 billion. However, the British were reluctant to commit themselves to this plan and some of the other member governments also expressed reservations. Britain wanted Germany to accept a higher rate of inflation to help British exports and some of the weaker EC countries (Italy and Ireland) hoped to bargain out economic aid for their agreement to participate in the EMS.(65) When, finally, all member states except the United Kingdom had agreed to participate in the EMS, a dispute broke out over the dismantling of the Compensatory Monetary Amounts (CMAs) which, with the introduction of a stable monetary system, seemed to have lost their rationale. France wanted to see the CMAs abolished as quickly as possible since its agricultural sector had not benefited from them as did the stronger currency countries. The Germans, on the other hand, had been major beneficiaries and, therefore, wanted to spread out abolition over seven years. Some of the Commission's legal experts asserted that introduction of the EMS would deprive the CMAs of their legal basis.(66)

These disagreements were the cause for a three-month delay in the inauguration of the EMS that had been scheduled for January 1, 1979, a delay which may not have displeased its critics in some of the central banks and finance ministries of the member states. The official action to block the start of the EMS was taken by France whose Prime Minister, Raymond Barre, stated that the new monetary system could not begin until West Germany and all other Common Market countries agreed to phase out the CMAs that existed and gave assurances that any new ones would be automatically eliminated at the end of each year.(67)

Barre's statement made it obvious that the CMA system had not only become a crucial factor in the implementation of the CAP, but also in the general process of European integration. Although basically an inducement to achieve economic and monetary union, the system's current unequal distribution of benefits had made it a worrisome obstacle to progress toward such union. Does all this mean that the introduction of the EMS was basically motivated by the desire to move unification or were there other motivations for this step? It appears that national interests played a major role. For France, fixed currency exchanges were always favored, and Giscard d'Estaing saw in the EMS a means to return to this system with the help of an affluent Germany and other financially strong EC neighbors. An important factor was also the existence of the Monetary Fund which set the EMS apart from the much less reliable "Snake" as a tool for currency stabilization. For Helmut Schmidt, the German Chancellor, the EMS provided protection against upward pressure on the D-Mark, which a slipping dollar was bound to exert. Hence, the EMS affected also German export business which was likely to suffer from a new revaluation of the D-Mark.(68)

Of course, the convergence of national interests in support of the EMS might have favorable implications for the political unification process, but it does not have the sustaining force of an ideological consensus on the creation of a European union and government. Indeed, converging interests may diverge again; and solidarity, even though a rational imperative as in the case of the 1973 oil debate, may give way to national egoism and disintegration. This brings us back to the disparity between professed goals regarding political integration and reality, a disparity for which the true causes have not been found.

Obviously, the reasons for the disparity between professed goals and reality are complex. Many individuals in the EC countries and, perhaps, beyond would like to see Europe "speak with one voice." Mass public opinion polls as recently as 1979 have indicated that the evolution of the Community toward political union is regarded favorably by a substantial majority of respondents (75 percent) in most countries, exceptions being Great Britain and Denmark.(69) However, public opinion can have a significant influence on the making of policy only if it involves an issue considered extremely important and strong pressures are exerted toward the desired objective. The low turnout for the European parliamentary elections suggests that this formal step forward toward union lacked political interest and excitement on the part of the public. And although a few of the issues associated with political integration have been politically highly controversial, an outstanding example being the nature and consequences of the CAP, there is no evidence that the politicization of the European farm problem, while related to concern about joint decision making in Europe, has led to an upward movement in political integration or in a shift of expectations and loyalty toward the European institutions.(70) Moreover, practical power considerations by influential elites such as national legislators and high-ranking civil servants also conflict with whatever aspirations may exist among the public for European union. Therefore, while "European" serves as a convenient label for Dutchmen, Frenchmen, Germans, and Italians when they are dealing with extracontinentals, nation state frames of reference emerge quickly when it comes to intracontinental relations. A united Europe is attractive because it allows small or medium powers to combine as one great actor – a role now largely played by Americans, Russians, and increasingly the Chinese and Japanese. But the nation state, even the smallest one, provides things even more basic to political elites and the general public: an identity, immediate access to available political power, and opportunities for more power.(71) For all these reasons, integrative tendencies remain weak and won't be strengthened until the Community system is able to fulfill the aspirations of political and other elites and receives broad-based support across national boundaries.

Integrative tendencies in Greece and the two candidates for EC membership, Spain and Portugal, are difficult to assess. Obviously, their economic interest in joining the Community is high, but whether the present political and administrative elites are prepared to turn over their newly-found positions of power to a central European government is open to doubt. Indeed, the Spanish and Portuguese democratic authorities are still engaged in building up their legitimacy, and this process may have to be completed before political union of the twelve member states can be seriously considered. On the other hand, one could argue that precisely because of the current relatively low level of legitimacy of these authorities, the people in these countries may be eager to turn to a hopefully effective European government. But this argument overlooks innate nationalism and the interests and goals of power-oriented national politicians and administrators. Moreover, from the perspective of the Nine, the disparity in economic levels and political cultures between the present and new EC members may make any attempt at political union an unlikely enterprise.

It is frequently said that for political unification to succeed, an outside force or an outside federator is required. It was the threat of Soviet aggression and United States prodding that initiated and sustained the movement of the Six toward political integration in the 1950s. The imposition of the 10 percent surcharge on imports in 1971 by the United States and the disintegration of the world monetary system triggered by the devaluation of the dollar eventually contributed to the establishment of the EMS, but how far this action will stimulate a renewed desire for unification is not clear at this time. The United States troop alert during the Arab-Israeli War in 1973 coupled with the quick accommodation of American interests in the Mideast with those of the Soviet Union(72) again seemed to demonstrate the need for unification to many Europeans,(73) but did not result in further progress towards political integration.

Prospects

In conclusion, it appears that the prospects for Western Europe's future are continued, increasing economic cooperation, and progress in economic integration, but only very small steps with unclear consequences toward political integration. There is a definite quest for coordinated foreign policies, but in essence these will continue to be guided by nationalist considerations and parochially conceived interests. The rising levels of economic development in all of Western Europe, due in part to the creation of an immense free trading area, may well be viewed by many as sufficient political pay-off of an exciting experiment in regionalism that has strengthened the stability of the participating political systems without necessitating governmental transformations whose final political effects would be uncertain and whose political risks for many major elites in Western Europe could be high.

In terms of regional integration theory, the following propositions may reflect the reality of developments and conditions in the Community.

1. Mass public opinion polls are unreliable indicators of attitudinal integration(74) and are only meaningful if the depth of the attitudes expressed can be determined. Unless the issues associated with integration generate sufficiently strong pressures for unification to be taken seriously by influential political and administrative elites, prointegrationist views of the public in general have saliency only when they coincide with the interests,

aspirations, and perceptions of these elites. So far, national legislators and administrators have rarely been exposed to such pressures and, in general, legislators have not regarded integration related issues as salient factors for their election.

2. Even when an issue related to joint decision making within the Community did become highly controversial and led to a widening of the audience interested in it, "spillover" in the form of "a redefinition of mutual objectives"(75) and an upward shift in the scope and level of commitment to integration did not occur. On the contrary, the groups involved, such as the European farmers, were primarily concerned with material gain without any ideological commitment to a politically unified Europe. Thus, the concept of politicization, which has been elaborated by some of the neofunctionalists as a variable for the promotion of spillover and political integration, may require rethinking since its validity has been put into question by the developments in the Community.

3. Both economic and monetary union imply constraints on the policymaking latitudes of the Community's member governments. Indeed, full monetary union cannot be accomplished unless major economic policies of the member states have been harmonized and, clearly, this is not the case, despite valiant efforts by the Commission. Hence, it is very doubtful that the introduction of the EMS can develop into a viable monetary union without complete harmonization of economic policies first. Domestic political considerations play a significant role in these decisions and it is certain that the interests, objectives, and aspirations of influential political and administrative elites constitute an important input into these decisions.

4. It would be idle speculation at this stage to make a judgment as to whether political integration in the European Community would lead to a confederal or federal structure. Clearly the attitudes and interests of many influential elites would suggest that minimum constraints on the exercise of national prerogatives are desired. The experiences of 1973 and 1974 indicate that nationalistic squabbles have come to the fore again despite the expressed desire in many quarters to see Europe "speak with one voice." Perhaps the best that can be expected is what Nye calls "policy integration."(76) The concern here is not with institutions or methods used in reaching decisions, but with the extent to which the Community can act as a group to produce joint decisions. It is much more a matter of intergovernmental cooperation than assigning specific powers for policymaking to central institutions. And from this point of view, considerable progress has been made in Western Europe which suggests a notable accomplishment in consensus building.

5. Finally, our discussion has made clear that for the understanding of the process of integration the focus must be on a continuing analysis of domestic/international policy linkages operating be-

tween the domestic political concerns in each country and the demands and aspirations for specific foreign, economic, and security policies. The constraints on national governments existing on the domestic scene and the responses necessary to be given to domestic political demands must be analyzed within the context of external pressures and demands when judgments are to be made about the likely prospects of political unification in Western Europe.

NOTES

(1) Louis J. Cantori and Steven C. Spiegel, The International Politics of Regions: A Comparative Approach (Englewood Cliffs, N.J.: Prentice Hall, 1970), pp. 25-26.

(2) Seymour Martin Lipset, Political Man (Garden City, N.Y.: Doubleday, 1963), p. 31.

(3) Cf. articles 85, 86 EEC Treaty; and 65, 66 ECSC Treaty.

(4) Agence Europe Bulletin, April 28/29, 1975.

(5) Regarding Eurovision, see Burton Paulu, Radio and Television Broadcasting in the European Continent (Minneapolis: University of Minnesota Press, 1967).

(6) See Gordon Smith, Politics in Western Europe (New York: Holmes and Meir, 1973), pp. 21-30.

(7) Ibid., p. 168.

(8) Commission of the European Community, Euro-Barometre, no. 10 (January 1979), pp. 74-78.

(9) Cf. Robert A. Dahl, ed., Political Opposition in Western Democracies (New Haven, Conn.: Yale University Press, 1966), pp. xvii, xviii.

(10) Lipset, Political Man, pp. 77, 78.

(11) Lectures on the Principles of Political Obligation (London: Longmans Green, 1941), pp. 144, 148-49, 207.

(12) Smith, Politics in Western Europe, pp. 9-10.

(13) Der Spiegel 31, no. 20 (May 9, 1977): 171.

(14) Ibid., p. 178.

(15) Time, (June 18, 1979), p. 37.

(16) See Smith, Politics in Western Europe, p. 76.

(17) Ibid., p. 71.

(18) For details see Joseph Palombara, Interest Groups in Italian Politics (Princeton, N.J.: Princeton University Press, 1964).

(19) Smith, Politics in Western Europe, p. 64.

(20) See Marguerita Bouvard, Labor Movements in the Common Market Countries (New York: Praeger, 1972), pp. 96-104.

(21) Leon N. Lindberg, The Political Dynamics of European Economic Integration (Stanford, Calif.: Stanford University Press, 1964), p. 99; see also pp. 333-39, and for a description of these organizations, pp. 96-105. It is not inconceivable that occasionally the consensus of a specific issue reached in an umbrella organization does not really represent the true intent of all national groups. One or more of these groups may have only agreed to the proposed common view because they knew that their governments would, in fact, oppose the endorsed Commission proposals in the Council of Ministers.

(22) See Leon Lindberg, "Decision Making and Integration in the European Community," International Organization, 19, no. 1 (1965): 56-80.

(23) The permanent missions also constitute excellent observation posts for the member governments to keep informed about the happenings in the Commission.

(24) Agence Europe Bulletin, June 11/12, 1979; and Wall Street Journal, June 11, 1979, p. 27.

(25) Cf. Werner J. Feld, "Diplomatic Behavior in the European Community: Milieus and Motivations," Journal of Common Market Studies, XI, no. 1 (September 1972): 18-35.

(26) Lipset, Political Man, pp. 64-81.

(27) Cf. David Easton, A Framework for Political Analysis (Englewood Cliffs, N.J.: Prentice-Hall, 1965), pp. 124-26.

(28) See Jerome T. Moomau, "The Concept of Legitimacy and the European Community," unpublished thesis, University of New Orleans, Summer 1975. He tries another standard for measuring effectiveness, mainly transfer of competences to the Community institutions.

(29) Cf. Werner J. Feld, "Subnational Regionalism and the European Community," Orbis 18, no. 4 (Winter 1975): 1176-92.

(30) Euro-Barometre, no. 10 (January 1979), p. 33.

(31) Department of State, Bureau of Public Affairs, Trade Patterns of the West, 1972, News Release, August 1973, p. 1.

(32) See Randall Hinshaw, The European Community and American Trade (New York: Praeger, 1964), pp. 51, 52, 102-05.

(33) OECD, Statistics of Foreign Trade, April 1979, pp. 40, 41.

(34) John D. Coppock, Atlantic Agricultural Unity: Is It Possible? (New York: McGraw-Hill, 1966), p. 135.

(35) For fruits and vegetables the Council of Ministers established in 1965 a "reference price"; however, the basic protection for these commodities is not the import levy, but traditional tariffs that are more loosely related to the reference price than the levies to the target and sluice gate prices.

(36) Le Figaro, July 6, 1973.

(37) International Herald Tribune, April 7-8, 1973, p. 1. Iran tried to follow the USSR's example a month later, but was refused (International Herald Tribune, May 29, 1973, p. 4).

(38) See Werner J. Feld, Transnational Business Collaboration Among Common Market Countries (New York: Praeger Special Studies, 1970).

(39) Donald J. Puchala, "Integration and Disintegration in Franco-German Relations, 1954-1965," International Organization 24, no. 2 (Spring 1970): 183-208. Puchala also presents limited statistics on other forms of communication such as mail and tourism.

(40) See pp. 111-12 infra.

(41) NATO Handbook (March 1978), p. 20.

(42) For example: "Committee 113," named after Article 113 of the EEC Treaty which authorizes its establishment.

(43) See Ralf Dahrendorf, "Possibilities and Limits of a European Communities Foreign Policy," The World Today (April 1971), p. 161. The commercial councilor of the embassy of the member state holding the presidency of the EC Council of Ministers prepares a report on these meetings.

(44) See Wall Street Journal, June 22, 1979, p. 4 for details. The United States reduced tariffs by 31 percent while the EC reduced theirs only 27 percent.

(45) Carl A. Ehrhardt, "EEC and the Mediterranean," Aussenpolitik 22, no. 1 (1971): 20-30, on 21-22.

(46) Agence Europe Bulletin, June 1979.

(47) For details see Werner J. Feld, "West European Foreign Policies: The Impact of the Oil Crisis," Orbis 22, no. 1 (Spring 1978): 63-88.

(48) Bulletin of the European Communities, No. 2 (1977): 65.

(49) Agence Europe Bulletin, July 1, 1977.

(50) See Agence Europe Bulletin, March 28/29, 1979.

(51) Interview with German foreign service officer involved in Political Committee activities.

(52) Times-Picayune (New Orleans), June 23, 1979.

(53) United Nations Statistical Office, Yearbook of International Trade Statistics (1972); and OECD, Statistics of Foreign Trade (April 1979), pp. 46-47. It should be noted that United States trade with the European Community since 1958 has, with the exception of 1972, always shown a surplus. In 1976 the favorable trade balance exceeded $7 billion.

(54) International Herald Tribune, June 29, 1973.

(55) See Werner J. Feld, The European Community in World Affairs (Port Washington, N.Y.: Alfred, 1976), p. 188.

(56) United States Department of Commerce, Survey of Current Business 58, no. 8 (August 1978): 16.

(57) Wall Street Journal, June 14, 1979, p. 8. If Japan is included, the percentage of those investments is 93 percent of total direct foreign investments.

(58) OECD, Statistics of Foreign Trade (April 1979), pp. 40-41.

(59) See Ernst B. Haas, The Uniting of Europe (Stanford, Calif.: Stanford University Press, 1958), passim.; and Philippe C. Schmitter, "Three Neo-Functional Hypotheses About International Integration," International Organization, 24, no. 4 (1970): 161-66.

(60) See Leon N. Lindberg and Stuart A. Scheingold, Europe's Would-be Polity (Englewood Cliffs, N.J.: Prentice-Hall, 1970), pp. 116-21, 150-63; and Schmitter, "Three Neo-Functional Hypotheses."

(61) The New York Times (International Edition), July 9-10, 1966, p. 1. The crisis was triggered by a dispute between France and her partners over the financing of the EEC agricultural policy. For a full account, see John Lambert, "The Constitutional Crisis 1965-66," Journal of Common Market Studies, 6, no. 3 (May 1966): 195-228.

(62) Cf. Agence Europe Bulletin, October 24, 1973; and Die Welt, October 4, 1973.

(63) In February 1972, Chancellor Brandt and President Pompidou called for the implementation of a "European Europe" and to proceed as quickly as possible with the creation of monetary and economic union (cf. Kolner Stadt Anzeiger, February 12, 1972). Similar declarations were made in the summer of 1973 by Chancellor Brandt and his foreign minister, Walter Scheel (Relay from Bonn 4, no. 135, August 29, 1973). The Christian Democratic members of the European Parliament which include the Christian Democratic parties of Germany, Italy, the Netherlands, and Belgium, as well as the Conservative Party of Great Britain,called for a "European Government" by 1980 during a meeting in October 1973 (Agence Europe Bulletin, October 2, 1973).

(64) See for example EC Commission, Twelfth General Report (1978), pp. 74-75.

(65) See International Herald Tribune, July 8/9, 1978; and The Economist, May 27, 1979, pp. 55-56.

(66) The Economist, November 25-December 1, 1978, p. 59.

(67) New York Times, December 30, 1978, p. 25.

(68) See Rainer Hellmann, "Das Europeische Waehrungs-system: Vorgeschichte und Motive," Integration, April 1978, pp. 140-47.

(69) See Euro-Barometre, no. 10 (January 1979), p. 64.

(70) Schmitter ("Three Neo-Functional Hypotheses") believes that increase in controversiality of joint decision making is likely to lead to "manifest redefinition of mutual objectives" which would trigger the spillover process and result in an upward shift in either the scope or level of commitment to integration. Joseph S. Nye ("Comparing Common Markets: A Revised Neo-Functionalist Model," International Organization 24, no. 4 (Autumn 1970): 796-835, on 823-24) is more cautious. He believes that timing is a crucial element. Clearly, politicization involves more groups in the problem of integration and may

increase the number of linkages among societal groups as well as lead to deliberate coalition formation. But there is also a risk that powerful political opposition in the member states will be mobilized which may make it impossible for low cost and quiet technocratic decision making to be effective in attaining integration goals. The final result may well depend on the degree of support that can be built up by legitimizing decision makers.

(71) Cf. Werner Feld, "The National Bureaucracies of the EEC Member States and Political Integration: A Preliminary Inquiry," in International Administration: Its Evolution and Contemporary Applications, edited by Robert S. Jordan (New York: Oxford University Press, 1971), pp. 228-44; and Werner J. Feld and John K. Wildgen, "Electoral Ambitions and European Integration," International Organization 29 (Spring 1975).

(72) The complaint by many NATO allies about insufficient consultation was answered by Secretary of State Kissinger that Britain and France were consulted extensively but proved to be most uncooperative while those consulted least were most cooperative (Time, December 3, 1973, p. 48).

(73) Ibid.

(74) See Joseph S. Nye, Peace in Parts (Boston: Little Brown, 1971), pp. 44-47.

(75) Schmitter, "Three Neo-Functional Hypotheses," p. 166.

(76) Nye, Peace in Parts, p. 41.

5 Eastern Europe
James A. Kuhlman

Despite much conventional wisdom, unfortunately reinforced from time to time by the combination of contemporary political issues and ideological rationalization of superpower postures in the international system, it is difficult, if not altogether impossible from an empirical point of view, to portray the East European region as a homogeneous entity. Though exact counting is complicated by inexact boundaries in time and space, Eastern Europe (including Albania, Bulgaria, Czechoslovakia, East Germany, Hungary, Poland, Romania, and Yugoslavia) may be seen incorporating as many as 27 linguistic groups, 25 ethnic communities, and nearly as many religious movements, all of which is compounded by the blurring and blending of these three social indexes as they are spatially and functionally distributed across the region. Parties, governmental administrative structures, economic systems, and other institutional sectors of these societies are hardly less complex a picture and hardly more conducive to the traditional practice of arriving at conclusions that imply commonality for behavior within, or for approaches from outside, the Eastern European region. Differentiation across the space that is Eastern Europe becomes even more acute when that dimension is put in a matrix with time. Empires, boundary changes, and nation state formations are historical events which seem to have extraordinary inertia in that East European setting.

To accurately depict the region and, more importantly, Eastern Europe's structure and function relative to other regions, it may be useful to lay a foundation of three general assumptions upon which further discussion can be built. The first of these assumptions is that physical proximity of states does not necessarily make for an identity of interests. In this sense, regions exist only when there is a community of interests in addition to mere vicinity; therefore, functional interest accommodation is usually a better basis for conflict management than any concept of region based solely on geopolitical or military criteria. This means that we necessarily must not look at the Soviet-East

European subsystem as a geographical region exclusive of other approaches that will lead to an awareness of issues that may, in their resolution and meaning, run counter to conclusions derived from a geographical perspective. Even the geographical approach is more complex than much of the traditional literature intimates when one goes beyond mere locational indexes of power politics (sphere of influence logic) into economic derivations of locational theory. The analysis of the Eastern European region in this chapter will not confine itself to geopolitical breakdowns such as "East-West" relations, but will attempt to extend explanation to include "North-South" configurations as they appear globally, regionally, nationally, and subnationally.

Logically, then, a second assumption upon which this analysis will proceed is that insight into behavior within and between regions is facilitated by a multidimensional approach. In simplistic terms, we will search for areas of complementarity in economic and political (to take just two dimensions for example) situations and policy responses, but at the same time be sensitive to the points of conflict among these dimensions as they are operationalized in the region and in the member states. How the region accommodates different dimensions of behavior across different countries is a key question. Periods of political flexibility may portend economic inflexibility and orthodoxy and not general liberalization as one might ordinarily expect over time. Similarly, we will take a complex view of the relationship between political and economic jurisdictions in policy across space as well as across time. As one might conceive of a period of economic change requiring a period of political maintenance of the status quo, one might also identify a parallel act of balancing the political and economic dimensions across jurisdictions. Internal flexibility may be matched with external inflexibility in regional and in national policy.

The third assumption is that issues, the formulating of issues, the processing of issues, and the resolution of issues, are the critical considerations in sorting out the convergence and divergence of interests and dimensions as they operate in regional and national contexts. Inevitably, even an analytical, as opposed to an intentionally political, approach to Eastern Europe will be involved with the identification of issues at each level of analysis, global and national as well as regional.

The issue of security as perceived by the core power of the Soviet Union in Eastern Europe has traditionally reinforced the geopolitical conceptions of East and West in Europe and the world. Yet from others' perceptions and different conceptions, the bloc advantage in strategic terms of the USSR is less obvious. The various countries of Eastern Europe, herein to include the Soviet Union or core as well as Albania and Yugoslavia or the periphery of the regional system, present a much more problematical element in the strategic balance. Just as the character and capability in foreign policy of a single nation are defined in large measure by domestic developments, so the impact of a community of nations in the overall balance of power in the global arena is, to a significant degree, determined by the nature of relationships within that community. Historical, cultural, social, economic, organizational, and elite perspectives point to a number of within-nation and between-nation differences in Eastern Europe which seriously limit standard assumptions about the position and meaning of the region in an assessment of the strategic balance.

Due in large part to the postwar ability of the two superpowers to shape the international system into Eastern and Western alignments, with mirror-image reflections appearing in critical theaters such as Europe in the form of NATO and WTO, the European Economic Community (EEC) and the Council for Mutual Economic Assistance (Comecon), Eastern Europe has become consigned to the Soviet sphere of influence. Whether by tacit acquiescence (the notion, incorrectly attributed but with inherent logic, of a "Sonnenfeldt Doctrine") or realpolitik pragmatism (the so-called "Brezhnev Doctrine," a parallel concept similarly disavowed by the Soviets), Eastern Europe has achieved the status of a foregone conclusion in United States foreign policy formulations.(1) Despite an acute awareness of flexibility and fragmentation within its own Atlantic alliance, the Western powers have taken for granted an ideological, political, and even socioeconomic uniformity and solidarity in Eastern Europe.

The issue at hand is the recognition of differences other than those of an East-West dichotomy which pertain to the nature of within-nation, within-region, and interregional relationships, particularly as these differences impact American foreign policy and the strategic balance between the United States and the Soviet Union. A simple shift of emphasis from East-West to North-South differentiation provides the vehicle for reexamination of Eastern Europe as it relates to United States foreign policy and US/USSR strategic postures. Of special importance will be the identification of issues made salient by the cross-cutting of North-South and East-West dimensions in the East European region.(2)

Differentiation within Eastern Europe is not and should not necessarily be correlated at all times and in every place with a foreign policy of differentiation on the part of the United States. However, the argumentation in this chapter will lead to a conclusion calling for a clearer understanding of the complexities involved in East European international relations and when and where they may accrue to the advantage of the United States in strategic competition and confrontation with the Soviet Union.

EASTERN EUROPE IN GLOBAL PERSPECTIVE

Despite a considerable range in rates and levels of development within the East European region, it is important to recognize that the European Communist Party-States represent a late-developing cluster of nations whose economic motivations have a good deal more in common with the Third and Fourth Worlds than with the advanced, industrial systems of the Western World.(3) As can be seen in Table 5.1 below, Eastern European shares of global population, production, and

Table 5.1. Shares of Global Population* and Production**
(percent)

	Population	Production
USA	5.3	25.1
Other developed noncommunist	12.9	36.9
USSR	6.3	12.8
Other developed communist	2.6	4.8
OPEC	8.4 (+OAPEC)	3.9
India	14.6	2.0
Other less developed noncommunist	25.1	9.8
PRC	22.9	3.7
Other less developed communist	1.9	1.0
	100.0%	100.0%

*1974 Population totaling 4,010 million.
**1974 GNP totaling 5,563 billion dollars. Data do not differentiate between high- and low-income OPEC and OAPEC members.

Source: Department of State.

consumption point to an unenviable position relative to other European actors in particular.

At the global and European-wide levels of analysis, one might expect that the same processes occurring throughout the international system with respect to social and political change in response to economic, ecological, and environmental stress will take place inevitably within Eastern Europe irrespective of the traditional structure of power.   As the superpowers themselves have simultaneously experienced increased economic and military advantage over middle and small powers on the one hand, and inability to exercise those capabilities in influence over developing nations on the other hand, a paradox of power exists for each superpower within traditional areas of influence.

Critical energy and economic problems in the United States have produced a changing balance of political power in Atlantic relationships. Economic development and political independence among West European allies has progressed to the point at which postwar political parallels of two, superpower-dominated blocs no longer hold essential meaning, at least for the West. Western Europe contains disparate types of socioeconomic systems, yet a market commonality persists among Atlantic partners. Similarly, in the East there exists a commonality in the form of planned, command-oriented economies, but, again, significant variations on the socialist model appear.

As East European systems attempt to redress the development imbalance vis-a-vis Western Europe, two simultaneous processes could occur: increased interaction and interdependence between Eastern and Western European countries; and accentuated differentiation and independence within the socialist community. The Soviet-sponsored political and military reinforcement of orthodox socialist administration within each country could well become susceptible to the same political impact of economic development as found in global relationships.

To be sure, the East European systems in relation to the Soviet Union are caught in the same sort of development paradox persisting among socialist and nonsocialist Third World countries alike; namely, that in economic interaction between advanced industrial systems and late-developing nations, the advantage for the former is quantitatively and qualitatively increased.(4) International economic relations within any context that includes vast development differentials gives ever-greater political and economic strength to the more developed partner in the interaction, especially in those instances in which the differentials may be attributable to the historical timing of development.

While the regional import of the development process within Eastern Europe may point to stable and ongoing power relations, clearly to the Soviet advantage, there may be global and pan-European possibilities for Western influence and amelioration of Soviet hegemony. The Eastern European regional configuration finds itself in a disadvantageous position in competition and interaction on key economic indicators such as productivity, trade, and a variety of commercial relationships.

Indications that global economic and, in particular, developmental indexes offer an advantage and potential influence of the West over the East may be underlined in the figures that follow in Table 5.2. At the very least, such levels of trade deficit and indebtedness to the West among East European socialist systems demystifies the popularized Marxist tenets concerning the contemporary decay of capitalist economic structures. It may be contested that continued granting of credits from the West to the East could prompt an abrogation of responsibilities on the part of socialist systems, but experience points more logically to increased levels of interdependence and long-term cooperation and flexibility in the solving of critical economic deficiencies which cannot be coped with in isolation from international economic realities.(5)

The Conference on Security and Cooperation in Europe (CSCE) culminating in the Final Act signed in Helsinki, which provided for a reconvening of the CSCE institutional framework in Belgrade during late 1977, provides a potential for linking such global processes to regional politics with special impact upon Eastern Europe. The territorial status quo granted the Soviet Union in the basket one provisions seemingly works toward the notion of a de jure as well as de facto recognition on the part of the Western countries of Soviet hegemony in the East. Yet, Helsinki itself rests upon a foundation of pan-European concepts in which national borders and entities become stabilized

Table 5.2. Current Comecon Economic and Trade Indicators*

	GNP	Trade Balance with West	Western Indebtedness
Bulgaria	13.0	-672	1.5
Czechoslovakia	37.4	-168	1.1
East Germany	40.4	-460	2.4
Hungary	19.5	-812	2.0
Poland	60.8	-2173	4.5
Romania	34.6	-657	2.5
Soviet Union	787.0		15.0
Yugoslavia	35.0		8.0**

*Compiled from U.S. Trade Status with Socialist Countries, U.S. Department of Commerce, Bureau of East-West Trade, Office of East-West Policy and Planning, monthly reports, 1974/1976. GNP is figured in billions of dollars at 1974 world market prices. Trade balance with the West is given in millions of dollars at 1975 world market prices. Indebtedness to the West is given in billions of dollars at 1974 exchange rates.

**This figure represents the total external debt, public and private, for Yugoslavia as of 1976, according to Morgan Guaranty Trust/New York Times estimate (New York Times, November 11, 1976, p. 60). The same estimates put the total Comecon external debt at $40 billion.

internally but, at the same time, become more flexible as actors externally. The basket two provisions of economic interactions reinforce nonbloc processes in European international relations.(6)

Even those areas in which the Soviet Union holds a long-term advantage in global development indicators, such as in key minerals and energy supplies, technological inferiority dictates dependence upon and openness to Western expertise. The crucial questions concern the Western (United States and European) strategies for the exploitation of points of weakness in these areas in the East. Global development indicators, describing ongoing economic and political advantages for the West over the East, especially in the context of Europe, offer an excellent example of a point at which North-South and East-West lines intersect and identify significant issues relating to the strategic balance. The concrete context in which these issues may be used to the advantage of the West must be explained in terms of Eastern Europe as a region. Before examining the socialist systems from a regional perspective, however, some preliminary hypotheses may be formulated on the basis of the global level of analysis:

1) Development differentials are correlated positively with political, economic, and military advantages, perhaps to the point of causal connection (i.e. greater differentials produce increased advantages over time).

2) International economic processes at the global level may be replicated at lower levels of the international system, such as the European-wide region.

3) Given West European developmental success to a degree greater than that found in Eastern Europe, economic interaction offers potential for extension of influence and advantage on a variety of dimensions from West to East.

4) The combination of global economic necessities and pan-European political processes under the framework of CSCE provides a mechanism by which such influence and advantage can be concretely realized.

EASTERN EUROPE IN REGIONAL PERSPECTIVE

The degree to which the medium and small countries of Eastern Europe represent an asset to the Soviet Union in the strategic balance with the United States depends upon the level of cohesion and degree of integration existing in the socialist community. Cohesion denotes the complementarity and similarity among systems on a variety of factors or attributes exhibited by the relevant social, economic, and political entities. Integration denotes an even more policy-relevant condition existing within a community of nations, a condition in which the whole becomes greater than the sum of its parts.(7) In other words, integration denotes political unification, the transference of loyalties and authority of each part to a higher-level political system.

The qualitative difference between cohesion and integration demands analysis not only of the number of ways in which each system complements every other system in the Soviet-East European subsystem but also analysis of the degree to which such complementarity determines a patterning of public policies at the community level. Further, the plotting of public policy variations in the region must be accomplished for both domestic and foreign policy issue areas. Finally, in order to ascertain openings for the intrusion of actors and processes external to the region, some attempt must be made at delineating the linkage between domestic and foreign policy patterning.(8)

For the crossnational (cohesiveness on a number of dimensions) and for the international (integration on a given dimension, predominantly economic in West European experience and political in East European experience) analyses of the East European regional setting, the major obstacle to understanding is the sheer complexity of the nine systems under consideration. A myriad of historical and cultural, social and economic, organizational and institutional, and leadership and elite factors characterize each country, despite the obvious pressure for public policy patterning emanating from the core system of the USSR. A close examination of the past and current behavior of the East European systems, from core to periphery alike, does point to the salience of certain factors in most situations. These critical factors may be listed as follows:

1) On the historical and cultural dimension, those factors which indicate at once the greatest variation across nations in the area as well as exert the greatest impact upon public policies in the region relate to ethnic, linguistic, and nationalistic diversity.(9) In particular, it is important to recognize not only the numbers of ethnic groups, especially those with recent and/or long-standing national independence (such as in the case of the Soviet Union itself), but also the degree of ethnic rivalry among a few, but clearly divided, groups (such as in the case of Czechs and Slovaks).   Of considerable impact upon policy variations are those ethnic situations which are reinforced on other historical and cultural indexes, such as periods of democratic experience in the case of Czechoslovakia in the interim war period or in the case of former national independence for several groups now included in the Yugoslav system.

2) On the social and economic dimensions, perhaps the most critical factor indicating a lack of cohesion and stress at the regional level due to enforced external economic uniformity by the Soviets is the variation along an economic continuum from industrial to pastoral base.(10) However, this factor has been modified to a considerable extent by the fact that the East European systems, with the possible exception of Albania, have all undergone an essential shift from agricultural to industrial emphasis in recent years. East Germany and Czechoslovakia, of course, had traditionally occupied advanced industrial status but also underwent modernization processes under Soviet control in postwar years similar to those experienced by the other systems. That factor which currently affects domestic policy variation centers on the ratio in both industrial and agricultural sectors of private to state owned forces of production.(11) A surprising degree of variance on this factor exists among even the most orthodox domestic systems, such as the case of Polish agricultural

holdings in contrast to those in Czechoslovakia. Less specific, but equally important, influences on policy variation can be seen in the varying rates as well as levels of development overall in the region.

3) On the organizational and institutional dimensions of cohesion and integration in the East European region, it is traditionally assumed that the commonality of Communist Party control internally in each nation and integrating force of the WTO and Comecon across the region serve as the means by which the Soviet core achieves the ends of political and ideological uniformity. A more microscopic examination of the organizations within and across the East European systems, however, pinpoints a number of variations from the organizational norm. The Party in each system inevitably reflects the internal historical, cultural, social, and economic factors operating in that system.(12) Similarly, the influence of institutions outside the formal political system in each society varies from country to country. In some cases, the Communist Party has attempted to incorporate all institutional facets of society into a controlled and hierarchical setting, such as in East Germany, while in other cases there are significant organizational loci outside the formal party structure, such as in Poland with the highly visible Catholic Church and in Yugoslavia with a variety of economic institutions.   Czechoslovakia signifies an especially important feature of many East European organizational frameworks for society in the cross-cutting of ethnic/administrative units and organizational loyalties with Czechs and Slovaks adhering to respective governmental and political organizational units.

4) The political elite and leaders in other sectors of society are necessarily treated as the most significant determinants of policy variation in systems which are characterized by authoritarian political structures.(13) Where the most interesting variations on these two dimensions appear is in the horizontal linkage between the two segments of policy-relevant opinion makers.   The traditional method by which the Communist Party has introduced new elites into the political system is through recruitment at the bottom of the political ladder and selective elevation of the most ideologically motivated to the top positions. Increasingly, however, East European systems have turned to a process of cooptation: the introduction of economic, administrative, and other technical experts at various levels of the political system in response to the requirements of modernization and resultant complexity and diversity. Still, traditional indicators among authoritarian elite structures in Eastern Europe maintain the greatest impact upon policy variation. Age in

particular, in cases as disparate as the Soviet Union at the core and Yugoslavia at the periphery, looms as the single most critical elite factor in contemporary Eastern Europe. Since it is virtually impossible to predict change in policy upon the basis of personality shifts as yet unknown, some indication of direction of change in the East European systems may be derived from an examination of the factions among elites of the various Communist Parties and, in particular, the basis upon which such factions, or more properly coalitions, are formed. In several cases, most noticeably the Soviet Union itself, elite factions seem built around patron-client relations, the Secretary-General depending, for the most part, on a number of personally sponsored members of the Politburo and Central Committee Secretariat for resolution of issues in his favor. On the other hand, there are cases, most extreme in Yugoslavia but increasingly apparent elsewhere in East Europe, where factions are built around issues as opposed to identities.

The simple identification of these four major sets of factors salient for the shaping of domestic and foreign policies in Eastern Europe only begins the process of regional analysis. More relevant is the interconnection among, and ranking of, factors in terms of policy relevance with respect to given issues under consideration by the political system. At the regional level, the single most policy-relevant issue before East European elites is integration involving the mix of political and economic options available in each national system.(14)

Figure 5.1 demonstrates the variation on several of the most significant factors determining policy differences in the region. What becomes apparent across these continua is the linkage existing and the pattern developing among the various factors as they interact with one another in the formulation of policy. For example, the ethnic heterogeneity in Yugoslavia, reinforced by historical experience of national independence in several cases, reinforces the significance of development levels and types from one ethnically homogeneous republic to another within the Yugoslav system which, in turn, has had tremendous impact on the party and nonparty organizational aspects of the society. Elite diversity, signified by a variety of issue-oriented factions within a Party, nevertheless is dominated by a single personality.

The regional significance of the horizontal flow and interaction of key indicators of policy variation rests in the degree to which such variations operate to create political distance between the several medium and small states in the region and the core system of the USSR. The foreign policy issue area serves to illustrate the impact that an underlying lack of cohesion (as outlined above) has had upon Soviet goals of economic, political, and ideological integration. Four broad dimensions of foreign policy behavior can be identified, each with critical factors for the determination of differentiation within the region:

Least Cohesive										Most Cohesive
				Ethno-Linguistic Composition[a]						
Heterogeneity	SU	YU	CZ	HU	BU	RO	AL	PO	EG	Homogeneity
				Economic Ownership[b]						
Private	YU	PO	HU	EG	CZ	RO	BU	SU	AL	State
				Organizational-Institutional Structure[c]						
Pluralism	YU	PO	CZ	SU	HU	EG	RO	BU	AL	Monolithism
				Elite-Leadership Structure[d]						
Discontinuity	YU	SU	CZ	PO	HU	EG	RO	AL	BU	Continuity

[a]Denotes number and intensity of differences.

[b]Includes industrial and agricultural sectors.

[c]Includes party factions and interest groups.

[d]Denotes rate and probability of turnover.

Fig. 5.1. East European arrays: policy-relevant indicators of cohesiveness.

1) The organizational focus to the regional goals of the Soviet Union on politico-military and socioeconomic dimensions are the WTO and Comecon, respectively.(15) The dual roles of the Warsaw Pact – external defense vis-a-vis the NATO alliance and internal policing within the bloc – are highlighted in the various postures of the East European systems with respect to military groupings. Albania and Yugoslavia eschew pact activities altogether, while Romania limits its relationship to observer status. Of some significance to the prediction of foreign policy behavior within the bloc is the actual use of Warsaw Pact intervention in internal affairs of its members, as in the case with Hungary and Czechoslovakia. Similarly, the economic mechanism by which the Soviet Union exerts integrative influence in the region is Comecon, an organizational network of bilateral economic associations among members that has demonstrated only minor successes at multilateral association. It is important to remember that Soviet resources and relative size place it in a position vis-a-vis any other East European system in such an advantageous manner as to be analogous to the global level relationship existing between advanced industrial systems and the Third and Fourth Worlds.(16) Again, the degree to which several of the East European systems have pursued alternative international economic paths to the Soviet dominated mechanism of Comecon only serves to accentuate the lack of integration on the critical economic dimension. Paradoxically, East European systems seem to demonstrate the least integrative behavior on that very dimension on which cohesiveness is most pronounced – economics. Conversely, the political and cultural diversity and lack of cohesiveness has been artificially sublimated by Soviet military might in the form of the WTO.

2) The entire range of economic, commercial, informational, and technological interactions undertaken by East European countries can offer evidence as to the distance of an individual system within the region from the core power. In two particular aspects, the ratio of bilateral to multilateral association with the Soviet system by a less-developed East European partner and the overall ratio of intra-bloc to extra-bloc interactions, the identification of integrative-disintegrative trends within the region may be facilitated. Of special importance in the future may be subregional groupings of East European countries outside the Soviet dominated organizations.(17)

3) Ideological orientation in foreign policy behavior offers another critical dimension on which significant variations between the Moscow model and national orientations elsewhere

in Eastern Europe exist. The most obvious divergence occurred in the case of Albanian support for the side of China
in the Sino-Soviet international communist split, but it is
equally significant that the Yugoslav national variation in the
direction of a distinctly different means of administration of
society and the economy has achieved the status of yet a
third model for the construction of socialism. The socialist
humanist movement in several East European countries, originating in Hungary and Poland among small intellectual
circles and continuing in Yugoslav philosophy and sociology in
general, has been reinforced internationally by some elements among West European socialism and communism.(18)

4) Orientation outside the region and roles played in the international system at large also point to foreign policy variation
considerably at odds with Soviet aspirations for the region.
Yugoslav involvement with the nonaligned nations of Afro-
Asia, to some extent pursued by Romania as well in recent
years, and the dual channels for non-Soviet association in the
international system provided in the Helsinki meeting of all
European states and the Berlin meeting of all European
communist parties evidence a regional flexibility previously
impossible and potentially exploitable by East European systems seeking a greater independence vis-a-vis Moscow and
West European systems seeking possibilities for a more
flexible structure for postwar Europe.

Figure 5.2 illustrates several of the dimensions of foreign policy
behavior variation across the region, a pattern which is most useful
when viewed both in terms of interconnection among the various
dimensions and in terms of linkage with domestic variations illustrated
in Fig. 5.1.

The regional perspective is crucial to the determination of significant variations between public policy patterns existing in the Soviet
Union on the one hand and among the other systems in the region on the
other, as well as to the identification of potential areas of impact
which the Western systems may have upon the Eastern region. Without
question, it would be misleading to suggest that political and military
realities in Eastern Europe mitigate Soviet power in relation to the
other members of the region, but equally misleading is the conclusion
that the West cannot, in some degree, influence the type of social and
economic evolution in the East European systems. Tables 5.3 and 5.4
indicate the simultaneous political equations operating in Eastern
Europe. Political power for the Soviet Union based upon military and
economic preponderance, with socioeconomic variability across the rest
of Eastern Europe (a factor not unimportant within the Soviet system
itself as will be pointed out below in the discussion of Eastern Europe in
national perspective), signals areas susceptible to influence from outside
the region.

Least Integrative   Most Integrative

Regional Organization[a]

Non-Participatory								Participatory
AL	YU	RO	PO	HU	EG	CZ	BU	SU

Bloc Institutionalization[b]

Extrabloc								Intrabloc
AL	YU	RO	PO	EG	HU	CZ	SU	BU

Ideological Movement[c]

Unorthodox								Orthodox
YU	AL	PO	HU	CZ	RO	EG	BU	SU

International Relations[d]

Nonalignment								Alignment
YU	AL	RO	PO	HU	CZ	EG	BU	SU

[a]Behavior with respect to WTO & Comecon.

[b]Core-periphery & intra/extrabloc relations.

[c]Sino-Soviet, Marxism-Leninism/humanism.

[d]East-West & North-South orientations.

Fig. 5.2. East European arrays: policy-relevant indicators of integration.

Table 5.3. Military Indexes and Rankings East European Socialist Systems, 1965/1970/1975

	I Deployed USSR Divisions	II Armed Forces (thousands)	III Armed Forces Per thousand people	IV Milex in millions	V Milex per capita	I-V Rank Order
AL	0	52/ 52/ 52	28/24.34/21.57	58/ 95/ 131	43.40/ 56.70/ 49.70	9, 9, 1, 9, 9
*BU	0	178/ 175/ 175	21.70/20.61/20.02	695/ 934/ 1680	118.00/140.00/176.00	6, 7, 2, 6, 4
*CZ	5	267/ 222/ 210	18.90/15.50/14.19	1680/ 1990/ 3180	166.00/177.00/197.00	3, 6, 4, 4, 3
*EG	20	205/ 202/ 220	12.10/11.83/13.03	1300/ 2380/ 3890	107.00/178.00/211.00	2, 4, 5, 3, 2
*HU	4	156/ 146/ 118	15.30/14.12/11.19	696/ 969/ 1420	95.00/119.00/123.00	4, 8, 8, 8, 6
*PO	2	302/ 314/ 435	9.68/ 9.65/ 12.80	1980/ 2820/ 5090	88.40/110.00/137.00	5, 2, 6, 2, 5
*RO	0	249/ 211/ 220	13.10/10.42/10.36	1120/ 1460/ 2230	81.80/ 91.90/ 96.00	7, 5, 9, 5, 7
*SU	64[c]	2780/4300/4600	12.00/17.70/18.10	52400/74600/119000	316.00/392.00/428.00	1, 1, 3, 1, 1
YU	0	310/ 257/ 270	16.00/12.62/12.65	453/ 772/ 1600	32.60/ 48.30/ 68.70	8, 3, 7, 7, 8
*WTO		4137/5570/5978	12.51/16.11/16.58	59.87/85.15/136.49[a]	252.15/313.92/346.73[b]	
NATO		5857/6311/5253	11.55/11.87/ 9.48	79.00/110.84/145.04[a]	216.98/265.46/239.33[b]	

[a] in billions
[b] average
[c] European USSR
*Indicates Members of WTO

Source: World Military Expenditures and Arms Transfers, 1965-1974 and 1966-1975. Washington, D.C.: US Arms Control and Disarmament Agency.

Table 5.4. Economic Indexes and Rankings East European Socialist Systems, 1965/1970/1975

	I Population in Millions	II GNP in Millions	III GNP Per Capita	I-III Rank Order
AL	1.860/ 2.136/ 2.411	600/ 900/ 1310	449/ 537/ 497	9, 9, 9
*BU	8.200/ 8.490/ 8.741	6750/ 10900/ 18500	1150/1640/1930	8, 8, 7
*CZ	14.100/ 14.319/ 14.804	22000/ 33000/ 54500	2180/2940/3370	6, 4, 1
*EG	17.000/ 17.070/ 16.885	26500/ 37100/ 60300	2170/2770/3270	5, 3, 2
*HU	10.200/ 10.338/ 10.541	10900/ 15100/ 25500	1490/1870/2210	7, 7, 5
*PO	31.200/ 32.526/ 34.022	30700/ 42900/ 85400	1370/1680/2300	2, 2, 4
*RO	19.000/ 20.253/ 21.245	14800/ 24200/ 46800	1080/1520/2010	4, 5, 6
*SU	231.000/242.757/254.300	333000/519000/870000	2010/2720/3130	1, 1, 3
YU	19.400/ 20.371/ 21.346	9590/ 18300/ 35300	688/1140/1510	3, 7, 8
*WTO	330.700/345.753/360.538	444.7/ 682.2/ 1161.0[a]	1874/2514/2946[b]	
NATO	507.214/531.817/554.166	1301.3/1913.6/2977.2[a]	3572/4589/4911[b]	

[a]in billions
[b]average

*Indicates members of WTO

Source: World Military Expenditures and Arms Transfers, 1965–1974 and 1966-1975. Washington, D.C.: US Arms Control and Disarmament Agency.

It is obvious from the preceding discussion that a policy of differentiation is necessary with respect to the Eastern European region, especially in the context of the strategic balance in which political and socioeconomic distance between the Soviet Union and other systems in the region offers advantages to the West.(19) Preliminary hypotheses based on a regional level of analysis can be formulated as follows:

1) Direct political and military influence in Eastern Europe on the part of Western powers will only act counter to objectives of independence and flexibility in East European/Soviet relations.

2) At the same time, socioeconomic differentials between the Soviet core and the remaining systems in Eastern Europe indicate not only the indigenous development of models based on national variations but also points of stress and susceptibility to Western influence in the area.

3) In particular, the West European countries may be the most economically appropriate and politically acceptable agents of intrusive influence into Eastern Europe.

4) The United States can most effectively exert influence in the area by a policy of differentiation which recognizes the Soviet and East European necessities of economic and technological interaction with the West, a recognition that includes awareness of Soviet deficiencies and demands as well as those in less-developed systems within the region.

EASTERN EUROPE IN NATIONAL PERSPECTIVE

Proceeding from the macro to the micro level of analysis of Eastern Europe, this chapter has attempted to outline a logical relationship and analogy between political and economic realities operating in global and regional configurations. Both globally and regionally the traditional East-West differentiation of the postwar era has given way to the policy relevance of North-South differentiation. Increasingly, economic status has accounted for political strategy. Even in a region characterized by traditional indexes of power, such as in postwar Eastern Europe, a variety of political models have arisen to achieve economic goals. It is appropriate that American foreign policy goals, especially in the crucial context of the strategic East-West balance, be attuned to the national political strategies of Eastern European countries. Specifically concerning the strategic balance between the Soviet Union and the United States, Eastern Europe may represent a test case for the ability of the United States and the Western world to take advantage of economic and technological superiority. Particular national strategies for economic development and political independence vis-a-vis Moscow are keys for the unlocking of doors previously closed to Western influence.

Figure 5.3 illustrates a simplistic matrix of political choices and system models available to Eastern European countries in their quest for flexibility in regional context, and support from the West in the international system at large. Here the crucial interconnection occurs between political and economic realities on the one hand, and internal and external dimensions of policy on the other. Two extreme cases – polar opposites in global, regional, and national contexts – are represented by Bulgaria and Yugoslavia, each system legitimately (and successfully, one might add) opting for contrasting models; the internally orthodox and externally inflexible for Bulgaria, and the internally unorthodox and externally flexible for Yugoslavia. More interesting in contrast, and more instructive in the long run for Western systems attempting to exert influence, are the Hungarian and Romanian models. The former system has exhibited an experimental attitude with respect to the market mechanism within socialism domestically (the NEM or New Economic Mechanism), but at the same time has adhered to the Moscow line in foreign policy without significant variation on a single issue. The latter system is recognized as one of the most orthodox internal systems in the bloc, yet, at the same time, has openly disputed Moscow on significant issues of foreign relations, especially in instances which would benefit Romanian development irrespective of Comecon directives for regional division of labor.

Just as the logic of global socioeconomic differentials argues for realignment of traditional political communities of nations, so do national aspirations for industrialization and sociocultural modernization argue for political models and choices in opposition to regional political and military powers. Hypotheses derived from the national perspective in Eastern Europe may be tentatively formulated as follows:

1) Even in cases of extreme variation from the Moscow core of the region, such as in Albania, wherein the deviation does not in any sense indicate a degree of cohesion with the West, such cases are important evidence in the assessment of the East-West and, in particular, the US/USSR strategic balance.

2) Where variations reflect a conscious choice of balance between internal and external flexibility, the greatest opportunities for Western influence exist with respect to the system possessing external independence of action, since the Soviet pattern of behavior and reaction to such flexibility is less extreme.

3) Where variations reflect a conscious choice of balance between political and economic flexibility, the greatest opportunities for Western influence exist with respect to the system possessing economic independence of action, since the mainstay of Soviet internal control is the authority of the Communist Party.

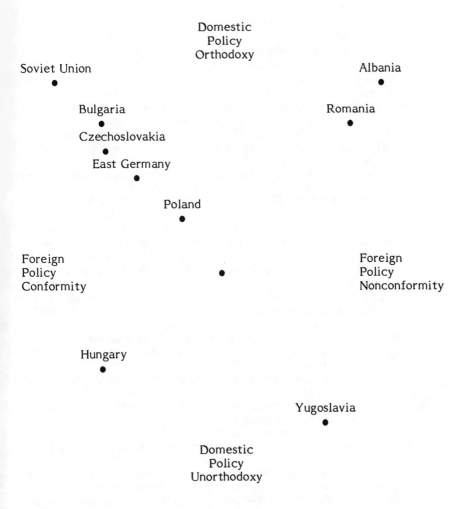

Fig. 5.3. Scattergram of public policy options in the Soviet-East European region.

4) In those cases where internal and external flexibility have been accomplished simultaneously on economic and political dimensions in relation to the socialist model exported by Moscow, the Western powers possess opportunities for the extension of influence into the periphery of the Eastern European region, a process which could potentially shift the strategic balance in favor of the Western world in general and the United States in particular.

CONCLUSION

Proceeding from the top downward and the bottom upward in the international system, socioeconomic change and its inevitable political impact indicate realignment at the global, regional, and national levels. In each instance, such realignment will accrue to the advantage of the system which is capable and willing to use social, economic, and technological strength, even in lieu of traditional indexes of power such as military might if available. The overall strategic balance between East and West can be best assessed in the total perspective of global, regional, and national levels.

The specific Soviet-American strategic balance, and the integral role played by Eastern Europe in that weighing of advantage in the international system, indicate not only an inherent economic and technological advantage for Western Europe and the United States, but also beckons an initiative on the part of the Western industrial countries for accentuation of those trends within the socialist community which tend toward development and stability in contradistinction to artificially imposed political uniformity and military solidarity under Soviet influence.

Change and its conceptual correlate "innovation," the latter denoting a departure, or break, in past patterns of incremental adaptation, seem to be proceeding apace in Eastern Europe in response to pressures from within and without the region.(20) Subnational sources of pressure on the political authority patterns of the past emanate from inevitable consequences of social and economic modernization.(21) The early general notions of coexistence and commerce in the East-West context have now developed to an extent that specific interactions with policy impact, such as in the case of technology transfer and resultant reorientation of the role of centrally planned change, can be discerned despite some dwindling support for detente.(22)

Neither core nor periphery countries are immune to agents of change operating at each level of the international system. The action between core and periphery may even serve to accelerate such processes. These East European systems, either independently or collectively as a region, may no longer be accurately termed "closed," but are better considered as being in constant flux in response to issues which are faced by all regions. Eastern and Western European regions may well be at the initial stages of regional reformulation at new levels in order to deal with new issues.(23)

NOTES

(1) See Charles Gati, "The Forgotten Region," Foreign Policy 19 (Summer 1975): 135-45: "In our persistent, if not desperate, search for detente, we have rightly abandoned our provocative 'forward strategy' toward Eastern Europe, but have wrongly adopted a policy of deliberate indifference" (p. 144).

(2) Evidence of East European intellectual and political awareness of the North-South impact upon the region may be seen in Bela Kadar, "Recent Trends in the Industrialization of the Developing Countries and the Global Strategy of the Leading Capitalist Countries," Trends in World Economy 14 (Budapest: Hungarian Scientific Council for World Economy, 1974).

(3) Elaboration of this point may be found in James A. Kuhlman, "Socialist Construction and the Steady State: Some Dialectics in the Debate," in The Sustainable Society: Implications for Limited Growth, edited by Dennis Clark Pirages (New York: Praeger, 1977), pp. 325-38. See also Phillip J. Bryson, Scarcity and Control in Socialism: Essays on East European Planning (Lexington, Mass.: D.C. Heath, 1976).

(4) A point developed at length with obvious implications for Soviet-East European economic interaction by Ferenc Kozma, "Some Theoretical Problems Regarding Socialist Integration and the Levelling of Economic Development," Trends in World Economy 6 (Budapest: Hungarian Scientific Council for World Economy, 1971).

(5) See Michael Kaser, "Soviet Trade Turns to Europe," Foreign Policy 19 (Summer 1975): 123-34; and Marshall I. Goldman, "The Soviet Economy Is Not Immune," Foreign Policy 21 (Winter 1975-76): 76-87. The Western academic community only recently has begun to devote attention to the impact of such interaction: see Robert W. Campbell and Paul Marer, eds., East-West Trade & Technology Transfer: An Agenda of Research Needs (Bloomington, Ind.: Studies in East European and Soviet Planning, Development, and Trade, May 20, 1974).

(6) This political outcome is stressed continually by the Romanians in particular. See Aurel Ghibutiu, "Pan European Economic Cooperation – The Essential Component of the European Security," Perspektiven und Probleme wirtschaftlicher Zusammenarbeit zwischen Ost – und Westeuropa (Berlin: Deutsches Institut fur Wirtschaftsforschung Sonderheft, 114, 1976).

(7) See Ernst B. Haas, The Uniting of Europe (Stanford, Calif.: Stanford University Press, 1958), p. 16.

(8) A preliminary framework and approach for this task has been developed in James A. Kuhlman, "A Framework for Viewing Domestic and Foreign Policy ·Patterns" in The International Politics of Eastern Europe, edited by Charles Gati (New York: Praeger, 1976), pp. 275-91.

(9) See Peter F. Sugar and Ivo J. Lederer, eds., Nationalism in Eastern Europe (Seattle, Wash.: University of Washington Press, 1969). The impact of ethnicity upon relations between states in Eastern Europe is discussed in Robert R. King, Minorities Under Communism: Nationalities as a Source of Tension Among Balkan Communist States (Cambridge, Mass.: Harvard University Press, 1973).

(10) See John P. Hardt, "East European Economic Development: Two Decades of Interrelationships and Interactions with the Soviet Union" in Economic Developments in Countries of Eastern Europe (Washington, D.C.: Subcommittee on Foreign Economic Policy, Joint Economic Committee, 91st Congress, 2nd Session, 1970), pp. 5-40.

(11) See Andrew Elias, "Magnitude and Distribution of the Labor Force in Eastern Europe" in Economic Developments in Countries of Eastern Europe, pp. 149-239.

(12) See H. Gordon Skilling and Franklyn Griffiths, eds., Interest Groups in Soviet Politics (Princeton, N.J.: Princeton University Press, 1971); and in particular H. Gordon Skilling, "Group Conflict and Political Change" in Change in Communist Systems, edited by Chalmers Johnson (Stanford, Calif.: Stanford University Press, 1970), pp. 215-34.

(13) Variability within and between national Communist elites is examined in R. Barry Farrell, ed., Political Leadership in Eastern Europe and the Soviet Union (Chicago, Ill.: Aldine, 1970). See also Carl Beck et al., Comparative Communist Political Leadership (New York: David McKay, 1973).

(14) See the section on "Policy and Planning" in Reorientation and Commercial Relations of the Economies of Eastern Europe (Washington, D.C.: Joint Economic Committee, 93rd Congress, 2nd Session, 1974), pp. 17-250.

(15) The standard works on the two regional organizations are Robin Alison Remington, The Warsaw Pact: Case Studies in Communist Conflict Resolution (Cambridge, Mass.: MIT Press, 1971); and Michael Kaser, COMECON: Integration Problems of the Planned Economies (London: Oxford University Press, 1967).

(16) See Dennis C. Pirages, "Global Resources and the Future of Europe" in The Future of Inter-Bloc Relations in Europe, edited by Louis J. Mensonides and James A. Kuhlman (New York: Praeger, 1974), pp. 121-44. See also Jeremy Russell, Energy as a Factor in Soviet

Foreign Policy (Westmead, England: Saxon House, Royal Institute of International Affairs, 1976).

(17) For instance George W. Hoffman, Regional Development Strategy in Southeast Europe: A Comparative Analysis of Albania, Bulgaria, Greece, Romania and Yugoslavia (New York: Praeger, 1972).

(18) This is one of the major reasons for the ambivalence toward Eurocommunism evidenced to date on the part of the Soviet leaders. Such channels of communication, even if only philosophical in nature, are perceived as political intrusions by the Soviets. Yet such nonbloc interactions in the ideological sphere are especially difficult to contain or curtail, given that the agents of such change fall within socialist and communist parameters.

(19) The point here is that the United States, or another region in relation to Eastern Europe, cannot and should not expect that lack of cohesion on the part of some systems in Eastern Europe necessarily will mean a realignment of those systems with the Western world. Despite the suggestions raised recently by Laurence Silberman, essentially putting forth the notion that basic change in communist societies should be an a priori condition for enhancement of economic, technological, and political interactions with the West, traditional Western strengths should be used in an ongoing attempt to reinforce processes of innovation. See "Yugoslavia's 'Old' Communism," Foreign Policy 26 (Spring 1977): 3-27.

(20) Essays on agents of change from within and without the individual systems and the collective region of Eastern Europe may be found in Andrew Gyorgy and James A. Kuhlman, eds., Innovation in Communist Systems (Boulder, Colo.: Westview Press, 1978).

(21) See Mark G. Field, ed., Social Consequences of Modernization in Communist Societies (Baltimore, Md.: The Johns Hopkins University Press, 1976); Charles Gati, ed., The Politics of Modernization in Eastern Europe: Testing the Soviet Model (New York: Praeger, 1974); Bogdan Mieczkewski, Personal and Social Consumption in Eastern Europe: Poland, Czechoslovakia, Hungary, and East Germany (New York: Praeger, 1975); and Jan F. Triska and Paul M. Cocks, eds., Political Development in Eastern Europe (New York: Praeger, 1977).

(22) The seminal volume by Samuel Pisar, Coexistence & Commerce: Guidelines for Transactions between East and West (New York: Mc-Graw-Hill, 1970), has been followed by several studies concerning the impact of such interaction; for instance see Carl H. McMillan, Changing Perspectives in East-West Commerce (Lexington, Mass.: D.C. Heath, 1974). For internal system adaptation and, in particular, its implications for the central planning model, see Michael Kaser and Richard Portes, eds., Planning and Market Relations (London: The Macmillan Press,

1971); Jan Marczewski, Crisis in Socialist Planning: Eastern Europe and the USSR (New York: Praeger, 1974, translated from the French by Noel Lindsay); and Robert Mayer, Robert Moroney, and Robert Morris, Centrally Planned Change: A Reexamination of Theory and Experience (Urbana, Ill.: University of Illinois Press, 1974).

(23) See, for instance, the volumes in the series East-West Perspectives; in particular James A. Kuhlman and Louis J. Mensonides, eds., Changes in European Relations (Leyden, The Netherlands: A.W. Sijthoff, 1976); and James A. Kuhlman, ed., The Foreign Policies of Eastern Europe: Domestic and International Determinants (Leyden, The Netherlands: A.W. Sijthoff, 1978). For examination of the regional interaction in the pan-European framework of CSCE, see Frans A.M. Alting von Geusau, ed., The External Relations of the European Community: Perspectives, Policies and Responses (Westmead, England: Saxon House, John F. Kennedy Institute, 1974); Charles Ransom, The European Community and Eastern Europe (Totowa, N.J.: Rowman and Littlefield, 1973); and Leuan John, ed., EEC Policy Towards Eastern Europe (Westmead, England: Saxon House, 1975).

6 North America

David Leyton-Brown

North America will here be considered to comprise Canada and the United States. Geographically speaking, Mexico is a part of the continent and could be included on those grounds. Indeed, some American political leaders (notably Governor Jerry Brown of California and ex-Governor John Connally of Texas) have treated Mexico as a significant potential, if not actual, interaction partner in recently calling for a continental common market in energy resources, to include the United States, Canada, and Mexico. Nonetheless, the cultural, political, and social affinities, and the relationship of complex interdependence(1) between Canada and the United States qualitatively qualify that pair of countries to be treated as a regional system.

REGIONAL CONFIGURATIONS

In the jargon of the North American academic community, this region is considered to be an asymmetrical dyad. By virtually any objective criterion except geographical size, the United States far surpasses Canada. The United States is a military and economic superpower, the home of the majority of the world's foreign direct investment and multinational enterprises, and has a population almost ten times greater than Canada's 22 million. But that disparity does not mean that Canada's own attributes are negligible. In the words of one American observer, "Only in comparison to the United States is Canada's economy small."(2) It is one of the world's top ten international trading nations, and is one of the seven leading economic powers of the Western world, with a bountiful resource base and a developed, though substantially foreign (American)-owned industrial economy. Canada's relative military might has dwindled since its height in the immediate post-World War II period, but it remains an active member of NATO and NORAD, and an invariable contributor to United Nations peacekeeping operations. Canada's armed forces number only about 80,000, but they are currently benefitting from a major reequipment program. It is plain that the conventional image of the relationship between the United States and Canada as one between an elephant and a mouse under-estimates Canada's relative position – perhaps a more appropriate image would be that of an elephant and a beaver.

There are no intrusive actors operating in the North American system, because the major global power is already within the region, and Canada is not an arena for superpower competition. Other impor-tant global actors, of course, maintain relations of all kinds with both Canada and the United States, but do not intrude in such a fashion as to penetrate the regional system.

Both the United States and Canada have relatively stable and cohesive societies. Both are countries of immigration, building upon early Western European, and principally British, settlement. The social treatment of immigrant groups has differed somewhat, however. The United States has culturally stressed assimilation and, while some identifiable ethnic groups remain, especially in the larger cities, the ethos of the melting pot has prevailed. In Canada, by contrast, cultural and ethnic diversity has been accorded far more legitimacy, to the extent that the Canadian Cabinet includes a Minister of State for Multiculturalism. This contrast is reflected in the conventional meta-phor of a mosaic rather than a melting pot.

One important social cleavage can be found in each country – in the United States on racial lines, and in Canada on linguistic ones. In the United States, generations of discrimination against blacks are now being redressed, but racial tensions have, in recent years, threatened the social fabric and are still not finally resolved. Issues of bilingualism and biculturalism have preoccupied Canadian politics for decades, and have arrived at the current "crisis of Confederation." The cleavage between anglophones and francophones is compounded by the fact that the vast majority of French-speaking Canadians reside in the province of Quebec. Long-standing, but scattered, support for Quebec separation was intensified by the election in November 1976 of a provincial government dedicated to Quebec independence. If such aspirations were to be realized, it would have profound implications for the United States as well as Canada.(3)

The political cultures of the two countries have many similarities. Both countries are advanced, open, pluralist democracies, with highly developed political institutions affording widespread opportunities for political participation, and with two dominant political parties (though a socialist party is a strong third force in Canadian politics, and has formed the government in several provinces). Differences flow primar-ily from the contrast between the separation of powers associated with the presidential political system of the United States and the re-sponsible government of the Canadian political system. The checks and balances of American political culture are broadly reflective of a distrust of government power, while Canadians are far more relaxed about government intervention in the private sector, and accord a far greater role to government in national life. Canada's informal mix of written and unwritten elements in its constitution is poorly understood in the United States, even by political leaders; and some cross-border conflicts have been fueled by American presumptions that Canadian acts which would be unconstitutional if committed in the United States, such as the nationalization of foreign-owned potash mines by the government of the province of Saskatchewan, or the issuing of regulations permitting the deletion of commercials from TV programs broadcast by United States stations but carried on Canadian cable systems, must be illegal, or at least unethical, in Canada also.

In each country, the ability of the executive to manage relations with the other is subject to an important domestic constraint. In the United States, that constraint is the Congress, whose authority to ratify agreements, appropriate moneys, and pass legislation can at times frustrate executive policy. In Canada, Parliament has similar powers but does not exercise the same degree of constraint because of the party discipline which is the other side of the coin of cabinet responsibility. The major constraint is from the governments of the provinces, which have constitutional authority over many areas under federal jurisdiction in the United States.

There is broad complementarity of values among primary and secondary elites in both countries. Fundamental ideological positions and basic foreign policy orientations have been held in common. Elite views on the Canadian-American relationship are also compatible. Interviews with members of the Canadian foreign policy elite conducted in connection with the Canadian International Image Study(4) showed that the senior government officials primarily responsible for Canada's external policies have a benign image of the United States and see a balance of benefits over costs in Canada's interdependent interactions with the United States. It is important to note that the elite does not hold a monolithic image of the relationship, however, and that dissensus among various bureaucratic groups could affect external behavior. For example, senior officials in the Department of External Affairs expressed the strongest support for policies designed to differentiate Canada from the United States and augment independence, despite a positive image of the United States; while senior officials in the Department of Industry, Trade, and Commerce were among the least likely to support such policies, even though they were more likely to see Canada's freedom of action constrained by interdependence with the United States.(5) Analysis of public opinion poll data suggests that nongovernmental elites also hold the relationship in high regard. More highly educated Canadians have been more likely to perceive relations between Canada and the United States to be good, though also to perceive American influence in Canada to be too great. Wealthy Canadians have been more likely than their low income counterparts to perceive the relationship to be good, and less likely to be concerned about the degree of American influence in Canada.(6) American elite views of Canada are hard to extract from the general opinion poll data available, but American public images of Canada when studied were more favorable than for any other country evaluated at the same time.(7)

The authority and influence patterns of the two countries are broadly similar – each is an established political system with highly developed political institutions, and each is polyarchic, with substantial subsystem autonomy. Each country is a federation, and the relatively autonomous pursuit of interests by various provinces and states can greatly complicate and delay negotiations on bilateral questions. Interest groups and other subnational nongovernmental actors are involved in the political process in both countries, but more so in the United States. The American political system is responsive to subnational pressures ranging from class action suits to congressional lobbying, with the occasional risk that national interest may be subordinated to special interests. Examples of that danger are harder to find in Canada. Relatively frequent transgovernmental contacts between governmental subunits (i.e. departments and agencies) add a further element to this picture of subsystem autonomy.(8)

We are thus left with the configuration of a region possessed of many affinities. The two countries emerged from a common colonial past with similar settlement patterns and ethnic composition. Apart from the francophones in Canada, citizens of the two countries speak the same language and share much of the same culture. Despite the best efforts of the Canadian Radio Television and Telecommunications Commission to foster Canadian content, many of the most popular television programs in Canada are American-made. Canadians watch American movies, read American magazines, and succumb to American advertising campaigns. Indeed, the growing closeness of the asymmetrical relationship has lead some scholars to ask whether North America is in the process of integrating,(9) and many Canadian nationalists decry American economic and cultural imperialism.(10)

REGIONAL INTERDEPENDENCE

It would be hard to find a more highly interdependent pair of countries than Canada and the United States. Keohane and Nye took Canadian-American relations as the case most likely to fit their three ideal conditions of complex interdependence: 1) multiple channels of interaction between societies, including interstate, transgovernmental, and transnational; 2) the absence of hierarchy among issues; and 3) the absence of military force as an instrument for achieving goals and resolving conflicts.(11) Though the relationship is an asymmetrical one in terms of the attributes of the two countries and the absolute and relative magnitude of interaction flows, the balance of sensitivities and vulnerabilities is often much more symmetrical.(12)

Interdependence is most evident in the economic area. The more than $50 billion of trade between the two countries is the world's largest bilateral trade flow. Each country is the other's best customer and supplier. Canada provides about 25 percent of United States imports and purchases about 25 percent of United States exports, with the total trade flow representing about one percent of the United States GNP. The United States accounts for about 70 percent of Canada's imports and exports, with mutual trade representing about 11 percent of Canadian GNP. Between 60 and 70 percent of the total trade between Canada and the United States is presently duty free, and when the tariff reductions agreed to in the Multilateral Trade Negotiations take full effect at the end of 1987, that duty free figure will rise to about 80 percent.

The $33 billion of American foreign direct investment in Canada is more than in any other single host country, and represents over 30 percent of all American direct investment abroad. It is not as widely known that Canadian per capita investment in the United States is greater than American per capita investment in Canada. Statistics Canada reported in 1978 that Canadian direct investments in the United States, coupled with the repatriation of profits on American investments in Canada, had risen to exceed the inflow of American investment capital into Canada, such that Canada was a net exporter of capital to the United States. Provincial governments in Canada have been frequent borrowers on the American capital market.

While Canada has depended on the United States for investment capital to develop its economy, and for sources of imports and markets for its exports, the United States has depended on Canada for profitable investment opportunities (to serve the Canadian market, the United States, and, in earlier years, Britain and the Commonwealth), for export markets, and for imports, especially of resources and raw materials. An enduring Canadian concern has been to avoid permanent assignment to the role of hewer of wood and drawer of water for the industrial heartland of the United States. In connection with resource trade, an interesting reversal has taken place in the last decade. Prior to the early 1970s, the thrust of American energy policy was to restrict imports of foreign oil through a quota system to protect American oil producers, and Canadian governments pressed repeatedly for increased quotas for Canadian oil in United States markets. Since the early 1970s, and especially since the onset of the energy crisis of 1973, official Canadian estimates of oil and gas reserves have shrunk, and American reliance on imports of foreign oil and gas has grown. As a result, the Canadian government has raised oil and gas prices and established export quotas, while American pressures are for increased imports from Canada. Energy interdependence is well demonstrated by the co-operative effort of the two countries to achieve at lower cost what was not attainable to either country acting alone, through the agreement to construct a northern gas pipeline to transport Alaskan natural gas to United States markets over Canadian territory, and ultimately to transport Canadian natural gas from the Arctic to Canadian markets. This massive and costly project is illustrative of efforts to find joint solutions of joint benefit, in situations where each country requires the cooperation of the other to achieve a positive outcome.

In terms of military interdependence, Canada and the United States have for many years constituted a pluralistic security community.(13) Though fears of American military threats against Canada had a basis in reality in earlier historical periods and were instrumental in bringing about Canadian confederation, in this century there has been no expectation that disputes between the two countries would be resolved by military force. Canada's "Defense Scheme No. 1," the last official military contingency plan for defense against an American invasion, was said to be unrepresentative of the state of Canadian-American relations when it was scrapped in 1931.(14) Since that time, Canada and the United States were allies in World War II, and are presently allied in both the North Atlantic Treaty Organization (NATO) and the North American Air Defense Command (NORAD). They have created a system of close, continental collaboration in the availability of defense facilities, interchanges of military personnel, and joint construction and manning of detection systems.(15) This military collaboration proceeds in an institutional setting unmatched in other areas of interdependence. Aside from the multilateral and bilateral alliance structures, Canada and the United States have created the Permanent Joint Board on Defense and such formal cooperative arrangements as the Defense Production Sharing Agreement.(16)

Beyond the obvious economic and military areas, there exist many other issues on which Canada and the United States are interdependent. Neither country can achieve its public policy goals unilaterally, and outcomes are jointly produced by the actions of both countries. An inexhaustive list of such issues can be taken from cases involving boundary and offshore waters. Construction of the St. Lawrence Seaway required the participation of both countries, as did the development and marketing of hydroelectric power along both the St. Lawrence and Columbia Rivers. Attempts to combat pollution in boundary waters often requires the action of governments in both countries. The Great Lakes Water Quality Agreements of 1972 and 1978 are the most notable examples, but there are others, such as the agreement to combat pollution in the St. John River Basin. On other occasions, developments in one country (such as the proposed Garrison Diversion Project in North Dakota or the proposed Poplar River thermal power generating plant in Saskatchewan) threaten to affect adversely the quality of waters flowing into the other country. Under the Boundary Waters Treaty of 1909, both countries have recognized the interdependent nature of effects on such waters, and have undertaken not to allow adverse effects on waters flowing into the other. Offshore, both countries find their interests interdependently linked on fisheries questions. Fish are no respecters of political borders, and Canada and the United States have found that efficient management of fish stocks requires collaboration, not only on a bilateral basis, but also multilaterally with distant-water fishing states whose boats fish off North American coasts. The extension of fisheries jurisdiction to 200 miles by both Canada and the United States has led to disputes over maritime boundaries, and has uncharacteristically resulted in the "fish war" of

1978, in which fishermen of both countries were denied access to the waters of the other until the negotiation of a permanent settlement.

Among the many transnational activities between Canada and the United States are the activities of multinational enterprises. American-owned enterprises are highly visible in Canada,(17) and the activities of Canadian-owned companies in the United States are increasing.(18) The actions of American-owned firms in Canada have directly or indirectly resulted in problems for public policy in seven issue areas:(19) 1) labor relations of the Canadian subsidiary; 2) attempts by American companies to take over existing Canadian firms; 3) attempts by American companies to establish new enterprises in Canada; 4) extraterritorial attempts by the United States government to control the export practices of the Canadian subsidiary; 5) extraterritorial attempts by the United States government to apply its antitrust policy to current or prospective American-owned operations in Canada, thus affecting the industrial structure of the Canadian economy; 6) attempts by the United States government to improve its balance of payments position by issuing guidelines concerning reinvestment, profit repatriation, purchasing, and production location decisions of American firms with subsidiaries in Canada; and 7) attempts by the Canadian government to affect the behavior of American-owned firms and their subsidiaries so as to achieve its own policy goals.

Recognition of these and other areas of interdependence has led to cooperation and coordination between the Canadian and American governments so as to manage fruitfully the interdependent relationship to the mutual benefit of both parties. It has not, however, led to the creation of collective decision making structures for that purpose. It has also led, at times, to great sensitivity to self-serving actions of the other government, and an occasional tendency to short-run maximization of special interests.

REGIONAL INTERACTIONS

In a relationship of asymmetrical interdependence, the greater volume of interactions originating in the larger party suggests that the larger party is more likely to initiate and the smaller party to respond. The balance of sensitivity and vulnerability may vary markedly from issue to issue. On questions of public policy, issues may be raised by either party, or by the involvement of third parties. In the Canadian-American case, the larger proportion of mutual business has moved on ad hoc Canadian initiatives. It has been conventional to suggest that, because of the preoccupation of the United States government with issues of global policy, the Canadian government has set the bilateral agenda.(20) Keohane and Nye have found that, in the postwar period, the Canadian government has initiated the interstate request more often than the United States, especially in socioeconomic issues; though the United States more often took the first governmental action which led to interstate conflict, again, especially in socioeconomic issues. "Thus the typical conflict pattern on these issues was for the United States (frequently the Congress) to take a unilateral, often 'domestic' action to which the smaller partners tended to respond by demanding redress through diplomatic channels."(21)

Legislative involvement in the relationship takes two main forms in the United States. When Congress passes laws of general application which have unanticipated or unintended side effects on Canada, bilateral issues are raised by Canada if Canadian interests are adversely affected. Other issues are raised, and pursued, through the responsiveness of Congress to pressures from electoral or special interest groups. This parochial concern on the part of some members of Congress leads to divisions between the legislative and executive branches that do not arise in Canada because of the cabinet system of government in which the distinction between the two branches is formal rather than real. Indeed, in Canada, public pressures on the government can contribute to an improvement in the government's bargaining position vis-a-vis the United States, and tactical politicization has proven to be a productive, though not always successful, technique.(22) Keohane and Nye observe that "Thus the pressures of democratic politics usually favor the smaller state in the bargaining process, because for them, politicization from below tends to lead to tough negotiating behavior and coherent stands by government, whereas for the United States such politicization leads to fragmentation of policy."(23)

Domestic constraints on policymakers, and especially legislators, are most influential when an election is upcoming. Under such circumstances, a government is normally less prone to make concessions than when it is not immediately to be accountable to the electorate. With some federal and state elections every two years and a presidential election every four years in the United States, and federal or provincial elections whenever the vagaries of parliamentary democracy dictate in Canada, there is rarely a time when an election is not imminent for at least one of the parties to an issue. The process of interaction, at least as it involves legislative performance, is, therefore, uneven and sometimes unpredictable.

In recognition of the important role of Congress, Canadians have endeavored to develop and maintain good congressional relations in two ways. On the legislative level, the Canada-United States Interparliamentary Group brings together delegations from both houses in each country for annual three-day discussions of problems of mutual concern, and for occasional brief meetings on single issues of particular concern.(24) The purpose of this group is to encourage better understanding of each other's politics and problems rather than to arrive at consensus or lead to specific legislative action. For years, the Canadian Embassy in Washington considered that relations with Congress were best left to Canadian parliamentarians, and emphasized their long-run interest in the maintenance of good relations with the executive branch to which it was accredited. Canadian diplomats feared the impairment of such relations if the embassy were seen to be going behind the backs of the administrators, especially at a time when the executive and legislative branches were at odds. Furthermore, it was widely believed that congressmen might resent the presumed "interference" of the Embassy, and that, in any event, Canadian effectiveness would be limited because congressmen were more responsive to constituency pressures and parochial concerns. As one Canadian official put it, "Canadians don't vote." Nevertheless, a modest increase in emphasis on contacts with Congress is now taking place on the bureaucratic level. Informational material is now being presented to American legislators, the Canadian Embassy has one full-time congressional relations officer (to deal with 535 senators and congressmen and their staffs), and congressional lobbying is being conducted on some issues, though with varying success.(25) In increasing the emphasis on studying congressional affairs and developing personal contacts with legislators, Canada is following the long-standing practice of the United States Embassy in Ottawa, but "Ironically, the U.S. Embassy in Ottawa is more active in a situation where the potential benefits are fewer than is the Canadian Embassy in Washington in an environment where the potential benefits are relatively much greater."(26)

On the administrative level, the United States Department of State and Canada's Department of External Affairs have been the main contact points, but a great many direct bureaucratic contacts between Canadian and American opposite numbers occur without going through foreign office channels. In the mid-1960s, about 31 American federal agencies and 21 Canadian counterparts dealt directly with each other, as did some state and provincial governments(27) and, since then, the proliferation of cross-border visits and long distance telephone calls by officials of both governments illustrates the transgovernmental nature of the bureaucratic relationship.(28) Sometimes, officials with technical or professional expertise and responsibilities may identify more with their professional counterparts in the other government than with other officials with competing bureaucratic perspectives in their own government. The archetypical example is the "Weather Bureau" case, in which American and Canadian meteorologists cooperated to overturn a ruling of the American Federal Communications Commission and wrest away authorized use of a particular radio frequency from the Defense Department in the best transnational interests of the world weather watch.(29) Nevertheless, despite the multiplicity of departments and agencies in the United States government involved in Canadian-American relations, the State Department remains the most sympathetic to Canadian concerns, the most interested in the maintenance of a cordial relationship, and the best spokesman for Canadian interests in the interplay of bureaucratic politics in the American policy process.

The Canadian-American relationship stands as an example of high interdependence without institutional integration. Canada has been determined not to create bilateral institutions which would restrict the freedom of Canadian decision making (though some have suggested that an institutional framework can protect the interests of the weaker party) or involve any loss of sovereignty. Neither government has shown any inclination to use regional institutions for serious decision making rather than for consultations and the exchange of information.(30) Legitimacy has not been attached to the forms of political integration, at least by most Canadians.

A survey of the 18 presently existing bilateral institutions established through treaties or agreements since 1909 showed that while there has been notable cooperation, policy coordination, and joint decision making on defense matters, boundary waters, and fisheries, there has been no bilateral institutional development in such areas as banking, science and technology, energy and resources, health, education, or transportation.(31) It was observed that the institutions featuring the highest degree of integration (as measured by the degree of joint decision making, permanence, staff, and research capabilities) were those designed to deal with technical and nonpolitical issues where interests converged, such as problems arising directly from geographical contiguity – border monuments and parks, boundary waters, fisheries,(32) pollution, and, to a lesser extent, defense. Those institutions with the least integrative features were concerned primarily with issues of divergent national interests, such as trade matters and balance of payments. Meanwhile, in those areas with virtually no shared interest, such as the allocation of airline routes and landing rights, there was no institutional growth at all. Institutions created to cope with specific problems fell into disuse once the problems were resolved. The Joint Ministerial Committees on Joint Defense, and Trade and Economic Affairs, ceased to meet as their respective members became disinclined to clear time in their busy schedules to listen to set piece speeches, and the issues one would have expected to see treated in those committees were once again handled through formal and informal ad hoc consultations.   The authors of the survey concluded "The list indicates no underlying commitment to increase institutionalization by either government, little spillover (except in regulatory commissions) from institution building in one area to another, and certainly no trend toward increasing the authority and powers of existing institutions."(33)

The outstanding example of a successful functional institution with an expanding agenda is the International Joint Commission, created under the Boundary Waters Treaty of 1909. Comprised of three commissioners from each government, it has such assigned tasks as approving applications by citizens or governments of either country to alter the level of cross-border flows of boundary waters and rivers, making recommendations to the two governments on any problem concerning boundary waters referred to it by both governments, and monitoring the progress of the Great Lakes Water Quality Agreement.(34)

Canada and the United States also participate in a wide variety of multilateral institutions. It is conventionally argued that Canada has preferred multilateral structures because they impose more restrictions upon the United States and make it less likely that issues may be linked to Canada's disadvantage. In many cases though, participation in multilateral institutions reflects a joint response to the problems of managing interdependence vis-a-vis third parties (e.g. the International Commission for the Northwest Atlantic Fisheries).

Regional cooperation and conflict reveal several clear patterns. The management of the relationship by officials of both governments is characterized by extensive consultation and advance notification, quiet diplomacy,(35) the avoidance of linkage of issues, policy coordination, and the search for solutions which are mutually advantageous in a nonzero-sum sense and thus do not involve winners and losers.

The linkage of issues has been resisted by Canadians who have expected it to be to Canada's disadvantage because of the disproportionate number of cards the United States could play. Nonlinkage of issues has been the norm in Canadian-American relations, perhaps because of the constraints of domestic politics wherein no group wishes to see its interests traded away,(36) and perhaps because of the compartmentalization and lack of coordination of bureaucratic interests wherein no agency is likely to be willing to give up something dear to it so other agencies could obtain something dear to them.(37) While officials are, of course, implicitly aware of the overall structure of relations, they tend to refrain from explicit linkage of issues. Politicians and members of the business community, however, sometimes favor the principle of linkage. Treasury Secretary John Connally departed from normal practice in pressing Canada to link a variety of trade matters in package negotiations.(38) Current Canadian efforts to gain relief from American tax legislation limiting tax deductions for expenses at conventions held outside the United States have been blocked by members of Congress who, responding to pressures from American border television station owners, have linked such relief to modification of Canada's bill C-58 which denies tax deductibility as a business expense for the cost of advertising on American television stations aimed at the Canadian market.

In a disjointed, incremental, and ad hoc fashion, the two governments have coordinated policies so as to manage their interdependence in a variety of areas – military, environmental, economic, and so forth. Sectoral free trade arrangements have been concluded, such as the Canada-United States Automotive Agreement which provides for duty-free trade by manufacturers in new automobiles and automobile parts. The Defense Production Sharing Agreements enable Canadian defense industries to compete for defense contracts on an equal basis with American firms, and provide for a rough equivalence of defense expenditures by each government in the other country. Policy coordination has resulted from a number of conflicts generated by American multinational enterprises operating in Canada, especially with reference to the extraterritorial application of American laws on American-owned subsidiaries in Canada.(39) Procedures not matched with any other country have been established whereby an American subsidiary in Canada will ordinarily be exempted from export controls upon application if the export in question is of significant benefit to the Canadian economy, and if the order could be filled in Canada only by a firm whose parent is subject to United States jurisdiction. A succession of similar agreements to depoliticize conflicts and lessen tensions have been concluded in the area of American antitrust law, to provide for prior consultations in the event of United States antitrust actions, but not to guarantee that the objectives of the Canadian government will be realized.

Policy coordination has been most pronounced in the area of monetary policy. Canada secured an exemption from the United States Interest Equalization Tax of 1963 in return for the acceptance of a ceiling on its foreign exchange reserves. It secured an exemption to the 1968 direct investment guidelines in exchange for a commitment to institute controls to prevent Canada from being used as a pass-through for United States capital and to convert one billion dollars of Canadian foreign exchange reserves into non-liquid United States Treasury securities. In both cases, Canadian negotiators successfully argued for an exemption on the grounds that a decreased capital inflow into Canada from the United States would lessen Canada's ability to purchase imports from the United States and would, thus, negate any benefit to the United States balance of payments.(40) That argument failed to win Canada an exemption from the August 15, 1971, United States 10 percent tariff surcharge which threatened Canada's exports of processed and manufactured goods. Treasury Secretary John Connally was preoccupied with the bilateral trade deficit, and treated Canada as a part of the problem, not a part of the solution. The unsympathetic response to Canada's request led not only to a decline in policy coordination, but also to a psychological adjustment regarding the relationship on the part of Canadian policymakers and a determination to lessen Canadian vulnerability to future United States actions. Many observers see August 1971 as a watershed in the development of Canadian-American relations, leading to a significant growth in Canadian resolve and capacity for autonomy.(41) Solutions to Canadian-American conflicts which had the effect of increasing policy coordination have become less frequent in the 1970s.(42)

The diplomatic culture of government officials in both countries disapproves of the notion of winners and losers in the relationship, but a major study which contrasts the issues and outcomes involved in all head-of-government level conflicts between Canada and the United States from the 1920s through the 1960s has shown that there is a surprisingly symmetrical attainment of objectives which does not accord with the relative power positions of the two countries.(43) Keohane and Nye found that the Canadian government achieved outcomes closer to its objectives than to those of the United States government in 25 percent of the prewar cases and in approximately 50 percent of the postwar cases, and did better in the 1960s than in the 1950s.   They attributed Canada's success to its ability to exploit American sensitivity while the regime governing the relationship between Canada and the United States held constant, to the symmetry of vulnerability to changes in the regime, and to the effects of complex interdependence. Outcomes of issues involving transnational organizations were more favorable to Canada because, in several cases, transnational organizations pursued autonomous interests which did not coincide with those of the United States government, and thus strengthened rather than weakened Canada's bargaining position. Outcomes of issues involving transgovernmental relations were even more likely to favor Canada, since Canada's greater cohesion and concentration in bilateral relations helps to redress its disparity in size.

REGIONAL DEVELOPMENT

In North America, the development of formal decision making institutions has been limited, though on most other dimensions the high and complex interdependence between Canada and the United States represents a substantial degree of integration.(44) Military cooperation is advanced. Policy coordination in a host of other areas is frequent and widespread. The level of bilateral social, economic, cultural, and political interactions is almost without equal. Consciousness of shared interests is fairly high because of alliance connections, similar foreign policies and sociocultural affinities. But attitudinal integration has not proceeded to the extent of creation of a sense of identity as a single regional political community. As has been found elsewhere, under conditions of asymmetry, rapidly rising transnational interactions can stimulate nationalism in the weaker party.(45) That certainly appears to have been the case in Canada where public awareness of the expansion of economic interactions with the United States (especially in the area of investment) was followed by a growing intensity of Canadian nationalism and a gradual increase in the number of government programs for greater control of transnational actors and interactions. One analyst has argued that the inevitable Canadian nationalist reaction to growing asymmetrical interdependence with the United States will prevent political union between the two countries.(46) The presumed logic of neofunctional integration spilling over into political unification appears to be resisted in North America.

Political integration with the United States has never enjoyed legitimacy in Canada, and in recent years the Canadian government has emphasized the symbolic and effective assertion of Canadian autonomy. In 1972, Canada's Secretary of State for External Affairs considered the future course of Canadian-American relations and rejected the options of continued ad hoc business as usual or increased integration. Official sanction was bestowed on the "Third Option" – to lessen Canada's vulnerability to the United States through a combination of domestic policies and international diversification of interactions.(47) International economic conditions have prevented any tangible payoff from the contractual frameworks painstakingly negotiated with the European Community and Japan, but Canada has continued to strive for increased international consciousness of its identity apart from the United States. Early French objections that Canada's economy was merely an adjunct of that of the United States have been overcome, and Canada now participates alongside the United States and five other Western countries in the annual economic summit meetings. Nevertheless, in a world of emerging regional economic blocs, Canada may find it increasingly difficult to maintain the appearance, and also the reality, of separateness from the United States.

THEORIES AND FUTURES

Canadian-American relations have been studied from a variety of theoretical perspectives, distinguishable by the presumptions made about the nature of the relationship, the questions raised, the variables identified, and the value interpretations made of empirical phenomena. The perspectives are not mutually exclusive, and some scholars implicitly or explicitly adopt more than one in the course of their work. There is no scholarly consensus about which perspective is most accurate or most analytically useful. The differing assumptions associated with the various perspectives can give rise to very different expectations about future developments in the relationship.

Those who write within the perspective of imperialism or dependency presume a condition of dominance and dependence, and question why the condition occurred and how it may be corrected.(48) They tend to focus primarily on economic interactions, and see increases in investment and changes in trade patterns as solidifying a relationship of economic domination.(49) The writings tend to be nationalistic in tone and prescriptive in character.

Those who write within the perspective of integration theory presume a process leading toward a defined dependent variable, and question whether the relationship is becoming more or less integrated along a variety of dimensions.(50) They examine a number of indicators of the process in progress to explain the effects on the level and direction of integration and predict future developments of that dependent variable.

Those who write within the perspective of transnational and transgovernmental relations posit certain independent variables (i.e., some of the indicators studied by integration theorists) and question what consequences flow from them.(51) They focus explicit attention on the effects of interactions involving nongovernmental actors and governmental subunits acting in a relatively autonomous fashion. Those who write about complex interdependence presume a particular configuration of those independent variables.(52)

While these perspectives have each attracted a cluster of writers, others have been adopted less frequently or explicitly, but may later become more widely used. Several approaches to systems analysis, treating North America as a regional system, have been proposed. The concept of a penetrated system, in which legitimacy is attached to the direct participation (but not control) by nonmembers of a national society in the allocation of the society's values, offers some promise.(53) Foreign policy analysis, bargaining theory, and events data analysis have all been applied with a variety of methodologies and conclusions, but with a principal purpose of comparing behavior and outcomes over time and with other countries.

The coming decade will offer evidence by which to judge the appropriateness of the expectations associated with these various theoretical perspectives. The responses to two major economic developments now beginning will indicate whether Canadian-American relations will develop in a cooperative or competitive direction. First, the recently concluded agreements at the Multilateral Trade Negotiations yielded for Canada greater improvements in access to the United States market than to the European Community or Japan. When the agreements are fully phased in at the end of 1987, about 80 percent of Canada-United States trade will be duty free, which approximates the level in many free trade areas. This suggests that Canada and the United States may slip unconsciously into the functional equivalent of a free trade area, unless corrective action is taken, or a formal agreement is negotiated. A free trade agreement has been opposed by those who fear that it would lead inevitably to political union or to the deindustrialization of Canada.(54) However, if negotiated carefully, it could contain sufficient safeguard provisions to guarantee the maintenance or expansion of the level of industrialization in Canada, and to maintain integrational equilibrium without spillover.

Secondly, the next decade will be a period of capital renewal in North America in which major investments will be made to expand and modernize industrial equipment. We are already seeing social and political considerations (i.e., neomercantilist concerns to maximize levels of employment) take precedence over economic efficiency in the scramble for those investments. (For example, the governments of Canada and Ontario provided a $68 million subsidy to the Ford Motor Company to locate a new engine plant in Ontario rather than in Ohio.) Whether this issue is approached in a zero-sum competitive fashion, or whether both countries can find an expansionary solution to further both their interests in the face of increasing competition for the location of investment from industrializing Third World countries, will be a strong signal about the future course of the North American regional system.

NOTES

(1) Robert O. Keohane and Joseph S. Nye, Power and Interdependence: World Politics in Transition (Boston: Little Brown, 1977).

(2) Annette Baker Fox, The Politics of Attraction: Four Middle Powers and the United States (New York: Columbia University Press, 1977), p. 110.

(3) R.B. Byers and David Leyton-Brown, "The Strategic and Economic Implications for the United States of a Sovereign Quebec," Canadian Public Policy (Spring 1980).

(4) R.B. Byers, David Leyton-Brown, and Peyton V. Lyon, "The Canadian International Image Study," International Journal 32, no. 3 (Summer 1977): 605-671.

(5) Peyton V. Lyon and David Leyton-Brown, "Image and Policy Preference: Canadian Elite Views on Relations with the United States," International Journal 32, no. 3 (Summer 1977): 653-61.

(6) Robert J. Drummond and Frederick J. Fletcher, "U.S.-Canadian Relations and American Investment in Canada," Preliminary Report #3 for the Canadian Attitude Trends Project, York University, June 1976.

(7) John H. Sigler and Dennis Goresky, "Public Opinion on United States-Canadian Relations," in Canada and the United States: Transnational and Transgovernmental Relations, edited by Annette Baker Fox, Alfred O. Hero, Jr., and Joseph S. Nye, Jr. (New York: Columbia University Press, 1976), pp. 57-58.

(8) Keohane and Nye, Power and Interdependence, p. 169. See also C. Robert Dickerman, "Transgovernmental Challenge and Response in Scandinavia and North America," International Organization 30, no. 2 (Spring 1976): 213-240.

(9) Andrew Axline, James E. Hyndman, Peyton V. Lyon, and Maureen A. Molt, eds., Continental Community? Independence and Integration in North America (Toronto: McClelland Stewart, 1974).

(10) Abraham Rotstein and Gary Lax, eds., Independence: The Canadian Challenge (Toronto: The Committee for an Independent Canada, 1972); Randy Morse and Larry Pratt, Darkness at the End of the Tunnel (Toronto: New Hogtown Press, 1975); Ian Lumsden, ed., Close the 49th Parallel, etc.: The Americanization of Canada (Toronto: University of Toronto Press, 1970).

(11) Keohane and Nye, Power and Interdependence, chs. 2, 7.

(12) Ibid., pp. 203-06.

(13) K.W. Deutsch et al., Political Community and the North Atlantic Area (Princeton: Princeton University Press, 1957), pp. 3-9.

(14) James Eayrs, In Defence of Canada, vol. 1 (Toronto: University of Toronto Press, 1964), pp. 74-77.

(15) R.D. Cuff and J.L. Granatstein, Canadian-American Relations in Wartime (Toronto: Hakkert Press, 1975); Fox, The Politics of Attraction, chs. 4, 5.

(16) John J. Kirton, "The Consequences of Integration: The Case of the Defence Production Sharing Agreements," in Continental Community, ch. 5.

(17) Canada, Gray Task Force, Foreign Direct Investment in Canada (Ottawa, 1972), pp. 17-18 (hereinafter referred to as Gray Report).

(18) See, for example, the acquisition of control by the Canada Development Corporation of Texasgulf, and the attempted takeover of F.W. Woolworth by Brascan.

(19) David Leyton-Brown, "The Multinational Enterprise and Conflict in Canadian-American Relations," in Canada and the United States; and "Canada and Multinational Enterprise," in A Foremost Nation? edited by Norman Hilmer and Garth Stevenson (Toronto: McClelland and Stewart, 1976).

(20) James Eayrs, "Sharing a Continent: The Hard Issues," in The United States and Canada, edited by John S. Dickey (Englewood Cliffs, N.J.: Prentice-Hall, 1964), p. 60.

(21) Keohane and Nye, Power and Interdependence, p. 200.

(22) Leyton-Brown, "The Multinational Enterprise and Conflict in Canadian-American Relations," p. 152.

(23) Keohane and Nye, Power and Interdependence, p. 206.

(24) Matthew J. Abrams, The Canada-United States Interparliamentary Group (Ottawa: Parliamentary Centre for Foreign Affairs and Foreign Trade and the Canadian Institute for International Affairs, 1973).

(25) Lobbying by the Canadian Embassy was instrumental in heading off a resolution condemning the Canadian seal hunt, but has been unable to achieve anything more regarding the income tax deductibility of expenses for conventions held outside the United States than to keep the issue alive.

(26) Peter C. Dobell, "The Influence of the United States Congress on Canadian-American Relations," in Canada and the United States, p. 334.

(27) Livingston T. Merchant and A.D.P. Heeney, "Canada and the United States: Principles for Partnership" (Ottawa: Queen's Printer, 1965) (hereinafter referred to as the Merchant-Heeney Report).

(28) Keohane and Nye, Power and Interdependence, p. 169; Dickerman, "Transgovernmental Challenge."

(29) Robert O. Keohane and Joseph S. Nye, eds., Transnational Relations and World Politics (Cambridge, Mass.: Harvard University Press, 1972), Conclusion.

(30) Maureen A. Molot, "The Role of Institutions in Canada-United States Relations," in Continental Community? ch. 7.

(31) Kal J. Holsti and Thomas Allen Levy, "Bilateral Institutions and Transgovernmental Relations Between Canada and the United States," in Canada and the United States, pp. 283-87.

(32) This finding did not anticipate the divergence of interests over maritime boundaries and fisheries in 1978, and the noninstitutional response to the dispute.

(33) Holsti and Levy, "Bilateral Institutions," p. 285.

(34) "The International Joint Commission: Seventy Years On," Proceedings of a Conference to Commemorate the 70th Anniversary of the International Joint Commission, Trinity College, University of Toronto, Toronto, Ontario, June 14-15, 1979.

(35) Merchant-Heeney Report.

(36) Keohane and Nye, Power and Interdependence, p. 214.

(37) Holsti and Levy, "Bilateral Institutions," p. 290; for example, suggestions that Canada should capitalize on American gratitude regarding Canadian participation in the International Commission for Control and Supervision in Vietnam by trying to obtain the removal of the countervailing duties imposed on Michelin tires were dismissed because it was realized that United States officials in the Departments of Commerce and Treasury were not interested in Canadian actions in Vietnam and responded to different domestic pressures.

(38) Fox, The Politics of Attraction, p. 140.

(39) Leyton-Brown, "The Multinational Enterprise and Conflict in Canadian-American Relations," p. 159.

(40) Gray Report, pp. 285-90.

(41) A.B. Fox and A.O. Hero, Jr., "Canada and the United States: Their Binding Frontier," in Canada and the United States, pp. 405-06.

(42) Keohane and Nye, Power and Interdependence, p. 210.

(43) Ibid., ch. 7.

(44) Peyton V. Lyon, "Introduction," in Continental Community? p. 3.

(45) Joseph S. Nye, Jr., Peace in Parts: Integration and Conflict in Regional Organizations (Boston: Little Brown, 1971), chs. 2, 3.

(46) Naomi Black, "Absorptive Systems are Impossible: The Canadian-American Relationship as a Disparate Dyad," in Continental Community? ch. 4.

(47) Mitchell Sharp, "Canada-U.S. Relations: Options for the Future," International Perspectives, Special Issue (Autumn 1972).

(48) See note 10 for an abbreviated list of such writings.

(49) Kari Levitt, Silent Surrender: The Multinational Corporation in Canada (Toronto: MacMillan of Canada, 1970).

(50) Axline et al., Continental Community?

(51) Fox, Hero, and Nye, Canada and the United States.

(52) Keohane and Nye, Power and Interdependence.

(53) James N. Rosenau, "Pre-theories and Theories of Foreign Policy," in Approaches to Comparative and International Politics, edited by R. Barry Farrell (Evanston: Northwestern University Press, 1966), pp. 52-71.

(54) Sharp, "Canada-U.S. Relations," p. 15; Peter C. Newman, "Economic Union with the U.S. Would Doom Canada," in Independence, pp. 48-53.

III

Globally Peripheral Regional Systems

7 East Asia
Gavin Boyd

East Asia is a mixed regional system at a low level of development. The attributes of states in this grouping vary more widely than those of the members of most other regions. The relations between East Asian states are mostly bilateral, but there is low level, subregional cooperation within the Association of Southeast Asian Nations (ASEAN), comprising Thailand, Malaysia, Singapore, Indonesia, and the Philippines. Outside their grouping these states relate principally to Japan, their main trading partner; and Japan interacts very substantially with China, supplying technology in exchange for primary products.

Japan's regional policy is restricted rather narrowly to economic interests, although it is influenced by major political and strategic concerns. In effect, this allows China considerable scope for political involvement in regional affairs, despite constraints associated with weaker resources. Chinese statecraft is directed mainly against the USSR, and seeks to enlist support from Japan and the United States. The United States is a constructive intrusive power in East Asia, and has a pervasive presence, based on high interdependencies with Japan and relatively strong links with the ASEAN members, and also on a coexistence relationship with China. In open opposition to the United States and China, the Soviet Union is active in East Asia as a state seeking engagement with Japan and with the ASEAN members, and as an ally of Vietnam.

Interdependencies within East Asia are developing mainly between the ASEAN states and Japan, and between Japan and China, and Japan and South Korea. The Indochinese states, North Korea, and Burma are relatively isolated because of their economic backwardness and autarkic policies. The Soviet Union trades with these states on a small scale; its only substantial economic interaction is with Japan, whose policy stresses the development of ties with China.

The pattern of relationships within East Asia is not strongly influenced by happenings in other regional systems. China, Japan, and the Southeast Asian states are separated by long distances from North America. Geography also separates most of Southeast Asia from the Indian subcontinent, and, although the distances are less than those across the Pacific, they are affected by strong cultural and ethnic differences and by India's disinterest in Southeast Asia. China's western neighbor is the Soviet Union, and the potential for interaction in this relationship is severely limited by mutual antagonisms.

CONFIGURATION

The characteristics of the East Asian states make up a diverse pattern that is not conducive to regional cooperation. Japan, a democracy operating at a high level of political development, contrasts with China's internally strained and institutionally underdeveloped revolutionary regime, while both China and Japan contrast, in different ways, with the weakly legitimized "soft states" of Southeast Asia. The most substantial forms of constructive foreign policy behavior in the region are Japan's, and they involve the use of large bargaining resources for interaction with China and the ASEAN members. Associated with these two interactive patterns are the main trade and investment flows of the region. Questions of political cooperation and strategic issues are posed for Japan in both contexts, but tend to be avoided by Tokyo because of a basic concern with maximizing the economic utilities of the relationships. China makes vigorous political efforts to promote change in the region and obstruct Soviet involvement, but with only modest results. The ASEAN states coordinate their policies on a small scale, but mostly endeavor to relate to Japan and China on an individual basis. They, thus, have to contend with the severe limitations imposed by their small resources.

The societal attributes of the East Asian states can be studied with reference to the qualities of their cultures, their value orientations, their degrees of internal unity, and the links between their social strata. There are some significant affinities, the most important being those which are felt with China at all levels of Japanese society.

The most advanced culture, which has evolved with a high degree of autonomy, is that in Japan. This is strongly insular, communal, and nationalist, but humanistic, and selectively open. There is a strong traditional dimension, and this makes for the preservation of a rather hierarchical society. Because of this quality, and the communal element, Japanese society sustains highly developed political and economic institutions. There is a very functional balance between leadership, secondary elite autonomy, and tertiary elite participation and support.(1)

Cultural uniqueness limits Japan's receptivity to foreign influences, and makes for intense consciousness of the need for self-reliant growth in all areas of national life. In the immediate environment, there is little scope for enriching exchanges because Soviet culture holds little attraction and the Southeast Asian societies are underdeveloped. Only

China has a highly developed traditional culture, and this is being slowly obliterated under the communist regime. Outside East Asia, Japan's main cultural contacts are with the United States, but interest focuses on the absorption of U.S. science and technology and little empathy is felt with the strong individualism of its society.

China's societal development has been less autonomous than Japan's, has involved more cultural and political strains, and has resulted in a less functional value orientation. The Chinese traditional culture, based on Confucianism, failed to provide direction for national development that would meet the challenge of Western imperialism, and was influenced by penetrations of European and North American culture in a semicolonial context during the first half of this century. After 1949, the communist administration used draconian methods to impose a revolutionary culture, hostile to "bourgeois" societies, and, more recently, to the USSR. The degree of emphasis on revolutionary values, however, has been a source of severe high level conflict.(2)

The Southeast Asian societies were deeply penetrated by Western cultures during the colonial period. Their traditional cultures, shaped mainly by religion, have been strongly influenced by those of their former colonial rulers. At the elite level, common elements of Western culture tend to facilitate understanding between these states, principally within ASEAN and between the ASEAN administrations and the United States, Britain, and Holland. The societies of the ASEAN states are moderately open, and are tending to absorb more Western culture through educational exchanges, communications development, and trade.

The Thai and Philippine societies are relatively homogeneous – ethnically and culturally – but the Thai people tend to be more passive in the acceptance of authoritarian rule and their society is more hierarchical.   Thai culture is strongly Buddhist and, thus, has a fatalistic quality, while Philippine culture is Christian and has been deeply affected by the liberal democratic ethos which was introduced during the period of U.S. rule from the beginning of this century until 1942, and for a short time after the Pacific war. In the Malaysian and Indonesian societies, there are deep cleavages which cause severe political strains, especially because they are manipulated by the ruling elites. In Malaysia, the principal division is ethnic and cultural – between the Malay and Chinese communities that are roughly equal in size. The Chinese control most of the modern sector of the economy, but leaders of the Malay community are politically dominant, and seek to use their power in order to redress the economic imbalance between the two main communities. In Indonesia, the line of division is religious and cultural, separating the abangan Moslems of Central and East Java from the orthodox Moslems of West Java and the outer islands. In the military elite which has been controlling the country since the mid-1960s the leading figures are abangan, and the main feature of their political psychology is a deep antipathy towards the orthodox Moslems.(3)

The traditional cultures of the ASEAN states have little in common. The only significant similarities are those between the Moslem Malay community in Malaysia and the two major Islamic communities in Indonesia. The Malay elite is more Westernized than its Indonesian counterpart, however, and accepts a degree of partnership with leaders of the Chinese community within the framework of a fairly representative system of government. In Indonesia's authoritarian system, the orthodox Moslems experience rather severe discrimination from the predominantly abangan leadership, and this is a source of political tension.

Outside ASEAN, the Indochinese states and Burma are culturally isolated, and their oppressive authoritarian regimes inhibit societal development. In each of these states, vigorous efforts are made to exclude outside influences and to build up socialist societies. Vietnam is the most homogeneous and most strongly organized polity, and Burma is the most deeply divided society, because of the presence of multiple ethnic and cultural cleavages. The Burmese and Indochinese economies, it must be stressed, are extremely backward in comparison with those of the ASEAN states. Burma has experienced serious internal disorders since the end of the Pacific war, and its economy (socialized since 1963) has been poorly managed. In Vietnam, modernization has been prevented by prolonged warfare and by the deficiencies of a command economy based on the Soviet model.(4)

Societal potentials for economic, cultural, and other interchanges with Japan are significant in the ASEAN countries. Each national political and economic elite is capable of relating effectively with its Japanese counterparts, and the interaction is extensive because of the large volumes of trade and of Japanese investment in this part of Southeast Asia. There are some societal antipathies toward the Japanese economic presence, however, and there are still some resentments toward Japan deriving from wartime experiences.(5) Attitudes towards the United States tend to be favorable, in part because the U.S. economic presence is less visible and is growing more slowly. There are no strong societal orientations toward interaction with China that can be compared with the positive feelings toward that country in Japan, but there is much consciousness in the ASEAN societies concerning the proximity of the Chinese regime and the penetration of its political influence.

POLITICAL CULTURES

The political cultures of the states in the main patterns of East Asian interaction are evolving in relative isolation. The highly self sufficient and distinctively national Japanese culture has little influence on the ASEAN members, and draws little from them. The Chinese culture, developing in ways that permit little contact with other societies, is influencing relatively small, affinitive, revolutionary movements in Southeast Asia, but is not stirring popular interest in the ASEAN states, and is viewed with hostility by Vietnam and its subordinate regimes in Cambodia and Laos.(6)

The Japanese political culture is the most advanced in East Asia, and it sustains a representative system that is dominated by the conservative Liberal-Democratic Party, which draws support from the middle and upper classes and the rural population. This political culture is nationalist, instrumental with some consummatory features, and participant, with strong social dependency orientations that hinder leadership development. The qualities of this culture are expressed in a highly coherent political economy directed, with great effectiveness, by political, bureaucratic, and economic elites in a highly consensual fashion, relying on the expertise of officials in the middle echelons who are constantly challenged to provide policy innovations. Prosperity through an export-oriented growth strategy is the most prominent instrumental value, and it has been pursued with some neglect of social justice. That is now being rectified by increasing allocations for welfare and infrastructure development. Democratic-socialist influence on the evolution of the political culture has been small because of conflicts between the leftist parties and a decline in the fortunes of the largest, the Japan Socialist Party, attributable in part to ideological extremism.(7)

The Chinese political culture has a narrow revolutionary orientation strongly influenced by opposition to the ideological "revisionism" which Peking claims has weakened the Soviet regime. A relatively simple faith in Marxism-Leninism is cultivated, with emphasis on equality in living standards and community service, but also with a new stress on scientific and technological advancement, through trade with and cultural borrowing from the West and from Japan. Continuing intra-elite conflicts tend to confuse this value orientation while raising questions about its permanence.(8) Appropriate institutional expression of the political culture, moreover, is made difficult by the effects of the high level conflicts over the past decade and a half and by problems of interaction between the primary and secondary elite, and between the secondary and the tertiary elite. The regime is "over-managed" and there appears to be considerable bureaucratic inertia in its structures.(9)

Of the ASEAN states, Malaysia, Singapore, and the Philippines have political cultures with fairly strong participant qualities, but in the Philippine case an authoritarian regime is attempting to impose a subject political culture. Such political cultures exist in Thailand and Indonesia and tend to be preserved because the military elites in those two states encounter little opposition from civilian leaderships advocating representative government.

In Malaysia, the participant quality of the political culture derives from the influence of liberal democratic ideas on the relatively Westernized elite. This political culture, however, reflects the deep communal division of Malaysian society. The anti-Chinese bias of the Malays severely modifies the participant dimension of the culture causing resentments that widen the gap between the two major communities.(10) Singapore has a more genuinely participant political culture but, as this island is predominantly Chinese, it does not serve as a model for Malaysia; rather, the vitality of its political culture tends to strengthen the motivation of the dominant Malay leadership to obstruct the growth of a vigorous political organization among the local Chinese. In the Philippines, the long-established political culture has a strong participant quality, but its failure to produce effective political institutions has resulted in generally passive acceptance of a corrupt and oppressive personalist autocracy.

Thailand and Indonesia have subject political cultures which induce relatively passive acceptance of the authority of their military regimes. These are "bourgeois" praetorian systems whose corrupt and autocratic military leaderships seek to administer depoliticized societies with little regard for social reform and little interest in the use of political methods to strengthen their legitimacy. Each regime promotes industrialization, relying heavily on the attraction of foreign private capital. The extensive parasitic association of officials with such capital affects popular attitudes toward the military elite.(11)

Among the more isolated states in East Asia, Vietnam has a relatively strong revolutionary-nationalist political culture which is perpetuated under an oppressive leadership. This culture has a strongly anti-Chinese quality. It exhibits considerable vitality, which appears to derive mainly from its nationalist component, and, thus far, it has not been affected by severe intraelite conflicts like those which have occurred in China. In particular, the Vietnamese leadership has not been divided by controversies over the relationship between revolutionary values and modernization such as those which split the Chinese ruling elite in the late 1950s and early 1960s. Economic failures, however, and problems in the relationship with the Soviet Union may well be causing strain in the Vietnamese political culture.(12)

The Burmese political culture is weak and confused. This state's military leadership has been unable to build up a strong political apparatus that would draw support for its ideology of Burmese Socialism, and has failed to give that ideology a significant appeal. These deficiencies have been made worse by failures to impose order, tendencies to rely heavily on force in coping with unrest, and acute incompetence in managing the socialist economy. The minorities in Burma have been seriously alienated and the political culture's lack of appeal for them represents a grave vulnerability.(13)

ELITE POLITICAL PSYCHOLOGY

As most of the East Asian states are authoritarian, their characteristics and external behavior are shaped mainly by their ruling elites. The capacities of these elites to build institutions and implement policies vary greatly, however, and so, also, do the contributions to statecraft from their secondary elites. In the few democratic states – Japan, Malaysia, and Singapore – the influence of elites on political processes is more constrained by societal factors and institutionalized forms of accountability.

In China, North Korea, and the Indochinese states, there are heavy concentrations of power in small primary elites which perpetuate themselves by selective recruiting among their secondary elites, who are kept in strict subordination. In each regime, the political psychology of the leadership is authoritarian and tends to be very much affected by isolation from spontaneous societal communications, dependence on uncritical information processing, and fears generated by intense desires for power. Each leadership's methods of operating generate stress at its own level and within the secondary elite. Continual efforts are made to consolidate the virtually absolute power which is possessed, but the purges used for this purpose have inhibiting effects on officials, causing less effective activation of the party and government structures. Leadership absorption in domestic power conflicts and in drives to maximize authority is usually intense, and this often has negative effects on attempts to transmit revolutionary values to other societies. There is, frequently, a compulsive articulation of complaints against internal enemies, particularly in China, and there is usually an incapacity to relate to other societies in terms of their own values.(14)

As in other industrialized democracies, elites in Japan are larger segments of their societies and function much more cooperatively than those in China. They have much autonomy, of course, under limited and accountable authority. These elites fulfill well-established roles within highly developed institutions in line with strong conventions for consensual decision making. Exercises of power by the leadership are regularly justified, assessed according to achievement criteria on the basis of widely distributed information, and are guided by much self-critical rationality, stimulated by opinion leaders independent of the ruling party. The nationalism and the distinctive culture of Japanese political elites, however, cause difficulties of comprehension and empathy in dealings with other states. More importantly, the primary elite's political psychology is so strongly conditioned by the pervasive neo-mercantilist consensus at the basis of the nation's very successful foreign economic policy that innovative departures from this are largely precluded.(15)

In most of the ASEAN states, elite political psychology is authoritarian, idiosyncratic, and relatively pragmatic, but influenced by primordial attachments and antipathies. In Malaysia, the Malay elite's authoritarian tendencies are moderated by concerns to avoid giving dangerous provocation to the Chinese community, and by awareness of Peking's interest in that community. Representatives of the Chinese population are given some participation in the Malaysian administration. In external policy, there is a positive orientation toward regional cooperation deriving mainly from confidence in the capacities of indigenous (mainly Chinese) firms and locally-based foreign enterprises to cope with competition from Thailand and the Philippines.(16) The Thai military leadership's political psychology, less authoritarian than that of the Indonesian ruling elite, is influenced by sensitivities to popular attitudes because of memories of the upsurge of mass hostility to the former military regime which was overthrown in 1973. This leadership, moreover, is anxious to avoid alienating sections of the population, especially students and workers, that might support communist terrorists in the northeast provinces who are receiving Chinese encouragement.   The longer-term threat posed by those terrorists preoccupies the Thai leadership, and tends to limit its interest in regional economic cooperation.(17) The more oppressive military leaders in Indonesia, who are much less sensitive to popular attitudes, do not have to contend with any major subversive elements, but tend to be much absorbed in the problems of drawing support from middle and lower level army factions. This leadership is little inclined toward regional cooperation, but appears to have some desire for a strong role in ASEAN and in Southeast Asia as a whole.(18) Finally, the very autocratic leadership in the Philippines, which is heavily dependent on the manipulative capacities of President Marcos and extremely vulnerable because of the heavy concentration of power in his person, has an inward looking quality because of its preoccupation with the management of domestic clientelist networks and its involvement in corrupt practices on a large scale.(19)

AFFINITIES

The significant affinities in the East Asian patterns of interaction are those felt toward China by a high proportion of the Japanese population. These derive from the premodern penetration of Chinese culture into Japan, and they tend to be strengthened by the strong emphasis on friendship with China in Tokyo's external policy. This friendship makes for some tacit identification with China as an adversary of the USSR, especially because there are strong traditional Japanese antipathies towards the Soviet Union. These antipathies, of course, tend to reinforce the established Japanese policy of reliance on U.S. military support for protection against the USSR. Since the United States now has a friendly relationship with China, Japan shows unrestrained interest in contributing to the Peking regime's industrialization program and, thus, in strengthening Chinese capabilities to resist Soviet pressures.(20)

Elsewhere in East Asia, there are some cultural affinities between the relatively Westernized elites of the noncommunist countries, principally those in the ASEAN group. These affinities facilitate understanding within that subregional grouping, and also assist the management of each ASEAN member's relations with Japan, because of the partial Westernization of that country's elites. As influences on policy, however, the cultural affinities at the elite level within ASEAN are relatively weak sources of motivation for regional cooperative activity.

Politically, in East Asia as a whole, dissimilarities and adversary relationships seriously limit the scope for regional cooperation. China and the Indochinese communist regimes have ideological affinities but are antagonists. China and North Korea have ideological bonds but their relationship is strained. Meanwhile, the Chinese attitude toward the USSR remains bitterly hostile. Burma, the only noncommunist East Asian state with a socialist philosophy, evidences no affinities with any of the communist regimes, and has an uneasy relationship with China because of Peking's support for the communist insurgents in its northern and eastern border areas.(21)

The various communist states are ideologically opposed to the bourgeois polities of East Asia, although, in the Chinese case, this is somewhat obscured by the link with the United States and the overtly friendly relationship with Japan. Identities of interest relating to strategic matters, with respect to the USSR, do not modify the Chinese ideological antipathy toward Japan and the United States as advanced capitalist societies, but certainly help to conceal it, and thus have only limited influence on Japanese and U.S. policies. Over time, the basic attitudes of the Chinese leadership may become more pragmatic and less influenced by ideology, because of satisfaction with U.S. and Japanese economic cooperation. But, for the present, the Chinese approach to these relationships is fundamentally manipulative.(22)

Of the noncommunist East Asian states, Japan, Malaysia, and Singapore have representative political systems but are not affinitive democracies. There are major differences between their political cultures, and also between their political parties; Japan, moreover, has attained a level of advancement which would prevent identification with any aspects of the Malaysian or Singaporean polities, even if there were strong similarities between the value orientations of the Japanese political elite and those of the leaderships in these Southeast Asian states. The Malaysian political parties are communal and, as such, are quite foreign to the moderately nationalist ruling Liberal Democratic Party in Japan. This party, moreover, has little in common with the democratic-socialist Peoples Action Party which dominates Singapore's politics.(23)

The military regimes in the ASEAN group – Thailand and Indonesia – have similarities but are not affinitive. Each army leadership has a parochial nationalist orientation, deeply influenced by the demands of solidarity building through patronage and the exploitation of particularistic attachments, in contexts of low institutional development. The officially sponsored political party of the Indonesian regime is a weak organization, for vote gathering purposes rather than the mobilization of support, and its only possible significance for Thailand's military leadership is that it illustrates the difficulties of infusing vigor into corporate structures that are designed for carefully controlled functional representation.(24) The personalist autocracy of President Marcos in the Philippines, of course, has no affinities with either the Thai or the Indonesian military regimes; it utilizes developmental rhetoric for public relations purposes, as is done in the other two states, but less convincingly because of its more blatant corruption, and this rhetoric does not express commitments that are shared with the other ASEAN members.(25)

There are some affinities between basic public policy orientations within ASEAN. The most significant are those between Malaysia and Indonesia which derive, in part, from cultural affinities between the Malay and Indonesian elites, and from somewhat similar concerns to promote modernization. In these two states and in Thailand, there is emphasis on private sector development and the attraction of foreign capital, although only in the Malaysian case is there an active and responsible policy of regulating economic growth in the interests of social equality. This, however, is pushed to excess because of the Malay bias against the Chinese community.

AUTHORITY AND INFLUENCE PATTERNS

Japan is the only politically advanced state in East Asia, and it maintains a high level of performance in the management of its political economy and its foreign economic relations. This nation's political institutions are well developed, and there is a broad elite consensus in support of the established direction of public policy.

The form of government in Japan is parliamentary, and cabinet stability is maintained by the strength of the ruling Liberal-Democratic Party which governs with the support of a small number of politicians in the lower house. This party has been experiencing a slow decline in its total vote, but it remains the country's largest political organization, and its parliamentary opposition is divided. The Japan Socialist Party, the leading force in that opposition, has also been experiencing a decline. The leadership of the Liberal-Democratic Party is closely identified with the business elite, and operates through a bureaucratic elite whose senior members move easily into the management of large corporations and high-level party positions. Highly coherent aggregation of interests results from the interlocking of the business, bureaucratic, and political elites, and the effective translation of these interests into policy sustains the broad consensus on export-oriented growth which has developed since the early 1950s.

The position of the Liberal-Democratic Party is, in part, dependent on the policy of friendship with China, through which it identifies with popular sentiments towards that country, while, in effect, denying political opportunities to the Japan Socialist Party. During the 1950s and 1960s that party was able to agitate against the Liberal-Democratic Party's association with the United States' East Asian policy, especially as affecting China; but the change in Sino-Japanese relations since 1971 has been an advantage for the Liberal-Democrats, and, as has been indicated, the Chinese evidently wish to see the Liberal-Democrats remain in power.

Because the Japanese polity manages its foreign economic relations with great effectiveness, it dominates the patterns of trade and investment in East Asia, while playing a very active role in the global economy. In dealing with the small developing states of the ASEAN group, Japan can utilize vast bargaining power, but its approach is cautious and considerate, aiming at the development of trust and goodwill. In this respect, however, Japanese government purposes are not always adequately served by the large business organizations which are associated with its economic policies and, in particular, with its efforts to develop basic processing industries in Third World countries. A special difficulty for those organizations is that their high standards of efficiency cannot be met without circumventing host country rules for the employment of local personnel.(26)

Of the ASEAN states, Singapore and Malaysia have attained significant levels of political development, and are well able to manage their complex interdependencies with Japan. The bureaucracies of these two states are quite advanced and their political decision makers are competent, although in the Malaysian case the leadership's task orientation is affected by a determination to use political power rather forcefully to upgrade the economic position of the Malays. The dominant Malay political party, the United Malay National Organization (UMNO), is in secure control of the political process and has demonstrated a capacity to cope with challenges from the communal right while securing cooperation from some of the small political parties that draw votes from the Chinese community.(27)

The praetorian regimes in Thailand and Indonesia function at low levels of development. They draw little societal support and have weak institutions. The ruling military groups are unstable coalitions of ambitious army leaders who have poorly defined links with incompetent and corrupt bureaucracies. There is little representation of public interests and nongovernmental policy inputs come mainly from economic elites interacting directly with army figures and bureaucrats. The oppressive methods of each regime encourage the growth of protest movements, especially in Thailand, where student agitation was largely responsible for removing the last military dictatorship in 1973.(28) In the Philippines, where the personalist autocracy seems likely to evolve into a military dictatorship, there is a narrower concentration of power at the top, in the corrupt presidency. This is unsupported by any active, officially-sponsored party, and there is no significant projection of leadership charisma. The level of institutional development is low, and government pressures on the trade unions to attract foreign investment are causing acute inequalities in the distribution of wealth.(29)

The small East Asian states outside ASEAN are all authoritarian and are extremely oppressive. Vietnam is the strongest of these states, and probably the most stable; its party and government structures were built up with much nationalist and ideological zeal during the long struggle against the French and the U.S.-supported regime in the South. The strong nationalism of this regime has been intensified by Chinese hostility since 1978, but its leadership may be experiencing some internal divisions over the policy of alignment with the USSR made necessary by Peking's animosity.(30) North Korea ranks next in terms of state strength; its basically similar political structure is more oppressive, if not despotic, and attracts less spontaneous popular cooperation. Difficult questions of external alignment confront this regime as it seeks both Soviet and Chinese support for unification of the country on its own terms. The threatened regime in the south is a tightly organized, military dictatorship which uses harsh measures to impose its control, but which is promoting rapid economic growth with emphasis on private sector development and the attraction of Japanese capital.(31)

The largest East Asian state, China, has political structures similar to those in Vietnam and North Korea. Like them, it is a revolutionary regime, hostile to influences that might deradicalize its system; but it has experienced more severe internal tensions, and has become open to dealings with the industrialized democracies, especially to secure advanced technology. The present Chinese ruling group comprises representatives of factions that have been in rivalry and conflict since the late 1950s. There is strong military involvement, attributable mainly to the severe purging of the party apparatus in the Cultural Revolution of 1966-1969. A difficult succession problem is facing the leadership because of the advanced age of the most influential figure, Teng Hsiao-ping, whose presence has been the outcome of serious high level conflicts: he was purged in the Cultural Revolution, and again in 1976, but was rehabilitated in 1973 and 1977.

The evolution of the Chinese regime is being affected by continuing intraelite differences and by a basic ambivalence toward modernization. Some elements of the leadership advocate more emphasis on revolutionary values and on self reliance, and less dependence on technocratic factors in China's industrialization. Others, especially Teng Hsiao-ping, stress the importance of administrative expertise and technology. There are also closely related issues concerning the utilization of the United States as a partial ally in the struggle against the USSR; involvement with the United States is repugnant to Chinese leaders who have a deep concern for the preservation of revolutionary values in their regime. The current drive to accelerate industrial growth lacks some impetus because of the high level differences, and also because of the presence of numerous officials in the administration who were appointed because of political rather than professional qualities during and after the Cultural Revolution. Because of the presence of these officials, and a lack of qualified personnel, the economy's capacity to absorb foreign technology is quite limited. Numerous large orders for Western and Japanese industrial plants were placed during 1977 and 1978, but some of these were cancelled during 1979, and a three-year period of readjustment was announced during which there would be only moderate growth.(32)

INTERDEPENDENCIES

East Asia has a pattern of economic relations centered on Japan, but that country's most substantial economic exchanges are extraregional, mainly with the other industrialized democracies, especially the United States, and with OPEC. Within East Asia, Japan is China's main source of technology and the principal trading partner of the ASEAN group, whose resources attract large volumes of Japanese investment. ASEAN trade with China is small and, accordingly, the trade policies of the ASEAN states give much attention to Japan, but also seek to expand commerce with other major industrial powers, especially the United States, in order to avoid excessive dependence on the Japanese market.

The Japanese economy is heavily dependent on imports of fuels and raw materials, and on revenue from exports of manufactured products and capital goods. A major proportion of the necessary imports is obtained from the ASEAN states, but large purchases of primary products are also made from other Third World countries, especially to secure access to their markets for manufactured goods. China is an additional source of fuels and raw materials, and has great importance as a trading partner because of its vast need for technology, which is a large factor in Japanese economic planning. For the present, however, trade with China is only a small proportion of Japan's total commerce.(33)

Roughly half of China's imports of plant, machinery, and manufactured goods come from Japan. This degree of Chinese dependence has resulted from a long process of trade expansion which began in the 1950s, and its acceptance appears to have been influenced by recognition of the dynamism of the Japanese economy and its high technological levels, awareness of the extent to which government credits and other forms of support help the expansion of Japanese exports, and appreciation of the political utility of commerce with Japan, insofar as it can influence Japanese business and political leaders, who see a great potential for economic partnership between the two countries. The present form of asymmetric interdependence has political and security dimensions for each side. China has to continue looking mainly to Japan for technology because the terms of trade and credit are favorable, and because geographic proximity makes Japan a more suitable supplier than the other industrialized democracies. A basic Chinese concern with diversifying sources of technology is moderated by factors which affect the significance of West Germany, France, Britain, and the United States as capital exporters. West Germany is China's largest supplier in the European Community, but its commercial policy is influenced by much more extensive trade with the USSR, and by political constraints relating to its Ostpolitik, which obligate caution regarding any policy that might antagonize Moscow. France is evidently regarded as a state with somewhat less advanced technology, and a foreign policy that is also influenced by concerns about detente, while Britain seems to be viewed as a country with a weak economy. The United States, while evidently recognized as the largest and most diversified exporter of capital goods, is apparently ranked after Japan as a trading partner because its terms of trade and credit are less attractive and are affected by some incoherence in its foreign economic policy, as well as by anxieties about its detente with the USSR.(34)

On the Japanese side, the priority given to the commercial relationship with China seems to be based on considerations of comparative advantage: Peking can keep down the prices of its primary exports and provide quantities of coal and oil that lessen Tokyo's dependence on the OPEC countries. Long-term trade prospects are relevant also, but in addition there are political and security factors. The domestic political fortunes of the ruling Liberal-Democratic Party depend, in part, on its demonstration of a capacity to maintain friendship with China, and that is also dictated by its external security interests, which require efforts to strengthen Chinese capabilities for resistance against Soviet pressures. Further, Japan's need for increased leverage in its strained economic relationship with the United States can be met, to some extent, by developing closer ties with China as a means of exerting indirect influence on the Sino-American connection. In varying degrees, all these considerations appear to affect Japanese elite opinion and will probably continue to do so unless there is a very favorable change in Soviet behavior which has been abrasive and erratic toward Japan over the past two and a half decades.(35)

The Sino-Japanese interdependencies appear to be managed on each side with little reference to either state's involvement in Southeast Asia. Before the development of the Sino-Japanese detente in 1972, China had shown strong opposition to Japan's "imperialistic" behavior in Southeast Asia in collaboration with the United States; but, subsequently, Peking began to show respect for Japan's economic and other interests in Southeast Asia and encouraged cooperation within ASEAN, especially to limit Soviet involvement in the area. China's exports to the ASEAN countries are small and consist mainly of low technology manufactures which do not compete effectively against Japanese products. Southeast Asian exports to China are quite small, and there is little optimism in the area that these will expand as China's main import requirements are seen to be capital goods. Japan's management of its interdependencies with the Southeast Asian states is almost entirely bilateral, because there is not sufficient cohesion between the ASEAN members to deal with Japan on a collective basis, although the Japanese government has shown interest in developing ties with these states as a group. The basic pattern of trade, in which primary products are exchanged for manufactured goods and technology, is being gradually diversified through medium to high levels of growth in the ASEAN economies. The commercial ties, moreover, are being strengthened by the spread of Japanese manufacturing and extractive industries in the ASEAN countries.(36)

ASEAN dependencies on Japan are growing faster than dependencies on the United States. Although smaller, the latter dependencies remain large enough to allow each state considerable scope for bargaining with Japan and with Japanese multinationals over the development of trade and investment relationships. Japanese bargaining strength is tending to increase and, although it is being used considerately, it inevitably will influence the growth policies of the ASEAN states, especially by affecting the options available to them regarding the industrialization of their economies. This is to be expected because of the comprehensive planning at the basis of Japan's regional involvement. United

States trade and investment activities in Southeast Asia are not coordinated under a regional strategy and do not involve long-term planning.(37)

Outside the Japan-ASEAN pattern, there are two other important economic relationships. Japanese investment in and trade with the rapidly growing South Korean economy is large, and so also is Japanese trade with Taiwan. Tokyo's interest in commerce with Taiwan is subordinated to the much larger interests of the China context. The economic relationship with South Korea is managed with much less restrictive concerns, but uncertainties about the future of the oppressive military regime in South Korea affect Japanese trade and investment planning.(38)

Of the other more isolated East Asian states, Burma trades on a small scale with Japan, and this commerce is not expanding significantly because the Burmese economy is extremely backward and the country's ruling military elite is reluctant to increase trade with industrialized states. Vietnam and the other Indochinese states conduct some trade with Japan, but Tokyo's interest in this commerce is small because of Vietnam's low level of development and China's hostile attitude towards the Hanoi regime.(39)

The Soviet Union's economic involvement in East Asia involves modest trade with Japan, aid to and commerce with the Indochinese states, and some trade with the ASEAN members. The most important relationship is that with Japan, and it has a considerable potential for expansion because of the USSR's interest in securing Japanese technology for the development of its Far Eastern territories. Soviet policy on this matter, however, has been indecisive, and Japanese interest is restrained because of the high importance given to the politically more useful connection with China(40)(See figure 7.1).

SECURITY

Security interdependencies form two patterns in which the United States and the Soviet Union are associated formally and informally with affinitive and dependent states. Formal military ties link South Korea, Japan, the Philippines, and Thailand with the United States; and the United States has a general commitment to assist Southeast Asian countries that may be threatened by communist direct or indirect aggression. In addition, the United States has an interest in ensuring that China is adequately protected against any major Soviet attack, and that there is no Chinese resort to force against Taiwan.

The Japan-U.S. military connection, based on a Mutual Security Pact, is the most significant interdependency in the regional strategic context. Large Soviet air, ground, and naval forces are based in the Kuriles and nearby parts of the USSR's Far Eastern territories, and this armed strength is often displayed in a threatening manner. Japan's small defense forces, with no nuclear capabilities, would be capable of offering only brief resistance against a Soviet attack. Such aggression is

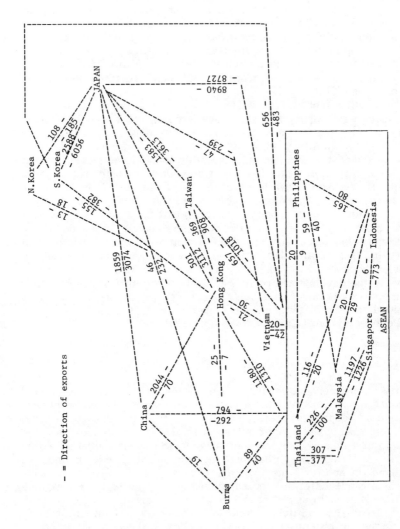

Fig. 7.1. East Asian trade (1978: US$ million).
Source: Direction of Trade Yearbook, 1979, International Monetary Fund.

not anticipated while the Soviet Union remains committed to detente; but, if relations between the superpowers deteriorate, Japan will have to reckon with the possibility of serious pressures from the USSR, including the use of Soviet naval power to disrupt shipments of Middle East oil en route to Japanese ports. The small Japanese navy could not cope with such a contingency, and Tokyo would need U.S. military assistance.(41)

To manage the immediate security issues, Japan seeks to maintain high degrees of rapport with Washington, strengthen ties with China, and implement a modest strategy of economic interdependence with the USSR, in order to give the Soviet Union inducements to accept genuine coexistence. Association with the United States' global strategic interests and policies is not sought because the operational context of Japan's security policy is regional. For the United States, Japan is an important ally whose defense has priority, after that of Western Europe, in the planning of a global deterrence strategy. Because this strategy requires carefully graduated responses in any escalatory events, there are uncertainties about the moves which the United States would make, and these give urgency to the Japanese policy of strengthening China's industrial power and gradual increases which are occurring in Japan's rate of military development.(42)

The security connection with the highest risk of conflict is the military link between the United States and South Korea. North Korea poses a serious security threat to South Korea. In the event of outright North Korean aggression against South Korea, or hostile military interactions along the frontier, the United States would be obliged to give South Korea active military support. A conflict on the peninsula would not be expected to spread into other areas, as both superpowers would have strong interests in restricting it, but this makes the danger of conflict rather high, in view of north Korea's hostility and the size of its military forces. The attitude of the United States in any of the likely contingencies involving North Korea, however, is likely to depend on the unity, effectiveness, and visible support of the South Korean regime. If that regime appears to be seriously lacking in legitimacy and administrative potential during a crisis or conflict, U.S. elite and popular willingness to support involvement on its behalf will be low.(43)

The informal U.S. security link with Taiwan (opposed by the Chinese Communist regime) is managed in a context of low risks and highly salient and complex political issues. The United States repudiated its Mutual Security Treaty with Taiwan at the end of 1978 in order to accord full recognition to Peking, but failed to obtain any assurances that there would be no use of force to assert Peking's claim to sovereignty over the island. The United States continues to provide some military aid to Taiwan in the face of Chinese Communist objections; but, if Peking were to apply military pressures against the island (for example, by interrupting its shipping), the United States administration would have no legal basis for threatening military intervention, and might not be able to secure sufficient Congressional and public support for any such intervention. In the broader Sino-

American security context, the United States has a strong incentive to build up goodwill in Peking, especially through a cooperative economic policy, in order to increase China's expectations that U.S. military support would be provided to assist Peking in repelling any major Soviet attack. To the extent that Peking's trust in this can be encouraged, it may be possible to diminish the Chinese leadership's interest in asserting control over Taiwan. On Peking's side there is clearly a strong desire to respond to what are seen as the positive elements in U.S. policy because of the additional security to be gained by drawing the United States into a stand that would raise Soviet assessments of the risks attached to any resort to force against China. There is a special interest in persuading the United States to sell arms to China, but for the present there is not sufficient support for this in U.S. administrative circles, although some defense-related equipment has been made available to the Chinese, and a favorable attitude has been shown to West European sales of military items to Peking.(44)

The security relationships between the ASEAN states and the United States are secondary features of the regional strategic pattern because the degree of interest on the U.S. side is moderate, and because the likely threats to these states are communist insurgencies, against which the United States would not likely plan to intervene, as a result of the strong domestic political constraints affecting U.S. policy in this area since the Vietnam War. The United States, thus, limits itself to the provision of economic and other forms of aid that directly or indirectly strengthen the internal security capabilities of the ASEAN states. In several cases, however, this has unfortunate consequences for it helps to build up the repressive apparatus of the weakly legitimized authoritarian regimes in Thailand, Indonesia, and the Philippines. Over time, the negative features of these regimes tend to encourage the growth of protest movements, often under radical leaderships.(45)

The network of East Asian security dependencies involving the United States is larger than the pattern of Soviet military links in the region, but the USSR has a larger and faster growing naval presence, operating from bases in the Soviet Far East and in Vietnam. The USSR's client states are Vietnam, Cambodia, Laos, and the North Korean regime; the degree of dependence is greatest in the Vietnamese case, because of the gravity of the Chinese military threat to this state. The strategic interdependence in this relationship is complex because, while the Vietnamese leaders evidently wish to have sufficient Soviet military support to deter Chinese attacks, they apparently hope to avoid becoming excessively dependent on the USSR, and seem unwilling to allow the Russians strong influence in their affairs. An important consideration for Hanoi is to minimize the danger of being drawn into a Sino-Soviet conflict in which the USSR's priority concern would be the security of its own Far Eastern territories. Yet to secure adequate Soviet support evidently requires substantial and increasing cooperation with the USSR in several areas of policy, including collaboration with Moscow's integrative designs in the Council for Mutual Economic Assistance, which Vietnam joined in 1978.(46)

The Soviet security link with North Korea appears to be stronger but less useful. While the USSR is apparently developing a presence in Vietnam that tends to influence the policies of the ASEAN states and Burma, its connection with North Korea adds little to the pressures which it exerts against Japan and China. In this relationship, moreover, the main Soviet interest, for the present, is to restrain North Korean aggressiveness, in the light of overall Soviet concerns with detente; whereas, in the Vietnamese case, the USSR's main incentive is to identify with Hanoi's efforts to consolidate its influence in Cambodia and Laos, and strengthen its defenses against China.(47)

For more than a decade, the USSR has been endeavoring to set up an Asian Collective Security Pact that would be directed against China. No noncommunist states have supported this, and the Vietnamese attitude has been unenthusiastic. The development of a strong military link with that state, however, in circumstances which rule out the former Vietnamese strategy of seeking ties with China as well as the USSR, has apparently altered Soviet perspectives. The USSR can now hope to receive more positive ASEAN responses to its proposals for increasing economic and cultural exchanges, and it can expect to influence ASEAN policies on the question of neutralizing Southeast Asia. For several years, the ASEAN members have been committed, in principle, to the neutralization of their area and some of them appear to envisage that this would exclude the armed forces of the super-powers from most of Southeast Asia. The Chinese have supported this proposal, apparently with expectations that their claims to the islands of the South China Sea would be recognized, and that their small naval presence based on those islands would entitle them to recognition as a regional power whose forces would not have to be withdrawn under a neutralization arrangement. In the current situation, the assertion of Chinese claims to islands that are not yet occupied by Peking in the South China Sea will be difficult; and the Soviet presence in Vietnam, of course, represents a danger to any Chinese air or naval forces operating in the areas east and south of Indochina.(48)

REGIONAL FOREIGN POLICY BEHAVIOR

The various forms of foreign policy behavior in East Asia are mostly expressions of leadership beliefs, values, motivations, and perceptions. In the Japanese case, these accord with and provide some direction for a broad elite consensus on most external issues; but in almost all the other noncommunist East Asian states, foreign policy is managed by an autocratic executive, relying on the expertise of a very subordinate external affairs bureaucracy, and accepting little informal accounta-bility to the secondary elite. Chinese, Vietnamese, and North Korean foreign relations are directed even more autocratically, but with a determination to impose general consensus about policy, with justifica-tions derived from Marxism-Leninism.

Japan

Japan's foreign policy is shaped by interpenetrating political, economic, and bureaucratic elites, in a highly consensual fashion, incrementally, in a context of stable administration by the ruling Liberal-Democratic Party, with broad societal support. The substance of this policy is mainly economic; it stresses export promotion and direct investment in nearby resource-rich developing countries. The principal external influences are the goodwill of the United States, expressed in relatively considerate management of a large trading relationship from which Japan benefits disproportionately, and cooperative Chinese behavior which, although accompanied by ideologically conflictual elements, encourages hopes for a growth of interdependence that will give the Chinese increasing incentives to accept coexistence. Conflictual behavior mixed with a considerable measure of cooperative activity is received from the Soviet Union, and this is viewed as a problem which requires the preservation of ties with that state as well as with China.(49)

Continued successes of a high order in the implementation of a neomercantilist foreign economic policy over the past two decades reinforce the Japanese elite consensus in favor of maintaining this policy and of maximizing its effectiveness by avoiding entanglement in political and security issues that might affect access to world markets. The practice of avoiding such entanglement developed in the 1950s and 1960s, when the Liberal-Democratic administrations were especially anxious to ensure that no opportunities for agitation were given to the opposition Japan Socialist Party for denunciation of a close partnership that was being maintained with the United States. The avoidance of security and political issues helped the penetration of foreign markets and, to some degree, assisted private Japanese groups seeking to develop trade with China. Since the opening of American diplomatic relations with Peking in 1972, strains in Japan-U.S. relations and uncertainties about the evolution of U.S. policy appear to have strengthened the determination of Liberal-Democratic administrations to concentrate on foreign economic affairs. This has meant rejection of suggestions that Japan should accept some of the responsibilities which the United States has been bearing for the support of Southeast Asian states coping with communist terrorism and insurgencies.

In the management of foreign economic policy, Japan is a highly coherent and effective actor, operating primarily to strengthen its powerful position through an enormous volume of trade, mainly with the world outside East Asia. There is an interest in developing comprehensive economic cooperation with the ASEAN states, but they lack the cohesion necessary for that, and Japanese policy appears to be adequately served through bilateral dealings with each of these Southeast Asian nations.(50)

Japan's economic role in East Asia encounters competition from considerably less coherent U.S. trade and investment policies. The United States' commercial and investment links with the ASEAN states are large, but smaller than Japan's, and, in relative terms, appear to be declining, although ASEAN administrations seem to look to the United States for aid in bargaining with Japan over terms of trade and investment. United States' competition is of smaller magnitude, but potentially more serious with respect to Japan's trade with China; and this rivalry appears to give impetus to Tokyo's efforts to strengthen its position as the main exporter of technology to China, especially by offering generous trade credits.(51)

China

China's foreign policy behavior ranks next as a major determinant of the regional pattern of interactions. This policy is shaped by a much smaller group of decision makers, comprising principally the Politburo of the Chinese Communist Party in a closed system with professional inputs from strictly subordinated officials. Basic orientation is derived from a version of Marxism-Leninism that has been adapted to the Chinese situation in a strongly nationalist spirit, but this orientation is somewhat confused by the present ruling group's repudiation of elements of Mao Tse-tung's Thought which had been the principal theoretical expression of that nationalist ethos. Marxism-Leninism provides the basic cognitive map for understanding the international environment, but under the influence of extreme antagonism toward the USSR which derives, in part, from what are felt to be authentic ideological values as well as from anti-Soviet nationalism.

Perceptions of interest and obligation relating to the development of China's power and the spread of revolutionary change are based on information processed by officials under exacting political discipline. They tend to sustain what is recognized to be the preferred content of the ruling group's psychological environment. Western and other non-communist news sources are utilized (but selectively), and their material is interpreted according to relatively constant ideological themes, especially concerning the growth of class struggles in the capitalist states, revolutionary movements in the Third World, and broad international opposition to the USSR. The scope for critical rationality in the policy process is also limited by the total absence of spontaneous societal observations on foreign policy issues, and by the survival of a Leninist concept of decision making by a ruling revolutionary elite as a process of authoritative prescription based on superior ideological wisdom rather than on the advice of professionals who are expected to be lacking in revolutionary zeal. Where the economic dimension of China's interests in a given area of foreign relations is large, however, there appears to be considerable scope for technocratic inputs into policy, and this is evident principally in relations with Japan and the United States.(52)

Chinese foreign policy behavior toward Japan is substantially cooperative, with an admixture of ideologically conflictual elements across a wide range of economic, political, and security issues; and it has a large supporting transnational component. The main Chinese objectives, clearly, are to strengthen the Liberal-Democratic administration's commitment to friendship with Peking, reduce its interest in ties with the Soviet Union, influence its relationship with the United States, and induce it to accept the growth of a stronger Chinese role in Southeast Asia. For these objectives, China's economic bargaining power is small, and is affected by Japanese estimates of the possibilities for trade expansion, which had to be revised downwards in 1979 with the slowdown in Chinese industrial growth. Peking's capacity for leverage, however, tends to be strong because of Japan's vital interest in preventing a Sino-Soviet rapprochement, and in maintaining a lead over the United States in the development of understanding and cooperation with the Chinese. Linked with all these considerations is China's tacit temporary interest in sustaining the dominant position of the ruling Liberal-Democratic Party, especially because Peking's strategic interests could be adversely affected by the emergence of a coalition government which might slow down Japan's rate of growth, weaken its ties with the United States, and become more open to dealings with the USSR – in response to Soviet displays of friendship that would have to be expected after such a government had emerged.(53)

The political and security dimensions of the relationship are matters of indirect rather than explicit interaction, and on these matters the Chinese tend to take the initiative, while Japanese behavior is reactive. The Chinese attach high importance to holding the initiative, especially through waging forms of international "struggle," through which they expect to influence the behavior of other states that are induced to collaborate. In their perspective forms of struggle, it is especially important to manipulate the activities of cooperating bourgeois administrations because these are seen to be ambivalent, especially with respect to the threat from the "main enemy" – the USSR. The Chinese are ready to denounce any new ventures in Japanese economic cooperation with the Soviet Union, especially if these have unfavorable strategic implications. Of course, Chinese hostility to Vietnam is intended to discourage Japanese aid to and trade with that state.(54)

Some of the ideologically conflictual elements in Chinese behavior amount to direct and indirect warnings that Tokyo must not neglect the necessity to identify closely with China's immediate interests and purposes, particularly in relation to the Soviet Union. But others concern Peking's long-term aims regarding the promotion of political change in Japan by contributing to the development of affinitive revolutionary groups in that country. For the present, the independent attitude of the Japan Communist Party is a serious difficulty, and the utility of the ideologically sympathetic Japan Socialist Party is in doubt because this organization has been losing strength and its leadership is divided over policy and doctrinal issues. There is, moreover, a very fundamental difficulty in that the Chinese leadership's capacity to provide ideological guidance is probably not adequate for comprehensive leadership of revolutionary groups in advanced open societies, where generally high levels of sophistication affect all except the most extreme leftist associations, thus limiting possibilities for uncritical acceptance of foreign ideological direction.(55)

Chinese behavior toward the ASEAN states comprises much less substantial cooperation and more conflictual elements. The Chinese have less influence over the policies of these states, notwithstanding their weaknesses, mainly because of an incapacity to hold out major advantages to them in a credible fashion, and because of Chinese identification with their underground communist organizations. At the state-to-state level, China seeks friendly relations with the ASEAN members on a basis of peaceful coexistence and opposition to the Soviet Union, while encouraging hopes for gradual expansion of the small-scale trade which is carried on with these countries. At what may be called the transnational revolutionary level, however, the Chinese Communist Party and "people" express militant solidarity with the affinitive Marxist-Leninist movements that are endeavoring to build up "peoples wars" against the ASEAN administrations. ASEAN government leaders appear to be conscious of such attempted political penetration, but show interest in developing links at the state-to-state level in the hope that the Chinese will be persuaded to accept genuine coexistence relationships, and that the friendships at the official level will help to undercut the appeals of the local communist movements.(56)

Because there is some cohesion between the ASEAN states, and because economically they are of interest to Japan and the United States, these relatively more developed Southeast Asian polities impose some caution on Chinese behavior, since any unexpected pressures exerted against one of them would evoke expressions of concern from the others. Peking, however, can be less restrained in dealing with Burma, the isolated noncommunist Southeast Asian state in which the Chinese are more actively identified with insurgent communist activities. Chinese interest in developing coexistence relationships with the Burmese regime is not very active, and this is understandable in view of that administration's weak bargaining power, its lack of external political support, the size of its domestic opposition, the disorder in its economy, and the ease with which the Chinese can provide military and other forms of aid to its communist insurgents who control large areas near the Chinese border. The Rangoon government could strengthen its position in relation to China by developing ties with the ASEAN members, but it appears to be inhibited by fears that links with these relatively pro-Western states would antagonize Peking and cause the Chinese to become more active in support of the insurgents. The development of links with the United States could be a further help, but the Burmese military leaders appear to share long-standing convictions that ties with the United States would make their regime more vulnerable to domestic leftist opposition, and could antagonize Peking since the Chinese have shown no disposition to regard Burma as a state in which the United States has any interests that deserve respect.(57)

The hostile relationship with Vietnam is managed as part of the wide-ranging struggle against the Soviet Union. Intense emotional antagonism strongly influences policy toward both Vietnam and the

Soviet Union. In the Vietnamese case, much of this appears to derive from historically-based beliefs that the country is a former part of the Chinese Empire that should be closely associated with China. Peking's anti-Soviet nationalism has a historical basis also. It is sustained by bitter feelings about tsarist seizures of territory from the former Chinese Empire, as well as by resentments at major contemporary expressions of Soviet animosity, including the termination of Soviet military and economic aid in 1960 and the mounting of vicious propaganda campaigns against China in order to weaken Peking's status and influence in the Third World. Ideological opposition to the USSR is a further source of Chinese motivation, and this appears to be based on rejection of the USSR not only as a regime that has lost its revolutionary qualities but also as a state whose relative levels of advancement and sophistication could weaken the domestic social controls of the Chinese communist regime if the relationship between the two states became normal.

The Chinese have no rational basis for expecting to promote political change in Vietnam, but they may believe that their intransigent hostility and military pressures will force the emergence of an accommodative Vietnamese leadership at some future stage, although the main effect of their animosity is to evoke intense hostility at all levels of Vietnamese society. The Peking leaders may well believe that demonstrations of their antagonisms are necessary to warn other Southeast Asian states against developing ties with the Soviet Union, and to diminish Southeast Asian fears of Soviet and Vietnamese capacities to pressure governments and support liberation movements in the area.(58) Chinese behavior toward the USSR, likewise, does not appear to be related to any rational expectations of encouraging favorable political change; this behavior, of course, arouses general resentment in the Soviet Union, and its ideological dimension is unappealing to Moscow's domestic critics. The Chinese hostility has a compulsive quality which suggests not only the absence of a coherent strategy but an unwillingness to recognize any need for such a strategy. There is a persistent refusal to engage in any meaningful interaction with the Soviet authorities; and this, together with the nondiscriminating quality of Chinese hostile behavior, suggests that there is little or no design to guide Chinese activity. In the global context, it is clear that the Chinese wish to encourage firmer United States opposition to Soviet policies, presumably in the expectation that China's security will benefit; but this appears to be mainly a matter of hope rather than design. The kind of animosity felt on the Chinese side is clearly evident in the extremism and the simplistic qualities of the communications that are intended to encourage U.S. hostility toward the USSR.(59)

The Soviet Union

The USSR's East Asian policy is totally hostile to China and evidently aims at imposing disruptive stress on the Chinese leadership. A generalized threat with apparently indefinite decision time is posed by large military deployments along the common frontier, and by warnings to Peking that it should return to the observance of proletarian internationalism and accept Soviet primacy among the socialist states. The Soviet authorities display a readiness to negotiate on the boundary question (which the Chinese evidently wish to leave open), but, understandably, reject Peking's demands that former parts of the Chinese Empire which were acquired by Tsarist Russia should be acknowledged as possessions obtained through unequal treaties. Soviet communications call on Peking to cease all hostile communications, but indicate that the basic demand for acceptance of Moscow's authority is not negotiable.   Few Soviet communications appear to be designed to persuade any sympathetic Chinese leaders, but accommodation might be forthcoming if there are signs of serious high level disagreements in Peking over policy toward the USSR.(60)

Japan is clearly intended to be dissuaded from continuing its pro-Chinese bias in its external policy, but the USSR's behavior toward this state is a somewhat confused mixture of proposals about large-scale economic cooperation, threatening displays of military power, and denunciations of Japanese collaboration with the United States.   The overall effect is to sustain, if not increase, Japanese antipathies toward the Soviet Union and, thus, to perpetuate Tokyo's emphasis on ties with China and the United States. The main alternative for the USSR is to make credible offers of large-scale economic cooperation which could greatly reduce Japanese interest in trade with China. But it must be stressed that the Soviet Union's management of its economic diplomacy toward Japan over the past two decades has been abrasive and erratic, and that strongly negative emotional factors as well as organizational problems affecting the direction of external relations make adoption of this second option rather unlikely.

The relationship with Japan, like that with China, has to be directed in line with overall objectives concerning the United States. As in other regional contexts, the USSR seeks to destroy U.S. influence and to promote the establishment of affinitive and client regimes so that the global balance of forces will be increasingly tilted in its own favor. For the present, however, Soviet objectives in relation to Japan are seriously hindered by the estrangement of the Japan Communist Party, which has become very critical of the Soviet Union's authoritarianism, and by the lack of rapport with the Japan Socialist Party, much of whose leadership is influenced by Chinese ideology.(61) In Soviet strategy, then, support for North Korea's hostile attitude toward South Korea is an important factor, because the establishment of an affinitive regime covering the whole Korean peninsula would increase the pressures against Japan. The USSR, however, has to contend with a somewhat independent North Korean regime that has been influenced by China, and evidently does not wish to see outright North Korean aggression against the South because that would involve the United States in hostilities. If the North Korean attitude were sufficiently friendly or submissive, Soviet purposes would be served by an insurgency in South Korea, directed and supported from Pyongyang; but this could be difficult to mount because of the strong security controls maintained by the South Korean regime. The promotion of such an insurgency could be made somewhat less difficult if Soviet coexistence diplomacy induced the United States to withdraw its forces from South Korea, especially as the removal of this psychological support would tend to weaken South Korean morale.(62)

Southeast Asia

In Southeast Asia, Vietnam is the focus of Soviet attention. While the USSR is endeavoring to gain influence in this state by supporting it against China, full rapport with the Vietnamese leadership has yet to be attained, and seems to be difficult to achieve because the Soviet Union tends to be overbearing in the use of its bargaining strength. The Vietnamese appear to be reluctant to become heavily dependent on the Soviet Union, and are evidently unwilling to provide it with extensive base facilities that would enlarge its military presence beyond what is required to deter the Chinese. Vietnam, of course, has an incentive to avoid provoking more serious Chinese hostility; but the Soviet Union, if it wishes to increase its military pressures against Peking, may encourage stronger Vietnamese expressions of anti-Chinese feeling, and assist a formidable Vietnamese military build up along the common frontier and in Laos.(63)

As a client state of the USSR, Vietnam is a challenge to the noncommunist Southeast Asian states; it has sought to develop good relations with the ASEAN members in competition with a similar Chinese policy, but the ASEAN administrations have been unwilling to antagonize Peking by responding. The external policies of the ASEAN members, of course, are quite limited in scope and are oriented to a considerable extent toward the development of coexistence relationships with China.

Substantively, the ASEAN members deal mainly with Japan and the United States with reference to trade, investment, and aid. Levels of understanding with and goodwill toward the United States appear to be high, and there are tendencies to view the expansion of these links as a policy that can help in the management of dependencies on Japan. There is little solidarity between the ASEAN governments, however, and their inability to manage relations with other states on a collective basis makes each one dependent on its own small bargaining power. Full utilization of that, moreover, is not usual because each administration's attention tends to be drawn away from regional and subregional affairs by difficult internal problems. In Malaysia, the predominantly Malay political elite is intensely preoccupied with the enormous problem of overcoming the economic disparities between its own community and the local Chinese. The military leaderships in Indonesia and Thailand are heavily dependent on unstable clientelist networks extending into their command structures for the mobilization of support in their armed forces, while the autocratic regime in the Philippines is dependent on very diverse and possibly even less reliable patronage connections.

REGIONAL INTERACTION

The patterns of interaction in East Asia are mainly dyadic rather than broadly inclusive, and they are not institutionalized except to a modest degree within the Association of Southeast Asian Nations, but they are influenced by fairly wide interdependencies. There are no serious antagonisms between the various noncommunist states, and all of them have friendly ties with the United States, the main outside power involved in the region. The persistence of strains and conflicts between the communist states of the area, moreover, limits their capacities to oppose subregional or regional cooperation.

Japan's position at the center of the principal dyadic relationships in East Asia is being strengthened by the growth of economic links with China and each of the ASEAN members. Japanese economic ties with states outside the region, however, are also expanding, thus limiting the degree of emphasis on East Asia in Japan's external policies. China's extraregional involvement is much smaller in economic terms, but politically has major dimensions, especially because of the relationship maintained with the United States on the basis of partially shared opposition to the USSR. This is a source of restraint on China's conflictual behavior. It leaves the way open for integrative activity by the constructively oriented states, without any of the political costs in terms of links with Peking, that would have had to be borne a decade ago.

The relatively restricted pattern of dyadic interactions is not tending to become more regionally inclusive. Levels of interdependence between China and the ASEAN states, and among these states themselves, remain low; Vietnam, Burma, and North Korea continue to be isolated, and trade between South Korea and the ASEAN members is growing only at a modest rate. The ASEAN members, moreover, do not have a strong political will to increase cooperation within their grouping.

The configuration of relations does not have any pronounced hierarchical features. There is no clearly dominant interactive process, although some do influence others. Neither the Sino-Japanese interchanges nor the Japanese-U.S. relationship has any significant influence on Japan's interactions with the ASEAN members. However, the tendency of the United States to limit its involvement in East Asia, together with the somewhat conflicting strand in this policy that emphasizes the strengthening of ties with China, amounts to a form of pressure on Japan. It challenges Tokyo to strengthen its links with China and, thus, produces a situation in which the Japan-China interaction will influence if not dominate the U.S.-China relationship.

Most of the dyadic interactions are interdependent to some degree. Shifts to more integrative, competitive, or conflictual behavior within any of these relationships will affect the others. In most cases, the forms of interacting behavior are relatively stable, but the probabilities of change in Chinese and Soviet regional activities appear to be significant.

The Sino-Japanese, Sino-American, and U.S.-Japanese relationships are asymmetrically interdependent. Any increases in Sino-American cooperation, it must be stressed, will give Japan stronger incentives to expand its collaboration with China, and it will be in Peking's interest to reciprocate. Depending on U.S. and Japanese dispositions, the Japan-U.S. relationship could become either more competitive and less trustful or more cooperative. The Soviet Union, meanwhile, will presumably be inclined to increase either its cooperative or its conflictual behavior toward Japan.(64) The relationships between Japan and the ASEAN states, however, are affected only in small degrees by continuity and change in the Sino-Japanese, Sino-American, and U.S.-Japanese interactions. The evolution of Japan's connections with each ASEAN member, on the other hand, is influenced by U.S. relations with the ASEAN states, and, of course, by the interactions within the ASEAN grouping.

The significant degrees of interdependence between the three major cooperative dyadic relationships of Northeast Asia result, in part, from each participating state's preference for maintaining the bilateral pattern. These preferences are due to expectations about maximizing control over and benefits from the dyadic interactions. The main explanation for the interdependencies between these interactions, however, is each state's capacity to derive benefits from the interchanges that increase its utility to the other members of the pattern. The interdependencies are relatively stable, moreover, except with respect to China's behavior, which could be affected by the continuing intraelite conflicts in that regime.(65) While increases or decreases in the utilities of China, Japan, and the United States to each other are of minor consequence for the ASEAN states in their mutual relations, theirs, of course, tend to be moderately significant with respect to ASEAN dealings with Japan and the United States. The ASEAN members have incentives to increase cooperation with both Japan and the United States, and to raise the levels of interdependence between their interactions with those states, but, as has been stressed, there is not sufficient political will to make this rational course a collective choice.

Within the various dyadic relationships there are diverse asymmetries with respect to levels of understanding, compatibilities and conflicts of interest, bargaining power, value orientations, capacities for coherent international behavior, and policy orientation. The main effect of the contrasts is to limit the development of the Japan-ASEAN pattern, and this is a problem which calls for regional political designing, especially to promote more equality in the bargaining relationships.

Levels of understanding are high in the Japan-U.S. connection, because of the large flow of communications between these two open societies, the high frequency of their interactions, the sensitivities to each other's behavior resulting from their complex interdependencies, their very substantial identities of interest, the compatability of their value orientations, the basic similarities between their forms of decision making rationality, and the substantial degrees of complementarity between their global policies. For the present, however, the bargaining related to their mutual behavior is competitive rather than integrative, due mainly to cultural dissimilarities and relatively long social distances. Nevertheless, the large and expanding interdependencies linking the two states, together with the factors that facilitate cooperation, have great potential significance for the development of collaboration between the various East Asian states.(66)

In the East Asian context, levels of mutual understanding within the ASEAN group are medium, but highest for the region. In this association, perceived identities and complementarities of interest are fairly extensive. There is rough equality in the distribution of bargaining power, value and policy orientations are moderately conducive to subregional cooperation, each state has a medium capacity for coherent external behavior, and each is relatively receptive to communications from the others. The development of a common resolve to undertake wide-ranging cooperation, however, is prevented mainly by characteristics of each ruling elite's political psychology and its perceptions of weakness, instability, and insufficient goodwill in its counterparts, from whom it desires cooperation.(67)

Levels of understanding in Japan's relations with the ASEAN members are medium, but lower than those within ASEAN; on the ASEAN side there is distrust and antipathy, limiting perceptions of identities of interest and causing desires to avoid dependence on Japan. The asymmetries in bargaining power are very great, and there is evidently little confidence on the part of the ASEAN group that the normative orientation of Japanese political and economic elites is sufficiently favorable. Cooperation in ASEAN-Japanese relations is expanding, in each case on a modified dependency basis, but with no significant increases in understanding and goodwill.(68)

DEVELOPMENTAL ISSUES

If there were wider collaboration between ASEAN members and Japan, and within ASEAN, East Asia would begin to develop as a regional system. The present configuration of interchanges could become more of a system whose members would be sensitive to and concerned with each other's interests, and who would tend to coordinate policies for mutual benefit. To the extent that all the participating states were benefiting equitably from growth and increased trade within the pattern, some of the relatively isolated East Asian states could be attracted to associating with the group, after which its members might have some influence on the evolution of those neighboring states. Current forms of cooperation in the Japan-ASEAN pattern, however, are not tending to reinforce the presently low levels of motivation to collaborate; instead, although the interdependencies are rising, anxieties and antipathies within the ASEAN states are tending to grow with rapid increases in the Japanese economic presence. Efforts are made by the Japanese to overcome such problems, but the difficulties resulting from cultural dissimilarities and economic disparities are very great. In each of the ASEAN states (except Malaysia and Singapore), moreover, a lack of indigenous talent for economic management limits the possibilities for effective local participation in the management of subsidiaries of Japanese firms, and restricts the development of local enterprises to levels well below those that might be expected in view of the multiplier effects of the foreign enterprises.

Regional development, clearly, would require changes in what may be called the terms of interaction within ASEAN, and between its members and Japan. Change in these terms is not likely to be initiated by either Japan or the ASEAN states, but could be promoted by a well-accepted outside state, and this represents a challenge for the United States. There is a potential for regional cooperation which is not likely to be realized unless there is considerable promotional activity by the United States with contributions to political as well as economic development in the area. For comprehensive and self-sustaining regional cooperation, the building up of goodwill, trust, and orientations toward integrative activity must be expected to require external support and leadership by an advanced state if the potential members of the regional system are underdeveloped nations, weak in bargaining resources and in capabilities for the management of external dependencies.

For the present there are no serious strains in Japan-ASEAN relations, but in the configuration of diverging, conflicting, and congruent interests, national decision makers are doing relatively little to promote integrative rather than competitive interaction, and to raise levels of understanding and trust. On the Japanese side, the highly coherent, functional, and comprehensive foreign economic policy which is being implemented quite vigorously is not being accompanied by sufficiently active diplomacy to evoke trustful cooperation by the ASEAN states, although a beginning has been made with the proclamation of the Fukuda doctrine, which expresses Japan's readiness to develop wide-ranging collaboration with ASEAN. As yet, there is no strong consensus among Japan's political, economic, and administrative elites that there should be a large commitment of energy and resources to integrative diplomacy addressed to the ASEAN members, and any efforts that might be made to promote such a consensus tend to be discouraged by demands from groups pressing more substantial interests relating to other parts of the Third World, as well as by the attitudes of ASEAN administrations.(69) For these governments, vigorous integrative statecraft toward Japan would be feasible only on a collective basis, in view of the weaknesses of their individual bargaining strength. Integrative activity directed at each other, while clearly in each one's interest, is not being undertaken because of the limited salience of long-term national and regional interests for ASEAN ruling groups, except in Singapore. To the extent that attention is given to the possible benefits of wider cooperation within the association, decision makers in most of the member states, particularly in the Thai and Indonesian military regimes, evidently tend to think in terms of the limited immediate gains and costs that would result from trade liberalization, rather than in terms of the benefits that could be realized through an integrative scheme providing for equitable redistribution of the benefits from market integration and for firm collective management of external dependencies. In the minds of most of those decision makers, the immediate gains from acceptable forms of trade liberalization are not large enough to obligate major efforts for market integration, and no solutions are seen for the problems of instability, distrust, and communal antipathy that affect each ASEAN member's relations with the others. Wide-ranging economic cooperation within ASEAN and between it and Japan, however, is imperative for modernization within this group. The economies of the ASEAN members are growing at rates averaging between five and eight percent a year, but in each, and especially in the Philippines, there is extreme maldistribution which imposes severe hardships on large proportions of each state's population, especially in the rural areas. The Philippine, Indonesian, and Thai administrations show little concern with the extreme injustices; but a significant acceleration of growth, resulting from an ASEAN-Japan integration scheme, would stimulate the development of industries producing for large local markets and multiply employment opportunities. An active role by the United States, moreover, could impose pressures on the ruling groups of the authoritarian ASEAN members to fulfill their distributive responsibilities.(70)

The ASEAN states tend to draw Japanese investment because of their proximity as Japan's Third World neighbors and on account of their rich resources. While these states hesitate to begin large-scale economic cooperation with Japan and achieve only modest, uneven, and imbalanced growth, substantial Japanese direct investment tends to flow to more distant parts of the Third World (especially Latin America) in pursuit of opportunities to produce for local markets. Japanese interest in the prospects for regional economic cooperation is given little encouragement by the ASEAN states, especially the authoritarian ones; while increasing social tensions generated by extreme distributive injustices and oppression within these states are endangering their very limited prospects for political development and are beginning to affect Japan's long-term regional security and political interests. The emergence of radical regimes in the ASEAN states that are aligned with or friendly to the USSR would make Japan more vulnerable to Soviet pressures, while increasing Japan's relative strategic and economic isolation.

THEORY AND DESIGN

There has been much less integrative activity in East Asia than in Latin America. East Asian elites capable of sophisticated advocacy and support of projects for regional economic cooperation have been much smaller and less influential, while in Southeast Asia antiimperialist economic nationalism has been much weaker than in Latin America and less oriented toward regional endeavors. Latin American ruling elites, moreover, appear to be somewhat less influenced by distrust and antipathies towards neighboring states.(71)

If there were major increases in integrative activity within ASEAN, Japan would probably seek partnership that would ensure privileged access to its markets and investment opportunities, as well as to compete more effectively against the United States for such access. Such a partnership would also tend to influence the policies of the ASEAN members. The United States, on present indications, would probably not seek a special and more active relationship with the groupings because of the extent to which U.S. foreign economic policy is influenced by groups with strong interests in trade with other Third World areas, especially Latin America.

A simple game theoretic proposition which emerges, then, is that movement toward market integration by a subregional or regional group of states gives incentives to their major external trading partners to seek preferential access, subject to costs which might be incurred in other national or regional markets. The making and implementation of choices with respect to those incentives will depend on the coherence of each trading partner's policy orientation, and the capacities of its decision makers to formulate consistent and functional policies. Japan is a much more coherent and rational international economic actor than the United States and Japanese choices with respect to ASEAN are influenced not only by geographic proximity but also by relatively short social distances.

The low probability of vigorous, spontaneous, integrative activity by the ASEAN states is to be explained in terms of common influences on Third World foreign policies, and of Southeast Asian national and subregional economic, cultural, and political factors, including leadership idiosyncrasies, personal and primordial attachments and antipathies, and administrative practices. In most developing states, authoritarian ruling elites are deeply absorbed in the problems of maintaining and consolidating power and influence relationships based on combinations of patronage and coercion, and tend to give only limited and intermittent attention to directing the overall performance of their regimes. Attention that is given to public policy is influenced by concerns with rewarding favored groups, and with obtaining resources from industrialized democracies and transnational enterprises in exchange for economic concessions. The benefits, in the form of economic or military aid, or monetary transfers from and shares in the ownership of foreign firms, are more substantial and of more direct use for the leadership's ambitions than the general economic gains to be expected from market integration with neighbors. The ruling elites, moreover, operate within quite parochial contexts. The politically more important elements among their secondary elites and supporters are mostly military officers and the managers of well-protected, indigenous firms who have long been totally immersed in local situations, have little acquaintance with neighboring countries, and whose political psychology is dominated by simple communal and nationalist attachments, and by distrust of as well as antipathies toward neighboring societies that are often cultivated, in the interests of solidarity, with leadership encouragement. Socialized by dependence on such secondary elites and supporters, ruling groups in developing states tend to rely more on affective and clientelist solidarity building among these social strata than on consensus building about matters of public policy, because of reluctance to permit secondary elite participation in and critical review of the policy process. While leadership political psychology tends to be oriented away from regional cooperation with neighboring states, the parochial domestic support structure tends to make any projected regional collaboration politically costly, since a leadership that takes initiatives in that direction can, thereby, expose itself to agitation by opposition elements appealing to narrow communal and nationalist sentiments. This, clearly, is a risk that can become more serious if a measure of trade liberalization leads to an influx of products from a neighboring country that places local interests at a disadvantage. Further, if leadership attention is given to questions of subregional or regional cooperation, despite the distractions of internal solidarity building and the constraints of parochial attachments, the evolution and management of regional policy is likely to be idiosyncratic, ambivalent, disjointed, and subject to drastic neglect or revision, especially because of the very limited accountability of the ruling group, its lack of exposure to critical review, and the weak political roles of its professional staffs.(72)

Domestic solidarity building in an authoritarian context, as a distraction from substantive policy issues, tends to be high in the case of a ruling elite affected by internal divisions, and by instability among the secondary elite. This problem is clearly more serious in Thailand, Indonesia, and the Philippines than in Malaysia and Singapore, where it has been reduced to moderate proportions by considerable institutional development. In the Indonesian and Thai military regimes, and even more in the blatantly corrupt Philippine autocracy, radically-oriented protest movements may well become more active, thus engaging greater leadership attention with mainly negative results.

The constraints of parochial communalism and nationalism on any tendencies towards regional cooperation are more serious in authoritarian developing states. The direct and indirect social controls which are imposed have restrictive effects on societal communications and, thus, tend to preserve strong and exclusive communal and nationalist attachments. In open modernizing polities, greater penetration by international communications and a growth of sophistication in the articulation of societal aspirations on policy issues tend to moderate narrow communal and nationalist attachments and facilitate transnational interactions that increase awareness of regional interests, at least in moderate degrees. Representative governments, of course, can seek to maximize domestic support by appeals to primordial feelings, but military regimes in the Third World tend to be quite consistently and actively nationalist in their policy orientations.

Psychological factors, of course, operate in conjunction with the dynamics of internal support building. Executives in the developing states, even more than their counterparts in advanced democracies, tend to keep their cognitive maps of the regional environment quite simple, conceptually and with respect to causal attributions and cost-benefit calculations. Simple images of the outside world facilitate communication of the meanings of external situations to associates and subordinates when making decisions or avoiding issues. In developing states, such simplicity is easier to maintain because there is less exposure to independent critical review, and domestic support groups are less informed and less sophisticated. The leadership's personal impressions and experiences, moreover, tend to have greater influence, as simplifying factors, than in the policy contexts of advanced states. Evaluations of the advantages of maintaining full national autonomy and avoiding substantial regional cooperation tend to be a matter of quite simple calculation for Third World ruling groups, especially because of uncritical neglect of the costs of self reliance and the potential benefits of integrative activity with neighbors; estimations of the utility of untrammeled autonomy tend to be high, and only superficially comparative.(73)

In Third World subregional and regional groupings, of course, leadership judgments on integrative issues do vary in relative sophistication. In the Andean Pact (Latin America's most significant venture in subregional cooperation), leadership perceptions of the benefits to be gained have been more complex and positive than those of ASEAN government leaders, in part, because of more substantial inputs from highly competent officials and academics. Andean Pact leaderships, moreover, have been less constrained by the parochial orientations of domestic support groups than their ASEAN counterparts, although these have certainly been significant.

Within ASEAN, the Indonesian ruling military elite appears to be more influenced and restricted by parochial domestic forces than the military leadership in Thailand, which relates to a somewhat more sophisticated audience that has more frequent and more extensive international contacts. The Malaysian administration is also less constrained in this regard and appears to be more positively oriented toward subregional economic cooperation, in part, because of confidence that its economy would benefit significantly.(74)

The influence of the international environment on regional foreign policy behavior has tended to discourage integrative activity within ASEAN, until quite recently. Fears of drawing Chinese or Soviet hostility by forming a political grouping have influenced the attitudes of the ASEAN members, despite the present Chinese leadership's overtly positive attitude; but no similar inhibiting factors have imposed restraints on integrative activity in Latin America. The ASEAN states confront numerous uncertainties because of the possibilities for change in Soviet-Vietnamese and Chinese behavior, as well as on account of the ambivalence and irresolution in U.S.-East Asian policy. Each national leadership's tacit preference seems to be to preserve maximum freedom for maneuver in case accommodative strategies become necessary and, therefore, to limit the acceptance of collective obligations with neighbors.

Japan's policy toward ASEAN, which is a major influence on the behavior of its members, has to be understood in a perspective that is sensitive to complex interplays between very distinctive cultural factors and fairly common patterns of demand articulation by major economic groups in an industrialized democracy, and that takes account of the effects of relative international isolation. Cultural distinctiveness limits the possibilities for identification with, understanding of, and penetration by foreign societies; and it can be a potent source of motivation for neomercantilist foreign economic policy, as well as a powerful aid in implementing such a policy. The transformation of interest group demands into neomercantilist statecraft, however, leads to confrontation with challenges to manage complex interdependencies with other industrialized democracies. Meeting these challenges entails more strains for Japan than for any other industrialized democracy because of the cultural barriers to rapport with the interdependent states, and because of the Japanese economy's critical need for export revenues to finance imports of food, raw material, and fuel.

Japan belongs to the small category of highly coherent international actors in which executive authority rests securely on support structures at high levels of institutional development, and there is a pervasive policy consensus with which the leadership is closely identified. In contrast with other rather strongly hierarchical polities, leadership capacities to innovate are limited by felt obligations to operate consensually; and, accordingly, there are tendencies to avoid external issues if these are likely to be divisive. In the absence of assertive leadership within culturally acceptable limits, the possibilities for change in external policy depend largely on broad elite and societal reactions to external events, while the general endorsement of neomercantilism in foreign economic policy remains constant. The basic societal reactive tendencies are simple, strongly affective, and, of course, influenced by media interpretations. These reactive tendencies are reciprocal in that friendly behavior received from another state evokes goodwill.   An accumulation of negative experiences causes alienation and a growth of strong sentiments in favor of self reliance and of assertions of national interest. But this reactive logic is influenced by the felt cultural affinities with China and, accordingly, negative reactions to any unfriendly Chinese behavior are moderated by desires for cognitive and affective consonance, thus giving rise to hopes for a better relationship.(75)

Japan's attributes and international situation cause much emphasis on self reliance in the management of the complex interdependencies built up through vigorous economic statecraft. The very distinctive culture, the long social distances from other industrialized democracies, and the absence of political and societal affinities with neighboring states tend to produce intense consciousness of the imperative to use the nation's resources with maximum effect in competing against other advanced nations in the international economy. Integrative activity tends to be precluded by the awareness of cultural uniqueness and discouraged by the negative culturally-based attitudes of other industrialized democracies. The strong neomercantilist orientation, because it is shaped by powerful domestic factors that are subject to little penetration by outside influences, is not being moderated by the nation's increasingly complex interdependencies and, indeed, is tending to become more pronounced in response to the perceived competitiveness of other industrialized democracies.

Regional design, then, cannot easily become a feature of Japan's East Asian policy. Although the subject interests some Japanese scholars, bureaucrats, and political figures, the simple but widely held view is that the nation's scope for independent economic statecraft should not be limited, even in a small degree, by participating in a multilateral decision process for the management of links with neighbors that have only moderate utility as trading partners. Yet, Japan's immediate and long-term economic and political interests clearly require stable and productive relationships with the ASEAN group. With the expansion of vital Japanese economic processes into those states, their friendship and performance are becoming more significant for Tokyo's overall external interests. What is needed is broad collaboration for complementary growth. But, on the Japanese side, motivation to engage in this is not likely to become strong unless it is identified with larger interests. This would be the case if the United States were to play an active role in support of such a venture for subregional cooperation, or of a more ambitious scheme such as the establishment of a Pacific Community. East Asia, because of the conflictual orientations of several of its states and the extreme differences between many of them in terms of size and levels of economic and military power, has quite unfavorable prospects for regional development. With regional designing for constructive involvement by acceptable outside states, however, and for identification with a larger grouping, the cooperatively-oriented East Asian states may well be able to undertake the building of a new economic community.

NOTES

(1) Bradley M. Richardson, The Political Culture of Japan (Berkeley, Cal.: University of California Press, 1974); Robert E. Ward, Japan's Political System (Englewood Cliffs, N.J.: Prentice-Hall, 2nd ed., 1979); and T. John Pempel, Policy Making in Contemporary Japan (Ithaca, N.Y.: Cornell University Press, 1977).

(2) Lowell Dittmer, "Bases of Power in Chinese Politics: A Theory and an Analysis of the Fall of the Gang of Four," World Politics 31, no. 1 (October 1978): 26-30; Kenneth Lieberthal, "The Politics of Moderniza-

tion in the PRC," Problems of Communism 26, no. 3 (May-June 1978): 1-17; and Allen S. Whiting and Robert F. Dernberger, China's Future (New York: McGraw-Hill, 1977).

(3) Robert O. Tilman, ed., Man, State, and Society in Contemporary Southeast Asia (New York: Praeger, 1969); Harold Crouch, "Patrimonialism and Military Rule in Indonesia," World Politics 31, no. 4 (July 1979): 571-87; and Gordon P. Means, "Malaysia," and Clark D. Neher, "Thailand," in Politics and Modernization in South and Southeast Asia, edited by Robert N. Kearney (New York: John Wiley, 1975), pp. 153-214 and 215-52, respectively.

(4) Marjorie Niehaus, "Vietnam 1978: The Elusive Peace," Asian Review 19, no. 1 (January 1979): 85-94.

(5) Franklin B. Weinstein, ed., US-Japan Relations and the Security of East Asia (Boulder, Colo.: Westview Press, 1978).

(6) Katsuji Nakagane, "The Chinese Model of Economic Development: Its Impact on and Influence from Foreign Economic Systems," in Japan, America, and the Future World Order, edited by Morton A. Kaplan and Kinhide Mushakoji (New York: Free Press, 1976), pp. 321-36; and Jay Taylor, China and Southeast Asia (New York: Praeger, 1974).

(7) Donald W. Klein, "Japan 1978: The Consensus Continues," Asian Survey 19, no. 1 (January 1979): 30-40.

(8) Lieberthal, "The Politics of Modernization in the PRC."

(9) This inertia is clearly due to insecurity caused by purging. See notes on the bureaucracy in Trong R. Chai, "Communist Party Control Over the Bureaucracy," Comparative Politics 11, no. 3 (April 1979): 359-70.

(10) Cynthia H. Enloe, "Ethnic Diversity: The Potential for Conflict," in Diversity and Development in Southeast Asia, edited by Guy J. Pauker, Frank H. Golay, and Cynthia H. Enloe (New York: McGraw-Hill, 1977), pp. 137-82.

(11) Geoffrey B. Hainsworth, "Economic Growth and Poverty in Southeast Asia: Malaysia, Indonesia, and the Philippines," Pacific Affairs 52, no. 1 (Spring 1979): 5-41; Crouch, "Patrimonialism and Military Rule"; and Ansil Ramsay, "Thailand 1978: Kriangsak – The Thai Who Binds," Asian Survey 19, no. 2 (February 1979): 104-14.

(12) Niehaus, "Vietnam 1978," pp. 85-94.

(13) Pauker et al., Diversity and Development.

(14) Parris H. Chang, Power and Policy in China (Harrisburg: Pennsylvania State University Press, 2nd ed., 1978); and Michael B. Yahunda, China's Rule in World Affairs (New York: St. Martin's Press, 1978).

(15) Robert A. Scalapino, ed., The Foreign Policy of Modern Japan (Berkeley: University of California Press, 1977); and T.J. Pempel, "Japanese Foreign Economic Policy: The Domestic Bases for International Behavior," International Organization 31, no. 4 (Autumn 1977): 723-74.

(16) Hans Indorf, "Malaysia 1978: Communal Coalitions Continue," Asian Survey 19, no. 2 (February 1979): 115-23.

(17) Ramsay, "Thailand 1978"; and H. Monte Hill, "Community Formation Within ASEAN," International Organization 32, no. 2 (Spring 1978): 569-75.

(18) Crouch, "Patrimonialism and Military Rule"; and Ronald M. Grant, "Indonesia 1978: A Third Term for President Sukarno," Asian Survey 19, no. 2 (February 1979): 141-46.

(19) Kit G. Machado, "The Philippines 1978: Authoritarian Consolidation Continues," Asian Survey 19, no. 2 (February 1979): 131-40; and Robert B. Stauffer, "Philippine Authoritarianism: Framework for Peripheral 'Development'," Pacific Affairs 50, no. 3 (Fall 1977): 365-85.

(20) Bernard K. Gordon, "Loose Cannon on a Rolling Deck? Japan's Changing Security Policies," Orbis 22, no. 4 (Winter 1979): 147-56.

(21) William L. Scully and Frank N. Trager, "Burma 1978: The Thirtieth Year of Independence," Asian Survey 19, no. 2 (February 1979): 147-56.

(22) Yahuda, China's Role in World Affairs.

(23) T.J. Pempel, "Political Parties and Social Change: The Japanese Experience," in Political Parties Development and Decay, edited by Louis Maisel and Joseph Cooper (Beverly Hills, Calif.: Sage 1978), pp. 309-42.

(24) Crouch, "Patrimonialism and Military Rule."

(25) Stauffer, "Philippine Authoritarianism."

(26) Franklin B. Weinstein, "Multinational Corporations and the Third World: The Case of Japan and Southeast Asia," International Organization 30, no. 3 (Summer 1976): 373-404.

(27) Indorf, "Malaysia 1978."

(28) Crouch, "Patrimonialism and Military Rule"; and Frank C. Darling, "Thailand in 1977: The Search for Stability and Progress," Asian Survey 18, no. 2 (February 1978): 153-63. See also David Morell and Chai-anan Samudavanija, "Thailand's Revolutionary Insurgency: Changes in Leadership Potential," Asian Survey 19, no. 4 (April 1979): 315-32.

(29) Stauffer, "Philippine Authoritarianism."

(30) See Niehaus, "Vietnam 1978," on factors responsible for Hanoi's dependence on the USSR.

(31) Dae-sook Suh, "North Korea 1978: The Beginning of the Final Push"; and Sungjoo Han, "South Korea 1978: The Growing Security Dilemma," Asian Survey 19, no. 1 (January 1979): 51-57 and 41-50 respectively.

(32) For a review of the Chinese economy shortly before the period of readjustment was announced see Jan S. Prybyla, "Changes in the Chinese Economy: An Interpretation," Asian Survey 19, no. 5 (May 1979): 409-35.

(33) Klein, "Japan 1978."

(34) See Gavin Boyd, "The European Community and China," paper given at Conference of Europeanists, Washington, D.C., March 1979.

(35) See Bhabani Sen Gupta, Soviet-Asian Relations in the 1970s and Beyond (New York: Praeger, 1976), chap. 7.

(36) Weinstein, "Multinational Corporations and the Third World."

(37) See the discussion of basic features of U.S. foreign economic policy in Stephen D. Krasner, "U.S. Commercial and Monetary Policy: Unravelling the Paradox of External Strength and Internal Weakness," International Organization 31, no. 4 (Autumn 1977): 635-72.

(38) See references to South Korea in Scalapino, The Foreign Policy of Modern Japan.

(39) Klein, "Japan 1978."

(40) Ibid., and Sen Gupta, Soviet-Asian Relations.

(41) See Donald C. Hellmann, ed., China and Japan: A New Balance of Power (Lexington, Mass.: D.C. Heath, 1976), pp. 1-50.

(42) Gordon, "Loose Cannon on a Rolling Deck?"

(43) See comments on U.S.-East Asian policy in Hellmann, China and Japan.

(44) See discussion of this issue in A. Doak Barnett, China Policy (Washington, D.C.: Brookings, 1977).

(45) Jyotirindra Das Gupta, "A Season of Caesars: Emergency Regimes and Development Politics in Asia," Asian Survey 18, no. 4 (April 1978): 315-49.

(46) See the examination of Soviet policy in CMEA by Arpad Abonyi and Ivan J. Sylvain, "CMEA Integration and Policy Options for Eastern Europe: A Development Strategy for Dependent States," Journal of Common Market Studies 16, no. 2 (December 1977): 132-54.

(47) This option should be seen in the context of issues that were posed for the USSR before the strengthening of its ties with Vietnam. See Donald Zagoria, "Into the Breach: New Soviet Alliances in the Third World," Foreign Affairs 57, no. 4 (Spring 1979): 733-54.

(48) See references to strengthening of Soviet military presence in Vietnam in Harlan W. Jencks, "China's 'Punitive' War on Vietnam: A Military Assessment," Asian Survey 19, no. 8 (August 1979): 801-15.

(49) Saburo Okita, "Japan, China and the United States: Economic Relations and Prospects," Foreign Affairs 57, no. 5 (Summer 1979): 1090-110.

(50) Weinstein, "Multinational Corporations and the Third World"; and Hill, "Community Formation Within ASEAN."

(51) Gordon, "Loose Cannon on a Rolling Deck?"; and Okita, "Japan, China and the United States."

(52) Gene T. Hsiao, The Foreign Trade of China (Berkeley, Calif.: University of California Press, 1977); and Chae-Jin Lee, Japan Faces China (Baltimore, Md.: Johns Hopkins University Press, 1976).

(53) See discussion of China's difficulties in dealing with the Japan Socialist Party in Chae-Jin Lee, "The Japan Socialist Party and China, 1975-1977," Asian Survey 18, no. 3 (March 1978): 275-89; and of the implications of the Sino-Japanese connection for the USSR in Avigdor Haselkorn, "Impact of Sino-Japanese Treaty on the Soviet Security Strategy," Asian Survey 19, no. 6 (June 1979): 558-73.

(54) Ibid.; and see Harlan W. Jencks, "China's 'Punitive' War on Vietnam: a Military Assessment," Asian Survey 19, no. 6 (August 1979): 801-815.

(55) This problem appears to be especially serious in the relationship with the Japan Communist Party. See Hong N. Kim, "Deradicalization of the Japanese Communist Party under Kenji Miyamoto," World Politics 28, no. 2 (January 1976): 273-300.

(56) Boyd, "China's External Security Policy"; and Sheldon W. Simon, "China and Southeast Asia: Security in Transition," in The Military and Security in the Third World: Domestic and International Impacts, edited by Sheldon W. Simon (Boulder, Colo.: Westview Press, 1978), pp. 223-86.

(57) Ibid.; Scully and Trager, "Burma 1978."

(58) Jencks, "China's 'Punitive' War on Vietnam."

(59) See, for example, the foreign affairs section of Hua Juo-feng's report to the National Peoples Congress, Peking Review 10 (March 10, 1978): 7-40. See also Yahuda, China's Role in World Affairs, chap. 10.

(60) See Gavin Boyd, "Sino-Soviet Relations: The Future," Asian Forum 8, no. 4 (Autumn 1976): 1-32.

(61) See Chae Jin-Lee, "The Japan Socialist Party and China, 1975-1977"; and Peggy L. Falkenheim, "Eurocommunism in Asia: The Communist Party of Japan and the Soviet Union," Pacific Affairs 52, no. 1 (Spring 1979): 64-77.

(62) For a discussion of the North Korea-South Korea relationship see Fuji Kamiya, "The Prospects for Peace in Korea," in Weinstein, US-Japan Relations, pp. 167-88.

(63) See the discussion of Soviet interests in Haselkorn, "Impact of Sino-Japanese Treaty."

(64) Okita, "Japan, China, and the United States"; Gordon, "Loose Cannon on a Rolling Deck?"; Haselkorn, "Impact of Sino-Japanese Treaty."

(65) Chang, Power and Policy in China.

(66) Okita, "Japan, China, and the United States"; and Leon Hollerman, "Locomotive Strategy and United States Protectionism: A Japanese View," Pacific Affairs 52, no. 2 (Summer 1979): 193-209.

(67) Hill, "Community Formation Within ASEAN."

(68) Weinstein, U.S.-Japan Relations; and Bernard K. Gordon, "Japan, The United States, and Southeast Asia," Foreign Affairs 56, no. 3 (April 1978): 579-600.

(69) Stuart Drummond, "ASEAN: The Growth of an Economic Dimension," The World Today 35, no. 1 (January 1979): 31-38.

(70) The possibilities for leverage can be envisaged in the light of comments by Richard Stuart Olson, "Economic Coercion in World

Politics: With a Focus on North-South Relations," World Politics 31, no. 4 (July 1979): 471-94.

(71) See Robert D. Bond, "Regionalism in Latin America: Prospects for the Latin American Economic System," International Organization 32, no. 2 (Spring 1978): 401-24.

(72) These problems have been especially apparent in ASEAN, as has been evident in Drummond, "ASEAN." They have been reflected also in studies of Latin American regional politics, including Bond, "Regionalism in Latin America."

(73) Hill, "Community Formation Within ASEAN"; Michael Leifer, "Southeast Asia," in Foreign Policy Making in Developing States, edited by Christopher Clapham (London: Saxon House, 1977), pp. 18-41; and Sheldon W. Simon, "The ASEAN States: Obstacles to Security Cooperation," Orbis 22, no. 2 (Summer 1978): 415-34.

(74) Indonesia's reluctance to accept trade liberalization reflects awareness of the weaknesses of the country's industrial establishment. Malaysia's is the fastest growing economy in ASEAN (11.8 percent in 1976), and the Malaysian share of world trade is growing rapidly. See J. Alexander Caldwell, "The Economic and Financial Outlook for Developing East Asia," paper for Pacific Forum Conference, Hawaii, December 1978.

(75) See references to China in Scalapino, The Foreign Policy of Modern Japan; and see also Chae Jin-Lee, Japan Faces China.

8 South Asia

Leo E. Rose
Satish Kumar

The South Asian subcontinent, comprised of the sovereign states of India, Pakistan, Bangladesh, Afghanistan, Nepal, Bhutan, and Sri Lanka, is probably about as well demarcated by physical features as any region in the world. The land frontiers of the region, approximately 4,000 miles in length, are dominated by mountain ranges that constitute a reasonably effective physical and ethnic/linguistic dividing line between the subcontinent and adjacent areas of Asia. While there are small tribal and ethnic communities that straddle the frontiers, these are generally peripheral to the dominant cultures on either side of the borders of the region.

Whether there is a regional "core culture" in South Asia is a very complex question. Certainly there is nothing like the Christian tradition in Europe, the Islamic tradition in West Asia and North Africa, or the Sinic tradition in East Asia that binds the societies of the subcontinent together. But it is also evident that there are some common characteristics that do distinguish the inhabitants of South Asia from their neighbors. Pakistani and Bangladeshi Muslims, for instance, share more common values and traditions with their Hindu neighbors than they do with the Muslims of West Asia and Southeast Asia. Most South Asians had a common historical experience for several hundred years under the Muslim Moghul dynasty and then under the British, which, in turn had been both superimposed on and influenced by the dominant Hindu Indoaryan culture that has thrived in the subcontinent for at least three millennia. While there are major religious, cultural, and linguistic divisions within South Asia that seriously complicate the interrelationships between the various subsystems in the region, there are important overlying commonalities as well.

Geographic factors have had a deep impact upon South Asia's relationship with the rest of Asia, physically and psychologically. The subcontinent, as the term implies, is peripheral to the main Asian land mass and the principal land channel of communications connecting West

237

Asia and Europe with East Asia. The result is that South Asia is part of but distinct from the rest of Asia, a dichotomy that is of considerable importance. The contests for the control of strategic areas in the intermediate Central Asian regions have occasionally overlapped into South Asia (as may be happening now in the Soviet Central Asian-Sinkiang-Afghan-Pakistan-Iran area), but, for the most part, the subcontinent has played a relatively minor role in the politics and wars of the vast areas to the north and west. Direct political, economic, and intellectual contacts between South Asia and China, for instance, are a modern phenomenon. Two great civilizations – the Chinese and the Indian – developed in quite close proximity for over 2,500 years without much awareness of each other's existence. That China and India fought their first war against each other in 1962 is indicative of the degree of their previous mutual isolation.

The subcontinent's position astride the major trade routes in the Indian Ocean and adjoining waters (the Bay of Bengal and the Arabian Sea) has made it an integral part of the southern Asian commercial and political system for many centuries. Indian commercial activities in Southeast Asia have been very extensive in some periods, while Indian intellectual and social values, both Hindu and Buddhist, permeated the societies to the north and east of the subcontinent. Later, it was from South Asian bases in India and Sri Lanka that the Portuguese, Dutch, and British established their commercial and political empires in Southeast Asia and conducted trade with China.

But while the subcontinent has been excluded from some of the turmoil and strife that has periodically engulfed other areas of Asia, it has had its own problems as regional political systems have been the exception during the approximately three millennia of recorded history in South Asia. As William J. Barnds has noted with reference to the post-1947 period:

> In contrast with South Asia's external boundaries, the political geography within the region follows no neat pattern. The three most important river systems – the Indus, Ganges, and Brahmaputra – cut across the boundaries of the principal countries in a way that has exacerbated the disputes between them.(1)

Intraregional conflicts and disputes have erupted on several occasions since 1947, and relations between the South Asian states, more often than not, have been marked by deep suspicions and antagonism even during periods of comparatively "normal" interaction. It is not too surprising, therefore, that no formal institutionalized regional system has emerged as yet. We will suggest, however, that there are certain aspects of interstate relations in South Asia that are essentially regional in character and that the present trends, while hardly unilinear, are in the direction of greater cooperation on a multinational basis in the subcontinent.

CULTURAL AND LINGUISTIC BASE

South Asia is comprised of a rich mosaic of religions and languages which often cross national boundaries and have a significant bearing on developments in neighboring countries in the region. Hindus constitute 83 percent of the population in India, 9 percent in Bangladesh, 90 percent in Nepal, 18 percent in Sri Lanka, 20 percent in Bhutan, and 0.5 percent in Pakistan. Muslims form 97 percent of the population in Pakistan, 11 percent in India, 80 percent in Bangladesh, 7 percent in Sri Lanka, 2 percent in Nepal, and 99 percent in Afghanistan. Buddhists constitute 67 percent of the population in Sri Lanka, 8 percent in Nepal, 80 percent in Bhutan, and 0.7 percent in India. The Christian communities are minorities in all South Asian countries – 8 percent in Sri Lanka, 3 percent in India, 1.4 percent in Pakistan, and 0.3 percent in Bangladesh.(2)

This scattered distribution of major religious groups all over the subcontinent has had multiple and contradictory implications for the development of a regional system. Most of the public discussion on this factor has focused on the negative consequences, primarily the conflicts and riots between religious communities in one country that then become issues in disputes between governments in the region. But the distribution of communities on a transnational basis has also promoted interaction between the people of South Asia on a massive scale, and this helps to remove misunderstandings between nations and to modify their negative perceptions of each other. This interaction occurs because of family ties between people from the same religious community living in neighboring countries, and because the places of pilgrimage and worship for a particular religious community are located in several countries in the region. Annually, hundreds of thousands of Muslims in India and Pakistan cross the borders between the two countries (when political conditions permit) in order to visit relatives in the other state. The same is true of travel by Hindus and Muslims between West Bengal and Bangladesh. Similarly, pilgrimages by thousands of Indian Hindus to Pashupatinath temple in Nepal, of Pakistani Muslims to Ajmer Sharif in India, of Indian Sikhs to Nankana Sahib in Pakistan, and of Sri Lankan, Bhutanese, and Nepali Buddhists to Bodhgaya in India are of major cultural importance in the subcontinent. This also has a political impact as many South Asians are familiar with neighboring societies and, thus, on balance, are less susceptible to the virulent campaigns launched by one government against another state in the region.

The multiplicity of religions, however, has, at times, led to communal strifes which have assumed gruesome proportions. Despite the professed commitment to secularism in the Indian political system, for instance, the actual behavior of Indians often falls short of this ideal. Hindu-Muslim riots have been a frequent occurrence in India and have usually had a negative impact on Indo-Pakistani relations. But while these receive intense publicity both in the region and outside, what is less often noted is that such confrontations are not necessarily indicative of the general trend in the relationship between religious communities in much of South Asia. One never hears of Hindu-Buddhist riots in Nepal or Buddhist-Hindu-Muslim riots in Sri Lanka. And even in India, Hindu-Muslim riots are the exception rather than the general rule, and directly involve only a minute proportion of the members of both religious communities.

The distribution of linguistic/ethnic communities in the various states of South Asia further complicates the problem caused by the religious heterogeneity. Bengalis, both Muslim and Hindu, constitute about 98 percent of the population of Bangladesh and are also the majority in the neighboring Indian states of West Bengal and Tripura and a substantial minority in Assam. Punjabis form 66 percent of the population of Pakistan and a majority in the Indian states of Punjab and Haryana. Urdu, the national language of Pakistan, is the home language of more families in India than in Pakistan. There are also substantial numbers of Hindi-speaking people in Nepal, Nepali-speaking people in India and Bhutan, Tamil-speaking people in India and Sri Lanka, and Pushtu-speaking people in both Pakistan and Afghanistan.

Indeed, there are at least 20 major languages and several hundred minor languages in South Asia. As an obstacle to regional integration, however, this diversity is somewhat modified by the fact that English is a common language of communication between most of the political and intellectual elites throughout the region. At the elite level, therefore, it is probable that communications between the different countries of South Asia are less inhibited by linguistic factors than is the case in Europe, Southeast Asia, or East Asia. Overall, religious, linguistic, and ethnic affinities probably help to promote social and cultural interaction between segments of the population in the different countries of South Asia and, when combined with the useful function that English plays in interelite relations, may contribute to a sense of regional identity.

Moreover, the distribution of major linguistic groups across national boundaries has a substantial impact on communications. While the percentage of literacy in most countries in South Asia is rather low, the infrastructure of the communication system is quite well developed. The distribution of newspapers on a population basis may not be high, but virtually every house in which members of the family are educated has access to newspapers. Similarly, throughout the subcontinent, most urban homes and rural community centers have a radio receiver. And while the newspapers cater to the needs and preferences of the educated elite, in a real sense, the radio serves as the communication channel for the vast masses of the people, even in the most distant sections of the subcontinent.

Radio broadcasting services in all the countries of South Asia are government controlled, and are usually employed to serve governmental purposes, both internally and externally. But one noteworthy fact is that radio programs originating in one country often have avid listeners in neighboring countries. There was a period, for instance, during which Radio Sri Lanka's broadcasts of Indian (mostly Hindi) film songs interspersed with commercials was the most popular service all over the region. To compete, All India Radio eventually had to sacrifice its elitist proclivity for classical Indian music, which has only a limited audience even in India, for the more popular filmi gane (film songs) in order to attract listeners.

Another consequence of the diversity of radio sources in South Asia is that censorship of broadcasts by the governments of the countries has only limited efficacy. When censorship is imposed too blatantly, the audience in that country can (and does) tune in the broadcasts from neighboring states, BBC, Voice of America, or the Soviet and Chinese radio systems which broadcast in the languages of the region. The communication infrastructure in the region, thus, serves as an effective form of information exchange between South Asian societies. The use to which it is put is, of course, a function of the political climate in the region. So far, communication systems have been used more often than not to exacerbate tensions and hostilities between states, but they could serve more constructive purposes on a transnational basis.

POLITICAL BASE

South Asia has a rich diversity of political systems, encompassing most varieties extant in Third World countries in the postcolonial period. Although most of the region emerged from its colonial past with a political elite that shared a common heritage of institutions and values, socioeconomic pressures and political vicissitudes have led to the evolution of distinctly different political styles and systems. India and Sri Lanka have continued to function as democracies that can be classified within the broader British tradition, although India's parliamentary system was put to a severe strain during "emergency" rule in 1975-1977 and Sri Lanka introduced a unique combination of presidential and parliamentary systems in 1977. During more than half of the period since independence in 1947, Pakistan has had a political system in which the military was the dominant institution; in other periods it has had a modified parliamentary system but always one that lacked certain of the essential ingredients required to make it a functioning democracy. Following its emergence as an independent state in December 1971, Bangladesh first experimented with a democratic parliamentary system modeled after that of India, but then introduced for a short period in 1975 a one-party authoritarian parliamentary system. Since the coup of August 1975, the military has been the dominant institution in a way not too dissimilar from that of Pakistan before 1971 and since 1977. The Himalayan kingdoms of Nepal and Bhutan have retained systems in which the monarchy is the dominant institution, but with very different kinds of political infrastructures underlying the royal authority. Afghanistan had a traditional limited monarchy until 1974, a limited military regime from 1974 to 1978, and has had a limited Soviet-type communist regime since 1978.

It can be assumed that some degree of consensus on political systems and values contributes to regional integration and capacity for cooperation. It was not coincidental, for instance, that India's relations with Nepal were best in the period before the royal assumption of absolute powers in 1960, and with Bangladesh while it had a functioning parliamentary system; the recent improvement in relations with Pakistan also began during the period when Bhutto headed the first and only popularly elected government in Pakistan's history.

Similarities between national political systems and values in the subcontinent, however, are unlikely to play a crucial role in regional integration, as these are almost as diverse as the number of countries involved. Secularism, democracy, and socialism have been the basic values underlying the Indian political system, and ones on which there is a broad national consensus. But Pakistan is avowedly nonsecular, with Islam defined as the basis of its political and social systems. Bangladesh included secularism as a fundamental principle in its 1972 constitution, but developments since the 1975 military coup have been in the direction of a revival of Islamic influences in its political culture. Nepal defines itself as a Hindu Indoaryan monarchy; Sri Lanka and Bhutan are Buddhist societies. While generally tolerant toward minority religious communities, the political institutions of these states are based on their dominant religious culture and they all specifically reject the concept of secularism.

Nor are democracy and socialism political values on which there is any broad agreement in South Asia. A number of regimes in the subcontinent have, on occasion, proclaimed their adherence to these principles, but have only rarely practiced what they preached. Democracy has been more an objective than a reality in South Asian societies other than India and Sri Lanka; developments in 1979 led to some liberalization of the political systems in Bangladesh, Nepal, and Pakistan, but not yet to their democratization. The Bhutto government in Pakistan, the Bandaranaike government in Sri Lanka, and the Mujib government in Bangladesh identified themselves as "socialist," but the successor regimes in these three countries are distinctly nonsocialist in policy and principle. For that matter, the Indian governments since the March 1977 elections have been more ambivalent in their attachment to socialism, but have not yet moved as far toward alternative economic, political, and social values as the regimes in neighboring states.

Tremendous diversity in national value systems, whether "traditional" or "modern," has certainly been a major obstruction to regional cooperation and integration. The religious heterogeneity in the different countries of the region is an obvious case in point. The maltreatment of Muslims in India or Hindus in East Pakistan before 1971 had been a constant issue in dispute between the two countries. The autonomy demands of the Hindu Tamil population in the Buddhist-majority country of Sri Lanka and of the Nepalis of Indian origin in southern Nepal complicate both states' relations with their giant neighbor. There is, thus, a strong cultural as well as a political and economic base to the evident concern with which all the other South

Asian states approach their relations with the "dominant power" in the region – India.

The hypothesis that similar political and cultural values are required for regional integration requires several qualifications, however, the most important of which are the dictates of pragmatism. When states are so situated that they impinge on each other's security and economic development, it becomes imperative for them to interact with each other despite fundamental systemic differences. For instance, while India's preferences for democratic regimes in South Asia is evident, New Delhi has, over the past three decades, learned – rather slowly at times – to come to terms with authoritarian systems in neighboring states. This is now a basic principle of Indian policy toward the region.

Another important factor in this respect is the elite structure in South Asia. Whatever their system of government, the elites in all the countries of the region are basically similar in composition. The extent of participation in the political process by the rural masses is marginal, even in those societies where the political system is parliamentary and democratic. The ruling elite is drawn from the landed class, the professional class, and/or the industrial and commercial class. In India, it is a combination of the three. In Pakistan, Bangladesh, Nepal, and Sri Lanka, it is the landed class and the "bourgeoisie." In Bhutan it has been the landed class but with the educated professional class assuming a more prominent role in recent years. While these elite groups are prepared to accept some changes that do not adversely affect their position, they all have a vested interest in the preservation of the status quo, both internally and regionally. In April 1971, for instance, when the government of Sri Lanka was seriously threatened by a revolt led by educated rural youth with radical objectives, both India and Pakistan quickly came to the assistance of the beleaguered regime in Colombo at a time when their own relationship was seriously deteriorating.

Given the affinity of interests among the ruling elites of the countries of South Asia, it may prove possible for them to interact and cooperate for common economic, political, and security goals if the disputes and tensions which impinge directly on their national interests can be resolved and a climate of confidence created. Moreover, most of their intellectual elite has been socialized in similar intellectual traditions, and the large majority in all these countries expresses support for such concepts as parliamentary democracy, "rule of law" rather than the personal whim of a ruler, and a more egalitarian society. There is, thus, a broad congruence in elite values and culture that contrasts with the broad differences in traditions and religion.

Moreover, there would appear to be basic similarities in the decision making process on foreign policy issues in all of the South Asian countries. In each of these states, including those with democratic institutions, foreign policy has been the preserve of a few top political leaders and the professionals in the foreign ministries on all but a few occasions. Only very rarely and under special circumstances have other political institutions – the cabinet as a body, the parliament or national assembly, or political parties – had any significant impact on decision making on critical foreign policy issues. Popular views and sentiments do set some outside limits on foreign policy, of course (e.g., no Indian government could make major concessions on Kashmir to Pakistan or on the boundary dispute with China without risking instant removal); but, for the most part, such parameters are so imprecise and easily manipulated that they do not constitute a serious limitation on foreign policy options.

This does not mean that foreign policy issues are not used for domestic political purposes, by both government and opposition forces. It has been a common phenomenon, for instance, for Pakistani regimes to raise the Kashmir dispute with India whenever the internal political situation was getting out of hand, presumably to distract the public from more immediate problems. But these issues are raised and then dropped with little evident concern for the "principles" so loudly proclaimed; similarly, one set of governmental leaders will replace another group that the former has strongly criticized on foreign policy issues, but then retain that policy virtually intact once in office. One case in point is the Janata government that replaced the Congress regime led by Mrs. Gandhi in March 1977. In opposition, the Janata had been strongly critical of the "too close alignment" with the Soviet Union and the abandonment of "true nonalignment"; in office, the new government did not significantly modify Indo-Soviet relations and, indeed, tended to use the same laudatory language as its predecessor in referring to the Russians.

From past experience it is not too clear if the similarity in foreign policy decision making styles has been a positive or negative factor in the improvement of relations between South Asian states. Until the early 1970s, the foreign policy elites in these countries were dominated by cliques that had learned their lessons in the strife-ridden postpartition era in the subcontinent and in the cold war period globally. On balance, therefore, the elitist character of the decision making process probably tended to prolong rather than resolve disputes. More recently, however, newer groups have emerged at the higher levels in the foreign ministries in South Asia, and these appear to be more concerned with the lessons to be learned from past mistakes and in correcting these where possible. The impression one receives is that the new elites are somewhat more open to alternative policies than were their predecessors, and that they are much less of an obstacle to bilateral or multilateral cooperation in the region.

REGIONAL FOREIGN POLICY BEHAVIOR IN
SOUTH ASIA

The whole South Asian region constituted an integrated foreign policy system until 1947. The area now comprising India, Pakistan, and Bangladesh was the core of that system, with Afghanistan, Nepal, Tibet, Sikkim, Bhutan, and Sri Lanka as peripheral territories important mainly because of their relevance to India's security. The British Indian Empire was the focal point of the entire region's foreign policy, as ultimately defined in London. The British representatives in adjacent areas, even while in direct contact with London, were supposed to coordinate their activities with New Delhi. And the primary goals of the foreign policies were the defense of the British Indian Empire and the preservation and promotion of British economic interests, as served from India. The objects of the foreign policies of the states of the region were the adversaries of Britain, actual or potential, such as France, Russia, or China. In other words, with regard to foreign policy, the region was outward looking.

The situation underwent a fundamental change in 1947 when the British withdrew from the subcontinent after partitioning the mainland into India and Pakistan. The region now consisted of five units – India, Pakistan, Afghanistan, Nepal, and Sri Lanka (for purposes of foreign policy decision making, Sikkim and Bhutan were the responsibility of India). In 1971, Bangladesh emerged as a sixth unit. The change pertained not merely to the number of units which were now responsible separately for their respective foreign policy processes, but more importantly to their perceptions of foreign policy environments. For each of them, the region itself became the primary element, and extraregional powers were relegated to a secondary position. And what loomed larger than anything else in the intraregional environment was the mutual distrust of India and Pakistan. India has been the single largest factor in Pakistan's foreign policy decision making. Indian foreign policy was also preoccupied with Pakistan, although there have been other global and regional issues important to New Delhi. For Afghanistan, Pakistan has been the primary foreign policy concern, although the Soviet Union, India, and Iran are major elements in its foreign policy environment. For Nepal and Sri Lanka, India has been the dominant factor, and their relations with China and other nonregional powers were determined by their relations with India. For Bangladesh, because of the circumstances attending its birth, India loomed large in its perspective until after 1975 when it started reaching out to the Muslim world, the West, and China as counterbalances to the Indian presence.

Since 1947, therefore, the countries of the region have become inward looking, with the region itself as the primary focus of their foreign policies. For the states other than India, the rest of the world was important primarily for the extent to which it helped limit their vulnerability to pressures from Delhi. Gradually, however, they have all been drawn into the nonaligned Third World movements and have identified themselves with these forces for the realization of some of their aspirations. Such identification helped the smaller units in South Asia to diversify international contacts in pursuit of their foreign policy objectives.

For the countries of South Asia, as for most others in the world, security and economic development are the twin goals of foreign policy. Security, however, has been defined in the broadest terms. Most countries of South Asia are as concerned about the security of their political systems as their national frontiers. Some ruling groups have felt their political systems threatened from within by dissidents allied with neighboring states. Such has been the concern of Nepal vis-a-vis India, Pakistan vis-a-vis Afghanistan and India, and more recently of Bangladesh vis-a-vis India.

Security as a primary goal of the foreign policies of South Asian countries has, at times, given rise to contradictions because of inequalities in the size and capabilities between India and the other states. Pakistan has invariably exhibited extreme apprehension of Indian objectives in the region, and this assumption of India's hostility has only recently been somewhat mitigated by the post-1971 Indo-Pak detente. India, in turn, has been critical of Pakistani alliances with extraregional powers which propped up its military capability. Nepal has also expressed concern over the possibility of Indian encroachment on its sovereignty, a sentiment shared to some extent by Bangladesh since 1975. The feelings of insecurity in the region derive mainly from this latent mutual distrust based on perceptions of behavioral patterns and basic attitudes.(3)

Economic development as a common foreign policy concern has led to a greater convergence of interests, in some respects at least. All the countries of the region belong to the lower segment of the underdeveloped world (even though India has developed a significant industrial base), with an average per capita GNP (1975) of $122 (ranging between $150 in India and Sri Lanka to $70 in Bhutan). All of them are still basically agrarian economies, and suffer from malnutrition, poor health, and illiteracy on a large scale. All need technology and capital to varying degrees, and in United Nations, Afro-Asian, or Third World forums pursue common bargaining strategies toward the developed world in their quest for a new international order, despite the fact that their immediate economic interests at times give rise to sharp contradictions between them. These contradictions are unavoidable, perhaps, in a short-term perspective, because of the enormous advantages enjoyed by India in terms of its resource base and level of development. Whatever reservations or suspicions the smaller states have about India, however, tend to be overshadowed by the fact that they are dependent on India in times of crisis. This is an economic reality which, in recent years, is beginning to give rise to an awareness that the best strategy for their own development, perhaps, might be cooperation with other states of the region.(4)

We shall analyze the foreign policy patterns of different states in the region in terms of their relations with India. The Indo-Pak relationship and its impact on the South Asian system will be considered first, not merely because India and Pakistan are the most important states of the region, but also because their intermittent conflicts have been the single largest obstacle to the evolution of a regional outlook. The two countries together comprised (until 1971) about 90 percent of the territory and population of the subcontinent. They gained independence in 1947 in the context of a bitter ideological conflict within British

India which continued to be a major determinant of their relationship in the postindependence period. The first violent symptom of this conflict was the Kashmir war which broke out within a few weeks of independence and lasted well over a year. The war, and Pakistan's nonacceptance of Kashmir's accession to India, set the tone for the subsequent 25 years of Indo-Pak relations. The essence of this relationship was distrust which, at times, was all-pervasive. Problems that should have been easily resolved in a few rounds of negotiations dragged on for years. The mainland of South Asia, already suffering from abject poverty and malnutrition, was subjected to a succession of wars between India and Pakistan.

The Kashmir war officially came to an end on January 1, 1949, through a UN ceasefire resolution, but the dispute has never been formally resolved. The subcontinent found itself engulfed in other Indo-Pak conflicts in April 1965, September 1965, and December 1971. War appeared to have become the principal symbol of relations between the two states. A perpetual concern with military preparedness led to an arms race between them which, in turn, provided foreign powers with a critical role in the affairs of the region. Pakistan became a member of the Central Treaty Organization (CENTO) and South East Asia Treaty Organization (SEATO), two American-sponsored military alliances in Asia, through which it acquired billions of dollars worth of arms, equipment, and training. India diverted a proportionate amount of resources (some acquired through American economic assistance) to the acquisition of arms and armament technology from diverse sources. In a sense, the cold war was injected into the subcontinent, hardly the kind of environment to encourage the states of South Asia to think in regional terms.

The 1971 war proved to be a watershed in Indo-Pak relations. The secession of East Pakistan as the independent state of Bangladesh brought about a basic structural change in the South Asian regional system. It affected the balance of power in the region by reducing the size and capability of Pakistan(5) and adding another actor on the eastern flank of India. At the same time, it removed a potent source of Indo-Pak conflict by eliminating a major internal contradiction in Pakistan which had often had spillover effects for India. More significantly, the decisive defeat of Pakistan in the 1971 war led to a basic rethinking in the minds of its ruling elites on the feasibility of armed conflict as a method of resolving Indo-Pak contradictions. The geographical boundaries drawn between India and Pakistan in 1947 (redesignated, on the eastern side, as Bangladesh in 1971) now acquired greater legitimacy in the regional context.

In the post-1971 period, India and Pakistan have dealt with each other in relatively constructive ways. The Simla Agreement of July 1972, which normalized relations in the aftermath of the 1971 war, can be interpreted as a compact of coexistence. The pace of normalization of relations, once the captured territories in each other's possession were vacated and the prisoners of war repatriated, has been mutually satisfying. One significant step, with long-term implications, was the redesignation of the ceasefire line in Kashmir as the Line of Control, and its redelineation and demarcation after some adjustments which took into account each country's strategic interests. By 1975, with the restoration of travel and communication links, trade between the two countries was resumed for the first time since 1965. The railway link between Lahore and Amritsar was restored and became the visible symbol of the improvement in relations. Soon the exchange of goods between the two countries, initially on an ad hoc basis, helped meet each other's immediate needs. With the improvement in relations, there have been occasional suggestions from both sides of complementary long-term trade arrangements or of limited industrial cooperation.

One significant effect of the detente has been an evident reluctance on the part of both countries since 1975 to comment on each other's internal political upheavals. Furthermore, they have begun to recognize significant similarities in their world outlooks which earlier had been ignored. This was apparent in India's readiness to accept Pakistan as a member of the nonaligned bloc of states in 1979, a significant policy reversal for New Delhi. Indo-Pak detente in the wake of the 1971 war, thus, brought about a qualitative change in the intraregional foreign policy environment that could prove conducive to the promotion of a regional outlook in South Asia if it should continue and deepen.

Afghanistan, though not integrally a part of South Asia, is of sufficient strategic importance as a peripheral country to have serious repercussions on the foreign policies of India and Pakistan. Historically, Afghanistan has always been regarded as of crucial importance to the defense of the subcontinent, situated as it is on the borders of Russia and Iran and directly opposite the famous Khyber Pass through which most of the land invasions from the northwest have entered the subcontinent.   The home of the sturdy and fiercely freedom-loving Pathans living in mountainous tribal settlements on both sides of the Khyber Pass, Afghanistan was a subject of special attention for the British. After the partition of British India, Pakistan inherited the difficult problem of contending with the Pathan's persistent demands for autonomy as most of them lived in the Northwestern Frontier Province (NWFP) and some in Baluchistan – the western and northern frontier provinces of West Pakistan. The problem of the NWFP was complicated by the fact that in 1947 an influential faction among the Pathans, led by Khan Abdul Ghaffar Khan, was opposed to the idea of Pakistan and partition. Their party lost the referendum on the question of whether the NWFP should join Pakistan, but they remained in the vanguard of the movement for Pathan autonomy – the demand for "Azad Pakhtunistan" (A "free" land of Pathans). The nature of this demand was never spelled out precisely, varying at times from a completely independent state to a democratically administered province with broad autonomy.

The Pakhtunistan question would have been an entirely internal problem of Pakistan but for the strong support it received from the successive governments of Afghanistan, and Pakistani suspicions of India's support for Kabul. The Afghan government's open support of the

Pathan cause, expressed frequently at the United Nations and else-where, reflected the interest of the dominant Pathan community in Afghanistan inhabiting the border regions with Pakistan. The import of this question on Pak-Afghan relations, which at times have been marred by violent raids on each other's territory, can be gauged by the fact that it once led to a breach of diplomatic relations and stoppage of trade. There were some signs that Afghanistan under Prime Minister Sardar Daud Khan (1974-1978) was trying to be more accommodative on this question. However, the 1978 coup in Afghanistan, resulting in a government headed by Prime Minister Taraki, introduced an element of uncertainty into the situation when the Soviet-supported Taraki govern-ment once again raised the Pakhtunistan question at the 1978 session of the UN General Assembly and, in 1979, alleged that Pakistan was assisting Afghan rebel forces.

India's sympathies for the Pakhtunistan demand have been generally known, and New Delhi has been acutely interested in the outcome of this question because of its strategic implications for the whole region. By the mid-1970s, however, the overriding concern of India would appear to have become the political stability of Pakistan, which has acquired added significance for New Delhi because of unstable condi-tions in neighboring Afghanistan and Iran.

The importance of Nepal and Bhutan in the region lies in their strategic location between India and China, a condition recognized by India immediately after independence when New Delhi clearly stated that it would not tolerate any threat to the security of the two Himalaya kingdoms in view of their direct relevance to the security of India. It was largely because of the strategic implications of the Chinese occupation of Tibet in 1950 that India felt constrained to intervene in Nepali domestic politics in 1951, and helped bring about a transition to a constitutional monarchy. This intervention was not welcomed by all sections of the Nepalese elite. After the 1955 death of King Tribhuvan (who had been the beneficiary of India's intervention), King Mahendra had grave reservations about India's role in Nepalese politics. Moreover, he was jealous of the rights of the monarchy and convinced of its relevance for the modernization of Nepal. His dismissal of the elected Nepali Congress government in December 1960, there-fore, brought him into conflict with New Delhi which criticized the king's action. India went to the extent of allowing Nepalese rebels to operate against the king from its soil, and Indo-Nepalese relations remained under tremendous strain for well over two years. During this period, Nepal tried to strengthen its relations with China in the fields of trade and communications as a counterbalance against India.

This phase of Indo-Nepalese relations coincided with a sudden deterioration in India's relations with China. The border war of October 1962 between India and China brought into sharp focus the strategic importance of Nepal (as well as Bhutan and Sikkim) and forced the government of India to a basic reconsideration of its policies toward Nepal. India made some accommodative gestures toward the Nepalese monarchy, and some ground rules were laid between the two countries for a mutually beneficial coexistence.

Although the Nepali anti-royalist elements were allowed to remain in India, New Delhi has prevented any substantial antiroyalist activity on its soil, even at the cost of displeasing its former friends, the democratically inclined Nepali leaders. India's repeated assurances in this regard, and evidence of compliance with them, improved the climate of relations in which the two governments sought to strengthen and expand their economic ties. The negotiations in 1976-1977 to revise the 1971 trade and transit treaty in the light of mutual experience also reflected Nepal's enhanced anxiety to assert its rights as a landlocked state. While the negotiations were dragging on, the change of government in New Delhi in March 1977 provided the requisite political climate for a compromise settlement. Two separate treaties on trade and transit, as desired by Nepal, were signed in 1978, paving the way for a much larger economic interaction between the two countries. Other areas in which cooperation between the two states is being seriously discussed on a larger scale than hitherto conceived are hydropower, irrigation, flood control, and joint industrial ventures. Thus, Indo-Nepalese relations are entering a phase which should be far more favorable to the development of a regional system than at any time since the mid-1950s.

The emergence of Bangladesh in 1971 constituted a basic structural change in the region. Bangladesh shares 2,500 miles of land frontier with India marked by few natural barriers. In part because of the decisive role that New Delhi played in the establishment of Bangladesh as an independent state, India is the dominant element in Dacca's geopolitical consciousness. Correspondingly, Bangladesh occupies an extremely strategic location for India because of its proximity to the Himalayan states, China, and West Bengal, and the turbulent northeastern hill tribes of India, making it highly relevant to the security of the northeastern section of the subcontinent.

Under the leadership of the Awami League, Bangladesh had declared itself a secular state. This, plus its adherence to nonalignment, democracy, and socialism, brought about a close relationship with India. The two countries signed a Peace and Friendship Treaty, resolved the longstanding and complicated boundary disputes, reached an interim agreement on the distribution of Ganges River waters by the Farakka Barrage project, entered into long-term trade arrangements, and drew up several schemes for industrial cooperation – all between January 1972 and August 1975. There was also evidence that the two countries shared a common perception of the nature of the international system and the role of the superpowers.

With the overthrow of the Awami League government in August 1975 and the eventual establishment of a military regime, Bangladesh began to perceive its interests differently. The charge of Indian dominance, a common feature in some other neighboring countries, was raised in certain circles. Secularism gave way to greater emphasis on the Islamic way of life. Relations with Pakistan were normalized, and Muslim theocratic influence increased through the enhanced presence of Arab money and Islamic religious leaders. This was accompanied by another spurt of migration of the Bangladesh Hindu minority community into India, and violent incidents on the India-Bangladesh border which were attributed to India's interventionist designs. This conflictual scenario was accompanied by a concerted propaganda campaign in Bangladesh against India's policy on the quantum of the Ganges River waters that would be diverted to Bangladesh through the Farakka Barrage during the dry season.

After a year and a half of drift in Indo-Bangladesh relations, the two governments realized the dangers involved and the need for consultation and cooperation on vital matters. Late in 1976, negotiations commenced on controlling the border incidents and resolving differences on the Farakka Barrage question, and the change of government in India in March 1977 facilitated the process. Later in 1977, the two governments reached a temporary settlement on the Farakka question, agreeing to discuss a long-term solution of the problem in the meanwhile. The border incidents were brought under control. In 1978, Bangladesh President General Zia-ul-Rahman visited India to discuss multilateral intraregional cooperation on such matters as jute marketing and joint river schemes for irrigations, flood control, etc. An interesting aspect of the changes in India's relations with Bangladesh and Pakistan was China's new interest in normalizing relations with India which, by implication at least, also must involve changes in Beijing's supportive role to other South Asian states.

India's relations with Sri Lanka since independence have never reached explosive points, but neither have they been particularly close. Both have shared some common perceptions of the international environment, particularly the relevance of the policy of nonalignment. But rapport is limited by Sri Lanka's concern over India's potential capacity to dominate the region.

One important question has been the problem created by hundreds of thousands of "stateless" persons of Tamil (Indian) origin, resident in Sri Lanka but not granted Sri Lanka citizenship. The negotiations on this issue dragged on for years. Eventually, it was settled in principle in 1964 between Lal Bahadur Shastri and Mrs. Bandaranaike, the prime ministers of India and Sri Lanka respectively. A second agreement in 1974 was welcomed by both governments, if not by the "stateless Indians" in Sri Lanka.

Sri Lanka's sizeable minority population of Tamil origin in its north and northeastern regions had become more vocal in demanding greater autonomy or even independence by the end of the 1970s. The Sri Lankan governments have occasionally expressed concern that India would exploit this Tamilian minority demand to its advantage. But India's "correct" attitude in discouraging support for Sri Lankan Tamils from India's large Tamil community has helped ameliorate Sri Lankan fears.

Both the countries have worked together in world forums on issues concerned with international order, within the general frame of nonalignment. They have publicly expressed similar attitudes on such questions as defining the Indian Ocean as a "zone of peace," although Sri Lanka has of late exhibited some reservations about identifying too

closely with India on this issue. However, the evident strengthening of
bilateral relations between India and Sri Lanka since the emergence of
new governments in both states in 1977, and an overall improvement in
the intraregional political climate have encouraged a movement toward
greater cooperation. Differences in perspectives remain, of course, but
the more important development is the evident interest on both sides to
expand and improve their relationship.

While there are still important differences on foreign policy positions and goals between the countries of South Asia, these no longer
appear as divisive as in the past. Indeed, their general positions on a
broad range of global economic and geostrategic questions are now
quite similar, and it is only rarely that they find themselves on opposite
sides in international forums on such matters as nonalignment vs.
alignment, East-West relations, or North-South economic issues.(6) On
regional security and economic issues, there are more substantial
disagreements between the states in the subcontinent, but, as we shall
note, even these are now less significant than at any time since 1947. A
regional "united front" on foreign policy may well be too much to
expect, but the serious divisions that once characterized the policies of
the South Asian states are much less evident.

REGIONAL ECONOMIC BASE

The British Indian Empire had what was, in theory, an integrated
economy, as policies for the entire subcontinent were set in New Delhi,
in consultation with London. In fact, however, the economic relationships between the different subregions of South Asia were of only
limited significance. The British were not interested in developing an
integrated economy and, indeed, tended to look upon movements in that
direction with some suspicion because of the possibility that these
would undermine the economic interests of the home country.(7)
Industrial development in British India was negligible until World War II,
and had been largely confined to two fields – textile and jute mills.
Despite the construction of an extensive and effective railway system,
the institutional structure for moving resources from one area of South
Asia to another was woefully neglected. Thus, famines could occur in
one area of British India in conjunction with surplus food production in
another; reasonably effective famine relief systems were established
only in the postindependence period. The economic system in British
India tended to be 1) subregional, 2) oriented toward trade with Britain
rather than other areas of South Asia, and 3) not much advanced beyond
a subsistence agrarian system.

Nepal, Bhutan, and Afghanistan were never part of the British Indian
empire and, thus, were never fully integrated into the British-controlled
economic system. Nepal bought a few luxury items from British India
and sold much of its food surplus across the border, but on a private ad
hoc basis. Kathmandu maintained its policy of economic isolation,
rarely allowing British or Indian firms to indulge in any economic

activities in Nepal except in the forest areas immediately adjacent to India. Bhutan's external economic relations were heavily oriented toward Tibet, both in exports and imports, except for a few luxury goods that had to be obtained from the British. Afghanistan's trade patterns were similar to those of Nepal and Bhutan – that is, some imports of luxury or manufactured products from British India – but most of its external trade was limited to exchanges within the tribal communities that straddled the Afghan-British Indian border.

Independence had quite different consequences for the various parts of British India. For West Pakistan, partition was not a particularly difficult problem economically. Some previously profitable relations, such as the sale of surplus food grains from west Punjab in Pakistan to chronically deficit areas (at that time) in east Punjab and Uttar Pradesh in India were terminated, but Pakistan had relatively little difficulty in finding alternative markets. The new manufactured products, mainly textiles, that had been provided by industries in India prior to 1947 were now available on at least as good terms on the international market, and domestic production of textiles increased fairly rapidly. A new source for tea also had to be found, but both Sri Lanka and East Pakistan provided all of this commodity that was needed. Thus, the separation of West Pakistan from India had only minimal economic consequences, and was virtually total by 1950. The main question with major economic implications concerned the division of the waters of the Indus River basin, vital to the agrarian economies on both sides of the border. This was largely resolved through the Indus Valley agreement of 1960 which not only set the terms for the division of water resources but also their development.

Partition was a much greater economic shock for East Pakistan (now Bangladesh), as it had formed an integral part of the prepartition regional economic system of Bengal and Assam but, in contrast to West Pakistan, on dependency terms. Cutting off East Pakistan from Calcutta, its port and principal source of supply for many critical goods, and from the jute mills in West Bengal in India that had processed the jute grown in the eastern wing, was a major problem. Food-grain shortages were also chronic in East Bengal once access to the normally surplus production areas in India and Nepal was closed.

At the time of independence in 1948, Sri Lanka was undoubtedly the most prosperous of the South Asian states. It was then a food surplus area and its major export crops, tea and rubber, found ready markets at good prices abroad. South Asia played a minor role in the Sri Lankan economy; Pakistan bought some Sri Lankan tea, but most of this commodity was still exported to the London market. When the world price for rubber began to decline in the mid-1950s, Sri Lanka found a reliable source in China through a series of agreements under which Sri Lankan rubber was exchanged for Chinese rice (by then a deficit crop in Sri Lanka). Trade with India was only a small proportion of Sri Lanka's total foreign trade and constituted a problem only because of the heavy imbalance in India's favor.

The post-1947 period has witnessed even greater changes in external economic policy in Nepal and Bhutan than in the former British colonies.   Under the British, the colonies had been part of the international economic order, although on different terms from sovereign states.   But Nepal and Bhutan had both followed autarkic economic policies deliberately designed to isolate their economies from surrounding areas, as well as the rest of the world. These policies were totally reversed by Nepal in the 1950s and, to a somewhat lesser extent, by Bhutan in the 1960s, in the process opening up their countries to an ever-widening range of international economic contacts. While this was not the objective in either case, the result in both has been an increasing economic dependence on India.

It was the introduction of programs directed at the development of their economies that led to the expansion of Nepal and Bhutan's contacts with the outside world. Both countries have become heavily dependent upon foreign aid – financial and technological – for their development programs, and have reached a situation where the only alternative to dependence would be the abandonment of their economic policies. Kathmandu has diligently tried to diversify its economic contacts abroad in order to reduce its dependence upon India, but with negligible success. Nepal is now an economic adjunct of the Indian economy and extremely vulnerable to any shifts and changes that may occur to the south. Bhutan has never even attempted a serious diversification policy, although some gestures in this direction, mainly involving UN agencies, have been made. Bhutan is probably somewhat less dependent upon India than Nepal, but only because its level of economic development is less advanced and its dependence upon outside resources and contacts is still of minimal importance for the living standards of the Bhutanese people. Bhutan has a self-sufficient subsistence economy for most of its basic requirements, something Nepal lacks.

Afghanistan's economic history is not too unlike that of Nepal and Bhutan, though the direction of its relationships are quite different. Afghanistan's external economic contacts with the outside world have increased substantially since 1947 but, because of both external and internal political developments, this has led to increasing dependence upon the Soviet Union for both trade and aid. Following the 1978 coup in Afghanistan, Kabul was virtually absorbed into the Soviet economic system, both through the provision of increased aid and, more important perhaps, the input of a large number of Soviet "advisers" into virtually every department of the Afghan government. The final results of this development are still unclear, but, in the short run, almost certainly will lead to a further diminution in Afghanistan's economic ties with South Asia and, possibly, to strains on Kabul's previously good political relations with the South Asian states other than Pakistan.

The South Asian regional economy, thus, has both complementary and competitive attributes, with neither predominating at this point in time. The critical factor in this respect is the central role of India in interstate economic relations in the region. While the other South Asian states do have limited economic contacts with each other, and are interested in expanding these, in all cases their main economic relations are with India and/or extraregional powers. Therefore, any analysis of the basis for a regional economic system must focus upon India's economic relations with the other South Asian states and upon their attitudes and policies toward the institutionalization of regional economic cooperation.

The complementary aspects of interstate relations in South Asia are most evident in India's economic ties with Nepal and Bhutan. In these two cases, there has been a relatively effective, if informal, division of labor and functions over the past three decades that amounts to a modified form of a common market. We can expect this to expand in the future whatever policies may be adopted by the respective governments, as both Nepal and Bhutan have no viable alternatives. Some Nepalis, including a few in high official positions, project China as a balancing factor in Kathmandu's external economic relations, but two decades of sustained effort to turn this wish into a fact have produced few concrete results, and prospects for the next decade do not seem more auspicious.(8)

However, there are problems in the Indo-Nepali relationship that must be resolved before a more institutionalized economic cooperative system will be possible. One chronic problem has been the terms under which Indian investment in Nepal's industrial and commercial development is allowed. While Kathmandu recognizes that Indian investment, both financial and technological, is essential to industrialization in Nepal, it has adopted policies that in net effect have tended to discourage investments by the more established and responsible Indian industrial and commercial enterprises. In the process, this has left the field open to Indian entrepreneurs who want to make a "quick rupee" and then get out. The results have not been satisfactory for Nepal (except for the few official and private Nepalis who are given a share of the profits) as it has not had lasting economic benefit; nor has it been a happy situation for New Delhi, since profits for the Indian investments in Nepal have often required the smuggling of imported goods across the border into the Indian market. Finally, in 1978, India and Nepal were able to agree upon new terms that should result in both larger and better structured Indian investment in Nepal's industrial development.(9) The economic consequences for Nepal are likely to be favorable, but some Nepalis object to the inevitable accompaniment to this policy – that is, a greater degree of economic integration with and dependence upon India.

More critical to both India and Nepal, however, are the terms on which the vast water resources that flow through Nepal into the Ganges River system are to be controlled and exploited. The floods that periodically inundate large sections of the Indian states of Uttar Pradesh, Bihar, and West Bengal – as well as Bangladesh – can never be tamed without Kathmandu's cooperation in the construction of river control facilities in the Nepal hill areas. There are wide differences between the two governments on certain technical aspects of the

proposed river development programs, but these are probably negotiable. Less susceptible to resolution are the differences between
Nepal and India on the institutional basis for such programs. New Delhi
has insisted upon bilateral agreements which exclude third powers,
including international organizations such as the World Bank. Nepal
prefers multilateral systems that would include not only other South
Asian states – Bangladesh and Bhutan, in this instance – but also
nonregional powers, as Kathmandu finds any kind of relationship with
India unpalatable unless there are balancing external forces.

This attitude is even more evident in Bangladesh's position on
regional water control projects. Bangladesh suffers only somewhat less
than India from the floods that inundate the Ganges plain, and, thus,
also has a vital interest in a river control system in the Himalayas. But
it has taken much the same position as Nepal on a regional water policy
for the northeast of the subcontinent, thus complicating even further
the process of negotiation on this issue. There were some hopeful signs
of more conciliatory positions by all sides in 1979, however, and the
prospects for a settlement based on a multilateral agreement involving
only South Asian states have improved.

India's economic relations with its most important neighbor, Pakistan, have been neither competitive nor complementary to any significant extent for nearly three decades, as the two societies have been
virtually isolated from each other since 1947. But there have been
several instances of mutually beneficial exchange. In 1975, for instance,
Pakistan had a large surplus of cotton, some of which was exported to
India on an ad hoc basis to meet a shortage. And in 1978 and 1979, India
had large wheat surpluses at a time that Pakistan was very short of this
vital food-grain. New Delhi offered to supply Pakistan with wheat on a
one-time basis, but also suggested a broader agreement that would
involve long-term policies to meet similar situations in either country
in the future. Islamabad expressed interest, but wanted time to consider
both the economic and political consequences of such a relationship.
Pakistan would probably still prefer to emphasize economic ties with its
Islamic neighbors to the west, but developments in Iran and Afghanistan
in 1978-1980 were certainly not encouraging to Islamabad in this
respect. The large quantities of foreign exchange that Pakistan earns
from remittances by Pakistani nationals employed in the oil-producing
West Asian states has eased, to some extent, Pakistan's chronic
economic crisis, but this cannot be considered a long-term solution.
Greater economic involvement in South Asia, which by necessity
involves increased interaction with India, may become increasingly
attractive to Pakistani decision makers if the government of India
maintains a liberal position on this and other questions concerning
relations with Pakistan.

India's role in the liberation of Bangladesh in 1971 seemingly set the
base for a cooperative, complementary economic relationship. India
needed and wanted Bangladesh's surplus fish and jute production, while
Bangladesh required massive food-grain imports and Indian manufactures. There were rather extensive economic relations between the

two countries for about three years, but on a crisis basis that did not establish institutional foundations. By 1975, it was obvious that there were serious differences between India and Bangladesh on economic and other issues. These became even more important with the assassination of President Mujibur Rahman (Mujib) and his replacement by a military-dominated government that wanted to end what it perceived as a client-state relationship to India. Dacca introduced an economic diversification policy that was primarily intended to reduce the economic dependence upon India. It has avidly sought foreign investment (other than Indian) for a wide range of ventures, including a revival of its own jute industries, the exploitation of natural gas resources, and the establishment of consumer industries.

Bangladesh's economic policies were, to some extent, the consequence of New Delhi's unfriendly and threatening attitude in the period between Mujib's assassination in 1975 and Mrs. Gandhi's electoral defeat in 1977. In that critical period, there were several alleged instances of covert Indian interference in support of antigovernment forces, as well as a hard-line approach on critical economic and development issues – e.g., the Farakka Barrage project. Since the change of government in New Delhi in March 1977, there has been a substantial improvement in Indian-Bangladeshi relations. But a number of difficult problems remain: a long-range agreement on a river control system for both the Ganges and the Brahmaputra; a trade agreement that would replace the present system of exchange based on smuggling; and the terms of investment for Indian firms in Bangladesh.

There can be no doubt that economic cooperation on a wide basis is essential to Bangladesh and important to India. Despite some success in Dacca's efforts to diversify its economic relations and attract a variety of external sources of support, it is unlikely that Bangladesh can become economically viable without a close working relationship with India, unattractive as this may be to many Bangladeshis for political and cultural reasons. Alternative sources of outside support are limited and, in any case, cannot provide much assistance in the resolution of some of Bangladesh's most critical problems such as control over water resources which, inevitably, require agreements with India. For India, Bangladesh is an integral part of the northeast section of the sub-continent, an extremely difficult and vulnerable area for New Delhi both politically and economically. Bangladesh as a "basket case," not an unreal prospect, would be an impossible burden for India.

A cooperative economic system that encompasses virtually all forms of interaction between the two states is important to both. But it would have to be a cooperative system in the true sense of the term for it to be acceptable to Dacca, and there is some question whether this is possible. It seems unavoidable that an expanded Indo-Bangladesh economic relationship would have certain neocolonialist overtones, as there is no way this could even approximate a relationship between equals. The vital questions for Dacca are: first, do the economic benefits of the Indian connection outweigh the political disadvantages; and second, will New Delhi maintain a comparatively liberal and cooperative attitude or revert to the more narrow self-interest policies that prevailed under Mrs. Gandhi. The trend has been toward more realistic appraisals of their economic and political relationships on both sides; while the obstacles to cooperation in a regional-based economic system are still formidable, the possibilities for significant changes in the direction of greater cooperation are encouraging.

Sri Lanka's economic relations with South Asia are similar to those of post-1971 Pakistan, limited in quantity but potentially of considerable importance. Trade with and aid from other South Asian states, including India, forms only a small proportion (approximately 10 percent) of Sri Lanka's total. This constitutes a continuation of the situation before 1947 when Sri Lanka's primary external economic contacts were directly with the colonial power. But while South Asia did not loom very large in Sri Lanka's economic policies, there were some important indirect factors. Competition with India in the world tea market, for instance, has been a major problem for Colombo since the mid-1960s when a buyer's market has generally prevailed. Several attempts in the 1970s to coordinate Indian and Sri Lankan tea exports in order to raise world prices were unsuccessful. Sri Lanka, which still earns about 60 percent of its foreign exchange from tea exports, has been much more adversely affected than India, but has also been more cautious in its response to proposed remedies. Once again, this would seem to be a case where political rather than economic factors have determined policy.

The government in Colombo is now seriously reconsidering the priorities previously set, as the high price paid for some of its economic relations with nonregional powers is more clearly comprehended. The rice-rubber agreements with China, for instance, are now viewed with some skepticism. There has been nothing particularly unfair to Sri Lanka in these agreements, as the prices Beijing has paid for Ceylonese rubber and charged for Chinese rice were not much out of line with the international market. There were, nevertheless, negative consequences for Sri Lanka in this commodity exchange system. The rubber could have been sold on the international market and the foreign exchange earned used to support a diversity of economic development programs. Instead, Sri Lanka received rice for its rubber, and this had two negative results: first, it discouraged a shift from rice to less expensive food-grains; and, second, and most destructively, it allowed the Sri Lankan government to continue the popular but economically disastrous program under which rice was distributed at highly subsidized prices.

The new Sri Lankan government elected in 1977 sought to revise economic development programs along lines quite different from those of its predecessors. Some of its policies, such as the "free industrial zones" program, are directed primarily at nonregional powers; but there is also a greatly expanded emphasis upon economic relations with other South Asian states, in particular India. Colombo hopes to create a more balanced trade relationship with India — in 1978 about 30-1 in the latter's favor — by persuading New Delhi to grant special treatment to some imports from Sri Lanka. Even more important, discussions on the expansion of Indian investment in Sri Lanka, through both the "free zone" program and joint projects, were held in 1978 with some encouraging results. The trend is toward greater Sri Lankan involvement in the South Asian regional economy. While it will be some time before a balance between regional and extraregional economic ties can be achieved, Colombo is now more receptive to regional economic cooperation, possibly even on an institutionalized basis, than at any time since 1947.

Prospects for Regional Economic Cooperation

Most of the popular and much of the scholarly literature on South Asia's economic potential is focused on the deficiencies in past performance and the supposedly bleak, sometimes horrifying, prospects for the future. What is often ignored is the fact that South Asia has a substantial resource base, both material and human, that provides some grounds for more optimistic projections. Mineral resources are only beginning to be developed, but already are becoming an important item in trade with the outside world – e.g., India's iron ore exports to Japan. There is even the prospect that South Asia may become a net food exporter (it already was in the late 1970s) rather than the great burden on the rest of the world forecast by the gloom and doom prophets. South Asia's record in this respect is not unimpressive, comparing favorably with that of China and only somewhat less so with the noncommunist societies in Southeast Asia. Bangladesh and Pakistan are the major problems at this time in food production, but their requirements can be met on a regional basis if production trends over the past two decades are at least maintained.

The situation with regard to human resources is even more encouraging, as the South Asian states have made intensive efforts to develop educational and training institutions. In contrast to most of the Third World, South Asia has a large surplus of highly trained, competent managerial and professional people; indeed, the "export" of this "commodity" has become a major source of foreign exchange earnings for India, Pakistan, and Bangladesh. The oil-producing West Asian states have been the principal beneficiaries of this particular resource exchange, but several Western states have also profited – e.g., the importance of Indian and Pakistani doctors to the nationalized medical system in Britain. While there has been some concern over this "brain drain," the fact is that there is still a plentiful supply of trained people available in the region for most developmental tasks.

Within the region, it will not be possible to promote extensive complementarity, and regionwide agreements on this issue will be difficult to achieve. But a fairly broad degree of complementarity is already evident, and increasingly important in some major fields. A regional food policy, for instance, would be beneficial to all, and would be complicated to only a minor extent by competitive national interests. Deficits in one area, common to regions in which production is still heavily dependent upon favorable weather, could usually be met by surpluses in other areas of South Asia. This would also have a positive effect upon another common problem in the region – temporary high inflation in prices due to localized shortages. Such cooperation has already been established on a de facto basis between some South Asian states – e.g., India and Nepal – and is capable of expansion on a regional basis.

A division of labor on rational resource and capacity terms in the industrial sphere is a greater problem, largely because of India's comparative advantage over the other South Asian states in industrial development and the latter's unwillingness to accept this as a permanent feature of the region's economy. But the Indian advantage in industrialization is still limited, and the capacity for extensive industrial development that either supplements Indian capacities or reaches into new spheres is still enormous. The psychological obstacles to agreement on an institutionalized regional system in this section of the economy, however, should not be underestimated. This would require acceptance by the other South Asian states of a broad degree of integration of their own industrial development with that of India, and this would be difficult for the elites in the other states. It would also require a willingness on the part of India to avoid intruding into industrial spheres critical to its neighbors, and the political and psychological underpinnings in India for such a policy of restraint are only now becoming evident.

It is unreasonable to expect a cooperative regional economic system in South Asia similar to the EEC or perhaps even the more modest ASEAN model. Nevertheless, the overall trend in the past few years has been toward expanding regional economic relations in South Asia. Whether this can be accomplished within the framework of a coordinated structure rather than the more informal approach now used will depend to a large extent on India. If New Delhi can learn to exercise restraint and develop a sense of regional responsibility, in the process expanding its vision of India's interest from the narrowly national to the regional level, the future may hold greater promise in this respect than anyone would now predict. The response of the other South Asian states is also very important, of course, but this depends largely upon their perception of India's policies and objectives.

SECURITY ISSUES

South Asian Perceptions

For an area well protected by formidable natural barriers, security is a major problem in the subcontinent. Much of the focus is on intraregional security problems, and in this respect South Asia is no different from other regions of the world. A millennium before Machiavelli, a great Hindu theorist on international relations had stated in precise language the operating principle for all states: don't trust your neighbor who is your natural enemy, but rather look for support from the states beyond who are your natural allies. Or, as a supplementary principle, if you happen to be surrounded by two or more larger states, play them off against each other.(10) The history of South Asia, up to and including the present day (e.g., India's supportive relationship with Afghanistan directed at their mutual "enemy," Pakistan; or Nepal's China-India balancing act), demonstrates that this advice has been heeded.

There is, however, also a well-developed consciousness in South Asia on extraregional security issues, determined primarily, as one would expect, by the subcontinent's historical experience. In the pre-Western colonialism period, the northwest of the subcontinent was the principal security problem. This was the case even for distant areas such as Bengal or central and southern India which, since the time of the Indoaryan invasions three millennia ago, have been the victims of aggression by forces that entered the subcontinent from the northwest. Traders and settlers came in by sea, but not invading armies. For the plains area, at least, the mountain ranges to the north and east were effective barriers; Assam was periodically overrun by tribal invaders from Burma, but they stopped there. It was only with the Chinese incursion into this area in 1962 that the government of India finally recognized the major security problems on the northeast as well as the northwest.

In the sixteenth century, European invaders began to intrude upon South Asia along the only possible route – by sea. This was a novel experience for the region and, since most of the Westerners first entered as traders, not too much attention was paid to them. They were perceived as a security threat only when it was too late – and the British Indian empire was the result. While the British rulers of India are often treated by South Asian historians as a unique phenomenon, in fact, their security perceptions were almost classically regional. The major threat to the British Raj came from the northwest because of the Russian expansion into Central Asia during the eighteenth and nineteenth centuries. The Himalayan barrier to the north and the status of Tibet as an autonomous buffer area made British Indian relations with China much less threatening. This may explain why the British were, at times, willing to make generous territorial concessions to the Chinese – for instance, on the Karakoram border in the northwest – if this strengthened their position in the buffer zone that separated India from the tsarist empire.

For the hill states of Nepal, Sikkim, and Bhutan (and to a lesser extent, Ladakh, which also had to contend with Kashmir valley), the major security problem in the pre-British period was with the north – Tibet. There were occasional armed intrusions into the hills from the plains area to the south, but these were short term and easily contained. Bhutan fought numerous wars with Tibetan invaders in the seventeenth and eighteenth centuries, and it was not strictly coincidental that Nepal's first major war with an external power after its unification under the Gorkha dynasty in the late eighteenth century was with China and Tibet. But what Nepal learned from this encounter was China's limited capabilities south of the Himalayas; from that time on, China was not seen as a serious threat to Nepal's independence but rather as a potentially useful, if limited, source of support.

Nepal's war with the British 25 years later was a very different matter, as this conflict could easily have ended with Nepal's absorption into the British Indian Empire. Kathmandu's security concerns, thereafter, were primarily directed to the south. Nepal first sought to establish working relations with possible counterforces to the British – China and the Indian princely states that were still independent. But by the mid-nineteenth century, China had virtually disappeared as a factor in Himalayan area politics and all the Indian princely states had made their submission to the British. Kathmandu then successfully sought an accommodation with the British that preserved Nepal's independence at the minimum price – cooperation with the British Indian security system. Both Bhutan and Sikkim adopted similar policy stances, Bhutan with considerable success; but Sikkim, which was vital to British Indian security and trade interests, was brought under direct British control in the 1880s.

As one would expect, the historical perspective of Sri Lanka on security issues is quite different from that of continental South Asia, as all of its invaders (Indoaryans, Tamils, Muslims, Portuguese, Dutch, and British) have come from the sea. Indian Ocean politics, thus, have decided the islands' fate, which may explain why it was Sri Lanka that sponsored the UN resolution calling for the declaration of the Indian Ocean as a "zone of peace."

In the post-1947 period, the nationalist elites that came to power in both India and Pakistan inherited, perhaps subconsciously, the basic British Indian views on security issues, but applied these in significantly different ways. For Pakistan, the northwest was the principal external security problem, and the Soviet Union was the major extraregional threat. The northwest was also a serious problem for India, but for quite different reasons; it was not under direct Indian control and, thus, was outside the Indian security system. New Delhi did not consider the Soviet Union as a major threat (at least as long as it made no direct expansionist moves into South Asia), but rather as a support base for the containment of United States and Chinese involvement in northwest frontier politics. Moscow played the role designed for it by India for the most part, earning Indian plaudits, if not always the expected expressions of gratitude (e.g., support of the Soviet's Asian Collective Security proposal) in the process.(11)

Indian and Pakistani views on northern frontier security issues were also borrowed virtually intact from the British, but again developed along quite different, indeed contradictory, lines. Until 1960, both India and Pakistan sought to neutralize the Chinese by limiting Beijing's involvement in South Asia and encouraging the maintenance of Tibet as a semiautonomous entity. However, the serious deterioration in Beijing's relations with both the Soviets and Indians became public around the same time, drastically altering both Indian and Pakistani perspectives.

For New Delhi, China became the major external threat to Indian security, particularly in view of Peking's developing relationship with Islamabad. The need for a Soviet counterforce was considered essential, and raised Indo-Soviet relations to a new level of strategic importance for both states. For Pakistan, China replaced the United States in 1963 as the major external support in its disputes with India and as a point of pressure upon Moscow to moderate its support of Afghanistan's expansionist ambitions and India's regional security policy. Pakistan exploited to the fullest the opportunity presented to play off China, the United States, and the Soviet Union on both its northwest frontier with Afghanistan and its western and eastern frontiers with India — with some success in the 1960s but with disastrous results in the 1970s.

The 1962 Sino-Indian border war also turned the northeast into a major security zone for India, again with temporary advantages for Pakistan. The existence of East Pakistan as a barrier to communication between the rest of India and its northeastern frontier posed serious problems for New Delhi, not only in terms of the Chinese military threat but also as a contribution to political insecurity and tribal rebellions in India's northeastern territories. The Chinese, for instance, were able to establish training camps for Naga and Mizo rebels in East Pakistan in the late 1960s with Pakistani cooperation. On the other hand, Sino-Indian hostility substantially improved Pakistan's extremely vulnerable security position in East Pakistan. Prior to 1962, the eastern wing of Pakistan had been considered indefensible, and had served as a virtual hostage to limit Pakistani ambitions in Kashmir.   It was understood by both sides that if Pakistan intervened successfully in Kashmir, India would counter by occupying East Pakistan. After 1962, however, China was seen as an effective check upon India in the northeast. During the 1965 Indo-Pakistani war, for instance, some Pakistanis credited China with having forestalled Indian intervention on the eastern front through a loudly publicized, if patently fraudulent, exercise in gesture-making (the Chinese had not reinforced or supplied their military force in Tibet to the extent necessary). Beijing's failure to do anything but console the Pakistanis in the 1971 war with India, however, finally persuaded knowledgeable sources in Islamabad that China is not an effective counterforce to India, much less to the Soviet Union.

In any case, it is apparent by now that the major external powers involved in South Asia have rarely been decisive, and that it has been the interrelationship between India and Pakistan that posed the major security problem for both countries and, indeed, for the subcontinent. Pakistanis long maintained that India would never accept the results of partition, and were determined to reunify the subcontinent. It has been argued that Pakistan's security policy must be based on this unfortunate "fact of life" even in other disputes (e.g., with Afghanistan), and that external balances to India's superior resources and capacities are essential to Pakistan's survival.

To New Delhi, Pakistan has been a channel for the intrusion of external security threats into the subcontinent, in the first instance the

United States and then later China. But the most frightening prospect for India would be a Pakistan that has been forced to accept a status as a Soviet client state, as Moscow has far greater capacities for effective intervention in South Asia than either the United States or China. The neutralization of Pakistan, the primary objective of Indian security policy, has strongly influenced New Delhi's relations with Washington, Beijing, and Moscow. The Indian objective, of course, has been to limit the involvement of external powers in South Asia to the greatest extent possible; where this was infeasible, the attempt was made to direct their involvement along lines that were least threatening to India or, even better if possible, supportive. India has been consistently success-ful in this endeavor only with the Soviet Union; but the United States and even China have come to play roles in South Asia that are much less objectionable to New Delhi, particularly in the context of develop-ments in Afghanistan and Iran in the late 1970s.

India and the Other South Asian States

The perspective on security issues in Nepal, Bangladesh, Sri Lanka, and Bhutan is similar to that of Pakistan in that the major problem for each is their relationship with India rather than with external powers. All except Bhutan have sought to use external powers as counterbalances to India. But it was apparent by the late 1970s that these states have had, at best, limited success in developing sources of external support that could be relied upon in any crisis with India. China's failure to support Pakistan effectively in 1965 and 1971 was indicative of the limits on Beijing's reliability; the United States is obviously not prepared to confront New Delhi on any South Asian issue except possibly the security of Pakistan; and the Soviet Union has been perceived as an Indian "client state," at least as far as its role in the subcontinent is concerned. Thus, some form of agreement with India on security as well as other regional issues is seen as unavoidable, although negotiable.

One fact little noted outside the region is that all of the South Asian states except Pakistan have already been brought within the matrix of an Indian security system which is regional rather than national in scope. In some cases, this is through formal agreements; in others through the unilateral extension of the Indian system to neighboring states. In the former category are Nepal and Bhutan, both of which have treaties with India that, in effect, bring them within the Indian security system. The 1950 Indo-Nepali treaty, and in particular the secret clauses attached to this agreement, provides for cooperation on security issues, and several subsidiary agreements (such as the 1965 secret agreement under which Nepal limited itself to India as a source of arms) have expanded this relationship. Nepal has tried on several occasions to opt out of these security arrangements or at least modify their terms, but with limited success. In 1969, for instance, the prime minister of Nepal announced unilaterally that the 1950 treaty was no longer operative since New Delhi had not consulted with Kathmandu on security issues as stipulated in the treaty. But the Indians rejected this interpretation in the strongest language possible, and Nepal has never reiterated this "private view" of its prime minister. More recently, Nepal has sought "neutralization" through international recognition of its status as a "zone of peace"; but this rather bizarre attempt to extend the zone of peace concept to an individual country has been dismissed by New Delhi as unrealistic, and India continues to insist that the 1950 treaty is still in force. Bhutan is also tied to India on security issues through several agreements as well as informal arrangements, such as periodic joint military exercises on Bhutanese soil. Bangladesh and Sri Lanka have not accepted roles in the Indian security system either formally or informally; nevertheless, they are included in Indian strategic calculations for the subcontinent.

South Asia, thus, has a "regional" security system of sorts through the extension of the Indian security system to all neighboring states except Pakistan; not a formal regional system to be sure, but one that is effective in certain situations. Collaboration with India on security issues by the other South Asian states is kept on the minimal level, but can be fairly extensive during crisis periods. In 1971, for instance, India supported the Sri Lanka government when it faced a serious internal insurrection. New Delhi was prepared to move in even more forcefully if necessary to prevent the establishment of what the Indians suspected would be a Chinese client regime. Thus, the Indian security system can be used against internal as well as external threats to the political system in neighboring states, although New Delhi's behavior in this respect has not been consistent – e.g., Nepal in 1950-51 and 1961-62 and Bangladesh in 1971.

While India's neighbors usually avoid any public commitment to the Indian security system, their own security policies are based upon the assumption of an Indian guarantee against extraregional aggression. This is the case even for Nepal, which has made the most public efforts to disentangle itself from the Indian security system on several occasions. Indeed, Kathmandu's enthusiasm for expanding its relationship with China is feasible and safe precisely because Nepal is assured of Indian support if Beijing should turn hostile or should support antiregime forces in Nepal. In 1967, for instance, when China was undergoing the trauma of the Cultural Revolution and the Chinese Foreign Office came under Red Guard control, Nepal was the recipient of several vituperative and threatening notes from Beijing. Rather than respond, Kathmandu waited it out until sanity had been restored in the Chinese government, but at the same time it sought reassurances from India in the event the Chinese would actually attempt to carry out the threats to "smash the heads" of the Nepali leadership.

The major obstacle to this limited and rather unique form of regional security system has been, of course, Indo-Pakistani relations. But there were some signs in the late 1970s that even this relationship was beginning to develop along lines that would make cooperation on security issues between the two powers no longer inconceivable. Basically, this involves a subtle but potentially significant change in perceptions on both sides. New Delhi has gone a long way toward accepting the proposition that Pakistan's viability as a nation state is vital to India's interest and must be sustained. Threats from outside to the integrity of Pakistan are increasingly seen as dangerous to India. The prospect of Pakistan becoming a client state to any outside power, including the Soviet Union, is repugnant to India, and its disintegration into several ministates is viewed as equally unacceptable. New Delhi has not assumed that Moscow, acting through an Afghan client, has designs upon Pakistan; but it no longer rejects this idea as forcefully as in the past when, in fact, it collaborated with the Soviet Union in supporting Afghan claims against Pakistan. A concerted Soviet drive directed at bringing tribal minority areas in Pakistan and Iran within the Soviet sphere of influence would pose a most perplexing and dangerous policy choice for New Delhi. It is now feasible, however, that India would decide to do what it could to support its neighbor to the west by the informal extension of the Indian security system to Pakistan, incredible as this may sound given the past history of relations between the two states.(12)

Pakistan has been slow in responding to the apparent changes in India's thinking on security issues, but has at least noted them. Old suspicions die hard, and there are still several major issues dividing the two powers. While New Delhi and Islamabad have both been comparatively restrained in their statements on the Kashmir issue in recent years, it is still there and capable of being revived by interested parties on both sides. Another option open to the Pakistan government is to seek an accommodation with the Soviet Union on the best terms possible as the most effective way to counter threats from that direction. If Islamabad should adopt this as policy, India's relations with both countries would be affected. At the very least, it would make Indo-Pakistani cooperation on security issues, even on very informal terms, far less attractive to both governments.

But with Iran no longer a reliable source of support for Islamabad, and the strong Pakistani suspicions of Soviet objectives in the Pak-Iran-Afghan triangle, an accommodation with Moscow may be unattractive to Islamabad if other options seem open. A favorable Pakistani response to recent Indian overtures on what are, in fact, security issues (though described in other terms) is one possibility. The result would be the transformation and expansion of South Asia's "regional" security system along lines that were unimaginable even in the recent past, and with consequences for major external power involvement in the region that no one could foresee.

One potentially serious problem for an Indo-Pakistani accommodation on security and other issues in the 1980s is the "nuclear proliferation" question — that is, the development of the capacity to produce nuclear weapons. India demonstrated such a capacity in its "peaceful nuclear explosion" in 1974. The response by Prime Minister Bhutto at the time was that Pakistan would make any sacrifice required to match India's accomplishment in this field. But not much more was heard on this matter from the Pakistan side for nearly five years, and the general assumption was that there had been no firm governmental decision on a nuclear bomb. Morarji Desai's assumption of the prime ministership of India in early 1977 seemingly diminished the importance of this question for Pakistan as Desai was known to be a strong opponent of a nuclear weapons program for India and he quickly made this the policy of his government.

Nuclear proliferation in South Asia assumed new and more dangerous proportions in early 1979 when allegations were made in the Western press − supported by some U.S. government revelations − that Pakistan was surreptitiously proceeding in the development of a nuclear weapons system. The Pakistan government strongly denied any such intention, but failed to persuade those making the allegations. The result was a crisis in Pakistan's relations with the United States and, to a lesser extent, other Western powers at a time when Pakistanis felt seriously threatened by revolutionary developments in Afghanistan and Iran.

One theme in the literature on Pakistan's nuclear weapons program is that India, if faced with a Pakistani bomb, would opt for a bomb itself. Given the history of Indo-Pakistani relations and the still strong suspicions in India of Pakistan's role in the region, this is reasonable. But one of the more surprising aspects of the Pak bomb scenario has been the relatively restrained response in india. Before his resignation in mid-1979, Prime Minister Desai asserted that India would not reverse its no-bomb decision, even if Pakistan acquired nuclear weapons. Charan Singh, shortly after assuming the prime ministership of India in mid-1979, did assert that India would have to respond to a Pak bomb decision but quickly modified his position by noting that this was not intended to imply that India would necessarily opt for a nuclear bomb itself.

Presumably, the reluctance in Indian official circles to challenge Pakistan on the bomb issue reflected the current concern in New Delhi with improving relations with its neighbor. Moreover, the "Pakistani bomb" has not generally been depicted in either Western or Indian sources (except for some pro-Soviet publications) as directed primarily at India, as would have been the case prior to 1977, but rather at West Asia − the so-called "Islamic bomb" concept. Nevertheless, with elections in India in December 1979 and a new government based upon an uneasy coalition of diverse political groups, it may be too much to expect Indian political leaders to forego exploiting so useful a political issue as the threat from Pakistan. Nuclear proliferation has become a major issue in both countries' domestic politics and in their relations with third countries; it may well also emerge as a major obstacle to the intensive efforts by both governments to reach a consensus on a wide range of subjects − including security questions.

THE MAJOR EXTERNAL POWERS AND SOUTH ASIA

The development of multinational regional institutions is not solely determined by internal factors, of course, as external powers also wield a significant influence in one way or the other. Indeed, most regional systems have had their origin in a commonly perceived external threat, and it is only at a later stage that the benefits of economic and political cooperation become evident to the participants. It can be argued that South Asia's failure to develop regional institutions has been due, in part, to the nonexistence of an external threat; or, more precisely, to a lack of agreement as to which of the several candidates for this status actually constitutes a serious danger. Pakistan has usually cast the Soviet Union in this role, while India has shifted back and forth between the United States and China. Moreover, all the other South Asian states have until recently considered India as the major threat to their security and national integrity, and the external powers have been viewed more as essential counterbalances to New Delhi.

For much of the time since 1950, the political and economic environment in South Asia has been ideally suited for intrusions by external powers, and the most effective limitations on their influence in the subcontinent have been the result of self-imposed restraints. The most important of these external powers – the Soviet Union, China, and the United States – usually see their interests in South Asia as important but rarely vital, and thus they have the option to expand, contract, or change the direction of their involvement at their own discretion.

The conditions under which the major external powers defined their roles in the subcontinent have provided them with the opportunity to influence in positive or negative ways the interactions between South Asian states. Since the mid-1950s, the Soviet Union has generally given India the highest priority in its policies in the subcontinent and has shaped its behavior toward the other states in the region on this basis. Since India would inevitably be the principal constituent in a South Asian bloc of states, Moscow's willingness to accept India's dominant status might be classified as a positive factor in the evolution of a regional system. At the same time, however, Soviet support of India in its disputes with other regional powers has greatly enhanced the latter's apprehensions over their interactions with New Delhi and has probably helped to deter or delay the resolution of these disagreements.

Since the late 1950s, China has defined its role in South Asia in terms directly opposite to those of the Soviet Union, another unwelcome byproduct of the Sino-Soviet dispute. Following the outbreak of a Sino-Indian border dispute in 1959, China sought to encourage the other states in the region to adopt antagonistic policies toward India as well as toward any regional-based systems. This policy was continued long after it had become counterproductive for Chinese interests in the subcontinent, probably because it was an integral part of Beijing's anti-Soviet stance throughout the Third World. Any trends toward regionalism in South Asia, thus, were anathema to Beijing. At the same time, however, the Chinese have carefully refrained from becoming too deeply involved in South Asia in order to avoid embarrassment over their incapacity to support friendly states in intraregional conflicts in the subcontinent.

There were some indications in the late 1970s that China was redefining its policies in South Asia along lines that would be appreciated by New Delhi, presumably in response to India's interest in a more balanced relationship between the great powers. There is even some congruence between Chinese and Indian perceptions of developments in the Afghanistan/Pakistan/Iran area as both powers would view with great concern an expansionist Soviet policy in the highly strategic frontier region between South Asia, Central Asia, and West Asia. Quietly, if not always consistently, the Chinese have been moderating their opposition to the expansion of ties between India and other South Asian states, and recently have even occasionally encouraged such developments. Beijing cannot yet be classified as a positive factor in the evolution of a regional system in South Asia, but it is no longer implacably hostile to the concept.

The role of the United States in South Asia over the past quarter century has been much less consistent than that of either the Soviet Union or China, primarily because American motivation for involvement in this region has been more complex and implicitly contradictory. Inconsistencies in the definition of American interests, for instance, were evident in the late 1950s when Washington discouraged Pakistan from seeking a political accommodation with India through its military aid program and, at the same time, strongly supported an economic accommodation between the two South Asian powers on the Indus River question through the promise of substantial financial assistance.

One can state as a general hypothesis that the United States has usually been supportive of broader cooperation on either a bilateral or regional basis in the subcontinent as long as South Asian factors were the main consideration. At times, however, American interests in adjacent areas of Asia have had a critical impact on the U.S. role in the subcontinent in ways that have contributed to interstate conflicts in the region. The military alliances and aid pacts between the United States and Pakistan in the 1950s were primarily motivated by Washington's interest in developing Pakistan as a support base for the "northern tier" states (Iran and Turkey) bordering on the Soviet Union. One consequence, however, was the gradual hardening of Pakistan's position in its dispute with India over Kashmir and an unresponsiveness in Pakistan to proposals – some from the U.S. – for a peaceful resolution of this issue. Or in December 1971, President Nixon could support Pakistan in the Bangladesh war with India, in part as one inexpensive way to improve American relations with China and the Islamic States in West Asia, and then three months later blandly accept India's emergence as the "dominant power" in South Asia as congruent with U.S. interests.

For some very good reasons, therefore, the United States is generally seen as an unreliable element in the subcontinent, earning ill will on all sides in the process. Indians criticize Washington for its support of

Pakistan; Pakistanis are disenchanted by the failure of the United States to support them sufficiently to achieve their objectives vis-a-vis India – or any other threatening power. But while the U.S. record is a mixed one, and thus subject to criticism from all sides, the general position of Washington in both theoretical and practical terms since the early 1970s has been supportive of cooperation on a regional level in the subcontinent even if the result is the emergence of India as a hegemonic power. The United States may not be doing much to encourage a regional system, but neither is it sabotaging developments in this direction any longer. One might even argue that American reticence to assume serious commitments in South Asia has become an important factor in the growing interest of Pakistan and Bangladesh to cooperate with India on a broad range of subjects.

In general, then, the major external powers were a less significant factor in the subcontinent by the end of the 1970s than at any time in the past quarter century. There is still some ambivalence and fluctuations in their policies toward the region, but none of them appear to feel threatened by a regional system or by more comprehensive bilateral relations between India and the other South Asian states. This could change rapidly and in unpredictable directions, however, if developments in West Asia, Southeast Asia, and the Indian Ocean are such as to increase dramatically the strategic importance of the subcontinent.

CONCLUSION

While neither the global environment nor the interventionist policies of the external powers in South Asia have been conducive to the establishment of regional institutions in the subcontinent, it is apparent that the major obstructions have their origin within the region. At any point in time, the external forces intruding on South Asia have worked at cross-purposes, and the result has usually been a precarious but reasonably effective balance. One can argue that the South Asian states, if so inclined, could always have found sufficient support from outside for regional organizations to counter the obstructionist position of some external powers. The fact is that the will has been lacking, and usually on all sides. No consensus on a regional system has been possible, and for a wide variety of reasons.

No doubt the most important internal factor has been the economic, military, and political capacities of India in comparison to the other South Asian states – either separately or together. Most regional systems, other than those based upon satellite relationships (e.g., the Soviet Union and Eastern Europe), do not have a core member of disproportionate size and power. Relevant examples are the European Economic Community, the Association of Southeast Asian Nations, the Arab League, and the Organization of African States. No regional system in South Asia, however, would be possible in which India was not the dominant force. Thus, the other South Asian states have always viewed any regional system as constituting the formal institutionalization of Indian hegemony in the subcontinent – not on the Soviet bloc model, perhaps, but, nevertheless, in ways that would seriously affect their autonomy. Only very recently has it been suggested by some of their own elite that they might be in a stronger position by bargaining with India on a regional basis rather than bilaterally.(13)

One might expect India to have a positive attitude toward regionalism, but this has not been the case. During the first decade after independence, to be sure, there were several half-hearted attempts by New Delhi to organize a regional system in South Asia, but these were all victims of Indo-Pakistani hostility.(14) By and large, India has preferred a bilateral relationship with each of the other states on the subcontinent; it has not even responded favorably to suggestions for a limited multinational (i.e., nonregional) approach to the resolution of a specific problem. One recent example is New Delhi's rejection of the proposal by Nepal and Bangladesh for a multinational system to control and regulate the river systems in the north and northeastern sections of the subcontinent. Apparently, India assumed that its interests were better served by negotiating bilaterally with the states involved. This was a very shortsighted position, presumably induced by the ill-conceived efforts of Kathmandu and Dacca to include China – an extraregional power – in the multinational system they were advocating. India is not likely to agree to any regional institution in which external powers play a major role; the other South Asian states, in turn, have been disinterested in any regional system from which external counterbalances to India are excluded. While the positions of all the states in the region on this subject would appear to be moderating, the situation is still best described as a stalemate.

We have suggested earlier that there have been significant changes in the attitudes of all the South Asian governments on their interrelationships in the late 1970s. To date, this trend has been primarily reflected in bilateral agreements that have substantially expanded relations between India and the other states in the region. But these bilateral agreements may well prove to be an important transitional stage, both substantively and psychologically, toward broader-based regional institutions since they are based upon novel perceptions of mutual interests and trust by the states of South Asia. This change in attitude is still very fragile and subject to a reversion to past hostilities and suspicions unless carefully nourished, particularly in India. But interstate relations in the South Asia of 1980 are qualitatively different from what they have been at any time since 1947, and there is now a foundation on which to build regional institutions.

NOTES

(1) William J. Barnds, "South Asia," in World Politics: An Introduction, edited by James N. Rosenau, Kenneth W. Thompson, and Gavin Boyd (New York: The Free Press, 1976), p. 501.

(2) There are also numerous "tribal" communities in South Asia that do not fit into any of these "great cultures." While some of these tribes occupy highly strategic areas on frontiers, they are relatively incidental to the political and social systems in the subcontinent.

(3) Baldev Raj Nayar argues that it has been the involvement of external powers that explains the inability of the South Asian states to resolve their differences. (Baldev Raj Nayar, "Regional Power in a Multipolar World" in India: A Rising Middle Power, edited by John W. Mellor (Boulder, Colorado: Westview Press, 1979), pp. 147-79). But most of the external involvement in South Asia has been the result of regional power disputes and of invitations to intervene from these states. Thus, the external powers did not initiate the disputes, though in some cases — but not all — their intervention helped prolong them.

(4) Several responsible Pakistani and Nepali officials expressed the view, in discussion with one of the authors in 1978 and 1979, that the economic and security interests of their countries require the establishment of regional institutions. This was very different from the views expressed earlier by the same officials or others in their positions. They realized that India would play a dominant role in such institutions, but accepted this as an unfortunate but unavoidable aspect of what was, in their view, the best option open to their governments.

(5) The 1971 Bangladesh war reduced the size and population of Pakistan substantially, but it is doubtful that the Pakistan Army has emerged any weaker — at least in terms of military capability. By the end of the 1970s, the Pakistan Army was larger and somewhat better armed than at any time since 1947 and, moreover, no longer was responsible for the impossible task of defending the eastern wing of the country. Nevertheless, the 1971 war did demonstrate convincingly that Pakistan was no match for India militarily without extensive outside support, and that such support was not likely to be forthcoming under the existing global power balance.

(6) Pakistan was the only South Asian state that had followed an alignment policy through its membership in SEATO and CENTO. Pakistan withdrew from SEATO following the victory of the communists in Indochina and from CENTO after the overthrow of the Shah of Iran in 1979. In mid-1979, Pakistan was formally admitted into the nonalignment club, with Indian support. What was even more unusual was the fact that Pakistan, India, and the other South Asian states adopted similar positions on all the critical issues at the September 1979

nonalignment conference in Havana. Previously, in almost any international forum, India and Pakistan were found on opposite sides of most issues.

(7) An interesting and somewhat "revisionist" view on the subject of British Indian economic policy is G.G. Jones, "The State and Economic Development in India 1890-1947: The Case of Oil," Modern Asian Studies 13, Pt. 3 (July 1979): 353-75.

(8) The Indian embargo on trade with Chinese-controlled Tibet had, in effect, been extended to Nepal in 1963 when, under strong Indian pressure, Kathmandu agreed to ban the reexport of products that were imported into Nepal from or through India. New Delhi also obtained Nepal's agreement to strictly limit the export of Nepali products (e.g., food-grains) which the Chinese wanted. The lifting of the Indian ban on trade with Tibet in 1978 revived Nepali expectations of a substantial expansion of economic relations with Tibet, but there has been no indication of this as yet.

(9) A novel economic agreement between the Nepal government and the Orissa state government in India was signed in 1979 providing for substantial industrial investments in Nepal by the Orissa government, in collaboration with private Indian companies (The Statesman Overseas Weekly, July 21, 1979).

(10) Kautilya, Arthasastra (translated by R. Sharma Sastry) (Bangalore: Mysore Printing and Publishing House, 1915), Book VII.

(11) Baldev Raj Nayar, "Regional Power in a Multipolar World," p. 155.

(12) Indian policy on Afghanistan in 1978-1979 appears to differ significantly from the role played by New Delhi in earlier Pakistan-Afghanistan confrontations. On the most recent occasion, according to some reports, the Indian government has sought to dissuade Kabul from pressing its territorial claims against Pakistan and has also encouraged the Soviet Union to moderate its policy toward Afghanistan.

(13) On this, see Sisir Gupta, India and Regional Integration in Asia, (New York: Asia Publishing House, 1964). The lack of a substantial literature on regionalism by South Asian scholars clearly reflects a situation in which regional institutions were seen as so implausible as not to warrant discussion.

(14) See Barnds, "South Asia."

9 The Middle East
James P. Piscatori
R.K. Ramazani

The peoples of the Middle East, a land rich in ancient civilizations, gained a regional consciousness only after centuries of conquest, religious antipathy, and economic exploitation by outsiders. More than a geographical notion, the area became a political concept to Alexander the Great, the Crusaders, and the British and French colonists. Together they distinguished it as a region apart from both the West, because it is not rooted in Greco-Roman civilization, and the rest of the Orient, because of its relative proximity to the great cities of Europe. The "Proche Orient" and the "Near East" were as much cultural attitudes as they were cartographic labels. Even the currently popular "Middle East," whether designed by the American Admiral Mahan or the British Army,(1) implies only a slightly less ethnocentric presumption that it lies on an international hierarchy topped by the Anglo-Saxons.

Though surely resenting the political implications, the area's peoples gradually accepted the externally generated categorization as convenient. The "Middle East" does make sense in three broad ways. In a geographical sense, the region becomes a unit when we view it as the intersection of the world's commercial lanes and as a strategic midpoint – in an era when it separated Europe from the treasures of the Indian subcontinent and today when it lies between the special spheres of the superpowers. The Middle East is also a unit in the cultural sense, for, although its peoples are divided into several ethnic groups and languages, they are tied together by common submission to Allah. Across the region, Islam is so pervasive a factor that it fashions the governing structures of some states, influences the legal order of others, and qualifies the work of the modernizers in all. The widely-shared belief that this area is the heartland of the Islamic umma helps to strengthen regional cohesion. This cultural consciousness, finally, has given shape to the history that also helps to weave the area's nations together. For a brief period the Arab conquerors and much later, and for much longer, the Ottomans gave to virtually the entire region an administrative

274

uniformity which, regardless of the persistence of local identities, helped to forge an ecumenic attitude. Even the Persian-Ottoman rivalry should not obscure that each shaped the other's course by political and cultural borrowings.

Geography, culture, and history, then, substantiate the idea of the "Middle East." The obvious exception to this sense of belonging, however, is Israel. As Leonard Fein says, though in the region, Israel is not of the region.(2) The future, with its domination by Oriental Jews, the presence of a growing Arab minority, and the experience of comity with at least Egypt, perhaps portends the Middle Easternization of Israel. But for the present, official Judaism, European cultural affinities, the political strength of the Ashkenazis, and the intimate connection with the United States make Israel unique in, and thus different from, the region. As a result, we define the Middle East as excluding Israel, but including eighteen Arab states, Iran, and Turkey.

CULTURAL DIMENSION OF REGIONALISM

Perhaps the most basic factor of regional cohesion in the Arab Middle East is the spirit of Islamic brotherhood. It is a spirit generated by the complete submission to Allah, who, in offering a rope (habl) to foundering mankind, admonished that it not be divisive.(3) Although their harmony was soon rent by partisan divisions, Muslims persist in believing that they belong to a community of faith and that the realm they inhabit is at peace among its own kind (dar al-Islam) and hostile to outlanders (dar al-harb). This sense of unity from time to time has taken more concrete political shape. Jamal al-Din al-Afghani (1839-1897) preached the need for cooperation among Muslims in order to insure the revitalization of their thought and civilization, particularly as the Western invaders made it seem that they were deficient in these areas.(4) Pan-Islam, then, was a way to respond to the European military success in and colonial penetration of the "holy land." The unfortunate sultan Abdulhamid II (1876-1909) also tried to stir pan-Islamic sentiments in order to counter the steady rise of ethnic loyalties eroding the strength of the Ottoman Empire. He found a measure of success in this ploy, for it muted some Arab criticisms of the Empire's orthodoxy, especially with the building of the Hijaz railroad, and it earned him a modicum of prestige as the defender of the faith in an era of apparent infidel ascendancy.(5)

Since the 1960s, pan-Islam has become a popular slogan in the sense of "solidarity" (tadamun) rather than of "unity" (ittihad). Even King Faisal, its most ardent proponent, did not believe that more than a loose form of cooperation was possible or desirable in the foreseeable future. While undoubtedly sincere in proposing greater Islamic rapprochement, Faisal, in his timing, also displayed his concern with Nasser's shrill criticism of feudal monarchies in the area and his constant appeals to pan-Arabism. The Egyptian president launched, in particular, a vitriolic campaign against the Saudi monarchy, which he accused of consorting with the enemies of Arabism. With the deposed king, Sa'ud, in Cairo, Egyptian troops still in the Yemen, and the outbreak of a few antiregime terrorist acts, Faisal was understandably concerned with the attraction of Nasser's rhetoric. The king's travels in late 1965 and throughout 1966 to garner support for Islamic cooperation, then, must be seen as part of a natural effort to counter the Egyptian delegitimating criticism.(6) Though no permanent "Islamic Pact" came out of this policy, it did help to reinforce the throne by reaffirming its intimate connection with the protection of Islam's best interests.

One institution that predates Faisal's policy, the League of the Islamic World, intensified its activities only in the mid-1970s with the oil price "revolution" and its enrichment of the oil-producing Muslim countries. Accompanying the League's new activism have been regular meetings of the foreign ministers of the Islamic states since 1970 and occasional meetings of their heads of state. The first of the latter convocations, which occurred in September 1969 after the burning of the al-Aqsa mosque, suggests that political rivalries even intrude upon discussions in the name of Islam: the summit in Rabat was marked by Saudi-Egyptian and Pakistani-Indian rivalries.   Though the second summit, coming after the Arab-Israeli war and oil embargo, had its fair share of dissension (notably, Algerian-Libyan), it was more successful in displaying a rough sense of solidarity. Indeed, the members agreed to establish an Islamic Solidarity Fund "to meet the needs and requirements for Islamic unity and Islamic causes, enhancement of Islamic culture, values, and universities."(7) In the wake of the meeting, they further agreed to establish an interest-free Islamic Development Bank with a projected capital of over two billion dollars, and the more fortunate pledged aid to the poorer members through a special fund of the Organization of Petroleum Exporting Countries (OPEC) and the Saudi Development Fund.(8)

Simultaneous with these structural developments has been the growth of Islamic fundamentalist movements – a growth that has been collectively, and erroneously, labeled the "Islamic revival."(9) It is doubly wrong to allude to a resurgence, because Islam has been an enduring, vibrant, transnational force in the Middle East and beyond without interruption since the seventh century; and because fundamentalism itself is not a new phenomenon. The modern nation state of Saudi Arabia, for instance, owes its existence to a conservative reform movement headed by Muhammad ibn 'Abd al-Wahhab, who in 1744 added religious fervor to the peninsula-wide ambitions of the Najdi Sa'uds.(10) In this century, the Muslim Brotherhood (Ikhwan al-Muslimin), founded by Hasan al-Banna in 1929, has been a potent force in Egypt and elsewhere urging the adoption of the Koran as the constitution for all modern believers. It has been a particularly vigorous movement, attracting millions to its cause and attacking those who opposed its ways. For example, the Ikhwan was responsible for the murder of the Egyptian Prime Minister, Nuqrashi Pasha, in 1948, and for attempted assassinations of Nasser himself in 1954 and 1965.(11)

Although the government suppressed it for these activities, the Brotherhood has endured, much as Eric Rouleau thought it would, because the basic frictions that nourished it originally have not disappeared.(12) In fact, the quickened pace of political, social, and economic development in the Islamic states, as a result of the increase in oil revenues generally, has intensified the modern Muslim's sense of unease and convinced him of the need to fasten himself to the most traditional and reliable of anchors – Islam. The phenomenon is found in all Islamic lands, and in many countries the sense of unease has organized expression. In Egypt, there have been several splits of the original Ikhwan movement, such as al-Tahrir al-Islami and al-Takfir wa al-Hijra, both of which have engaged in notable acts of terrorism. In the Sudan the National Front exerts pressure for a more Islamic polity than that of President al-Numayri, and the revolution of Ayatollah Khomeini, of course, stands as a testament to the strength of traditional religious sentiment in modernizing Iran. Even Turkey, which developed along the secularist lines of Ataturk, has been making concessions in education and social policies to the many devout among its people since the Democratic Party victory of 1950.

While there is no evidence that these groups and attitudes are coordinated, it is clear that Islam serves as a natural attraction for the believer whose nation, town, and family are experiencing rapid and confusing changes. A New York Times commentary on the Ikhwan in 1952 is relevant to the present situation: "Student fascination with the Muslim Brotherhood is concerned with. . .his desire to discover himself. . . .What the Muslim Brotherhood offers is primarily a sense of intimacy within the common home of Islamic faith, which Western influence and modern industry and commerce were destroying."(13) It is a concern for more than the student and beyond Egypt's border; indeed, the concern is one which permeates the region.

We would be remiss, however, if we left the impression that Islam is a source of unity in the Middle East. Though it provides a considerable measure of cohesion, it is limited in its unifying potential because of divisions within the faith. The Sunni-Shia split, the most basic of them all, has been a constant source of tension since the murder of Ali in 661. Shia Islam is aptly characterized as oppositional, since its adherents have played the role well, in the Umayyad and 'Abbasid dynasties of Sunni Islam.(14) The classic rivalry was between the Sunni Ottoman Empire and the Shia Persian Empire, which has left its legacy today in a suspicion shared across the Persian Gulf – the very name of which is a subject of some controversy since the Arab states prefer "Arabian Gulf." The reaction to the success of an Islamic revolution in Iran demonstrates this suspicion, for the Saudis in particular have been uncertain as to how they should greet the nearby developments. On the one hand, they have not been unhappy to see the exile of the Shah, who had been bothersome in his overbearing policies and ostensible lack of devotion; on the other hand, they are uncomfortable with the triumph of a Shia movement, whose rites and clerical hierarchy are alien and sometimes offensive to them.

The Sunni-Shia tension also poses more immediate problems to national decision makers. The Middle East has few countries that are homogeneous and many that have significant ethnic and religious heterogeneity. The Kurds, for example, are a Sunni group whose loyalty to Shia Iran is only questioned anew by the deposition of the Shah. Shias also constitute a majority of Iraqis, but the Sunni governors have so far effectively kept them from exercising dominant power. The situation is far different in Syria where the 'Alawis are a Shia minority who, due to their cohesiveness and the clever leadership of President al-Asad, have been able to control the government. The Alevis of Turkey have had violent engagements with the dominant Sunnis, and the case of war-torn Lebanon is a timely reminder of the many divisions between Sunnis and Shias and within each fold. The intrareligious conflict gives rise not only to difficulties in building modern nation states but also to complications in foreign policy, precisely because of the transnationalism of Islam. The victory of Khomeini has undoubtedly worried the Ba'thists in Baghdad who must ponder the political effect on their own Shias. It has had a discernible effect already in Lebanon where yet another group, the Sadriyin, has emerged, named after the local Shia leader who mysteriously disappeared in 1978.

There are, finally, differences in approach to the great public issues that face the Islamic states. While most allow, and some encourage, birth control, for example, Saudi Arabia has proscribed its practice as an offense to Islam.(15) Divergence is also found in the approach to women's rights in general. Egypt has made great strides since the 1952 revolution in advancing the political and economic positions of women, and under the inspiration of Jihan al-Sadat the post-Nasser era portends even greater advances. Women have the right to vote, several have served in the People's Assembly, and occasionally there is a woman minister in the cabinet.(16) There is still, however, significant opposition to radical changes in the status quo, as evidenced by the inability of the government to enact a liberal law of personal status, similar to those found in Algeria, Iraq, Morocco, the People's Democratic Republic of Yemen (PDRY), Syria, and Tunisia. The latter has gone the furthest in directly outlawing polygymous marriages, but the others have also liberalized the provisions on women's rights in marriage and inheritance. In Iran the Shah imposed similar legal changes with the Family Protection Act of 1967, revised in 1975;(17) in light of the revolutionary government's denunciation of this law as contrary to the spirit of Islamic law, the title now appears ironic. In the PDRY, women successfully demonstrated against the veil; and Islam, though deferred to, is buried in the constitution in Article 46.(18) The clearest contrast to these examples are the countries of the Arabian peninsula where the Shari'a remains the most important part of their constitutional orders, with one result: the circumscribing of women's roles in society.

It is clear that Islam contributes positively and negatively to regional cohesion. On the one hand, its universality provides a common bond of attachment that transcends race, ideology, and place. As the broadest and most fundamental bond, it partly forms personal and national identities in the region. This attraction of Islam also renders it a handy legitimating device for rulers who must contend with diverse and often shrill demands for changes in social planning and in political development. The appeal of Islm for legitimation is both a recognition of its tremendous vitality in the area and, at the same time, an enhancement of its special significance to life there. On the other hand, Islam cannot contribute any more certainly to regional order because of ancient divisions of rite and jurisprudence and contemporary differences over the Islamic way of modernizing.

The contributions of Arabism are similarly mixed. Arabs have for a long time responded to appeals for broad unity. This qawmiyya nationalism plays on the kindred spirit of those who speak a common language and share comon heroes, but it matured only after the first signs of weakness in the Ottoman Empire. Unable to call on Islam to stir a revolt against their fellow believers, Arab intellectuals gradually inspired an "awakening" by reminding the Arabs of their special role in Islamic history and of their great and early achievements in science, philosophy, and medicine.[19] They received their inspiration from the nation states of Western Europe, and they tirelessly agitated for liberation of their eastern lands from Turkish control and their western lands from the domination of their liberal tutors. After independence, Arab nationalism continued to serve as a rally against the "neoimperialists" of the West and the new "imperialism" of Zion.

The most vibrant form of pan-Arabism has been Nasserism, the collective thinking and policies of the Egyptian leader. Eschewing a single philosophical base and suspicious of idle theorizing, Nasser gradually evolved an ideology for his country and his times. A pragmatist ever, he came to appreciate the need for the inspirational message and the symbolic gesture, and with his inexhaustible energy and mesmerizing voice, he provided both for his own people and for all who could hear him. First the protagonist of the British, then the hero of Suez, and later still the Salah al-Din of Arab unity, he seemed to become by the early 1960s the arbiter of the Arab political future. It was an extraordinary testament to his charisma, the permeability of national borders in the region, and the attraction of pan-Arab sentiment that at his command Jordanians, Syrians, Lebanese, and others would demonstrate against their governments and in behalf of some vaguely defined though passionately pursued goal.

Despite the intense emotion often associated with qawmiyya, there have been few successes at making it concrete. Attempts during the later years of World War II to unify the Arabs resulted rather in the interstate Arab League. Reality could not supplant the rhetoric of Arab unity because of significant inter-Arab rivalries, such as between Faruk of Egypt and Nuri al-Said of Iraq and between 'Abd Allah of Jordan and 'Abd al-Aziz of Saudi Arabia. The latter was perhaps most honest in his attitude: while allowing that Arabs are brothers, he made it clear that he would not tolerate any ruler above him.[20]

The League has proven itself to be a marginally effective instrument for resolving disputes when cooperation breaks down. It was unable to resolve differences between Egypt and Syria after the dissolution of the United Arab Republic (UAR), between Egypt and Saudi Arabia during the Yemeni civil war, between Egypt and Libya during their 1977 border war, between Algeria and Morocco over the Western Sahara, and between North and South Yemen in the 1972 and 1979 fighting. It has been most united recently against South Yemen, whose leadership stands implicated in the 1978 assassination of the North Yemeni president, and against Egypt, which broke Arab ranks to conclude a separate peace treaty with Israel; already, the isolation of Egypt has strengthened opposition to Israel. The current threats to remove the League headquarters from Cairo remind us of the fragility of the organization's quest for cooperation and harmony among all Arab states.

There have also been efforts at more circumscribed forms of Arab unity. Various leaders, notably King 'Abd Allah and Nuri al-Sa'id, advanced the Greater Syria Plan for the unification of Syria, Iraq, Jordan, and Palestine under a common, preferably Hashemite, government. The plan was never a serious possibility, however, because of rivalries among the principals and British-French opposition. In 1958, Nasser allowed himself to be persuaded that a union of Egypt and Syria under his leadership was workable. In fact, it was not, given the vast differences in economic, social, and political institutions and styles. The experience of this union only served to strengthen the animosity between the two pan-Arabist ideologies of Nasserism and Ba'thism. Banned as a political party of the UAR, the Ba'th reconfirmed its faith in the drive for "unity of ranks" while insisting on more democratic leadership than that furnished by Nasser in the years of the Egyptian-Syrian Union (1958-1961).(21)

Subsequent efforts at union have been equally fruitless. Egypt, Syria, the Sudan, and Libya (1971); Tunisia and Libya (1972); and North and South Yemen (1972) have agreed to unify their countries. None has so far done so. The most recent flurry of announcements on unity comes from Damascus and Baghdad whose rapprochement has generated plans for the gradual meshing of their political and economic structures. Opposition to Egypt's policy toward the Arab-Israeli conflict makes a diplomatic entente between Syria and Iraq understandable, but the vast differences in economic conditions and the bitter disagreements in interpreting their ostensibly common Ba'thism render these plans as problematical as the earlier ones in the Arab world.

In addition to the political rivalries that have stymied programs of Arab unity, there is the fact that particular nationalisms are everywhere being solidified. While qawmiyya is a potent attraction for Arabs, wataniyya is also an increasingly important way by which Arabs identify themselves; the individual is now both an Arab and a Bahraini, a Muslim and a Libyan, a Druze and a Syrian, a Christian and a Palestinian. The nation-building efforts of Sultan Qabus of Oman, the Egypt-first policies of President Sadat, and the socialization activities of the Palestine Liberation Organization confirm the great importance today of identities below that of the general Arab World. Finally, if the "great

Arab caravan"(22) takes second place to more particular loyalties for most Arabs today, it makes no demands on the loyalties of the area's non-Arabs – notably, the Turks and Iranians. For all these reasons, pan-Arabism has limited potential for stimulating regional integration.

SOCIOLOGICAL DIMENSION OF REGIONALISM

Perhaps the most noteworthy aspect of Middle Eastern societies is their ethnic diversity. This heterogeneity is doubly complicating, for it makes not only national but also regional integration difficult.   The Kurds exemplify these problems. Distinct in language, traditions, and history, they are a stubbornly rugged people who have resisted efforts by the Arabs, Turks, and Persians to assimilate them. Least successful have been the Iraqis who do not suffer their two million Kurds gladly. Alternating between a policy of cohabitation and violent campaigns, the Iraqi authorities have tried to control these descendants of the ancient Medes inhabiting now the oil-rich sectors of Kirkuk and Mosul. Most frequently, the government's efforts have met with opposition from the legendary mullah Mustafa al-Barazani, and his tribal militia, the Pesh Merga. Although the Kurds of Iraq lost their international support with the Iranian-Iraqi agreement of March 1975, and their leader with al-Barazani's death in early 1979, it would be premature to conclude that they are being successfully included in the nation-building efforts of Ahmad al-Bakr and Saddam Husayn al-Takriti. Indeed, even the pan-Arab Ba'thist ideology of the Baghdad rulers can hardly be seductive to the non-Arab Kurds.

Iran has been similarly dogged by the question of Kurdish loyalties. There was an independent Kurdish state in 1946, made possible by the weakness of the Shah and the assistance of Russian soldiers.(23) Though short-lived, this republic in northwestern Iran was tangible evidence that a significant portion of the inhabitants of Iran did not feel Iranian, and that outside powers were able to interfere easily in the fragile domestic order. If the Kurds seemed less of a problem in the past two decades, it is now clear that it was due to the autocratic policies of the central government in Tehran. The relative surface placidity quickly disappeared with the overthrow of Muhammed Reza Shah. In fact, one major problem that challenges the revolutionary government of Iran is accommodating the political demands of the Kurds without encouraging the dissolution of the nation state itself.

The Kurdish problem is essentially a transnational one, for the ethnic borders of the Kurdish nation fall in five states – Syria, Iraq, Turkey, Iran, and the Soviet Union. The abortive Treaty of Sevres had provided for an independent Kurdistan that would have covered the area of the Mosul province of the Ottoman Empire. Although there have been no efforts to unite all the Kurdish lands and peoples, there are continuing cross-border influences. The Kurdish revolt against the Iraqi government, for example, received until 1975 substantial aid from the Shah, who risked discontent among his own Kurds for the greater goal of tying down Iraqi troops. Since the change of government in Iran, the Kurdish unrest there has ramified in the Kurdish regions of Turkey and Iraq.

There are other minorities who have intimate ties with their kin in neighboring yet separate states. Iranian Arabs have been a worrisome population in the sensitive, oil-rich region which they prefer to call "Arabistan." The Baluchis of southeastern Iran also have intimate ties with the Baluchis of Pakistan, thereby affecting bilateral relations. Additionally, the Berbers of North Africa (Maghreb) are a non-Arab group whose relationship to the Arab majority has been uncertain and whose sympathies sometimes transcend present state frontiers. Constituting some 33 percent of the Moroccan population and about 25 percent of the Algerian population, they are unique in language, tribal organization, and colonial history. The Maghrebi Arab elites have actively and rather successfully sought their cooperation, but they have also aroused their suspicion and often their enmity by attempting to Arabize them along with the French-educated Arabs. While the latter lose in accent and style, the former do so in language and culture. The Sudan, furthermore, is illustrative of the difficulties of nation-building when there is significant ethnic heterogeneity. With at least one third of the Sudanese population black and, naturally, feeling closer to Africans to the south than to the Arab elite of the north, Khartoum has had to wage a costly civil war from 1955 to 1972 to preserve unity. Finally, the Armenians and Jews are, in the countries we are examining, small minorities now, due to their suffering from brutal and forced moves, severe discrimination, and extensive emigration. Though small in number, they are people along with others, whom Syria, Lebanon, and Iran have yet to integrate fully.

In addition to these intranational and transnational ethnic divisions, there are other social conditions inhibiting regional integration. One is demographic. Although census data are highly unreliable in the Middle East, it is clear enough that there are vast differences in population size. The countries range from the most populous states of Turkey, Iran, and Egypt, to the medium-range states of Morocco, the Sudan, Algeria, and Iraq, to the small population states of Syria, Saudi Arabia, Tunisia, the Yemens, Libya, Lebanon, and Jordan, to the ministates of Bahrain, Kuwait, Qatar, and the United Arab Emirates (UAE).(24) The rough coincidence of great oil wealth with low populations is a source of friction in the region, particularly as it makes the populous and poor states dependent for their basic development on the few sparsely settled and rich states. For instance, four countries of the Arabian peninsula — Saudi Arabia, Kuwait, the UAE, and Qatar — which had a current account surplus of $30 billion in 1976,(25) had, by 1978, become responsible for giving almost a billion dollars worth of aid a year to Egypt alone. When the recipients begin to resent their loss of autonomy, and when the donors demand too much, confrontation is possible, as in the rift between Egypt and its Gulf patrons in 1978-1979.

Another factor to note is the rural-urban population split. Monroe Berger concluded almost 20 years ago that three-fourths of all Arabs are inhabitants of the countryside and are tied to agriculture.(26) The main observation is valid still, although the preponderance of rural dwellers is definitely declining. One example of the change is Egypt where in 1960, 37.4 percent of the population was urban whereas 62.6 percent was rural; in 1966, 40.5 percent was urban and 59.5 percent was rural; and in 1976, 43.9 percent was urban while 56.1 percent was rural.(27) In the mid-1970s 44 percent of Iran and Turkey's populations were urban, whereas 52 percent of Algeria's and over 60 percent of Lebanon's populations were urban. Clearly, cities like Cairo and Tehran are at the point where they are unable to absorb significantly greater numbers of rural emigrants. The gradual movement from countryside to urban centers portends ill for the economic and social development of Middle Eastern countries, since they are unable to employ gainfully the new city dwellers, and the departure of workers from their rural jobs further enervates the valuable agricultural sector.

The movement could also complicate the always tenuous political stability of these states. Clement Moore, though referring to a particular historical pattern in Morocco, describes well the delicate nature of politics balanced between the blad al-makhzan or area of government control and the blad al-siba or area of the outlying dissidence:

> Protected by the Rif and Atlas Mountains, the Atlantic plains — and more especially the triangle defined by the capital cities of Fez, Marrakesh, and Rabat-Casablanca — constituted a governable core capable of sustaining a patrimonial construction and sufficiently isolated to withstand traditional external threats from Europe or from the eastern Maghreb. The blad al-makhzan often did not cover more than one-fifth of Morocco's actual geographical expanse, but the plain constituted a civilization with which the mountain tribesmen considered themselves to be linked even when they refused to pay taxes to, and hence be an integral part of, the makhzan. The blad al-siba, or outlying territory of dissident tribesmen, was an effective buffer against internal invasions. Its expanse dilated or contracted in proportion to the extractive capabilities of the dynasty, these capabilities being a function of the sultan's military power and network of tribal alliances.(28)

Even today, central governments must work hard to satisfy both rural and urban constituencies for the sake of national integration — their natural priority.

Another social factor is the degree of literacy. Although all the Middle Eastern countries suffer by comparison to the developed states, there are significant variations within the region. Lebanon, for instance, has the most impressive record with 20 percent of its men and 40 percent of its women illiterate, whereas in Saudi Arabia and North Yemen somewhere between 80 and 90 percent of their populations are illiterate. Turkey has an illiteracy rate of approximately 35 percent, but Iran's is around 60 percent. Egypt has made great strides in its educational program, reducing illiteracy from 70.5 percent in 1960 to 56.5 percent in 1976, and this very success stands in contrast to its erstwhile union partners, Libya and the Sudan, whose illiteracy is substantially higher.(29)

There are, finally, variations of class that make transnational, class-to-class relations difficult. The ruling class, for instance, differs markedly in structure and content from Libya and Iraq with their military-dominated Revolutionary Command Councils, to Syria with its ethnic and nepotistic solidarity, to the Arabian peninsula states with their patrimonial and institution-poor rule, to Algeria and the PDRY with their pervasive single-party apparatus, to Turkey with its parliamentary and democratic format. The traditional cleric class also varies. In Egypt, for instance, the 'ulama' (religious scholars) contribute intermittently to great affairs of state, and the government controls their training and selection carefully; in securalist Turkey, they are excluded from public affairs almost entirely. In Saudi Arabia, however, they exercise great influence and independence. The mujtahids in Shia Iran had divided between the collaborationists and the opponents of the Pahlavi dynasty, and this fact combined with the Shah's modernizing intentions accounts for the relatively low clerical influence until the revolution. The rise of Khomeini suggests that the religious class generally will exercise a profound impact on the future of the country.

The professional middle class in all of these countries is, at best, an inchoate group, facilitating modernization, yet tenuously joined together by standards of efficiency in a region where connections and status are more important. Bill and Leiden estimate that these doctors, lawyers, professors, engineers, and mid-rank military officers constitute about ten percent of a total Middle Eastern population including Israel, Afghanistan, and Pakistan in addition to the countries discussed here.(30) Although it is safe to conclude that no state in the area lacks an emerging middle class, it is also clear that their size and impact vary greatly. The Egyptian, Syrian, Moroccan, Turkish, and Iranian middle classes, for example, are fairly large and entrenched, whereas the comparable groups in Saudi Arabia, the Yemens, and the Sudan are small and relatively limited in influence.

In addition to the variations of structure, size, composition, and impact, there are two reasons why class-to-class cooperation across the region is unlikely. First, consciousness of class at any level is fairly underdeveloped. Other affinities – family, tribe, province, and ethnic group – qualify constantly class membership and so mitigate its importance. The suq merchant of Riyadh is more likely to feel a member of the 'Anayza tribe than he is of a profession that includes the bazaar merchants of Tehran. Secondly, although perhaps making an intellectual association with similar job-holders in other countries, class members are unlikely to feel any shared sentiment with those who live in widely divergent political, social, economic, and cultural milieus. For example, professional class members may "prefer professionalism to personalism, justice to wealth, intellectual freedom to imposed stability and effective political participation to political cooptation."(31) But this view obscures the fact that middle class members seem to be influenced more by the local conditions of their country than by abstract professional and class expectations. It is hard to believe, for instance, that the Turkish journalist shares many political goals with the Qatari journalist, regardless of their common employment; and it is clear that the intelligentsia of Iran had less in common with their counterparts in, say, Egypt or Morocco than they did with the clerical class of their own country during the 1978-1979 revolution.

POLITICAL DIMENSION OF REGIONALISM

If there are significant differences of ethnicity, demography, literacy, and class that militate against regional integration, there are also political factors that do not encourage regionalism. There are, first, noteworthy variations in the political cultures of the area. The peoples and elites of Libya, Saudi Arabia, Kuwait, the UAE, Qatar, Bahrain, and new Iran place a great deal of emphasis on Islam, which, in turn, helps to define their perspectives on political changes and particular policies. In the Arabian Peninsula states, the Islamic imperative of consultation (shura) combines with the tribal notion of consensus among elders to produce polities whose institutional developments are slow. Operating in consummatory political culture, then, these dynastic and traditional regimes subsist on, and rarely advance beyond, low levels of regular and structured political participation. By way of contrast, in Algeria, Egypt, Syria, Iraq, and Turkey, Islam plays a circumscribed role in shaping political attitudes, though it persists as an affective influence in private, daily life.

Moreover, each of these countries has proclaimed itself revolutionary in some way, and years of socialization and ideological persuasion have led their peoples to expect major changes and even to demand greater political responsibilities for themselves. Our point is not that some Middle Eastern countries are more participatory than others, and certainly not that Islam inhibits democracy. It is, rather, that the possibilities of structural development in each country depend on particular melanges of traditional norms and modern demands. There is little ground for arguing, therefore, that there is an evolving Middle Eastern political culture.

The common element that does permeate all the region's political cultures is personalism, whether it refers to individuals or groups. Though the force of personal leadership is present throughout the world, it is particularly strong in the Middle East where imposing character, eloquent speech, and selfless courage are virtues long enshrined in its histories and literatures and where, at any rate, few ideologies and parties exist to mobilize the masses. Examples abound: Nasser of Egypt, Faisal of Saudi Arabia, Qaddafi of Libya, Ataturk of Turkey, Bourguiba of Tunisia, Khomeini of Iran. In many cases, the appeal of a leader's baraka (special grace) and the charm of his demeanor have earned not only the affection of the common man but also the jealousy and sometimes enmity of rival heroes, as in Nasser's rivalry with King Faisal, Qaddafi's with Sadat, and King Hassan's with Boumedienne.

Personalist groups, based on interpersonal ties rather than impersonal structure, so dominate the political life of most states in the Middle East that they are taken for granted by the natives and often unrecognized by outsiders. A key element of Iranian political life has been the informal group, the dawra, often associated with the bazaar; and central to Lebanese politics have been the zu'ama who control access to national authorities and distribute political and social goods, much in the manner of local "godfathers" or ward bosses. The royal families of Morocco, Jordan, Kuwait, and Saudi Arabia function, because of their centrality, cohesiveness, and sometimes size (particularly in the Saudi case with its several thousand princes), to aggregate political interests for the consideration of the kings and few preeminent princes. Even in these monarchical regimes, there is room for other informal associations (shilal), whereby individuals of like education, ethnic group, or trade meet regularly to exchange information and ideas, occasionally to galvanize political opposition, and, rarer still, to plot a coup.

Informal group activity in the Middle East has manifested itself in a myriad of ways. From tiny dyads that plug in and out of one another depending upon mutual needs, to enormously complex coalitions of individuals who come together on the basis of kinship, these group structures have little in common beyond their personal, informal nature. Personal homes have served as the more exclusive locales for group meetings, while mosques, coffeehouses, teahouses, common rooms, and bazaar shops have existed as more inclusive locus points for group interaction. Informal groups operating in these kinds of settings act as the nodes of a communication grid that constantly relay information through the various societies. It is on the basis of much of this information that personal and political decisions are made.(32)

The Middle Eastern pattern of formal decision making is similarly variegated. Most states of the region have a parliamentary body, yet their legislative experiences vary widely. Turky has the most independent parliament in the Middle East, the Grand National Assembly, which is responsible for passing all legislation and for electing the president of the republic every seven years. Apart from intermittently severe crises, such as the period of the military's political ascendancy in 1960 and the creation of the National Union Command, the Assembly acts much as any national legislature of Europe. The Lebanese parliament has been similarly powerful and central to national political life, in spite of, and perhaps because of, its sectarian proportionality. Reflecting the severe splits in the Lebanese polity, the National Pact of 1943 ordained a "confessional" order, whereby political positions are distributed in a sectarian ratio that has favored Christians over Muslims generally and Sunni Muslims in particular over Shias.(33) Often to the disbelief of observers, the very predictability of confessionalism allowed a functioning political order. But there were profound resentments which, when paired with the challenge of the Palestinians' presence and the damaging Israeli strikes, erupted into the civil war of 1975-1976. The continuation of occasional fighting, the failure so far of national leaders to work out a new compromise constitution, and the presence of 30 thousand Syrian troops indicate that the Lebanese parliament, like all institutions of state currently, lacks any real efficacy.

Egypt's National Assembly has been, from time to time, a significant forum for lively political debate, but it has rarely opposed major policies and, most often, it has been the constitutional vehicle through which the elite have validated their reforms and foreign policies. The Assembly has found a new, albeit still wan, vigor under Sadat, who undoubtedly remembers his leisurely days as Assembly Speaker under Nasser. Jordan's bicameral parliament exercised its power several times. In 1956, for example, it put considerable pressure on the king to renounce the Anglo-Jordanian Treaty of Alliance and to join Syria in a federal union; and several times it voted no confidence in the king's Prime Minister and Council of Ministers, as in April 1963 with the Rifa'i government. There was a basic shift after the Rabat summit conference of 1974 at which Hussein renounced his right to represent the Palestinians. The king dissolved the parliament and revised the constitution to prohibit Palestinian representation. Since then, he has governed without benefit of an elected legislature, although he created an appointed Consultative National Assembly in April 1978.

To a more limited extent, the Kuwaiti Consultative Assembly functioned as a restraint on the Sabah family from 1963 to 1976 when the amir dissolved it. In 1965, members of the Assembly soundly criticized policies of the regime, and in the years before its dissolution, it vocally contributed to national discussions on the best way to take over full control of the oil consortium. The National Assembly of Bahrain and the Consultative Assembly of Qatar have proven to be more docile, as was the Shah's parliament. Although the Majlis of Iran was independent when the monarch was weak, such as when the Shah refused to ratify the oil concession with the Soviet Union in 1947(34) and generally in the Massadegh era of 1950-1953, it was reduced to a mere appendage of the Shah when he regained his power with American connivance in August 1953. Saudi Arabia stands in contrast to all these varying examples by the absence of a legislature. While Crown Prince Faisal had promised to create a consultative assembly after his accession to full powers in November 1962, and while Crown Prince Fahd similarly indicated after his elevation in 1975 that the government would allow national and regional assemblies, none is yet in existence.

There are also differences in the political parties of the region. In Libya, Kuwait, and Saudi Arabia, for example, there are no officially recognized political parties; whereas Turkey, Lebanon, and Morocco support multiple parties. Once again, the Turkish case contrasts markedly with the other Middle Eastern countries, for there has been a lively competition for power between the two main parties, the Republican Peoples Party (RPP) and the Democratic (now Justice) Party. The electoral victory of the Democratic Party in 1950 was an indication that the Turkish political culture would allow effective and rival parties to operate in the polity so long guided by the RPP. Lebanon seemingly has had an excess of parties, with each organized about a religious or ethnic group and led by a za'im. The Kata'ib of the Maronite Christian Pierre Gemayel and the Progressive Socialist Party of the Druze leader Kamal Jumblat are but two examples. King Hassan has allowed several parties to operate, among them the Istiqlal, the Socialist Union, and the Communist Party.

Most countries of the Middle East are effectively single-party states. Though they allow other parties to exist, the Ba'th parties of Syria and Iraq are the primary power holders; the National Liberation Front in Algeria, its namesake in the PDRY, and the neo-Destour Party in Tunisia retain exclusive power from the days when they spearheaded the struggles for independence; and the Rastakhiz Party in Iran replaced the Shah's earlier "official" two-party system. Modern Egyptian political history has been characterized by single party rule, whether it be the nationalist Wafd Party or the National Liberation Rally and the Arab Socialist Union (ASU) of Nasser. Sadat, experimenting with electoral innovations, allowed in 1977 the formation of three "platforms" within the ASU, which have evolved into separately organized parties. The centrist, majority platform has become Sadat's own National Democratic Party, the overwhelming winner in the local elections of June 1979.

Another significant factor of power in the Middle East is the military. There probably are no states where it has refrained from taking an occasionally direct role in decision making, but we might suggest the cases of Morocco, Tunisia, Jordan, Saudi Arabia, and prerevolutionary Iran as examples of where military men have, by and large, eschewed interventionist policies. In each, they have only rarely departed from their background role of supporting the regime and, then, more often to buttress it in times of attack than to try to improve it. At the opposite end of the spectrum are the instances of direct and persistent military intervention. If there is a pattern, it is that revolutions launched by military coups tend to institutionalize the political influence of the revolutionary army and air force officers. Egypt, Algeria, Libya, Syria, and Iraq have done so in their versions of the now familiar organization, the Revolutionary Command Council (RCC) or the National Progressive Front. Through such a collective body, the primary architects of the revolution guarantee their place in national policy formation and serve as a check on the primus inter pares who emerges as central leader. Each of the instances cited, however, is unique. The Egyptian RCC successfully translated itself into a civilian government, to the point where 25 years after the coup d'etat, military interference in politics seems improbable. Algeria is in the process of "civilianizing" its government, but much is uncertain in the wake of

Boumedienne's death. The Libyan RCC remains controlled by the enigmatic Qaddafi and the more pragmatic Jallud, both military men. In Syria, the military (at least the air force under al-Asad's command) has so effectively captured the Ba'th organizations that observers call government there "proctorian,"(35) whereas the Ba'thist leadership in Iraq, like Qasim before it, has cleverly coopted the military for support of its own goals and at the expense of would-be political rivals.

Between the alternatives of law and very high politicization, there is intermittent, perhaps idiosyncratic political involvement. Examples are the military interventions in Lebanon and Turkey. In the former, the army, steadfastly refusing to become involved in the civil war of 1958, gradually became active in "police actions" against the unruly Palestinians in the 1970s. As the civil war of 1975 gained its brutal intensity, the temptation to act was too great to resist. The predictable result was its splintering into confessional groupings and its destruction as a viable institution of state. The creation of the pro-Muslim Lebanese Arab Army of Lieutenant Ahmad ad-Khatib and the supposed coup of Brigadier General 'Abd al-'Aziz al-Ahdab seemed to be, when measured against the unfolding Greek tragedy, burlesque subplots.

The political interferences of the Turkish military have been more decisive. Civilian control was ostensibly well accepted by 1950, but suffering from inflation and increasingly disagreeing with the policies of Prime Minister Menderes and his Democratic Party cabinet, a group of military men staged a coup on May 27, 1960. Since their return to the barracks at the end of 1961, they have continued, nevertheless, to exercise political influence. There was a coup threat in 1960; the top brass warned the political parties to end their bitter dissension in 1964; the presidency was occupied again by a member of the General Staff in 1966; a "coup by memorandum" occurred in March 1971, leading to Prime Minister Demirel's resignation; and the military have issued subsequent memoranda throughout the 1970s. Although its prestige is high since the Cyprus invasion of the summer of 1974, the military is unlikely to become more directly and permanently involved in the governance of Turkey for three reasons: military officers are deeply committed to the "six arrows" of Ataturk and consider themselves the guardians of his republican, populist, and securalist revolution; they well remember their internal bickering after the 1960 coup; and they are acutely sensitive to the deleterious effect on national security such political involvement would likely have at a time of external challenge (in varying ways from Greece and from the Soviet Union) and relative weakness (due to the United States' arms embargo).

Bureaucracies, finally, are remarkably similar throughout the Middle East in that they are developing and transitional. None has yet attained the level of administrative efficiency and managerial rationality theorists would have us believe exists in the developed states, and all are affected still by traditional influences such as family ties and social hierarchies. In all these states as well, professional cadres are emerging to advise on, and often to help direct, the process of modernization; and everywhere bureaucratic experience advances political socialization by strengthening the bureaucrat's identification with the national unit. Yet there are, of course, differences in the size and efficiency of bureaucracies in the region. Egyptian bureaucracy is huge, overstaffed, and often inefficient, whereas Jordan's administration is smaller and better organized. Staffed principally by Palestinians, the Jordanian bureaucracy is highly centralized and controlled by an upper echelon of loyal tribesmen, former military men, and members of old Palestinian families attached to the Hashemite crown. The Saudi bureaucracy, nonexistent only thirty years ago when 'Abd al-'Aziz governed directly and the national treasury could fit under an advisor's bed, is now growing to the point where there are twenty ministries and a number of related, specialized boards and administrative tribunals.(36)

While we have only briefly touched on major political factors, we believe it is safe to conclude that no common pattern emerges with regard to any one and to the interaction among them. The peculiarities of personalist leadership and the variations of parliaments, political parties, military roles, and, to a lesser extent, bureaucracies suggest that there are few political cultures and institutions whose compatibility is sufficient for the emergence of effective organized linkages among them.

ECONOMIC DIMENSION OF REGIONALISM

It is even more difficult to find any basis for real economic integration. The differences are simply overwhelming. In addition to the demographic and rural-urban problems we have already discussed, there are important differences in wealth. Iran, for instance, had a Gross Domestic Product (GDP) in 1976 of over $66 billion and Saudi Arabia had a GDP in 1977 of $55 billion, whereas Algeria's 1976 figure was $15 billion and Libya's $13 billion in 1975. The differences are dramatic if we compare any of these oil-producing states to the non-oil producing ones. For instance, Jordan's 1977 GDP was $1.5 billion, Morocco's 1976 figure was $8 billion, the Sudan's 1975 figure was $4 billion, and Syria's 1976 GDP was $5.8 billion. It is easy to grasp the great differences in wealth and to understand why political resentments flow from them when we consider that Tunisia's GDP in 1977 was about $5 billion while Kuwait, with about one-fifth the population and one-eighth the land size, had a GDP in 1976 of $12.8 billion – almost two and a half times that of Tunisia a year later.(37) There is no wonder that a loose confederation such as the UAE faces problems of integrating the oil-rich sheikdoms like Abu Dhabi, Dubai, and Sharjah with the non-oil producing ones of Fujayrah and Umm al-Qaywan.

We hasten to add that there are also resentments among the oil producers stemming from differences in reserves. Although new sources are frequently found, it is clear that the fortunate are not equally favored. Saudi Arabia, with 150 billion barrels in reserve, is clearly the region's – and the world's – leader. Iraq may well have as much as Saudi Arabia, but based on current figures, it is generally thought to rank behind Kuwait and Iran, whose reserves are each over 60 billion barrels. Further down the scale are Libya with 25 billion barrels, Egypt with under 20 billion barrels, Oman and Qatar with about 5 billion barrels apiece, and Bahrain with about a billion barrels.

The extent of oil reserves is one factor in a complex calculus determining the pace and extent of economic development. The Shah felt capable of embarking on an ambitious development program because of the vast oil reserves and Iran's wealth in other valuable resources. Although Saudi Arabia's $142 billion Five Year Plan is also extensive, the government has had to take into account that it largely has a "one-crop economy" and that it must defer to traditional values. Algeria possesses a rich stock of minerals and some excellent agricultural land, but its rival, Libya, finds itself in a similar situation to that of Saudi Arabia. Egypt, with a population of 37 million and an economy weakened from years of heavy military spending, has had to turn to Western investors in the hope of developing.

This policy of "opening" (infitah) makes Egypt dependent on outside sources for aid and investment more than any other country in the Middle East, save perhaps Turkey. That country, currently suffering from high unemployment and inflation, low labor productivity, and poor management of state industries, has had to turn for assistance to the International Monetary Fund and Western allies. The economic development of Morocco and Tunisia is also troubled to the extent that they are heavily dependent on the world price of phosphates. Indeed, one reason prompting King Hassan to covet seriously the Western Sahara was the fact that there was a quadrupling of prices of the valuable minerals abundantly found there. The development of both Syria and Iraq, moreover, depends on an equitable sharing of the Euphrates waters, used by both for irrigation and power generation. In these instances and others, economic development is often precariously a function of scarce internal resources and ephemeral international cooperation. In most instances, needed resources are not available in other Middle Eastern states or are inferior to Western ones; and when geography and nature demand bilateral economic arrangements, the interaction is as likely to stimulate conflict (for instance, between Syria and Iraq over the Euphrates, and between Iraq and Iran over the Shatt al-'Arab) as it is some form of regular cooperation.

The facts of intraregional trade, furthermore, are not encouraging. Very few countries trade mostly in the Middle East, and the great majority prefer European, American, and Japanese trading partners.(38) Only Jordan, with 72 percent of its 1977 exports going to Middle Eastern countries, and Lebanon, with 50.4 percent of its 1973 exports going there, rate high in intraregional trade. But even these countries preferred non-Middle Eastern imports: 17.9 percent of Jordanian imports and 10 percent of Lebanese imports came from the region. The Maghreb states have close economic ties with Western Europe and the United States. Algeria imported 0.3 percent from the Middle East in 1976 and 14.7 percent from West Germany, its principal supplier, and exported 0.2 percent of its total to the region and 42.5 percent to the

United States, its principal buyer. Morocco imported 7 percent of its 1977 total from the Middle East and exported 2.2 percent of its total to the region, whereas it imported from France 27.3 percent of its total and exported to it 24.7 percent of the total. Libya's trade pattern for 1976 indicates that its regional trade was 1.2 percent of its total imports and 2.8 percent of its exports, with Italy the largest source of its imports and the United States its largest purchaser. Neither Ba'thist Syria nor Iraq does better in intraregional trade, since Syria's 1975 imports from the Middle East were 11.5 percent and Iraq's 3 percent, while 8.4 percent of Syrian exports and 12.2 percent of Iraqi exports went to the Middle East. In the Syrian case, West Germany was the main source of imports and Italy the principal purchaser, while Iraq bought most heavily from Japan and sold most to Italy. Among the non-Arab states, Turkey does more trade in the region, accounting for 16.3 percent of its imports and 10.6 percent of its exports in 1976. By way of comparison of Iran's total imports in the same year, 1.4 percent was from the region, and of its exports only 0.5 percent was destined for the Middle East. The record is clear that Middle Eastern states look outside the region to sell their wares and to buy what they cannot produce.

The lack of effective regional economic institutions reflects differences in wealth and development problems. The Arab Common Market came into existence in 1965, but it has failed to develop because tariff reductions have not occurred and because key states such as the Sudan have opted to remain apart from the grouping in order to be able to protect nascent industry and to collect needed revenues from customs payments. The Arabian Gulf states are supposedly working toward a common currency zone; the Council on Arab Economic Unity (CAEU) encourages broader-based unity; the Arab Fund for Social and Economic Development (AFSED), created in 1972 to advance the economic development of the region, is planning a massive aid scheme for the Sudan; and the Arab oil producing states hope to sponsor ventures beyond the coordination of their petroleum policies. John Waterbury summarizes well the success of these efforts:

> The CAEU, the Arab Fund for Social and Economic Development, and the Organization of Arab Oil Exporting States, while not entirely sharing like philosophies, have been promoting an integrationist formula founded on publicly funded, multinational Arab companies one variant of which is AFSED's proposed Authority for the Sudan. . . . The hope is that tanker fleets, fertilizer industries, steel complexes, aluminum smelters, and agricultural production can be rationally and profitably distributed among states. The emphasis is on the development of natural and human resources to overcome the major impediments to increased production and interaction. . . . The CAEU would like, for instance, to help create the conditions in which the Arabs can create their own technology. So far, however, these ideas have yet to move very far toward implementation.(39)

A further reminder of the tenuousness of these plans is the fact that the Arab arms industry, set up in Cairo in 1975 through the largess of Saudi Arabia, Qatar, and the UAE, is destined to become moribund since its financial backers have withdrawn to punish Egypt. If pan-Arab economic union seems remote, we can only conclude, on the basis of this experience and the general trends we cite, that there is no prospect for wider Middle Eastern economic integration.

EXTERNAL DIMENSION OF REGIONALISM

Outside threats, which often abet integration, have stimulated some regional institutions in the Middle East. One was the controversial Baghdad Pact, which began as bilateral treaties between Turkey and Pakistan and Turkey and Iraq. Iraq's participation in a security web backed by the United States and Great Britain provoked widespread condemnation of it by the other Arab states. Undeterred, Nuri al-Sa'id formally entered into the 1955 arrangement that became the Central Treaty Organization (CENTO), designed like the North Atlantic Treaty Organization to serve as a collective defense mechanism against external, presumably Soviet, pressure. With the revolution of July 14, 1958 in Baghdad, CENTO lost a principal member and its headquarters, but Iran was determined to maintain some life in the organization. Despite the Shah's efforts, CENTO was never very vigorous because the United States never became a full member; it consisted of only four countries after Iraq's withdrawal, and several of the members pursued independent policies toward the Soviet Union. With the revolution in Iran, CENTO became a dead organization.

The threat of the Soviet Union may prove to be more instrumental in the creation of other limited arrangements. For years the Shah urged the formation of a Persian Gulf collective security system, but Iranian-Iraqi and Iranian-Saudi rivalries rendered such prospects slim. Saudi Arabia also was ill-suited for a major role because of its low population, relative military weakness, and historical reluctance to pursue an activist foreign policy. The situation has now clearly changed: the 1975 rapprochement between Iran and Iraq reduced tensions in the area; the fall of the Shah in 1979 removed a powerful figure of great suspicion in the Gulf and brought Iran to the brink of chaos; the Soviet Union, with successes in Afghanistan, Ethiopia, and the PDRY, has become more menacing to Gulf states, especially since it will soon become a net importer of oil; and Saudi Arabia has grown stronger and more assertive. The combined effect is a general sense of unease in the Gulf and some sentiment that the time is auspicious for regional organization.

There are, indeed, good reasons for believing that organization is possible. The Gulf, as an "arm" of the Indian Ocean and a "finger" of the Middle East, is an easily delineated and compact region; the littoral states have clear interests in promoting external stability so that they can get on with their internal modernization; they all need to have navigation through the Strait of Hormuz unhindered; they are similarly vulnerable to internal political challenges, which might be exacerbated in a period of external pressure; and each wishes to be its own master, close to the West out of fear of the Soviet Union, but independent of both.(40) But these are factors that might favor the creation of <u>security</u> arrangements, not regional integration.

Soviet activism, new-found interest in seabed resources, and fear of Israeli interference have prompted the Red Sea states to ponder their mutual interests. The Horn of Africa conflict has visibly worried Saudi Arabia, the Sudan, and North Yemen, because of the implications of Cuban-Soviet assistance for the PDRY and for internal movements within their own countries. Incidents of Israeli war planes threatening shipping in the area also cause alarm, especially among the Saudis who fear that it might provide the pretext for greater Soviet involvement. Meeting in Ta-izz in March 1977, the presidents of the Sudan, Somalia, North Yemen, and South Yemen discussed stability in the area, particularly as it involves passage through the Bab al-Mandad Straits. Although Egypt and Saudi Arabia did not directly participate in this meeting, they have endorsed the search for cooperative arrangements.(41) However, simply because the stakes are relatively lower (57 percent of the world's oil trade passes through the Strait of Hormuz), Red Sea states are less likely to feel it necessary to form a security pact than are the Gulf states.

The Israeli threat generally has had little integrative effect. Created before the establishment of the state of Israel, the Arab League has, through most of its history, sponsored summit meetings and meetings of its military committee to encourage a united stand against that state. League meetings have been unable, however, to make their inter-Arab security pact work due to sovereign rivalries and suspicions. Ironically, the Arab states are most united, not against Israel, but against Egypt, the major Arab combatant in the Arab-Israeli wars. It is probable that the challenge of Israel has more divided the Arab states, on intentions and strategies, than it has united them; only in rhetoric and passion are they consistently united.

There is a final, economic threat which comes from the fact that Middle Eastern states cannot compete with the developed world in terms of sophisticated technology. The fear of being left behind has given rise to the Euro-Arab Dialogue, involving Arab League states and members of the European Economic Community (EEC). Though the results are not overwhelming, greater intra-Arab cooperation has resulted in some areas. For instance, the Arabs have had to think out their comparative advantages within the region and as a group interacting with the EEC. As Louis Turner and James Bedore explain:

> For one thing, the Euro-Arab Dialogue has spawned one subcommittee which has specifically concentrated on how the two sides might collaborate in the chemical and refining industries. Chances are small that any deal will come out of this debate with, say, the Europeans agreeing that the Arab side should

specialize in certain products, but the Arabs have been forced to examine the cumulative impact of all their national plans, particularly in the light of the ever more pessimistic market projections for the 1980s.(42)

Considerations of military, political, and economic security, then, have inspired some cooperation among regional states. In terms of major external challenges, they have much in common, yet to date they have rarely seen their common interest clearly and persistently enough to sustain long-term institutional developments.

CONCLUSION

We find three broad conclusions of note. First, there is a sense of the Middle East as a region because of its geographical place and cultural wholeness. Long described as Middle Easterners, the diverse peoples of the area now are comfortable with the designation. They are conscious of their shared religion and intertwined histories, and they understand when scholars contrast their civilization with others. Like it or not, they accept that they are part of a political destiny only partly controlled by them. When the Soviet Union seems to get close or when the United States talks too menacingly of its economic lifeline in the region, all states share the same shudder. And when Israel seems intransigent and expansionist, no state, not even prerevolutionary Iran and Turkey, can afford to appear too conciliatory.

Secondly, this regional sentiment does not translate into regional cohesion and is unlikely to advance regional integration. Though we acknowledge some transnational cooperation, we are unable to pinpoint any discernible trends toward greater regularity of interaction and institution building. To the contrary, our review suggested that the staggering differences of social, political, economic, and even cultural factors make integration improbable. The Middle East is characterized by vivid heterogeneity, in each country and from land to land. National elites there have the unenviable tasks of consolidating their own country's independence while advancing economic and social development and satisfying political demands. It is a tough enterprise that often produces partial and uneven success. But if nation-building is formidable, region-building seems the stuff of utopians or at least the work of distant generations. Faced with integrating the Berbers and reversing the pattern of dependence on France, the Algerian socialist leadership has little in common with the royal family of homogeneous and uncolonized Saudi Arabia, let alone with democratic, non-Arab Turks, or better still, with the Islamic movement of neighboring Libya. Diplomatic coalitions are possible and are, indeed, likely in a region where the adversary of the moment is most often within, but detentes and even ententes are far from the depth and range of interaction that would characterize an integrated unit. The requisite interdependence and will are lacking in the Middle East.

Finally, we suggest that the Middle East must stand as an exception to the contributions of regional systems theory. It is a part of the world that defies the application of rigorous methodologies. Data are hard to come by and they are often wrong, attitude surveys are almost impossible to take except among limited groups in few countries, and trends are difficult to discern amidst the rapidly shifting current. We are troubled, moreover, by the very notion of a regional system itself, for we suspect that, formulated so abstractly, it obscures the vibrancy of concrete situations and so runs the risk of becoming more a logical construct than a depiction of a particular history. Told that the Middle East's contours are best seen from above and afar, the student might mistake a reified concept for a difficult reality. In so doing, he is led to overlook that the Middle East is best known in the details. The notion of a regional system, more importantly, might be misleading because of a built-in bias. Intended or not, there is an unmistakable assumption that a proper system is one promoting integration. The very systemic idea encourages us to think of a closely-knit unit, and while it is true that there are various levels of systemic integration, we naturally tend to take as our standard the most developed. The comparison with Western Europe is inevitable; it is also damaging when it leads to the assumption that other areas are but in pre-EEC condition.

If the Middle East is a regional system, it is so metaphorically – that is, it is like a unit with subcomponents in regular interaction. "Subsystemic" elements, however, portend to be more revealing of how states of the area cooperate with each other, coordinate their interests and polities, and disagree with each other. The Middle East, already burdened with its own mysticisms, hardly needs the added burden of identificaton with "an almost mystical wholeness."(43)

NOTES

(1) Bernard Lewis credits the terror to the ingenuity of Mahan in The Middle and the West (New York: Harper & Row, 1966) p. 9. But Carleton S. Coon believes it was the work of the Cairo command of the British Army: Caravan: The Story of the Middle East (New York: Holt, Rinehart and Winston, rev. ed., 1958), p. 1. For a discussion of the development of the Western reception of the Middle East, see Edward W. Said, Orientalism (New York: Pantheon Books, 1978), pp. 58-73.

(2) Leonard J. Fein, Politics in Israel (Boston: Little, Brown, 1967), p. 65.

(3) Koran, Book III, p. 103.

(4) Majid Khadduri argues that Al-Afghani did not significantly urge the unification of Muslim countries. See Political Trends in the Arab World: The Role of Ideas and Ideals in Politics (Baltimore: The Johns Hopkins Press, 1970) p. 57, especially Fn. 1. For the standard work on the

subject, see Nikki R. Keddie, An Islamic Response to Imperialism: Political and Religious Writings of Sayyed Jamal al-Din "al-Afghani" (Berkeley: University of California Press, 1968).

(5) See Bernard Lewis, The Emergence of Modern Turkey (London: Oxford University Press, 2nd ed., 1968), pp. 340-43.

(6) Malcolm H. Kerr, The Arab Cold War: Golamal 'Abd al-Nasir and His Rivals, 1958-1970 (London: Oxford University Press, 3rd ed., 1971), p. 110.

(7) Nizar Obaid Madani, "The Islamic Context of the Foreign Policy of Saudi Arabia: King Faisal's call for Islamic Solidarity, 1965-1975" (unpublished Ph.D. dissertation, The American University, 1977), pp. 97-128, at 124.

(8) Ragae El Mallakh and Mihssen Kadhim, "Arab Institutionalized Development Aid: An Evaluation," The Middle East Journal 30, no. 4 (Autumn 1976): 472-75.

(9) See, for example, "Islam: The Militant Revival," Time (April 16, 1979), cover story.

(10) For the classic work on this movement see George S. Rentz, "Muhammad ibn 'Abd al-Wahhab (1703/04-1792) and the Beginnings of Victorian Empire in Arabia" (unpublished Ph.D. dissertation, University of California at Berkeley, 1948).

(11) For a detailed history of the Ikhwan, see Richard P. Mitchell, The Society of the Muslim Brothers (London: Oxford University Press, 1969).

(12) Le Monde, September 1, 1966.

(13) New York Times (August 3, 1952), p. 33.

(14) Bernard Lewis, The Arabs in History (New York: Harper Torch Books, rev. ed., 1966), pp. 71-114.

(15) Arab News, 1, no. 24 (May 16, 1975): p. 1.

(16) Two percent of the 1975 Assembly seats were held by women. The first woman cabinet member was appointed in 1962, and most recently, Dr. Aisha Ratab has served as Minister of Social Affairs.

(17) For information generally on law reforms, see Norman Anderson, Law Reform in the Muslim World (London: The Ashlone Press, 1976).

(18) Michael C. Hudson, Arab Politics: The Search For Legitimacy (New Haven: Yale University Press, 1977), p. 357.

(19) For standard works on Arab nationalism see George Antonius, The Arab Awakening (Philadelphia: Lippincott, 1939); Sylvia G. Haim, ed., Arab Nationalism, An Anthology (Berkeley: University of California Press, 1962); and Albert Hourani, Arabic Thought in the Liberal Age, 1798-1939 (London: Oxford University Press, 1970).

(20) For background on the Arab League, see Robert W. MacDonald, The League of Arab States: A Study in the Dynamics of Regional Organization (Princeton: Princeton University Press, 1965). King Abd al-Aziz's attitude was reported by Ambassador Moose in Dispatch No. 97: Decimal Files, 1940-1944, Department of State, Washington, 890B.00/319, Moose to Hull, January 12, 1944.

(21) Kerr, The Arab Cold War, pp. 26-76.

(22) The phrase is Richard Nolte's in his "From Nomad Society to New Nation: Saudia," in Expectant Peoples: Nationalism and Development, edited by K.H. Silvert (New York: Random House, 1963), pp. 89-90.

(23) See William Eagleton, Jr., The Kurdish Republic of 1946 (Oxford: Oxford University Press, 1963).

(24) This rough listing, from the most populous to the least, is based on figures found in the United Nations Statistical Yearbook, 1977 (New York, 1978), pp. 68-74. We have chosen not to give exact figures since we doubt that any are indeed available, but to give some idea of the range. Turkey is reported as having a population of 40,197,670 and the UAE a population of 179,126. (No figure is listed for Qatar).

(25) Abbas Alnesraw, "Arab Oil and the Industrial Economies: The Paradox of Oil Dependency," Arab Studies Quarterly 1, no. 1 (Winter 1979): 13.

(26) Monroe Berger, The Arab World Today (Garden City, N.Y.: Doubleday, 1964), p. 59.

(27) John Waterbury, Egypt: Burdens of the Past/Options For the Future (Bloomington: Indiana University Press, 1978), p. 79.

(28) Clement Henry Moore, Politics in North Africa: Algeria, Morocco, and Tunisia (Boston: Little, Brown, 1970), pp. 14-15.

(29) Literacy figures are derived from UNESCO Statistical Yearbook, 1977 (Paris, 1978), pp. 42-51. Compare with Charles Lewis Taylor and Michael C. Hudson, World Handbook of Political and Social Indicators (New Haven: Yale University Press, 2nd ed., 1972), pp. 232-35.

(30) James A. Bill and Carl Leiden, The Middle East: Politics and Power (Boston: Allyn and Bacon, 1974), p. 86.

(31) Ibid., p. 87.

(32) Ibid., p. 66.

(33) For an excellent overview of Lebanese politics, see Michael C. Hudson, The Precarious Republic: Political Modernization in Lebanon (New York: Random House, 1968).

(34) For a description of this event, see R.K. Ramazani, The Foreign Policy of Iran, 1941-1973: A Study of Foreign Policy In Modernizing Nations (Charlottesville: University Press of Virginia, 1975), Chaps. 5 and 8.

(35) Hudson, Arab Politics, p. 261; Itamar Rabinovich, Syria Under the Ba'th, 1963-1966; The Army-Party Symbiosis (Jerusalem: Israel Universities Press, 1972). For information on the situation in Iraq, see Majid Khadduri, Socialist Iraq: A Study in Iraqi Politics Since 1968 (Washington, D.C.: The Middle East Institute, 1978).

(36) For information on the bureaucratic structure of Saudi Arabia, see Fuad al-Farsy, Saudi Arabia: A Case Study in Development (London: Stacey International, 1978), pp. 92-127.

(37) These figures are based on those reported in the World Almanac and Book of Facts, 1979 (New York: Newspaper Enterprise and Association, Inc., 1978), pp. 513-95. Here, as elsewhere, the years cited are not consistent because of data unavailability.

(38) The following data are culled from the United Nations Yearbook of International Trade Statistics, 1977, Vol. I: Trade By Country (New York, 1978).

(39) Waterbury, Egypt, pp. 269-70.

(40) R.K. Ramazani, "Security in the Persian Gulf," Foreign Affairs 57, no. 4 (Spring 1979): 827-30.

(41) Middle-East Intelligence Survey, 4, no. 24 (March 16-31, 1977): 191-92.

(42) Louis Turner and James Bedore, "The Trade Politics of Middle Eastern Industrialization," Foreign Affairs 57, no. 3 (Winter 1978-79): 319.

(43) Ernst B. Haas, "On Systems and International Regimes," World Politics 27, no. 2 (January 1975): 148.

10 Latin America
Yale H. Ferguson

CONFIGURATION OF THE REGION

For the purposes of this essay, the Latin American region will be taken to include the 25 member states of the Organization of American States (OAS)(1) (excluding the United States but technically including Cuba), plus the independent states of the Bahamas and Guyana, as well as various colonial entities with close economic and political ties to the foregoing. For example, British-associated Antigua, Belize, Dominica, Montserrat, St. Kitts-Nevis-Anguilla, St. Lucia, and St. Vincent are among the members of the Caribbean Community (CARICOM). Because of their colonial status, such entities might be regarded as relatively peripheral to the core nation states of the region; or one might wish to reserve the core designation for the three states – Brazil, Mexico, and Venezuela – that, by almost any measure, are the three "superpowers" in the region. Some would certainly add Argentina to the core; others, Cuba.

However the core is defined, it is noteworthy that the boundaries of the region have been greatly expanded in relatively recent times, with the progress of political independence in the English-speaking Caribbean, to embrace the Bahamas (1973), Barbados (1966), Grenada (1974), Guyana (1970), Jamaica (1962), and Trinidad and Tobago (1962). The earlier movement for political independence from Europe began in Haiti about 1791 and achieved success in most of present-day Latin America by 1824. Cuba severed its connection with Spain in 1898, and Panama was "liberated" from Colombia in 1903. Most of the countries in the region are, therefore, not "new" states in terms of the possession of formal sovereignty.

Formal political independence and sovereignty notwithstanding, no basic description of the region could fail to mention the intrusive roles, especially of Great Britain in the mid-nineteenth century and the United States in the late nineteenth and twentieth centuries. The U.S.

role – variously described as "hegemony," "penetration," "neocolonial-ism," or "imperialism" – has been declining since the mid-1960s(2), and the international relations of Latin America have become much more complex. Efforts by many Latin American countries to "diversify dependency" have led to increasing economic and political ties with Europe, Japan, and the Eastern bloc (the dominant external link for Castro's Cuba). Simultaneously, Latin Americans have looked to greater cooperation within the region and with the rest of the developing world.

Subregions in Latin America are difficult to delimit precisely. Geography, as we shall observe, has been more of a barrier than a unifying factor. Perhaps the most distinct subregion is Central America, including Guatemala, El Salvador, Honduras, Costa Rica, and Nicaragua. These were grouped into a political federation from 1823 to 1938 and are today linked by the Central American Common Market (CACM). However, Mexico to the north and Panama to the south, although contiguous with and influential in Central America, are not members of the CACM and have traditionally been more interested in their bilateral ties with the United States. Of late, Venezuela has also begun to extend its influence into Central America.

It is even more difficult to establish the exact boundaries of a Caribbean subregion. William G. Demas of the Caribbean Development Bank finds three separate but overlapping definitions in widespread use.(3) One is the English-speaking Caribbean – Barbados, Guyana, Jamaica, Trinidad and Tobago, Grenada, and the seven British colonies mentioned previously – plus entities informally linked to CARICOM – the Bahamas, British Virgin Islands, Cayman Islands, and Turks and Caicos Islands. Another definition is the Caribbean archipelago, including the CARICOM grouping plus Cuba, the Dominican Republic, Haiti, Puerto Rico, the Virgin Islands, Surinam, the Netherlands Antilles, and the three French departments of Martinique, Guadeloupe, and Cayenne. A third conception is the so-called Caribbean basin, adding to all the above Mexico, Central America, Panama, Colombia, and Venezuela.

Venezuela, on the other hand, is an important member of the Andean Common Market (ANCOM). Apart from ANCOM and a mountain range, the six Andean countries – Venezuela, Colombia, Peru, Ecuador, Bolivia, and Chile – have little in common; and Chile withdrew from ANCOM in 1976. Bolivia, an increasingly discontented member of ANCOM, has historically been under the political and/or economic sway of either Argentina or Brazil. The La Plata Basin countries of Brazil, Argentina, Uruguay, and Paraguay have long been intertwined political-ly and economically, but Brazil is distinguished by its Portuguese heritage, immense geographic size, and extraordinary economic perfor-mance. Equally as significant as subregional patterns in the La Plata Basin area over the years have been bitter territorial conflicts between Bolivia and Paraguay and between Argentina and Chile.

Therefore, rather than searching for clearly defined subregions, it may be more realistic to recognize that these vary to some extent by issue and that bilateral relationships are often as significant as sub-regional – indeed, as regional or extraregional – relationships.

AFFINITIES AND DIVERGENCES

Political Geography

Latin America stretches some 7,000 miles north to south from the Rio Grande to the Tierra del Fuego and is up to 3,200 miles wide across South America. The region's total land area is about 8 million square miles, 19 percent of the world's total or roughly the same as the United States and Europe combined. South America represents some 7 million square miles and Brazil, alone, about 5 million, an area larger than the continental United States excluding Alaska. Most of South America lies east of the United States, which helps account for a stronger European orientation in the Southern Cone countries and for Brazil's longstanding interest in Africa (just 1,600 miles from the Brazilian bulge).

National boundaries in several cases are about as unsettled as the boundaries of subregions. Guatemala claims Belize. Venezuela claims over half of Guyana's territory. Guyana claims some 6,000 square miles in the southwest corner of Surinam. France claims 780 square miles in Surinam's southeast corner for French Guiana. Ecuador claims the Maranon area in Peru. Bolivia demands a corridor to the Pacific, which would most likely come from territory won by Chile in the nineteenth century War of the Pacific. Argentina claims the Falkland Islands (Islas Malvinas). Argentina and Chile are at an impasse over title to several small islands in the Beagle Channel.

South America contains four of the largest river systems in the world — the Amazon, La Plata, Orinoco, and Magdalena — but great distances and rugged terrain have inhibited exploitation of natural resources and general communication both within and among the countries of the region. Approximately 25 percent of Latin America is mountains, another 25 percent is tropical dense forest, and another 10 percent is desert or semiarid. Hence, only about 40 percent of the region is relatively easy to transverse or is attractive for settlement. Climate tends to be a function of altitude, and many population centers lie in highland plateaus close to the seacoast. For this reason, the fact that most of the region is in the tropical zone is a little misleading. All of Uruguay and only part of Mexico, Argentina, Chile, and Paraguay are in the temperate zone. The temperate Pampas are uniquely suited to grain and cattle; the tropical coastal regions, to crops like sugar, bananas, and cocoa; and the tropical highlands, to coffee.

There are abundant mineral resources in the region, e.g., bauxite in Jamaica, Guyana, Surinam, Venezuela, Haiti, and the Dominican Republic; nickel and copper in Cuba and the Dominican Republic; nitrate and copper in Chile; iron and coal (for steel) in Venezuela and Brazil; tin in Bolivia; emeralds in Colombia; and so on. However, like the affinity of the land for certain types of agriculture, some mineral resources have proved to be a mixed blessing, in that they have been exploited for short-range profit (beginning with the gold and silver that lured the conquistadores) and have tended to encourage overdependence on a single commodity for economic development.

Oil is found in major quantities in Venezuela and Mexico, where recent discoveries suggest potential reserves greater than Saudi Arabia's.(4) Net exporters of oil in 1977, in addition to Venezuela and Mexico, were Bolivia, Ecuador, and Trinidad and Tobago.(5) Argentina, Barbados, Brazil, Chile, Colombia, and Peru also have some proven reserves.(6) Petroleum consumption in Brazil represents almost 30 percent of the region's total consumption, but that country currently produces only about 20 percent of the amount required to meet internal demand.

Political Economy

The combined gross national product (GNP) of Latin American countries (in 1976 dollars) increased from about $129 billion in 1960 to circa $334 billion in 1977. Growth averaged some 5.8 percent a year in this period, and an unusually high 7.3 percent from 1968 to 1974. From 1960 to 1976, as a proportion of the combined GNP of the developed countries (DCs), Latin America's GNP increased from 6 to 7.6 percent.(7) During the same period, Latin America's exports and imports rose, respectively, from 11.2 to 15.2 percent and from 11.9 to 13.7 percent of world totals.(8) Also from 1960 to 1976, Latin America's share of the combined GNP (OPEC members excluded) of the developing or less-developed countries (LDCs) remained relatively constant at about 26 percent.(9)

By other standards, however, Latin America as a region continues to be much more developed than the balance of the LDC world. This is a factor making Third World cooperation somewhat more difficult and hampering Latin America in competition for bilateral and multilateral aid funds which are increasingly aimed at the "poor majority" among the developing countries. Again excluding OPEC, per capita GNP in Latin America of $1029 in 1976 was nearly twice that of the combined LDC figure of $542.(10) Only Bolivia, Haiti, Honduras, and Paraguay fell below the LDC average.(11) The above-mentioned percentages for Latin America's 1976 exports and imports, as a proportion of world totals, represent the lion's share of combined LDC percentages of 19.8 and 27 respectively.(12) In the early 1970s, Latin America's rate of literacy – one rough indicator of socioeconomic development – was estimated at 69 percent, compared with 57 percent in noncommunist East Asia, 28 percent in the Near East and South Asia, and only 19 percent in Africa.(13)

Statistics for the overall region should not obscure the fact that there is tremendous variation country-to-country in Latin America. Brazil's gross domestic product (GDP) in 1977 (preliminary estimate) of $123,431 million was about twice that of Mexico ($63,851 million), three times Argentina's ($44,841 million), four and a half times Venezuela's ($26,532 million), 53 times Bolivia's ($2,321 million), and over 300 times that of Barbados ($402 million). On the other hand, calculating GDP for 1977 on a per capita basis yields strikingly different

results: Brazil ($1090) ranks close to Mexico ($991) and well behind
Venezuela ($2083), Argentina ($1721), Barbados ($1654), Uruguay
($1331), Trinidad and Tobago ($1329), Chile ($1313), Panama ($1271),
and Jamaica ($1204). At the opposite end of the spectrum is Haiti with
a per capita GDP of $189.(14) While GDP for Latin America as a whole
grew in 1977 at an annual rate of 4.5 percent, the rate of increase by
country ranged from a high of 8.6 percent in Chile to a low of minus
five percent in Jamaica.(15) Even within countries, there are significant
variations among different social sectors and geographic areas. Per
capita GDP statistics are very misleading. In Venezuela in the early
1970s, for instance, the top 10 percent of income earners accounted for
40 percent of the national total; the top 20 percent, 65 percent of the
total; and the lowest 40 percent, only 8 percent of the total. Moreover,
urban wage earners as a group were much better off than rural
workers.(16) In Brazil in 1970, the richest five percent of the population
received 36.3 percent of total income, a share comparable to that of
the poorest 80 percent (36.8 percent).(17) In no area of Brazil did more
than 50 percent of urban workers' incomes fall below the poverty level,
but 90 percent of the incomes of rural workers in the Northeast were in
this category.(18) A 1968 study focusing on Mexico indicated that the
upper five percent of families had 28 percent of the nation's disposable
income, whereas the bottom 50 percent of families had a mere 18
percent.(19) Thus, if aid funds are directed at "the poor" regardless of
country averages, Latin America remains eminently eligible!

Latin America has traditionally been an exporter of primary commodities and an importer of finished goods, technology, and capital.
This dependent arrangement originated under the classical mercantilism
of the European colonizers of the region and persisted after independence under British and eventually United States economic hegemony.
Spain, Portugal (in a much more lackadaisical fashion because of
Brazil's initial apparent lack of gold and other natural resources), the
British, and other colonial powers parceled out the land and mining
resources of the New World in generous measure. The large hacienda or
plantation became the principal form of landholding, and came with the
labor of local Indians or, where this was insufficient, utilized slaves
brought in from Africa.   Mining was also an important economic
activity supported primarily by Indian labor in colonial Mexico, Peru,
and Bolivia. These patterns persisted in only slightly modified form for
many years following independence, with most of the economies of
Latin America being increasingly geared to the production of one or
two commodities for the world market. During the second half of the
nineteenth century, there was a large inflow of foreign capital and
technology to expand the infrastructure and processing facilities for
commodity exports.

Industrialization began in several countries − including Argentina,
Brazil, Chile, Uruguay, Colombia, and Mexico − in the late nineteenth
and twentieth centuries ancillary to commodity export (e.g., meat-
packing in Argentina and Uruguay) and gradually diversified. The
industrialization process was greatly stimulated throughout most of the

region by the trade dislocations attending World Wars I and II and the 1930s worldwide depression. Accustomed external sources of finished goods often proved undependable, and with fluctuation in the demand for commodities, foreign exchange was often hard to come by in any event. Infant Latin American industries expanded to fill the vacuum. Echoing the primacy of the Spanish state in colonial economic enterprise, and to a much greater extent than was the pattern in North America, many governments took an active role in promoting, regulating, and participating directly in industry and other commercial ventures.

In the 1950s the single most important influence on Latin American thinking about matters of development was the U.N. Economic Commission for Latin America (ECLA), whose executive secretary was the prominent Argentine economist, Raul Prebisch. ECLA doctrines were to a postwar generation of technicos what "order and progress" positivism had been to turn-of-the-century cientificos in countries like Mexico. ECLA maintained (the "Prebisch thesis") that the "terms of trade" between the LDCs and the DCs were steadily worsening, that the prices for primary commodity exports on the average were not rising as rapidly as the prices for finished-good imports. Unless there were changes in development strategy, the inevitable result, according to ECLA, would be that the rich countries would continue to get richer and the poor countries would gradually lag further and further behind.(20)

ECLA's multifaceted program for remedying this situation helped set the agenda for national and international development initiatives into the Alliance for Progress and UNCTAD decade of the 1960s. ECLA urged planned development at the national level and international cooperation to make development a more feasible endeavor. One recommendation was for international commodity agreements to end "boom and bust" cycles for traditional commodity exports. However, ECLA stressed reducing dependence on the export of primary commodities by boosting import-substitution industrialization and, over the longer term, also by the export of manufactures and semimanufactures. Another recommendation, regional and subregional economic integration, was conceived mainly as a means of insuring wider markets and tariff protection for fledgling Latin American industries. Moreover, the developed countries were to be petitioned to reduce or eliminate tariff and nontariff barriers to expanded Latin American trade. In ECLA's view, a vast increase in public financial assistance from abroad would also be required to supplement foreign private investment, for infrastructure projects, and to support social reforms. Social reforms – in areas such as land tenure, education, housing, and health – not only were necessary for reasons of simple social "justice" but also made good economic-development sense. They would result in bringing more of the Latin American masses into the mainstream of national economic life as workers and consumers.

Some of ECLA's vision has been fulfilled in the ensuing decades, but this has not proved wholly salutory and certainly has not been uniform country-to-country.

Import-substitution industrialization has proceeded apace. Indeed, manufacturing has been the most consistently dynamic sector of national economies in the region, growing at an average annual rate of 7.3 percent between 1967 and 1975.(21) The share of regional GDP represented by manufacturing increased from 22.6 percent in 1960 to 26.6 percent in 1976. In individual countries the percent of GDP contributed by manufacturing ranged in 1976 from 36.7 in Argentina, 28.9 in Brazil, and 28.2 in Mexico; to more than 20 percent in Peru, Uruguay, Nicaragua, and Costa Rica; to less than 12 percent in Haiti, Trinidad and Tobago, and Barbados. Brazil is by far the region's leading manufacturing country, accounting in 1976 for nearly 40 percent of the value added by manufacturing to regional GDP. In that same year, Mexico and Argentina together accounted for 38.7 percent. Brazil increased its share by about one-third from 1960 to 1976, while Argentina's fell from 25.4 to 18.3 percent during this same period.(22) Part of the expansion in manufacturing in Latin America has involved a growth in the volume and competitiveness of goods produced for export. Growth of such exports was at an annual rate of 14.9 percent from 1967 to 1970 and 29.5 percent from 1972 to 1975. The rate rose an amazing 46 percent in 1974 (manufactured goods were nearly 19 percent of total regional exports in that year), fell to 12.7 percent in 1975 in the wake of the oil crisis, and then appeared to rebound somewhat as world demand gradually recovered. Once again, Brazil, Argentina, and Mexico are the clear leaders, together accounting for some 70 percent of the region's manufactured exports.(23) Brazil's phenomenal expansion in this regard has owed substantially to the military regime's innovative policy of the "crawling peg" (frequently adjusting exchange rates for the cruzeiro to assure the competitive pricing of the country's exports).

If manufacturing has been the region's most dynamic economic sector, agriculture has been the weakest. Agricultural productivity is low as a consequence of land tenure patterns, antiquated technology, government neglect, and occasionally deliberate downgrading in national development schemes. For example, the first Juan Peron regime in Argentina (1946-55) financed industrial expansion primarily by buying beef, grain, and other primary commodities from domestic producers at low prices and selling them abroad at much higher prices through a state monopoly. In any event, in 1976 there were only two countries (Haiti and Paraguay) where agriculture contributed more than 30 percent of GDP; whereas agriculture's share was 10 percent or less in six countries (Brazil, Chile, Jamaica, Mexico, Trinidad and Tobago, and Venezuela). For Latin America as a whole, the figure was 16.5 percent in 1960 and 11.1 percent in 1976.(24) This decrease has obviously reflected a growth in the importance to GDP of industry and services as well as stagnation in agriculture.

Agriculture has not been the only problem evident in postwar Latin American development. Planning has been difficult because of political instability but also because of the continued price vicissitudes of key primary-commodity exports. Effective commodity agreements have been hard to design and even harder to negotiate with the DCs.

Economic integration in the region has not advanced nearly as far as some of its original proponents had hoped (more on this subject later).

Inflation has continued to soar out of control in many countries, reaching an incredible 506 percent in Chile in 1974 and 443 percent in Argentina in 1976. Seven countries had high inflation in 1977: Mexico (26 percent), Colombia (30 percent), Peru (38 percent), Brazil (44 percent), Uruguay (58 percent), Chile (92 percent), and Argentina (176 percent).(25)

The external public debt has also increased rapidly, at an annual rate of 26.2 percent for the region in 1976.(26) Since 1973, private creditors have steadily taken the lead over bilateral and mutilateral creditors: in 1976, respectively, 58.6 versus 41.4 percent of total indebtedness.(27) Not entirely coincidentally, the principal lender countries – less Uruguay and plus Venezuela – are the same as those listed above as having high inflation. The ratio of debt service payments to the value of exports of goods and services for Latin America as a whole in 1976 was 15.6 percent, close to that for Brazil (15.2 percent) and well above Venezuela's 4.1 percent. However, the ratio was much higher in Mexico (33.2 percent), Chile (33 percent), and Peru (21.6 percent).(28) Peru, in particular, hovered on the brink of default in the late 1970s, any many countries found themselves in the position of borrowing anew to help meet the payments on old loans. Debt servicing, of course, has aggravated what is already in many countries a chronic balance-of-payments problem.

Beginning in the late 1960s, so-called dependency theorists leveled new fundamental criticisms at prevailing development patterns in the region and, directly or implicitly, at some of ECLA's earlier prescriptions.(29) The main criticism was that import-substitution industrialization, rather than alleviating dependency, had actually increased it, since much of the expansion in industry took place under the aegis of foreign multinational corporations (MNCs). That the MNCs played a significant role is undeniable; for example, a study for a United States Senate subcommittee found that, in 1972, MNCs controlled 50 percent of the total net assets of the 300 largest manufacturing corporations in Brazil and owned 32 percent of the 300 largest nonfinancial firms in Mexico.(30) Dependencistas accused the MNCs, also with considerable foundation, of a variety of evils: dominating some of the most strategic, dynamic, and profitable market sectors; preempting local capital; meddling in politics; cheating on their taxes; utilizing foreigners in principal managerial posts; worsening the balance of payments through a high propensity to import goods (especially "finishing touch" industries), services, and technology; unduly constraining the dissemination of technology; using capital-intensive instead of labor-intensive technology; producing "luxury" or at least unnecessary consumer items; curbing exports in some cases to avoid competing with the parent company or other subsidiaries abroad; and so on. Moreover, dependency writers warned that unless preventive measures were adopted, it would be the MNCs – not member governments – that would benefit most from the wider markets envisaged in regional economic integration plans. Finally, MNCs were charged with coopting the "modern" sector of Latin American societies into an international hierarchy, under which the local elites who benefited from this arrangement had their attention focused away from the socioeconomic needs of the "marginalized" countryside and urban poor.(31)

Dependency theory has really been not just one, but at least two different schools of thought – for want of better labels, Marxist and non-Marxist schools. The latter – technico writers like Osvaldo Sunkel, Constantine Vaitsos, Miguel Wionczek, Anibal Pinto – have been more influential in government circles, arguing the need for more national and international controls over the MNCs (an argument which, we shall see, has borne some practical fruits). Marxists tend to blame all or most of the problems of Latin American development on "imperialism," are very dubious about accommodating with the MNCs, and usually insist that the only hope for economic progress with social justice lies in socialist revolutions.(32) In their view, the prominent Soviet role in the Cuban model of socialism is indicative of "international socialist fraternity" rather than another imperialism or dependency.(33)

Quite apart from its political implications, the Cuban model stands at one pole of what might be termed the ideologies of socioeconomic development in Latin America on the issue of economic progress versus social justice.(34) The Castro Revolution opted for much greater equality in income, health care, housing, and so forth (for all except the exiled oligarchy and middle class) with strikingly little regard for the economic development consequences. Indeed, for several reasons – but, none the least, the relative "leveling" of Cuban society – there was little real economic growth in Cuba for a decade after the revolution and the economy of the country today still relies primarily on sugar exports. At the opposite ideological pole stands the military government of Brazil, which has advanced the view that the wisest course is an initial strong emphasis on economic development over social justice, including massive public investment in infrastructure and industry, and even a somewhat greater concentration of income in the upper classes to encourage private investment. Investment in economic development now, the reasoning goes, will eventually mean a much larger "pie" than would otherwise be possible, which can then be more equitably "sliced." Most governments, like Mexico's, have adopted (for better or worse) an intermediate ideological course, seeking to find a balance between the demands for economic growth and social change. Even in relatively stable political systems, the balance actually struck has tended to vary from one administration to another.

Closing this subsection, we might refer to some statistics regarding Latin America's general role in the international economy that are subject to different interpretations. Like the optimist or pessimist who sees the glass half-full or half-empty, respectively, one may conclude either that "the more things change, the more they remain the same," or vice versa. As we noted previously, Latin America has traditionally been an exporter of primary commodities and an importer of finished goods, technology, and capital. From 1970 to 1975 – despite the

significant 18.3 percent of regional exports represented by manufactures – exports of food, raw materials, and fuels accounted for 81
percent of the total.(35) Moreover, most countries continued to be
overwhelmingly dependent on the export of just one or two commodities. During the same 1970-75 period, manufactures accounted for
62.9 percent of Latin American imports (fuels were 21.6 percent).(36)

We also noted previously that the United States in the twentieth
century succeeded the British as the dominant economic power in the
region, and that a stronger orientation toward Europe has historically
been characteristic of the Southern Cone countries. Direction-of-trade
statistics suggest that these generalizations still hold, although the
"diversifying dependency" campaign of recent years has had some
impact. In 1978, the United States' share of Latin American export
trade worldwide was 32.9 percent, compared with Europe's 25.7 percent, the 8.8 percent directed to countries with "centrally planned
economies" (CPEs), Japan's 4 percent, and 19.3 percent for intra-Latin
America. However, from 1975 to 1978 Latin America's export trade
with Europe increased 49.2 percent, compared with an increase of 22.6
percent for trade with the United States (for a respective value added
of $5.4 million versus $3.8 million). Trade with CPEs was up 37 percent
($1.5 million), and intra-Latin America trade rose 26.6 percent ($2.6
million).(37) Among some of the major economies in Latin America, the
export and import trade of both Mexico and Venezuela are most closely
linked with the United States; Argentina with the EEC; and Brazil with
the EEC in terms of exports and the U.S. and EEC on a roughly equal
basis as regards imports.(38) Latin America's export trade in manufactures 1972-75 offered a slightly different picture from the region's
total export trade; 30.9 percent went to the United States; 23.2 percent
to Europe; and 25 percent stayed in Latin America.(39) Incidentally, as
a result of trade agreements signed by the second Peron administration,
Cuba in the mid-1970s suddenly became the largest single foreign
customer for Argentine manufactures.

Political Sociology

Contemporary society in Latin America is the legacy of the confluence
over time of four main groups of peoples: 1) the indigenous Indians; 2)
the Spanish, Portuguese, French, English, and Dutch who conquered and
colonized the New World; 3) blacks who were brought as slaves from
Africa, and East Indians who came as indentured servants; and 4)
Europeans (primarily Italians, Germans, Polish, Spanish, and Portuguese)
who came as immigrants in the nineteenth and twentieth centuries.

The confluence of these peoples and others has resulted in an ethnic
structure in Latin America today that is far from uniform. Sizeable
Indian populations remain where the conquistadores encountered relatively dense native settlement and often advanced Indian civilizations
like the Aztec, Maya, Chibcha, Inca, and Aymara – in Mexico, Guatemala, Colombia, Ecuador, Peru, Bolivia, and northern Chile; where a

policy of extermination was not adopted, as it was in Argentina; or where the Indians were simply far removed from the "progress" of European colonialization, as (at least until recently) in Panama's San Blas Islands or in the upper reaches of the Amazon. Large numbers of blacks and mulattoes reside in the Caribbean island states and coastal areas bordering the Caribbean, and in Brazil. East Indians are mainly in Guyana and Surinam. Argentina, Uruguay, most of Chile, and southern Brazil are basically European societies which have derived much of their character from later waves of immigrants. The rest of the countries of Latin America may be classified as predominately mestizo (Indian admixture). In addition, all Latin American societies include people of other ethnic backgrounds, such as several hundred thousand Japanese in Brazil and Javanese in Surinam.

The consequences of this broad ethnic gamut are not easy to pinpoint. Internationally, it both hampers and facilitates cooperation. The Portuguese language, for example, has always been something making Brazil "different" from Spanish America; on the other hand, a partially black ethnic heritage is another factor helping to explain Brazil's longstanding interest in Africa, as well as Castro's recent African interventions. Looking inward at Latin American societies, ethnicity has contributed to what W. Raymond Duncan has called (with only some exaggeration) the "absent nation" phenomenon. Ethnic heritage is even more fragmented than we have indicated, dividing horizontally from one another even persons whom the casual observer would be likely to regard as similar. For instance, Duncan comments: "(Indians) differentiate between highland and lowland Indians in Bolivia or village identities in Guatemala or Peru. Linguistic differentiation between Quechua, Aymara, and Guarani throughout the Andean countries also fragments the Indian community. . . .At least 73 languages are spoken (by Indian groupings in Latin America) and more than 355 separate tribes have been identified."(40) Ethnicity is also a consideration in social stratification. De jure racial discrimination has never been practiced to the extent it was in, say, Southern United States, but de facto discrimination is widespread. An individual of color is much less likely to achieve relatively high social status and material rewards. Nevertheless, racial lines tend to be somewhat indistinct and, at any rate, are only one of many bases for stratification. Consider what Charles Wagley says about "systems of social race" in Brazil and the Caribbean, which he identifies as "actually a continuum from Caucasoid through the various degrees of mixed physical appearance to Negroid":

They do not in themselves form social groups that act vis-a-vis one another as do Indians and mestizo in Mexico, and Negro and white in the United States. They are a way of describing and classifying individuals according to physical appearance, but this is just one way these societies classify people. The position of an individual in the hierarchy of social race combined with education, economic status, occupation, family connections, even manners and artistic abilities places one in his or her proper rank.(41)

Latin America as a region has the highest rate of population growth in the world, an average of 2.8 percent annually from 1970 to 1977. Most of the region is in that stage of demographic transition when death rates fall and birth rates remain high. In an IDB survey,(42) Mexico's 3.5 percent annual increase in population over the 1970-77 period was the highest. Only seven countries had a rate of increase of less than 2 percent: Barbados (0.2), Uruguay (0.9), Jamaica (1.5), Trinidad and Tobago (1.5), Argentina (1.7), Haiti (1.7), and Chile (1.9). Three of these countries are European-style societies of the Southern Cone, and the others are Caribbean islands with high to very-high existing population densities; all have very-low to moderate birth rates, and Haiti also has a high death rate. Bolivia has the dubious distinction of having both the highest birth rate and the highest death rate in the region (for a net 3.1 percent annual increase).

Latin America's rapid growth in population is a problem of very serious proportion. It tends to offset gains in GNP, generates unemployment and underemployment, and makes for grave shortages of housing, health care, transportation, and social services generally. Birth control, thus, remains a critical issue, one that has long been complicated by the Catholic Church's official opposition to artificial means of contraception. Birth control devices are readily available in most countries for upper-income groups, so it is the masses that are most affected by the dearth of government programs. A number of governments – including, most recently, Mexico – have decided to move ahead with programs despite the sensitivity of the issue. At the other end of the spectrum is Brazil, which has adopted the goal of greatly expanding its population to help fill its vast backlands. Argentina has also announced its intention to increase its rate of population growth, not to be outdone by its northern rival.

As the Brazilian case indicates, there is still a great deal of open land in Latin America. Much of it is tied up in large estates, and some is unattractive for settlement, but a great amount could be utilized with appropriate government initiatives combined with pioneering ventures on the part of private citizens. Only the four Caribbean countries mentioned above, plus Grenada and El Salvador, have unusually high population densities. However, beyond the burden of more mouths to feed, a major part of the population problem in much of Latin America is the fact that many more persons are joining the great migration to the cities than are staying in, or moving to, relatively empty land. Latin America's urban population has grown from 49.4 percent of the total population in 1960 to 63.4 percent in 1977.(43) A recent study of some 700 cities in twelve countries indicates that whereas the total population in those countries will increase by a factor of four between 1950 and 2000, the population of the cities will increase by a factor of seven.(44) In 1960, Mexico City had a population of 8.5 million; the current estimate is about 14 million; and the population estimated for the year 2000 is 32 million.

The vertical structure of Latin American societies has become considerably more complex, a matter of major political significance (as we shall see later). From colonial times until the late nineteenth and early twentieth centuries – and later in some countries that were less developed economically – Latin America was essentially a two-tier society made up of the landed oligarchy and the masses who worked the plantation or the mine. However, in the second half of the nineteenth century and into the twentieth, the growth and modernization of Latin America's export trade, the gradual development of industry, urbanization, immigration, and related factors helped to create new intermediate social strata. These included an amorphous middle group of government bureaucrats, small businessmen, white collar employees, military officers, students, clerics, and others; an increasingly skilled and organized working "class" in the cities and countryside (in the more modern production-for-export sector); and an unskilled urban labor (lumponproletariat) element made up largely of peasant migrants from rural areas.(45) The old oligarchy itself spawned a new industrial-commercial elite, which maintained a close relationship with a growing population of their foreign counterparts. Despite this differentiation, however, much of the traditional two-tier society remained, albeit in a somewhat disguised form. Contemporary analysts stress the relative economic well-being, upward mobility, and "modern" values of the urban middle sectors and "islands of privilege" in Latin American labor – compared with the urban and rural peasantry.(46)

Political Culture

Attempting to discuss values in Latin America is not an easy matter, considering the diversity of ethnic backgrounds in the region, variations by country, contrasts between urban and rural life-styles (not to mention the primitive Indian or "bush Negro"), the several social strata, the wide spectrum of occupations Latin Americans engage in, and the differential contact between Latin American citizens and foreign influences. Nevertheless, it does seem possible to define some "core" values that are characteristic of those citizens most actively engaged in politics, at least in the Hispanic countries of the region. The English-speaking Caribbean has had its culture much more shaped by mother England and by the blacks, East Indians, and others who have come to inhabit those countries. Haiti is also unique because it is formerly French and almost completely black, and multiethnic Surinam is a-typical as well.(47)

We will be referring here primarily to the common culture that the military conquerors, governors, Church, and colonists from Spain and, to a lesser extent Portugal, very effectively transplanted to the New World. They were as successful as they were in this transplant because the New World when they came was either nearly empty land or inhabited by Indian civilizations whose values, in certain key respects, were not entirely different. For example, Spain merely substituted its own authoritarian rulers for Indian authoritarian rulers, and Christian saints and priests, for Indian gods and priests. This "traditional"

Hispanic culture over the years has had a fundamental impact on the political and socioeconomic development of the region. As Carlos Rangel writes:

> In this New World, it was the historic good luck of the North Atlantic seaboard to be colonized by England, the European nation then endowed with the greatest energy and creativity in all fields, and particularly in science, technology, economics, and political theory. . . .By contrast, it was Latin America's destiny to be colonized by a country that, although admirable in many ways, was at the time beginning to reject the emerging spirit of modernism, and to build walls against the rise of nationalism, empiricism, and free thought – that is to say, against the very bases of the modern industrial and liberal revolution, and of capitalist economic development. . . .The Spanish American New World was the Spanish Old World, with a few serious additional problems.(48)

An awareness of the persistence of Hispanic culture is absolutely crucial to understanding contemporary Latin America. However, it is also important to recognize that the traditional culture, almost from the beginning, has been regularly challenged by ideas from abroad – the European Enlightenment, the American and French Revolutions, the rise of industrial capitalism, positivism, twentieth-century technocracy, liberal democracy, fascism, Marxism-Leninism, and so on. "Cultural imperialism" has been far more extensive than ads for Coca-Cola or Arrow shirts; and it continues even as a Latin American government economist studies at Harvard or Chicago, a businessman socializes with a Volkswagen executive, a military officer takes advanced training at the Inter-American Defense College, a student reads Mao, or an Indian going home from market turns on his transistor radio. On the one hand, isolated Indian communities live and think much as their ancestors did several hundred years ago. On another, the life-styles and values of a narrow stratum of upper-class elites are, in significant respects, indistinguishable from the "jet set" the world over. Middle groups share different mixes of traditional and other values.

A central value in the Hispanic tradition is personalismo or la dignidad de la persona, the "dignity" of the individual, including his/her "inner worth" which is not dependent upon material assets or social status. Closely related to this value is another, machismo, the quality of strength combined with sexual appeal that is supposed to characterize the Latin American male. Taken together, personalism and machismo help explain the Latin American predilection for strong executives and charismatic leaders. Personalism makes cooperation for the goals of society at large more difficult, but it has never implied a rejection of family. On the contrary, extended kinship ties are extremely important and, in turn, are partly responsible for nepotism and corruption in government – one is expected to do well by one's family.

Perhaps the most directly politically-relevant values are those of hierarchy, authority, and order, which hold that society and the political system are rightly organized in a pyramidal fashion, each person occupying his/her "appointed place." The Catholic Church, at least until the advent of "liberationist" sentiments in some quarters, bolstered such a hierarchy by its own organizational structure, "render unto Caesar" doctrine, and attitude that the earthly life is but an insignificant anteroom of eternity. Other supports for hierarchy have been the inner-worth dimension of personalism – "I am who I am, regardless" – and the widespread acceptance by the masses of the fatalistic maxim "Que sera, sera." Patron-client ties (clientelismo), originating in the compadrazgo (godfather) relationship between land-lord and laborer, have also been important to hierarchy; advancement in the system is not so much by merit as through "whom one knows." A similar arrangement undergirds the political "families" in urban slums and, writ a bit larger, the "corporatist" links in some present-day authoritarian regimes between bureaucracies and their "approved" interest-group clienteles.

In addition, Latin Americans tend to lay great emphasis on transcendental values – that is, on the existence of a spiritual dimension to life – and there is much interest in educated circles in philosophical questions, literature, and the arts. This is the basis of the oft-repeated Latin American claim (arielismo) that their "humanistic" culture is far superior to North American "materialism" (however disdainful some Latin American elites are about their fellow humans of a lower social class or desirous of accumulating material possessions). To the Latin American mind, "ideals" (as Plato or Don Quixote might have reasoned) need have little relation to observable "reality"; legal niceties, to the actual state of affairs; and the well-turned phrase, to the crux of the debate at hand. An emotional attachment to ideas, as well as persons, is to be expected. Pragmatism and compromise, familiar values to North Americans, are regarded by many Latin Americans as more than faintly immoral. Hence, the regional penchants for political ideology, "nominal" constitutionalism, factionalization in political parties and interest groups, and rhetoric.

Another traditional value is a disdain for manual labor. This speaks volumes about the continued existence of a two-tier society in Latin America and, therefore, about some of the strains that have often been encountered in political reform movements seeking to forge an alliance between the middle and lower social sectors against an entrenched oligarchy. Wagley states:

> (The "middle class") who have climbed socially and economically out of the inert mass tend to identify themselves with the aristocracy. The upper class tries to live up to what Gilberto Freyre, the famed Brazilian social historian, calls the "Gentleman Complex." Just as manual labor was the lot of slaves, peons, and Indians in the past, today it is considered the work for the lower classes. The upper and even the middle class prefer white-

collar jobs at any cost. This group feels disdain for those aspects of professional occupations which involve physical labor. . . .

Many Latin Americans are now doing difficult technical field jobs – wading through swamps, caring for patients in hospitals, and fighting disease in rural districts – but these technicians are still exceptional. Most technicians. . .do not like to carry bundles or packages. . . .Members of the lower class expect this behavior from the upper class. They often feel uncomfortable when a North American visitor insists on carrying a package or participating in manual labor.(49)

Political Systems

Until the 1960s, most scholarly analyses of Latin American political systems emphasized constitutions and the legal institutions of government.   The tacit assumption seemed to be that there was gradually evolving in the region some form of democratic pluralism along North American lines. However, more recent analyses have focused on "real" rather than nominal constitutions – that is, on actual patterns of political behavior in the region.(50)

There have been two basic insights, both of which coincide with present-day popular stereotypes of Latin America and, thus, might not seem particularly startling to the reader. They, nevertheless, were extremely significant in reorienting academic thinking about the area away from legalism and supposed "emergent properties."   The first insight is that most of the Latin American region historically has had many more authoritarian governments than democratic ones. Dictatorship has been the norm rather than the deviant case. Second, many of the countries of Latin America have suffered from long and recurrent – in some countries, almost perpetual – periods of political instability.

There have been numerous factors favoring authoritarianism, including, at root, the Hispanic colonial legacy of political and ecclesiastical authoritarianism, social hierarchy, and values that we have already mentioned like personalism and machismo. The fifty years or so following independence was a period of political tumult, but there was gradual consolidation beginning in the late nineteenth century and extending well into the twentieth. The consolidation took the form of two main patterns that often were intertwined – rule by a union of landed and commercial oligarchs (e.g., Argentina, Brazil, Chile) and/or rule by an order-and-progress caudillo (e.g., Mexico, Venezuela, Guatemala).(51) Thus, the colonial legacy was reinforced after independence by an additional historical experience of authoritarianism.

Another factor contributing to authoritarianism has been the appearance of ideologies – some more concrete and durable than others – justifying it. Although Latin American dictators frequently excused the "limited" democracy they permitted by asserting that their country was not "ready" for full democracy, and although military establishments

often intervened at least ostensibly to restore or guarantee constitutional rule, it was not until the post-1930 era that certain regimes arose
which set themselves up frankly as alternatives to democracy. Getulio
Vargas modeled his O Estado Novo ("New State") in Brazil from 1937 to
1945 partly on Italian fascism. Even though he was popularly elected
Peron also billed his initial autocratic regime in Argentina as something
new in the political universe, justicialismo. Marxism-Leninism provided
an ideological framework for Castro when he decided not to go through
with his pledge made before the revolution to hold elections, arguing
that such a course would restore bourgeoisie corruption in national
politics. Finally, when the Brazilian military seized control of their
country's political system in 1964, they raised the ideological flag of
"developmental nationalism cum internal security." They insisted that
economic development without intolerable social strains – and, therefore, the nation's "destiny" as a great power – could never be realized
except in the context of technocratic authoritarianism. The so-called
Brazilian model subsequently had a major influence on military takeovers in Bolivia, Argentina, Uruguay, and Chile.

This brings us to a related explanation of authoritarianism in the
region which has received increasing scholarly attention, the "corporatist" or "bureaucratic authoritarian" institutions that the modern state
has forged to link citizens and government.(52) One of the most often
quoted definitions of "corporatism" is Philippe Schmitter's:

> Corporatism can be defined as a system of interest representa-
> tion in which the constituent units are organized into a limited
> number of singular, compulsory, noncompetitive, hierarchically
> ordered or functionally differentiated categories, recognized or
> licensed (if not created) by the state and granted a deliberate
> representational monopoly within their respective categories in
> exchange for observing certain controls on their selection of
> leaders and articulation of demands and supports.(53)

For example, in Mexico (under Lazaro Cardenas, 1934-40), Argentina
(under Peron), and Brazil (under Vargas) labor was unionized or "re-
unionized" and, thereby, essentially "captured" by the government.
Labor functioned not as a pluralist interest group, negotiating independently with employers, but presented its demands mostly through
the channel of government bureaucracies. In Mexico, labor was given
the additional status of formal representation in the party of the
Revolution (today the PRI). In Brazil, the link between labor and the
state remained one of the few features common to all of the regimes
that followed Vargas, even those of Janio Quadros and Joao Goulart in
the early 1960s and the military regime after 1964.(54) The Argentine
case was somewhat different, with labor forming the principal support
for the outlawed Peronist movement after Peron's overthrow. Argentina
moved toward pluralist democracy under Arturo Frondizi (1958-62),
making it exceedingly difficult for the military regime that assumed
power in 1966 to bring labor back under control.

We must be grateful to a recent book by Alfred Stepan(55) for further clarification of the nature of corporatism in Latin America. First, he points out that, though there are some definite similarities, corporatism differs from the now-discredited fascisms of post-Versailles Europe in that it has not encouraged large-scale paramilitary organizations, adopted the "leader principle" (except Vargas and Peron), romanticized violence, or been particularly aggressive internationally. Second, Stepan makes a key distinction between "inclusionary" and "exclusionary" corporatism, the former seeking to integrate new social groups into the bosom of the state before they have become organized on an autonomous basis, and the latter attempting to bring groups under control after they have become accustomed to acting independently. Inclusionary corporatism (e.g., Mexico, Argentina under Peron, Brazil roughly from 1937 until 1964, the Bolivian MNR after the Revolution of 1952, and the "leftist" military government in Peru headed by Juan Velasco Alvarado from 1968 to 1975)(56) is obviously the easier of the two forms to create, because it represents a positive response to emerging social sectors (like Peron's descamisados) and at an earlier stage of the national development process. Exclusionary corporatism (e.g., military regimes in Brazil after 1964, Argentina after 1966, Uruguay in the 1970s, and Chile after Salvadore Allende's overthrow in 1973)(57) is inherently more difficult to impose. As in Brazil, if adequately maintained, institutional linkages created initially by inclusionary corporatism may later serve exclusionary purposes; on the other hand, the Argentine experience indicates what happens when earlier linkages are not maintained.

Stepan also emphasizes that corporatist experiments have normally been a response to real or imagined political crises. It might be expected that the magnitude of the precipitating crisis is likely to have some relationship to popular tolerance of the response. For example, the chaos of the Goulart and Allende years badly frightened the middle sectors as well as the upper class, and the resulting "something must be done" attitude provided an atmosphere for severe repression and harsh economic austerity measures.

Lastly, Stepan observes: "There are no fully corporate systems, but rather there are political systems, in some sectors of which (usually the working class) corporatist rather than pluralist patterns of interest representation predominate."(58) As Stepan suggests, labor has been the principal target of corporatist organization since the days of Vargas and Peron. Vargas and Peron both attempted to set up national confederations of industry and business, but the extent of control of labor was much greater. In authoritarian systems today, despite the existence of some state-approved and regulated associations, the business elite remains largely autonomous and is not always supportive of government economic policies.(59) On the other hand, the authoritarian state generally has more means of influencing business than the other way around. There is, of course, a common interest in keeping organized labor and the unorganized masses in bounds. The Mexican PRI and Bolivian MNR made an effort to organize and incorporate elements of the peasantry. Indeed, the peasant link with the MNR held up even as labor, especially the tin miners, repeatedly challenged the regime and, finally, precipitated a military takeover in 1964.

Further contributing to political instability and authoritarianism in the region over the years has been the changing nature of Latin American societies and economies. During most of the nineteenth century, most countries were dominated by a landholding and nascent commercial elite, and instability reflected primarily personalist struggles at the top of the social pyramid. Even in this period, however, the military was a critical variable in national politics. After independence the military for a time was a "predator" force, intervening to support the personalist political ambitions of a member of the elite or one of its own officers. Later, the military helped national governments, including order-and-progress caudillos who were often recruited from their own ranks (like Porfirio Diaz in Mexico), to establish order and rein in regional caudillos and private armies.(60)

In the late nineteenth and early twentieth centuries, as we have seen, economic modernization and urbanization in Latin America created a much more complicated society. This period saw the rise of a diverse middle stratum and urban labor, both of which came to demand greater political participation and an increased share of the fruits of development. Of primary significance were the middle sectors, which rallied labor and some peasant support in a political assault against oligarchical rule. The military, the officer corps of which was itself largely middle-class, paved the way at key junctures in most countries for the middle sectors to come to power.(61) Howard Wiarda and Harvey Kline observe: "Indeed, it could be said that since 1930 virtually all institutions in Latin America – armed forces, Church, parties, universities, bureaucracy – have come to be dominated by the middle sectors, and that, hence, politics in Latin America is essentially middle-class politics."(62)

In Vargas' Brazil and Peron's Argentina, we have noted, the political transformation went a bit further, to include labor as an integral component of an authoritarian corporatist state. However, in these two countries after Vargas and Peron, and in many other countries as well, the predominant pattern was intermittent democratic pluralism, which was refereed by the military in the role of self-styled "guardians of the constitution." The middle sectors had grave difficulty meeting their promises to their supporters lower down on the social scale. This was partly because of continued resistance to change from the upper class and partly because of the middle sectors' own latent conservatism when forced to sacrifice for social reform, but none the least because of the "revolution in rising expectations" that swept the developing world after World War II.

Although accelerating demands were generated to some extent by domestic modernization, they were also the product of a "demonstration effect" from abroad. Improved communications brought to the masses a greater awareness of external political events and living standards.   In the 1950s and especially the 1960s, "development" became an international watchword and one focus of the Cold War rivalry between the two superpowers. Latin America was thus pressured, from outside as well as inside, to achieve levels of political, economic, and social development in the space of decades that it had taken countries like the United States and England centuries to achieve. Most governments in the region lacked the capacity to institutionalize demands, and, in any event, the capacity to meet them. In Brazil after the mid-1960s and in Venezuela, rising demands were to some extent satisfied by sheer "trickle down" from unusually prosperous economies. Elsewhere, there has been a pressing need to consider at least some painful redistribution of existing resources.

Some observers of the Latin American military predicted that as the military establishment became more "professional," it would gradually withdraw from playing such a prominent role in domestic politics. This prediction ignored the pull of tradition and several other important considerations. A central fact is that, except in instances of border conflicts and during World War II, the Latin American military has never had a genuine mission of national defense against an external threat. After the war, large sums were devoted to the armed forces to prepare them for a possible conventional war against communism, but the war failed to materialize. Hence, the military had to find a mission in keeping domestic order and, as in the past, in refereeing national politics. Advanced military training stressed anticommunism and, when strategic doctrines shifted in the late 1950s, counterinsurgency. Many officers, not surprisingly, tended to see a threat of communist subversion lurking behind popular demands for change, and their fears were immensely heightened by the Cuban Revolution and the guerrilla uprisings of the 1960s. Events in Cuba appeared to indicate that, were the communists to take over, the very existence of the armed forces might be jeopardized. Moreover, increasingly, military officers in the better training schools received sophisticated instruction about the socioeconomic and political problems of their countries. Many came to believe that they were at least as qualified as civilians to run the country, and there was widespread impatience with civilian corruption, "indiscipline," and "bungling."

Officers continually received appeals from disgruntled civilians urging them to "save the country" by unseating this-or-that administration. Customarily, the military had responded to appeals of this kind by intervening to "clean house," scheduling new elections, and then returning to the barracks. In the mid-1960s, however, exclusionary corporatism derived from the decision of the armed forces in some countries to stay on in the presidential palace for the duration or, minimally, until the political process had been completely "reformed." Characteristic of these regimes has been collective rather than individual leadership, although some specific presidents have made a personal imprint on the policies of their administration (such as Gen. Ernesto Geisel in Brazil and Gen. Juan Ongania in Argentina). Perhaps it is most accurate to view these individuals as representative of one faction in the military.(63)

Yet another factor that helps to account for endemic political instability is the incapacity of Latin American governments to institutionalize foreign "constituents." This is the political dimension of dependency.(64) Decisions made in foreign offices and corporate boardrooms abroad – mainly but certainly not exclusively in the United States – have often had serious domestic political repercussions. Political ideologies and issues have regularly been imported from abroad. There have been even more direct linkages between domestic and foreign elites, as illustrated by the extreme case of Allende's Chile. United States military attaches plotted with Chilean officers; the CIA supported opposition parties, unions, and newspapers; nationalized MNCs undertook legal action in Europe to block sales of Chilean copper; and the IMF, the World Bank, and foreign private banks had a major influence on the state of the Chilean economy.(65) The recently deposed dictator of Nicaragua, Anastazio Somoza, might also testify to the extent of foreign influence. When the Sandinista rebel movement reached sufficient proportion to attract moral and material support from abroad,(66) Somoza found the United States, several Latin American governments, and the OAS publicly demanding his resignation.

A final factor making Latin American authoritarian governments unstable has been the challenge posed by a less prominent, but nonetheless real and significant, alternative, democratic ideal in the region. Liberal aspects of the United States, British, and 1812 Spanish constitutions found their way into the constitutions of Hispanic countries after independence. Also, parliamentary democracy was the form of government that the British bequeathed to the English-speaking Caribbean countries, however imperfectly it is sometimes practiced. Democratic pluralism, as an aspiration that has some basis in practice, thus, has a long history in Latin America. Over the years, numerous statesmen and political parties – most notably, the reformist "democratic left," "national revolutionary" (APRA-type), and Christian Democratic parties, which looked like the political wave of the future in the late 1950s and early 1960s – have passionately defended the concepts of free elections and civil liberties. Even dictators of the old school like Fulgencio Batista (Cuba), Rafael Trujillo (Dominican Republic), or today's lone survivor, Alfredo Stroessner (Paraguay) have felt sufficiently intimidated by the democratic ideal to pay it lip service, allowing at least token opposition and an occasional rigged election. "Papa Doc" Duvalier's proclaiming himself president of Haiti for life was generally regarded as a breach of etiquette, about which, unfortunately, nothing much could be done. (the Kennedy administration and Juan Bosch of the Dominican Republic made abortive attempts to oust him.)

The democratic ideal continues to undermine the legitimacy of authoritarian regimes. Whenever a military regime begins to lose its grip, demands for more political freedom and free elections immediately start to escalate. Currently, in mid-1979, there has been dictatorial rule in many countries for about 15 years – since the ebb of the democratic-left wave. Outside of the English-speaking Caribbean, only

Venezuela, Costa Rica, and possibly Colombia (with frequent "states of seige") have pluralistic democracies that would pass muster by North American standards. Venezuela's open and stable system (since 1958) can partially be attributed to that country's exceptional oil wealth. However, there appears to be a modest revival of interest in a gradual transition to civilian rule and democratic institutions in Argentina, Brazil, Chile, Bolivia, Ecuador, and Peru. Also, after the Carter administration insisted, the results of a free election were honored in the Dominican Republic, the 12-year rule of Joaquin Balaguer ended, and the PRD opposition was allowed to come to power.

If there is a principal reason for this trend, it is, perhaps, that in most countries military rule and corporatist institutions have ultimately been no more successful than democratic processes in meeting the tasks of political institutionalization and social development. An exception as regards political institutionalization is Mexico, where corporatist institutions were forged over 50 years ago, before the onset of major industrialization; where the ideology of the revolution continues to serve a legitimizing function; and where elites have remained extraordinarily flexible in adjusting to changing conditions. One wonders how effective the institutionalization mechanisms in post-1964 Brazil would have proved in the intervening years had not the "economic miracle" bought the regime time. Although the economic record of technocratic-military regimes has generally been good, the lesson appears to be that (short of a miracle) economic performance is not in itself enough to compensate for lagging social development and a lack of political freedom.

FOREIGN POLICY AND INTERNATIONAL RELATIONS

Regional Foreign Policy Behavior

We will confine this subsection to a few general observations about Latin American foreign policies and the foreign policymaking process.(67) Later, we will focus in more detail on the foreign policies of particular Latin American countries and on bilateral and multilateral relationships both within and without the region.

Nationalism is the predominant characteristic of Latin American foreign policies, and it has been on the rise over the last decade. One factor accounting for this rise is the progress of nation-building in the region. National integration is far from complete, the "absent nation" phenomenon mentioned earlier. However, more and more citizens have gradually become politically socialized into responding to national symbols. Moreover, nationalist appeals are a useful diversion for governments that find it hard to meet domestic demands, including demands for the full integration of marginal social sectors. Another boost for nationalism has been the fact that economic development has proceeded in several countries – particularly in Brazil, Mexico, and Venezuela – to a point where major or at least middle-power status on the world scene appears to be a reasonable objective. Another related consideration is the decline of U.S. hegemony, which has allowed and even encouraged the more important Latin American states to pursue their own national destinies. Some national goals, however, are clearly not obtainable (or are much more difficult to achieve) without reforms of the international economic system. This, in turn, prompts Latin American governments to define their national destinies as involving an element of "continental nationalism" or tercermundismo (Third-World-ism). On the other hand, nationalism, more narrowly defined, has been a perennial impediment to the establishment and smooth functioning of regional integration schemes. Brazil, especially, has been leery of any multilateral arrangement that would substantially reduce its own options.

Observers of Latin American affairs have long emphasized the strong linkages between foreign and domestic policies in the region. There are, of course, domestic determinants of any state's foreign policies, but the linkages are, perhaps, more obvious in Latin America. Some of our comments about nationalism suggest the two main reasons for this pattern. First, dependent states find that internal development rests, in large part, upon trends in the external universe. Second, when a government lacks the resources or the will to engineer adequate domestic change, a "radical" and/or nationalist foreign policy can help to salvage its prestige. A familiar interpretation of Mexican politics, for example, is that successive administrations have tended to adopt relatively "independent" and even radical foreign policies in order to bolster the PRI's "revolutionary" image, while pursuing relatively conservative domestic policies.(68) In 1973, not coincidentally, Peron combined the removal of leftists from his cabinet with the negotiation of trade deals with Cuba and the Eastern bloc.

Rhetoric, we have already noted, is a feature of Latin American politics, and, although so much is primarily for domestic consumption, it characterizes foreign policy as well. Castro's marathon speeches are legendary. Rhetoric reached a recent high (low?) during the administrations of Luis Echeverria of Mexico (1970-76) and Carlos Andres Perez of Venezuela, when each attempted to outdo the other in championing the NIEO cause. Both men were well-known to have sizable egos and, whatever the political rewards, to derive great personal satisfaction from the adulatory media coverage of their speeches on NIEO topics at home and during their many state visits around the world. While not accusing Perez of insincerity, various analysts have pointed out that Venezuela has little to gain from the projected NIEO and that all the rhetoric did was function as a useful smokescreen or partial "compensation" for Venezuela's role in OPEC's continued hiking of oil prices.(69)

The strong ideological dimension present in Latin American domestic politics also characterizes foreign policy. No one has suggested that Castro's dedication to exporting revolution is strictly rhetorical, however modest his material contributions to subversive movements in the region have been over the years. Venezuela's role as a defender of the Third World, as Robert Bond explains, derives at least in part from that country's protracted struggle with foreign oil companies. Moreover, the identification of Costa Rica and Accion Democratica (AD) governments in Venezuela with democracy and human rights in Latin America stems as much from the personal moral convictions of political leaders as it does from their realization that their countries are among the isolated examples of liberal political systems in the region.

All of the foregoing ideological stances are quite consistent with, and even to some extent have their roots in, domestic political ideologies. However, the NIEO, "dependency," and related themes are sufficiently vague and have such transcendent popular appeal, as well as practical utility, that they have attracted varying amounts of support from a wide gamut of political regimes. A remarkable degree of Latin American and Third World unity has been achieved in this ideological context on certain issues of international economic relations; for example, both authoritarian and democratic regimes have a stake in greater access to the markets and technology of the developed countries. At the same time, there has been considerable variation country-to-country in the militancy with which NIEO themes have been advanced. Moreover, it has always proved much easier to hammer out compromise positions to present for negotiation in international forums than to move beyond rhetoric to concrete regional development projects, effective domestic measures to reduce dependency, and so forth.

Pragmatism is not a value that is held in high esteem in most of Latin America. Since the late 1960s, among the major powers in the region, Brazil alone has followed a self-consciously pragmatic course.(70) This helps explain Brazil's support for Arab international positions beginning with the energy crunch of 1973-74 and its surprisingly early recognition of the Soviet-backed Popular Movement for the Liberation of Angola (MPLA). Nevertheless, ideological orientations in other countries have been flexible enough to allow for a great deal of compromise and inconsistency. For example, Venezuela's criticism of repression in Brazil was not allowed to stand in the way of the successful conclusion of an Amazon Pact (more on this to come). Castro's ritualistic railing against capitalist imperialism did not dampen the welcome he extended to a visiting delegation of executives of U.S. companies interested in doing business with Cuba.

Let us now turn to the policymaking process. One might expect that the process would be highly centralized in the many authoritarian regimes in Latin America and much less centralized in the few democratic governments. This is the situation in some respects: in Venezuela, for instance, the national legislature has a role, interest groups function openly and in a largely autonomous fashion, and foreign policy issues are mentioned by rival presidential candidates in national election campaigns. Moreover, especially in regimes with charismatic leadership (e.g., Cuba) or in military regimes in less-developed countries when the armed forces are not themselves factionalized (an important qualification), foreign policy decision making approaches the unified process posited by the "rational" model. However, there are several factors normally at work that tend to blur the distinctions between political systems. Democracies are more unified than might be anticipated, and dictatorships less so. The resulting process – centralized but not entirely – does not fit neatly into the rational, bureaucratic, or any other scholarly model.

As in the United States and other countries, foreign policy in Latin America is primarily the responsibility of the executive branch of government. Executive dominance of foreign policy is strengthened in the Hispanic countries by the tradition of authoritarian personal or coporatist leadership, which has left something of an imprint even in a democratic country like Venezuela. In Mexico at the outset of each sexenio (six-year presidential term) there is a major turnover in bureaucratic and party posts, giving the Mexican president a degree of control over his administration never achieved in the United States. In the more democratic countries, the national legislature customarily devotes most of its attention to domestic issues and these are the main concerns in elections. The press usually echoes the official government line or the positions of an opposition party, and rarely engages in the kind of independent investigative reporting which might usefully inform the attentive public. Interest groups relevant to foreign policy in democratic systems are principally the military and the business community. The military is the key voice on matters of national defense and internal security. Business is influential, although almost never controlling, on issues of international economic relations. An exception was the opposition of the Venezuelan business community which for several years was an insurmountable barrier to that country's participation in ANCOM.

On the other side of the coin we find the numerous factors working against unified foreign policy decision making, even in authoritarian regimes. The presidential office itself has expanded to include a large staff. Bureaucracies concerned with foreign policies have also proliferated with the growth of the state and the increasing complexity of international economic relations. For example, Ronald Schneider writes of Brazil: "Whereas only a generation ago foreign policy decisions were the preserve of the foreign ministry and the president, these decisions are now influenced by a variety of interministerial councils, a half-dozen military-security organs, and at least a score of economic and financial agencies."(71) The foreign ministry in most countries not only does not control foreign policy but also is usually one of the least prominent of all the bureaucracies concerned with foreign affairs. Among the major states, the quality of foreign ministry personnel ranges from highly professional in Brazil to almost completely non-professional in Venezuela.

Under authoritarianism, the business community makes its desires known mainly through corporatist and personal channels, which are but a little less effective than those available in democratic systems. The military, of course, is more than just another interest group in most authoritarian regimes (except Mexico). However, the armed forces are themselves divided. Today, the old interservice rivalries tend to be less significant than factions within the dominant service, the army. There have been several internal power struggles in the course of military rule in Brazil, Argentina, Chile, Bolivia, Peru, Ecuador, Honduras, and elsewhere. These struggles have not been primarily over foreign policy, rather over questions of the amount of repression required to maintain internal security, the advisability and timing of a return to civilian rule, and/or the radical transformation of domestic socioeconomic structures (Bolivia and Peru). Nevertheless, as in Latin American democracies, foreign policy under authoritarian regimes immediately becomes very much a concern of the military whenever they perceive it as impinging on national security. For example, Schneider reports that the Brazilian military have been uneasy about foreign ministry actions in the Angola case and Cuba's renewed international activism.(72) As for Cuba, Edward Gonzalez distinguishes between the policy priorities held by three political elite groups: Castro and his closest associates (fidel-istas), the technocrats, and the military (the raulistas, headed by Fidel's brother Raul). According to Gonzalez, a "ruling coalition" of fidelistas and raulistas has emerged and both factions found their priorities served by intervention in Africa.(73) The military in Cuba – probably the best trained and equipped in Latin America – may become a much more important policymaking actor once charismatic leadership passes from the scene.

Relations with the United States

We must pause at this juncture to examine the evolution of Latin America's special relationship with the United States, because this has been one of the major factors giving impetus to Latin American nationalism, intraregional cooperation, efforts to diversify dependence, and tercermundismo.(74)

What Arthur Whitaker has termed "the Western Hemisphere Idea" originated with the Monroe Doctrine in 1823. However, during the early nineteenth century the United States was neither able to enforce the Doctrine nor keenly interested in doing so. A surge of isolationist sentiment aborted U.S. participation in the 1826 Panama Congress that was convened by Simon Bolivar, and proposals of various Latin American governments for an alliance with Washington met with a cool reception. Monroe had considered making the doctrine a joint declaration with England, and, in fact, it was the substantial British presence in the New World that was the primary (if imperfect) deterrent to interference from other European quarters.

Bolivar envisaged a Pan-Latin American association and had to be persuaded by associates even to invite U.S. representatives to the Panama Congress. Subsequently, rumors of European plots occasioned periodic meetings among different groups of Latin American governments, but none of the alliances and other treaties emanating from these meetings were widely ratified. England was the dominant military and commercial power in the region, and France was the principal source of cultural inspiration.

Manifest Destiny ambitions led the United States into a war with Mexico from 1846 to 1848 and, thereafter, toward a greater interest in what was perceived as its natural sphere of influence in the Caribbean and Latin America generally. By the time the United States emerged triumphant from the brief Spanish American War (1898), the Caribbean had become "an American lake." Meanwhile, beginning in 1889, Washington inaugurated a new series of inter-American meetings to encourage trade and investment and to resolve outstanding political questions. Latin American resistance to discussion of substantive issues soon limited the agendas of these meetings to noncontroversial "technical" matters, but this had the unforeseen advantage of allowing them to continue despite rising resentment over U.S. Roosevelt Corollary interventions in the Caribbean. Out of these meetings evolved an institutional structure for a fledgling "inter-American system." The Pan American Union was established in 1910 as a sort of permanent committee and secretariat for the ongoing conferences.

In the 1920s, Latin American governments discovered that the inter-American system could be used as a forum to criticize U.S. interventions in the name of Pan-Americanism. The Franklin Roosevelt administration in 1933 formally accepted the principle of nonintervention, which became a legal cornerstone of the system (albeit a vague principle and, by any definition, one honored as much in the breach as in the observance). The Roosevelt "Good Neighbor" policies were shaped, in part, by Washington's interest in putting the inter-American house in order, so that the hemisphere might be united in its response to the looming threat of war in Europe. As hostilities escalated, the inter-American system served first as a consultative mechanism and then provided the institutional framework for a wartime alliance. At least in symbolic terms, the Monroe Doctrine was "multilateralized." With the exception of friction over a pro-Axis regime in Argentina and the accession to power of what was incorrectly feared to be a Nazi-influenced MNR faction in Bolivia, the World War II period involved unprecedented cooperation between the United States and Latin America. In addition to less tangible rewards, Latin American governments received substantial material aid for their participation in the Allied cause. At the conclusion of the war, Latin American governments and supporters of Pan Americanism in the U.S. Congress prevailed upon the Truman administration to accept a conversion of the inter-American alliance into a genuine collective security system, to plan for the establishment of a formal hemisphere organization, and to see to it that the new United Nations Charter made appropriate allowances for "regional organizations and agencies."

The inter-American system was consolidated with the signing of the Rio Treaty (1947) and the Charter of the Organization of American States (1948). Although an additional Treaty of Bogota, detailing peaceful settlement procedures, was not widely ratified, the OAS was able to investigate and defuse several disputes that arose in the Caribbean through the 1950s. Most of these disputes stemmed from the conflict between prodemocracy exile groups and dictatorships in the area. The OAS success in this regard may be attributed primarily to the fact that the United States now had a multilateral institution through which to bring its influence to bear, without necessarily raising charges of intervention.

Be that as it may, intervention was the charge directed by some Latin American governments at U.S. efforts to use the OAS as an anticommunist alliance. Particularly controversial was the "Dulles Doctrine," which was embodied in a resolution of the Tenth Inter-American Conference (Caracas, 1954). Plainly directed against the Arbenz government in Guatemala, the resolution stated that the "domination or control" of an American state by "international communism" would occasion inter-American consultation and possible sanctions. The Eisenhower administration subsequently blocked United Nations involvement while a CIA-assisted exile invasion overthrew Arbenz. There was widespread suspicion that U.S. hostility toward Arbenz was prompted mainly by his government's expropriation of some United Fruit properties, an interpretation that gives too little weight to Dulles' personal crusade against communism and the Cold War climate of the time. Later, similar suspicions hampered the Eisenhower and Kennedy administrations' initial efforts to elicit OAS expressions of concern about developments in Castro's Cuba.

Another source of friction in the United States-Latin America postwar relations was the fact that the wartime partnership had raised Latin American hopes that Washington would continue to strengthen hemispheric cooperation for economic development. However, the Truman and Eisenhower administrations were preoccupied with recovery and containment of communism in Europe and Asia. There was no Marshall Plan for Latin America, and the United States for many years also turned a deaf ear to Latin American pleas for commodity agreements and other trade concessions. The prevailing view in Washington was that Latin America could secure nearly all the capital needed for development if governments in the area would only move decisively toward the free enterprise economic model and foster the conditions necessary to attract foreign private investment.

In the late 1950s, with the rise of the Latin American democratic left, Vice President Nixon's poor reception on a Latin American tour, and the Cuban Revolution, U.S. policies began to shift on a number of fronts. The Eisenhower administration acceded to Latin American demands for an Inter-American Development Bank (IDB) and, in 1960, established a small additional Social Progress Trust Fund. Moreover, despite their earlier record of support for Latin American dictatorships, Eisenhower decision makers acquiesced in, and then strongly implemented, an OAS decision to levy sanctions against the Trujillo regime in the Dominican Republic. Although this was partially a trade-off for Latin American votes on the Cuban issue, it was also a reflection of Washington's new assessment that Trujillo was another Batista who might be succeeded by another Castro unless constructive change could be engineered in the Dominican Republic.

The Kennedy administration was no less concerned about a perceived Communist threat in Latin America than its predecessors. Attempts to overthrow Castro (the Bay of Pigs and subsequent CIA plots) were combined with a largely successful campaign through the OAS to isolate his government diplomatically. The United States and the Soviet Union went to the brink of nuclear war in the Cuban Missile Crisis of 1962. U.S. military aid programs in this period were mainly directed at increasing counterinsurgency and civic action capabilities.

However, the administration firmly believed that the only viable alternative to more Castroist revolutions was evolutionary socioeconomic change under the aegis of the Latin American democratic left. From this assumption flowed both a posture of opposition to unconstitutional regimes and the Alliance for Progress, which was designed to provide the public and private capital that the democratic left needed for economic and social development. In its incorporation of large-scale public aid and its emphasis on national planning, the Alliance embraced some of the prescriptions which had been advanced by the Economic Commission for Latin America (ECLA) during the Eisenhower years. The Kennedy administration also endorsed ECLA goals of import-substitution industrialization and Latin American economic integration, promised to lower barriers to expanded Latin American trade and to rethink the U.S. position on commodity agreements, and ended a previous almost-categorical refusal to fund state enterprises in Latin America.

The Alliance for Progress goals of democratic government and social reform were frustrated by a series of "technocratic" military coups in the early 1960s, and these goals were greatly deemphasized by the Johnson administration. What was left of the Alliance became a traditional-style aid program largely for economic development, with an increasing proportion of assistance channeled through multilateral lending agencies. U.S. bilateral assistance to Latin America as a percentage of total U.S. bilateral and multilateral assistance steadily declined from 53.9 percent in the 1960-65 period, to 43.1 percent during the years 1966 to 1970, to a mere 28.2 percent in 1971-75, and 20.4 percent in 1977.(75) President Johnson earned plaudits in Latin America for his willingness to begin negotiations toward a new Panama Canal treaty when riots broke out in the Canal Zone in 1964. However, the following year, fear of "another Cuba" led the United States to intervene militarily in the Dominican civil war, an action which generated even more controversy than the 1954 Guatemalan episode. Although the OAS subsequently "multilateralized" the operation by creating an Inter-American Peace Force, it did so only after an acrimonious debate and by a narrow vote.

United States-Latin American relations entered a new divergent phase in the late 1960s. The Johnson administration became preoccupied with the war in Indochina, and hemisphere affairs received considerably less priority. Under the Nixon administration, Washington policymakers made the conscious decision to strive for a "lower profile" in Latin America and what Henry Kissinger called a "mature partnership." This decision was partly a reflection of the demands of the extrahemisphere environment (e.g., ending the war in Vietnam, negotiations with the Soviets on arms control and other matters, the trade and monetary crisis involving Europe and Japan, efforts to achieve a settlement in the Middle East), and partly a result of changing conditions within Latin America. Che Guevara's death in Bolivia in 1967 and Castro's muting of his appeals for "armed struggle" after 1968 seemed to signal a substantial diminishing of the threat of additional Castroist revolutions. For their part, the Soviets appeared to be exercising a restraining influence both on Castro and Latin American leftists generally, lobbying for a "peaceful road to power" strategy, and cultivating "respectable" diplomatic and trade relations with Latin American governments of all ideological persuasions. Another reason for the lower profile was rising economic nationalism in Latin America, which was itself partially a response to what Latins perceived as neglect from Washington.

The Nixon administration angered Latin Americans by not exempting their goods from a temporary 10 percent surcharge imposed on all imports in 1971. Nevertheless, the administration made a determined effort, with considerable resistance from Congress, to respond to Latin American demands for a generalized system of trade preferences that was projected by UNCTAD II (1970) for developing country manufactured and semimanufactured goods, continued development aid, and unrestricted military arms sales. A Special Negotiating and Consulting Commission (CECON) was established in 1970 under the OAS Economic and Social Council to serve as the first permanent forum for United States-Latin American trade negotiations. Paralleling a similar emphasis that had emerged at the World Bank, U.S. bilateral assistance through AID was reoriented in 1973 (at congressional insistence) to stress the needs of the poor majority in developing countries.

However, the administration's lower profile was, to some extent, frustrated by the adoption of a hard line in response to expropriations of U.S. companies in Peru, Chile, and several other countries. In 1972, the White House officially declared that such expropriations must be "nondiscriminatory," for a public purpose, and followed by "prompt, adequate, and effective compensation"; failing this, the United States would withhold "new bilateral economic benefits" and also oppose the extension of additional multilateral assistance to the country in question. This policy was incorporated into the Gonzalez Amendment to U.S. foreign assistance legislation.(76) Treatment of U.S. enterprises was one of several factors motivating the Nixon administration's economic and political pressures against the Allende government. Other concerns were Allende's extraordinary challenge to U.S. prestige and his example of the "peaceful road to power," which Washington feared might encourage similar electoral movements on the left in Europe and possibly elsewhere in Latin America.

Following the onset of the energy crisis, at meetings of hemisphere foreign ministers in early 1974, Secretary of State Kissinger announced his intention to undertake a "new dialogue" to revive the United States "special relationship" with Latin America. This was widely interpreted as an attempt to woo Latin Americans away from participation in any Third World bloc. In any event, despite Kissinger's concessions on the Panama Canal issue (a joint statement with Panama regarding principles to be incorporated in the new treaties), the new dialogue died aborning. Congress finally passed the generalized preferences scheme affecting Latin American industrial exports, but pointedly denied benefits to governments that are members of commodity cartels (including OPEC members Venezuela and Ecuador). This provision was particularly irksome to Venezuela, which had not supported the Arab boycott and had even postponed a planned cutback in production to accommodate U.S. needs during the worst of the shortages. With the atmosphere poisoned, it was decided not to go ahead with a hemisphere foreign ministers meeting scheduled for Buenos Aires early in 1975.

That same year the United States acquiesced in an OAS decision to lift sanctions against the Castro regime, leaving relations with Cuba to the discretion of member states. However, Castro's involvement in Angola derailed what had appeared to be gradual movement toward a normalization of U.S. relations with Cuba. There was additional friction in the OAS, culminating in 1976, over the Latin's desire to have the OAS formally subscribe to the concept of "collective economic security." The United States cast the sole negative vote against a draft convention on this subject and also refused to support several articles concerning the exclusively domestic character of a country's treatment of foreign investment in the draft Inter-American Convention on Cooperation for Integral Development.[77] Finally, Kissinger's conclusion in 1976 of a special consultative agreement with Brazil seriously disturbed rival governments and advocates of democracy and human rights generally.

The Carter administration has given Latin American affairs more attention than any U.S. administration since Kennedy, but not in the context of a revival of the special relationship. Administration spokesmen have stressed that, in their view, such a relationship between the United States and Latin America is no longer either desirable or feasible. Rather, Latin America is best addressed in the framework of "global" policies, which, in turn, are adjusted to reflect important bilateral ties. Most observers[78] have given Carter credit for negotiating new treaties for the Panama Canal and achieving the even more difficult task of getting them ratified (and largely implemented) by Congress; reidentifying the United States with democracy and human rights in Latin America;[79] increasing ties with Cuba through the exchange of diplomatic interest sections (although Castro's African involvement continues to stall full normalization); and maintaining reasonably good relations with socialist governments in Guyana and Jamaica.[80] On the other hand, little came of the Carter administration's promise to undertake new initiatives in the Caribbean; and there has been no major progress on the remaining items on the NIEO agenda. Several governments expressed dismay that the Carter administration – after openly criticizing the Somoza regime – sought a negotiated settlement ostensibly under OAS auspices after civil war erupted in 1978. As they saw it, Washington was unduly cautious about Somoza's possible violent overthrow because of the leftist ideology of some of the Sandinista rebels.

Residues of the hegemonic relationship obviously remain. For example, the Carter administration has been more sensitive about the possible emergence of a radical-left regime in Nicaragua than it might have been in many places outside of Latin America (especially the Caribbean). The probable U.S. domestic political uproar was simply too much to contemplate, particularly when the Panama Canal treaties were hanging in the balance. Otherwise, the Carter administration has been more active and successful in pursuing human rights violations in Latin America than outside the traditional U.S. sphere of influence. Nevertheless, some analysts would no doubt regard U.S. human rights pressures on many Latin American dictatorships as, conversely, an indication of the region's "expendability" from the U.S. viewpoint – and point to Carter's rather tentative policy toward Somoza as evidence of what happens when there is a higher level of concern.

As for bilateral ties, the Carter administration has not officially renounced the special consultative agreement with Brazil, but relations with Brazil were initially strained by the human rights issue and U.S. opposition to a nuclear sharing agreement that Brasilia concluded with West Germany.(81) Greater priority has been given to relations with Mexico and Venezuela because of the oil wealth and better record on human rights in these two countries.(82)

Regional and Subregional Institutions

The idea of Pan-Latin American association harks back to Bolivar, but it began to be realized only after World War II, indeed, mainly since 1960 and to date only to a modest extent. ECLA was the ideological progenitor of postwar regional and subregional cooperation. The United States was (and is) a member of ECLA; however, it was Prebisch and the Secretariat that shaped Latin American – and eventually Kennedy administration – thinking about development. After the Alliance incorporated many of ECLA's prescriptions, though the organization continued in existence, it ceased to be a leading regional actor. Prebisch himself went on to the post of Executive Secretary of UNCTAD. UNCTAD, dependency theory, OPEC, and NIEO proposals have all provided an ideological foundation for post-ECLA regional organization. However, as we have stressed, the decline of the special relationship with the United States also had an important – possibly a critical – impact. Latin America was forced to explore other alternatives, including intraregional association, which itself appeared to be a precondition for dealing successfully with a less-receptive United States and with extrahemisphere DCs and LDCs.(83)

LAFTA

The Latin American Free Trade Association was one of two regional economic integration efforts (the other was CACM) launched directly by ECLA's vision of wider markets mainly to support import-substitution industrialization.(84) The 1960 Montevideo Treaty established the organization; its members are Argentina, Brazil, Chile, Colombia, Ecuador, Mexico, Paraguay, Peru, Uruguay, and Venezuela. The original plan was to achieve a free trade area by 1973, but by 1967 it was clear that this deadline was not going to be met. It was then decided to aim for a common market by 1980 that would incorporate the CACM. This deadline, too, is not going to be met, and the goal of an all-Latin America common market may never be reached.

In 1978, a mere 13 percent of LAFTA members' exports went to the zone.(85) A sore issue over the years has been one that has usually plagued integration experiments, the matter of an unequal sharing of benefits. Most benefits have plainly accrued to the three leading exporters of manufactured goods – Argentina, Brazil, and Mexico – and primarily to foreign multinationals operating in these and other countries. Hopefully to speed integration, LAFTA in 1967 also authorized the formation of "subregions." The Andean Common Market (ANCOM) emerged from this provision and proved somewhat more successful than its parent. Since the late 1960s there have been only relatively minor trade concessions within the LAFTA framework proper.

CACM

The other integration scheme directly fostered by ECLA was the Central American Common Market (CACM), created in 1960 with a membership of Guatemala, El Salvador, Honduras, Nicaragua, and Costa Rica.(86) During the 1960s, the CACM did achieve a common external tariff and eliminated most intrazonal tariffs. Then almost all momentum was lost in 1969 with the "Soccer War" between El Salvador and Honduras. Honduras withdrew from active participation, although at the same time concluding bilateral agreements with the other governments (except El Salvador) to preserve some gains in intrazonal trade. Currently, about a fifth of all CACM exports stay in the zone, making the CACM the most integrated subregional trading system in Latin America. There have, nevertheless, been complaints from Honduras and Costa Rica that Guatemala, El Salvador, and (to a lesser extent) Nicaragua have been reaping most of the rewards from the expanded market. More precisely, all parties recognize that it has been foreign multinationals in the more industrialized countries which have been the principal beneficiaries.

For some years, Mexico has been attempting to increase its influence in the subregion, and Venezuela succeeded in doing so after 1974 when Central America was hard-hit by the increase in oil prices. Venezuela loaned back oil payments made in local currencies, bought bonds of the Central American Bank for Integration, and offered to finance a plan to create a buffer stock to support the price of Central American coffee (to be discussed below).

CECLA

The Special Commission for Latin American Coordination (CECLA) was established on an informal basis to develop a common Latin American position on issues of international economic policy that were likely to arise at the first UNCTAD conference in 1964. A common position was largely achieved and had considerable impact at this conference. CECLA continued to meet sporadically and in 1969, its finest hour, presented the United States with a detailed list of Latin American demands (the "Consensus of Vina del Mar"). In 1971, CECLA roundly condemned the Nixon administration's 10 percent surcharge.

The creation of CECLA was an exceedingly important milestone, not only because it excluded the United States but also because, as Mary Jeanne Reid Martz points out, it was "one of the few organs of the developing world which. . .made a concerted attempt to present a common economic front in negotiations with developed nations."(87) However, the organization never established a permanent secretariat or headquarters, and it began to fade in the early 1970s. Chile (the Eduardo Frei and Allende administrations) and Peru (the Velasco government) had been among CECLA's strongest supporters, and shifts to more conservative regimes in those two countries had a definite dampening effect.

OPANAL

The product of a Mexican initiative, the Treaty of Tlatelolco (the Treaty for the Prohibition of Nuclear Weapons in Latin America) was signed in 1967 and is now in full force for 22 Latin American countries. Parties to the treaty pledge not to develop, test, or import nuclear weapons. They are obliged to establish safeguards in conjunction with the International Atomic Energy Agency for nuclear development and are subject to "challenge inspections" by an organ of the Agency for the Prohibition of Nuclear Weapons in Latin America (OPANAL). Additional Protocol I, pledging countries with territorial possessions in the Americas not to introduce nuclear weapons therein, has been, or is in the process of being, ratified by all the relevant parties (France, the United Kingdom, the Netherlands, and the United States); likewise, Protocol II, pledging countries which already possess nuclear weapons (United States, Soviet Union, France, the United Kingdom, and China) not to use them against parties to the treaty. Four key Latin American countries (Argentina, Brazil, Chile, and Cuba) have neither ratified the world Nuclear Nonproliferation Treaty nor are, as yet, full parties to Tlatelolco. Brazil and Chile have ratified Tlatelolco but have elected to exercise a treaty option whereby it will not come into full force for them until all relevant parties have ratified both the treaty and the protocols. Argentina has indicated its intention to ratify on the same terms.

Although the prospects for the Tlatelolco Treaty's coming into full force eventually are good, there is a serious gap in the treaty: it does not unambiguously forbid "peaceful nuclear explosives" (PNEs). (India's entrance into the nuclear club has been through the PNE back door.) Argentina and Brazil have evidenced strong interest in PNEs. These two countries and Mexico should have one or more nuclear power reactors in service by the early 1980s; in addition, Chile, Colombia, Cuba, Peru, and Venezuela have nuclear energy programs in various stages of development. An even more ominous trend is that there appears to be a growing desire among those countries in Latin America developing nuclear energy to incorporate the full fuel cycle, including enrichment, reprocessing facilities, and breeder reactors. The Carter administration's main objection to West Germany's 1975 agreement with Brazil was that it involved enrichment and reprocessing without, in Washington's view, adequate safeguards that nuclear development would not ultimately be used for military purposes.

Considering the potential linkage between nuclear energy development and weaponry, John Redick has suggested that Latin Americans and the United States should consider at least two institutional changes.(88) The first would be a merger of OPANAL with the OAS Inter-American Nuclear Energy Commission (CIEN), which is essentially a technical agency that was designed to encourage the development of nuclear power. The second would be the possible establishment of regional nuclear energy centers, including one owned and controlled jointly by Brazil and Argentina but located in a "neutral" country like Paraguay. Such a facility might offer greater safeguards than a strictly unilateral program. However, whether two countries that have long been bitter rivals could cooperate in such a sensitive area is doubtful, unless the threat of a local nuclear arms race were to become sufficiently frightening.

CARIFTA/CARICOM

The Caribbean Free Trade Association (CARIFTA) was formed in 1968 and in 1973-74 was converted into a common market, the Caribbean Community (CARICOM). Members include Barbados, Guyana, Jamaica, and Trinidad and Tobago, plus Grenada and several colonial entities. Intrazonal exports in recent years have ranged from about 8 to 11 percent of total exports. One of the more interesting aspects of CARICOM has been its use of the public international corporation. This involves the joint participation of two or more states in particular projects, in the fields of agriculture and food processing as well as industry. For example, a Regional Food Corporation – with several subsidiaries engaged in various aspects of production, processing, and marketing – is just going into operation, and joint aluminum smelters are being planned.(89)

Nevertheless, CARICOM has had numerous problems, and its future is still not entirely secure. Socialist Jamaica and Guyana have applied for membership in COMECON (the communist regional trade association) and of late have experienced such severe balance-of-payments difficulties that they have drastically curtailed imports from CARICOM. The subregion has also been hard-hit by agricultural shortages and rising oil prices, a source of resentment against oil-producing Trinidad and Tobago. Furthermore, CARICOM's common external tariff makes no allowances for the different import requirements of divergent economies: tourism (Barbados), industry (Trinidad and Tobago), and agriculture (Guyana, Grenada).(90)

Things temporarily seemed to look up for the subregion when the Carter administration, in 1977, indicated that it was going to undertake a new initiative for the Caribbean. Later that year, a Caribbean Group for Cooperation and Economic Development (CGCED) was formed under the chairmanship of the World Bank. However, hopes fizzled when it became apparent that the White House was primarily concerned with coordinating existing economic assistance from several quarters and would not authorize any major new spending for either multilateral or bilateral aid. A modest consolation was that the IDB modified its regulations to allow it to lend to CARICOM's Caribbean Development Bank, which then could extend credit to CARICOM members who otherwise have no access to the IDB. Also, Venezuela – as evidence of its growing interest in the subregion – gave $25 million to Caribank. On the negative side, Trinidad and Tobago's Prime Minister Eric Williams warned that the increasing activities of Venezuelan private companies and the Venezuelan government in the subregion were a form of "imperialism."

ANCOM

The Cartagena Agreement that created The Andean Common Market (ANCOM) was signed in 1969. Founding member states were Colombia, Ecuador, Peru, Bolivia, and Chile; Venezuela joined in 1973, and Chile withdrew in 1976. At the outset, ANCOM was by far the most ambitious Latin American regional integration scheme, and it remains so despite major setbacks.(91)

ANCOM's claim to fame has never rested primarily on its trade measures. Full liberalization of intraregional trade is scheduled to be completed by 1982 (1987 for the less-developed members, Bolivia and Ecuador), but there has been some grumbling that this schedule is too demanding. There has also been only slow progress converting a minimum common external tariff into a full-fledged tariff because of the desire of Venezuela for more protection than Bolivia, Chile, and Colombia have wanted to provide. The level of intrazonal trade, mainly on agricultural items, has stalled at just about five percent since the early 1970s.

A more innovative and controversial aspect of ANCOM was Decision 24 of the Andean Commission which established a common policy on foreign investment. The goal was to avoid the error made by LAFTA and the CACM of having foreign multinationals gain the most from a lowering of tariff barriers. Accordingly, certain economic sectors were reserved for national and ANCOM development; foreign multinationals already operating in those sectors were to "phase out" over a period of 15 years; and existing and new foreign enterprises in the nonreserved sectors were to establish majority local ownership and management within the same time frame. This policy proved too confining for the new military government of Chile, which was anxious to reattract foreign investment after the turmoil of the Allende years. The Andean Junta, a group of ANCOM technocrats with advisory and planning functions, ruled that Chile's laws were incompatible with Decision 24; and Chile, after making some efforts to comply, finally decided to withdraw from the organization. There is a considerable division of opinion among the remaining members of ANCOM as to whether the common investment code should be liberalized with regard to lesser matters such as the allowed rate of profit remittance. Venezuela, which has enacted a foreign investment code that, in some respects, is even more restrictive than Decision 24, has supported a hard line, while Colombia has argued for a more liberal policy.

Another important innovation was ANCOM's plan to conclude a series of industrial sectorial development agreements, allocating new plants and production lines for specific products among the member countries. Decision 46 provided for the creation of ANCOM multinationals which would have majority investment from one or more member states (perhaps some minority foreign investment as well) and enjoy special terms of access to the common market. The Junta, in 1972, drafted a general plan for industrial development within the subregion. To date, agreements have been concluded covering metal-mechanical (1972), petrochemical (1975), and automobile (1977) industries. Because negotiations over the automobile agreement were so protracted, they delayed Commission consideration of several other proposed programs, including fertilizers, steel, electronics and telecommunications, chemicals and pharmaceuticals, food processing, ship building, and pulp and paper.

Now that Chile has withdrawn, Bolivia is the most troublesome member of ANCOM. In 1977, Bolivia protested officially, with some justification, that it was getting less out of ANCOM than the other four members. Because of the country's limited industrialization, tariff cuts are of little direct benefit, and Bolivia claimed that it was neither receiving sufficient assignments under sectorial programs nor were the exclusive assignments which had been received being honored by all of the other members. ANCOM's response was a special aid program to Bolivia to promote existing industries and to explore new opportunities for the country in the sectorial programs.

An additional issue for ANCOM has been its external relationships. ANCOM tariff policies and sectorial agreements have, to some extent, conflicted with LAFTA decisions, and vice versa. Mexico made early overtures to ANCOM, including the extension of a $5 million credit to ANCOM's Andean Development Corporation, but has neither asked nor been asked to join. Argentina has asked to become a member, but Colombia and Venezuela are apparently unalterably opposed.

La Pla Basin

In 1969, the same year that ANCOM was established, another treaty formed Argentina, Bolivia, Brazil, Paraguay, and Uruguay into a Plata Basin Group for the purpose of developing subregional hydroelectric power and water resources. The group was to act in cooperation with a consortium of international organizations chaired by the Inter-American Bank. However, cooperation gave way to mutual recriminations beginning in 1973, when Argentina raised strenuous objections to a Brazil-Paraguay agreement to construct the Itaipu Dam on the upper Parana River (the world's largest hydroelectric project). Argentina insists that the project threatens damage to Argentina-Paraguay projects downstream. Today there is little left of what was initially a promising arrangement except several bilateral agreements.

OLADE

A Latin American Energy Development Organization (OLADE) was proposed in 1972 by Venezuela, primarily as a means of marshaling regional support for OPEC. The following year, the Arab oil boycott and attendant price increase occasioned a meeting of Latin American energy ministers, where it became apparent that there were grave differences of opinion as to exactly what kind of organization OLADE should be. Many ministers argued for an organization that would control prices and supplies and facilitate negotiations between the region's oil-exporting and oil-importing countries. Peru and Ecuador wanted to see an even broader organization that would control prices and supplies of raw materials generally. Venezuela, by this time having second thoughts, only proved willing to offer financial assistance for an energy development fund. Moreover, Cuba's presence at the meeting was particularly irksome to military regimes in Chile and Brazil.(92)

Consequently, although OLADE was officially launched, it was effectively (in Edward Milenky's words) "stillborn." "OLADE was to be little more than a framework for voluntary joint development projects, it was hoped with Venezuelan financing, and an opportunity for Latin American oil-importing countries to express their solidarity with each other and with OPEC in the hope that they might at best escape from dependence on Arab oil and at least become preferred customers."(93) Mexico gave strong moral support to the organization, but Argentina and (ironically) Venezuela were slow in ratifying the founding treaty. Indeed, Venezuela channeled its financial assistance elsewhere: $500 million to the IDB for development loans; additional sums to subregional banks in Central America and the Caribbean; and strictly bilateral arrangements with the Central American countries, Jamaica, and several other countries for oil and/or deficit financing.(94)

Commodity cartels

The spectacular success of OPEC encouraged Latin American efforts to form other cartels, none of which has been nearly as significant. One for bananas failed completely. Another for mild coffees will be discussed below. A sugar cartel with a permanent secretariat was created in 1976, despite the nonparticipation of Latin America's two largest exporters, Cuba and Brazil. Its aims are to present a common position at meetings of the International Sugar Organization, to negotiate price agreements with consuming countries, and to ban sales below the daily market price.(95)

SELA. By the mid-1970s the time seemed ripe for the establishment of a new institutional mechanism for regional consultation and action. For reasons mentioned previously, CECLA was no longer adequate. Although there was no strong support for the notion of abandoning the OAS – still useful for negotiations with the United States and for peaceful settlement – it was clear from such indications as the 1975 Trade Act and Washington's determined opposition to the principle of collective economic security that Kissinger's "new dialogue" was not going to revive the old special relationship. Opportunities for cooperation with Third World organizations also appeared to be increasing. This, then, was the context out of which the Latin American Economic System (SELA) gradually emerged.(96)

The concept of SELA was initially advanced by President Echeverria of Mexico in July 1974, and it attracted the almost immediate backing of President Perez of Venezuela. The organization was created in August 1975 with a Council of Ministers and a Permanent Secretariat. Its mission, couched in rather hazy terms, is essentially threefold: (a) to develop and advance common Latin American positions on issues of international economic relations; (b) to increase the production and supply of basic commodities (especially food); and (c) to promote the establishment of Latin American multinational enterprises.

There is some background for the third function in both CARICOM and ANCOM and in the recent establishment of two major companies in coffee and shipping, respectively. With the financial support of Venezuela and the cooperation of Mexico, Costa Rica, Ecuador, El Salvador, Guatemala, Honduras, Nicaragua, and Panama, La Compania Cafe Suaves Centrales was founded in early 1975. This is a marketing agency through which it was hoped to help stabilize prices for mild coffees by controlling exports. In addition, a Caribbean shipping enterprise – a cooperative venture of Colombia, Venezuela, Costa Rica, Jamaica, Cuba, Nicaragua, Panama, and Mexico – started operations in February 1976. SELA was not responsible for either of these companies, but its Action Committees are examining the prospects for others in a variety of economic sectors.

SELA may facilitate joint enterprises and serve as a latter-day CECLA; however, it is extremely unlikely to amount to much more. There are now new, less internationally-inclined administrations in Mexico and Venezuela. Nationalism is also less pronounced now than it was in Panama, Peru, and Ecuador. Brazil has traditionally preferred bilateral diplomacy to Latin American multilateralism and – with other Latin American conservative regimes – is not happy about Cuba's involvement in SELA. Argentina has never been a particularly enthusiastic supporter of the organization.(97)

Amazon Pact

The Amazon Pact is basically a mechanism for the loose coordination of the development by each sovereign nation of its own Amazon territory. The pact was signed in July 1978 by representatives of Bolivia, Brazil, Colombia, Ecuador, Guyana, Peru, Surinam, and Venezuela. An Amazon Cooperation Council will meet annually and foreign ministers biannually to consider the implementation of various principles included in the accord. These principles concern such matters as free navigation of rivers, protection of flora and fauna, improvement of health conditions, and promotion of tourism and scientific research.

The pact derived from an initiative by Brazil's President Geisel late in 1976 and, as Martz remarks, "has been seen by many Latins as an attempt (by Brazil) to shortcircuit integration arrangements while at the same time not isolating herself."(98) It was also an effort by Brazil to assure its uneasy neighbors that projects like the Trans-Amazon Highway were not intended to lay the groundwork for military expansion. Moreover, as Robert Bond has stressed, the agreement was additionally significant in that it signaled at least a slight warming in Brazil's relationship with Venezuela, which had been badly strained by Venezuela's resentment over Brazil's decision (in the early 1960s) to switch to lower-priced Middle Eastern oil, criticism of repression in Brazil, and an abortive campaign (by President Rafael Caldera) to organize an alliance of Spanish-speaking countries to contain possible Brazilian imperialism.(99)

Relations with Extrahemisphere DCs and LDCs

As we have observed, Latin America's trade with Europe has increased in recent years at a faster rate and more in terms of value than Latin America's trade with the United States. Though the patterns vary greatly from country to country, the overall value of Latin America's trade with Europe is now only a little less than its trade with the United States. Latin America's trade with Japan and the Eastern bloc has also increased, but these levels are still quite modest – roughly 4 and 9 percent of the total, respectively.(100)

More intensive trade ties with Europe are more the result of the increasing dynamism of Europe and a Latin American policy of diversifying dependency than European generosity in receiving Latin American exports. EEC protectionism has been a continuing problem. The 1975 Lome Agreement gave 46 African, Pacific, and Caribbean states special access to the EEC in competition with most of Latin America.

Outside of trade, a more encouraging trend in the mid-1970s was that many of the European states became members of the IDB. This was all the more significant because, under a system of weighted voting, it vastly reduced U.S. influence over lending decisions.(101)

Latin America as a region is, almost by any standard, more developed than Africa, Asia, and the Middle East. Yet, as the special relationship with the United States has declined and the North-South cleavage in world affairs has more clearly emerged, Latin American governments have increasingly aligned themselves with the South. Indeed, they have been one of the most cohesive and responsible elements in the South's coalition, providing leadership and often a degree of realism and moderation that otherwise might have been lacking. As early as 1959, OPEC itself was the brainchild of Venezuela's oil minister, Pablo Perez Alfonso, and Prebisch was the logical choice to be the first Executive Secretary of UNCTAD.

Latin American governments have played a prominent role in the United Nations General Assembly; successive meetings of UNCTAD, the so-called Group of 77, and the Nonaligned Countries; and the ongoing UN Conference on the Law of the Sea.(102) The framework of generalized preferences for LDC manufactures and semimanufactures which has been at least partially implemented by the DCs, as well as the shift away from the traditional three-mile limit for territorial waters to a formula of 12 miles for territorial waters plus a conservation zone extending to 200 miles, are directly attributable to the Latin Americans.(103) Presidents Echeverria and Perez were among the architects of the NIEO and certainly two of its most eloquent spokes-men. In 1974, Latin America joined the rest of the Third World in: UN General Assembly approval of a Declaration on the Establishment of a New International Economic Order, an action program on the NIEO, and the Echeverria sponsored Charter of the Economic Rights and Duties of States. Many of the NIEO themes were foreshadowed by the 1969 Consensus of Vina del Mar. Depending upon one's point of view, possibly less constructive has been the switch, most notably of Mexico and Brazil (not coincidentally, beginning in 1973-4), to a pro-Arab position in the Arab-Israeli conflict.(104) An extreme example of this switch was Mexico's subscription to the 1974 UN General Assembly "anti-Zionist" resolution, which subsequently proved rather embarrassing to Echeverria because of a Jewish tourist boycott.

Within the general context of the NIEO, Latin American countries have several major goals. High on the list of priorities is the international support of "just" prices for food and raw materials, through such devices as buffer stocks and/or control of exports. Equally important is access to DC markets, which is still restricted despite widespread acceptance of the concept of generalized preferences. For example, U.S. trade law not only discriminates against members of cartels but also protects domestic manufacturers from "unfair" competition from goods that have allegedly been "dumped" or that have received a government subsidy. Given the heavy involvement of the states in economic life, the latter is a common practice in Latin

America. In addition, agricultural goods may face stiff health requirements, quotas, or bans because of claims of "hardship" on the part of domestic producers.

Another Latin American goal is the continued flow of adequate levels of international financial assistance for development projects, energy deficits, and other balance-of-payments problems. Many countries are also experiencing an urgent need for debt relief, which may involve a rescheduling of debt payments, a temporary moratorium, and/or new tide-over capital from public-international or private sources.(105) Yet another issue is adequate access to DC technology, in part through the elimination of existing restrictions on the dissemination of technology that have been imposed by multinationals already operating in the region. This issue is closely related to the broader question of the regulation of foreign investment. The major Latin American countries have all been revamping their laws affecting the multinationals in recent years and, as we have noted, this has been one of the preoccupations of ANCOM. However, there is also a worldwide NIEO dimension to the debate, as Latin American and other Third World spokesmen have pressed for formal international affirmation of the sovereignty of individual states over their natural resources and the exclusively "domestic" character of disputes arising from nationalizations and expropriations. Moreover, some effort has been made to draft a code of conduct for the multinationals.

If there is a trend in the continuing North-South negotiations over the NIEO agenda, it appears to be a decrease in ideological posturing and a corresponding increase in pragmatism. The same might be said for the policies many governments are applying at home. Fire-breathing speeches and confrontation tactics seem to be giving way to hard bargaining. Certainly, the current absence of Allende, Velasco, Peron, Echeverria, and Perez from the scene has contributed to this trend; however, something more profound in the realm of what might be termed international social learning has also been involved. Latin Americans are fond of saying that one cannot meaningfully discuss "interdependence" until there is greater equality in the balance between North and South. Nevertheless, more parties to the North-South negotiations have seemingly come to recognize that economic interdependence, albeit limited, is real; that leverage on both sides, albeit limited, is also real; and that confrontation, except in rare cases, only hardens positions. In the jargon of game theory, North-South negotiations are increasingly viewed by the players as a nonzero sum game.

THE FUTURE OF THE REGION

Barring intervening factors like a major world war or depression, virtually the only foreseeable future for the Latin American region appears to be "more of the same."

Current patterns of domestic politics and socioeconomic development will persist, including considerable variation country-to-country.

Apart from extraregional relationships, the future will be shaped primarily by the policies of several key states.

As Schneider observes: "Brazil is nearing the ill-defined but generally recognized point at which it can claim to be a ranking power – the first Southern Hemisphere state in the world galaxy and the first new major power to emerge on the international scene since the rise of China after World War II."(106) Mexico and Venezuela are also guaranteed important international roles by virtue of their oil wealth, although Venezuela's reserves are declining. If Venezuela is to remain in the spotlight, it will have to find a commercially viable means of utilizing the Orinoco tar belt (which is probable). Brazil, Mexico, and Venezuela all have a domestic liability, a growing gap between the rich and poor, which sooner or later could result in social strife and political instability. A full-scale social revolution in any case is unlikely, but trouble at home would militate against international prestige and an effective foreign policy.

Partly because of political turmoil and also uneven economic performance, Argentina has gradually been losing ground in its race to keep pace with the "Big Three," especially Brazil. Cuba will no doubt continue to be a source of controversy in Latin America, until and unless Fidel ceases to try to export revolution and normalizes relations with the United States.

Rivalries among the major Latin American powers, differing ideologies, and smoldering territorial disputes will continue to undermine the processes of institution-building at the inter-American, regional, and subregional levels. The OAS(107) will probably remain an adequate peaceful settlement mechanism, supplemented by ad hoc mediatory efforts by the United States, Latin American governments, and others (the Vatican defused the recent flare-up of the Beagle Channel dispute). The OAS Inter-American Commission on Human Rights has been useful in publicizing some abuses, and the OAS as a whole has condemned extreme examples of repression in Chile and Nicaragua. However, at least for the present, the presence of so many dictatorships in the organization rules out collective action in most instances.(108) We have examined the limited accomplishments and problems of Latin American economic integration experiments and of regional institutions like SELA and OPANAL.

Were one a "regional manager," one might insist that much greater intraregional and subregional unity be achieved – especially in economic integration – as the best means of realizing the internal potential of Latin America and enhancing the region's bargaining power vis-a-vis external actors. Nevertheless, a Bolivarian vision of this kind is simply not going to be fulfilled. In the future as in the recent past, we will see a remarkable degree of Latin American consensus on many issues of international economic policy, a very gradual growth in intraregional trade, and the establishment of more Latin American multinationals. This outlook is not particularly exciting, but it is enough to give Latin America a continuing claim to being more of a "region" than any other in the developing world.

APPENDIX: LIST OF ACRONYMS

AD – Accion Democratica (Venezuela)
ANCOM – Andean Common Market
APRA – Alianza Popular Revolucionaria Americana (Peru)
CACM – Central American Common Market
CARICOM – Caribbean Community
CARIFTA – Caribbean Free Trade Association
CECLA – Special Commission for Latin American Coordination
CECON – Special Negotiating and Consulting Commission (OAS)
CGCED – Caribbean Group for Cooperation and Economic Development
CIA – Central Intelligence Agency (US)
CIEN – Inter-American Nuclear Energy Commission (OAS)
COMECON – Council of Mutual Economic Aid
DCs – developed countries
ECLA – Economic Commission for Latin America (UN)
EEC – European Economic Commission
GDP – gross domestic product
GNP – gross national product
IDB – Inter-American Development Bank
IMF – International Monetary Fund
LAFTA – Latin American Free Trade Association
LDCs – less-developed (developing) countries
MNC – multinational corporation
MNR – Movimiento Nacionalista Revolucionario (Bolivia)
MPLA – Popular Movement for the Liberation of Angola
NIEO – New International Economic Order
OAS – Organization of American States
OLADE – Latin American Energy Development Organization
OPANAL – Organization for the Prohibition of Nuclear Weapons in Latin America
OPEC – Organization of Petroleum Exporting Countries
PRD – Partido Revolucionario Dominicano (Dominican Republic)
PNE – peaceful nuclear explosion
PRI – Partido Revolucionario Institutional (Mexico)
SELA – Latin American Economic System
UN – United Nations
UNCTAD – United Nations Conference on Trade and Development

NOTES

(1) Argentina, Barbados, Bolivia, Brazil, Chile, Colombia, Costa Rica, Dominican Republic, Ecuador, El Salvador, Grenada, Guatemala, Haiti, Honduras, Jamaica, Mexico, Nicaragua, Panama, Paraguay, Peru, Surinam, Trinidad and Tobago, Uruguay, and Venezuela.

(2) For a provocative discussion of the terminology used in characterizing the U.S. role, see Jerome Slater, "The United States and Latin

America: The New Radical Orthodoxy," Economic Development and Cultural Change 25, no. 4 (July 1977): 747-61.

(3) William G. Demas, "The Caribbean and the New International Economic Order," Journal of Interamerican Studies and World Affairs 20, no. 3 (August 1978): 229-64.

(4) For detailed information on Mexico's resources, see: United States Library of Congress, Congressional Research Service, Mexico's Oil and Gas Policy: An Analysis (Washington: Government Printing Office, 1979).

(5) Inter-American Development Bank, Economic and Social Progress in Latin America: 1977 Report (Washington: IDB, 1978), Table I-19. This volume hereafter cited as IDB.

(6) Ibid., Table 70.

(7) Ibid., p. 4.

(8) Ibid., Table II-4.

(9) Ibid., p. 4.

(10) Ibid., Table I-1.

(11) Ibid., Table 3.

(12) Ibid., Table II-4.

(13) USAID statistics, cited by Edward J. Williams and Freeman J. Wright, Latin American Politics: A Developmental Approach (Palo Alto, Cal.: Mayfield, 1975), p. 20.

(14) IDB, Table 3.

(15) Ibid., Table I-2.

(16) Studies summarized by Loring Allen in his Venezuelan Economic Development: A Politico-Economic Analysis (Greenwich, Conn.: JAI Press, 1977), p. 120.

(17) Calculations by Jose Carlos Duarte, mentioned by Peter Evans in his Dependent Development: The Alliance of Multinational, State, and Local Capital in Brazil (Princeton, N.J.: Princeton University Press, 1979), p. 97.

(18) Douglas H. Graham, "The Brazilian Economy: Structural Legacies and Future Prospects" in The Future of Brazil, edited by William H. Overholt (Boulder, Col.: Westview Press, 1978), pp. 122, 124.

(19) Banco de Mexico study cited by Lorenzo Meyer in his "Historical Roots of the Authoritarian State in Mexico," in Authoritarianism in Mexico, edited by Jose Luis Reyna and Richard S. Weinert (Philadelphia: ISHI Press, 1977), p. 18.

(20) For an analysis and critique of the "Prebisch thesis" and other ECLA doctrines, see P.M. Fontaine, Functionalism and Regionalism in the United Nations: The Economic Commission for Latin America (Lexington, Mass.: D.C. Heath, 1972); and Albert O. Hirschman, "Ideologies of Economic Development in Latin America," in Latin American Issues, edited by A.O. Hirschman (New York: Twentieth Century Fund, 1961).

(21) IDB, p. 26.

(22) Ibid, Table I-4 and p. 25.

(23) Ibid., pp. 26-29.

(24) Ibid., Table I-9.

(25) Ibid., Table I-5.

(26) Ibid., Table III-20.

(27) Ibid., Table III-21.

(28) Ibid., Table III-24.

(29) Cf., Osvaldo Sunkel and Pedro Paz, El subdesarrollo latinoamericano y la teoria del desarrollo (Mexico: Instituto Latinoamericano de Planificacion Economica y Social, Siglo XXI Editores, 1970); Osvaldo Sunkel, "The Crisis of the Nation State in Latin America: Challenge and Response," in Continuing Issues of International Politics, edited by Yale H. Ferguson and Walter F. Weiker (Pacific Palisades, Cal.: Goodyear, 1973), pp. 352-69; Osvaldo Sunkel, "Big Business and 'Dependencia': A Latin American View," Foreign Affairs 50, no. 3 (April 1972): 517-31; Constantine Vaitsos, Intercountry Income Distribution and Transnational Enterprises (Oxford: Clarendon Press, 1974); Miguel S. Wionczek, Gerardo M. Bueno, and Jorge Eduardo Navarrete, La transferencia internacional de tecnologia: el caso de Mexico (Mexico: Fondo de Cultura Economica, 1974); Celso Furtado, Obstacles to Development in Latin America (Garden City, N.Y.: Doubleday, 1970); Andre Gunder Frank, Capitalism and Underdevelopment in Latin America (New York: Monthly Review Press, 1969); James D. Cockcroft, Andre Gunder Frank, and Dale L. Johnson, eds., Dependence and Underdevelopment: Latin America's Political Economy (Garden City, N.Y.: Doubleday, 1972); Fernando Henrique Cardoso, Dependencia y desarrollo en America Latina (Mexico: Siglo XXI Editores, 1969);

Theotonio dos Santos, Dependencia y cambio social (Santiago, Chile: Centro de Estudios Socio-Economicos, Universidad de Chile, 1970); and essays by Octavio Ianni, Anibal Quijano Obregon, Anibal Pinto, and others in Latin America and the United States: The Changing Political Realities edited by Julio Cotler and Richard R. Fagen (Stanford, Cal.: Stanford University Press, 1974).

(30) Richard S. Newfarmer and Willard F. Mueller, Multinational Corporations in Brazil and Mexico: Structural Sources of Economic and Noneconomic Power, Report to the Subcommittee on Multinational Corporations of U.S. Senate Committee on Foreign Relations, 94th Congress (August 1975). See also especially: Sylvia Ann Hewlett, "The State and Brazilian Economic Development: The Contemporary Reality and Prospects for the Future," in Overholt, Future of Brazil, pp. 149-210; and Richard S. Weinert, "The State and Foreign Capital," in Reyna and Weinert, Authoritarianism in Mexico, pp. 109-28. Weinert, who (like Hewlett) uses Newfarmer and Mueller statistics, nevertheless cautions against the direct reading of "control" from unrefined ownership figures.   He maintains that one should also know whether foreign ownership is minority or majority participation in particular firms and what shares of sales in what market sectors those firms have that are clearly under foreign direction. Making these distinctions, Weinert concludes that the influence of the MNCs in Mexico has often been overrated.

(31) On this point see especially the various works by Sunkel; also Evans, Alliance.

(32) For example, writings by Frank, Quijano Obregon, and dos Santos. See also Vassilis Droucopoulos, "Radical in Spite of Itself: (review of Vaitsos)" Latin American Perspectives 3, no. 11 (Fall 1976): 86-96.

(33) Cf. Agustin Cueva, "A Summary of 'Problems and Perspectives of Dependency Theory'," Latin American Perspectives 3, no. 11 (Fall 1976): 12-16. For more balanced views on this issue, see Cole Blasier, "The Soviet Union in the Cuban-American Conflict," in Cuba in the World, edited by Blasier and Carmelo Mesa-Lago (Pittsburgh: Univ. of Pittsburgh Press, 1979), pp. 37-51; Richard R. Fagen, "Cuba and the Soviet Union," The Wilson Quarterly 2, no. 1 (Winter 1978): 69-81; and Frank T. Fitzgerald, "A Critique of the 'Sovietization of Cuba' Thesis," Science and Society 42, no. 1 (Spring 1978): 1-32.

(34) See Charles W. Anderson, "The Changing International Environment of Development and Latin America in the 1970s," Inter-American Economic Affairs 24, no. 2 (Autumn 1970): 65-87.

(35) IDB, Table 64.

(36) Ibid., Table II-5.

(37) Statistics derived from those in United Nations, Monthly Bulletin of Statistics 33, no. 6 (June 1979), Special Table C.

(38) Useful statistics on Latin America's trade with the major industrial countries can be found in Carlos Regunaga, "Exporting Industry in LAFTA: Policies and Trends," in Latin America Annual Review: 1979 (Saffron Walden, England: World of Information, 1979), p. 42.

(39) IDB, p. 29.

(40) W. Raymond Duncan, Latin American Politics: A Developmental Approach (New York: Praeger, 1976), p. 121.

(41) Charles Wagley, The Latin American Tradition (New York: Columbia University Press, 1968), p. 171.

(42) IDB, Table 1.

(43) Ibid., Table 2.

(44) Ibid., p. 17.

(45) See especially John J. Johnson, Political Change in Latin America: The Emergence of the Middle Sectors (Stanford, Cal.: Stanford University Press, 1958); and Samuel P. Huntington, Political Order in Changing Societies (New Haven, Conn.: Yale University Press, 1968).

(46) Cf. Richard N. Adams, "Political Power and Social Structures," in The Politics of Conformity in Latin America, edited by Claudio Veliz (London: Oxford University Press, 1967), pp. 15-42. "Islands of privilege" is Henry Landsberger's term.

(47) We have drawn heavily on John P. Gillin, "The Middle Sectors and Their Values," as reprinted in Latin American Politics, edited by Robert D. Tomasek (Garden City, N.Y.: Doubleday, rev. ed., 1970), pp. 55-73. See also Wagley, The Latin American Tradition; William Lyle Schurz, This New World: The Civilization of Latin America (New York: E.P. Dutton, 1964); and Julius Rivera, Latin America: A Sociocultural Interpretation (New York: Halsted Press, rev. ed., 1978).

(48) Carlos Rangel, The Latin Americans: Their Love-Hate Relationship with the United States (New York: Harcourt, Brace, Jovanovich, 1977), p. 34.

(49) Wagley, The Latin American Tradition, p. 53.

(50) A seminal work was Charles W. Anderson, Politics and Economic Change in Latin America (Princeton, N.J.: Van Nostrand, 1967).

(51) Howard J. Wiarda and Harvey F. Kline, eds., Latin American Politics and Development (Boston: Houghton Mifflin, 1979), p. 27.

(52) See especially Frederick B. Pike and Thomas Stritch, eds., The New Corporation: Socio-Political Structures in the Iberian World (Notre Dame, Ind.: University of Notre Dame Press, 1974); James Malloy, ed., Authoritarianism and Corporatism in Latin America (Pittsburgh: University of Pittsburgh Press, 1977); Guillermo A. O'Donnell, Modernization and Bureaucratic-Authoritarianism: Studies in South American Politics (Berkeley, Cal.: Institute of International Studies, University of California, 1973); Alfred Stepan, The State and Society: Peru in Comparative Perspective (Princeton, N.J.: Princeton University Press, 1978); Reyna and Weinert, Authoritarianism in Mexico; Wiarda and Kline, Latin American Politics; Robert R. Kaufman, Transitions to Stable Authoritarian-Corporate Regimes: The Chilean Case? (Beverly Hills, Cal.: Sage, 1976); and David Collier, ed., The New Authoritarianism in Latin America (Princeton, N.J.: Princeton University Press, forthcoming).

(53) Philippe C. Schmitter, "Still the Century of Corporatism?" in Pike and Stritch, The New Corporatism, pp. 93-94.

(54) See Kenneth Paul Erickson, The Brazilian Corporative State and Working-Class Politics (Berkeley, Cal.: University of California Press, 1977).

(55) Stepan, State and Society.

(56) In addition to works previously cited on corporatism and others on the military to be cited later, see especially Marvin Goldwert, Democracy, Militarism and Nationalism in Argentina 1930-1966 (Austin, Tex.: University of Texas Press, 1972); Donald C. Hodges, Argentina, 1943-1976: The National Revolution and Resistance (Albuquerque, N.M.: University of New Mexico Press, 1976); Peter H. Smith, Argentina and the Failure of Democracy: Conflict Among Political Elites, 1904-1955 (Madison, Wis.: University of Wisconsin Press, 1974); Philippe C. Schmitter, Interest Conflict and Political Change in Brazil (Stanford, Cal.: Stanford University Press, 1971); Thomas A. Skidmore, Politics in Brazil, 1930-1964 (New York: Oxford University Press, 1967); Christopher Mitchell, The Legacy of Populism in Bolivia: From the MNR to Military Rule (New York: Praeger, 1977); James M. Malloy, Bolivia: The Uncompleted Revolution (Pittsburgh: University of Pittsburgh Press, 1970); Abraham F. Lowenthal, ed., The Peruvian Experiment: Continuity and Change under Military Rule (Princeton, N.J.: Princeton University Press, 1975); and David Chaplin, ed., Peruvian Nationalism: A Corporatist Revolution (New Brunswick, N.J.: Transaction Books, 1976).

(57) In addition to works previously cited, see especially Ronald M. Schneider, The Political System of Brazil: Emergence of a "Modern-

izing" Authoritarian Regime, 1964-1970 (New York: Columbia University Press, 1971); Alfred Stepan, ed., Authoritarian Brazil (New Haven, Conn.: Yale University Press, 1973); Riordan Roett, Brazil: Politics in a Patrimonial Society (New York: Praeger, rev. ed., 1978); Peter Flynn, Brazil: A Political Analysis (Boulder, Colo.: Westview Press); Martin Weinstein, Uruguay: The Politics of Failure (Westport, Conn.: Greenwood, 1974); and Edy Kaufman, Uruguay in Transition (New Brunswick, N.J.: Transaction Books, 1978).

(58) Stepan, State and Society, pp. 70-71.

(59) Cf. Peter H. Smith, "Does Mexico Have a Power Elite?" in Reyna and Weinert, Authoritarianism in Mexico, pp. 129-51; Ronald M. Schneider, Brazil: Foreign Policy of a Future World Power (Boulder, Colo.: Westview Press, 1976), pp. 127-36; and Edward S. Milenky, Argentina's Foreign Policies (Boulder, Colo.: Westview Press, 1978), pp. 83-86.

(60) An excellent study of the social background and historical political roles of the Latin American military is John J. Johnson, The Military and Society in Latin America (Stanford, Cal.: Stanford University Press, 1964).

(61) See Jose Nun, "The Middle-Class Military Coup Revisited," in Armies and Politics in Latin America, edited by Abraham F. Lowenthal (New York: Holmes & Meier, 1976), pp. 49-86.

(62) Wiarda and Kline, Latin American Politics, p. 37.

(63) On the contemporary role of the military, in addition to country studies already cited, see especially Lowenthal, Armies and Politics; Brian Loveman and Thomas M. Davies, eds., The Politics of Antipolitics: The Military in Latin America (Lincoln, Neb.: University of Nebraska Press, 1978); and John Samuel Fitch, The Military Coup as a Political Process (Baltimore, Md.: Johns Hopkins University Press, 1977).

(64) See Douglas A. Chalmers, "Developing on the Periphery: External Factors in Latin American Politics," in Linkage Politics, edited by James N. Rosenau (New York: Free Press, 1969), pp. 67-93.

(65) See especially Paul E. Sigmund, The Overthrow of Allende and the Politics of Chile, 1964-1976 (Pittsburgh: University of Pittsburgh Press, 1977).

(66) Reportedly, mainly from Costa Rica, Panama, and Venezuela; and apparently very little from Castro, who has for some years been extremely cautious about offering much direct assistance to guerrilla groups in Latin America.

(67) Relevant general works (in addition to some others cited in the next subsection) include Harold Eugene Davis and Larman C. Wilson, et al., Latin American Foreign Policies: An Analysis (Baltimore, Md.: Johns Hopkins University Press, 1975); Neil R. Richardson, Foreign Policy and Economic Dependence (Austin, Tex.: University of Texas Press, 1978); and Vaughn A. Lewis, ed., Size, Self-determination and International Relations: The Caribbean (Mona, Jamaica: University of the West Indies, 1976).

(68) Cf. Mario Ojeda, Alcances y limites de la politica exterior de Mexico (Mexico: El Colegio de Mexico, 1976); Olga Pellicer de Brody, "Las relaciones commerciales de Mexico: una prueba para la nueva politica exterior," Foro Internacional 17, no. 1 (July/September 1976): 37-50; Yoram Shapira, "Mexico's Foreign Policy under Echevarria: A Retrospect," Inter-American Economic Affairs 31, no. 4 (Spring 1978): 29-61; Wolf Grabendorff, "Mexico's Foreign Policy – Indeed a Foreign Policy?", Journal of Interamerican Studies and World Affairs 20, no. 1 (February 1978): 85-92.

(69) Robert D. Bond makes this point in his "Venezuela's Role in International Affairs," in Contemporary Venezuela and Its Role in International Affairs, edited by Robert D. Bond (New York: New York University Press, for the Council on Foreign Relations, 1977), pp. 244-45.

(70) Schneider, Brazil: Foreign Policy, pp. 151-52. See also Wayne A. Selcher, Brazil's Multilateral Relations: Between First and Third Worlds. (Boulder, Colo.: Westview Press, 1978).

(71) Schneider, Brazil: Foreign Policy, pp. 14-15.

(72) Ibid., pp. 74-75.

(73) Gonzalez's statement (along with the useful testimonies of other Latin American specialists) appears in United States House, Committee on International Relations, Subcommittee on Inter-American Affairs, Impact of Cuban-Soviet Ties in the Western Hemisphere, Hearings before the Subcommittee...(March 14, 15, April 5, 12, 1978), 95th Congress, 2nd Session, Committee Print (Washington: Government Printing Office, 1978), pp. 145-66. Gonzalez incorporates an earlier essay on his in the record: "Complexities of Cuban Foreign Policy," Problems of Communism 26, no. 6 (November/December 1977): 1-15. This essay was itself a revision of yet another essay of his in Blasier and Mesa-Lago, Cuba in the World, which is an excellent compendium of writings on recent Cuban foreign policy. See also Martin Weinstein, ed., Revolutionary Cuba in the World Arena (New York: New York University Press, 1979); Jorge I. Dominguez, "Cuban Foreign Policy," Foreign Affairs 57, no. 1 (Fall 1978): 83-108; and Jorge I. Dominguez, "The Cuban Operation in Angola: Costs and Benefits for the Armed Forces," Cuban Studies 8, no. 1 (January 1978): 10-21.

(74) For historical background on inter-American relations and the international relations of Latin America generally, see Gordon Connell-Smith, The United States and Latin America (New York: Halsted Press, 1974); Harold Eugene Davis, John J. Finian, and F. Taylor Peck, Latin American Diplomatic History (Baton Rouge, La.: Louisiana State University Press, 1977); Arthur P. Whitaker, The Western Hemisphere Idea (Ithaca, N.Y.: Cornell University Press, 1954); Bryce Wood, The Making of the Good Neighbor Policy (New York: Columbia University Press, 1961); R. Harrison Wagner, United States Policy Toward Latin America: A Study in Domestic and International Politics (Stanford, Cal.: Stanford University Press, 1970); Jerome Slater, The OAS and United States Foreign Policy (Columbus, Ohio: Ohio State University Press, 1967); Cole Balsier, The Hovering Giant: U.S. Responses to Revolutionary Change in Latin America (Pittsburgh: University of Pittsburgh Press, 1976).

On more recent patterns, see (in addition to items cited later): Richard R. Fagen, ed., Capitalism and the State in U.S.-Latin American Relations (Stanford, Cal.: Stanford University Press, forthcoming); Abraham F. Lowenthal and Albert Fishlow, Latin America's Emergence: Toward a U.S. Response, Foreign Policy Association Headline Series No. 243 (February 1979); Mark W. Zacher, International Conflicts and Collective Security, 1946-77 (New York: Praeger, 1979); chap. 3; John Bartlow Martin, U.S. Policy in the Caribbean (Boulder, Colo.: Westview Press, 1978); Joseph Grunwald, ed., Latin America and the World Economy: A Changing International Order (Beverly Hills, Cal.: Sage, 1978); G. Pope Atkins, Latin America in the International Political System (New York: Free Press, 1977); Yale H. Ferguson, "The Ideological Dimension in United States Latin American Policies," in Terms of Conflict: Ideology in Latin American Politics edited by Morris Blachman and Ronald G. Hellman (Philadelphia: ISHI Press, 1977), pp. 193-235; Yale H. Ferguson, "Through Glasses Darkly: An Assessment of Various Theoretical Approaches to Inter-American Relations," Journal of Interamerican Studies and World Affairs 19, no. 1 (February 1977): 3-34; Abraham F. Lowenthal, "The United States and Latin America: Ending the Hegemonic Presumption," Foreign Policy no. 55 (October 1976): 199-213; James Theberge and Roger W. Fontaine, eds., Latin America: Struggle for Progress (Lexington, Mass.: Lexington Books, 1976); Commission on United States-Latin American Relations (Linowitz Commission), The Americas in a Changing World (New York: Praeger, 1975); also the Commission's The United States and Latin America: Next Steps (New York: Center for Inter-American Relations, 1976); and Ronald G. Hellman and H. Jon Rosenbaum, eds., Latin America: The Search for a New International Role (New York: Halsted Press, 1975).

(75) Figures extrapolated from IDB, Table III-14.

(76) See Jessica P. Einhorn, Expropriation Politics (Lexington, Mass.: D.C. Heath, 1974); and Charles H. Lipson, "Corporate Preferences and

Public Policies: Foreign Aid Sanctions and Investment Protection," World Politics 28, no. 3 (April 1976): 396-421.

(77) See Benoit Otis Brookens, "Diplomatic Protection of Foreign Economic Interests: The Changing Structure of International Law in the New International Economic Order," Journal of Interamerican Studies and World Affairs 20, no. 1 (February 1978): 37-67.

(78) Cf. Abraham F. Lowenthal, "Latin America: A Not-So-Special Relationship," Foreign Policy no. 32 (Fall 1978): 107-26; and Richard R. Fagen, "The Carter Administration and Latin America: Business as Usual?" Foreign Affairs, 57, no. 3 (Special issue on "America and the World 1978"): 652-69.

(79) The emphasis has obviously been on political and civil rights rather than economic and social matters.

(80) See J. Daniel O'Flaherty, "Finding Jamaica's Way," Foreign Policy no. 31 (Summer 1978): 137-58.

(81) See Albert Fishlow, "Flying Down to Rio: Perspectives on U.S.-Brazil Relations," Foreign Affairs 57, no. 2 (Winter 1978/79): 387-405.

(82) On energy and U.S.-Mexico relations, see Congressional Research Service, Mexico's Oil; Edward J. Williams, "Oil in Mexican-U.S. Relations: Analysis and Bargaining Scenario," Orbis 22, no. 1 (Spring 1978): 201-16; and George W. Grayson, "Mexico and the United States: The Natural Gas Controversy," Inter-American Economic Affairs 32, no. 3 (Winter 1978): 3-27.

(83) Recent surveys include Edward S. Milenky, "Latin America's Multilateral Diplomacy: Integration, Disintegration and Interdependence," International Affairs (Royal Institute of International Affairs) 53, no. 1 (January 1977): 73-96; F. Parkinson, "International Economic Integration in Latin America and the Caribbean: A Survey," The Year Book of World Affairs no. 31 (1977): 236-56; and Joan Pearce, "Regional Integration: A Balance Sheet," in Latin America Annual Review, 1979, pp. 27-34. We have drawn heavily from Milenky.

(84) See Edward S. Milenky, The Latin American Free Trade Association (New York: Praeger, 1973).

(85) U.N. Monthly Bulletin, June 1979, Special Table C.

(86) See especially Thomas L. Karnes, The Failure of Union: Central America, 1824-1975 (Tempe, Ariz.: University of Arizona Press, 1976); Royce Q. Shaw, Central America: Regional Integration and National Political Development (Boulder, Colo.: Westview Press, 1979); William R. Kline and Enrique Delgado, Economic Integration in Central America

(Washington: Brookings Institution, 1978); and Jeffrey B. Nugent, Economic Integration in Central America: Empirical Investigations (Baltimore, Md.: Johns Hopkins University Press, 1974).

(87) Mary Jane Reid Martz, "SELA: The Latin American Economic System 'Ploughing the Seas'?" Inter-American Economic Affairs 32, no. 4 (Spring 1979): 37.

(88) John R. Redick, "Regional Restraint: U.S. Nuclear Policy and Latin America," Orbis 22, no. 1 (Spring 1978): 161-200. See also Conference on Energy and Nuclear Security in Latin America, April 25-30, 1978, St. Johns, Antigua, West Indies: Vantage Conference Report (Muscatine, Iowa: The Stanley Foundation, 1978).

(89) Parkinson, "International Economic Integration," pp. 252-53.

(90) Ibid., p. 242.

(91) See especially Milenky, "Latin America's Multilateral Diplomacy"; Parkinson, "International Economic Integration"; Ricardo French-Davis, "The Andean Pact: Model of Economic Integration for Developing Countries," in Grunwald, Latin America and World Economy, pp. 165-93; and D. Morawetz, Economic Integration Among Developing Countries: The Andean Group (Cambridge, Mass.: MIT Press, 1974).

(92) Milenky, "Latin America's Multilateral Diplomacy," p. 87.

(93) Ibid., pp. 87-88.

(94) Ibid., p. 88.

(95) Ibid., p. 89.

(96) See Martz, "SELA"; and Robert D. Bond, "Regionalism in Latin America: Prospects for the Latin American Economic System," International Organization 32, no. 2 (Spring 1978): 401-23.

(97) Martz, "SELA," pp. 58-60. See also Selcher, Brazil's Multilateral Diplomacy.

(98) Martz, "SELA," p. 89.

(99) Robert D. Bond, "Venezuela, Brazil and the Amazon Basin," Orbis 22, no. 3 (Fall 1978): 635-50.

(100) On Latin America's economic relations with Europe and Japan, see Grunwald, Latin America and World Economy, chaps. 1, 3-5.

(101) See R. Peter DeWitt, Jr., The Inter-American Development Bank and Political Influence (New York: Praeger, 1977).

(102) See Felipe Herrera, "Latin America and the Third World," in Grunwald, Latin America and World Economy, pp. 223-36.

(103) See Bobbie B. Smetherman and Robert W. Smetherman, Territorial Seas and Inter-American Relations (New York: Praeger, 1974); Ralph Zacklin, ed., The Changing Law of the Sea: Western Hemisphere Perspectives (Leiden, The Netherlands: A.W. Sijthoff, 1974); and Richard C. Bath, "Latin American Claims on the Living Resources of the Sea," Inter-American Economic Affairs 27, no. 1 (Spring 1974): 59-87.

(104) Following the Soviet lead, Cuba has also become more militantly anti-Israeli. See Yoram Shapira and Edy Kaufman, "Cuba's Israel Policy: The Shift to the Soviet Line," Cuban Studies 8, no. 1 (January 1978): 22-35.

(105) See Albert Fishlow, Richard S. Weinert, et al., "The Third World: Public Debt, Private Profit," Foreign Policy no. 30 (Spring 1978): 132-69.

(106) Schneider, Brazil: Foreign Policy, p. xiii. See also Riordan Roett, "The Political Future of Brazil," in Overholt, The Future of Brazil, pp. 71-102.

(107) See Tom J. Farer, ed., The Future of the Inter-American System (New York: Praeger, 1979).

(108) See Lawrence J. LeBlanc, The OAS and the Promotion and Protection of Human Rights (The Hague, The Netherlands: Martinus Nijhoff, 1977).

11 Africa*
Timothy M. Shaw

Africa is not only the largest regional subsystem in terms of size of territory and number of states,(1) it is also the least industrialized and the most unequal. Its colonial inheritance – "dualistic" economies, authoritarian regimes, and high levels of ethnic and racial consciousness – was not a promising one, and its future prospects are rather gloomy if current projections materialize in terms of both its continued inability to meet basic human needs and the incidence and impact of growing inequalities.(2) Nevertheless, despite its unhelpful inheritance and mixed performance, Africa has emerged as an important actor and arena in contemporary world politics.

Although the African nations share a certain geographical identity, their commonality derives more from colonial experience than from racial composition. Its place in the world system, brought about initially by incorporation through trading, slaving, and colonizing, is characterized essentially by dependence on external exchange, finance, technology, skills, and tastes. But there are significant differences in degrees of dependence and incorporation; and these differences are likely to increase as a few African states come to achieve a greater degree of growth and order than the majority. Nevertheless, the continent as a whole remains characterized by poverty, instability, and disunity. Its more than 50 states share, in general, low levels of income, basic human need satisfaction, and life-expectancy, as well as high levels of malnutrition, early death, and illiteracy.

If the continent consists essentially of highly balkanized, very poor, rather small, and typically weak states it is not because it lacks reserves. Africa is rich in unexploited mineral, agricultural, and human resources. But these have yet to be tapped and turned to the benefit of

---

*An earlier version of this chapter was presented as a paper entitled "Towards a Political Economy of Regional Integration and Inequality in Africa" at an Inter-University Seminar on International Relations, Montreal, March 1979.

the continent's own peoples. Rather, its considerable potential stands in marked contrast to its contemporary impoverishment. Because of Africa's peripheral place in the world system, its potential has so far not been turned into production for its own development. Rather, it continues to display the essential qualities of a colonial-type system: it exchanges raw materials for manufactured goods at unfair prices. The resultant continuing crisis of underdevelopment has meant that the continent as a whole has been unable to easily escape from dependence to achieve a higher degree of self-reliance. Instead, its weakness exposes it to external political and economic manipulation, diverting its attention and depleting its reserves. Unless and until these underlying features of its political economy are addressed, Africa will continue to be exposed to divisive external forces, and will postpone any transition to improved rates of internal development.

Africa contains 30 million square kilometers – 25 percent of the earth's surface – but it produces only three percent of the globe's annual output of goods and services. Although it includes a higher proportion of the world's states than any region – one-third – it also has the lowest per capita income of any region – $425 per annum. While its population growth rate is rather high – almost three percent per annum, its economic growth rate is very low – either minimal or negative since independence. The continent's population, presently 10 percent of the global total, is expected to almost double by the year 2000, from 450 to 800 million. Adding to the already considerable problems of unemployment and underemployment, 45 percent of its peoples are under 15 years of age; and life expectancy remains stubbornly low at just over 40 years.

Yet Africa is rich in agricultural, energy, and mineral as well as human resources. It already produces 15 percent of the world's oil and possesses 40 percent of the globe's hydroelectricity potential. It is the origin of 70 percent of the world's diamond production, 50 percent of its gold and phosphates, 40 percent of its chrome, and 20 percent of its copper. And it holds 35 percent of the international uranium reserves not controlled by the superpowers.

However, Africa's manufacturing output remains marginal in global terms – up from 6.7 percent of world production in 1960 to 8.1 percent in 1972 – and its contribution to world exports is just around four percent. Meanwhile, the continent's debt jumped from $7 billion in 1970 to almost $19 billion in 1975, so that external financial obligations constitute up to 20 percent of some African states' annual exports. Overall, then, Africa's past, present, and prospects are all rather gloomy unless significant and fundamental changes occur in its political economy. As of now, according to the United States Overseas Development Council's Physical Quality of Life Index, Africa has the lowest regional rating (31) compared with other Third World areas (Asia-41 and Latin America-65). This inability to satisfy basic human needs either now or in the future has profound effects on and implications for continental politics.

Africa's vulnerability and instability is revealed in the checkered history of the continent's international institution, the Organization of Africa Unity (OAU). Its sixteenth annual heads of state summit was held in the Liberian capital of Monrovia in July 1979; but its agenda was remarkably similar to that of previous years. The OAU is still largely preoccupied with political crises – Southern Africa, the Middle East, border wars (Somalia-Ethiopia, Algeria-Morocco), sovereignty issues (Western Sahara, Nigerian civil war, Tanzania's involvement in Uganda, Shaba), and the OAU's own structures and goals (an association of states or a movement for integration). It has little time or effort left to tackle the continuing structural problems of economic dependence and underdevelopment, in part, because of members' divergent development and foreign policies and, in part, because the UN's own regional organization – the Economic Commission for Africa (ECA) – is charged with such responsibilities. But as a topical editorial in Africa magazine suggested before the 1979 summit, without structural unity Africa is doomed to continued dependence and humiliation. After reviewing Africa's enormous reserves and potential and contrasting these with its past and present impoverishment, Raph Uwechue argues that unity is a prerequisite for development since economic union based on political agreement is the only way to remove the "root of evils":

> What is needed now is a political covenant irrevocably commit-ting the peoples of Africa to an agreed economic objective. The OAU's role is to provide the psychological atmosphere and the political framework that would make the acceptance of Africa's common economic burden easy for African peoples. The OAU Secretariat and the ECA have taken the commendable initiative of inviting African experts to a series of preparatory confer-ences. . .to study and recommend ways and means of integrating Africa's economy. These experts have done their job and have produced specific recommendations, including what is in essence the establishment of an African Common Market. Thus, for the first time, a blueprint for Africa's economic development has been prepared for the consideration of our leaders. They now have the way to our survival in security and dignity.(3)

The ambiguities or contradictions in the past and present political economy of Africa are rather characteristic of the place of the South in a global system still dominated essentially by the interests and actions of the North. The discontinuities and dilemmas of economic dependence and political interdependence are revealed most poignantly in the very tenuous and vulnerable form of independence presently achieved by the countries and continent of Africa. The uneven rates and results of development – with its interrelated political, economic, social and strategic components – have served to exacerbate inequalities and tensions both within and between the states of Africa as well as between continental and global actors.(4)

The position and prospects of Africa in an unequal world order pose problems for analysis and action as well as for perception and prediction. This chapter is concerned, therefore, not only with the comparative study of Africa as a regional subsystem but also with alternative approaches to analysis as well as alternative development strategies. In particular, it will consider and contrast the more orthodox and more radical modes of analysis and modes of production, recognizing the interrelationship between theory and policy. The paradoxes and dilemmas of Africa's role in the world system are of relevance, then, for comparative analysis of regionalism, comparative explanations of integration, and comparative policy choices.

The essential characteristics of African regionalism are portrayed in strikingly different ways by these two approaches. The dominant, orthodox perspective is based on the premise of decolonization: Africa is a continental system of equal (both amongst themselves and between themselves and non-African countries) state actors who have sufficient sovereignty to determine their own individual and collective foreign policies. By contrast, the emerging, radical critique is based on the premise of dependence: Africa is a continental subsystem of unequal (both amongst themselves and between themselves and non-African institutions) mixed actors(5) (i.e. consisting of both state and nonstate actors) who lack sufficient autonomy to determine their own individual and collective political economies. The two approaches vary, therefore, in terms of the premises, actor types, ranking of relations and degrees of freedom that they attribute to the region. As indicated in table 11.1, the orthodox perspective deals primarily with continental and national institutions whereas the radical approach considers Africa in the context of a global system which includes important transnational as well as state actors and relationships. For the former, then, Africa is a regional system with its own claim to autonomy whereas for the latter, Africa is a dependent subsystem possessing minimal autonomy.

The essential distinctions between the orthodox and radical approaches are twofold. The primary distinction centers on level of analysis, with the orthodox perspective concentrating on the regional while the radical mode situates the region in the context of the world system. A secondary, and related, distinction occurs over the balance and direction of forces treated, with the orthodox perspective focusing on cooperation and integration while the radical mode concentrates more on conflict and incompatibilities. There are, of course, several other major differences between these two approaches, some of which are indicated in Table 11.1

At the risk of oversimplifying, the orthodox perspective is largely a derivative of structural-functional and systems analysis, whereas the radical mode is quite closely related to dependence and Marxist approaches. The former focuses on current relations, particularly in the diplomatic and strategic issue areas, and envisages a future characterized by development and cooperation; whereas the latter exhibits a greater historical awareness, particularly of economic and conflictual relationships, and envisages a future characterized by a continuation of

Table 11.1. Alternative Approaches to the Analysis of African Regionalism

Phenomenon	Orthodox	Radical
level of analysis	continental/national	global/transnational
primary focus	OAU/states	world systems/classes
major issue areas	diplomatic/strategic	economic/conflict
central assumptions	decolonization/interdependence	dependence
current processes	development	underdevelopment
regional characteristics identified	cohesion/integration/equalities	fragmentation/contradictions/inequalities
ideological preferences	Pan-Africanism/nationalism	self-reliance/disengagement
mode of analysis	structural functionalism/systems	dependence/Marxist
future projections	neofunctionalism/federalism	confrontation/restructuring

359

underdevelopment and contradiction.(6) The orthodox approach is large-ly compatible with the decolonization perspective identified by I. William Zartman in his examination of Eur-Africa, whereas the radical mode is more compatible with his alternative dependence viewpoint.(7) These two rather different and distinctive modes of analysis will be employed throughout this chapter as a means of furthering inquiry into regionalism in Africa. At times the dichotomy and contrast may be somewhat overdrawn, but the implications for future policy and devel-opment are substantial; the alternatives, no matter how stark, need to be recognized and examined so that appropriate and informed choices can be made to overcome Africa's colonial heritage and to enhance its prospects in the future.(8)

The intent here to consider and contrast two rather divergent modes of analysis is complicated further by the dominance of scholarship within the orthodox tradition by comparison to the paucity of work in the radical genre. Just as writing on the relationship between the European Economic Community (EEC) and Africa (particularly the majority African component of the African, Caribbean, and Pacific States (ACP)) is dominated by classical modes and positive perceptions (rather than critical approaches and negative opinions),(9) so research on regionalism in Africa is largely ahistoric, uncritical, and permissive of continued dependence. Indeed, even in comparison with the case of EEC-ACP relations, analysis of African regionalism is almost exclusive-ly within the structural-functional and systems analysis traditions.

This dominant mode is best represented by the series of essays on the African subordinate state or regional system by Zartman.(10) The alternative perspective does not yet really exist as a set of coherent assumptions, concepts, and conclusions, in part because it sees Africa as just one component in a broader global system characterized by increasing inequalities and dependencies.(11) The scholar who has gone furthest in articulating such a radical critique for both Africa and other dependent regions is Lynn Mytelka.(12) We turn initially to a description and comparison of the continental African system or political economy as presented by Zartman and Mytelka, who are taken to be representa-tive of the orthodox and radical approaches respectively.

CONFIGURATION

The configuration projected by the orthodox approach essentially is one of interdependence at both the continental and global levels in which interrelatedness is assumed to be mutual and contemporary; notions of imbalance and history are eschewed. However, in response to this rather uncritical and ahistoric approach, the radical perspective em-phasizes dependence, particularly at the global level, in which integra-tion into the system is taken to be unequal and well-established; ideas of balance and contemporary mutuality are rejected, replaced by concepts of inequality and evolution within the world system.(13)

Zartman's recent characterization of Africa is typical of the dominant orthodox perspective. He asserts that "the African regional system is distinguished by its relatively egalitarian power distribution, the recent origin of many of its states, its island-continental territorial base, it high sense of unity, and its search for appropriate tasks."(14)

Earlier, Zartman had reflected the concern of students of subsystems for autonomy in a way that symbolizes the fundamental differences of assumption and perspective of the two approaches considered here.   Rather than conceiving of Africa as a dependent formation, he suggested that one central continental "characteristic is intrarelatedness or autonomy. . . .Relations between African states are primarily governed by intra-African stimuli. . .African solidarity and support behind the struggle for independence in various countries have had the dual effect of breaking ties with the metropole and strengthening relations between African states."(15) Zartman did, however, recognize that there was a negative interrelationship between continental integration and external dependence, admitting that any deficiencies at the regional level would encourage external intervention, although eschewing any notion of such involvement being structural and continual, an issue to which we shall return.(16)

By contrast, the radical approach conceives of Africa as just another dependent part of the world system. It recognizes certain distinctive features of the continent's incorporation into this system but would avoid any idea of Africa being "special." While open to some notion of the particular role of Africa in the international division of labor and world politics, it largely bases its conception of Africa on the global impact of colonialism and capitalism, with the continent's fate being but one aspect of the ongoing process of integration and differentiation. Africa, from this perspective, constitutes just one section of the world periphery, separate from and dependent upon the center.

From this world system perspective, then, according to Steven Langdon and Lynn Mytelka, any analysis of Africa's emerging political economy has to commence with the global capitalist economy, emphasizing "historical processes, international dependency relationships, and class analysis."(17) Compared with the orthodox approach to development and regionalism,

A political economy approach for investigation is likely to be far more valid, in that it recognizes the complex intermeshing of so-called political, economic, and social factors that a process of broad social change involves. Second, it suggests that one cannot isolate the process of change in any given Third World country from that occurring in the world economy as a whole.(18)

The explanation offered by Langdon and Mytelka of the roots of underdevelopment concentrates on modes of production, transnational class integration, and the constraints of dependence. These factors together are seen to account for the growing problem of structural inequality and violence on the continent:

The focus of analysis is on the external pressures and ties created for the periphery African societies by the expansion and adjustment of the capitalist world economy. These pressures and ties, it is argued, have generated certain socioinstitutional effects that influence contemporary change. Furthermore, such ties in the contemporary context influence both internal class structure and class consciousness within Africa. And finally, such external realities constitute a continuing constraint on rapid transition to new internal structures, even in cases where regimes emerge with some independence from transnational integration and some commitment to escape from historical legacies. The fundamental argument, then, is that the structural change and capital accumulation taking place in interrelationship with these strong external links have led and are leading to increasing segmentation and inequality in many African countries, to growing employment problems, and to ongoing poverty for most Africans.(19)

The world system assumptions and critical analyses of the radical school allow for more critical comparisons between dependent regions or subsystems than are possible within the orthodox approach. A subfield within the systems analytic tradition has emerged of late concerned with comparative regionalism. In general, this subfield seeks to compare and contrast "structure" and "texture" between regions or "subordinate state systems," particularly those in the Third World, or periphery. In addition to the contributions of Michael Brecher and Leonard Binder,(20) the major, explicitly comparative work in this mold has been that of Louis Cantori and Steven Spiegel.(21) Their comparative framework consists of a typology of states for each region (core, periphery, and intrusive), pattern variables (cohesion, communications, power, and relations), and system types (integrative, consolidative, cohesive, and coherent). Using these three typologies, Cantori and Spiegel can proceed to compare the different degrees of autonomy and varieties of direction for international regions.

By contrast, the radical approach can also compare regions, not so much in terms of types of states and regional processes as in variations of incorporation in and response to the world system, particularly in terms of time, process, and impact. In other words, the radical perspective can also be employed to advance comparative regionalism, although its primary goal is to explain types and impact of the incorporation of the periphery into the world system. The radical approach would also conceive of regional and extraregional actors in more critical and dynamic terms than the orthodox one.

Cantori and Spiegel distinguish intrusive actors that affect regional relationships. However, the radical perspective would treat these countries and corporations as imperialistic rather than just intrusive, whose impact on the periphery is fundamental to any explanation of underdevelopment. In the latter approach, external involvement in the periphery is conceived of as intrinsic and structural rather than incidental and sporadic; a characteristic feature of an unequal world system.

Within the orthodox approach, the role of intrusive actors is not seen to be necessarily incompatible with the development of regionalism; indeed, external threats or supports are usually seen to be positive for regional integration. By contrast, the radical perspective sees a fundamental incompatibility between regionalism and the world system, advocating regional integration as an alternative to global incorporation. Likewise, the political economy approach sees dependence as a fundamental cause of national disintegration and fragmentation. At both national and regional levels, then, the response of the dependentistas to continued global integration is national and collective self-reliance.(22)

By contrast, the orthodox school sees no necessary incompatibility between continental and "subregional" groupings in the parlance of the Economic Commission for Africa (ECA), the "regional" (continental) institution associated with the UN system. In its early years, the mid-1960s, the OAU was somewhat jealous of its continental supremacy, seeking the demise of any potential competition such as the Organization Commune Africaine, Malgache et Mauricienne (OCAM) to ensure its own "organizational pre-eminence."(23) Since then, however, with the growth of OAU-ECA links as well as with the multiplication of regional groupings, a de facto "division of labor" has been arrived at, with the myriad regional organizations being mainly functional, economic, and societal in orientation while the continental system concentrates on strategic, diplomatic, and political questions. In other words, "high" politics are handled mainly at the continental level with "low" politics being the preserve of regional institutions, many of which are no more than rhetorical flourishes or moribund agencies.

The radical perspective on regional compatibility tends to distinguish not so much between interactive levels and issue areas as it does between intent and orientation. In general, continental and regional groupings are assumed, from this perspective, to be largely inconsequential for the operation of the world system. They only become of consequence if they attempt either to disengage from the global community or to generate changes in the world system itself; i.e., if they practice self-reliance and/or call for a New International Economic Order (NIEO). In general, they are associated with the latter claims within the North-South dialogue(24) rather than with the former espousal of some variety of extra- or noncapitalist path.(25) This is the only way in which dependent ruling classes can, on the one hand, demand external change and, on the other hand, be sure of external support, as necessary.

The new class is, then, characteristic of much of the continent; and it is caught in a dilemma. As part of a transnational network, it cannot conceive of disengagement without being prepared for major changes in the national political economy. On the other hand, unless it continues to espouse vocally the "new nationalism" it cannot maintain crucial patron-client relations.(26) Its only recourse is to call for external redistribution while ensuring that an equivalent level of internal re-distribution does not undermine its own hegemony. In any event, the NIEO debate has profound implications for different groups of African states, and so for continental unity and advocacy.(27) We shall return to the issue of inequalities in Africa. Meanwhile, we turn to the nature of political sociology and culture on the continent.

POLITICAL SOCIOLOGY

The development of regionalism in Africa has been closely associated, at least within the orthodox model, with the ideologies and movements of nationalism and Pan-Africanism. Independence and unity have long been considered the prerequisites for development and stability. They have served to legitimize various policies of national liberation and integration, and few leaders have abandoned or denied them, at least at the declaratory level.(28) Moreover, the OAU forum has served as a regular and symbolic confessional at which the "myths" of the continent's struggles are revived and perpetuated.(29) It has also been conceived of as an arena within which a collective and consensual "African" foreign policy is forged, the externalization of continental unity.(30)

If the record of the OAU has been at best mixed for orthodox analysts, the expectations of the radical school have been even less sanguine. The radical approach, based as it is on Africa's position in the international division of labor, conceives of the OAU as an association of dependent ruling classes whose basic common interest lies in holding onto power in the interests of themselves and their external associates. Nationalism and Pan-Africanism are dismissed from this perspective as bourgeois ideology that serves to camouflage the class nature of African regimes and organizations. So, any move toward a common foreign policy is taken to be further evidence of shared class interest rather than of an emergent continental community. The revival of myth is treated as a collective exercise in "defensive radicalism." Radical rhetoric on Southern Africa and NIEO is designed to defuse criticism and divert opposition from both national regimes and conti-nental institutions while avoiding fundamental change toward some form of socialist society.(31) "Progressive" ideology may, therefore, lead away from rather than toward, a basic transformation in Africa's political economy.

However, the prospect of most OAU members continuing to follow a common development path and adopting a common foreign policy stance has receded in the second half of the 1970s. Changes in the world system as well as in the African subsystem have served to undermine the tenuous unity and to revive the factionalism that characterized the continent in the early 1960s. But contemporary differences are likely to have a longer and more intense impact as they revolve around basic issues of political economy, not around alternative styles of leadership or rhetoric. Choices, constraints, and contradictions at the national level come to affect interactions at both the regional and continental levels and are inseparable from broader issues of inheritance and response, dependence and development. Although the focus here is on regional and higher levels of interaction, divergencies at the national level are coming to affect these increasingly.

The majority of African regimes have continued to follow an orthodox development strategy that is compatible with established notions of regionalism and growth. However, a few have always questioned the assumptions of the majority, redefining development in terms of disengagement not incorporation, basic human needs not growth, and relevance not grandeur, all of which challenge the established conceptualization of regionalism and continentalism. And this grouping of more radical states has grown in size in the later 1970s as disillusion with orthodox approaches has spread and as liberation struggles have led to the emergence of new regimes. The alternative radical faction in continental affairs today is, therefore, larger, more stable, and more determined than in the early 1960s.

Although most African states have relied, since independence, on state involvement in the economy to stimulate activity – typically through the proliferation of ubiquitous "parastatal" organizations – the majority have remained state capitalist countries; only a few have advanced toward (let alone beyond) a state socialist political economy. The majority have only reformed, and not transformed, the colonial societal and economic systems they inherited, although they may have superimposed a distinctive African political superstructure over continuing social substructures. By contrast, the minority have sought to transform the political economy as a whole, attempting to transcend inherited contradictions and establish, instead, new and more equitable modes and relations of production. No state in Africa has yet achieved a high level of socialist organization, but several have begun to move toward state socialism and to contemplate (and debate) steps beyond this stage.

Elsewhere, we have suggested, given the salience of a few new forces in postindependence Africa – especially the roles of the transnational bourgeoisie and the labor aristocracy as well as of those factions which control the state apparatus – a new typology is necessary for the continent, one that reflects essential differences in political economy and external linkages.(32) In particular, a fundamental distinction needs to be made and sustained between those regimes that encourage private capital, both national and international (Egypt, Ivory Coast, Kenya, Morocco, Nigeria, Senegal, and Zaire) and those that insist on some form of community ownership (Algeria, Angola, Mozambique, Somalia, Tanzania, and Tunisia). And within the latter grouping, a set of states may be tentatively identified that might attempt to go beyond state socialism toward some form of socialist system (Mozambique and Tanzania).(33)

By following a noncapitalist path, this minority of state socialist countries has had to confront fundamental choices about linkages with regional, continental, and global structures. Instead of accepting most forms of external interaction and integration as beneficial, they have begun to selectively distinguish between more and less equal forms of exchange; in particular, they have attempted to reduce their contact with capitalist-oriented institutions, whether they be regional organizations, major states, or global corporations. They have also attempted to identify their own development goals and to design their own resources, skills, and technologies. By trying to escape from dependence, they not only challenge external interests but also threaten common assumptions about the forms and bases of regionalism in Africa.

State socialist regimes confront the comfortable collaboration between state capitalist interests at all levels. They further expose and erode the myth of Pan-Africanism and the deficiencies of defensive radicalism. They have begun to offer a cohesive and comprehensive set of alternative values and policies at both national and regional levels – national and collective self-reliance – and have expressed a different understanding of the continent's political culture.

POLITICAL CULTURES

The orthodox view of Africa's political culture is that it is both pluralistic and elitist: pluralistic in terms of official recognition of a rich variety of ethnic, racial, religious, and regional social groups; elitist in terms of consisting of a small self-appointed set of rather jealous leaders. The OAU system has attempted to bridge the gap between pluralism and elitism by broadening the scope of its activities to embrace a diverse range of interests and activities. The tension between different groups remains, however, and the exclusiveness of the OAU system has been only marginally moderated by some more popular involvement in certain specific activities.

By contrast, the radical perspective considers contradiction and tension to be inherent in the OAU because of Africa's position in the world system, and the unwillingness of most of its members to recognize the class content of their states and regimes. Rather than seeking accommodation and amelioration, then, the alternative perspective advocates self-consciousness and self-criticism for African leaders, expecting that an awareness of the historical and material bases of conflict will lead not to orthodox measures of conflict resolution but rather to structural change both within the continent and between it and the global system. But the structural changes envisaged by the radical school are very different from any demand for NIEO; transformation rather than reform is sought in which socialism as well as self-reliance is the basis of social relations. This issue of degree of pluralism and exclusivity is no longer merely an analytic one but, with the appearance of more radical regimes, is now on the agenda of regional institutions.

State capitalist and state socialist regimes differ, then, in terms of how they perceive the nature and role of the state and how they define nation-building and national unity. The former still concentrate on political superstructures, designing alternative constitutional forms to deal with continuing ethnic, regional, and religious differences. By contrast, the latter focus on social substructures, seeking alternative forms of political economy to deal with emerging class-type inequalities and tensions. State capitalist governments — whether they be multi-, one-, or nonparty military or praetorian regimes — attempt to resolve factional conflicts based on nonclass distinctions, whereas state socialist governments — usually one-party or military regimes — recognize and attempt to overcome class contradictions first. The latter tend, therefore, to be more centralized and _dirigiste_ than the former, defining participation in a more profound way.

The different emphases and policies of these two distinct types of regime are reflective of different, perhaps even dialectical and incompatible, approaches to political economy and development strategy. They also affect the degree of consensus and cohesion on the continent and reduce the amount of commonality in foreign policy. Moreover, their divergent approaches to development and external associations mean that regional institutions can no longer obscure nuances of policy, but tend to fragment overtly along the cleavage between state capitalist and state socialist governments. The notion of "we are all Africans" has worn rather thin as a characterization of continental political culture. In particular, the differential treatment of national and regional inequalities has disturbed common assumptions about the right of the new class to rule. While orthodox governors and analysts still recognize the need for hierarchy and order, more radical (and populist) leaders and scholars question the basis of and necessity for distance between citizens. They are critical of elitist values and behaviors and call for a removal, rather than the glorification, of social and material differentiation. They define participation in terms of popular control over the means of production and availability of basic human needs, not just in terms of access to the political process.

ELITE POLITICAL PSYCHOLOGY

In a sense both orthodox and radical approaches focus on the OAU as the centerpiece of integrative efforts. They diverge, however, in their evaluations of the intent and impact of such efforts, with the orthodox perspective considering them to be essentially benign and the radical school conceiving of them as more malignant. The former, extending its interest in Pan-Africanism, considers interelite interaction to merely facilitate cooperation, mediation, and liberation; whereas the latter, consistent with its critique of African ideology, conceives of contact amongst the ruling classes to be counterproductive for fundamental change.

The orthodox mode, based as it is on the premise of interstate equality, is supportive of cohesion and integration as means toward development. By contrast, the radical mode, founded on the alternative premise of mixed actor inequalities, is skeptical about attempts to prevent fragmentation and reduce contradictions. Continental efforts at negotiation and mediation are seen to be integrative by the former and counterrevolutionary by the latter.

The prevailing psychological preferences of Africa's elites can be deduced from the Charter and resolutions of the OAU.(34) These, together with the revival of certain precolonial forms and the customs of diplomatic exchange, constitute the bases of regional international law.(35) Zartman has identified three particularly salient aspects of regional norms that reflect the Pan-African ideology and assumptions of Africa's contemporary leadership: ". . . .(I)ntrasystem solutions are to be preferred over extrasystem solutions. . . .(T)he successor state is the basic, sovereign, inviolable, legitimizing unit of intra-African politics. . .A third rule is that white minority. . .rule is the greatest evil. . . ."(36)

Chime presents salient characteristics of the African system comparable to that of Zartman:

> a common colonial experience, which was continentwide, continuing, and fundamental in its impact on Africa's political economy; underdevelopment and nonindustrialized condition; widespread feeling of nationalism and unity, being most potent in terms of furthering liberation in Southern Africa; and highly penetrated states that have minimal freedom because of external spheres of influence.(37)

In other words, African regional norms reflect and reinforce the nationalist, statecentric and Pan-Africanist values of the majority of leaders and institutions. They have been expressed most clearly in regional debates and activities over secession,(38) mediation, and liberation. OAU-related involvement in, say, the Nigerian Civil War, a variety of bilateral "border" disputes, and change in Southern Africa have all occurred within the context of regional norms.

Yet, the evolution of a collective set of norms and procedures has not yet excluded individual initiatives that bring credit and status to particular statesmen and states. The radical approach tends to emphasize either the irrelevance or contradictions in African regional law or the role of single statesmen in salvaging the system. On the one hand, therefore, critics argue that African values are contradictory in both conception and implementation (contrast, for instance, unsuccessful Somali "irredentism" in the Ogaden and Northern Kenya with successful Moroccan "adventurism" in the Sahara; or compare attitudes toward "secessionist guerillas" in the Southern Sudan, Shaba, or Eastern Angola with "liberation movements" in Southern Africa) and, on the other hand, that they are the function of just a few "great men" who engage in "shuttle diplomacy" to prevent the inevitable disintegration of continental structures.

One particular variation in the orthodox genre is offered by Adda Bozeman who, in her continuing quest for distinctive regional sources of international law, has identified conflict as inherent in African culture and hence, characteristic of the regional system.(39) She argues that this precolonial cultural heritage has led to an escalation and intensification of conflict in the postcolonial era, producing "distinct and acrimonious competitions for continental and international leadership."(40) Bozeman conceives of conflict as a cultural trait, leading to customary resolution procedures characteristic of contemporary African regionalism:

> Since conflict is traditionally accepted in Africa as ongoing or latent in social and interstate affairs, negotiations, too, are apt to be continuous or protracted – an enmeshment of activities which explains, incidentally, why stamina in the face of feuds and wars is matched by patience when it comes to conciliatory consultations.(41)

For the orthodox analyst, then, continental norms and laws are but one aspect of an emerging African identity and authenticity, reflective of regional culture and psychology. From a radical perspective, however, these beliefs and behaviors are merely the superficial indicators of more basic difficulties that are characteristic of the contradictions arising from Africa's place in the world system. The radical school considers most efforts at mediation and integration to be attempts to perpetrate Africa's dependent status by states and statesmen closely involved in the current global order. So actions considered to be attempts at conciliation by the orthodox approach are conceived of as further forms of collaboration from a radical perspective.

AFFINITIES

Given the elitist and ethnic sensibilities expressed in regional forms in Africa, societal variables have not been important factors, notwithstanding formal homage paid to more popular notions of Pan-Africanism and participation. On the other hand, political affinities and cleavages that appeared to have been transcended in the first decade of the OAU have revived in the middle 1970s, disturbing the relatively tranquil, consensus politics of the OAU and other continental forums. Both analytic approaches recognize the diversities of Africa; but whereas the orthodox perspective tends to view them all as equally salient, the radical mode places most emphasis on structural characteristics of the continent's political economy, such as social class and political stratification.

Zartman identifies several affinities considered to be important from an orthodox angle: rather exclusive regimes that tend to reflect the interest of the more educated, urbanized elites, certain cultural and religious traits and cohesion as well as division between Arab and African.(42) He also tends to underestimate the causes of ideological conflict, conceiving of them as superficial rather than structural, although recognizing the demise of consensus.(43)

The radical approach recognizes a range of affinities and contradictions, emphasizing the exclusivity and dominance of national leaders, the ambiguities of ethnic and religious affiliations, tensions of race and religion and, above all, the emergence of class politics based on relationship to the means of production and on an increasingly unequal division of labor and income. Divisions based on social class and development preferences are intensifying as growth is increasingly uneven and problematic. This intensification has been revealed in African demands for NIEO and for Afro-Arab dialogue.

Moreover, it has served to revive the hitherto tranquil ideological scene in Africa that had, until the early 1970s, been relatively quiescent following the frantic factionalism of the early 1960s preceding the founding of the OAU. Zartman's comment about the passing of the "age of ideology in Africa" may have been premature.(44) For, as James Mayall has noted in a recent revision of the orthodox viewpoint, in the 1970s a "new threat to Africa's political order came with the revival of ideology. The coexistence for more than a decade of the two opposing elements in the OAU Charter had been very largely the result of an ideological ceasefire in 1963."(45) But by the mid-1970s, following the liberation of Mozambique and Angola and with the growing disillusionment over orthodox development strategies, coexistence among different political economies on the continent began to fade. Mayall suggests that:

> The undermining of the OAU consensus was the work of forces beyond the Organization's control. . . .The three most critical developments. . .are the collapse of two empires, that of the Portuguese in Southern Africa and that of Haile Selassie in Ethiopia, and the emergence since October 1973 of the Arab States as a major force in African diplomacy.(46)

A radical analysis of this revived "moderate" versus "progressive" divide would look below the surface of organizational disputes and border conflicts to examine basic differences among the political economies of African states. Rather than focusing on external involvement or post-OPEC petro-diplomacy, it would concentrate on changes within the center and periphery as well as in their interrelations. Together, the uneven impact of changes in the world system, changes in growth rates on the continent, and changes in development strategy have revived the ideological debate or dialectic in Africa, with profound implications for regional cohesion and consensus. These will further reinforce the imperative of a redefinition and reconceptualization of Pan-Africanism to reflect not only an awareness of racial oppression and colonial dominance but also a sense of economic exploitation and social alienation.

AUTHORITY AND INFLUENCE PATTERNS

The revival of ideology in Africa is one aspect of a broader trend toward divergent political economies because of the highly uneven character and impact of incorporation into the world system. The myth of equality dies hard among scholars as well as statesmen, yet the emergence of a few leading powers on the continent is forcing a reassessment in both perception and policy. Nevertheless, the orthodox school sticks doggedly to the assumption that the continental system consists of essentially equal and similar actors, while the radical approach attempts to relate novel concepts – such as that of "subimperialism"(47) – to changes in Africa's position in the world order. Both modes of analysis retain their currency in a global system characterized by a return to realpolitik and power politics. However, Zartman continues to assert that "it is simply not possible to understand the relations of the continental system through a study of the few states which might be counted as the powerful of the continent."(48)

Nonetheless, the orthodox approach has moved some way toward recognition of the growing inequalities on the continent, conceiving of them, however, as changeable and unstable phenomena rather than as reflections of a gradual evolution in Africa's substructure. Instead of treating Africa's new group of "middle powers" as indicative of changes in the international division of labor, Zartman views them merely as centers of momentary conflicts and coalitions. According to him, the three major features of the leading African states are: ". . .temporary initiatives on the regional level, delicate positions of predominance within a subregion, and limited arrays of resources available as a power base. . . ."(49)

By contrast, the radical mode sees regional powers as being less transitional, not restricted to strategic issues alone, and more structurally defined. From this viewpoint, the emergence of subimperialism on the continent is related to the evolving international division of labor in which some limited forms of industrialism can take place, albeit under the auspices of the multinational corporations, in the "semiperiphery." Although production is restructured within corporations and center states so certain countries may advance from periphery into the semiperiphery, technological, financial, and administrative controls are largely retained in the center.(50)

Internationalization of production does not mean internationalization of control. Rather, the center is able to secure favorable terms and attitudes by offering some limited degree of semiindustrialization to cooperative regimes or countries with particularly valuable natural or organizational resources. According to the world system framework of Wallerstein, a few African states, either by invitation or by accident, will come to enjoy upward mobility in the international hierarchy, whereas the majority will continue to stagnate and underdevelop in the periphery.(51) The possibility or prospect of advancing into the semiperiphery serves to reinforce confidence in orthodox development theory as well as encourage quiescence in established spheres of influence. In turn, a few semiindustrial states get to partially dominate their own regions of the continent on behalf of center interests.

The depth and persistence of such new divisions in Africa has been apparent in OAU meetings, actions, and issues since the mid-1970s. On major issues involving extracontinental interests and interventions, the semiindustrial states have tended, along with some of the poorer countries, to take a more permissive stance whereas the noncapitalist regimes have generally expressed resistance to such forces. On a range of interrelated questions (concerning Angola, Ethiopia, Sahara, Shaba, and Uganda) and the broader issues that they represent (collective security, integrity, border secession, and political change), the more conservative and capitalist countries (especially Egypt, the Ivory Coast, Kenya, Malawi, and Morocco) have encouraged Western involvement in crises as well as its capital in infrastructure. By contrast, the radical faction – especially Algeria, Benin, People's Republic of the Congo, Mozambique, and Tanzania – has opposed further Western intervention, seeking instead either autonomy or nonalignment through the judicious use of socialist forces. A few mixed economies have opted for a more intermediate position – especially Cameroon, Nigeria, and Zambia – but they have been unable to secure enough votes to form an alternative faction, although they tend to reflect, in the mid-1970s, the OAU's consensus of the mid-1960s.(52)

Given the tenacity with which the conservative and radical factions hold their positions, it seems unlikely that this particular source and variety of disunity will disappear readily. Rather, it is likely to intensify in the next decade as inequalities grow under the impact of continued scarcities and recession.(53) In the longer-term future, the structural constraints of semiindustrialization may appear and limit the activities of the semiperiphery. However, for the immediate future, and at the level of superstructural relationships, the new visibility and dominance of the nouveaux riches seem assured.

In the midterm future, semiindustrialism in the semiperiphery may, then, reinforce confidence in orthodox development strategies and in the continent's ability to maintain order. However, in the longer term, as Langdon and Mytelka suggest, the subimperial "solution" may generate its own contradictions and demise because of its association with the established capitalist international division of labor:

Export manufacturing in Africa, then, will undoubtedly increase – as the signs of change in such countries as the Ivory Coast, Senegal, Ghana, and Kenya suggest. But this manufacturing is likely to be largely under the direction of foreign enterprises and integrated into the structure of internationalized production. In consequence, the linkage, employment, and income effects of such manufacturing will be fairly limited within Africa – and probably will be enjoyed mainly by those local elites who will extend their import-substitution symbiosis to the export sector. Significant restructuring of African economies, with wide dynamic advantages for African majorities, cannot be expected to emerge from this export-manufacturing growth.(54)

INTERDEPENDENCIES

The emergence of inequalities and regional powers on the continent may, paradoxically, serve to increase the level of interaction in Africa, at least in the short run and among the group of emergent middle powers. To date, the proportion of intra- versus extracontinental exchange has been very limited, because of Africa's dependent status within the world system. Economic interaction and military relations have been concentrated at the subregional level, increasingly under the dominance of a few regional centers and cities – such as Dakar, Abidjan, Lagos, Nairobi, and Cairo – that serve as intermediaries between metropoles and peripheries.

Interdependencies based on integration in Africa remain largely an aspiration rather than a reality. Despite resolutions, declarations, constitutions, and diplomacy, integration (as measured in terms of economic, communications, and social transactions) remains at a stubbornly low level. The orthodox view of this situation is that integration takes time and that, given African's colonial inheritance, its post-independence performance is quite promising. By contrast, the radical perspective sees extracontinental economic dependence as an essential characteristic of the capitalist world system; it does not expect high levels of continental integration while Africa remains incorporated within global networks.

So, whereas the orthodox approach sees no necessary incompatibility between global, continental, and regional integration, the radical school considers continental and regional self-reliance to be incompatible with global and transnational integration. The data on regional exchange shows a rather mixed record, with inter-African trade rising less slowly than extra-African; i.e., inter-African exchange continues to fall as a percentage of total African trade. Moreover, most of this trade is either transit of non-African goods to land-locked states or the export of manufactures by multinational branches located in regional centers such as Abidjan, Lagos, and Nairobi.

Intra-African trade is unlikely to increase much until the continent escapes from its colonial heritage of North-South links and develops products with markets on the continent as well as outside. But to maximize compatibility and exchange, a regional industrialization policy is necessary; yet, this cannot be designed or realized until decisions made by foreign countries and corporations are transcended. This, in turn, requires a degree of autonomy that can be achieved only through collective action. Hence, the vicious circle of exogenous rather than endogenous growth, of a highly open rather than relatively closed continental system. Jonathan Chileshe points to this paradox:

Cooperation in the promotion of intra-African trade is a challenge which promises better lasting results insofar as the region's rate of economic growth is concerned than continuous dependency on foreign aid and trade with outside economic blocs.(55)

The elusiveness of intra-African exchange is reflected in the under-developed state of the continental infrastructure. Communications by land, sea, air, and telegraph are improving but still by no means balance extra-African connections. Moreover, this is so despite the major efforts of external agencies to enhance Africa's infrastructure, even if only to improve extracontinental links. The prevalence of nationalism in a balkanized continent does not improve the prospects for infra-structural development. Nevertheless, successive OAU and ECA meet-ings along with a variety of functional organizations have provided plans for a network of road, rail, sea, and air routes, such as the Trans-Sahara, Trans-African, Trans-Sahelian, and Cairo-Gaborones high-ways.(56) But the use to which such routes will be put is problematic until Africa's development strategies are clarified. Moreover, like other aspects of regionalism, they tend to reinforce rather than reduce inequalities, with Lagos, for instance, being the terminal of three continental routes – Trans-African, Trans-Sahara, and Trans-Coastal. And, as has already been indicated, semiindustrial growth in the semiperiphery may not produce a change in Africa's global position but merely reflect a modification in the essentially unequal international division of labor.

REGIONAL FOREIGN POLICY BEHAVIOR

The established African response to colonialism and underdevelopment has been advocacy of nationalism at the state level, Pan-Africanism at the continental level, and nonalignment at the Third World level. All of these reactions called for a redistribution of authority and resources without involving a real transformation in Africa's world position. These three clusters of values have constituted the core of Africa's collective foreign policy and have led to current demands for NIEO. However, with the emergence of inequalities on the continent and the reap-pearance of ideological cleavages, common international positions have tended to fragment. The espousal of alternative development strat-egies, such as the noncapitalist path and various forms of socialism, inspired by Marxist-Leninist rather than traditional thought, have undermined the continent's ideological consensus and led to a variety of foreign policy orientations and emphases.(57)

The orthodox approach, recognizing Africa's common heritage and transition, still emphasizes commonalities in the continent's foreign policies. The radical approach, reflecting changes in the political economy of parts of the continent, accepts and examines contradictions in the foreign relations of participating state and nonstate institutions. The orthodox perspective, based on certain sociological, cultural, and psychological affinities already identified, conceives of Africa's foreign policy as being singular and consensual. It appreciates the imperative of unity if Africa's voice is to be heard, and recognizes the importance of externalization for continental integration as well as extracontinental effectiveness. Under the impact of various associations, however, it has begun to accept that there may be different foreign policy emphases or nuances, particularly based on membership in, say, the Commonwealth or Francophones, the Arab League, or Islamic States. "The recognition of overlapping systems in interpreting foreign policy alternatives and possibilities for states with dual membership is both a more helpful and more realistic way of looking at foreign policies than is the attempt to force such states exclusively into one area or the other."(58)

While African states may belong to a variety of international institutions, their foreign policy "choices" may be quite limited, particularly by their selection of a development strategy. The comparative study of foreign policy in Africa remains rather embryonic, although a few frameworks for analysis now exist.(59) One major factor in foreign policy making is, of course, choice of development strategy which, given Africa's dependence and openness, means essentially how to respond to external pressures and opportunities. Donald Rothchild and Robert Curry have proposed a trilateral typology of such responses that may also serve as a framework for comparative foreign policy analysis.(60) They identify three policy options – accommodation, reorganization, and transformation – which span the spectrum from acquiescence to resistance respectively. But, compatible with the general tenor of the orthodox school, they treat these as mere policy responses rather than as political strategies that reflect underlying structural contradictions.

In contrast, the radical perspective concentrates on development alternatives rather than foreign policy and attempts to relate these to mode of production and incorporation rather than to international associations and ideologies. More radical African scholars such as Micah Tsomondo and Teti Kofi argue that Pan-Africanism is representative of bourgeois interests and needs to be transcended in both analysis and practice by a more scientific variety of socialism. Moreover, they see the adoption of socialism at the continental level as a prerequisite for effective unity based on an appreciation of class politics and the adoption of a continental industrial strategy. In other words, they conceive of socialism as a response to fragmentation and functionalism on the one hand and dependence and underdevelopment on the other hand.(61)

The orthodox approach, however, still sees Pan-Africanism as a reaction to colonialism and does not go much beyond the re-Africanization of the continent as an objective. It still has faith in orthodox theories of development – convergence and "trickledown" – and extroverted strategies of growth. The radical approach, however, has largely abandoned the assumptions and remedies of the orthodox perspective in favor of an approach that is more introverted and self-reliant, based on an appreciation of the international division of labor as it affects Africa.(62) This debate or dichotomy over foreign and development policies has begun, in turn, to affect regional politics.

REGIONAL INSTITUTIONS

The orthodox approach has analyzed attempts at regional integration in Africa as part of a diplomatic strategy to improve the balance of forces between the continent and the rest of the global system. It conceives of regionalism, then, not so much as a development strategy or attempt to restructure the international division of labor but rather as a diplomatic tactic designed to enhance Africa's visibility and autonomy – a collective form of decolonization. Its focus has been on regional constitutions and institutions – the form rather than the relationship – and on mediation and liberation rather than structural transformation. From this perspective, the process is as important, if not more so, than the results. And although one motive of the Pan-African movement has been to reduce balkanization and transcend nationalism, in fact, the record of the OAU to date has served to reinforce fragmentation and to reify the state:

> From the start the existence of the OAU has been far more important to African statesmen and politicians than any functional role it may perform in promoting economic cooperation or even the alignment of foreign policies. . . .By merely being there, the OAU does, indeed, perform one vital role in African diplomacy – it bestows legitimacy on its members and on the movements and causes which they choose to recognize. . . .It has always been the OAU's main task to set the seal of legitimacy on both the distribution of power within African states and on those liberation movements, mainly in Southern Africa, which were contesting power with colonial or minority regimes.(63)

In contrast with the focus on diplomacy and legitimacy of the orthodox school, the radical approach considers the developmental and economic impact of regionalism. And, whereas the former may produce relatively positive evaluations, the latter leads to essentially negative conclusions. The OAU network may have served to stabilize the continental system in terms of decolonization, mediation, and consultation. But the ECA and its "subregional" associates have not yet begun to escape from a position of economic dependence on the world system.

The OAU has shown a remarkable resilience in its ability to weather the storms of dialogue and detente with South Africa; of conflict in Katanga/Shaba, Southern Sudan, Nigeria, Eritrea, Chad, and Western Sahara; and of OPEC and Afro-Arab divisions.(64) But these rather ephemeral, diplomatic crises are seen by the radical school as merely reflections of fundamental contradictions that the OAU-ECA system has yet to confront seriously. Despite a growing range of proposals, meetings, and institutions – such as the OAU Declaration on Cooperation, Development and Economic Independence; the African Development Bank and Fund; Ministerial Conferences on Trade, Development, and Monetary Problems; and participation in EEC-ACP negotiations, UNCTAD preparations, and CIEC debates – regional interactions have

not yet led to significant economic advances.(65) As Zdenek Cervenka
laments in his latest book on African regionalism,

> Compared with the progress made by the OAU on decolonization,
> and the success of its international campagin against apartheid,
> its performance in the economic field has been disappointing.
> After fourteen years of the OAU, the real struggle for the
> liberation of the continent of Africa from economic domination
> by outside powers has hardly begun.(66)

The reason for this condition advanced by the radical school is the
continued integration of Africa into the world system. Whereas at the
level of diplomacy and ideology the OAU can score Pyrrhic victories at
the level of exchange and capital, the ECA cannot advance development without a fundamental restructuring of the continental political
economy, with profound implications for both metropolitan and African
elite interests. Given the close transnational links between the new
class and foreign countries, corporations, and other classes, such a
prospect is unlikely. Continued economic dependence combined with
diplomatic activeness pose problems for both statesmen and scholars.

In an attempt to make Africa's powerlessness and assertiveness
compatible, Zartman has recognized the discontinuity between continental dependence and demands while ignoring the structural contradictions that generate such ambiguity: "(I)n a world where Africa does
not have the power to protect itself and promote its own goals,
it. . .emphasizes its rights and deemphasizes the classical means to
attain them. The inherent contradiction. . .is typical of an idealistic
view of international relations."(67) If the orthodox approach, with its
emphasis on the new diplomacy, is idealistic in tone, then the radical
perspective, with its emphasis on the old dependence, is realistic in
orientation. This analytic and existential dichotomy is also reflected in
patterns of contemporary regional cooperation and conflict.

REGIONAL COOPERATION AND CONFLICT

The OAU system, established to reflect and advance the interests of
national leaderships on the continent, seeks to achieve cooperation
without further reducing sovereignty and to minimize conflict without
resolving fundamental issues. It has to avoid both progress toward
supranationalism and escalation toward warfare. This would be a fine
line, even if the region as a whole had a higher level of autonomy, but,
given its dependent status, the achievement of satisfactory levels of
cooperation and conflict control is quite problematic. The continent
continues to be the target of two distinct types of external pressures,
one of which is recognized by the orthodox school, the other of which is
emphasized by the radical school.(68)

The orthodox approach conceives of extracontinental intervention in
essentially strategic and diplomatic terms, focusing on the role of

foreign bases, troops, diplomats, and intelligence networks.(69) Like the nonalignment movement, it overlooks any constraints imposed by Africa's position in the international division of labor, and conceives of cooperation as a collective diplomatic response to external threats. And it emphasizes intervention from the socialist states, particularly Russia and Cuba but also China, as endemic, whereas the role of capitalist powers is assumed to be more benign.

Because of the pervasiveness of external involvement in Africa, however, some students within the orthodox tradition have attempted to treat at least some, albeit the more superficial, aspects of dependence and underdevelopment. Nevertheless, they continue to see the processes of intervention and conflict as sporadic and crisis-related, rather than structural and normal. Raymond Copson, for instance, has recently argued that: "The persistence of conflict on the African continent is deeply rooted in the underdevelopment of African states and of the African system of states. . . .Political and economic underdevelopment (is) a cause of international conflict in Africa. . . ."(70) Copson attempts to explain the absence of regional order and the regularity of boundary disputes, regional power centers, and diplomatic disagreements in terms of national underdevelopment (insecure regimes, limited capabilities, economic stagnation, and colonial borders) and regional underdevelopment (absence of strong organization, regional imbalances, and local arms races). He avoids notions of political economy, such as dependence and class, and opts, instead, for a more critical form of systemic and realist analysis, concluding that "Conflict is the unavoidable consequence of the underdevelopment of the African states and of the African state system."(71) Chime also conceives of foreign intrusions in these terms, appreciating the history of bloc politics and feudal networks in the international system. He characterizes external intervention as "the Godfather syndrome" in which foreign actors capriciously determine events and outcomes on the continent through activating their spheres of influence.(72)

The radical perspective on intervention and blocs is that they are the result of Africa's historical incorporation into the world system and of current transnational linkages between rulers on the continent and those in the center. External involvement from this viewpoint is neither capricious nor sporadic but structural and routine, one aspect of Africa's part in the international division of labor. It sees cooperation against such a status being either idealistic or merely part of a continual quest for a better bargain by African leaders caught between cautious foreign associates and impatient national constituencies. The emphasis from this perspective is not on strategic and diplomatic disputes but, rather, on structural constraints imposed not by socialist armies and advisers but by corporate branches, foreign technology, and external exchange. Such extracontinental involvement cannot be readily resisted, particularly given the ubiquitous transnational class linkages that maintain global interdependence rather than continental integration.(73) Any response involves not only African cooperation – a somewhat unlikely prospect given different transnational orientations and expectations – but disengagement and restructuring – also unlikely prospects unless intranational pressures come to demand it.

To date, much regional cooperation in both strategic and economic issue areas has advanced rather than reduced external involvement. The arms trade with Africa and the continuing associations with Western and Eastern armies – particularly those of France(74) and Cuba – reflect not only foreign interests but also the insecurity of regimes and states.(75) And much regional economic cooperation – from the entente and ECOWAS to ECA and ADB – serves the interests of foreign aid agencies, consultants, and corporations (from both socialist and capitalist states).(76) Many of the benefits of such regional integration have flowed back to centers of foreign investment, aid, and technology; most dependent industrialization is by corporate branches rather than by indigenous institutions and has served to advance the symbiotic interests of semiperipheral and center states rather than those of the region as a whole. As Langdon and Mytelka note, reflecting the radical approach,

> The contemporary crisis of regional integration in Africa is not, however, a purely nationalistic affair in which states are pitted against each other in conflicts over the interstate distribution of the gains from integration. Rather, this interstate conflict is a reflection of more fundamental problems that are associated with the distribution of gains between national and international capital as the MNC seeks to structure not only national but also regional markets around its own needs and interests.(77)

The difficulties and dilemmas of regional cooperation in Africa have led to the decay as well as the creation of institutions (e.g., the now-defunct East African Community); it has also led to a new awareness of different forms and strategies for regionalism on the continent.

REGIONAL INTEGRATION

Regional integration at the subcontinental level has had a rather checkered history in Africa, with disintegration and decay being as common as regional initiatives and successes. Regionalism by declaration (such as the Guinea-Ghana-Mali Union of African States) common in the 1960s, has been superseded by regionalism through evolution in the 1970s, along the lines of the francophone with African Economic Community (CEAO). Regionalism in Africa is no longer merely declaratory, as in the case of the abortive East African Federation; neither is it simply egalitarian, federal, or colonial as in the instance of the Central African Federation. Rather, it is increasingly characterized by neofunctionalism, i.e., by a judicious blend of economic self-interest, political activism, and functional purpose. Moreover, recent attempts at regional cooperation on the continent have been influenced by earlier failures and so have tried to avoid the twin pitfalls of naivete and overambition. They have also begun to transcend established damages of colonial or linguistic inheritance. And furthermore, they are characterized increasingly by the growth of compatible, even if overlapping, institutions, many of which are functionally specific.

Regionalism in Africa at this level is still a major subject of political as well as intellectual debate, related to the broader question of collective self-reliance and incorporation. Instinctively, the origins of regionalism on the continent either lie in colonial administrative convenience (i.e., anglophone East Africa and francophone north, west, and central Africa) or settle economic ambitions (i.e., anglophone southern and central Africa). Some of these early arrangements have survived the nationalist period and emerged as more Afro-centric institutions (e.g., Customs and Economic Union of Central Africa (UDEAC), the entente, and Afro-Mauritanian Common Organization (OCAM), as well as the CEAO which still awaits the final liberation of the continent before being further reformed, and the Southern African Customs Union (SACU). Others are essentially postcolonial creations (e.g., the now-defunct East African Community) which at least represent hopes for a successful revival of regionalism as a form of pan-Africanism, and the Economic Community of West African States (ECOWAS) that includes Portuguese as well as francophone and anglophone states among its sixteen members.

But the major level of innovation and success has been in the more specific (in activity) and restricted (in membership) organizations. Such trilateral or bilateral institutions include the Great Lakes Economic, Kagera River Basin, Senegal River Development, Gambia River Development, Mano River, and Liptako-Gowma Development Organizations. These are all designed to improve infrastructure among members and to advance development as well as growth in particular geographic areas. Their achievements have given them a certain resilience but their compatibility with larger forms of regionalism such as ECOWAS remains problematic and controversial.

The more ambitious and uncertain projects such as EAC, CEAO, and the Entente have all tended to suffer from partisan politics and unequal distribution of grants. So they have failed to achieve sustained and balanced levels of development and have been dominated by a few corporate or national interests. The EAC failed, for example, despite repeated attempts at restructuring and revival, because of divergent ideologies, regimes, and growth. In particular, the economic achievements of Kenya, based on its symbiotic links with certain multinational corporations, were both unacceptable to, and at the expense of, the other East African partners, Tanzania and Uganda.(78)

Despite the elusiveness of industrialization, development, and self-reliance through regionalism in Africa, repeated attempts are still being made to advance both unity and exchange through this strategy.(79) The ECA is actively encouraging such subcontinental institutions and experiments; e.g., an association of Southern African states without the present Republic of South Africa, despite the regions' diverse languages, structures, origins and struggles, in part as a counterattraction to the long-established SACU. Regional organizations can be incompatible and competitive, as well as compatible and reinforcing.

The most ambitious, comprehensive, and contemporary scheme — designed to be compatible with established bi- or trilateral arrangements — is ECOWAS, which largely coincides with ECA's west African sub-region. The form of its structure has benefited from earlier failures such as EAC, for it includes a sophisticated secretariat and a well-endowed Fund for Cooperation, Compensation, and Development.(80) ECOWAS is intended to facilitate joint projects, comprehensive industrialization, and labor migration, in addition to increasing the exchange of goods and commodities.

ECOWAS is illustrative of the need for and dilemmas of regional integration in contemporary Africa. Horizontal exchange could usefully supplement and overcome an inheritance of vertical integration with former metropolises, leading toward greater self-reliance at both national and collective levels. But the major beneficiaries of such integration to date have been multinational corporation branches and the leading states of each region.(81) If integration is to continue and evolve, meeting basic human needs and permitting more autonomous development, then it needs to be redefined along more radical lines, taking into account Africa's historical incorporation within the world system. This would require basic agreement among member states not only on developmental and industrial strategies but also on technological, financial, and agricultural issues.

Unless regional integration in Africa is based on recognition of the need for disengagement and reorientation of political economies, it may serve to facilitate rather than to challenge the established pattern of trade and division of labor. To this end, proposals for integration in Southern Africa among more radical countries may advance development and self-reliance further than can be done in West Africa with cooperation among a group of more orthodox regimes. In any case, regional integration at the subcontinental level cannot be seen in isolation but has to take into account the prospects and constraints of interaction at other levels — interregional, continental, global, and transnational.

DEVELOPMENTAL ISSUES

The two schools of analysis for regionalism in Africa diverge, then, over explanations of regional efforts and recommendations for regional strategies. The orthodox approach, still retaining its confidence in laissez-faire theories, asserts that local political rather than global structural difficulties have produced the demise of integrative efforts to date but that further functional attempts will be successful. By contrast, the radical approach, with its focus on dependence and underdevelopment from a global perspective, asserts that regional efforts to date have been misplaced because they have not recognized

Africa's place in the international division of labor. It advocates a fundamental restructuring of both national and regional political economies as the prerequisite for integration and development. Whereas the orthodox prescription calls for more of the same (more regional cooperation among open, mixed economies), the radical recommendation is for greater national and collective self-reliance combined with a transition toward some form of socialist political economy.

The claims of the respective orthodox and radical approaches and strategies have recently been subjected to various sorts of empirical tests as one way of assessing their reliability. However, as James Caporaso notes in his review of this burgeoning literature,(82) most quantitative evaluations of dependence do not adequately operationalize the richness of the theory, usually relying for data instead on macro, external and static indicators. Therefore, the attempts by Patrick McGowan and others(83) to discuss or dilute the claims of dependency should not be taken too seriously. Moreover, they do recognize that variables other than the concentration of external links may be crucial, pointing in particular to the superior economic performance of the better-endowed states. This idea receives some support in a recent paper by Michael Dolan and his colleagues in which the more affluent states of Africa are seen to exhibit the greater level of dependence on and association with superordinate actors; growth may lead, at least in the short term, to conformity and intensified linkages despite the asymmetrical nature of the relationship.(84)

This continued, even expanded, intimacy between a few semi-peripheral states and a few major powers may further exacerbate inequalities on the continent by generating cumulatively unequal rates of growth. On the other hand, semiindustrial states may come to challenge their mentors and flex their muscles once they have secured sufficient privileges and growth from their manipulation of dependence. Nevertheless, the perpetuation of a few "special relationships" on the continent – often involving substructural as well as superstructural links (France with the Ivory Coast, Britain and Kenya, United States and Egypt, Soviet Union and Ethiopia, Cuba and Angola) – will continue to facilitate external involvement and regional inequalities. The potential of such divisive "bloc politics" for disunity and conflict on the continent continues to worry and preoccupy many African leaders and institutions.(85)

The ECA, for instance, has projected increased inequalities among the richer and poorer states over the next decade unless corrective action is taken.(86) It has called for the acceptance of "another way" so that Africa as a whole can avoid further inequality, disagreement, and underdevelopment. Indeed, recent ECA statements have suggested the discarding of orthodox approaches and theories and the adoption of alternative perspectives and strategies:

> ...an increasing measure of self-reliant and self-sustaining development and economic growth is an essential accompaniment of political independence, two of which are of particular

concern to the ECA: the reduction of mass poverty and mass unemployment. . . .Self-reliance is considered in terms of:
- the internalization of the forces of demand. . .;
- increasing substitution of factor inputs derived from within the system for those derived from outside;
- increasing participation of the mass of the people in the production and distribution of the social product.(87)

The ECA's concern for self-reliance and self-sustainment – as with the analytic concerns of the radical approach described in this chapter – has implications for external relations as well as for internal structures. In particular, it leads to a reconsideration of the place of international exchange for extra-Africa actors at the level of both theory and praxis. So the ECA has called for a reevaluation of such international economic relations:

Their significance lies in the role they play in facilitating or inhibiting a) the establishment of self-reliance, i.e., the substitution of domestic for foreign factor imports, and b) the promotion of self-sustainment, i.e., the substitution of internally generated for externally generated forces determining the speed and direction of economic growth. . . .

It is the Secretariat's conviction that what is being sought through extra-African trade are those components of development and economic growth processes which are available only outside the system for combination with those that are known to be available within the system. . . .(88)

In other words, for both the ECA and the radical school, extra-African trade should be conceived of only as a supplement to, and not as a cause of, national or regional exchange. This new ECA policy perspective on trade also has its counterpart in the radical approach to regionalism in which collective self-reliance is seen to be preferable to continued extraregional dependence. On the other hand, the conservative school still views regionalism uncritically by refusing to situate it in the context of broader international forces and inequities.(89)

Based on such orthodox analysis, state capitalist governments in Africa and elsewhere seek a new interstate order in which the resources of national leaderships are augmented so that their powers of patronage at the national level are reinforced. By contrast, radical leaders as well as scholars advocate a new global order in which both national and international structures are changed so that development can be facilitated at all levels. They do not want change only in the external terms of trade; rather they seek new global modes and relations of production in which basic human needs can be satisfied and inequalities at all levels reduced.(90) The radical approach recognizes and seeks to transcend contradictions at all levels; the conservative approach concentrates largely on constraints in the external system.

The orthodox school remains concerned, therefore, with regional cohesion, constitutions, and identities so that trends and correctives can be proposed. Zartman, for instance, examines the evolution of regionalism since independence as one means of discerning the future of regional interaction and integration: "A checkerboard, or Kautilian, pattern of interlocking alliances. . .turned into a balance-of-power structure, between 1960 and 1963, between two competing and basically ideological alliances, but this competition was merely the prelude to the establishment of a concert pattern of relations within the OAU after 1963. Since 1963, the concert pattern of relations has persisted. . . ."(91)

A counterpattern may already be in process, with the emergence of a regional bloc committed not merely to African socialism but to a fundamental restructuring of national political economies in the world system. The independence of Angola, Guinea-Bissau, and Mozambique, combined with "revolutionary" states such as Algeria, Guinea, Somalia, and Tanzania, has produced a continental faction that seeks development through disengagement rather than incorporation. Its espousal of alternative development strategies has undermined both continental consensus and the regional concert. But over time it may lead toward higher levels of development and integration once Africa's position in the world system has been transformed.(92) Moreover, the new radical caucus may come to shift the values and priorities of the regional system away from order and growth and toward change and development, neither of which can be achieved without a fundamental restructuring of Africa's political economies, and, hence, of the world system of which it is but a part.

THEORY AND DESIGN

This chapter has examined the claims of the radical as well as orthodox approaches to African regionalism — despite the dominance of the latter and the tentativeness of the former — because of a growing skepticism about traditional analysis and policy and because of the growing strength of the alternative strategy in both intellectual and political circles. Given the difficulties and deficiencies of both theory and policy associated with the orthodox school, the alternative framework has to be considered seriously. Contemporary analytic and empirical "experimentation" with it tend to support its claims to being considered as a powerful alternative approach.

The contrasting frameworks for African regionalism identified in this chapter offer not only alternative analyses, explanations, and policies but also different views of the future. As indicated in table 11.1, the dominant, orthodox school envisages a continual, gradual move toward functional and federal integration, whereas the radical perspective projects increased conflict in the midterm leading to fundamental restructuring in the longer-term future. The orthodox view consists of an extension and improvement of the present state of neofunctionalism in Africa whereas the radical view consists of an escalation and intensification of contemporary contradictions, producing an historical conjuncture out of which will emerge a fundamentally "new" Africa. These two alternative scenarios for the continent's future are, as we have seen, based on very different assumptions about Africa's current global position. The orthodox approach assumes that political decolonization has already been won whereas the radical approach assumes that the process of economic decolonization has hardly begun. The former asserts, therefore, that regional integration and autonomy are already possible if functional and federal strategies are successful, whereas the latter argues that no amount of cooperative action can produce integration and autonomy if the prerequisite of independence is absent. Zartman has captured the essentials of this debate in his characterization of the twin "decolonization" and "dependence" approaches.(93)

The orthodox, decolonization perspective, then, envisages a future for Africa characterized by continued integration within the world system as well as further integration at the continental level resulting in higher degrees of interdependence and interaction at both levels. By contrast, the radical, dependence approach projects a future characterized by growing tensions both within and between the states of Africa as the uneven incidence of growth exacerbates inequalities, leading away from African unity and toward revolutionary change at national, continental and, eventually, global levels. The adoption of either a continental or global level of analysis leads, therefore, to markedly different explanations and expectations.

While particular events and results are not amenable to confident prediction, certain structural trends and projections are now available for Africa.(94) We can now foresee some basic economic and ecological features that will pose problems for Africa's leaders in coming decades. Continued population pressures, including urbanization, food shortages, and proletarianization, are inevitable; continued economic difficulties, including overreliance on mineral exports, capital imports, foreign technology and skills, and external food reserves, are also highly likely; and the incidence of instability caused by uneven and unstable rates of change both within and between states is unavoidable.(95)

The real question for Africa is not whether these discernible trends are avoidable but rather how to respond to them: by reviving established methods of repression that would involve external strategic and economic assistance, or by recognizing inevitable contradictions and so facilitating a reshaping of society. The former reaction involves further dependence, whereas the latter is compatible with notions of greater self-reliance. Obviously, each of these divergent responses also involves its own ideological formulation and developmental preferences, with the former being most compatible with nationalism, depoliticization, and state capitalism; and the latter with self-reliance, participation, and state socialism.(96) Both are in response to a third possible scenario, namely that of anarchy, the breakdown of order in both political economy and society. It is this fear of the specter of anarchism that yields a degree of compatibility between the orthodox and radical perspectives, forcing both in the direction of some redistribution and restructuring, albeit in varying degrees. For as Claude Ake cautions, "It would appear that the choice for Africa is not between capitalism and socialism after all, but between socialism and barbarism."(97) Given Africa's present involvement in the world system, such a scenario would have implications for extracontinental interests as well; so it serves to reinforce their concern for the future(s) of Africa, making them aware of the continued interrelationship between continental cohesion and global integration.(98)

Projections about the future of the continent also serve to undermine the assumptions of the orthodox school regarding the equality of actors and development prospects. This has already produced some rethinking within this genre about both African inequalities and extra-African influences. Zartman, for instance, concludes his latest tour d'horizon by recognizing that: "By the 1980s, the spread in the level of power sources is certain to increase, even dramatically. Within the decade, Algeria or Nigeria may be more developed economically than South Africa, and Zaire might also be included in the list."(99) Uneven rates of growth in the future have serious implications for intrusive powers, regional dominance, and internal inequalities all centered around the notion of subimperialism. Again, Zartman has begun to recognize these and fit them into a revisionist orthodox framework for the 1980s that still avoids taking the world system and political economy as its starting points.(100)

Given the related changes in the global and continental systems projected to the year 2000, the African region is likely to be characterized by growing economic inequalities, ideological differences, social strains, and political changes in the midterm future, many of which will be expressed in the growing and intensifying debate between orthodox and radical approaches to analysis and praxis. Langdon and Mytelka foresee, for instance, an increasing demand for fundamental economic change arising in Africa, particularly in the real periphery, analogous to earlier forms of political nationalism, with profound implications for dependence and development on the continent:

> Just as the constraints of colonialism ultimately were challenged and rejected through political struggles, so we expect many other African countries to be pushed, by domestic political forces in the 1980s to similar reactions against the constraints of periphery capitalism. Not all African countries will move in that direction: those few privileged nations that are deeply incorporated into the international capitalist economy – such as the Ivory Coast or Kenya – may find the symbiosis between local and foreign capital powerful enough to resist radical change. But for most African countries, the incapacity of the present international capitalist system to adjust sufficiently to draw most Third World people much more comprehensively into the international division of labor can be expected to force such peoples to adopt more imaginative and creative strategies, with unhappy

human costs of transition but long-run developmental advantages.(101)

This new creative tension is likely to spill over into new forms of continental and regional integration that take account of the radical critique and go beyond rationalization of the global division of labor toward some form of collective self-reliance and socialist strategy, some distance from the essentially laissez-faire assumptions of the founders of the Pan-African movement and the OAU.

This possibility may be especially appealing to the 20 African states presently classified as "least developed," as they have gained little if anything from incorporation into the world system. However, like the followers of a noncapitalist path, they may be able to turn their privileged inheritance and status to good advantage if, as the periphery of the periphery, they are less subject to external pressures now and in the future. With innovation and determination, a note from the ECA Secretariat suggests:

> ...Least developed countries are in a position to establish a more substantial and relevant basis for accelerated development and diversified growth in the long run than others now considered more fortunate...to develop as a matter of urgency a profounder grasp of the nature and dynamics of the processes of socioeconomic change which will lead to accelerated self-reliant and self-sustaining development and economic growth. This will not be easy because of the very great intellectual pressures to conform to conventional notions characteristic of the age of high finance capitalism, because of aid offered on those terms, and because of the risk of social and political instability.(102)

The appeal of "another way" may not be limited to the very poor, Fourth World states of Africa,(103) but may also be of relevance to the continent's most advanced (if highly uneven) economy – South Africa. The process and impact of change in the remaining white-ruled state, following the independence of Namibia and Zimbabwe, will have profound implications for the rest of the continent in terms of industrial, as well as military, capability and of an indigenous model of partial industrialization. Langdon and Mytelka situate this struggle for Southern Africa in the context of the broader debate between state capitalist and state socialist protagonists over alternative development paths for the region in the future:

> Armed conflict in Southern Africa, though, is likely to be no more than the most dramatic African form of confrontation between dependence and self-reliance in the 1980s. We expect the contradictions of periphery capitalism in Africa to become more acute in most countries on the continent in the next decade, and we expect the struggles for change in such countries to become more bitter as a result. We are confident, however,

that out of such conflict can come more equitable and self-reliant development strategies that benefit the great majority of Africans.(104)

Such change in Southern Africa would not only affect the rest of the continent, but, given the place of South Africa and the continent as a whole in the world system and the interplay of dependence and interdependence, would come to affect us all.

NOTES

(1) See Leon Gordenker, "The OAU and the UN: Can They Live Together?" in Africa in World Affairs: The Next Thirty Years, edited by Al. A. Mazrui and Haru H. Patel (New York: Third Press, 1973), pp. 105-19.

(2) For a description of and debate about Africa's future(s) see Timothy M. Shaw and Malcolm J. Grieve, "The Political Economy of Resources: Africa's Future in the Global Environment," Journal of Modern African Studies 16, no. 1 (March 1978): 1-32.

(3) Ralph Uwechue, "Root of Evils," Africa, 95 (July 1979): 11.

(4) For an introduction to these see Timothy M. Shaw, "Discontinuities and Inequalities in African International Politics," International Journal 30, no. 3 (Summer 1975): 369-90.

(5) On the mixed actor system in Africa see Timothy M. Shaw, "The Actors in African International Politics," in The Politics of Africa: Dependence and Development, edited by Timothy M. Shaw and Kenneth A. Heard (New York: Africana, 1979), pp. 357-96.

(6) For succinct and suggestive introductions to Africa from a critical world system perspective see Samir Amin, "Underdevelopment and Dependence in Black Africa: Origins and Contemporary Forms," Journal of Modern African Studies 10, no. 4 (December 1972): 503-24; and Immanuel Wallerstein, "Dependence in an Interdependent World: The Limited Possibilities of Transformation Within the Capitalist World Economy," African Studies Review 17, no. 1 (April 1974): 1-26.

(7) Cf. I. William Zartman, "Europe and Africa: Decolonization or Dependency?" Foreign Affairs 54, no. 2 (January 1976): 325-43. For a more general discussion about two related modes of analysis, types of policy, and forms of ideology see Timothy M. Shaw, "From Dependence to (Inter)Dependence: Issues of the (New) International Economic Order," paper presented at a meeting of the International Political Science Association, Moscow, August 1979; and Kal J. Holsti, "A New International Politics? Diplomacy in Complex Interdependence," International Organization 32, no. 2 (Spring 1978): 513-30.

(8) For projections and prospects see Timothy M. Shaw, ed., Future(s) of Africa (Boulder, Colo.: Westview, 1979).

(9) For reviews of this literature and relationship see Michael Dolan, "The Lome Convention and Europe's Relationship with the Third World: A Critical Analysis," Review d'integration europeene 1, no. 3 (May 1978): 369-94; and Timothy M. Shaw in association with Ali A. Mazrui, "EEC-ACP Interactions and Images as Redefinitions of Eur-Africa: Exemplary, Exclusive, and/or Exploitative?" paper presented at a meeting of the International Political Science Association, Moscow, August 1979.

(10) See, in particular, I. William Zartman, "Africa as a Subordinate State System in International Relations," International Organization 21, no. 3 (Summer 1967): 545-64; and "Africa," in World Politics: An Introduction, edited by James N. Rosenau, Kenneth W. Thompson, and Gavin Boyd (New York: Free Press, 1976), pp. 569-94.

(11) It is not, for instance, reflected in the otherwise comprehensive and comparative analysis of four approaches to integration examined in the latest major studies of African Regionalism. For example, Chimelu Chime identifies pluralism, functionalism, federalism, and neofunctionalism as the major approaches, omitting any reference to a more radical, political economy perspective (Integration and Politics Among African States: Limitations and Horizons of Mid-term Theorizing, Uppsala, Sweden: Scandinavian Institute of African Studies, 1977, p. 33).

(12) See, for instance, the following articles by Lynn K. Mytelka: "The Lome Convention and a New International Division of Labor," Revue d'integration europeene 1, no. 1 (September 1977): 63-76; "A Genealogy of Francophone West and Equatorial African Regional Organizations," Journal of Modern African Studies 12, no. 2 (July 1974): 297-320; and "The Salience of Gains in Third World Integrative Systems," World Politics 25, no. 2 (January 1973): 236-50. Mytelka is representative of an emerging and critical "Carleton" school on the political economy of Africa in the world system.

(13) See Immanuel Wallerstein, "The Three Stages of African Involvement in the World Economy," in The Political Economy of Contemporary Africa, edited by Peter C.W. Gutkind and Immanuel Wallerstein (Beverly Hills, Calif.: Sage 1976), pp. 30-57.

(14) Zartman, "Africa," p. 569.

(15) I. William Zartman, "Africa as a Subordinate State System," p. 548.

(16) Ibid., p. 549.

(17) Steven Langdon and Lynn K. Mytelka, "Africa in the Changing World Economy," in Africa in the 1980s: A Continent in Crisis, edited by Colin Legum et al. (New York: McGraw-Hill, for Council on Foreign Relations 1980s Project, 1979), p. 123.

(18) Ibid., p. 124.

(19) Ibid., p. 127. For a particular case of a center state affecting and conditioning African underdevelopment see Steven Langdon, "Canada's Role in Africa," in Foremost Nation: Canadian Foreign Policy and a Changing World, edited by Norman Hillmer and Garth Stevenson (Toronto: McClelland and Stewart, 1977), pp. 178-201; and "The Canadian Economy and Southern Africa," in Canada, Scandinavia, and Southern Africa, edited by Douglas Anglin, Timothy Shaw, and Carl Widstrand (Stockholm: Almqvist & Wiksell, and New York: Africana, 1978), pp. 15-27.

(20) See Leonard Binder, "The Middle East as a Subordinate International System," and Michael Brechner, "International Relations and Asian Studies: The Subordinate System of Southern Asia," in Falk and Mendlovitz, Regional Politics and World Order, pp. 355-382.

(21) Louis J. Cantori and Steven L. Spiegel, The International Politics of Regions: A Comparative Approach (Englewood Cliffs, N.J.: Prentice-Hall, 1970), especially pp. 1-40 and 381-89.

(22) On this mode of analysis and prescription see Timothy M. Shaw and Malcolm J. Grieve, "Review Article — Dependence or Development: International and Internal Inequalities in Africa," Development and Change 8, no. 3 (July 1977): 377-408; and "Dependence of Development: International Inequalities in Africa," in Problems of Socialist Orientation in Africa, edited by Mai Palmberg (New York: Africana, 1978), pp. 54-82.

(23) Immanuel Wallerstein, "The Early Years of the OAU: The Search for Organizational Pre-eminence," International Organization 20, no. 4 (Autumn 1966): 772-87.

(24) See, for instance, Economic Commission for Africa, "The African Region and International Negotiations: A Note by the Secretariat," ECA 19th Executive Meeting, Arusha, October 1978, E/CN.14/ECO/158.

(25) On this strategy see Palmberg, Problems of Socialist Orientation in Africa; and Marina Ottaway, "Soviet Marxism and African Socialism," Journal of Modern African Studies 16, no. 3 (September 1978): 477-85.

(26) On these, particularly on their role in maintaining an unequal global system, see Bruce J. Berman, "Clientelism and Neo-colonialism: Center-Periphery Relations and Political Development in African States," Studies in Comparative International Development 9, no. 2 (Summer 1974): 3-25.

(27) On the emergence of a fourth, very poor, world, much of which is concentrated in Africa, see Timothy M. Shaw, "The Elusiveness of Development and Welfare: Inequalities in the Third World," in The International Law and Policy of Human Welfare, edited by Ronald St. John Macdonald, Douglas M. Johnston, and Gerald L. Morris (The Netherlands: Sijthoff and Noordhoff, 1978), pp. 81-109.

(28) On current Pan-African sentiments see Resolutions and Selected Speeches from the Sixth Pan African Congress (Dar es Salaam: Tanzania Publishing House, 1976).

(29) See James Mayall, "African Unity and the OAU: The Place for a Political Myth in African Diplomacy," Year Book of World Affairs (London: Stevens, 1973), Vol. 27, pp. 110-33.

(30) See Colin Legum, "The OAU – Success or Failure?" International Affairs, 51, no. 2 (April 1975): 208-19.

(31) See Claude Ake, Revolutionary Pressures in Africa (London: Zed Press, 2nd ed., 1978), pp. 89-94.

(32) See Grieve and Shaw, "The Political Economy of Africa," pp. 614-22.

(33) Colin Legum suggests that "There are now ten African countries which adhere to the Marxist system – Mozambique, Angola, Guinea-Bissau, Cape Verde, Sao Tome e Principe, Madagascar, Congo, Benin, Ethiopia, and Somalia. However, there are considerable differences in the systems established in these ten countries, with only the first three conforming to the classical Marxist pattern" ("The Year in Perspective," Africa Contemporary Record: Annual Survey and Documents, Volume 10, 1977-1978 (New York: Africana, 1979), p. xxiii).

(34) The "Principles" of Article III, for instance, are all supportive of the African state system (see Zdenek Cervenka, The Unfinished Quest for Unity: Africa and the OAU, New York: Africana, 1977, Appendix 2, p. 229). Most of the resolutions of the latest summit are concerned with national independence, integrity, and authority (see OAU, Resolutions of the Thirty-First Ordinary Session of the Council of Ministers, New York: Executive Secretariat of the OAU to the UN, July 1978). See also B. David Meyers, "The Organization of African Unity: An Annotated Bibliography," Africana Journal, 5, no. 4 (1974): 308-21.

(35) See R.A. Akindele, "Reflections on the Preoccupation and Conduct of African Diplomacy," Journal of Modern African Studies 14, no. 4 (December 1976): 557-76.

(36) Zartman, "Africa as a Subordinate State System," p. 589.

(37) Chime, Integration and Politics Among African States, pp. 92-93.

(38) O.S. Kamanu, "Secession and the Right of Self-determination: An OAU Dilemma," Journal of Modern African Studies 12, no. 3 (September 1974): 355-76.

(39) Adda B. Bozeman, The Future of Law in a Multicultural World (Princeton, N.J.: Princeton University Press, 1971); and Conflict in Africa: Concepts and Realities (Princeton, N.J.: Princeton University Press, 1976).

(40) Bozeman, Conflict in Africa, p. 45.

(41) Ibid., p. 370.

(42) Zartman, "Africa," pp. 579-81.

(43) Ibid., p. 529.

(44) Ibid., p. 580.

(45) Mayall, "The OAU and the African Crisis," Optima 27, no. 2 (1977): 86.

(46) Ibid., p. 87.

(47) See Timothy M. Shaw, "Inequalities and Interdependence in Africa and Latin America: Subimperialism and Semiindustrialism in the Semi-periphery," Cultures et Developpement 10, no. 2 (1978): 231-63.

(48) Zartman, "Africa," p. 571.

(49) Ibid., p. 574.

(50) See, for instance, Timothy M. Shaw, "Kenya and South Africa: 'Subimperialist' States," Orbis 21, no. 2 (Summer 1977): 375-94; and "International Stratification in Africa: Subimperialism in Eastern and Southern Africa," Journal of Southern African Affairs, 2, no. 2 (April 1977): 145-65.

(51) Wallerstein, "Dependence in an Independent World."

(52) Cf. the bases of OAU mediation in its first decade in B. David Meyers, "Intraregional Conflict Management by the Organization of African Unity," International Organization 28, no. 3 (Summer 1974): 345-73.

(53) Cf. Ruth W. Arad and Uzi B. Arad, "South-South: Regional Powers and Natural Resources," in Sharing Global Resources, edited by Ruth W. Arad, Uri B. Arad et al. (New York: McGraw-Hill, for Council on Foreign Relations 1980s Project, 1979), pp. 87-97.

(54) Langdon and Mytelka, "Africa in the Changing World Economy," p. 204.

(55) Jonathan H. Chileshe, The Challenge of Developing Intra-African Trade (Nairobi: East African Literature Bureau, 1977), p. 151.

(56) See Guy Arnold and Ruth Weiss, Strategic Highways of Africa (London: Friedmann, 1977); and "Land Transportation," Africa 80 (April 1978): 69-70.

(57) For overviews of foreign policy in Africa see Christopher Clapham, "Sub-Saharan Africa," in his collection on Foreign Policy Making in Developing States: A Comparative Approach (Farnborough: Saxon House, 1977), pp. 75-109; W.A.E. Skurnik, Sub-Saharan Africa: Information Sources on International Relations (Detroit: Gale, 1977); and Mark W. DeLancey, "Current Studies in African International Relations," Africana Journal 7, no. 3 (1976): 195-239, and "The Study of African International Relations," in Aspects of International Relations in Africa, edited by Mark W. DeLancey (Bloomington, Ind.: Indiana University African Studies Program, 1979), pp. 1-38.

(58) Zartman, "Africa," p. 581.

(59) For a review of these see "Conclusion" in Douglas G. Anglin and Timothy M. Shaw, Zambia's Foreign Policy: Studies in Diplomacy and Dependence (Boulder, Colo.: Westview, 1979). For an empirical overview see Patrick J. McGowan and Thomas H. Johnson, "The AFRICA Project and the Comparative Study of African Foreign Policy," in DeLancey, Aspects of International Relations in Africa, pp. 190-241.

(60) Donald Rothchild and Robert L. Curry, Scarcity, Choice and Public Policy in Middle Africa (Berkeley: University of California Press, 1978), pp. 91-148 and 301-35.

(61) See Micah S. Tsomondo, "From Pan-Africanism to Socialism: The Modernization of an African Liberation Ideology," Issue 5, no. 4 (Winter 1975): 39-46; and Teti A. Kofi, "Principles of a Pan-African Economic Ideology," Review of Black Political Economy 6, no. 3 (Spring 1976): 306-30.

(62) See Mytelka, "The Lome Convention and a New International Division of Labor."

(63) Mayall, "The OAU and the African Crisis," p. 84.

(64) See Zdenek Cervenka, "The Organization of African Unity in 1976," in Africa Contemporary Record: Annual Survey and Documents, Vol. 9, 1976-1977, edited by Colin Legum (London: Rex Collings, 1977), pp. A68-A75, and The Unfinished Quest for Unity.

(65) See Timothy M. Shaw, "Inequalities and Conflicts in Contemporary Africa," International Perspectives (May/June 1978), pp. 44-49, and "The Organization of African Unity: Prospects for the Second Decade," International Perspectives (September/October 1973), pp. 31-34.

(66) Cervenka, The Unfinished Quest for Unity, pp. 186, 190.

(67) Zartman, "Africa as a Subordinate State System," p. 390.

(68) For a powerful comparison and critique of both, see Tanzania Rejects Western Domination in Africa: Statement by President Mwalimu Julius K. Nyerere (Dar es Salaam: Government Printer, June 1978).

(69) See, for instance, Robert M. Price, U.S. Foreign Policy in Sub-Saharan Africa: National Interest and Global Strategy (Berkeley, Calif.: Institute of International Studies, 1978). Cf. Tom J. Farer, "Soviet Strategy and Western Fears," Africa Report 23, no. 6 (November-December 1978): 4-8.

(70) Raymond W. Copson, "African International Politics: Underdevelopment and Conflict in the Seventies," Orbis 22, no. 1 (Spring 1978): 228.

(71) Ibid., p. 245.

(72) Chime, Integration and Politics Among African States, pp. 391-97.

(73) Timothy M. Shaw and M. Catherine Newbury, "Dependence or Interdependence? Africa in the Global Political Economy," in DeLancey, Aspects of International Relations in Africa, pp. 39-89.

(74) See James O. Goldsborough, "Dateline Paris: Africa's Policeman," Foreign Policy 33 (Winter 1978-79): 174-90.

(75) Cf. the rather unfortunate and premature prediction of Zartman made in the mid-1970s, perhaps the period of greatest continental cohesion and autonomy:

Nor are there outside agents – peripheral or intrusive members of the system – that appear willing and able to exert decisive influence for change. Even before the detente of the early 1970s, Africa had lost its position of the early 1960s as a cold war battlefield, and outside of some noisy skirmishes in various nonaligned conferences the Sino-Soviet schism has not had much effect on regional relations. These characteristics too seem unlikely to change in the short run (Zartman, "Africa," p. 593).

(76) See Timothy M. Shaw," Regional Cooperation and Conflict in Africa," International Journal, 30, no. 4 (Autumn 1975): 671-88.

(77) Langdon and Mytelka, "Africa in the Changing World Economy," pp. 178-79.

(78) See Agipah T. Mingomba, "Regional Organizations and African Underdevelopment: The Collapse of the East African Community," Journal of Modern African Studies 16, no. 2 (June 1978): 261-72.

(79) See John P. Reninger, "The Future of Economic Cooperation Schemes in Africa, With Special Reference to ECOWAS," in Shaw, The Future(s) of Africa.

(80) See John P. Reninger, Multinational Cooperation for Development in West Africa (Elmsford, N.Y.: Pergamon Press, for UNITAR, 1979).

(81) See Timothy M. Shaw, "The Actors in African International Politics," in Shaw and Heard, The Politics of Africa: Dependence and Development, pp. 357-96.

(82) James A. Caporaso, "Introduction to the Special Issue of International Organization on Dependence and Dependency in the Global System," International Organization 32, no. 1 (Winter 1978): 9-12.

(83) Patrick J. McGowan and Dale L. Smith, "Economic Dependency in Black Africa: An Analysis of Competing Theories," International Organization 32, no. 1 (Winter 1978): 179-235; Patrick J. McGowan, "Economic Dependence and Economic Performance in Black Africa," Journal of Modern African Studies 14, no. 1 (March 1976): 25-40; and Robert Kaufman et al., "A Preliminary Test of the Theory of Dependency," Comparative Politics 7, no. 3 (April 1975): 303-31.

(84) Michael B. Dolan et al., "Foreign Policies of African States in Asymmetrical Dyads," paper presented at a meeting of the Canadian Political Science Association, Saskatoon, May 1979, pp. 26-30.

(85) See Paul Goulding and Timothy M. Shaw, "Alternative Scenarios for Africa," in Shaw, The Future(s) of Africa.

(86) See Adebayo Adedeji, "Africa: The Crisis of Development and the Challenge of a New Economic Order," Address to the Fourth Meeting of the Conference of Ministers and Thirteenth Session of the ECA, Kinshasa, 1977. ECA, Addis Ababa, July 1977, and "Development and Economic Growth in Africa to the Year 2000: Alternative Projections and Policies," in Shaw, The Future(s) of Africa.

(87) Biennial Report of the Executive Secretary of the United Nations Economic Commission for Africa 1977-1978 (Addis Ababa, February 1979). E/CN.14/695, p. 1.

(88) Ibid., p. 12.

(89) For a plea to examine African regionalism critically in the context of an unequal global division of labor, see James A. Sackey, "West African Integration: Some Further Reflections," paper presented at a meeting of the Canadian Association of African Studies, Winnipeg, May 1979.

(90) Cf. Roger D. Hansen, Beyond the North-South Stalemate (New York: McGraw-Hill, for Council on Foreign Relations 1980s Project, 1979), especially pp. 167-279.

(91) Zartman, "Africa," p. 587.

(92) Timothy M. Shaw, "The Political Economy of African International Relations," Issue 5, no. 4 (Winter 1975): 29-38.

(93) Zartman, "Africa," pp. 583-84.

(94) See Timothy M. Shaw and Don Munton, "The Future(s) of Africa: A Comparison of Forecasts," in Shaw, The Future(s) of Africa.

(95) See "Africa 2000," special number of Issue 8, no. 4 (Winter 1978).

(96) Cf. Raymond Hall, "Africa 2000: Thinking About the African Future in the Modern World System"; Sanford Wright, "Africa and World Economy: Prospects for Growth, Development, and Independence"; and Ann Seidman, "Africa and World Economy: Prospects for Real Economic Growth," in Issue 8, no. 4 (Winter 1978): 3-9, 43-45, and 46-49 respectively; and Andrew M. Kamarck, "Sub-Saharan Africa in the 1980s: An Economic Profile"; and Philippe Lemaitre, "Who Will Rule Africa by the Year 2000?" in Africa: From Mystery to Maze, edited by Helen Kitchen (Lexington, Mass.: D.C. Heath, 1976), pp. 167-94 and 139-76.

(97) Ake, Revolutionary Pressures in Africa, p. 107.

(98) See Legum et al., Africa in the 1980s; and Jennifer Seymour Whitaker, ed., Africa and the United States: Vital Interests (New York: New York University Press, 1978). Cf. Davidson Nicol, "Africa and the USA in the United Nations," Journal of Modern African Studies, 16, no. 3 (September 1978): 365-95.

(99) Zartman, "Africa," p. 592.

(100) Ibid., p. 593. Cf. quote in note 75 above.

(101) Langdon and Mytelka, "Africa in the Changing World Economy," pp. 207-08.

(102) ECA, "Development Issues of the Least Developed African Countries: A Note by the Secretariat," ECA 19th Executive Meeting, Arusha, October 1978. E/CN.14/ECO/159.

(103) On alternative development strategies for Africa, see Timothy M. Shaw and Malcolm J. Grieve, "Dependence as an Approach to Understanding Continuing Inequalities in Africa," Journal of Developing Areas 13, no. 3 (April 1979); and "Chronique Bibliographique – The Political Economy of Africa: Internal and International Inequalities," Cultures et Developpement 10, no. 4 (1978): 609-48.

(104) Langdon and Mytelka, "Africa in the Changing World Economy," p. 211.

IV
Regions and World Order

12 Political Change in Regional Systems

Gavin Boyd

Few states in the various regional systems are static societies. Most of them are modernizing, with varying degrees of stability and stress, and a high proportion of those in the globally central regions are experiencing changes associated with problems of advanced political development. Interactions in all the regional systems are being affected, and states in these systems are, in some cases, changing their behavior toward each other in ways that are not directly related to happenings within their political economies.

Most of the processes of change in the modernizing and advanced states are issue-related, in a dual sense. They are associated with contests between groups over policies, appointments, and the institutionalizing of power; and they have developmental aspects affecting the unity, cohesion, representative qualities, structural capabilities and performance of national political systems. Changes in regional configurations, moreover, attributable to changes in the characteristics of their members and in the behavior of those members towards each other, also tend to be issue-related at the regional level. Questions of regional and subregional cooperation are evaded or engaged with in varying degrees, and problems of regional political development are made more difficult or are resolved.

In the globally central regions, the most significant forms of political change at the national level are associated with problems of governability and performance. The political processes of many industrialized democracies are affected by pluralistic stagnation, as performance in public policy is made difficult by the aggressive and forceful articulation of conflicting and diverging interests which cannot be appropriately aggregated because of institutional overload and inadequate leadership. At the same time, pressures to satisfy a large proportion of the allocative demands cause governments to overextend their distributive resources, producing chronic inflation, thus stimulating those demands while making their longer term satisfaction more difficult.

Forms of national political change in Third World regions are mostly transitions from one authoritarian regime to another. Incumbent regimes generally fail to solve their legitimacy problems and become vulnerable to takeovers. In many cases, such regimes are dependent on resources provided by industrialized democracies and by transnational enterprises based in those democracies. Such resources are necessary for modernization, but are also utilized, directly and indirectly, to strengthen each administration's coercive apparatus. Incoming regimes usually continue the practice of relying on such available external resources, but this can become controversial if counterelites mobilize nationalist sentiments against such dependence. Developmental issues are highly salient in these Third World states, and their forms of political change are, in most cases, directly related to intractable problems of allocation: allocations of power and allocations of resources.

In the configurations of the globally central regions, the West European interactive pattern is exhibiting the most important forms of change. Expanding complex interdependencies are setting larger and larger requirements for policy integration, which are being met, to some extent, through slow and disjointed collective decision making. At the same time, states within this region are becoming more intensely competitive in the management of their regional and global economic policies, and this competitiveness reflects domestic pressures for more effective direction of internal economic policies.

Regional and subregional patterns of interaction in the Third World concern smaller interdependencies that are growing more slowly. Felt imperatives to cooperate with neighbors are weak, especially as ruling elites tend to give high priority in their foreign policies to the management of dependencies on industrialized democracies and transnational enterprises. The most important attempts to promote regional and subregional cooperation are being made in Latin America, but these are only moderately successful; and there are significant failures to continue forms of collaboration that have been initiated. In this region, as in other Third World groupings, the most common form of political change at the national level (i.e., a transition from one authoritarian regime to another) is a serious hindrance to sustained regional and subregional cooperation.

CONCEPTS AND ANALYSIS

Political change is normally conceptualized as a national process affecting structures, functions, values, and societal involvement in the polity. Such change can be stabilizing or destabilizing and may enhance or weaken performance. Further, the dimensions and speed of such change may vary greatly, and it may be coherent and more or less controlled or ordered, or it may be quite unpatterned.

Whatever its character and scale, political change at the national level amounts to a significant alteration of the polity as a system.

Overall, political growth or decay may result; and, with such change, a state may become more or less coherent and purposeful as a regional actor. If a national political system becomes more integrated and the level of its performance rises, however, this may not contribute to greater cooperation in the regional group to which it belongs; its external policy may become, on the whole, more competitive and less integrative. France, under de Gaulle, became a more coherent but much less constructive member of the West European region.

Structural change in a national political system tends to make power more concentrated or dispersed, stronger or weaker, more functional or less functional, and more accountable or less accountable. Major structural changes are rare in industrialized democracies because the high degrees of consensus that would be necessary are very difficult to build up in pluralistic contexts, and because elites generally lack incentives to attempt the difficult tasks of promoting support for such changes. In Western Europe the most significant structural change at the national level over the past few decades has been the establishment of a very strong executive in France – with a drastic reduction in legislative authority. This change was effected by plebiscite in an emergency atmosphere, and to a large extent it expressed popular acceptance of de Gaulle as a leader.(1) In the developing areas, where national authority patterns mostly have weak legitimacy, structural change is fairly common and usually occurs as one authoritarian regime replaces another. Incoming administrations are usually disinclined to continue any forms of regional cooperation undertaken by the governments which they have replaced; the outlooks of the new ruling groups tend to be more parochial, and often favor the exploitation of popular nationalist sentiments in order to mobilize mass support.

Change in influence relationships can affect the national authority structure. In industrialized democracies, shifts in the distribution of economic power cause changes in influence relationships based on such power, depending on the scope for interest group activity. Such activity can be restricted by strong political parties and by strong executives. The United States' executive is significantly vulnerable to pressures from interest groups, and these pressures change with the emergence of new centers of economic power and the weakening of others which have been long established. In some advanced open states, notably West Germany and Japan, dominant influence patterns based on concentrations of economic power are closely linked with the national authority structure, through intimate association with ruling political parties, and with the higher levels of the bureaucracy. In these cases, highly competitive management of foreign economic policies becomes possible.(2) Ruling groups in Third World states, operating mostly on an authoritarian basis, usually seek to build up strong influence relationships through which large sections of their societies can be dominated, through patronage and threats of coercion. Such influence relationships rarely become institutionalized because the leaderships are not gifted for institutional development, and successor elites, thus, seek to establish their own influence patterns. The normal consequence, for external policy, is that resources for the development of those influence patterns are sought from industrialized democracies and transnational enterprises, with varying degrees of concern for modernization and the maintenance of economic sovereignty.

Change in authority structures can be related to issues of participation and performance. The concentration of authority in the French executive by de Gaulle was intended to overcome an acute problem of legislative irresponsibility in the Fourth Republic, and to make possible high levels of achievement in the management of public policy.(3) In the United States, assertions of legislative power over external security policy during the Vietnam War were expressions of resentment over what was seen as a lack of executive accountability. The principal effect, it can be argued, has been to lower the level of performance in U.S. defense policy. Attempts to strengthen executive authority, of course, raise questions of accountability, and their significance is likely to depend on the value orientation of the political culture. Mrs. Indira Gandhi's attempts to establish a virtual dictatorship in India during the early 1970s evoked widespread hostility at all levels of society and increasing demands for effective participation in the policy process.(4)

Functional change can occur without structural change, but may set requirements for such change. In an industrialized democracy, a multiplication of competing societal demands for allocations can hinder and discourage executive decision making, causing this to become very incremental and disjointed. At the same time, increased executive concern with the comparative political utility of alternative policy choices may cause pronounced sectoral bias in the adoption of such choices. Regional foreign policy behavior, then, may become less coherent, less integrative, and less effective as a means of aiding the realization of domestic goals. Structural change to facilitate more coherent policymaking may be desired, but may not be feasible because of popular resistance to suggestions for the development of stronger aggregating institutions.(5) In developing states, functional change is, of course, mostly attributable to elite choices and conflicts. Allocations of authority within the primary and secondary elites, based often on clientelist considerations, are typically changed to prevent the emergence of threats to the dominant group; and the functional consequences vary with the expertise and value orientations of the new office holders, and, of course, their relationships with the top decision makers.

Normative change, at elite or mass levels, may amount to overall shifts of motivation toward more cooperative or more conflictual behavior (domestically and externally) and toward greater concern with national and/or regional order and equity, or with individual advantage. Several scholars see tendencies toward more active pursuit of personal advantage at the expense of common interests in the industrialized democracies: a general displacement of consummatory by instrumental values, contributing to alienation and to problems of governability.(6) In developing states, administrative corruption, repression, and poor performance tend to present nonruling elites with challenges for radical normative change. Administrations in both advanced and developing states may promote normative change by stirring nationalist feelings, and may have strong inclinations to do so if their legitimacy is weak. The effects on schemes for regional cooperation are negative, of course, and the most significant illustration of this has been the disruption of integrative activity in the European Community by assertive French nationalism during de Gaulle's period in office.(7)

Political change normally varies in character, scale, and pace through the structural and other dimensions of a polity. Achievements and failures in economic performance, that may be related to structural changes, can produce shifts in popular attitudes and demands. Regionally, the patterns are quite diverse, and their consequences for regional politics depend largely on the sensitivities of the national political economies to each other's statecraft and to the activities of transnational enterprises that are in varying degrees associated with that statecraft.

Satisfactory experiences of regional cooperation in one area of policy tend to encourage wider collaboration by the participating states, as the perceived advantages activate their interest groups. The working out of this neofunctional logic, however, is affected by past and ongoing processes of political change at the national level.(8) If an administration is strongly committed to the mobilization of popular support through appeals to nationalist sentiments, it will have little motivation to accept wider interdependencies with neighboring states. What is of more general significance, however, as the recent history of the European Community indicates, is the probability that ventures in regional cooperation by industrialized democracies, while providing benefits that encourage wider collaboration, will also tend to increase competitiveness between the states in the grouping because the benefits from integrative activity will not be evenly distributed, but will be secured in large proportions by the states with more dynamic economies and more actively neomercantilist policies.(9)

In Third World regions, the working out of neofunctional logic is hindered even more seriously, and is necessarily weaker because the interdependencies that require management between developing states are smaller. Ruling elites tend to be deeply absorbed in problems of support mobilization, particularly within segments of the armed forces; they can cope effectively with demands from indigenous business interests that are usually protectionist and, thus, opposed to regional trade liberalization. Demands from local branches of transnational enterprises are less easily dealt with, and these often involve conflicting preferences on questions of regional cooperation. The most significant limitation on leadership interest in regional cooperation in most Third World states, however, is dependence on trade with and aid from industrialized democracies, and on investment by transnational enterprises.(10)

The analysis of political change at national and regional levels must begin with the sources of such change. The types of sources which can operate in a given polity, and their scope, depend on the degrees of hierarchy in the authority structures and influence patterns, and the congruence of these with the political culture. If the level of subsystem autonomy is low, the ruling elite will be in a strong position to impose change, provided it enjoys a significant degree of legitimacy and has adequate leadership capabilities. If the degree of legitimacy is low, as in many authoritarian Third World regimes, there may be growing popular hostility to the ruling group, and this animosity may be intensified whenever the authorities resort to repression. Change in an industrialized democracy is usually an expression of high subsystem autonomy, and this can often involve a weakening of institutions for the representation of broad national interests. In regional politics, the various sources of change at the national level are expressed, directly or indirectly, through behavior that differs in coherence and integrative or competitive purpose. The regional foreign policy behavior of states can also change in response to new external situations and to differences in behavior received from neighbors and more distant states.

The forms of political change, while affecting structures, functions, and values, may be spread in various ways through these dimensions of a national polity. These forms of change can affect a polity's degrees of integration, its legitimacy, the building of its institutions, its processes of participation, and its performance. The relationships between patterns of economic and political power are likely to be affected as well, with consequences for the state's foreign economic policy that will have regional significance. At the regional level itself, change may mean the growth of greater cohesion between states in the grouping, and more cooperative behavior, or shifts toward more competitive or even conflictual activity.

Political change tends to be more significant for a region if it occurs in a large state rather than in a small one. Large states have greater scope for the use of inducements and pressures to cause change in a regional interactive pattern. Further, if an administration in one large state strengthens its capabilities for the management of foreign economic policy, this will be to its advantage in dealing with other large states. In Western Europe, the Federal Republic of Germany has strengthened its capacity for economic statecraft over the past two decades and has, thereby, increased its bargaining capabilities vis-a-vis France and Britain.

SOURCES OF POLITICAL CHANGE

In advanced open states, stability and growth depend on achievements in public policy which can be made possible by leadership with holistic purposes, the maintenance of a functional consensus about objectives and values, and institutional development which ensures aggregation and ordering of societal demands. The quality of leadership, the utility of the policy consensus, and the level of institutional development are interdependent; and they tend to be threatened mainly by aggressive interest groups seeking narrowly conceived economic advantages through political leverage. Political change can result from the weakening of legislatures and political parties by interest groups, and from consequent deviations of public policy from the general interest. Further changes may follow, as the management of public policy becomes more difficult because of the pressures associated with interest group demands, and as those demands are stimulated by failures in performance. Alternatively, strong leadership may promote a functional policy consensus, build up institutions, ensure the aggregation of demands, and raise the level of performance.(11)

In Britain, chronic inflation and economic stagnation (attributable to pressures from strong interest groups and to persistent allocations in excess of resources by administrations with narrow majorities) have produced serious problems of governance, while exposing the weak national economy to severe competition from the more dynamic members of the European Community. Institutional failures, meanwhile, have contributed to acute instability in the Italian political system. In West Germany, however, stability has been maintained by high performance in the management of the political economy, the preservation of a sound policy consensus, and the maintenance of well developed institutions for the aggregation of interests.(12)

Because of differences of performance in their economic policies, some industrialized democracies benefit much more than others from their mutual trade and openness to investment and, thus, from any forms of market integration. Efforts by advantaged states to preserve their benefits, and by disadvantaged states to overcome their difficulties, can be major sources of change in a regional pattern of interaction. Trade liberalization without arrangements for redistribution of the resultant benefits tends to be favored by the stronger states, which are more capable of managing neomercantilist policies, while the weaker states tend to resist such liberalization.

The regional behavior of industrialized democracies may also change because of shifts in the political rather than economic objectives of their administrations. The negative change of French policy toward the European Community which was effected by de Gaulle was primarily an assertion of national status and autonomy, and was intended to generate stronger nationalist support for the administration.(13) With the continual expansion of interdependencies between most of the industrialized democracies, however, the requirements of managing these interdependencies are imposing significant constraints on the adoption of strategies to further interests associated with the legitimacy, status, and international influence of national administrations.

In developing states, the sources of political change are mainly intraelite conflicts, and the challenges of counterelites. Both reflect the power ambitions of authoritarian personalities, in most cases, as few of these states have representative systems. Opportunities for the seizure of power are usually presented by losses of leadership charisma, the alienating effects of gross failures in performance, and the disintegration of supporting factions caused by unfulfilled expectations of patronage and habits of intrigue. All these factors, of course, aggravate the problems of institution building, which are fundamentally very serious because of leadership reluctance to accept any of the elements of accountability, however informal, that might be associated with the institutionalizing of authority. In effect, leadership efforts to monopolize power and to retain the capacity to use it at will cause most developing states to be vulnerable to change through conflicts within and between the primary and secondary elites, as these conflicts are not moderated by accepted rules or by institutional loyalties.(14)

Many administrations in developing states, aware of their internal vulnerabilities, are disinclined to regard each other as reliable partners in schemes for regional cooperation. Perceptions of instability and of likely causes of instability impose caution on the often moderate motivations to collaborate with neighbors in the common regional interest. Incoming administrations, moreover, are often unwilling to assume any regional obligations that have been accepted by the governments which they have replaced. These new administrations are usually very eager to secure economic and military support from industrialized democracies, and thus can be prepared to outbid each other in offering inducements to such democracies and to transnational enterprises that are more or less associated with the policies of those democracies.

A problem of both national and regional significance in Third World contexts is that external dependencies can weaken the political strength of developing states, directly and by contributing to economic imbalances and inadequate growth. Ruling elites securing foreign investment, developmental aid, and, sometimes, military assistance, tend to neglect problems of social reform and the political tasks of mobilizing support; excessive reliance is placed on favored elements of the secondary elite and on the use or threat of coercion to repress dissent. Protest movements can, thus, gain ground, while the administration's reliance on force becomes more pronounced. Meanwhile, dependence on the markets of industrialized democracies for sales of primary products, in highly asymmetric bargaining relationships, entails only slow acquisition of resources for industrialization. More importantly, the extractive ventures of transnational enterprises often result in inadequate benefits for the local economy. More benefits are secured when such enterprises engage in manufacturing, but inefficient regulation of such enterprises, together with weak capabilities for bargaining with them, usually prevent the realization of sufficient gains for the modernizing economy.(15)

The problems of coping with external dependencies and the tasks of modernizing can challenge ruling elites to initiate political change and to engage in regional cooperation. This is not common, because it requires strong political will and cohesion at the leadership level and holistic regional perspectives that ordinarily do not develop in the rather parochial contexts of Third World elite politics. When leaders in developing states do become strongly committed to the promotion of economic growth and diversification with equity on a basis of full sovereignty, and attempt responsible regulation of the local subsidiaries of foreign enterprises, success depends to a considerable extent on compromise with the interests of those organizations and on the cultivation of trust among their managements. The need for the technology of the transnational enterprises is always urgent, their bargaining positions are strong, and, if faced with threats of strong regulation, they may shift their activities to weaker states with more compliant administrations. Developing states can strengthen their bargaining power and promote complementary industrialization within their regions or subregions by agreeing on common policies toward transnational enterprises, as has been attempted by members of the Andean Pact. As the experience of that group has shown, however, the necessary collective political will is difficult to maintain.(16)

The various communist states have some similarities with the authoritarian Third World regimes, but are affected by different sources of change. There are heavy concentrations of power in the leaderships of the communist states, and these generate intraelite conflicts, which are subject to few restraints because the levels of institutional development are low and there are no established rules for the making of appointments and the shaping of policies. Political change can result from the emergence of new leaders, but the most pervasive source of change is deradicalization, a weakening of ideological beliefs and of commitments to ideological values. This is due to rises in the general level of sophistication with the growth of education systems and increasing international contacts, to the increasingly technocratic orientation of much of the elite, and to disillusionment with the utopian appeals of Marxism-Leninism.(17)

Deradicalization tends to weaken a communist regime's social controls and opens the way for unofficial interest group activity, but, seen as a threat, can motivate a ruling elite to work for a greater concentration of power in its own hands. In the USSR, political change results from a complex interplay between deradicalizing influences and leadership attempts to maintain highly centralized controls. Because deradicalization weakens the ruling elite's capacity to build up the political culture, the efforts made to tighten controls tend to be mainly coercive, and they stimulate the growth of an underground counter-culture. In the East European states that are closely associated with the USSR, deradicalizing tendencies are more active, principally because they are tolerated by the national administrations. Although under strong Soviet pressure, these ruling groups tend to permit some liberalization in order to improve the performance of their systems, and evidently wish to have some deradicalizing influence on the Soviet regime so that its policies toward them will become more reasonable. The Soviet leadership, while attempting to strengthen its own influence on the affinitive East European states, seeks to promote regional change by drawing these regimes into closer association with itself, in a scheme integration under the auspices of the Council for Mutual Economic Assistance. Such integration tends to be resisted because it entails linking each European partner individually with the USSR's economy, on the basis of a division of labor that is designed to strengthen the Soviet Union's position as the core of the group.(18)

Political change in China is also resulting mainly from deradicaliza-tion, but with stresses associated with high level conflicts over the values threatened by a decline of ideology and those awaiting realiza-tion through technocratic modernization. The cleavages are linked with questions of national pride and self reliance, and also with policy issues relating to the USSR and the United States. These complex sources of political change are further complicated by a succession struggle, of large dimensions, which has arisen because of the advanced ages of the presently dominant group in the higher levels of the Chinese Communist Party.(19) A major succession problem is also being posed in the USSR, but the rivalries which it is engendering appear to be less potent sources of political change than the conflicts which seem to be deciding the issue in China.

Altogether, the various sources of change in regions of industrial-ized democracies, developing states, and communist regimes show a lack of coherence and direction. Few ruling elites are able to control processes of such change, nor is this possible for leaderships of opposition and protest movements. In the West European case, however, political change tends to be limited and oriented in varying degrees by high interdependencies and by a general, although uneven, consensus that these interdependencies must be managed collectively. Regional politics is, thus, a source of some restraints on forms of national political change. On the other hand, those forms of change generally tend to limit the possibilities for greater regional cooperation.

FORMS OF REGIONAL CHANGE

The most common forms of political change in industrialized democ-racies tend to aggravate their problems of governability. Stronger demand articulation, stimulated by poor performance in public policy and by elite competitiveness, overloads and weakens institutions. At the same time, elite competitiveness inclines decision makers toward sectorally-biased and disjointed incrementalism to secure comparative political benefits at costs to the community as a whole. These common problems of what may be called advanced political development are serious in Britain and Italy, and they have significantly negative effects in the United States; but in West Germany and Japan, for the present, they are of modest proportions.

In Western Europe, the major differences in performance levels that are associated with current forms of political change are enabling West Germany to consolidate its position as the economic core of the European Community, while the British and Italian economies assume a peripheral character. France, lagging behind West Germany but main-taining its lead over Britain and Italy, has the choice of aligning with the weaker economies against West Germany, or with West Germany against those disadvantaged members of the Community. Since there is no collective will to redistribute the benefits from market integration (except to a small degree through a common development fund), the general effect is that each state tends to become more active in the defense of its own interests, and more reluctant to coordinate its policies with those of other members of the Community. Basic requirements to integrate policies more widely for the collective management of interdependencies are recognized, but practical concerns focus on the comparative costs and benefits in conditions of uncertainty and intense competitiveness. The basis of the Community remains a form of laissez-faire market integration, but the policies of the competing members are shifting toward neomercantilism. With this kind of change, national elites are disinclined to accept the logic of working toward structural integration for the more effective management of common interests. Decision making within the Community, then, remains confederal.(20)

In the Third World, the main form of political change is the replacement of one military regime by another. Most of these regimes are relatively conservative or bourgeois praetorian systems which lack stability and fail to attract popular support. Incoming leaders from the military usually have sufficient force at their disposal to prevent resistance, as the bulk of the population are dispersed in rural areas and have little capacity to organize in protest movements because of their poverty, lack of education, and the oppression they endure under local elites. In the urban areas, the relatively small number of industrial workers and students are usually discouraged from asserting their interests by sizable concentrations of military strength near the capital and the main towns. The maintenance of relatively large armed forces is often assisted by industrialized democracies whose political, economic, and strategic interests can be served by the goodwill of the military rulers.

Change in the military regimes may be initially developmental, but this is often followed by political decay which critically weakens the legitimacy of the incumbent administration and opens the way for a coup. Military elites generally have subjective preferences in conflict with their needs for popular support; they are inclined to impose authority rather than generate power through the development and use of capabilities for political leadership. If they recognize the need for representative structures, they seek to meet this requirement through forms of corporatism that serve as mechanisms for controlled functional representation, and these alienate the masses that are intended to be given a sense of participation. To reinforce the political appeal of experiments in corporatism, or to substitute for them, new military regimes typically display energetic commitments to industrial development. Over time, however, the implementation of their policies for industrialization tends to lose impetus and coherence, especially because of the effects of intraelite conflicts and of low accountability. At the same time, an intensification of social inequalities caused by the army leadership's dependence on local elites and its repression of trade unions reduces the appeal of its public commitments to modernization.(21)

In reaction to the failings of bourgeois praetorian systems, some military leaders in developing areas establish radical regimes. These offer scope for mass participation in politics, under army direction, and are oriented toward modernization with much emphasis on public sector development. They often become unstable, however, because the ideological principles of their leaders tend to become divisive, their controlled forms of popular participation cause alienation, and their economies tend to stagnate due to overmanagement and bureaucratic inertia. Burma is the most significant example of economic failure in a radical praetorian regime. As there are relatively few of these regimes, however, their developmental problems are much less significant for the regional systems of the Third World than those of the relatively conservative or bourgeois praetorian systems.(22)

One-party systems in the developing areas undergo different kinds of change. The vitality of the ruling party tends to decline; vigorous at first and, therefore, quite different from the officially sponsored parties of praetorian regimes, such a party loses strength because of the political strategy adopted by its leadership. The ruling elite becomes unwilling to accept formal and informal accountability to its secondary elite in the party, and relies more on the state bureaucracy for the implementation of policy. State officials are more compliant and have more expertise than most party officials. Any talented party figures tend to move into government posts in which they lose contact with their political followings and are socialized in ways compatible with leadership preferences.(23)

Interactive patterns in Third World regions are affected by political change at the national level and by the challenges of modernization and dependency. In general, the instability perceived in neighbors discourages new states from promoting or cooperating with schemes for regional collaboration and, as has been stressed, incoming administrations are often reluctant to continue ventures in regional cooperation that have been started under the governments which they have replaced. Moreover, new administrations tend to give priority to the acquisition of economic and other resources from industrialized democracies in order to consolidate their authority. Further, new authoritarian governments in large developing states tend to exhibit a narrow nationalistic outlook, and prefer to deal with small neighbors individually rather than in the multilateral context of a regional organization.

However, the challenges of modernization and dependency which activate some influential academics, opinion leaders, and politicians in Third World states, particularly in Latin America, are evoking some attempts at regional cooperation. Such attempts, as Axline has shown, can take three basic forms. Laissez-faire schemes for market integration following the European Community model result in unequal gains for the participating states because of differences in their levels of industrial development and in the capabilities and attitudes of their indigenous and foreign enterprises. The inequalities in the gains derived from such regional cooperation can be overcome or prevented by redistributive mechanisms; if these can be set up, their operation will require much political cooperation, but, of course, the collective political will to undertake such redistribution and continue it will often be lacking. A third type of regional scheme will include redistributive arrangements but will also provide for cooperation in managing and reducing dependencies on industrialized democracies and transnational enterprises. Quite resolute political cooperation will be needed between the partners in this kind of venture. When such cooperation fails, as has happened in the Andean Pact because of Chile's unwillingness to discourage foreign investors, subregional or regional integration becomes very difficult.(24)

In negotiating arrangements for economic cooperation, less developed modernizing states tend to seek protectionist understandings and redistributive provisions, while the more developed states usually seek as much market expansion as possible. Large-scale market expansion, while opposed in many cases by well protected indigenous industries, is usually supported by transnational enterprises, unless their managements view cooperation between the participating governments as threats to foreign enterprises, or see comparatively greater monopolistic advantages in the avoidance of market integration.(25)

The potential advantages of trade liberalization, even without redistributive arrangements, are being recognized by growing numbers of academics, bureaucrats, opinion leaders, and politicians in the Third World due to awareness of the achievements of the European Community, and of the importance of developing exchange networks that will stimulate local industries while reducing dependence on the industrialized democracies. The influence of advocates of regional and subregional trade liberalization on their governments varies greatly, however, and, overall, is modest in Latin America and weak in the rest of the Third World. Such influence fluctuates with changes of regime, and especially because of the parochialism and idiosyncrasies of new military administrations. For the present, there are no indications that this influence will become sufficiently potent to sustain attempts at market integration even in the relatively favorable Latin American context. Further, it is unlikely that influence of this kind will become strong enough to produce the collective will that would be needed for schemes to redistribute the gains from any market integration, in Latin America or elsewhere. A collective resolve to impose some regulation on transnational enterprises can be produced more easily, as was evidenced in the formation of the Andean Pact, although each participating state in such an arrangement will tend to be very sensitive to factors that may affect the attractiveness of its investment climate for foreign enterprises.(26)

The complex relationships between external dependency and political change at the national and regional levels in the Third World are, to some extent, reflected in the evolution of the East European-Soviet region, although in this context the unique factors of Soviet coercion and use of ideology have effects that are not paralleled in the developing areas. The most extensive and most significant forms of change in the East European-Soviet system are transformations of the imposed Marxist-Leninist political cultures that are in conflict with the power ambitions of the Soviet ruling elite.

The values of· the political culture which the USSR has been endeavoring to promote in its affinitive East European states have been tending to lose appeal because of their identification with Soviet hegemonic controls, the growth of new cultures based on professional achievement and material rewards, and elite toleration of some degree of intellectual freedom. Problems of performance in these states, moreover, have been aggravated by the deficiencies of the over-centralized controlling institutions which are maintained at Soviet insistence. Yet, pressures from the USSR and from within each East European society for improved performance have been increasing. The principal consequence, for this regional system, is a growth of tensions between the USSR and the East European states under its influence. Within the USSR, the ruling group is attempting to increase the concentration of power in its own hands, and improve the effectiveness of this power. With this orientation, moreover, it is seeking stronger influence over the East European regimes, and these are accepting, with evident reluctance, deeper incorporation into the Soviet-centered scheme for regional integration of the socialist states.(27)

The Soviet ruling elite's symbolic capabilities are not adequate for the tasks of invigorating its own political culture and spreading this more effectively in Eastern Europe. The emergence of a leadership that would be suitably gifted for these tasks has been made difficult by a pervasive high-level unwillingness to permit substantial ideological innovation, by the leadership's own isolation from potential sources of intellectual challenge and stimulation, and by the effects of factional politics associated with the current succession struggle, which tend to draw elite energies into conspiratorial activities in support of favored candidates for office.

The tensions between East European regimes and the USSR, that are evidently tending to grow with increases in Soviet pressures for integration within the Council for Mutual Economic Assistance, are probably rousing East European nationalism, but are certainly contrib-uting to strains within the East European leaderships. A general growth of East European antipathies toward the USSR is to be expected as the Soviet authorities make increasing use of their bargaining power to impose forms of economic specialization that link the East European economies individually and unequally to the Soviet system. As this becomes the dominant feature of the regional pattern of interaction, the ideological issues and questions of national interest which it poses are becoming more divisive for East European ruling elites, and there are no indications that Soviet policy is likely to become more pragmatic and liberal.(28)

The East European states, of course, cannot diversify their depen-dencies, as is possible for states in the developing areas; they are members of a hierarchical regional system, in which the possibilities for change are predicated on what may shape the evolution of the hege-monic power. The pattern of relations does not serve as a model for regions of developing states, although the modernization problems of those states, because of their magnitude, may seem to require very strong governmental involvement in each economy, with vigorous mobilization of popular energies. Regional and subregional groups of Third World states can seek to profit from the experience of the European Community, as this is the most significant example of regional cooperation in contemporary world politics, and is gradually evolving into a more integrated system through policy coordination, although disjointedly and with strains over the distribution of benefits from the common market.

DEVELOPMENTAL ISSUES

As international polities, with some potential for providing collective benefits, regional systems can develop. Their members may become more cohesive and more oriented toward cooperation in the common interest; regional institutions for such cooperation may be established; and, through such cooperation, interdependencies between such states may grow and may be managed in more orderly and equitable ways. If such relatively comprehensive development occurs, problems analogous to those encountered in the growth of national polities will be overcome. These are problems of identity, integration, participation, legitimacy, institution building, and performance.

The degrees of support for collective decision making in a regional context will depend on how much elites and masses within each national society identify with the group, and are satisfied with the conditions under which their administrations can participate in its affairs and with the outcomes of the regional policies that are adopted. If satisfactory outcomes are to be provided on a continuing basis, regional institutions will be needed, and they will require leadership for the promotion of consensus regarding the substance of common policies.

Industrialized democracies experience problems of advanced political development under conditions of complex interdependence, and these problems affect the management of their regional interdependencies. The most common problems, which are associated with forms of political change, concern the relationships between societal demands for allocations, the aggregating capabilities of institutions, and leadership choices with respect to opportunities for political advantage and the requirements of overall performance. Difficulties of aggregation resulting from high levels of popular demand, as has been seen, tend to have paralyzing effects, and also cause leaderships to engage in disjointed and incremental decision making. Such decision making, moreover, is often influenced more by concerns for political advantage than by considerations of the general welfare. Policies toward other states in a regional system are affected, and all the more so because of rising interdependencies which increase with trade and investment flows. In the West European system, then, problems of advanced political development at the national level are linked with problems of regional development.(29) A further complication is that, in both the more developed and coherent and the less developed and less integrated industrialized democracies, the competitive management of complex interdependencies can rouse nationalist motivations. These tend to be given expression in neomercantilist policies which work against common needs for policy coordination and integration. At the same time, the various forms of nationalism prevent the development of positive societal attitudes toward existing and projected regional institutions.

External challenges can stimulate integrative activity in a region of industrialized democracies, but can also intensify their competitive pursuits of national interests. The oil crisis of the mid-1970s, because of its magnitude and degree of surprise as well as its urgency, had the latter effect in the European Community. The problems of the international monetary system, caused by inflationary pressures on the American dollar, together with U.S. balance of payments difficulties, have, in effect, allowed longer decision time but have had even greater salience and have evoked significant policy coordination for the development of a European Monetary System. In this case, a crucial factor has been a substantial identity of views and preferences between the French and West German administrations.(30)

Collective decision making in the European Community has been institutionalized on a confederal basis, and this, because of its low political risks and costs for each administration, can be considered the natural preference for any industrialized democracies attempting regional cooperation. Functionally, however, it has disadvantages because the outcomes depend on protracted bargaining, and there is little scope for flexibility in negotiations with outside states. Unresolved issues concerning the management of regional interdependencies tend to accumulate, and the gaps between the more dynamic economies of the core states and those of the peripheral members tend to widen, thus increasing strains within the system. The problem of institutional development at the regional level, then, is a problem of collective decisional efficacy for a common public policy, and it can be argued that this requires the setting up of a federal authority with significant transfers of power from the national governments. Societal support for this, however, tends to be lacking because of the competitive ethos with which regional interdependencies are managed.

The developmental issues posed in the European Community raise questions about the capacities of executives in industrialized democracies to provide regional leadership for societal, structural, and policy integration, in the general interest. A basic difficulty is that the national processes of elite socialization cause absorption in the tasks of maximizing comparative political advantage through the favoring of sectoral interests, with competitive behavior toward neighboring states that can draw general domestic support. Questions of regional interest tend to be excluded. If strong transnational bonds were to develop between the major political parties, the elite socialization processes would produce concerns with regional welfare. The West European experience indicates, however, that political leaders are generally not motivated to promote such bonds, and that the interest groups with which they interact are primarily concerned with exerting leverage on national policies, especially because of the expanding role of each administration in the direction of its economy.(31)

In Third World regions, the developmental issues are even more serious. Most of the states in these regions function at low levels of political development; a high proportion of these states accordingly lack stability; and, in many cases, their leaders feel antipathies toward and distrust of neighboring administrations. Further, as the levels of interdependence between these new nations are low, their governments have only weak incentives to engage in regional cooperation.

Awareness of weak legitimacy, it must be stressed, causes most Third World ruling groups to be deeply preoccupied with the mobilization of support through clientelist networks. Due to the lack of institutional development, these networks need constant attention, and factional activities by dissatisfied groups must be thwarted. Because of the intensely personal character of clientelist interactions, moreover, distrust, rivalries, and resentments tend to develop, with destructive effects.

While the motivations of Third World governments to undertake regional cooperation are weak, their capabilities for such cooperation are also weak, principally because of deficiencies in their executive establishments and bureaucracies. Executive skills are often unrelated to executive power and responsibilities, the allocation of such power and responsibilities typically lacks coherence and permanence, and the bureaucracy is usually affected by inertia that results from autocratic direction. Yet, the management of even modest schemes for regional cooperation by developing states requires high degrees of political resolve and rather comprehensive use of each national government's administrative resources. Where the resolve is lacking, or is not sustained over time, the regional venture will achieve little, as has been illustrated by the experiences of ASEAN and the Andean Pact.(32) The difficulties which must be overcome are that trade liberalization measures are hard to negotiate and implement because they tend to benefit the larger and relatively more advanced states; that inequalities in the distribution of benefits from market integration cause rifts between developing countries; that any support for redistributive measures is usually inadequate; and that some transnational enterprises, in the pursuit of their own narrow interests, can attempt to exert influence on the policies of one or more of the participating states.

Third World states with democratic systems are likely to be more positively oriented toward regional cooperation than their authoritarian neighbors. This is suggested by the contrasts between the regional policies of the democratic Latin American states in the 1960s and those of the military dictatorships now controlling those states.(33) Military regimes tend to be more exclusively concerned with the development of their own armed strength and economic power, more distrustful and antipathetic toward neighbors, and more inclined to accept dependencies on industrialized democracies, especially those willing to provide weapons under grants or loans. Yet, it cannot be denied that democratic Third World states can have unstable and ineffective governments, and that even those with well-established administrations can be rather indifferent to the possibilities for regional cooperation, as India was under Nehru.(34)

Basic advances in political development are difficult in Third World states because, fundamentally, elite value orientations and forms of rationality are unfavorable. The mixes of traditional values and instrumental Western cultures do not produce active concerns with community welfare, but make for intensely personal pursuits of self interest. The advancement of such interests through rationally organized cooperation in large economic and political institutions is largely precluded by distrust, corruption, and incapacities for developing regulatory mechanisms that would ensure continuous achievement. These problems call for more substantial and constructive Western contributions to political development in Third World nations, and, certainly, more responsible Western control over flows of resources to military regimes in these nations.

Socialist regimes in developing states can build up strong political structures and mobilize popular support, but most of them exhibit the defects of the Soviet and Chinese models of revolutionary modernization. The heavy concentrations of power in the ruling elite generate severely divisive high-level conflicts by stimulating personal ambitions, rousing fears of insecurity, and posing ideological issues. The overmanaged system becomes afflicted with bureaucratic inertia which causes grave inefficiencies in the large public sector. Virtually all possibilities for collaboration with transnational enterprises in the industrialized democracies are rejected and, accordingly, the foreign technology that can aid industrialization is not acquired. Trade with industrialized democracies tends to slacken for complex reasons, including the disruption of commercial links with those states, and commercial exchanges with the large advanced socialist states bring only limited gains. Over time, perceptible, economic deterioration weakens the appeal of the ideology, leadership charisma declines, and unrest provokes increasing repression. The difficulties of political development in such contexts are especially serious because supporting socialist states, including the USSR, can provide resources to increase the repression, and there is tight closure against the penetration of cultural influences from open societies that could inspire liberalization.(35)

In the East European-Soviet region, where problems of advanced socialist political development are encountered, issues of legitimacy, participation, institution building, and performance have to be seen in two contexts. There are questions of system dominance and subsystem autonomy which are primarily functional; performance in these industrialized states requires more subsystem autonomy than the Soviet ruling elite is willing to allow. This is the most basic reason for slow growth in the Soviet economy, and for the weakening legitimacy of the regime's political structures. Secondly, there are questions of state building that can be posed if the leadership's value orientation becomes adaptable. There are strong impediments to this in elite political psychology, but, if there is such a shift in value orientation, authority can be spread out, made accountable in some measure, and given more legitimacy. This could become feasible on a corporate basis, with partially controlled functional representation.

The issues of political development in the USSR and its East European regimes have ramifications that affect the East European-Soviet system, as has been stressed. The form of integration which is being imposed in this system can be made acceptable only if there is a great improvement in the methods of exporting the USSR's political culture to its affinitive states, and this is not likely. The rational choice for the Soviet authorities would be to promote integration on a more equal basis, allowing for the autonomous development of exchanges among the East European regimes. Yet, this solution would not be feasible without basic changes in the Soviet and East European economies to permit large-scale trade without the presently serious obstacles of arbitrary pricing, currency inconvertibility, and commodity inconvertibility.

Choices that are relatively favorable to the East Europeans and that affect basic features of the Soviet economy, even if considered seriously by elements of the USSR's leadership, are not likely to be welcomed among the concerned segments of the secondary elite, especially in the party and the military establishments, and are not likely to be advocated by contenders for power in the current succession struggle. Such contenders may well expect to strengthen their positions by identifying with the nationalist and parochial feelings of elements in the secondary elite, with promises to impose more effective controls in Eastern Europe.(36)

REGIONAL DESIGNING

The growth of interdependencies between industrialized democracies, the expansion of largely unregulated transnational economic activity, and the difficulties of modernization in the Third World call for what Andrew Schonfield has termed "a new dimension of international public power."(37) This can be argued also on the basis of numerous observations by scholars about the lack of holistically directed interaction in regional and global politics.

Industrialized democracies in geographic proximity, with more or less affinitive and open cultures, can work for the management of their complex interdependencies through regional cooperation. Geographic proximity provides a natural basis for collaboration in resource, environmental, communication, transport, industrial, labor, education, health, and trade policies; and the advantages of collaboration in all these fields tend to become increasingly significant with the growth and diversification of each national economy. While frequent interactions between neighboring states over very substantial issues can increase antipathies and distrust between them, if one or more are seen to be excessively concerned with their own interests, the possibilities for restraint in bargaining and for the growth of a regional consensus on developmental issues will be increased if the openness of their cultures facilitates the growth of an international community of leaders of opinion, scholars, politicians, bureaucrats, and industrialists, who critically review the policies of their own and other administrations, and who engage in continuous debate on policy questions. To the extent that such a community evolves, each national administration is likely to become transnationally accountable, and the influence of its own elites on its policies is affected by trends in regional thinking.

Comprehensive regional cooperation is also necessary in the Third World for the management of dependencies, as well as for growth with appropriate distributive arrangements. Because of the underdevelopment of these states, and because most of them have small territories and populations, extensive collaboration on a basis of geographic proximity is needed for adequate utilization of shared resources, the management of common environmental problems, and the development of complementary industries, transportation systems, and communication networks. More importantly, the resolute political cooperation that is needed between developing states for comprehensive management of their dependencies on the industrialized democracies and the multinationals has to develop, to a large extent, on a basis of geographic and cultural identity. Because of the asymmetries in bargaining power which the developing states must reckon with in their relations with industrialized democracies and transnational enterprises, the formation of quite large regional systems in the Third World seems necessary, although the multiplicity of states, their relatively closed cultures, and the social distances between them tend to make cooperation very difficult.

The most advanced regional political economy is the European Community, and its achievements and failures have much significance for its own future and for developing states. The Community is also important as a major force in international politics, as its size and economic strength challenge Third World states to combine in associations large enough to offset, at least partially, the great bargaining power which it can bring to bear in negotiations on trade, investment, and aid.

The recent history of the European Community indicates how ventures in policy integration, undertaken confederally on an intergovernmental basis, cause national policies to become more sensitive to issues of national interest that are raised by disparities in the gains from collaboration, especially with respect to market expansion. Heightened concerns with national interest tend to perpetuate the confederal character of the collective decision making process preventing movement toward structural integration, although the confederal management of interdependencies tends to be increasingly inadequate because of its requirements for unanimity, and fails to correct inequities since any advantaged state can veto distributive and developmental proposals that are seen to be against its own interests. The confederal management of interdependencies is also inadequate because, while national administrations tend to be acutely sensitive to matters affecting their perceived interests, their regional behavior tends to reflect the sectorally-biased, disjointed incrementalism in their public policies, their lack of concern with high order value questions, including matters of regional interest, and the organizational procedures of their foreign affairs output structures that make for concentration on the disaggregated components of immediate policy issues.

Neofunctional theorists anticipated movement toward structural integration in the European Community as interest groups pressured their national administrations to seek the benefits of more complete unification. Such expectations were based on assumptions about the political psychology of ruling elites in industrialized democracies which reflected insufficient awareness of the extent to which these leaderships were inclined toward sectorally biased incrementalism rather than comprehensively rational statecraft with high order value integrations.(38) The degree to which such integrations are excluded and political useful sectoral interests are favored is considerable, and is a reflection of a fundamental shift in value orientations – a major displacement of consummatory by instrumental values which has been evident in most of the industrialized democracies. Community, national, and, of course, regional considerations have given way to preoccupations with maximizing the political utility of allocations favoring diverse interests whose support is desired. This basic problem (viewed in different ways by Apter, Bell, Beer, Crozier, and Huntington(39)) causes not only a neglect of national welfare and regional interests but also an incapacity to recognize such concerns, and insensitivities to anxieties about them that may be expressed by opinion leaders.

Problems of normative development at the national level in advanced open states, then, are linked with problems of normative development at the regional level, with negative implications for neofunctional logic. The scope for this logic in Third World regional cooperation schemes is also limited, principally because ruling elites in developing countries tend to be distrustful and antipathetic toward neighboring states, as has been seen, and, in many cases, are not strongly motivated to expand and manage more effectively their low-level interdependencies with their neighbors. Moreover, the attention of many elites in the developing states is drawn away from regional questions by very demanding internal legitimacy problems. In a majority of cases, the value orientations underlying these concerns and the rather negative dispositions toward neighbors are, of course, instrumental rather than consummatory, and saction much corrupt and rather oppressive behavior. Surviving traditional consummatory values tend to be weak, few consummatory values relating to social reform and social justice are absorbed from the industrialized democracies, and the ideals invoked by communist regimes tend to have little appeal, except for a minority of radically inclined modernizers.

Neofunctional logic does have some relevance for the problems associated with inspiring more integrative activity by industrialized democracies. While the demands of interest groups tend to be too divergent to push national administrations toward wider policy coordination, and while the sectoral concerns of national leaders as political rather than rational actors tend often to be opposed to forms of cooperation in the regional interest, the expanding interdependencies between the advanced, open political economies do set functional requirements for policy coordination. Holistic considerations, thus, tend to command some attention, despite the dominant inclinations toward sectorally biased incrementalism. Determination to achieve more comprehensive management of interdependencies, however, to the extent that it develops at the national level, does not lead to support for structural integration above that level, unless there is confidence that strong influence can be exerted on the functioning of the integrated structures, and that national interests will be advanced through the outputs of those structures.

Within the European Community, more extensive policy coordination on an intergovernmental basis, within the confederal framework and with occasional contributions from summitry, can be expected to be the main regional response to the increasingly complex interdependencies linking states in that area. Any movement toward the establishment of a federal-type authority is likely to be possible only if a common political will for this develops among the members. That does not seem likely because of the present orientations of the national administrations, but it could develop if there were intensive leadership activities to promote the necessary consensus. The emergence of a suitably gifted and motivated leader is not probable; but, if such a leader did begin to influence elite and popular attitudes, the attitudinal integration which resulted would help to form the common political will for structural integration. Such a leader would have to make vigorous and sustained use of symbolic capabilities, define persuasively the significance of the Community's situation, project appealingly the values that would be realized through political unification, and inspire support for the realization of those values. At present, Community institutions and programs fail to generate any symbolic attachments among elites and masses in the member states, and Community processes are, to a large extent, isolated from major political activities in those members – in line with the tacit preferences of the national administrations.

A design for more advanced region building in the European Community could, therefore, include plans for private organizations (including institutes for higher learning) that would seek to inspire regional leadership activities for the promotion of structural integration, using capacities for what may be called transnational symbolic interaction. Such leadership activities could be directed, in part, toward strengthening the role of the European Parliament, especially by promoting bonds between its major political groups, and encouraging them to demand the formation of an executive body, with significant powers, which would be responsible to that assembly.

For the building of international political communities in the Third World, intensive use of symbolic capabilities by national leaders seems even more necessary; because the pressures to manage interdependencies are weak, high degrees of commitment are necessary for comprehensive regional development, and the tasks of modernization are urgent. Concerned private organizations that support Third World development could endeavor to stimulate supranational community formation efforts by national leaders in developing states, especially by sponsoring informal seminars on regional issues for such leaders.

Structurally, designs for region building can be based on the present confederal model of the European Community, or on the federal concept envisaged as its eventual achievement by the promoters of that Community. The confederal model, because it safeguards state interests, is the easier to negotiate, but tends to resist transformation into a federal arrangement.

The main elements of the confederal model are a collective decision making unit, comprising representatives of the member governments, and an international bureaucracy for the provision of common services. There may also be an international assembly, with directly elected or appointed members. In such a system, representatives of the national administrations in the decision making unit tend to restrict the competence of the bureaucratic structure, to limit the expansion of its common services and its opportunities to provide inputs into policymaking, while the national administrators tend to restrict the role of the international assembly, if it exists or is being planned.

In confederal policy coordination, because the requirements for unanimity tend to be exploited by the member governments, there is considerable issue avoidance and deferral, and methods of engaging with issues tend to be inadequate. Yet the intense preoccupations with national interest that result in this type of coordination prevent the development of a consensus for further political unification through structural integration. The costs, in terms of interdependencies that are inadequately managed, can be borne without serious difficulties by industrialized democracies, but the disadvantages in the case of a Third World grouping, with reference to the neglect of dependency problems, are likely to be substantial. Regional cooperation ventures by developing countries, therefore, should aim at the early establishment of federal structures, although the degree of authority to be vested in the supranational executives can be expected to cause serious differences.

The range of choices in region building between strong and weak federal structures, and confederal arrangements that facilitate leadership or make it difficult, is fairly extensive. The full significance of these options depends, of course, on the political cultures, the internal cohesion, the bargaining strength, and the overall performance of the states that are attempting to cooperate. Certain general principles of structural-functional design, however, can be set out on the basis of what can be generalized about the experiences of industrialized democracies and Third World states in regional ventures.

Balanced distributions of bargaining power among the participating states are desirable and can be attained by fostering the growth of subregional groups of coalitions to reduce asymmetries in size, population, level of economic development, and degrees of internal unity. If this is not done, smaller and weaker states that are in danger of being pushed into peripheral roles will tend to slow and obstruct the confederal or federal process in order to extract maximum benefits from their cooperation, although the extent to which this is done consistently will depend on the degrees to which the administrations of these states are inclined to disjointed incrementalism with sectoral biases. Equitable arrangements for participation in collective decision making processes, however, must be accompanied by provisions for the aggregation of interests and demands that will be both representative and appropriately oriented toward regional policymaking. These requirements, moreover, must be closely linked with the need for balance between the level of participatory activity and the level of institutional growth in the regional structures, and also with the need for another kind of balance between leadership functions and the autonomous provision of inputs into the regional process by member states. The coherent aggregation of inputs, of course, requires a significant level of institutional development in the regional organizations, and depends very much on leadership activities that are self critical, sensitive to feedback, and accountable not only in formal contexts but also, more widely, to critically and constructively-oriented elites in the participating states. To foster such leadership and discourage narrowly conceived incrementalism, together with the idiosyncratic authoritarianism common in the Third World, structural arrangements may be devised to limit a federal executive's vulnerability to pressures from within the states in a regional system, or, in a confederal context, to strengthen the power of the regional bureaucratic structures, as well as of any regional assembly.

Functionally, regional designing must provide for strong direction in the collective management of interdependencies. This will be necessary to raise levels of societal support for the emerging community, and to establish a regional policy consensus on the basis of which adjustments can be made to redistribute the gains from integration after its initial stages. Strong direction, of course, may increase strains between members of the region, but low decisional efficacy at the regional level will prevent the supranational institutions from gaining legitimacy and diminish confidence in the potential for regional collaboration. Because strong direction in the regional interest is so important, it can be argued that very active partnerships of bureaucratic and political leaders are necessary, that the high bureaucrats should be members of a permanent regional civil service, and that they should be given comprehensive and fundamentally irrevocable administrative mandates. The political leadership, which hopefully would be constitutionally directed to respect the competence of the permanent regional civil service heads, would be responsible for the supervision, adjustment, and expansion of the ongoing collective administrative process.

From all this, more explicit principles of regional design can be set out with detailed references to the attributes and foreign policy orientations of participating states and potential members. But it must be stressed that the solution of problems of regional design is conditional on successful political designing at the national level. This is especially true with respect to groups of industrialized democracies. The dispositions towards sectorally biased incrementalism that have been stressed in references to these states reflect general acceptance of interest group pluralism as the major source of public policy. In such polities, performance is largely determined by the competitive configurations of group demands, appraised by executives on a basis of comparative political advantage. For greater equity in public policy, with a holistic developmental thrust, officially structured or corporate interest representation, according with criteria laid down in the public interest, can be persuasively advocated.(40) This dimension of the connection between national and regional problems of political development indicates a need for stress, in theory and policy prescription, on the supreme importance of leadership and, thus, of associations and institutions that can contribute to elite formation. The building of open and integrated regional systems has to be a democratic responsibility, and the building of advanced democracies, as constituent elements or sponsors of such systems, requires political innovation of a high order. Leadership for this task, it can be hoped, will assist progress in the development of Third World regions, in which the heavy burdens of dependency relationships are serious hindrances to the growth of sovereign political economies.

NOTES

(1) Jean Blondel, The Government of France (New York: Thomas Y. Crowell, 4th ed., 1974).

(2) Michael Kreile, "West Germany: The Dynamics of Expansion"; and T.J. Pempel, "Japanese Foreign Economic Policy: The Domestic Bases for International Behavior," International Organization 31, no. 4 (Autumn 1977); 775-808, and 723-74, respectively.

(3) Blondel, The Government of France.

(4) Francine R. Frankel, India's Political Economy, 1947-77, (Princeton, N.J.: Princeton University Press, 1978).

(5) Michel Crozier, Samuel P. Huntington, and Joji Watanuki, The Crisis of Democracy, (New York: New York University Press, 1975); Samuel H. Beer, Adam B. Ulam, Suzanne Berger, and Guido Goldman, Patterns of Government (New York: Random House, 3rd ed., 1973), pp. 104-116; and Norman J. Vig and Rodney Stiefbold, eds., Politics in Advanced Nations, (Englewood Cliffs, N.J.: Prentice Hall, 1974), pp. 3-76.

(6) Ibid., and see David E. Apter, The Politics of Modernization, (Chicago, Ill.: University of Chicago Press, 1965), pp. 422-64. See also George Moyser; "Political Culture and Political Change in Western Europe and the USA: An American Perspective," Government and Opposition 13, no. 4 (Autumn 1978): 497-509.

(7) See Jack Hayward, The One and Indivisible French Republic, (London: Weidenfeld and Nicolson, 1973), pp. 227-68.

(8) See Charles Pentland, International Theory and European Integration, (New York: Free Press, 1973), pp. 100-46.

(9) See Jurgen Wohlfahrt, "The European Economic Community: Expectations and Realities of Integration," in State and Society in Contemporary Europe, edited by Jack Hayward and R.N. Berki (London: Martin Robertson, 1979), pp. 203-17; and Barry Bracewell-Milnes, Economic Integration in East and West, (London: Croom Hlem, 1976).

(10) Constantine V. Vaitsos, "Crisis in Regional Economic Cooperation (Integration) among Developing Countries: A Survey," World Development 6, no. 6 (June 1978): 719-70; Robert D. Bond, "Regionalism in Latin America: Prospects for the Latin American Economic System," International Organization 32, no. 2 (Spring 1978): 401-24; and Peter Robson, Economic Integration in Africa, (Evanston, Ill.: Northwestern University Press, 1968).

(11) Crozier, Huntington and Watanuki, The Crisis of Democracy. See also Jack Hayward, "Interest Groups and the Demand for State Action;" and Neil Elder, "The Function of the Modern State," in Hayward and Berki, State and Society in Contemporary Europe. On the possibilities for leadership achievement, see Georg H. Kuster, "Germany," in Big Business and the State, edited by Raymond Vernon (Cambridge, Mass.: Harvard University Press, 1974), pp. 64-86.

(12) Hayward and Berki, State and Society in Contemporary Europe.

(13) Hayward, The One and Indivisible French Republic.

(14) Samuel P. Huntington and Jorge I. Dominguez, "Political Development," in Handbook of Political Science, edited by Fred I. Greenstein and Nelson W. Polsby (Reading, Mass.: Addison-Wesley, 1975), pp. 1-114.

(15) Richard Stuart Olson, "Economic Coercion in World Politics," World Politics 31, no. 4 (July 1979): 471-94; and Richard Rubinson, "Dependence, Government Revenue, and Economic Growth," Studies in Comparative International Development 12, no. 2 (Summer 1977): 3-28.

(16) Elizabeth G. Ferris, "National Political Support for Regional Integration: The Andean Pact," International Organization 33, no. 1

(Winter 1979): 83-104; W. Andrew Axline, "Underdevelopment, Dependence, and Integration: The Politics of Regionalism in the Third World," International Organization 31, no. 1 (Winter 1977): 83-106; and Constantine V. Vaitsos, "Crisis in Regional Economic Cooperation."

(17) Samuel P. Huntington and Clement H. Moore, eds., Authoritarian Politics in Modern Society, (New York: Basic Books, 1970), pts. I & III; and Hayward and Berki, State and Society in Contemporary Europe, pt. II.

(18) Arpad Abonyi and Ivan J. Sylvain, "CMEA Integration and Policy Options for Eastern Europe: A Development Strategy of Dependent States," Journal of Common Market Studies 16, no. 2 (Dec. 1977): 132-54.

(19) Lowell Dittmer, "Bases of Power in Chinese Politics: A Theory and an Analysis of the Fall of the Gang of Four," World Politics 31, no. 1 (Oct. 1978): 26-60; and Joyce K. Kallgren, "China 1979: The New Long March," Asian Survey 19, no. 1 (Jan. 1979): 1-19.

(20) Paul Taylor, "Confederalism: The Case of the European Communities," in International Organization, edited by Paul Taylor and A.J.R. Groom (London: Frances Pinter, 1978), pp. 317-25; and Helen Wallace, William Wallace, and Carole Webb, eds., Policy Making in the European Communities, (New York: Wiley, 1977).

(21) Harold Crouch, "Patrimonialism and Military Rule in Indonesia," World Politics 31, no. 4 (July 1979): 571-87. See also Samuel P. Huntington, Political Order in Changing Societies, (New Haven, Conn.: Yale University Press, 1968).

(22) William L. Scully and Frank N. Trager, "Burma 1978: The Thirtieth Year of Independence," Asian Survey 19, no. 2 (Feb. 1979): 147-56.

(23) Immanuel Wallerstein, "The Decline of the Party in African Single-Party States," in Political Parties and Political Development, edited by Joseph LaPalombara and Myron Weiner (Princeton, N.J.: Princeton University Press, 1966), pp. 201-14.

(24) See Ferris, "National Political Support for Regional Integration," and Bond, "Regionalism in Latin America."

(25) See Vaitsos, "Crisis in Regional Economic Cooperation," and Axline, "Underdevelopment, Dependence, and Integration."

(26) Ibid.

(27) See Abonyi and Sylvain, "CMEA Integration."

(28) Ibid.

(29) See Stuart A. Scheingold's discussion of the European Community as an instrument of public policy in "The Community in Perspective: Public Policy and Political Structure," The Annals of the American Academy of Political and Social Science (Nov. 1978), pp. 156-68.

(30) See Michael Brenner, "Monetary Policy: Processes and Policies," The Annals of the American Academy of Political and Social Science (Nov. 1978), pp. 98-110; and Jocelyn Statler, "The European Monetary System: From Conception to Birth," International Affairs, 55, no. 2 (April 1979): 206-25.

(31) See Wallace, Wallace, and Webb, Policy Making in the European Communities and Susan Strange, "The Management of Surplus Capacity: Or How Does Theory Stand Up to Protectionism 1970's Style?" International Organization 33, no. 3 (Summer 1979): 303-34.

(32) Stuart Drummond, "ASEAN: The Growth of an Economic Dimension," The World Today 35, no. 1 (Jan. 1979): 31-38; and Ferris, "National Political Support for Regional Integration."

(33) Bond, "Regionalism in Latin America."

(34) See William J. Barnds, "South Asia" in World Politics edited by James N. Rosenau, Kenneth W. Thompson, and Gavin Boyd (New York: Free Press, 1976), pp. 501-27.

(35) See Roger E. Kanet and Donna Bahry, eds., Soviet Economic and Political Relations with the Developing World (New York: Praeger, 1975); and Alvin Z. Rubinstein, ed., Soviet and Chinese Influence in the Third World, (New York: Praeger, 1975).

(36) For a discussion of the succession problem see R. Judson Mitchell, "The Soviet Succession: Who, and What, Will Follow Brezhnev?" Orbis 23, no. 1 (Spring 1979): 9-34.

(37) Andrew Schonfield, Europe: Journey to an Unknown Destination, (Middlesex, Eng.: Harmondsworth, Penguin Books, 1972), pp. 16-17.

(38) See J. Steinbrunner, The Cybernetic Theory of Decision, (Princeton, N.J.: Princeton University Press, 1974); and observations by Leon N. Lindberg, "Energy Policy and the Politics of Economic Development," Comparative Political Studies 10, no. 3 (Oct. 1977): 355-82.

(39) Apter, The Politics of Modernization; Daniel Bell, The Cultural Contradictions of Capitalism (New York: Basic Books, 1976); Crozier, Huntington, Watanuki, The Crisis of Democracy; and Beer, Ulam, Berger, Goldman, Patterns of Government.

(40) Charles W. Anderson, "Political Design and the Representation of Interests," Comparative Political Studies 10, no. 1 (April 1977), 127-52.

13 Patterns of Transregional Relations*
Donald E. Lampert

Discussing patterns of transregional relations inherently requires inquiry about the nature of interaction in global politics. The conceptual meaning of a region is grounded in a sense of "boundary" or "discontinuity,"(1) suggesting that interactive patterns which can be considered regional stop somewhere. The various chapters in this volume all assume that, at the very least, geography is critical to this demarcation, and such demarcations allow us to take note of the patterns interaction forms when it occurs across them. If the patterns which these transregional interactions display could be aggregated or summed, the result would provide a "system map" of the world. It is critical to point out, however, that this result would _not_ constitute a "single international system."(2) A concentration on regions and the relationships among them makes it especially clear that assuming the existence of a single international system as a kind of grand container into which the multitude of events that compose global politics somehow can be thrown is of limited analytical utility. The substantive issues connected with these events are simply too diverse.

The approach employed herein stresses the importance of issues for understanding systems in global politics (unique concatenations of actors and issues recognizable through behavior). In certain contexts, this will mean going beyond the conventional wisdom of much regional analysis. Regional affinities, influence patterns, interdependencies, political cultures, and so forth are among the many sources of issues in

*This research was supported in part by a Faculty Grant-in-Aid from Arizona State University. It was completed in spite of the idiosyncracies manifested by Arizona State's Univac 1100, and the assistance of Academic Computing Services in overcoming them is gratefully acknowledged. Thanks are also due Bruce Bowen, Larry Falkowski, Pat McGowan, Greg Pollock (especially), John Rockfellow, Frances Rotter, Shell Simon, Steve Walker, and George Watson for their various contributions.

world politics. Whether behavior involving them remains within the confines of a single region, transcends them, or engenders impacts felt around the world is really an empirical question. This implies that certain regions correspond to some of the "multiple systems" evident in global politics. The composition of other systems may represent linkages between two or more regions, and it is such transregional linkages that serve as our primary focus.

Nonetheless, investigation of transregional relations is not just an inductive process. Alternative theoretical frameworks exist that can be used to condition our expectations about those regional and transregional patterns which are found. Each of these models is somewhat broader than what traditionally may be thought of as a regional focus, but they contain important implications for transregional relations. Since we are considering transregional relations as largely equivalent to world politics itself, these models provide a useful initial backdrop against which regional and transregional systems can be analyzed. Although a rigorous comprehensive test of each of these models is beyond the scope of the present research, the transregional patterns that are identified will shed some light on their respective strengths and weaknesses.

MODELS OF TRANSREGIONAL RELATIONS

It has become commonplace to observe that world politics are growing more complex. One result of this complexity is that the models applicable to transregional relations emphasize different kinds of variables for explaining regional and global outcomes. Distinctions can be drawn among models which emphasize the political as opposed to the economic, those which do just the opposite, models emphasizing institutional decision making, those which regard decision making as the outplay of aggregate attributes, and so forth. This theoretical cacophony largely reflects the world with which analysts are trying to come to grips, and one of its primary characteristics is that the consequences of various foreign policy actions seem to be increasingly unintended. As Andrew Scott has pointed out:

> (T)he number of pathways by means of which processes can link with one another multiplies so rapidly with increases in the permeability of functional boundaries. The essential point is. . .entire trains of consequences can link up with one another, and all without deliberate collective calculation or management because the linking takes place at the process level rather than at the structural level.(3)

This implies one of the difficulties posed by the different models of transregional relations. It sometimes seems as if there is almost a one-to-one correspondence between the analysts discussing a given global phenomenon and the number of approaches that are used, with a similar problem apparent when attempts are made to categorize various approaches. This is because models, virtually by necessity, emphasize structural characteristics as a key to the understanding of processes. Scott's argument suggests that, for purposes of explaining current world politics, a sort of reversal of this ordering should be considered. Thus, the key element of our first model becomes processes of politico-economic exchange rather than the depiction of a splintered liberal American world order. In the second model, decision making processes producing integrative, disintegrative, and a variety of other outcomes take precedence over various discontinuities and institutional contexts. Finally, exploitation and/or imperialism become the basis on which centers and peripheries exist.

Exchange: The Liberal American Order

It may seem strange at first to think of the transregional processes encompassed by the characteristically American approach to world politics as those of "exchange." Our use of the term is intended to evoke a certain segment of social scientific theory which provides "an explanation of the act of giving or taking one thing in return for another."[4] Stephen Walker summarizes exchange theory as involving four basic propositions, "rationality, deprivation-satiation, aggression, and approval," to which may be added an additional "modeling proposition: If an activity is learned through modeling, then the observer is likely to repeat it in similar circumstances (provided the model's behavior was reinforced)." While the meaning of the various propositions themselves need not concern us, it is the metaphor of modeling which provides the key for understanding exchange theory's relevance to this view of transregional relations.

Put in its most simple form, the American view of world politics and, hence, of transregional relations is that the patterns which exist across regions can be conceptualized with reference to the costs and benefits accruing to the actors involved. The American way of life provides the yardstick in terms of which these costs and benefits are assessed. By the 1980s, this yardstick has had to be adjusted somewhat due to manifold situations representing global interdependencies, but whether they are conceived as involving politics or economics, or some combination of the two, interdependencies still may be summarized through the interplay of costs and benefits. In Robert Gilpin's words, "The intermeshing of interests across national boundaries and the recognized benefits of interdependence now cement the system together for the future. Therefore, even though the power of the United States and security concerns may be in relative decline, this does not portend a major transformation of the international economy and political system."[5]

The essential assumptions of this model are derived from a generalization of the American experience. Foremost among them is that there should be as little interference as possible with "model" transregional relationships. "Free markets" for political ideas and/or economic transactions are looked upon with approval. They provide contexts in which exchanges lead to desirable outcomes for the actors participating in them through quasirational attempts to maximize utilities. The modeling metaphor is critical because this assumption is viewed as having been reinforced very positively in the case of the United States and its closest allies. Communist governments and Third World statist regimes are antithetical to varying degrees because they deliberately interfere in exchange processes. Third World statist regimes attempt to violate the virtue of what has been termed "the domestic weakness of the American state,"(6) despite the fact that various interdependencies have rendered this factor somewhat of a mixed blessing for the United States. The Soviet Union and its Eastern European allies are currently less troublesome because of their relatively higher modernization as well as the fact that they are more consonant with the "bigness bias" implicit in the model itself:

> The United States has often been accused of attempting to remodel the rest of the world in terms of American social, economic, and political institutions. As a continental power, organized as a political federation to form the world's largest economy, we have implicitly also attempted to get other nations to measure up to American standards of size.(7)

A second assumption involves the extent of what may be termed "transitivity" between politics and economics, as well as the ways in which certain transregional patterns can be generalized. The meaning of this assumption has undergone an interesting historical development. Related to the free market idea, the traditional American conception was that the political and economic aspects of a liberal international order were largely separable, hence "intransitive." Yet, after 1945, this assumption was progressively undermined as the globalization of the Cold War and the liberal economic regime founded at Bretton Woods came to be institutionalized.

The spread of the Cold War to the Third World meant that transregional relations became largely transitive. Economic tools like foreign aid and assistance programs could be used for political purposes to prevent newly independent countries from "going communist." Politics and economics assumed a transitive quality, with the latter subservient to the former, as did transregional relations involving diverse actors. In other words, the catalytic effects of the Cold War cast all transregional interactions in a similar light. Detente, failure in Vietnam, and especially the economic dislocations of the 1970s led the characteristic American perception of the primacy of politics and its potential separation from economics to undergo further major adjustments. Transregional relations became less transitive, due largely to the persistence of related energy and monetary crises. Attempts were made to treat specific kinds of interactions with particular regions as unique for purposes of preserving declining American global advantages.

At the same time, transitivity greatly increased between politics and economics to a point where they were literally inseparable. Cold War "power politics" were replaced in the 1970s by a transitive "political economics" with little precedent in the American experience. Despite these altered transitivities, the American basis for viewing the world remains one which emphasizes exchange relationships. Greater political/economic transitivity has allowed declining transregional transitivity to be employed almost as a tactic against a newly assertive Third World. This can be illustrated through considering three of the five categories identified by Robert Cox in reviewing literature relevant to the New International Economic Order (NIEO) which represent variants of the American model.(8) First, "the establishment perspective: monopolistic liberalism," envisions transregional relations as remaining on the First World's terms by means of exchanges determined through market mechanisms. The second, a "social democratic perspective," is closely related to the first because it rests on similar assumptions about exchange processes:

> (It) shares with it a basic commitment to the normative preference for a world economy with relatively free movement of capital, goods, and technology as well as an acceptance of the rationality of conventional economics, while putting more stress upon the needs of the poor. It represents, in other words, a broader and somewhat more generous view of the adjustments that can be made without fundamentally disturbing the existing hegemony. . . .They share the same fundamental assumptions about the progressive nature of world capitalism bringing about a new international division of labor, and both recognize the need in addition for an international welfare program to be carried out as far as possible by the poor themselves.(9)

A third of Cox's viewpoints is that of the "neomercantilists." Neomercantilism also rests upon notions of exchange but, unlike the first two perspectives, it emphasizes the extent to which the United States is relatively shortchanged by current global patterns. Neomercantilism almost seems to hearken back to the Cold War in the sense of arguing for a recasting of economic exchanges in terms of American political advantage. In a word, neomercantilists would confront NIEO, and virtually all other transregional issues besides, from the classic realpolitik paradigm. Politics must come again to dominate economics, and from one analyst's perspective: "(P)roliferation of economic interdependencies is largely a dependent variable, subject to management or reversal, which has derived from a condition of stalemate at the level of the 'muted' bipolar relationship of major tension, and which has impacted more upon U.S. policy elites than upon those of the Soviet Union."(10) The neomercantilists, then, are angry because three decades of American global leadership did not result in the rewards anticipated.

Both modeling and transitivity represent "givens" for purposes of a third assumption which, in many ways, is a response to the altered circumstances of both the United States and the world in the 1970s. "Relativity" allows time to be treated as a variable dependent upon the nature of the transregional relationships being considered. Within the context of developed regions, the contributions of American foreign policy in the post-World War II era, at least implicitly, are supposed to count for something. For example, the fact that the American restoration of the West German and Japanese economies was so successful means that these countries' economic strength should now be used to assist the United States in trying to escape from its economic doldrums. The American efforts had been premised on the idea that, "(I)f a fully developed regionalism could take hold in several areas of the world, providing economic, political, and military strength on a local basis, the United States would be left with little to do. After 'winding up the clocks' it could watch them run, safe and secure in its North American redoubt."(11)

Thus, when it comes to exchanges with the more developed world, time is regarded in cumulative terms based upon a tacit ledger reflecting the costs and benefits which have accrued to the United States and its allies. Even in somewhat altered global circumstances, the temporal dimension of what has become American "leadership without hegemony"(12) involves certain compensations. Yet Richard Rosecrance suggests: "(T)he United States cannot hope that the world can be run on the basis of the regional 'clock-universes'. . . .The erroneous Cold War conception of the past was that American military power conjoined with economic aid could determine the future in one geographic context after another."(13) The emphasis on economic considerations in transregional relations has provided a coherence for the Third World that the Cold War policies of the United States based upon regional transitivities failed to create. The American view, however, is that similar compensatory effects based upon a cumulative temporal weighing of costs and benefits does not apply to the Third World.

What is at issue, really, are the Third World's claims that it has been "exploited" by previous transregional relations still in evidence today. Charges of exploitation acquire their coherence through a comparable notion of time viewed cumulatively, and the United States serves as the prime target because of its key role in establishing and maintaining these global patterns. In this context, the American position becomes one of denying that time has cumulative effects, emphasizing instead that free market choices most closely approximate "rationality" when they are made with reference only to present circumstances. Richard Cooper's treatment of "a new international economic order for mutual gain" provides an excellent example of the role relativity plays vis-a-vis the Third World in the American model.(14) Having offered a definition of exploitation, Cooper uses a kind of temporal reductio ad absurdum going as far back as the seventh century for purposes of negating the possibility that exploitive practices can be cumulated precisely. This leads him to conclude:

(T)he existence, on any scale, of economic exploitation in the sense defined above remains an open question, but the bits and pieces of evidence are far from overwhelming. Combined with the questions that can be raised about the nature of rectification claims, they hardly provide a solid base from which to launch claims to repayment.(15)

The time frame employed by the Third World in advancing claims of exploitation is, of course, much more exact than Cooper allows, dating from the age of European imperialism in the nineteenth century. Following World War II, the era of the most dramatic growth in multinational corporations (MNCs),(16) these actors became the source of neoimperialistic transregional processes which no longer were, nor needed to be, under the direct control of developed governments. The American model views MNC activities benignly, not as exploiters but rather as the potential engines of transregional development. In so doing, the American model accepts the idea that MNCs have a temporal perspective of their own which must also be understood in relative terms. Over the long haul, MNC activities produce a more efficient globalization of the world economy, eventually generating benefits that will trickle down to the disadvantaged. In the short term, this means as little interference as possible with MNC activities by Third World (or other) governments.

Ultimately, relativity becomes a means whereby the status quo of transregional exchanges can be maintained through the manipulation of their temporal dimension to the advantage of actors adhering to the American model. Relativity lends itself to devious uses, and one analyst even suggests: "(T)here are practical calculations which argue strongly in favor of accepting the Southern call for reform of the world economic system. . . .The most obvious is the opportunity to change what would appear to be concessions to the South into leverage over it."(17) In other words, acceptance of cumulative temporal effects for the future could be converted into a potent bargaining chip for the present in order to prevent too much change.

A final premise involves the "interactive" quality of the goals which state actors pursue within the context of the American model. Transitivity between politics and economics makes it possible to generalize what Stephen Krasner calls "a state-power theory of international trade" involving "four basic state interests – aggregate national income, social stability, political power, and economic growth."(18) The interactive effects of these variables provide an explanatory mechanism above and beyond simple hubris for the key role of the modeling proposition in the American approach to transregional exchange. The greater the extent to which transregional relations remain open (governed by as free a market as possible), large and/or developed states (like the United States and its allies) reap political advantages. This is because, despite the possibility that exposure to global forces can increase internal social instability, the effects of involvement in open exchanges vary inversely with size and development.

For large and/or developed states, the costs of insulation from open exchanges are less, leaving those lacking these traits more vulnerable. This potential vulnerability of the less developed to free global exchange reinforces the effects of relativity. As long as both the small and the large maintain their technological advantages, they remain comparatively protected. In the case of the large, factors of scale render exchanges less important. The small are vulnerable to global circumstances anyway, but through keeping up technologically they can, in effect, "ride the coat tails" of larger actors. On the whole, then, Krasner's description of "the hegemonic state" provides an excellent summary of how modeling, transitivity, relativity, and interactive effects combine to make the exchange model of transregional relations quintessentially American:

> At the symbolic level, the hegemonic state stands as an example of how economic development can be achieved. Its policies may be emulated, even if they are inappropriate for other states. Where there are very dramatic asymmetries, military power can be used to coerce weaker states into an open structure. . . .Most importantly, the hegemonic state can use its economic resources to create an open structure.(19)

Integration: Regional Discontinuities

The concepts, hypotheses, and theories subsumed under the integration model are more directly recognizable as applicable to regional contexts than those associated with exchange. Integration concerns "how national units come to share part or all of their decisional authority with an emerging international organization," and the dependent variable of this process "focuses upon an attempt to specify and predict the conditions under which the consequences generated by prior joint decisions will lead to redefinitions of actor strategies vis-a-vis the scope and level of regional decision making."(20) Integration does not really conflict with the exchange model, although there are differences in emphasis which derive basically from a simple fact — the exchange model represents a generalization of the American case while integration focuses upon the post-World War II experience of Western Europe.

By the late 1960s, the integration model was virtually synonymous with the study of regionalism.(21) This was due in part to the inclusiveness of the neofunctional approach, described succinctly by Michael Sullivan as based on a premise "which maintains that people who cooperate on a small, nonideological noncentral issue-area are very likely to build up, over time, patterns of cooperation that will carry over to matters of rather crucial concern."(22) By concentrating on the effects of political decision making as their dependent variable, the neofunctionalists were able to incorporate the findings of the other major school of empirical integration research, one that emphasized cybernetic "transaction" processes. Transactions became one of several "process mechanisms" impacting upon "integrative potential" which was then outplayed in various decisional outcomes.(23) Furthermore, the possibility of variable integrative outcomes surmounted the criticism that had been leveled at earlier functional theories stressing the automaticity of integrative processes.

The integration model is really a rather elegant set of explanations for the success of a single case, Western Europe. The model is somewhat applicable with much reduced explanatory power to Eastern Europe.(24) It proceeds from a dominant set of assumptions likening regional integration to the integration of the nation state itself.(25) Critical variables include various structural correspondences involving common codes of communications, culture, and compatible value orientations, all of which are reflected in high levels of transactions. Particularly important is the expansion of the "multifunctionality" of economic markets. Over time, learning processes produce a psychological identification with the integrated system and its symbols, altering popular habits of compliance with authority. It is when this point has been reached that the neofunctional decision-making processes have their most profound effects through a constant interplay of official policies and popular attitudes. Karl Deutsch summarizes this interplay as follows:

> Maintaining political integration, and particularly the integration of loyalties, may depend, in the long run, on some combination of two system capacities: to respond adequately – and hence sometimes quickly, massively, and single-mindedly – to short-term emergencies; and to remain sensitive and open-minded towards a much wider range of challenges from the human and natural environment.(26)

When the model is applied elsewhere in the world, however, its use yields, at best, mixed results. For example, the Central American Common Market (CACM) or the Association of Southeast Asian Nations (ASEAN) largely lack the conditions for successful integration.(27) Transregional implications thus remain somewhat unclear, due, in part, to the fact that they are derivable from the integration model rather than constituting an integral part of it. Louis Cantori and Steven Spiegel highlight one aspect of this problem when they refer to "the apparent insularity neofunctionalists attach to the regional integration process in their failure to make theoretical provisions for extraregional powers."(28) Nonetheless, some propositions exist for assessing transregional relations in terms of the integration model. A useful starting point is Ernst Haas' summary of "empirical generalizations: the external world," even though their implications are ambiguous:

● Perceptions of being victimized by the global system tend to spur integration as a way of "getting out from under."
a) Economic unions among late developing countries are designed to change a situation in which prosperity depends on commodity exports to developed nations. . .

b) But perceptions of dependence on a larger system may be so pervasive as to be a disincentive to regional efforts. . . .

● The role of extraregional single states (or their elites) is indeterminate in explaining regional integration.
a) A hegemonic extraregional actor can use his payoff capacity to undermine the will to integrate, as has been alleged of the United States. . .
b) But economic unions among late developing countries sometimes survive largely as a result of support from an exogenous actor. . . .

● Extraregional counterunions are a definite — but temporary — aid to integration.
a) Regional groupings with a military purpose survive only as long as they face a rival external grouping. The same is true of diplomatic groupings which do not take the form of an alliance.
b) Economic unions among industrialized countries may survive only because they seek united strength in dealing with another such union.(29)

By design, Haas' dependent variables relate to integrative outcomes. Yet, because of the indeterminacy in obtaining them, a picture of global politics emerges in which some regions are integrated, or on their way to being so, while others are not. This is why the structural implications of integrative processes can be summarized with reference to Oran Young's model of "political discontinuities" in global politics.(30) A "discontinuity" is basically equivalent to a system boundary, but has an additional connotation concerning communications patterns. If we represent a discontinuity in physical terms (which does not necessarily have to be the case), such as a river or other geographic border, then transactions on either side of it flow in the direction of different "core areas." Since integration ultimately is concerned with the development of such cores, its global effects would be to produce discontinuities of varying strengths. The more advanced the integration process in a given region, the more noticeable the discontinuity in global terms.

From a politico-economic perspective, this description has an interesting and nonobvious implication. In regions where degrees of integration are minimal (which is to say everywhere but Europe and the North Atlantic, including other developed countries with strong attachments to them like Japan or Australia), more amorphous discontinuities are penetrated through processes of linkage politics.(31) If such processes are looked upon as undesirable, then the most apparent way out is the strengthening of regional discontinuities with the rest of the world. This brings us to the formulations advanced in the 1950s and 1960s by Raul Prebisch, Executive Secretary of the Economic Commission for Latin America.(32) Prebisch's analysis was based on the "terms of trade" problem of less developed regions exporting primary goods and having to import manufactured products, with the prices of the latter always rising faster than those of the former. The original proposal for escaping from this vicious cycle was import substitution whereby needed products could be provided through local industrialization. Had it worked, the end result would have been a more encapsulated regional system with greater degrees of discontinuity vis-a-vis the rest of the world.

The possibility of integration producing regional systems that are encapsulated, or those which "spillover, spill-around, muddle-about, spill-back," and so forth,(33) leads to a key consideration for transregional relations raised by the model: Will its end result be the world of 1984 with large regional blocs opposing each other in some macabre balance of power? The other side of the coin is implied by those who stress the basic isomorphism between national and international integration – namely, that regional integration is itself only a stage in the evolution of some kind of world state. Similar questions were raised more than a decade ago by Bruce Russett in predicting "some further integration in certain regions" which would have minimal effects on global patterns, although he hastened to add:

> If not accompanied also by stronger global ties, regional integration in itself is a choice against the cross-pressures or cross-cutting solidarities that bind, however weakly, the diverse nations from all parts of the world. The role of cross-pressures in preventing rigidity in political alignments has long been recognized as crucial.(34)

Unfortunately, the integration model does not provide direct answers for questions concerning its more long-term transregional and global effects. James Caporaso's scrupulous attempt to address some external consequences of European regional integration in terms of systemic variables including "inequality, dependence, polarization, and symmetry" was largely inconclusive.(35) Employing data on shared organizational memberships for various European regional groupings from 1945 through 1972, periods of "structural decline" (1945-1955), "structural increase" (1956-1963), and "leveling off" (1963-1972) were identifiable, as well as the fact that the European Economic Community (EEC) countries ranked first in terms of comemberships. EEC members' self-preoccupation was also reflected in rising systemic concentration and an increase in structural polarization during the early 1960s. Treating several indicators of politico-economic integration as independent variables in regression equations for the systemic variables, however, yielded few substantive results (although the majority of the equations were statistically significant).

Treatments of the diplomatic effects of the integration model on transregional and/or global patterns are more common, but similarly inconclusive. Werner Feld has found limited support for Philippe Schmitter's "externalization hypothesis" (that integrative strategies increase the degree of influence over third parties) without the expected intra-European effects.(36) The Lome Convention of 1975 linking various less developed countries with the EEC has been suggested as producing an economic pattern of specialization which "could be detrimental to some of the dynamic gains envisaged" by the Economic Community of West African States (ECOWAS).(37) EEC attempts to insure energy supplies through discussions with the Arab members of the Organization of Petroleum Exporting Countries (OPEC) have met with only partial success, due, in large measure, to the close external ties between the EEC and the United States, the external power whose impact is explained poorly by the integration model itself.(38)

What all of this adds up to for patterns of transregional relations remains somewhat unclear. The integration model itself is more theoretically sophisticated than that of exchange, but lacks precision in its transregional implications. When the interface between politics and economics is accounted for, the two models have much in common, resulting in a largely status quo world with profound discontinuities between "haves" and "have-nots" persisting. In policy terms, integration is, perhaps, the European "social democratic perspective" to America's "monopolistic liberalism," something manifested by official positions regarding NIEO.(39) Both regions are advantaged by current global processes, and the failures of integration in the Third World suggest the limitations of trying to generalize the European experience (or the American one for that matter). Successful integration would create those economies of scale envisioned by the American model, but in and of itself the integration model does not provide ways for transcending historical circumstances with the same degree of assurance implied by its American counterpart. The transregional patterns apparent from the integration model rely a great deal on practical linkages established in the colonial era prior to most of the third World's independence. Accepting this basis for transregional relations, the integration model does allow us to isolate certain key variables, but at the same time does not provide for the aggregation of their global effects. The final model of transregional relations rests on exactly this kind of aggregation.

Exploitation: Centers and Peripheries

A final model for transregional relations stands in marked contrast to the previous two. In the first place, exchange and integration are ultimately "political" in the sense of emphasizing the effects of actions undertaken by official (usually governmental) decision makers. Exploitation, however, views these actions as more or less derivative from an "economic" calculus. In the second place, exchange and integration imply that those less advantaged by current global processes will eventually be able to "develop" through careful imitation. Exploitation argues this is highly improbable, if not impossible, because advantages can only exist at others' expense. In the third place, the economic orientation of integration and especially exchange is a capitalist one, and that of exploitation is Marxist, although with varying degrees of orthodoxy. A final interesting contrast is that the exploitation model only recently has been accepted within the broad confines of the social scientific "mainstream."

A critical role in this acceptance has been played by the body of dependency theory which emerged from the context of United States-Latin American transregional relations. Raymond Duvall points out: "The term 'dependence' is heard frequently in discussions of contemporary national and transnational relations. The popularity is, in part, a result of a widespread acceptance and voguish adoption of theories of contemporary capitalist imperialism, of which the term is a common element. Indeed, an important part of imperialism theory is denoted by the term. . . ."(40) Yet, along with this voguishness and acceptance has come a proliferation of terminology with fuzzy interconnections, among which are "dependence," "dependency," "interdependence," and "imperialism." James Caporaso has clarified the first two concepts with implications for the third, and his comments merit citation at length:

> From the literature on dependence, one can abstract two predominant usages: dependency as the absence of actor autonomy and dependence as a highly asymmetric form of interdependence. With respect to the former usage, one frequently hears of dependency as reflecting nonautonomous developmental possibilities (especially in the Latin American literature), as the lack of true independence from foreign or transnational influences, or as the presence of a series of related domestic, external, and transnational influences, or as the presence of a series of related domestic, external, and transnational characteristics. . . .However, we often hear the term dependence used in a different way, as an imbalance in the relationship between two actors. In this definition, the opposite of dependence is interdependence – not autonomy. While autonomy rests on the idea of self-control, interdependence rests on the notion of mutual control. . . .Dependence as asymmetric interdependence is immediately a dyadic concept and a "net" concept, i.e., it is measured by looking at the differential between A's reliance on B and B's reliance on A. The concept of dependency, however, requires that we look at a unit in relation to all external influences or, as a variant of this, the most important external influences.(41)

Whatever nuances surround the concepts in the dependency tradition, they exhibit a common analytical underpinning with reference to global processes that result in the exploitation of one region by another. Moreover, as long as the present capitalist world economy persists, there are few avenues of escape for the exploited because the various processes are mutually reinforcing. The structure of international trade creates export enclaves in less developed regions.(42) Incentives do not exist for the less developed to produce for their own needs, but rather those of the more prosperous, reflected in the terms of trade emphasized by Prebisch. This global inequality has intranational effects. A relatively small elite segment prospers as a result of the export enclaves, and this exacerbates conditions of domestic inequality, increasing sociopolitical distortions. The inability to produce what is really needed for economic modernization in the less developed regions creates further reliance on the export enclaves to maintain international liquidity, allowing relative economic disadvantages to snowball. Thus, a vicious cycle of ever-growing inequality is apparent both within and between countries and regions.

From the perspective of exploitation, the global processes emphasized by the exchange and integration models become thinly disguised attempts to preserve Euro-American dominance. Not only do Latin American relations provide fertile ground for the exploitation model, but also American global preeminence in the post-World War II era. Two points are worthy of emphasis in this latter regard. First, the United States was the principal architect of the Bretton Woods economic regime, and even its post-1971 disarray had more disastrous effects for the less developed. "Petrodollar prosperity" may have some symbolic value with respect to at least parts of the Third World being able to bargain more equally, but its real effects have been to worsen the lot of those who can least afford higher oil prices. Second, the United States is most closely identified with the global proliferation of MNC impact. MNCs are more significant to exploitive processes than their home governments, even that of the United States. The controversy involving MNC activities has been cogently summarized within the context of dependency by Theodore Moran:

> The benefits of foreign investment are "poorly" (or "unfairly" or "unequally") distributed between the multinational and the host, or the country pays "too high" a price for what it gets, or the company siphons off an economic "surplus" that could otherwise be used to finance internal development. . . .Multinational corporations create distortions within the local economy. . . .Foreign investors pervert or subvert host country political processes 1) by coopting the local elites; and/or 2) by using their influence in their home countries to bring pressure to keep host governments "in line"; and/or 3) by structuring the international system to respond to their multinational needs to the detriment of host authorities.(43)

Exploration of these and related propositions have so far yielded inconclusive results. As one reviewer points out, "Although there is mounting evidence in support of dependency theory, the research cannot be labeled as definitive owing to the inconsistencies and limitations uncovered."(44) Various attempts have been made to summarize the global impacts of these processes in structural terms, and they all lead in the direction of what has been called the shared core of imperialism theory. . .that unequal global realization of social values results from a complex of structured asymmetric relations among societies, the most basic of which are various forms of dependence, domination, and exploitation. The many variants and different particularizations of this core argument emphasize different social values whose unequal realization is of interest (although economic development is most standard) and, especially, different forms of mechanisms of relational asymmetry.(45)

A particularly important formulation of the exploitation model has been advanced by Johan Galtung in his "structural theory of imperialism." For Galtung, imperialism is "a dominance relation between collectivities, particularly between nations. . .that splits up collectivities and relates some of the parts to each other in relations of harmony of interest, and other parts in relations of disharmony of interest, or conflict of interest."(46) Nations are classified as being either "Central" or "Peripheral," and within each nation "centers" and "peripheries" also exist. The structure of imperialism is such that there is harmony of interest between the centers of both Central and Peripheral nations. This is established through a system of "bridgeheads" which have been constructed by Central nations in the Peripheries (as in export enclaves dependent upon more developed regions). Since there is a greater net disharmony of interest within Peripheral compared to Central nations, disharmony of interest exists between the Central peripheries and the Peripheral peripheries. The processes of imperialism involve two "mechanisms," the "vertical interaction relation" and the "feudal interaction structure." Global patterns are monopolized by the various Central nations. Peripheral nation peripheries do not interact meaningfully with Central peripheries or with the centers of Central nations to which they are not significantly related. This means that transregional interaction remains "feudal," with its vertical quality reinforced because each Peripheral nation is related to only one Center.

Terminological differences aside, up to this point the Galtung formulation does not really vary that much from the classical theories of Lenin or Hobson. What differentiates it from them, however, making it extremely significant as a model of transregional relations, are two implications Galtung draws when he begins discussing imperialism in temporal terms. First, Galtung considers there to be an inherent similarity among all kinds of international organizations, be they governmental (IGOs), nongovernmental (NGOs), or those encompassing a mixed constituency. This is because their raison d'etre is to provide links between centers and peripheries. Thus, the activities of MNCs (his example is General Motors) and those of the "International Communist Movement" (involving both governmental and nonstate actors) are fundamentally analogous. Second, in contradistinction to the exchange model's emphasis on free markets for political ideas and that of integration on decision making within international organizations, Galtung suggests: "Instead of seeing democracy as a consequence or a condition for economic development within certain nations, it can (also) be seen as a condition for exercising effective control over Periphery nations."(47) The reasoning is straightforward – Central peripheries have a greater stake in what is going on than Peripheral peripheries.

While the Galtung model and the dependency theories to which it is closely related have not been proven, they so far have resisted wholesale falsification. Taken together, they emphasize simultaneously the profound inequalities existing within and between countries and regions. This does create something of a data problem for assessing transregional relations because the causal mechanisms postulated are largely reciprocal and operationally complex, as is recognized by Richard Fagen when he points out:

> The logic of the international relations of capitalism both stems from and leads back to the logic of capitalist production and distribution at the national level. . . .(A)lthough peripheral capitalism may, under certain circumstances, be relatively successful in accumulating capital, it cannot solve the linked problems of national disintegration, widening socioeconomic gaps, relative and even absolute poverty, and the coming penetration and distortion of national economies and societies.(48)

As a result, empirical tests of the exploitation model have produced widely varying results. Most often the effects of exploitation are operationalized in terms of the dependent less developed regions, and the kinds of causal mechanisms emphasized in the overall model are assessed only indirectly. The attempt by Robert Kaufman and his colleagues to test Latin American dependency in the 1960s employing data that, in some cases, went back through the 1930s yielded mixed findings.(49) Modernization as envisioned by the exchange model had more significant sociopolitical effects than dependency. This led Patrick McGowan and Dale Smith to suggest rather than dependency a more orthodox "Marxist interpretation of the Kaufman paper: capitalist trade and investment (so-called dependency) stimulate economic growth which, under the capitalist mode of production, leads to income inequality."(50) This is surely ironic since the entire complex of theories subsumed by the exploitation model, including dependency and imperialism, has Marxist roots. McGowan and Smith's own research best supported the more orthodox Marxist model among the various competitors considered, and they concluded: "(C)ross-national variations in economic performance in tropical Africa during the 1960s have two causes: 1) economic development potential directly enhances performance, and 2) potential leads to market dependency – or integration into the international capitalist economy – and this pattern in turn enhances economic performance."(51)

Here again, however, it is not possible for the research design to incorporate the various actions and/or policy decisions which contribute to the transregional patterns the aggregate data reflect. Nor is it demonstrated directly that those in the more developed regions, whether they be MNC employees or more peripheral citizens, are profiteering as a result of the existence of these patterns. Marx's original notion of exploitation was a humanistic one, involving the difference between the value produced by labor and the actual value workers received. Asserting that transregional patterns ultimately reflect the greed of individual actions undertaken by those who are relatively well-off involves the postulation of an operationally problematic social scientific universal which, because it either cannot be measured directly or does not vary, ceases to be very interesting theoretically.

Nonetheless, the transregional patterns explained by the exploitation model alert us to relationships between the more and less developed that are either not dealt with or glossed over by exchange and integration. All three models, perhaps, could prove to be complementary rather than contradictory, with one or another supplying better descriptions for particular global patterns. Any model involves simplification of what are increasingly complex global phenomena, and, in this regard, it is a good idea to remember the place of models in scientific inquiry: "Models are undeniably beautiful, and a man may be justly proud to be seen in their company. But they may have their hidden vices. The question is, after all, not only whether they are good to look at, but whether we can live happily with them."(52)

REGIONS AS SYSTEMS: SOME COMMENTS AND CRITICISMS

To this point the three models and the particular formulations they encompass have been presented more or less in their own terms. In this section we shall discuss various criteria with reference to which they can be evaluated. It was pointed out initially that systems in global politics may be defined as "unique concatenations of <u>actors</u> and <u>issues</u> recognizable through <u>behavior</u>." Each of the key concepts in this definition is useful as a category for bringing international relations theory to bear on the models. Two related problems are raised by this evaluation. They are the meaning of "an empirical systems model" and the ways in which regions should be defined.

The Models and International Relations Theory

"Actors" are simply any entity with a capacity for undertaking autonomous behavior which, when such behavior crosses the borders of a state or has an impact beyond them, is part of global (rather than the somewhat misnomered "inter<u>national</u>") politics. Two research foci summarize theoretical developments in the last decade relevant to how actors are conceived: 1) "nonstate actors" (variously called "transnational actors," "NGOs," and so forth) behaving with transregional and/or global impact; 2) nation states not constituting unitary wholes, but rather congeries of bureaucracies and organizations, any of which can be capable of independent global action.(53)

The exchange model is weakest on the basis of these considerations. Rationality connotes governmental ability to act as a unitary whole. Modeling is so general that what the rest of the world is supposed to be able to emulate involves the totality of the American experience. The benefits of global interaction somehow will be distributed to the advantage of all members of the national society. Even recognition of MNC activities within the American model is partly compartmentalized as "nonpolitical" through the idea of transivity.

In contrast to the American model, exploitation deals more directly with the role of MNCs. Yet recognition of particular nonstate activities is not necessarily tantamount to adequate treatment of various actor types. The argument that governmental policies have economic interests as their underlying cause is a debatable way of simplifying uncertainty. In fact, it tends to distort the extent to which governmental policies represent bureaucratic and nonstate inputs, and this is not only true for the more developed world. Finally, the suggestion in Galtung's imperialism model that the overriding purpose of all IGOs and NGOs is providing arenas for further center-periphery domination must be subjected to careful scrutiny. In the first place, this proposition implies such actors are all of a piece, seemingly denying the functional logic normally used for differentiating among them.(54) In the second place, the idea of IGOs as arenas for intermixing national interests discounts their autonomous impacts by rendering them mere resultants of state-centric political forces.

The integration model, therefore, proves most satisfactory in its treatment of actors. Nonstate actors, including MNCs, reflect transnational processes that are explained by the functional logic which not only gives the neofunctional approach its name, but also produces the very IGOs that are its reference points. Yet a peculiar development has occurred within regional integration theory. Ernst Haas, one of its veritable "intellectual godfathers," has labeled it "obsolescent."(55) His reasoning in doing so is related to the second of the theoretical foci mentioned above and is worth examining in some detail because of its implications for the remainder of our argument.   .

Haas is concerned with three "properties of the familiar theories of regional integration. . .1) the presumed predictability of the institutional outcomes of the integration process; 2) the tendency to treat the region undergoing integration as a self-contained geographical space; 3) the parallel tendency to regard that region's practices of increasing the centralization of joint tasks and concerns as an autonomous process following its own unique rule."(56) All of these properties are related to the regional and transregional milieus in which actors behave, and such milieus have now come to be "turbulent fields:"

> Turbulence is the term we bestow on the confused and clashing perceptions of organizational actors which find themselves in a setting of great social complexity. The number of actors is very large. Each pursues a variety of objectives which are mutually incompatible; but each is also unsure of the trade-offs between

the objectives. Each actor is tied into a network of inter-dependencies with other actors that are as confused as the first. Yet some of the objectives sought by each cannot be obtained without cooperation from others. A turbulent field, then, is a policy space in which this type of confusion dominates discussion and negotiations.(57)

Turbulent fields imply newer conceptions of actor rationality which are more in line with recent decision-making models like John Stein-bruner's than with earlier ones based on the incrementalism so im-portant to functionalism.(58) "Fragmented issue linkage" means that any problem must be approached piecemeal on an issue-by-issue basis leading to often unintended and relatively unpredictable outcomes. This requires that the systemic picture presented by earlier integration theory be opened more widely from the perspective of actors, issues, and behavior. In Haas' words, "The paradox of all this is that as we increasingly subordinate the discussion of regional integration to the consideration of overall interdependence, we undermine the theoretical and ideological tenets which in the past seemed to point toward increasing regional integration."(59)

These tenets remain, however, and, especially if not understood deterministically in terms of increasing integration, contribute to a more accurate view of both actors and issues. "Issues" are <u>what</u> behavior is about, subject matters involving a diversity of possible outcomes. They represent incentives for action while, at the same time, serving as the substantive building blocks of regional, transregional, and global systems. Where the integration model previously had been restricted largely to political outcomes involving the economic, tech-nical, and scientific issues emphasized by its functional logic, Haas' criticisms suggest an even greater possibility to account for complex-ities brought about through issue diversity. This possibility remains fairly implicit within the exchange model, and the recent tendency of American decision makers to rally around the catch phrase of "inter-dependence" introduces a cautionary note. The key relates to just how broadly transitivity may be conceived. On the one hand, the Cold War perspective was that just about all issues could be aggregated by a power-political logic, in a sense transforming everything into what Stanley Hoffmann called "high" as opposed to "low" politics.(60) On the other, if the exchange model is seen as ultimately producing what Wolfram Hanrieder terms "the domestication of international pol-itics,"(61) then a greater variety of issues should be able to be encompassed by it.

The exploitation model actually may be best when it comes to accounting for issue <u>diversity</u>. Indeed, Galtung's treatment encompasses five different "types of imperialism – economic, political, military, communication, and cultural."(62) Yet it introduces a further complica-tion for considering issue <u>complexity</u>, or the tendency of various issues, such as those involving energy or the environment, to be associated with unintended consequences. Because issues serve only as opportunities for the relatively advantaged to continue their exploitation of those who are less so, the idea of unintended consequences makes little sense from this model's point of view.

Finally, there is the concept of "behavior," which we shall conceptualize along lines derived from the perspective of "event data" as including actors, targets, and observable actions. All three models have different pretheoretic expectations in this regard. The integration model is the most severely constrained, not only limited to what are by and large institutional contexts, but also because within them cooperation is supposed to be the norm. Haas' eschewal offers some hope regarding the latter, but does not really even begin to question the institutional bias. Exploitation is the most interesting theoretically, but this very quality involves operational dilemmas. The model's Marxist underpinning would seem to skew it in the direction of conflict, although contemporary formulations allow for behavioral variety (as in Galtung's "harmony, disharmony, and conflict of interest"). The difficulty is that "what one sees may not necessarily be what one gets" because center cooperation eventually may lead to the conflictful overthrow of the entire structure.

The assumptions involved in the exchange model, therefore, appear comparatively superior, perhaps in part due to their minimalistic nature. "Tit-for-tat" interaction implies that both conflict and cooperation involve largely self-reinforcing processes, a proposition supported by the relative potency of "action-reaction models" in empirical international relations research.(63) Exchange, however, brings with it the additional connotation that both parties benefit from interaction, making it fair to conclude that a covert skew toward cooperation, or at least for the persistence of extant patterns, is in evidence.

Empirical Systems and Transregional Relations

The system construct, made relevant for international relations more than two decades ago, is responsible for much of the theoretical sophistication in the study of regional systems. Our use of it so far, while it may seem a bit idiosyncratic from the perspective of Morton Kaplan's original formulation,(64) is, nonetheless, within this tradition. Yet the system construct has, in some ways, posed complications for regional analysis. This has been due largely to the fact that the attempt to draw a macroanalytic "big picture" is bound to introduce some distortion. Such distortion may not have seemed particularly important during the height of Cold War bipolarity, but, in a world of multiple systems, the peculiarities of each can be crucial. "Mice that do not roar" could one day, and as Jorge Dominquez has suggested:

Research in the field of international politics has often focused on the "center" of the international system. . . .(T)he dominant traits of international politics in the peripheries arise from characteristics of subsystems in the peripheries. These traits are not mere extensions of the center. When systemwide issues arise (e.g., communism, economic growth, colonialism), the policies of countries in the peripheries are still strongly shaped by "local" or subsystemic factors.(65)

Dominquez' argument, which rings true enough, does raise a significant terminological problem – the existence of regions as "subsystems" with reference to "the international system." Virtually all treatments of regions assume that they constitute separable "levels-of-analysis" which can be interposed between the nation state and the international system.(66) Michael Brecher speaks of "subordinate state systems," Louis Cantori and Steven Spiegel's earlier work of "subordinate systems," Bruce Russett of "international subsystems," and William Thompson summarizes the literature dealing with "the regional subsystem."(67) Even when Cantori and Spiegel later refine their "empirical systems approach" they remark: "A focus upon the region permits theoretical formulations that interpose a unit of analysis between that of the discreteness of the nation state and an undifferentiated international system."(68)

The underlying difficulty with viewing regions as a rigid level-of-analysis can in many ways be traced back to Kaplan's separation of "system dominance" from "subsystem dominance" with reference to his various models.(69) Theorizing from the perspective of a largely bipolar world which had replaced that of the balance of power through historical processes involving various fits and starts, the empirical occurrence of subsystem dominance must have been hard to contemplate. Harder still would be a world of "complex interdependence" in which dominance was of questionable relevance with multiple channels connecting societies, issues demonstrating an absence of hierarchy, and military force being less in evidence.(70) "Dominance" implied "subsystems" which could be swallowed up within "larger systems." Today such a swallowing appears increasingly unlikely empirically and unprofitable theoretically because the critical concern has become the ways in which systems are linked to one another.

Cantori and Spiegel's regional analyses recognize these linkages, although they end up being unable to take this recognition to its logical conclusion because of the way systems theory is itself understood. Dividing the world into 15 regions, each with a "core sector," a "peripheral sector," and an "intrusive system," they deal with basically two kinds of linkages – those between cores and peripheries, and those which are due to activities originating in the intrusive system.(71) In the case of the former, the primary relationship reflects alienation, but this creates problems because it is defined in terms of four Parsonian (and hence tautological) pattern variables ("level of cohesion, nature of communications, level of power, and structure of interrelations").(72) In the case of the latter, the linkage is identified by "the politically significant (as opposed to <u>insignificant</u>) participation of external powers in the international relations of the subordinate system."(73) Yet the methods of participation by which intrusive system linkages are operationalized do not reflect such political significance/insignificance.(74)

Besides providing the basis on which core-periphery linkage is defined, the pattern variables also are used to construct a typology of "integrative, consolidative, cohesive, and coherent" regional systems.(75) The different systems are then connected with conflict and competition among intrusive powers, but in a fashion that muddies the possibility of intuiting the <u>direction</u> of the causal connection. Is it the pattern variables or the types of linkage which cause intrusive competition, and what of the conflict's effects on the pattern variables themselves? This problem later was clarified somewhat when Cantori and Spiegel argued that "the assignment of independent variable status to the regional system is premature," and that "contextual variables (for example, social, economic, political, and organizational cohesion) become intervening variables between the independent variable of state behavior and the dependent variable of the regional system."(76) If this formulation provides a sense of causality, however, it is obscured soon again when they turn to sample explanatory hypotheses in which what were supposed to have been separate independent and dependent variables are all mixed together:

1) When a great power achieves hegemony over an area, the level of international conflict is reduced, international cooperation intensifies, and domestic tensions increase. . . .2) "Balkanization," or the division of areas into comparatively small units, delimits international conflict by reducing the capacity of the resulting states to engage in war and by reducing the interest of great powers in the outcomes should international tensions increase, thereby isolating the conflict from global outcomes.(77)

We have dwelt upon Cantori and Spiegel's efforts not only because they are largely representative of more sophisticated regional analyses, but also because they reveal some of the underlying difficulties relevant to comprehending transregional relations. These difficulties include three interrelated points. First, transregional relations represent a specific kind of connection between polities and aspects of their global political environments, better known as "linkage politics." James Rosenau's formulation of this concept allowed for the possibility that linkages could become "fused" – "certain outputs and inputs continuously reinforce each other and are thus best viewed as forming a reciprocal relationship."(78) Such fused linkages are appropriately regarded as systems in their own rights, and this raises the second point: how systems can best be understood theoretically.

There are basically two ways of doing so – what can be called "system as theory" and "system as framework." Both are "empirical" in the sense of identifying entities which exist in a "real world." The former, however, approaches the world <u>deductively</u>, tending to "close" the system by viewing <u>it</u> as "reality," and Ernst Haas points out such systems have a teleology which "is built in: it is to adapt in order to survive."(79) This is Kaplan's legacy and, despite some disclaimers,

Cantori and Spiegel as well as most other regionalists are heirs to it. In contrast, a more inductive logic conceives of systems as "open," with reality represented by behaving actors. Citing J. David Singer's view that a system is "nothing more than an aggregation of human beings (plus their physical milieu) who are sufficiently interdependent to share a common fate. . .or to have actions of some of them usually affecting the lives of many of them," Haas contends: "Systems, as Singer defines them, have no purpose. They are taxonomies devised by the researcher to permit the specification of hypothesized non-random events and trends in the hope of gradually mapping reality. If everyone used the construct in this sense, we would have no problem."(80)

Yet analytic problems persist, especially those connected to our final point. Whether linkage politics or systems represent the explicit substantive focus, theorists have to select some way of representing the reality with which they are dealing. Almost invariably they have done so on the basis of <u>national</u> geography, and the result is illustrated well by reference again to Cantori and Spiegel: "(T)he relation between the emerging study of transnational politics and regional systems theory. . .is probably closer than students of both subjects have generally recognized. Though empirical systems theory is more sympathetic to the 'state-centric' approach than Keohane and Nye, it encompasses the types of relations covered by them."(81) The way Cantori and Spiegel would have it do so, however, is by continuing to assume the primacy of the nation state construct as the benchmark against which transnational (and transregional) relations are gauged. This actually ignores the implications of the nonstate and bureaucratic research foci mentioned in the previous section. In other words, Cantori and Spiegel, and others as well, may present solid regional analysis, but the conception of systems on which they base it leaves something to be desired.

The nation state itself constitutes a system rather than an actor. By constructing regions that are mere aggregations of nation states, reality is transformed so that transregional relations are not engaged in by actors whose geographic origins embody one among many classification devices. Instead, the globe is characterized by hulking continents moving to and fro. Thus, most empirical propositions relevant to transregional relations seem to rest on a somewhat contrived basis. This is, indeed, unfortunate since transregional relations reflecting intrusive-penetrative behavior can be considered, by one reckoning, the most popular focus of regional analysis.(82) In order to discover an appropriate underpinning for approaching transregional relations that encompasses transnational politics in a more suitable fashion, therefore, it becomes necessary to inquire about the ways regions themselves are defined.

The Definitional Dilemma Revisited

The regional definition dilemma can be stated quite succinctly. On the one hand is an apparent geographic reality that inspection of a map reveals. On the other is Bruce Russett's well-known conclusion of more than a decade ago:

> There is no region or aggregate of national units that can in the very strict sense of boundary congruence be identified as a subsystem of the international system....(S)uch a subsystem must be identified empirically by the agreement of several different criteria....Even allowing for this arbitrariness, how- ever, there is in our findings no area where the inclusions and the exclusions are the same over all criteria.(83)

Russett's study remains the leading example of an "open" per- spective on regional systems. With an inductive factor analytic meth- odology, he attempted to delineate regions based on five criteria, "social and cultural homogeneity, political attitudes or external behav- ior, political institutions, economic interdependence, and geographical proximity,"(84) and reached the conclusion cited above. After exam- ining various clusters through paired comparisons, however, Russett did sound a more cautiously hopeful note:

> For there is indeed, for each major aggregate, a core, a limited number of states found in each of the clusters. Nor is the disagreement from one criterion to the next so violent that we cannot expect to find the same states associated from one analysis to the next....Thus, in a general sense the regional labels we use when discussing international relations or compara- tive politics do hold.(85)

The question remains, though, of what such labels reflect. William Thompson's review of the regional literature listed 21 different at- tributes, demonstrating apparently little consensus about anything save the common regional label.(86) The average mean for "interanalyst agreement" was a dismal .21. Nonetheless, 86 percent of the analysts did include at least two attributes which Thompson was able to suggest "come closest to supplying the necessary and sufficient conditions for applying the concept of a regional subsystem: 1) proximity or primary stress on a geographic region, 2) actors' pattern of relations or interactions exhibit a particular degree of regularity and intensity."

This may appear little more than a starting point, perhaps not a very good one at that. It is obvious that, before we can talk about transregional relations, some handle is needed for deciding what consti- tutes a region, but all that seems to exist is a morass composed of scholarly disagreement, state-centricity, and confusion over the "sys- tem master-concept." Yet Thompson's two attributes do end up pro- viding a way out when they are employed in conjunction with the constructs of "actors, issues, and behavior" which have been introduced previously. The first attribute, geographical proximity, will be invoked arbitrarily as providing the definition for region. (Notice that we are not using the term "regional system" here.) Keeping with the practice followed in this volume, eight such regions can be identified — Western Europe, Eastern Europe-USSR, North America, East Asia, South Asia, Middle East, Latin America, and Africa.

Thompson's second attribute approximates what is meant by a system, although recall that the definition employed herein includes issues as well as actors and behavior. This will make it possible to operationalize systems in a fashion that avoids the pitfalls which have been discussed. The definitional dilemma vanishes, and the following kinds of questions can begin to be answered: What regions are themselves systems? Which transregional patterns constitute systems in their own rights? What are the linkages among regional/transregional systems? We shall turn to this task in the next section.

REGIONAL AND TRANSREGIONAL PATTERNS: THE MULTIPLE SYSTEMS IN GLOBAL POLITICS

Having suggested systems to be "unique concatenations of actors and issues recognizable through behavior," it remains to give this definition operational meaning. Based upon a random sample of 48 dates for the year 1975, a data set was generated composed of 3,169 individual "events." Each event included at least an actor, a target, a behavior, and an issue. The actors, targets, and issues were coded as specifically as possible based upon the news report provided by the New York Times. To correct for the possible distortion that reliance upon a single American coding source might introduce, the following procedures were adopted. Those "foreign" events (that is, involving actors, targets, and indirect targets none of which were American) were coded automatically. Events in U.S. foreign relations were not coded unless the actor, target, or indirect target had origins outside of the geographical confines of the United States.(87)

Undigested and unanalyzed, such data are of little utility, especially given the specificity with which actors, targets, indirect targets, and issues were coded. Treating issues as the unit of analysis yielded 4,839 divided into more than 250 categories. The names of more than 1,000 separate actors/targets/indirect targets appeared. Hence, it was necessary to aggregate these data for meaningful analysis to take place. Actors and targets were divided into 72 categories (indirect targets do not play a part in the current analysis), and the issues placed into 61 different groups (see Table 13.1).

Because as full a picture of global interaction as possible was desired, dyadic combinations based upon the 72 actor/target categories were generated. There turned out to be 874 such dyads, and these were then aggregated into 80 dyadic categories. The decision rules employed reflected the raw number of issues (rather than their distribution) with which the dyad was involved (with 40, approximately 10 percent of the total number of issues found in the events, serving as a flexible lower boundary). An informal, step-wise procedure was followed whereby each part of a dyad was named as specifically as possible ("President:Con-

Table 13.1 Factor Analysis Used for

VARIABLES:	1	2	3	4	5	6	7	8	9	10	11	12
Arms Sales	.81											
W Eur & Thrd Wrld	.93											
Western Solidarity	.75											
Consumer Organiz	.90											
Superpower Aid		.34	.52									
Indochina Refugee		.85										
Indochina Military		.66										
US in Indochina		.76										
Individual Norms		.59										
Indochina Pol Rel		.60										
Information Exchg			.47									
Business-State			.88									
Global Crime			.52									
Glo Econ Interdep			.83									
Sinai				.68								
US Aid to Israel				.72								
Superpow in Mid E				.63								
Lebanon Civil War				-.32								
US Exec-Cong Rel				.32								
Race & Ethnic Div				.48								
Mid E as Glo Prob				.54							.47	
Energy					.90							
Raw Material					.37							
Sea Bed					.92							
E Bloc Cohesion						.96						
Global Communism						.78						
W Eur Detente						.63						
Port Civil Control							-.95					
Port Polit Conf							-.91					
Domest Labor/Decay								.88				
UK Global Role								.46				
Other Dem Pol Iss								.75				
Foreign in Angola									.95			
Control Angola Gov									.92			
Post Peron										.80		
Terror & Control										.59		
Latin Instability										.91		
Cuban Communism											.87	
US in Latin America											.88	
PLO Recognition												.85
Israel N Front												.32
UN Role												
Thrd Wrld Develop												
India Subcont Instab												
US in Asia												
Othr Major in Asia												
Global Inflation												
Rout Intragov												
African Instability												
Detente SALT												
Islamic Unity												
Arab Economic Role												
Culture Sports												
Cyprus												
Trade & Money												
Colonialism												
Spanish Instability												
Rout Transact												
Church & State												

*All insignificant factor loadings (below .30) have been omitted to make Table
one factor, constituting "system linkages." Two issues ("Israel E Front" and "S
(eigenvalues greater than unity) was employed to control the number of factors
was 78.3%. The factors with their amounts of total variance explained be

Deriving Issue-based Systems*

	13	14	15	16	17	18	19	20	21	22	23
Arms Sales	.81										
W Eur & Thrd Wrld											
Western Solidarity			-.51								
Consumer Organiz											
Superpower Aid								.34			.34
Indochina Refugee											
Indochina Military											
US in Indochina											.35
Individual Norms											
Indochina Pol Rel											
Information Exchg											
Business-State											
Global Crime									-.38		
Glo Econ Interdep											
Sinai											
US Aid to Israel											
Superpow in Mid E											
Lebanon Civil War											
US Exec-Cong Rel											.57
Race & Ethnic Div	.64										
Mid E as Glo Prob						.37					
Energy											
Raw Material		-.39									
Sea Bed											
E Bloc Cohesion											
Global Communism											
W Eur Detente											
Port Civil Control											
Port Polit Conf											
Domest Labor/Decay											
UK Global Role							.31				
Other Dem Pol Iss											
Foreign in Angola											
Control Angola Gov											
Post Peron											
Terror & Control							.40				
Latin Instability											
Cuban Communism											
US in Latin America											
PLO Recognition											
Israel N Front	.46										
UN Role	.72										
Thrd Wrld Develop		-.71									
India Subcont Instab		-.55									
US in Asia			.74								
Othr Major in Asia			.67								
Global Inflation				-.74							
Rout Intragov					.90						
African Instability					.35						
Detente SALT						-.55					
Islamic Unity						.54					
Arab Economic Role						.42					
Culture Sports						-.33					
Cyprus							.77				
Trade & Money							.69				
Colonialism								-.62			
Spanish Instability								-.55			
Rout Transact									.61		
Church & State									.73		

ore readable. Underlined issues and factor loadings were significant to more than
trica") did not load significantly on any factors. The "rule of thumb" criterion
are rotated. The amount of the total variance accounted for by the factor analysis
tation and common variance after rotation are given in percentages in table 13.2.

Table 13.2

FACTOR	TOTAL VARIANCE	COMMON VARIANCE	FACTOR	TOTAL VARIANCE	COMMON VARIANCE
1	7.5	10.4	13	2.7	3.4
2	6.2	8.7	14	2.6	3.2
3	5.7	7.7	15	2.5	3.1
4	5.1	6.9	16	2.4	2.8
5	4.6	6.2	17	2.4	2.7
6	4.5	6.0	18	2.1	2.5
7	4.1	5.6	19	2.1	2.3
8	3.6	4.9	20	1.9	1.9
9	3.6	4.7	21	1.8	1.8
10	3.3	4.3	22	1.7	1.8
11	3.2	4.1	23	1.7	1.6
12	2.9	3.7			

gress," "American Actors:Egypt," "Minor Europeans:EEC Countries"). Where this was not possible at least one part of the dyad (which could be named most specifically) provided a criterion ("UK Bureaucracies:Most Others," "PLO:Non-Middle East," "MNC:Developed Governments," "Southern Africa," "South Korea:All Others"). Finally, there were several residual categories ("Other US Societal," "Residual Western Interaction"). It is at this point that the system definition employed herein acquires operational significance.

A matrix was generated for which the 80 dyads served as the rows. The colums were the 61 grouped issues. Each cell in the matrix represented the number of actions along a given dyad that were concerned with a particular issue. Therefore, the matrix included actors (the rows), issues (the columns), and behavior (the individual cell entries). The notion of "unique concatenation" was operationalized through the use of factor analysis.(88) An R-factor analysis employing orthogonal (varimax) rotation was performed on this matrix, meaning that the factors were based on the correlations between the columns (issues) and that the resulting factor axes were themselves uncorrelated. Each factor, then, represented "a unique concatenation of actors and issues recognizable through behavior." In other words, each factor constitutes a system, and the results of the analysis (given in Table 13.1) reveal a "world of multiple issue-based systems."

The next analytic task was to decide what each system (factor) represented in substantive terms on the basis of the issues which loaded significantly (greater than .30) on it. These "system names" (see Fig. 13.1) demonstrate that, from the perspective of regional international politics as they are conventionally understood, some of our results raise questions. Can an individual country really be considered a region in and of itself ("7. Portugal," "9. Angola")? Certain systems represent patterns of interaction to be sure, but are they relevant for "international politics" ("22. Church-State Relations," "23. American Executive-Con-

1. Western Europe in World Politics

2. Indochina War

3. Global Economics

4. Middle East Conflict

5. Energy and Resources

6. The Communist World

7. Portugal

8. Western Democratic Politics

9. Angola

10. Latin American Instability

11. Latin America in World Politics

12. The Middle East in World Politics

13. The United Nations in World Politics

14. Third World Development

15. Asia in World Politics

16. Global Inflation

17. African Instability

18. Great Powers vs. Emerging Powers

19. Unconventional Politics

20. Trade and Currency

21. Colonialism

22. Church-State Relations

23. American Executive-Congressional Relations

Fig. 13.1. The multiple systems in world politics, 1975

gressional Relations")? Such questions necessitate exploring in greater detail the assumptions on which our analysis rests.

The methodology employed herein reflects an "open" approach to systems. This does introduce the possibility (perhaps probability) of results that appear anomalous at first glance (a la Russett) because issues reflected in behavior (rather than any explicit geographical considerations) constitute the variables on which the systems are based. The systems do not necessarily have to covary with a particular conception of national, regional, or transregional geography; and a key question becomes to what extent does <u>any</u> geographical construct correspond to patterns of systemic interaction? Given a sufficiently high degree of actor/issue/behavioral relationship, all sorts of permutations and combinations are possible. Actors having origins in national systems gripped by the throes of instability may be so confined that they have little interaction with those from their own broader geographic regions, let alone any other (Portugal, Angola).

Another possibility is transnational relations which exist with respect to nonobvious kinds of issue-systems ("Church-State Relations," "American Executive-Congressional Relations"). The logic here is similar to Karl Kaiser's view of "transnational society. . .as a system of interaction in a specific issue area between societal actors in different national system," and he goes on to argue:

> Transnational society cannot be understood geographically; nor does it comprise the whole of the societies of the nation state systems involved. That means, first, that a transnational society can exist between geographically separate societies and, second, that it must be understood functionally, i.e., that it is circumscribed by the issue areas which are the object of transnational interaction.(89)

Kaiser considers such transnational society as the prerequisite for "(t)ransnational politics – the third ideal type of multinational politics – (which) can be loosely defined as those political processes between national governments (and international organizations) that have been set in motion by interaction within a transnational society."(90) Unfortunately, this produces another manifestation of the "closed system problem" because the identification of systemic patterns proceeds by a deductive logic with reference to nation states.

All of this suggests the necessity for providing some relevant means of differentiating among the systems discovered through our "open" methodology. The obvious first dimension would be the nature of the geographical reality to which a given system corresponds. A clue for how to go about this is Russett's conclusion that, although "neat" regional systems did not exist, certain "cores" were identifiable. Employing the factor scores of the significant outlying dyads for each system, it is possible to assess whether it has a core composed primarily of actors from one of the eight geographic regions (not "regional systems") mentioned above.(91) Therefore, we shall define "regional systems" as those possessing such a core (even if the given system is not "region-wide" in conventional terms), demonstrating that a correspondence exists between a single geographical area and an issue-system. If such a core cannot be found, meaning that the actors are drawn from more than one of the eight geographic regions, the system will be considered "transregional." In other words, for our purposes "regional" and "transregional" merely denote the nature of the match between geography and interaction. This explains why Portugal and Angola can be considered regional systems. Actors were drawn overwhelmingly in the first case from a part of Western Europe and in the second from a part of Africa to the exclusion of those from other regions.

A second dimension for classifying systems emerges when the "system map" of what our world looked like in 1975 is drawn. It will be noticed that certain of the issues in Table 13.1 are part of more than one system. These (underlined) issues represent the "linkages" connecting some of the systems in fig. 13.2. Such linkages reflect two kinds of phenomena which characterize interdependent world politics. The first is the logical connection existing between the substantive nature of various issues. For instance, the "Israel N Front" issue provides a linkage between Systems 12 and 13 ("The Middle East in World Politics" and "The United Nations in World Politics") because its substance involves different UN activities related to the Lebanese Civil War, conflict between Israel and Palestinians in Lebanon, and maintaining the uneasy truce between Israel and Syria. The second is "actor sharing" whereby actors participating in different systems literally forge the linkages between them through their behavior. Thus, the complexities of the "UK Global Role" entailed actor behavior (such as by the Irish Republican Army, British authorities, and other British nonstate actors) which created the less substantively obvious linkage between Systems 8 and 19 ("Western Democratic Politics" and "Unconventional Politics"). These linkages are shown in the fig. 13.2 "system map," with the numbers of the various sytems corresponding to those in fig. 13.1.(92)

Combining the dimension of linkage with that of geography/system match ("regionality") yields the following fourfold classification of the multiple systems in world politics (table 13.3). The system identification numbers again correspond with those of fig. 13.1.

The predominant type of system is that of the "linked transregional" variety in terms of both frequency and the amount of variance for which they account (39.9 percent of the common variance after rotation). These systems represent our explicit research focus, implying that those analysts who stress the importance of interdependence for understanding global outcomes have much to recommend their positions. The substantive bases of these systems reveal an intuitively obvious sense of interdependence (something which does lend an air of "face validity" to our approach), although there are some surprises:

3. Global Economics
4. Middle East Conflict
5. Energy and Resources
12. The Middle East in World Politics
13. The United Nations in World Politics
14. Third World Development
16. Global Inflation
18. Great Powers vs. Emerging Powers
20. Trade and Currency
23. American Executive-Congressional Relations

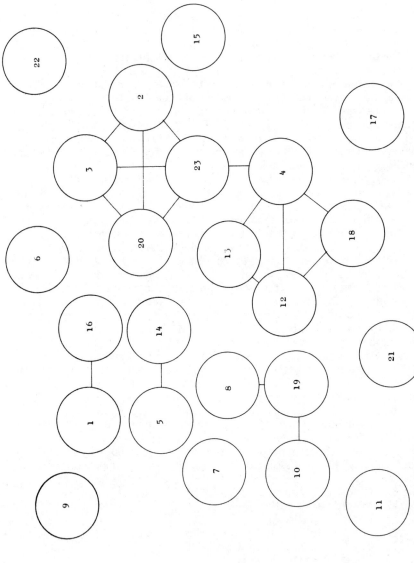

Fig. 13.2. System Map of world politics, 1975.

Table 13.3. Types of Systems

Linkage

	No	Yes
Regional	Encapsulated Regional Systems 6,7,9,11,15	Linked Regional Systems 1,2,8,10,19
Transregional	Encapsulated Transregional Systems 17,21,22	Linked Transregional Systems 3,4,5,12,13,14, 16,18,20,23

Half of these systems are broadly economic, bringing together regional actors from literally every area in the world as well as MNCs and other nonstate actors. Two different issues link Systems 3 and 20, "Superpower Aid" and "Global Crime." The former represents the state dimension of economic interdependence, while the latter provides a linkage involving charges of MNC bribery, price-fixing, and so forth. Systems 5 and 14 are linked so directly through the importance of "Raw Materials" in Third World developmental terms that they constitute a separable pattern dominated by the activities of the less developed. This stands in sharp contrast to the concentration of activity on the part of the more developed nations ("Western Solidarity") as they sought to institutionalize various ways of coping with inflationary pressures. Indeed, System 16 centers around an American-European axis (hence its link with System 1), with peripheral involvement emanating from the Middle East and Africa.

The other major source of linked transregional systems originates in the interdependencies of Middle Eastern politics. The Middle Eastern region is so penetrated that it becomes impossible to speak of it as a single geographical regional system. System 4 is based on the core of the Arab-Israeli conflict, including the Lebanese Civil War, as what here (appropriately) might be called a "subsystem." Its transregional quality comes from the prevalence of "North American-Middle East" dyads concerned with American aid and other support for Israel as well as American diplomatic initiatives that bore fruit subsequent to our sampling period. The linkage supplied by "Race and Ethnic Division" in global terms provides a conceptual key for understanding the UN's heavy involvement in specific activities (System 13). The unique significance of the Middle East in World Politics (System 12) is reinforced further by the actions of the Palestinian Liberation Organization (PLO) outside the region in forums such as those supplied by the UN, a linkage based upon "The Middle East as a Global Problem."

"The Middle East as a Global Problem" also supplies the linkage for what is perhaps the most unique of the linked transregional systems. System 18 consists of two separable but interrelated patterns of issues. One concerns "North American-Eastern European(USSR)" dyadic inter-action involving Strategic Arms Limitation Talks (SALT) and various forms of cultural exchange. The other includes political ramifications related to the "Arab Economic Role," particularly various efforts at "Islamic Unity" centering around petrodollar rich Iran and Saudi Arabia. What we appear to have here, therefore, is a clear case of "actor sharing," with American activities forging linkages among what were seemingly unrelated issues.

Actor sharing also provides an explanation for System 23 ("American Executive-Congressional Relations"), suggesting how transnational pol-itics can exist without regard for traditional geographic compartments. With reference to geography alone, Washington, D.C. constitutes "the tiniest transregion in the world." What has been most often in recent years the Executive-Congressional battleground allows for linkages among apparently diverse systems based upon the advantages certain issues are seen as presenting for different American governmental actors. During 1975, these issues were "Superpower Aid" and "US in Indochina," creating a strange linkage in geographical terms among East Asia, the Middle East, and Western Europe which existed because actors were shared in Washington. The former issue also brought about a linkage to systems of an economic variety (Systems 3 and 20), serving as a reminder that heavy American involvement in Vietnam had always entailed "guns vs. butter" choices.

These same two issues constituted connections to the next kind of systems, "linked regional" ones. Five in number, linked regional systems are second most significant in terms of the variance for which they accounted (30.6 percent of the common variance after rotation):

1. Western Europe in World Politics
2. Indochina War
8. Western Democratic Politics
10. Latin American Instability
19. Unconventional Politics

Where the majority of linked transregional systems reflect the substantive logic of various issues, the interdependencies of linked regional systems rest more upon actor sharing. Integration may have become a "turbulent field," but a reservoir of reciprocal interaction exists among Western European actors that gives this geographic area coherence as a regional system. While each of the issues significant to System 1 have seemingly transregional implications, they are framed in European terms, providing some loose support for the idea of "external-ization."(93) The linkage of System 2 with those of a transregional variety also reflects an actor sharing, this time with regard to "North American-East Asia" dyads. As evidenced since the withdrawal of the United States from Vietnam, the Indochinese regional system is dependent for its linkages on the activities of extraregional actors. (In other words, had the data been sampled several years later, Indochina might have joined the rest of Asia as part of a largely encapsulated regional system.)

Systems 8, 10, and 19 suggest a more general point about the nature of linked regional systems and phenomena of actor sharing. Because the linkages of regional systems appear to rely more upon actor sharing than the substantive nature of the issues involved, such linkages are probably more transitory than those of transregional (or transnational) systems. What, after all, do Western Europe and Latin America have in common with a system for which "Cyprus" is the most significant issue? The answer can be found only with reference to the activities of a particular kind of nonstate actor, terrorists, and the efforts of various governments to control their activities. Terrorists may act primarily for local reasons, but the confluence of the Irish Republican Army ("UK Global Role"), the Italian Red Brigades, Greek and Turkish Cypriotes, and various Latin bands ("Terror & Control") has come to be viewed in global terms. Were such groups to disappear overnight, European strikes and electioneering as well as Latin America's chronically unstable politics would return to being largely regional phenomena.

There is an underlying uniqueness to both the actors and issues characterizing "encapsulated regional systems." Five such systems also can be identified, but they are of less significance to global patterns (23.5 percent of the common variance after rotation):

6.   The Communist World
7.   Portugal
9.   Angola
11. Latin America in World Politics
15. Asia in World Politics

The first three of these systems reveal the different picture of the world which emerges when regions are viewed in conjunction with issues rather than only in geographical terms. System 6 includes "Global Communism" and its Eurocommunist analogue, but its core centers around "East Bloc Cohesion" and almost solely involves "Eastern Europe (USSR)" dyads instead of any implicit transregional ramifications. Thus, it seems fair to say that the Soviet Union and its Eastern European satellites constitute a coherent regional system. There may be coherence and an interactive intensity surrounding Systems 7 and 9, but they would certainly not reflect regionality in its conventional sense. Some more broadly "Western European" dyads appear with regard to System 7, and "North American" ones owing to United States governmental actors with regard to System 9. Yet the core of these systems is overwhelmingly national rather than even regional, suggesting the extremely limited leverage that any outside actors can have over areas undergoing extreme unrest.

Despite what might be considered the transregional implications inherent in their names, Systems 11 and 15 are again recognizable as primarily regional systems. Even with the expected North American presence ("US in Latin America"), the interactive core of System 11 is overwhelmingly regional without directly involving any other geographic area (a finding from which dependency theorists probably can take heart). Interestingly, no matter what causes for alarm the Cuban presence in Africa may have set off within the United States, the issue of "Cuban Communism" is confined to its Latin American context. The Asian regional system does reflect an American presence, and that of "Other Major in Asia" as well. Here again, though, the interactive core is mostly regional, a finding supported also by the fact that the People's Republic of China has its single highest factor score in this context (rather than with regard to systems involving communist- or Indochinese-oriented issues).

Lastly, and least importantly (only 6.3 percent of the common variance after rotation), are three "encapsulated transregional systems:"

17.   African Instability
21.   Colonialism
22.   Church-State Relations

The notion of an "encapsulated transregional system" at first may appear to be a contradiction in terms. Such systems exist, however, largely because of the idiosyncracies inherent in various issues. Examining the nature of these issues suggests that such systems are quite amorphous, categories for actor participation on a somewhat hit-or-miss (as opposed to shared) basis. More than any other kind of global activity, System 17 reflects those largely ceremonial occasions such as symbolic cabinet shufflings or the trappings of Third World independence. The frequency of such "Routine Intragovernmental" issues in many respects lent whatever coherence existed to the regional aspects of this system. System 21 appeared to lack a substantive basis, too, something which gave to it a quality of being a "container" into which actors poured their behavior rather than action undertaken on a consistent, substantive basis. "Colonialism" is certainly a transregional issue, but its manifestations are subtle and particularistic, often expressed only in ideological terms. Various events involving the Spanish Sahara and their implications for the unsettled politics of post-Franco Spain figured heavily. Thus, situational peculiarities were of greater importance to behavior in this system than the ideological connotation its name implies. Finally, no system could be more unusual, and transregional at the same time, than one oriented around the role of the Catholic (and various Protestant) church(es) in different regional contexts. System 22 is transregional (or better still "transnational") to be sure, but its connections with regional international politics and more prevalent transregional interactions remain heavily obscured.

Summary

Viewing both transregional and regional systems in conjunction with the issues on which they are based has yielded a mixture of results. Evidence exists for considering Western Europe, Eastern Europe (USSR), and Latin America as coherent regional systems. Despite the idiosyncracies introduced by Indochina, some sense of an East Asian regional system emerges, although Russett's cautionary note must be taken into account: "Our moral is that for purposes of generalization one should not refer to Asia unless one specifically means to refer to countries with a certain physical proximity to each other and distance from the rest of the world."(94) Discounting Angola, the remainder of Africa would seem to constitute a loose and not very important regional system. The nature of South Asia or the Middle East as conventionally understood regional systems is not apparent in our analysis. In the case of the former, this is due to the extremely infrequent behavior regarding issues which are focused on this region. In the case of the latter, the reasoning is just the opposite. Middle Eastern politics are so much a part of transregional and transnational patterns that it becomes difficult to focus in on the regional core of actors or issues. Last, and far from least, if there is a North American regional system in the stricter sense of the term, then it is the most profoundly transregional system in the world due to the massive involvement of American actors in global politics.

TRANSREGIONAL RELATIONS AND REGIONAL POLITICAL DEVELOPMENT

It has been argued that especially in regional terms:

> Changes in a political system may be considered developmental to the extent: (1) actor behavior reflects systemic rather than internal determinants; (2) it is more difficult for the behavior of any single actor to change the patterns and procedures characteristic of the system; and (3) the demands on the system represented by actor behavior are more successfully met. In other words, regional political development is a process of political change producing a system structure characterized by greater (1) interdependence; (2) predictability; and (3) balance.(95)

This conceptualization allows for many of the variables emphasized by political development and integration theory to be assembled within a common framework. These variables are based upon the functional logic which largely underpins such theories, and the nature of behavioral interaction can be considered their primary indicator. In a sense, interdependence is both the most important and the most qualitative of the variables, having been defined recently by one theorist as "the direct and positive linkage of the interests of actors such that when the position of one actor changes, the position of others is affected, and in the same direction."(96) Interdependence has profound implications for the other two developmental variables. Too much interdependence can "imbalance" a system, making the adequate management of the issues it includes unlikely, even through the most cooperative of actor behavior. Furthermore, the issues with regard to which interdependencies exist may be more or less predictable; and, when they are less so, efforts to build collective decision making structures are inhibited.

The mere existence of effective regional (or transregional) organizations represents the kind of institutionalization which can take place once behavior has become somewhat predictable. This is not the only reason why predictability is, in many ways, the most straightforward of the developmental variables to operationalize. Predictability is higher when fewer patterns exist with reference to which greater amounts of actor behavior can be explained. This conveys the idea of a "predictability ratio" constructed on the basis of dividing the number of systems of a given type into the amount of (common) variance (after rotation) they explain (treated as a whole number).(97) Employing this ratio, it is clear that regional systems are more predictable than those of the transregional variety (a ratio of 5.4 for all regional systems compared to 3.6 for all transregional ones). The underlying reasons for this finding would seem to entail the nature of regional as opposed to transregional interdependencies.

In fact, linked regional systems turn out to be the most predictable of all (a ratio of 6.1). The idea of linkage itself connotes interdependencies involving other systems. Some of the reasons such interdependencies do not prove more complicating factors for linked regional systems are conveyed by Cantori and Spiegel's suggestion:

> Intrusive powers are relatively weak in their ability to alter social cohesion, and only slightly stronger with respect to economic cohesion. . . .When internal communications have already been developed, intrusive powers tend to concentrate on aiding regional instruments of interaction. When the nation states in a subordinate system distinctively lack internal communications, intrusive powers tend to concentrate on the domestic arena and support few regional projects.(98)

Both of these kinds of variables are quite important to regional interdependence in either a positive (Western Europe) or largely negative (Indochina and Latin America) sense.

Interdependence in Western Europe arises within a highly balanced context reflecting overwhelming amounts of cooperative as opposed to conflictual behavior. This is so in two respects, even bearing in mind "the necessity of taking domestic politics into account in any discussion of the dynamics of European integration."(99) First, Western European domestic politics include relatively low levels of conflict. Labor disputes and parliamentary name-calling fall far short of other kinds of conflictual events, such as riots, in both their scope and intensity. When the latter kinds of events do occur, for example involving the Irish Republican Army or the Red Brigades, the interdependence arises not because of the substantive nature of the essentially local issues related to the behavior, but, rather, with regard to the efforts of governmental actors to maintain civil control. Thus, within Western Europe, there are highly predictable relationships based upon the fact that even the most conflictual events have their cooperative sides.

Second, and perhaps more importantly, European regional conflict has come to take place within a transregional or transnational context, especially as far as economic issues are concerned. Unpredictability and conflict effectively are funneled outside of a purely regional setting through the "Western Solidarity" linkage for which the United States is critical: "At the end of 1978. . .belief in the American economy and the dollar as the mainspring of the Western economic system was badly undermined in Europe; and although Europe's overriding reliance on U.S. arms for protection was undiminished, the reassertion of the power and rights of Congress vis-a-vis the Carter Administration created funda-mental doubts about the stability of American foreign policy."(100) Western Europe remains the most highly developed regional system, which does, however, create complications insofar as the predictability of linked regional systems is concerned. The finding that linked regional systems are the most predictable is certainly plausible, but we cannot really know whether this is due overwhelmingly to the fact that Western Europe constitutes such a system.

Yet, there is also a logic to the predictable nature of both the Latin American and Indochinese linked regional systems which is reinforced by the finding that encapsulated regional systems rank second in predictability (a ratio of 4.7). Regional encapsulation can engender a good bit of predictability, whether the case is that of the broader Asian role in world politics (for which Indochina itself may not necessarily be that critical) or that of Latin America. "Encapsulation" is one possible reaction to the exigencies of transnational politics, and Karl Kaiser has spoken of it in national terms as follows:

This would mean, first, that connections and channels of interactions with transnational society would have to be cut by restricting the free movement of persons, capital, currency, information, ideas, etc. National encapsulation requires, second, that the nation states involved change to some extent the goals and organizations of their internal sociopolitical system and redefine the nature of their links with the outside world.(101)

While the analogy is somewhat imperfect because regions themselves do not "act," such patterns are characteristic of Latin and Asian politics. Encapsulation can result in comparatively high predictability because of relative isolation from outside forces. In such cases, however, the predictability derives from patterns of interdependence and balance that contrast sharply with those of Western Europe.

The massive American presence in Indochina catalyzed inter-dependence there in a fashion which reminds us that the most highly interdependent type of relationship is the one found in crisis when there are great amounts of interaction during a short time among relatively few actors. As such, the highly negative interdependence forged through "Superpower Aid" and "US in Indochina" further imbalanced what was already a highly unstable system where "ancient conflicts have existed for centuries among the various peoples which now inhabit the area."(102) The removal of the American presence did little to alter the essentially negative character of Indochinese interdependence, although its level was reduced. Negative interdependence and imbalance expressed through conflict have remained highly predictable, a conclusion for which no better evidence can be given than the Vietnamese-Cambodian War.

In terms of East Asia as a whole, predictability is not so high as simply with regard to Indochina alone. This is because interdependence itself is somewhat lower, which is consistent with the idea that "East Asia is not one system, but a series of overlapping groups of states interacting in political, economic, and military issue areas."(103) Balance also varies greatly on a regional basis with relatively cooperative interaction among the ASEAN countries, a continuation of the Sino-Japanese detente, and persistent antipathy between the Koreas. Predictability is, therefore, occasioned by the region's encapsulated status, with more or less a persistence of intraregional patterns and a reactive, as opposed to active, involvement with transregional relations.

The predictability of Latin American politics derives from what has been called its "stable pattern of instability."(104) Instability characterizes the regional system whether we are considering the traditional linkage unconventional politics provide or its encapsulated involvement in global patterns. Latin American interdependence appears somewhat unique, its relatively low levels and negative nature more a reflection of commonality of situation than conscious activities: "Rapid population growth, rapid rates of urbanization, high migration rates, soaring demands for education, uncertain labor markets, and unrewarded aspirations for social participation are seen to one or another degree everywhere."(105) The system chronically seems to exist on the border-line of balance. When, in the aftermath of the Cuban Revolution, regional interdependence rose rapidly, not even United States-induced cooperation could restore a high degree of balance or prevent the widespread impression of political decay.(106) Of course, the history of the United States-Latin American "special relationship" might be looked upon as transregional, but only in a most formalistic sense. It would seem much more accurate to consider the United States as an integral part of the Latin American regional system. This presence, while contributing to the image of uniqueness, does little to alter the predictable nature of Latin America's encapsulation.

Angola and Portugal both demonstrate the relatively predictable nature of an encapsulated system undergoing developmental crises fraught with the possibilities of political decay. In such situations, interdependence reaches extremely high levels as the system polarizes. Imbalance is expressed by high amounts of conflict. The encapsulated nature of these systems, however, apparently prevented their becoming more embroiled in regional (let alone transregional) patterns, despite both communist and rightist militance in Portugal and the presence of Cuban troops in Angola. As a result, these systems subsequently have remained predictable on the basis of their own patterns, largely without reference to transregional relations.

The encapsulation of the communist system around its Soviet-Eastern European core might have reflected greater predictability were it not for the fact that <u>within</u> the region transregional issues are managed in an idiosyncratic fashion. After all, intraregional interdependence and balance are at a fairly high level, no matter what their undercurrents. As James Kuhlman has argued:

> The cohesiveness of the community in the East strains toward a bloc, rather than just an alliance or cooperative grouping. Economic interdependence and organizational networks outweigh the centrifugal forces inherent in an area concerned with sovereignty, ethnicity, and legitimacy. The economic dominance of a single-state core also contributes to regional cohesion.(107)

It is the regional core, the Soviet Union, which is at the root of predictability, as well as interdependence and balance, for the regional system as a whole. The Soviet Union itself becomes involved with various transregional patterns, although similar actions on the part of fellow bloc members are seen as requiring orchestration. This is particularly true with regard to ties with the West that could be engendered through greater participation in the world economy. A logical course such transregional participation could take involves the EEC, but it has proceeded with various fits and starts. John Pinder summarizes the overall result as follows:

> Trade negotiations between the Community and its Eastern partners might, then, lead on to major developments in the relationship between them in the long term, as well as being useful in alleviating some of the East Europeans' economic difficulties in the near future. The obstacles that stand in the way are political, but are reinforced by the lack of immediate material interest in such negotiations on the part of the Community and the Soviet Union.(108)

Little wonder that the encapsulation of the Eastern European regional system renders it less predictable, if perhaps more independent and balanced, than it would be if stronger linkages existed with various transregional and transnational systems.

Turning to linked transregional system, there is some lack of predictability, though not an overwhelming one (a ratio of 4.0). This is, no doubt, due to the high levels of interdependence which exist in the two major sets of linked transregional systems that have been described — those involving global economic relations and those centered around the Middle East region. In the case of the former, interdependence is by and large of a positive nature, while, in the latter, it is predominantly negative. There is a strong cooperative bias inherent in the inter-dependent relationships among the developed industrialized countries. Furthermore, their control over economic relations persists, despite the significant shifts which have occurred, sometimes on an almost year-by-year basis:

> Immediately after the "oil shock" of 1973-74, the payments deficit which mirrored the massive surplus of the OPEC nations was shared among virtually all petroleum-importing nations, both industrialized and developing. By 1975, widespread recession among the industrialized countries had reduced their external deficits and increased the pressure on the payments positions of oil-importing developing countries. With the uneven economic recovery of 1976-78, however, the payments position of the oil-importing developing nations improved and the largest payments imbalances were concentrated among the industrialized group of nations.(109)

What most complicates the predictability of linked transregional systems, however, are the interdependencies which exist between the two different sets. An "oil war" has not occurred, and seems highly unlikely, but it comes as no surprise that Middle Eastern politics are profoundly interrelated with global economics. This has been especially true since 1978-79 turmoil in Iran brought about the Shah's overthrow and dislocations in world oil supplies, as well as the unprecedented conclusion of a peace treaty between Egypt and Israel. The result has been a kind of scurrying about, particularly as United States foreign policy attempts to bring a permanent end to the imbalance in Middle Eastern transregional relations and, at the same time, restore greater balance (and American advantage) in global economic relations. It, therefore, can be anticipated that the predictability of linked trans-regional systems remains a bit unclear. Broad developmental outcomes would seem likely because high levels of interdependence present incentives for creative diplomatic strokes. Yet the causal mechanisms determining their success or failure are extremely difficult to gauge.

Finally, encapsulated transregional systems are the least predictable of all (a ratio of a mere 2.1). The reason would appear to be their intractability in terms of any meaningful developmental outcomes. Interdependencies exist with regard to these systems because they are, after all, transregional or transnational. Such interdependencies, however, seem to have little impact on the broader spectrum of global interaction. "Church-State Relations" are clearly important at the Vatican, but the uneasy "live-and-let-live" relationship with Eastern European governments is not very likely to cause a reversal of balance in the latter. "Colonialism" so intimately relates to the practicalities of

North-South economic relations that its ideological implications remain unconnected and subservient to them, except with regard to how various NIEO issues may be framed. The framing of issues, of course, is far from equivalent to their resolution.

The encapsulated transregional system centering around Africa is the most problematic from a developmental perspective. The diversity of Africa is certainly comparable to Asia and would seem to be characterized by an even lower level of interdependence. At the same time, its lack of balance is more in line with that of Latin America since it has proved resistant to intrusive attempts to catalyze the region, even during the height of the Cold War. Barring a possible, though not necessarily probable, racial conflagration involving the white supremist regimes in Southern Africa, William Zartman's conclusion about Africa's developmental prospects as a region are still in order:

> In the short run, it is unlikely that any of these characteristics of the regional system will change appreciably. This is so, partly because the system has not long been in its present stage of relations and partly because the characteristics of the system do not lend themselves to rapid alteration, and even militate against it. . . .Nor are there outside agents — peripheral or intrusive members of the system — that appear willing and able to exert decisive influence for change.(110)

CONCLUSIONS: THE MODELS RECONSIDERED

Transregional relations have been treated as largely equivalent to the patterns characterizing global politics in general. Three different models (exchange, integration, and exploitation), each of which entails various pretheoretical assumptions, were introduced at the outset with reference to which global phenomena could be viewed. These models were all found lacking in one respect or another, prompting examination of formulations with a more explicitly regional focus. Difficulties also were discovered here, however, although a synthesis involving a model of multiple issue-based systems provided the means for surmounting many of them. This model, then, was operationalized, leading to a typology of global systems based upon two considerations — geographical area/issue correspondence, and such systems' linked or encapsulated status. Having discussed briefly each type of system from a developmental perspective, it is, therefore, appropriate that we return to the models which served as our initial point of departure. Unfortunately, our evaluation of them must remain somewhat impressionistic due to the kinds of gaps which almost inherently exist between pretheoretic assumptions and operational results.

A first, if not particularly shocking, conclusion is that global politics is the scene of significant discontinuities (or as partisans of exploitation would have it, centers and peripheries). Systems of a linked transregional variety pervade global politics with actors from the industrial-ized North, including those representing the highly developed linked regional system of Western Europe, dominating such systems. While the less developed countries participate in some of these transregional systems, these actors do so largely on the North's terms, and those systems in which Southern participation has greater effects on trans-regional patterns tend to be of lesser importance. The exchange model is weakest here because such structural differentiation is only taken into account implicitly at best.

A second conclusion involves the unique place of Latin America and, particularly, the Middle East among what are commonly recognized as the world's less developed regions. The integration model does not do a very good job of explaining the linkages which are critical to the developmental prospects for these regions. The exploitation model appears to do best in the former context because the economic connection with the United States along with the sporadic linkages brought about by chronically unstable politics have largely encapsulated Latin America. The exchange model provides no real mechanisms for why such encapsulation should occur. The relative strength of the models is reversed, however, with regard to the Middle East. Here more blatant economic explanations simply will not do. The linkages of what are actually the Middle East's transregional systems (on one hand through the politics of Arab-Israeli conflict, and on the other through the economics of oil) involve extremely complex, though imperfect, exchange processes.

Thirdly, with regard to the 23 systems as a whole, not more than the merest trace of the Cold War was found. It may be suggested that this is the primary nonindigenous reason for the encapsulation of Africa and Asia, although whether this has a direct bearing upon the models is questionable. The integration model could rely on the lack of "condi-tions favoring integration," but this is tautological. The exploitation model must demonstrate the dominance of a center before the encap-sulating mechanism can be invoked.

Finally, and most importantly, we seem to be living in a world of transregional rather than regional systems. Those regions which actual-ly do meet empirical criteria for constituting meaningful regional systems are those most significant for transregional patterns of linkage and interdependence. This is not to say that the study of regional politics is unimportant, far from it. It is to suggest strongly that the ways we conceptualize the place of regions in interdependent world politics should be cast in a new light.

NOTES

(1) See Raimondo Strassoldo, "The Study of Boundaries: A Systems-Oriented, Multidisciplinary, Bibliographical Essay," The Jerusalem Jour-nal of International Relations 2, no. 3 (Spring 1977): 81-107; and Oran R. Young, Systems of Political Science (Englewood Cliffs, N.J.: Pren-

tice-Hall, 1968), pp. 5-6, and "Political Discontinuities in the International System," World Politics 20, no. 3 (April 1968): 369-92.

(2) This point is discussed more fully in Donald E. Lampert, Lawrence S. Falkowski, and Richard W. Mansbach, "Is There an International System?" International Studies Quarterly 22, no. 1 (March 1978): 143-66.

(3) Andrew M. Scott, "The Logic of International Interaction," International Studies Quarterly 21, no. 3 (September 1977): 436 (emphasis in original).

(4) Stephen G. Walker, "The Congruence Between Foreign Policy Rhetoric and Behavior: Insights From Role Theory and Exchange Theory," paper at the International Society of Political Psychology Annual Meeting, 1979, p. 4 (emphasis in original). The remainder of our discussion of exchange theory per se is derived from Ibid., pp. 5-6.

(5) Robert Gilpin, "Three Models of the Future," International Organization 29, no. 1 (Winter 1975): 40.

(6) See Stephen D. Krasner, "U.S. Commercial and Monetary Policy: Unravelling the Paradox of External Strength and Internal Weakness," International Organization 31, no. 4 (Autumn 1977): 641-56.

(7) Nathaniel H. Leff, "Bengal, Biafra, and the Bigness Bias," Foreign Policy 3 (Summer 1971): 129.

(8) Robert W. Cox, "Ideologies and the New International Economic Order: Reflections on Some Recent Literature," International Organization 33, no. 2 (Spring 1979): 255-302.

(9) Ibid., pp. 261, 302.

(10) James P. O'Leary, "Envisioning Interdependence: Perspectives on Future World Orders," Orbis 22, no. 3 (Fall 1978): 536 (emphasis in original).

(11) Richard Rosecrance, "New Directions?" in America as an Ordinary Country, edited by Richard Rosecrance (Ithaca, N.Y.: Cornell University Press, 1976), pp. 245-46 (emphasis in original).

(12) Marina V.N. Whitman, "Leadership Without Hegemony: Our Role in the World Economy," Foreign Policy 20 (Fall 1975): 138-60.

(13) Rosecrance, "New Directions?" pp. 245-246.

(14) See Richard N. Cooper, "A New International Economic Order For Mutual Gain," Foreign Policy 26 (Spring 1977): 66-120, esp. 81-90.

(15) Ibid., p. 90.

(16) See, for example, the tables in Werner J. Feld, International Relations: A Transnational Approach (Sherman Oaks, Calif.: Alfred, 1979): 318-21.

(17) Tony Smith, "Changing Configurations of Power in North-South Relations Since 1945," International Organization 31, no. 1 (Winter 1977): 26 (emphasis in original).

(18) Our discussion here is based on Stephen D. Krasner, "State Power and the Structure of International Trade," World Politics 28, no. 3 (April 1976): 317-47.

(19) Ibid., p. 323.

(20) Philippe C. Schmitter, "A Revised Theory of Regional Integration," in Regional Integration: Theory and Research, edited by Leon N. Lindberg and Stuart A. Scheingold (Cambridge, Mass.: Harvard University Press, 1971), pp. 232, 236-37.

(21) See, for example, Joseph S. Nye, Jr., ed., International Regionalism (Boston: Little, Brown, 1968).

(22) Michael P. Sullivan, International Relations: Theories and Evidence (Englewood Cliffs, N.J.: Prentice-Hall, 1976), p. 208.

(23) See J.S. Nye, Peace in Parts (Boston: Little, Brown, 1971), Chaps. 2 and 3, esp. pp. 64-86; also Schmitter, "A Revised Theory of Regional Integration."

(24) See Andrzej Korbonski, "Theory and Practice of Regional Integration: The Case of Comecon," in Lindberg and Scheingold, Regional Integration, pp. 338-73.

(25) From a neofunctional perspective Karl Deutsch is something of a maverick owing to his championing of transactional research. Nonetheless, he was virtually the "founding father" of the national/international metaphor for empirical integration studies. As a result, his recent thoughts on integration provide the basis for the current discussion. See Karl W. Deutsch, "National Integration: Some Concepts and Research Approaches," The Jerusalem Journal of International Relations 2, no. 4 (Summer 1977): 1-29.

(26) Ibid., p. 25.

(27) See, for example, J.S. Nye, "Central American Regional Integration," in Nye, International Regionalism, pp. 377-429; and Sheldon W. Simon, "The ASEAN States: Obstacles to Security Cooperation," Orbis 22, no. 2 (Summer 1978): 415-34.

TRANSREGIONAL RELATIONS   475

(28) Louis J. Cantori and Steven L. Spiegel, "The Analysis of Regional International Politics: The Integration Versus the Empirical Systems Approach," International Organization 27, no. 4 (Autumn 1973): 472 (emphasis in original).

(29) Ernst B. Haas, "The Study of Regional Integration: Reflections on the Joy and Anguish of Pretheorizing," in Lindberg and Scheingold, Regional Integration, pp. 16-17.

(30) See Young, "Political Discontinuities in the International System."

(31) See James N. Rosenau, "Pre-Theories and Theories of Foreign Policy," and "Toward the Study of National-International Linkages," in The Scientific Study of Foreign Policy, edited by J.N. Rosenau (New York: Free Press, 1971), pp. 95-149 (esp. 116-32) and 307-38, respectively.

(32) The reason the present discussion has been termed "nonobvious" is that Prebisch, despite the fact that he did not present himself in Marxist terms, usually is looked upon as a forerunner of dependency arguments because of his concern with the "international division of labor." See Raul Prebisch, The Economic Development of Latin America and Its Principal Problems (New York: United Nations, 1950), and Towards a New Trade Policy for Development (New York: United Nations, 1964). In the latter work he analyzes some of the reasons why import substitution failed.

(33) Schmitter, "A Revised Theory of Regional Integration," p. 241.

(34) Bruce M. Russett, International Regions and the International System (Chicago: Rand McNally, 1967), pp. 226, 229.

(35) James A. Caporaso, "The External Consequences of Regional Integration for Pan-European Relations: Inequality, Dependence, Polarization, and Symmetry," International Studies Quarterly 20, no. 3 (September 1976): 341-92.

(36) See Werner J. Feld, The European Community in World Affairs (Port Washington, N.Y.: Alfred, 1976), Chap. 9; and Schmitter, "A Revised Theory of Regional Integration," p. 244.

(37) Sam Olofin, "ECOWAS and the Lome Convention: An Experiment in Complementary or Conflicting Customs Union Arrangements?" Journal of Common Market Studies 16, no. 1 (September 1977): 71.

(38) David Allen, "The Euro-Arab Dialogue," Journal of Common Market Studies 16, no. 4 (June 1978): 323-42.

(39) See Branislav Gosovic and John Gerard Ruggie, "On the Creation of a New International Economic Order: Issue Linkage and the Seventh Special Session of the UN General Assembly," International Organization 30, no. 2 (Spring 1976): 309-45. See also Cox, "Ideologies and the New International Economic Order."

(40) Raymond D. Duvall, "Dependence and Dependencia Theory: Notes Toward Precision of Concept and Argument," International Organization 32, no. 1 (Winter 1978): 51. Certainly one index of "mainstream acceptance" was the devotion of this entire journal to "dependence and dependency in the global system."

(41) James A. Caporaso, "Introduction: Dependence and Dependency in the Global System," International Organization 32, no. 1 (Winter 1978): 18.

(42) Duvall, "Dependence and Dependencia Theory," pp. 69-72, provides the basis for the current discussion.

(43) Theodore H. Moran, "Multinational Corporations and Dependency: A Dialogue for Dependistas and Non-Dependistas," International Organization 32, no. 1 (Winter 1978): 80, 85, 93 (emphasis in original).

(44) R. Dan Walleri, "The Political Economy Literature on North-South Relations: Alternative Approaches and Empirical Evidence," International Studies Quarterly 22, no. 4 (December 1978): 619.

(45) Raymond D. Duvall and Bruce M. Russett, "Some Proposals to Guide Research on Contemporary Imperialism," The Jerusalem Journal of International Relations 2, no. 1 (Fall 1976): 9-10 (emphasis in original).

(46) Johan Galtung, "A Structural Theory of Imperialism," Journal of Peace Research 2 (1971): 81 (emphasis in original). The remainder of our discussion is taken from pp. 81-117.

(47) Ibid., p. 100 (emphasis omitted).

(48) Richard R. Fagen, "A Funny Thing Happened on the Way to the Market: Thoughts on Extending Dependency Ideas," International Organization 32, no. 1 (Winter 1978): 289-91 (emphasis omitted).

(49) Robert R. Kaufman, Harry I. Chernotsky, and Daniel S. Geller, "A Preliminary Test of the Theory of Dependency," Comparative Politics 7, no. 3 (April 1975): 303-30.

(50) Patrick J. McGowan and Dale L. Smith, "Economic Dependency in Black Africa: An Analysis of Competing Theories," International Organization 32, no. 1 (Winter 1978): 193.

(51) Ibid., pp. 226-28.

(52) Abraham Kaplan, The Conduct of Inquiry (Scranton, Pa.: Chandler, 1964), p. 288.

(53) For a representative treatment of the first focus, see Richard W. Mansbach, Yale H. Ferguson, and Donald E. Lampert, The Web of World Politics: Nonstate Actors in the Global System (Englewood Cliffs, N.J.: Prentice-Hall, 1976); and of the second, Graham T. Allison, Essence of Decision: Explaining the Cuban Missile Crisis (Boston: Little, Brown, 1971). The "definitional misnomer" is, of course, that "international" connotes both state-centricity and the unified "rational actor model."

(54) See, for example, the breakdown given in Werner J. Feld, "The Impact of Nongovernmental Organizations on the Formulation of Transnational Policies," The Jerusalem Journal of International Relations 2, no. 1 (Fall 1976): 63-95.

(55) Ernst B. Haas, "Turbulent Fields and the Theory of Regional Integration," International Organization 30, no. 2 (Spring 1976): 173-212.

(56) Ibid., p. 175.

(57) Ibid., p. 179.

(58) See John D. Steinbruner, The Cybernetic Theory of Decision (Princeton, N.J.: Princeton University Press, 1974). This point is made by Haas, Ibid., p. 184.

(59) Haas, Ibid., p. 208.

(60) See Stanley Hoffmann, "Obstinate or Obsolete? The Fate of the Nation-State and the Case of Western Europe," Daedalus 95 (Summer 1966): 862-915.

(61) Wolfram Hanrieder, "Dissolving International Politics: Reflections on the Nation-State," The American Political Science Review 72, no. 4 (December 1978): 1276-87.

(62) Galtung, "A Structural Theory of Imperialism," pp. 91-94.

(63) See, for example, Raymond Tanter, Modeling and Managing International Crises (Beverly Hills, Calif.: Sage, 1974).

(64) Morton A. Kaplan, System and Process in International Politics (New York: John Wiley, 1957).

(65) Jorge I. Dominguez, "Mice that Do Not Roar: Some Aspects of International Politics in the World's Peripheries," International Organization 25, no. 2 (Spring 1971): 175-76.

(66) The original problem was posed only to include "the international system" and "the national state" in J. David Singer, "The Level-of-Analysis Problem in International Relations," in The International System: Theoretical Essays, edited by Klaus Knorr and Sidney Verba (Princeton, N.J.: Princeton University Press, 1961), pp. 77-92.

(67) Michael Brecher, "International Relations and Asian Studies: The Subordinate State System of Southern Asia," World Politics 15, no. 2 (January 1963): 213-35; Louis J. Cantori and Steven L. Spiegel, The International Politics of Regions (Englewood Cliffs, N.J.: Prentice-Hall, 1970); Russett, International Regions and the International System, p. 7; and William R. Thompson, "The Regional Subsystem: A Conceptual Explication and a Propositional Inventory," International Studies Quarterly 17, no. 1 (March 1973): 89-117.

(68) Cantori and Spiegel, "The Analysis of Regional International Politics," p. 467.

(69) See Kaplan, System and Process in International Politics, pp. 16-18.

(70) Robert O. Keohane and Joseph S. Nye, Power and Interdependence (Boston: Little, Brown, 1977), 24-25.

(71) Cantori and Spiegel, The International Politics of Regions, pp. 8-10. They represent the "bipolar center" as having neither peripheries nor an intrusive system in the case of the U.S.S.R., and the "North American core" as composed of both the United States and Canada with a Caribbean periphery and no intrusive system.

(72) Ibid., pp. 20-25.

(73) Ibid., p. 25 (emphasis added).

(74) Ibid., pp. 26-30.

(75) See ibid., pp. 382-88. The four types of systems reflect rankings on the pattern variables.

(76) Cantori and Spiegel, "The Analysis of Regional International Politics," pp. 483-84.

(77) Ibid., p. 489.

(78) Rosenau, "Toward the Study of National-International Linkages," p. 324.

(79) See Ernst B. Haas, "On Systems and International Regimes," World Politics 27, no. 2 (January 1975): 152-53.

(80) Ibid., p. 150.

(81) Cantori and Spiegel, "The Analysis of Regional International Politics," p. 490.

(82) Thompson, "The Regional Subsystem," pp. 107-10, lists twenty propositions in this category, six more than the number in the next most frequent ("intrasubsystemic interaction").

(83) Russett, International Regions and the International System, p. 168 (emphasis in original).

(84) Ibid., p. 11 (emphasis omitted).

(85) Ibid., p. 182.

(86) See Thompson, "The Regional Subsystem," pp. 93-101.

(87) On the whole, the procedures followed for data collection were largely analogous to those followed in Mansbach, Ferguson, and Lampert, The Web of World Politics (see "Methodological Appendix"). Overall intercoder reliability was a quite satisfactory, .90. Further methodological details are available directly from the author.

(88) The actual program employed was the SPSS PA2. For further information on factor analysis, see Jae-On Kim, "Factor Analysis," in Statistical Package for the Social Sciences, edited by Norman H. Nie et al. (New York: McGraw-Hill, 2nd ed., 1975), pp. 468-514; and R.J. Rummel, Applied Factor Analysis (Evanston, Ill.: Northwestern University Press, 1970).

(89) Karl Kaiser, "Transnational Politics: Toward a Theory of Multinational Politics," International Organization 25, no. 4 (Fall 1971): 802-03.

(90) Ibid., p. 804.

(91) Note that the term "actor" is now being used generically because dyads obviously include both actors and targets. The procedures involved for core identification were as follows. Since the factor scores were normalized, "outlying dyads" were defined as having factor scores greater than $+$ .68 in the direction of the factor (meaning that they would fall within the extreme 25 percent of a normal distribution). The outlying dyads were then classified according to the geographic region (or transregion in the case of dyads like "North America-Middle East") and summed for each region. A "regional core" was defined to exist if

the sum of the outlying factor scores for a given region was at least
twice the sum of the outlying factor scores for all of the other regions
(or transregions) for a given factor.

(92) Certain methodological considerations at least should be raised
here. There is nothing sacrosanct about the factor names, and they may
be looked upon "as descriptive of the interrelationships in the data. The
factor structure is then a typology, and the factors are classifications
to which descriptive names have been assigned" (Rummel, Applied
Factor Analysis, p. 473; emphasis in original) Because the factors are
being treated largely in descriptive terms, our ensuing comparisons
among them are consciously somewhat limited. The systems are discussed only in terms of the typology in table 13.3 and the amounts of
variance accouanted for by each type. Thus, we are "punting" certain
theoretical comparisons on the basis of operationalized explanatory
variables. One such particularly important variable that has a bearing
on the representation in fig. 13.1 is system "size." At a further stage of
the "multiple systems analysis" each of the systems will be regenerated
to contain _all_ those events involving issues that are part of a given
system. (Due to linkage phenomena this means that the same event can
appear in several different systems because of the issues it involves.) A
pretest of these procedures as well as the resulting systemic comparison demonstrated that system size, interdependence, coalition patterns,
and so forth were not merely artifacts of the procedures employed and
produced theoretically meaningful results. (See Donald E. Lampert,
"The Utility of a Multiple Systems Model for the Explanation and
Prediction of Nonstate Behavior: An Illustration from American-West
German Relations," (paper at the Annual Convention of the American
Political Science Association, 1977.) For present purposes, however,
such analysis was not deemed essential and, therefore, all of the
systems in fig. 13.1 are depicted as being of equivalent size.

(93) See Feld, The European Community in World Affairs; and Schmitter, "A Revised Theory of Regional Integration."

(94) Russett, International Regionalism and the International System, p.
182 (emphasis in original).

(95) This has been adapted from Donald E. Lampert, "The Developmental Bases of Nonstate Behavior: Nonstate Actors and Regional
Political Development in Westen Europe and Latin America," (Unpublished Ph.D. Dissertation, Rutgers University, 1975), pp. 55-56.

(96) The word "actor" has been substituted for "state" in this definition
because of the state-centricity inherent in the original formulation.
See R. Rosecrance et al., "Whither Interdependence?" International
Organization 31, no. 3 (Summer 1977): 426-27 (emphasis in original).

(97) This procedure was introduced in Lampert, "Developmental Bases
of Nonstate Behavior," pp. 145-48.

(98) Cantori and Spiegel, The International Politics of Regions, p. 293 (emphasis in original).

(99) Donald J. Puchala, "Domestic Politics and Regional Harmonization in the European Communities," World Politics 27, no. 4 (July 1975): 519 (emphasis omitted).

(100) David Watt, "The European Initiative," Foreign Affairs 57, no. 3 (America and the World 1978): 573.

(101) Kaiser, "Transnational Politics," p. 806.

(102) Cantori and Spiegel, The International Politics of Regions, p. 292.

(103) Sheldon W. Simon, "East Asia," in World Politics, edited by James N. Rosenau, Kenneth W. Thompson, and Gavin Boyd (New York: Free Press, 1976), p. 550.

(104) See Charles W. Anderson, Politics and Economic Change in Latin America (New York: Van Nostrand, 1967), Chap. 4.

(105) Kalman H. Silvert and Morris J. Blachman, "Latin America," in Rosenau, Thompson, and Boyd, World Politics, p. 567.

(106) See Lampert, "Developmental Bases of Nonstate Behavior," Chapters 5 and 6.

(107) James A. Kuhlman, "Eastern Europe," in Rosenau, Thompson, and Boyd, World Politics, p. 458.

(108) John Pinder, "Economic Integraiton and East-West Trade: Conflict of Interests or Comedy of Errors?" Journal of Common Market Studies 16, no. 1 (September 1977): 20.

(109) Marina v.N. Whitman, "A Year of Travail: The United States and the International Economy," Foreign Affairs 57, no. 3 (America and the World 1978): 528 (emphasis in original).

(110) I. William Zartman, "Africa," in Rosenau, Thompson, and Boyd, World Politics, p. 593.

14 Regional Organizations and the Global System
Werner J. Feld

This chapter will focus on interactions between regional organizations in various parts of the world and the global system that may affect either the operation of the latter or influence actions and functions of the former. Regional organizations are characterized by discernible patterns of activities carried out for one or more purposes (economic, security, political, technical) through some kind of institutional framework (ranging from primitive to highly sophisticated) in a geographically definable part or parts of the world. Some organizations may have only one purpose and, thus, are functionally specific; while others may have several purposes, making them almost general purpose regional organizations.

Contiguity of countries that are members of the organizations is not essential. I am not concentrating on regions per se,(1) because my concern with interaction presupposes some kind of distinctive organizational behavior and, perhaps, dynamics. This also bypasses the troublesome problem of boundary identification of regions since the extent of the region covered is defined in the underlying international treaty.(2)

There are many concepts of the global system and its operations, but this is not the place for comparative analysis.(3) As defined here, the system consists of parts that are, in varying degrees, interdependent and that function together as a whole. Every system may have subsystems that exist and function within the larger system. The global system is no exception, and regional organizations are here viewed as subsystems of the global system.

In both the global system and the regional subsystems the predominant actors are nation states, but nongovernmental entities such as multinational corporations and influential interest groups also participate as actors. In the global system, intergovernmental organizations (IGOs) influence the interaction process and, thereby, have actor status.

The global system is prismatic in character: it operates in several spheres or domains (military, economic, political, and others) and in each of these spheres the maintenance of an equilibrium is sought. If the equilibrium is disturbed as a result of the interaction process, the system will attempt to return to the equilibrium state through various adjustments and, if unsuccessful, major system changes will occur or the system may decay.

Inputs into the global system may come not only from states, universal and regional IGOs, and powerful nongovernmental organizations (NGOs), but also from the physical environment such as the exhaustion of raw materials. Inputs may cause disturbances in the global system, affect its equilibrium, activate an "equilibrating" mechanism, or may lead to important changes in particular spheres of the system. Disturbances may also be caused by the creation of new regional IGOs or their disbandment, by the formation of new alliances to counter perceived military or economic threats, and the dissolution of old ones. As a consequence, the power distribution within the global system may be altered. Outputs of the global system in the form of particular initiatives in reaction to various inputs may have differing impacts on the regional organizations, with the implications for the operations of these organizations often difficult to foresee. What is obvious, though, is the dynamic nature of the global system, to which interactions between it and regional organizations have major consequences.

For our inquiry, the economic, military, and political spheres of the global system are most interesting since these are the issue areas for which regional organizations have been created. What kind of interactions take place between these organizations and the global system, and what are the effects of these interactions?

We can identify several categories of such interaction effects. In some of these categories, the cause-effect thrust produces changes in the global system while, in others, global system outputs may contribute to changes in existing regional organizations or to the creation of new ones. In the first cluster of categories, we list the following regional organization activities:

1. Common management of relations with outside states, organizations and the global system;

2. Market integration and separation, with consequent diversion of international trade;

3. Regional monetary cooperation;

4. Regional investment regulations;

5. Regional military cooperation; and

6. The setting up of multipurpose (political-economic-security) regional organizations.

In the cause-effect relationships through which the global system affects regional organizations, the patterns of interaction are more diffuse, and the impact less clear, than in the opposite flow of effects. Nevertheless, we can discern two categories of interaction: Behavior stimulated by multilateral and unitary global actors; and effects of resource scarcities and consequent economic imbalances.

REGIONAL EFFECTS ON THE GLOBAL SYSTEM

Common Foreign Policy Formation Within Regional Organizations

The European Community is the prime example of institutionalized intergovernmental foreign policy formation by member states. The three EC treaties contain a number of foreign policy competences that have been assigned by the member states to the Community institutions. Most prominent among these is the negotiation of trade agreements regulating tariff and nontariff barriers. The participation of the EC as a unit in the Kennedy and Tokyo rounds of trade negotiations is an example of this regional organization's pervasive influence on international trade. In addition, the Community has signed a growing number of trade and economic cooperation agreements with countries throughout the world which have left their distinctive mark on the world economy.(4) Many nonmember countries have been eager to negotiate such agreements in order to improve their economic relations with the most powerful unit in world trade. Their interest has demonstrated the economic magnetism of the Community and has expanded its political influence.

A particularly significant foreign policy instrument with implications for the global system has been the Community's capability to create associations with nonmember states, giving them preferential treatment through tariff advantages and financial aid. Greece and Turkey were the first countries to become associates in the early 1960s. However, the greatest impact of the association instrument has been in Africa, which we will discuss in the next section.

In addition to the specific EC external competences, the member countries have also developed a foreign policy coordination device to "speak with one voice" on certain international issues. We have discussed some of the details of this mechanism in chapter 4. The center pieces of this mechanism are the Political Committee composed of the political directors of the foreign ministries and the periodic meetings of the foreign ministers of the Nine.

There is no question that the combination of the EC external competences and of the foreign policy coordination mechanism has materially increased the impact of the Community countries on the global system. Their cooperation and the consequent leadership role assumed by the EC member states in the CSCE negotiations, which was accepted by the United States, strengthened the position of the West and led to concessions by the Soviet Union and her satellites. Of global significance, also, has been the stand taken by the Nine toward Israel's policies in the occupied Arab areas which tends to strengthen the hand of the United States in the crucial Middle East peace negotiations, and which, of course, has aided the Community's image in the Euro-Arab Dialogue.(5) The high level of collaboration of the Nine with respect to economic policies in various United Nations forums has made successful outcomes for their foreign policy objectives more likely. It is difficult to measure the effects on the power distribution within the global system that results from both the policy coordination efforts and the common policies carried out under the EC competences. Multi-directional shifts of power, however, have benefited the EC countries, while affecting the Soviet Union negatively overall, and the United States more negatively in the economic sphere, but positively from a political point of view.

In Latin America, the economic regional organizations such as LAFTA, CACM, and the Andean Pact (which, to varying degrees, have been unsuccessful in their own integration efforts) have shown some concordance in foreign affairs, especially in United Nations voting; and, as far as CACM is concerned, in support of regional (OAS) over global (UN) peacekeeping endeavors.(6) But these policy coordination manifes-tations had hardly any effects on the global system. One of the purposes of the Caribbean Common Market was external policy coordination,(7) but its Standing Committee of Ministers of Foreign Affairs has not been significantly active.

On the other hand, CECLA, the Special Latin American Coordi-nating Committee designed for unified economic bargaining with ex-ternal powers and international organizations, scored some successes vis-a-vis Europe and the United States in the early 1970s. In 1971, the United States government exempted Latin America from the 10 percent trade surcharge imposed on U.S. trading partners by the Nixon adminis-tration and the EC agreed to explore ways to improve its trade relationship with Latin America.(8) SELA, the Latin American Econom-ic System, organized in 1975 and counting among its extensive member-ship some Caribbean countries, has as one of its purposes the formula-tion of common regional positions prior to attending international meetings and, therefore, may compete with or replace CECLA. Such coordination sessions were held prior to UNCTAD conferences, but common positions adopted are not binding(9) and, therefore, their impact on the global system, if any, is likely to be very minor.

For Afrifca, despite a plethora of regional economic organizations since the early 1960s (the latest entry being the West African Economic Community), the prospects for _effective_ cooperation and integration are dim. Nevertheless, in the negotiations with the European Com-munity on Lome II, all African states managed to adopt a common position, although some of their governments were not fully satis-fied.(10) The policy stand of the African countries, most of whom are members of the African regional organizations, did, indeed, have a significant impact on the European Community and, thus, on the global system; but the individual African organizations, so far, have not had any significant effects on that system.

In Asia, ASEAN (Association of South East Asian Nations) has emerged as a regional organization which has used its rather informal collective decision making procedures for foreign policy coordination. This has been potentially significant in ASEAN's relations with Japan, with implications for the global system to be discussed in the next section.

We have purposely omitted Comecon in our discussion. Although qualifying as a regional organization, its decisions are determined by the wishes of the Soviet Union and, therefore, any interactions with the global system are primarily echoes of Soviet decisions and policies.(11)

Market Integration and Separation

The creation of a substantial trade bloc, especially if it comprises major parts of one or more continents, has a significant impact on the distribution of economic and political power in the global system and could alter its operation. International trade diversions can be serious, national economies may suffer, and national governments may take protective measures, leading to a sharp deterioration of international relations. The final outcome could be vicious competition between continents and an increasingly inefficient use of the world's economic resources.(12)

The expansion of the European Community's market beyond the member states through various free trade arrangements with former EFTA countries, and its Mediterranean policy of special trade agreements with countries rimming this body of water have made Western Europe and the Mediterranean region into a huge trading area where tariff barriers on most manufactured goods have been dismantled. The Lome Conventions have extended this trading area into much of Africa, with industrial, technological, and financial measures such as the European Development Fund and Stabex. As we have seen in chapter 4, ties are supplemented by institutional and political links with parliamentarians and civil servants of the EC member states playing major roles in this endeavor.(13)

It is not difficult to imagine that the long-run implication of this EC trading bloc and extensions of West European influence will be a weakening of the current U.S. power position in both economic and political terms. But, paradoxically, it will probably also adversely affect the other superpower, the Soviet Union, whose influence and interests in Africa and the Middle East may face growing opposition as many states benefiting economically from the Lome Convention may be unreceptive to Soviet aid and intervention. Of course, as the negotiations for Lome II have shown, the African affiliates have deplored the "negative and rigid" attitude of the EC representatives, but the increase of financial aid from $5 billion to nearly $7.5 billion, expanded Stabex support, and increased industrial cooperation are generally satisfactory results.(14) Without doubt, the reinforcement of the EC-African trade bloc by Lome II and the consequent rise in power of the EC countries is a significant change in the global system. It is likely to gradually alter the system's operation and may change the economic and political equilibrating forces without, however, affecting its ability to regain and then maintain a sound equilibrium.

The relationship between ASEAN and Japan may carry within it the seeds for an arrangement similar to the EC-Lome link. Japan has always looked toward Southeast Asia as a market for its manufactured goods and as a source of essential raw materials. Indeed, the region is heavily dependent on Japanese products, investment capital, and Japanese purchases of raw materials. As a consequence, Japan has been able to establish an economic hegemonial position in Southeast Asia and particularly over the member states of ASEAN – Indonesia, Malaysia, the Philippines, Singapore, and Thailand – as illustrated by the trade figures for 1976. During that year Japanese exports to the area amounted to $6.1 billion, while the United States shipped only $3.7 billion and all of the EC less than $3.5 billion to that area. Japan was also the best customer, purchasing nearly $9 billion, mostly in raw materials and oil. United States imports from that area were somewhat less than $6 billion and those of the Community countries about $3.7 billion.(15)

During the 1977 ASEAN meeting of heads of government, Japan's Prime Minister was invited to participate. In contrast to a visit in 1974 to some of the ASEAN countries by then Prime Minister Tanaka who became the target of anti-Japanese demonstrations – perhaps memories still lingered on of Japan's attempts to establish the "Great Asia Co-Prosperity Sphere" during World War II – the climate during the Fukuda visit was friendly, probably in part because of ASEAN expectations of financial support from Japan.(16)

Interchanges begun with the Fukuda visit may eventually lead to an agreement similar to the Lome Convention. Such an agreement may give the ASEAN countries preferred access to the Japanese market, although actual tariff preferences may have to overcome GATT objections. In addition, these countries may be offered a stabilization scheme for raw material prices and receive assistance for technology transfers and development aid in general. Other Third World countries may object to the special treatment for the ASEAN states by Japan. However, if the Japanese government were to double its currently rather low foreign aid as announced, it might mollify the Group of "77."

For Japan, a Lome-type arrangement would not only bolster its markets for the export of manufactured goods, but it would also offer great supply security for needed raw materials. But for the United States, such a development would be the creation of another trading bloc that might well impair American exports to the ASEAN area. Moreover, as in the Lome Convention, intensified Japanese economic ties would engender greater political influence, perhaps at the expense of American foreign policy objectives. If the United States government were to give its blessing to such an arrangement, some ASEAN countries might see in it a signal that U.S. interests in Southeast Asia were waning, and Japan was being given a surrogate role to ensure peace and stability in the region through its economic power and influence. For all these reasons, the impact on the global system flowing from such an arrangement by ASEAN and Japan would be considerable, and the power position not only of the United States but also the Soviet Union, with its extensive interests in the Pacific, would be affected.

Regional Monetary Cooperation

The introduction of a monetary system by a regional organization holding the currencies of the member states to a narrow range tends to have repercussions beyond the territory of the organization since it affects many currencies throughout the world. And this impact is all the greater the more economically powerful the member states of the organization. It is, therefore, not surprising that when the European Community initiated the EMS in March 1979, it sent shock waves through the global economy, although the range of fluctuations permitted was the same as the "snake," and although Great Britain remained outside the system for the time being. But this new system was much more than the "snake," since it was bolstered by an impressive reserve fund in which U.S. dollars and 20 percent gold were included and was directed at the ultimate creation of a new monetary unit, the ECU.

The EMS modifies the existing, though already weakened and altered, Bretton Woods system; and it may end the role of the U.S. dollar as the main international reserve currency. There is, of course, little doubt that the erosion of world confidence in the dollar provided the major impetus for setting up the EMS and creating the ECU, an accounting device that may become a new money. But whether the ECU ever achieves world reserve currency status may well depend more upon actions by the United States than by the European Community and its member states.

In the meantime, EMS policy with respect to the dollar remains uncertain, and so does the role of the dollar in the all-important trade in crude oil. If the Arab oil producers were to replace the dollar with a basket of currencies such as the EMS, the repercussion for the global economic system would be explosive, especially considering the billions of Eurodollars floating around the world. With the dollar thus wounded and suspect, international capital movements would be impeded and international trade would falter. A basket of currencies would be no easy substitute because none of the countries behind the EMS has a sufficiently large economy, and common economic policies in the EC remain difficult to achieve. Thus, the introduction of the EMS poses serious problems for the economic, and to a lesser degree political, spheres of the global system which could severely upset its equilibrium if the dollar's position as a world reserve currency is undermined.

Regional Investment Regulations

Although many developing countries have attempted to regulate foreign investment capital in order to assure that its operations conform to national policies, the Andean Common Market (ANCOM) scored a first by drawing up a comprehensive investment code for all member governments of this organization. This code is embodied in the famous Decision 24, which places great value on "independence from foreign influence" and aims at increasing the bargaining power of the members, without discouraging the influx of useful foreign investment. The member states are to be prevented from adopting beggar-my-neighbor policies to attract investment by MNCs.(17) The code contains a comprehensive program of industrialization and envisages strong political direction by the leadership of the ANCOM countries.

Under the code, foreign manufacturing firms must convert their subsidiaries step-by-step into mixed enterprises with at least 51 percent ownership in local hands by 1986 (by 1991 in Ecuador and Bolivia). However, foreign companies exporting as much as 80 percent of their production to nonmember states are exempted. New foreign investment entering the region must start with at least 51 percent local ownership. The code freezes all new foreign investment in banking and finance, public utilities, insurance, transport, communications, and advertising. But several exceptions have been made by some of the member states, especially Peru, Ecuador, and Chile (now disassociated), and new waivers of the code's strict provisions continue to be made, considerably reducing its effectiveness.(18)

In spite of the failure of some of the features contained in Decision 24, its provisions have had a global impact. It has provided most of the intellectual and motivational sources of demands by the Third World leaders for a global code of conduct for MNCs, which is now being negotiated in the United Nations under the auspices of the Commission on Transnational Corporations. But Decision 24 contributed to more than the code of conduct negotiations; control over MNCs sought by the Third World has become part of an overall strategy to transform the market orientation of the world economy and establish a New International Economic Order (NIEO).(19) Moreover, the investment control model devised by ANCOM has also induced a number of Third World governments to put in place similar provisions for the acceptance of foreign investment and for the establishment of subsidiaries by MNCs. Thus, ANCOM as a regional organization may well be, at least in part, responsible for bringing about, indirectly of course, changes in the economic dimension of the global system.

Regional Military Cooperation

It is generally recognized that global peace has been maintained during the last two decades by the strategic balance between the superpowers. Whether this benign equilibrium in the global system will continue may well depend on the ability of one of the superpowers to achieve an invulnerable first strike capability. In the meantime, can this equilibrium be affected by decisions and actions of regional security organizations? Obviously, the chief actors for such a development would be NATO and the Warsaw Treaty Organization (WTO).

NATO's decisions and actions, up to now, may not have influenced much the strategic balance between the United States and the Soviet Union, but have had an impact on the overall military, and perhaps political, equilibrium of the global system. The three percent increase in expenditures for NATO forces to which the member states committed themselves in 1978 is strengthening the European theatre power of NATO and, to some extent, counterbalances the effect of the enormous Soviet deployment of tanks and missiles in Eastern Europe. Without this NATO action, the global balance would have been tilted in favor of the Soviets.

The Eurogroup coordinating actions aiming at procurement rationalization (discussed in chapter 4) also may have long-range effects on the central balance. It will enhance NATO's conventional capabilities and reduce duplication of weapons, equipment, and spare parts.

Finally, expanding consultation among the allies strengthens NATO vis-a-vis the Soviet Union and East European satellites. The consultations preceding the signing of the CSCE Final Act and in preparation for the review sessions regarding the application of this Act in Belgrade in 1978 and in Madrid in 1980 have strengthened the pursuit of NATO objectives and helped its position in its continuing confrontations with the WTO.

On the other hand, intra-NATO quarrels (such as the Greek-Turkish dispute over Cyprus and the United States Congressional mandate to cut the flow of military supplies to Turkey) weaken NATO in its relationship with the East. The withdrawal of France from the integrated structure of NATO had a similar effect.

The impact of WTO decisions and actions is essentially different from those of NATO because the satellite governments are under strict control of the Soviet Union. WTO decisions and actions are really those of the USSR, and it is not proper to regard them as emanating from an independent decision making process within a regional organization. In other words, whatever effect a WTO decision or action may have on the global system is actually an effect caused by Soviet policy.(20)

The security functions performed by the Organization of American States (OAS) have been significant – examples are sanctions against Cuba, the Dominican Republic intervention in 1965, and the Honduras-El Salvador football war – but their concrete effects on the global system have been minimal. Only one aspect of the OAS security functions could be viewed as globally relevant, and that is the priority given to the organization's peacekeeping efforts over those of the United Nations. In the event of disturbance of the peace in the OAS area, the OAS peacekeeping mechanisms are utilized first, and only if ineffective, is the United Nations resorted to for assistance. Although this priority accords with article 52 of the United Nations Charter, it reduces the worldwide peace maintenance responsibility of the United Nations organs, particularly, of course, of the Security Council.

The security functions carried out by the Organization of African Unity (OAU) also have had only minor significance at the global level and, at least so far, have only minimally affected its interaction processes.

The Establishment of Multipurpose Regional Organizations

The OAS and OAU have purposes and functions other than security. Both are concerned with political and, in varying degrees, economic matters. In addition to serving as a forum for political consultation and cooperation, the OAS has been increasingly supportive of programs for Latin American economic and social development. It provides specialized training for thousands of Latin Americans each year in a wide variety of development related fields. The OAS institutions were also to be utilized by the ill-fated Alliance for Progress launched by the United States in the early 1960s. Had it succeeded, major beneficial changes in the economic, social, and administrative patterns of Latin America and, perhaps, in the political systems of some of the states in the region may have been achieved. In such a case, the consequent transformation of economic and political life in Latin America may have had a significant impact on the interaction process of the global system. However, as events have unfolded during the last two decades, the relationship between the United States and Latin America within and outside the OAS has stagnated. There are indications that South Americans are strengthening their economic and political links with Western Europe in response to greater economic penetration efforts by some of the EC countries. Considering the longstanding cultural ties between South America and Western Europe, such efforts are likely to fall on receptive ears. If, as a consequence, the thrust of relations on the part of individual South American states were to shift from the United States to Europe, it would materially affect the economic and political equilibrium of the global system and tend to reduce the influence of the United States in the OAS.

While the economic concerns of the OAU are less pronounced than those of the OAS, its political interests are more intense and relate to the termination of colonial and neocolonial forms of control in the region. The OAU's Liberation Committee, directly under the control of the General Secretariat, coordinates military aid to African liberation movements in Zimbabwe (former Rhodesia) and in South Africa. If this endeavor is fully successful, the effect on the political equilibrium of the global system could be considerable. White intransigence could arouse an extensive radical protest movement which eventually may lead to the establishment of radical regimes, supported by the USSR. Even if the persistent OAU pressures were to lead only to gradualist solutions in Zimbabwe and Namibia, and later perhaps in South Africa, at least partial responsibility for whatever changes might occur in the global system has to be attributed to the OAU.

The Arab League, with broad membership of Arab states in the Middle East and North Africa, has political and economic aims. However, despite the fact that many of its members are oil producers who have formed a separate unit – the Organization of Arab Petroleum Exporting Countries (OAPEC) – the Arab League itself has not been a very effective organization and has often been rent by serious dissension. In the Euro-Arab Dialogue, in which the League was the principal party for the Arab states, little significant progress has been made. The Arab Common Market, inaugurated in 1965 with great expectations, has also been largely a failure. Hence, the League has had little, if any, impact on any dimension of the global system; although, in view of the key position which Arab crude oil holds in the world economy and in the strategic relations of the major powers (especially considering the volatile and complex Middle East situation), its impact could be enormous.

Finally, a few comments need to be made about the Council of Europe, which has broad-ranged concerns which include political, social, economic, and legal matters. While nearly a hundred conventions have been concluded under the Council's auspices, covering such diverse fields as social security, patents, extradition, medical treatment, automobile insurance, and others, its effect on the global system has been minimal. The main reasons are that most of the problems with which the Council has dealt are primarily of a technical nature; and its political clout, not extensive even within Europe, is even smaller in worldwide affairs.

GLOBAL EFFECTS ON REGIONAL ORGANIZATIONS

It is easier to identify the effects of regional organizations on the global system than to determine the reverse flows. The patterns of activities in most regional organizations (excepting perhaps the EC) are more easily discernible and less complex than in the global system, with its several spheres of interactions and large numbers of actors. Yet two cases can be identified where actions or reactions of regional organizations were caused by parts of the global system and these will be briefly examined in the following pages.

Behavior Stimulated by Multilateral and Unitary Global Actors

As a universal organization, the United Nations and its subordinate agencies are part of the global system, and their decisions, recommendations, and actions provide inputs into the interaction process of the system. In the 1950s the United Nations Economic Commissions for Europe and Latin America (ECE and ECLA) began, through pervasive studies and recommendations, to stimulate regional cooperation schemes to overcome problems of economic development. Although other factors were much more responsible for the establishment of the European Communities than the ECE studies, ECLA gave much impetus to the creation of LAFTA and the CACM.

The Economic Commission for Africa (ECA) also played a major role during the 1950s and early 1960s in arousing interest in regional arrangements and, in spite of the poor record of making various intra-African common markets and free trade areas a success, regional cooperation continues to be a persistent aspiration.(21) Indeed, during the Lome II negotiations, the African countries insisted that 15 percent of the Community financial aid program be allocated to existing and new regional cooperation schemes.(22)

In other United Nations bodies concerned with economic development, regional cooperation also continues to be emphasized. For example, the United Nations proposed draft of the Code of Conduct for Multinational Corporations contains provisions urging support of MNCs for regional cooperation arrangements.(23) The proposed UN code for the transfer of technology expreses itself in a similar vein. Thus, we find an effective interaction pattern between the global and regional systems which has contributed to the establishment of regional organizations in the past and may do so in the future.

In the strategic-political sphere of the global system, the change from a tight bipolar configuration to polycentrism in the late 1950s was reflected in changing control of the superpowers over their respective alliance systems. As a consequence, France could assert increased independence from the United States as symbolized by its withdrawal from NATO's integrated command structure. Some of the East European satellites also showed manifestations of deviations from Soviet policies, but the USSR recaptured control through the swift and effective employment of military force as events in Poland, Hungary, and Czechoslovakia demonstrated.

Exhaustion of Natural Resources and Reactions
by Regional Organizations

The physical environment is a crucial part of the global system and furnishes significant system inputs. A critical pattern of interactions in the economic and political spheres of the system and its subsystems has been caused by the exhaustion of certain raw materials, with the dwindling crude oil supplies being, of course, the prime example.

The regional organization which has been most active in devising plans, policies, and actions to counter the decline of oil supplies has been the European Community. Having at its disposal an extensive institutional framework and mechanisms for intergovernmental collaboration among its member states, the Commission, the Council of Ministers, and the member governments have launched a variety of initiatives. The EC participated in the establishment of the International Energy Agency (IEA) and played a prominent role in the formulation of contingency measures and policies. The Community also took an active part in the establishment of the Conference on International Economic Cooperation (CIEC) which, however, turned out to be a failure with respect to the hoped-for assurance of oil supplies. In addition, the EC initiated the Euro-Arab Dialogue, with very meager results so far. The Community's Mediterranean policy of granting preferences to qualifying Middle East countries was used subtly to show West European sympathies with the Arab cause, and the good relations engendered by the Lome Convention with the African countries were seen as a potential aid in the supply of not only oil, but also other critical raw materials. And finally, within the context of an anticipated, but not yet fully realized, common energy policy, more use was to be made of nuclear resources. We can see, thus, an array of wide-ranging actions undertaken by a regional organization in response to events coming from the global system, actions which, if they were not to achieve their objectives, could, in turn, lead to serious imbalances in the existing economic equilibrium of the international system, and eventually produce an equilibrium of forces quite different from those making up the balance in the global economic system now.

Obviously, the EC with its economically advanced member states, with the critical energy needs of its vast industries, and with demanding consumers was almost compelled to react vigorously to the threat of oil shortfalls. There are no indications that other regional organizations (LAFTA, CACM, OAS, OAU, ASEAN) have shown a similar concern. The following reasons may explain the difference in reactions: 1) the economic needs and different lifestyles of the bulk of the populations in the member states of these organizations which mostly fall into the Third World category, and 2) with the exception of the CAMC, these organizations have as members one or more crude oil producing countries.

CONCLUSIONS

The foregoing discussion demonstrates the existence of a variety of interactions between regional organizations and the global system. The majority of actions originate in the regional organizations and affect different spheres of the system and the prevailing equilibrium therein.

In terms of effectiveness of the actions emanating from the regional organizations as well as their reactions to global system output, one can generalize that the wider the availability of economic resources and the higher the degree of institutionalization of the organizational decision making process, the greater are the effects on the global system. Therefore, the European Community and NATO decisions and actions have a much greater capability to influence various domains of the global system than the regional organizations in the Third World. In turn, reactions and policy responses to system events by the regional organizations of advanced countries have a greater potential of success than those of Third World counterparts. We have disregarded the decisions and actions of Comecon and WTO because they seem to be nothing more than echoes of the policies of the Soviet Union.

Decisions and actions emanating from both the regional organizations and the global system have brought about some changes in sphere equilibria and affected the worldwide distribution of power. But precise measurements are impossible and, therefore, the degree of input can only be judged impressionistically.

The interaction processes described and analyzed in this chapter are evidence of the complex interpenetrations and the plethora of actors which generally characterize the operation of the global system and its subsystems. With such richness of reality compounded by the emergence of new power centers (witness OPEC), the increasing salience of economic factors, and the rapid advance of mind-boggling technologies, Oran Young's "discontinuities" model of the international system(24) becomes increasingly attractive to capture this reality.

NOTES

(1) See also Louis J. Cantori and Steven L. Spiegel, The International Politics of Regions (Englewood Cliffs, N.J.: Prentice-Hall, 1970), pp. 1-5.

(2) See William R. Thompson, "The Regional Subsystem: A Conceptual Explication and a Propositional Inventory," International Studies Quarterly 17, no. 1 (March 1973): 89-117.

(3) A recent concise survey of various concepts is found in Donald E. Lampert, Lawrence S. Falkowski, and Richard W. Mausbach, "Is There an International System?" International Studies Quarterly 22, no. 1 (March 1978): 143-66.

(4) See Werner J. Feld, The European Community in World Affairs (Port Washington, N.Y.: Alfred, 1976), pp. 21-62 and 161-262.

(5) For details see chapter 4, this book.

(6) See Philippe C. Schmitter, Autonomy or Dependence as Regional Integration Outcomes: Central America (Berkeley, Calif.: Institute of International Studies, University of California, 1972), pp. 59-67.

(7) G. Pope Atkins, Latin America in the International Political System (New York: The Free Press, 1977), p. 301.

(8) Ibid., p. 303.

(9) Ibid., p. 304. For a comprehensive analysis of SELA see Robert D. Bond, "Regionalism in Latin America: Prospects for the Latin American Economic System," International Organization 22, no. 2 (Spring 1978): 401-23.

(10) Agence Europe Bulletin, June 28, 1979.

(11) See Andrzej Korbonski, "Theory and Practice of Regional Integration: The Case of Comecon," in Regional Politics and World Order edited by Richard A. Falk and Saul H. Mendloritz (San Francisco: W.H. Freeman, 1973), pp. 152-78; especially pp. 166-70.

(12) See Ernst H. Pregg, Economic Blocs and U.S. Foreign Policy (Washington, D.C.: National Planning Association, 1974), especially p. 11.

(13) For an excellent analysis of Lome II see Michael B. Dolan, "Lome 2 (or Khartoum 1): The Evolution of EC-ACP Relations," paper presented at a Conference of Europeanists, Washington, D.C., March 29-31, 1979.

(14) See Agence Europe Bulletin, June 28, 1979.

(15) OECD, Statistics of Foreign Trade, July 1977.

(16) See D. Davis, "A Marriage is Being Arranged," Fareastern Economic Review, 97, no. 30 (1977): 18-23.

(17) See David Morawetz, The Andean Group: A Case Study in Economic Integration Among Developing Countries (Cambridge, Mass.: The MIT Press, 1973), p. 46.

(18) Ibid., p. 304; and Atkins, Latin America in the International Political System, p. 295.

(19) See Werner J. Feld, Multinational Corporations and U.N. Politics: The Quest for a Code of Conduct (New York: Pergamon Press, 1980).

(20) See Richard F. Staar, The Communist Regimes in Eastern Europe: An Introduction (Stanford, Calif.: The Hoover Institution, 1967), pp. 266-69.

(21) See Constantine V. Vaitsos, "Crisis in Regional Economic Cooperation Among Developing Countries," World Development 6, no. 6 (June 1978): 719-70.

(22) Agence Europe Bulletin, June 25/26 1979.

(23) See U.N. Document E/C.10/AC.2/8, p. 4.

(24) Oran R. Young, "Political Discontinuities in the International System," in International Politics and Foreign Policy edited by James N. Rosenau (New York: The Free Press, Rev. Ed., 1969), pp. 336-49.

15 Whither Regional Integration Theory?

Charles A. Duffy
Werner J. Feld

As regional integration developed in Western Europe and other regions in the post-World War II period, so, too, did attempts to explain and predict the rise of this phenomenon in theoretic terms. Regional integration theory evolved into a cornucopia of explanations for the development of governmental institutions which seemed to go beyond the nation state. But, as integrative activities in Europe slowed with the emergence of DeGaulle and regional organizations based upon free trade areas or common markets in Central and Latin America and East Africa went into eclipse, the salience of regional integration theory seemed to decline. One of the more disheartening aspects of the study of regional integration was the 1975 pronouncement by the godfather of theory, Ernst Haas, that much of the body of theory was obsolete.(1) Independent observation of regional integration efforts in the second half of the twentieth century seemed to bear him out.

Although the geographic scope of regional integration in Western Europe had broadened, neither the scope nor the level of institutional power in the European Community had grown significantly, as neofunctionalists had predicted. In the Third World, regional integration efforts in East Africa, Latin America, and Central America were foundering on the reefs of distrust, noncooperation, and parochial nationalism. In the early 1970s, the promise of regional integration as a means of regional development seemed moribund in contrast to the political clout of a producer cartel known as OPEC.

Integrational malaise and the apparent power of the producer cartels were brought to the fore with the spectacular rise of OPEC to global prominence through the Arab oil embargo of 1973. Rather than stimulating solidarity and integrative activity in Western Europe, as the role of crisis had been perceived by many theorists, the oil crisis precipitated a go-it-alone attitude in the EC countries as a means to resolve their energy problems. Many of the member states displayed a "me first" policy of making individual agreements with the oil producers instead of seeking a common resolution of this international problem.

But can it truly be said that regional integration and regional integration theory are obsolete? The European Community survived the 1973 crisis diminished but intact. Recent movement toward a common monetary policy in the form of the EMS and continuing Community discussions with the ACP countries on the topics of trade, aid, and development seem to indicate a movement toward some form of communal foreign policy and the reinvigoration of Community institutions. The recent transition from an appointive to an elective European Parliament augurs well for the continued vitality of regional integration in Western Europe.

As to regional integration theory, Haas' perception that it is obsolete is a very qualified view. His essential distaste for conventional theories (functionalism, neofunctionalism, and pluralism) appears to be that they have proved inadequate in the explanation and prediction of real world events, the essential task of any theory.(2) He notes that a problem endemic to regional integration theories is "not properly identifying the spatial focus of the process."(3) In other words, the theories tend to overlook the importance of events and actors external to the region or regions under examination. He does suggest, however, that existing theories have correctly identified the incremental nature of the integration process, in terms of both the scope of integration and the motives of the actors.(4)

Haas suggests that the incrementalism of earlier theory is not continuous but disjointed in nature, moving along from one crisis or problem to another as the occasion arises. Moreover, he states that a new "syndrome" of actor perceptions, based upon perceptions of interdependencies is, perhaps, more appropriate for the study of European integration in the 1970s, which he identifies as fragmented issue-linkage.(5) As a process of regional integration, Haas notes that: "Issue linkage occurs when older objectives are questioned, when there is a clamor for satisfaction of new objectives, and when the rationality accepted as adequate in the past ceases to be a guide to future action."(6) Additionally, fragmented issue linkage is more than a process mechanism, it is the driving force or "engine" for regional integrative efforts, and it becomes the context which molds and shapes; its outcomes:

An initial commitment to policies of regional integration presupposes some notion among the participants as to their interdependence. Their initial commitment includes a shared conception on how and why they need one another. But this commitment is fragile. A reassessment of interdependencies in trade, financial flows, and migration may occur as "sensitivities" are perceived differently.

If the costs of increased sensitivity appear to be greater than the initially assumed benefits of interdependence, governments are likely to have second thoughts about integration.(7)

Though still within the confines of neofunctionalist thought, Haas portrays a much different perception of regional integration. Rather than blind automaticity, it is a fragmented, disjointed process, heavily dependent upon the motives of actors and their ability to link the solution of one problem with the solution of prior problems.

Regional integration theory, then, has reached a critical juncture in its development. The general body of knowledge lumped under the rubric of regional integration theory appears to have failed to live up to its promise. The redirection of interest and pressure groups away from national centers of authority to regional centers of authority, with the concommitent growth in regional authority and legitimacy, as foreseen by the neofunctionalists, has not proceeded with any undue haste. The growing web of international organizations, slowly undermining state sovereignty, has not yet appeared, as the functionalists predicted. The federalist United States of Europe, what Hoffman refers to as the "new Jerusalem,"(8) is yet to appear on the global stage.

This chapter continues what Haas started. We will examine the problems and pitfalls of regional integration theories, and their inability to "scientifically" predict the pathways of regional development. Additionally, we will posit a pretheoretical paradigm of regional integration which takes into account fragmented issue-linkage and disjointed incrementalism within the foreign policies and national interest of the member states. Lastly, we will show the paradigm within the European context, both in the development of the European Communities and in its ongoing growth.

WHAT IT IS

A problem which plagues the entire body of regional integration theory is the failure to reach an agreed upon operational definition of the concept. According to Haas (in his early masterpiece, The Uniting of Europe), integration is

> ...the process whereby political actors in several distinct national settings are persuaded to shift their loyalties, expectations, and political activities toward a new center, whose institutions possess or demand jurisdiction over the pre-existing national states.(9)

Later, Haas abandoned this strict process-oriented definition based upon the activities of subnational actors, now insisting that regional integration theory is

> ...concerned with explaining how and why states cease to be wholly sovereign, how and why they voluntarily mingle, merge, and mix with their neighbors so as to lose the factual attributes of sovereignty while acquiring new techniques for resolving conflict between themselves. Regional cooperation, organiza-

tions, systems, and subsystems may help describe steps along the way; but they should not be confused with the resulting definition.(10)

Karl Deutsch, on the other hand, neatly sidesteps both the political nature of integration and the manner of process. For Deutsch, it is a matter of "community building" which is a social process, dealing primarily with the attitudes of individuals. Rather than a process, integration becomes a terminal condition or, more precisely, ". . .the attainment, within a territory, of a 'sense of community' and of institutions and practices strong enough and widespread enough to assure, for a 'long' time, dependable expectations of 'peaceful change' among its population."(11)

In a similar fashion, Etzioni somewhat evades the thorny problem of defining integration, switching his focus to unification, which is a "process in which the integration of a system is increased. . . ."(12) Thus, integration as well as such mechanisms as the "kinds of integrating power" become subsumed within the greater flow of the process of unification and community building.

The problem of defining integration rests upon its perception: is it a process, a terminal condition, an intermediate condition leading to some other terminal condition, or, a mechanism for building toward unification? Similarly, does it concern the attitudes and sentiments of a population, the interests of various political actors, or the desires of states for a peaceful means of conflict resolution?

FUNCTIONALISM AND NEOFUNCTIONALISM

Functionalism, one of the bases of the greater part of regional integration theory, oddly enough did not originate as a theory of regional integration, but as a means of peaceful change through international organization and system transformation. The logic of functionalism rests upon the premise that the nation state, as presently constituted, is incapable of solving economic and social problems of a border-crossing nature. In essence, functionalism seeks to improve the economic and social conditions of man and to eventually replace the present order of obsolete states. Despite a certain determinist flavor, functionalism is more than "vulgar Marxism" as Raymond Aron has referred to it.(13)

Functionalism attempts to identify common international economic and social problems and create regional or global organizations to deal with them. The organizations themselves would be monofunctional in that their sole task would be the addressing of a single international problem and its ultimate solution. The logic is that, in a highly interdependent world society, the scope of certain social and economic problems overwhelms the capacity of the individual nation state to satisfactorily deal with them. As a result, these monofunctional organizations are required. The end result is a conglomeration of border-crossing organizations which, through control over the administration of a certain sector of social or economic life, have removed layers of sovereignty from the state, as well as redirected the sentimental attachments of individuals toward the new organizations. As the role and number of these functionally specific organizations grows, the state system slowly fades. The process is best described by the "father" of functionalism, David Mitrany, who states:

> By entrusting an authority with a certain task, carrying with it command over the requisite powers and means, a slice of sovereignty is transferred from the old authority to the new; and the accumulation of such partial transfers in time brings about a translation of the true seat of authority.

> (Functionalism is a method) which would. . .overlay political divisions with a spreading web of international activities and agencies, in which and through which the interests and life of all the nations would gradually be integrated.(14)

Functionalism rests upon two fundamental assumptions: the first refers to the nature of human perceptions and motivations; the second upon the perceived nature of politics and sovereignty.

Initially, for functional integration to proceed, there is a heavy reliance upon the ability of individuals, both as elites and nonelites, to perceive the rational need for international institutions to deal with problems of an interrelated and interdependent nature. In other words, once people are able to perceive increased benefits and the greater ability and efficiency of regional or global problem solvers, demands will be raised for the solution of other problems with other functionally specific organizations. This process, "spill-over" in a broad sense of the term, will result in ever-widening circles of social and economic integration, and is seen to be a natural evolutionary process of expansion.

The second assumption deals with a perception of sovereignty and politics, a distinction which Hoffman refers to as high politics and low politics.(15) High politics are those most closely associated with the concept of sovereignty: defense, foreign policy, administration of justice. Low politics, on the other hand, embraces the social welfare and economic functions of the body politic. Low politics are perceived to have a low salience in the minds of the public in terms of association with the concept of sovereignty and nationalistic attachments. Since this low salience of association exists, according to functionalist theory, the individual will have little cognitive difficulty with the redirection of his attention to the international organization as the focus of problem solution and disperser of benefits. Dove-tailed with the spill-over phenomenon,(16) the logic of the transfer of "slices of sovereignty" is evident.

Although the development and evolution of the ECSC appeared to have fulfilled the functionalist philosophy (in fact, pro-ECSC arguments were couched in functionalist phraseology), events were to prove that what functionalism lacked was a healthy dose of political realism to counteract the political idealism of the theory. Member states, both of the ECSC and other intergovernmental institutions, were unwilling to share even the smallest degree of sovereignty with these newly created international institutions. With the possible exception of the ECSC, most, if not all postwar regional institutions were considerably more intergovernmental than supranational. In other words, true decision making power lies in the hands of governmental representatives rather than with the members of organizational bureaucracies. The efficiency of monofunctional technocracy did not always spawn legitimacy and redirection of sentiment; the spirit of nationalism, like the nation state itself, was not nearly as archaic as perceived.

This paucity of political input prompted a major critique of the functionalist approach, The Uniting of Europe, by Ernst Haas.(17) The major bone of contention was the question of political involvement in the process. According to Haas, and the neofunctionalist school of thought which developed in his wake, politics was the essence of the process of regional integration. It was not the politics of international power, however, but of the pluralistic democratic society in the member states of the ECSC. The key actors were not the regional institutions of the functionalists, but national and regional elites and pressure groups. The high politics/low politics dichotomy, began to be abandoned.

The "spill-over" concept of growth was maintained and broadened within the neofunctionalist framework. Rather than the simple re-direction of sentiment, the neofunctionalist model portrayed the political impact of groups and elites and their bargaining as contributing to the incremental growth of supranational institutions. Regionally-based elites and interest groups, with memberships formed along the dimension of interest rather than nationality, would develop and bargain within the supranational framework. Through this bargaining, the incremental growth of supranational institutions would be stimulated to deal with related sectors of the economy. Thus, spill-over became related to both the perceived level of authority and the scope of integrated institutions. Incremental growth rather than evolutionary process was stressed.

Although neofunctionalism was perceived to be a hybrid composed of elements of both functionalist and federalist theory,(18) the model changed with major revisions of the central concepts of spill-over and pluralism.

The first major theoretical revision came from Lindberg and Schein-gold, who suggested that spill-over may not have the deterministic quality which functionalism posited and neofunctionalism tacitly accepted in its incremental pattern. With an emphasis upon process rather than end-state, they argued that other possibilities exist, that the process may result in plateaus of "spill-back" or "encapsulation."(19) Further elaboration of this theme came from Philippe Schmitter, whose revised neofunctional model envisaged a myriad of outcomes which could occur along the way, depending upon the scope and level of integration. In other words, the process may result in "encapsulation," which Schmitter describes as a "self-maintaining international sub-system"; or "spill-back" may occur, "whereby in response to tensions actors consequently withdraw from their original objective, down-grading their commitment to mutual cooperation."(20)

The second major area of revision dwelt upon the framework of the process, the pluralist model. Although Haas originally noted that heroic actors such as a DeGaulle or a Monnet may have an impact upon the process, the impact of external actors and/or events was originally thought to be minimal. This possible variable was explored by Nye,(21) who came to the conclusion that, indeed, both external actors and events should be included as a "process mechanism" within the evolution of integrative schemes, with the emphasis placed upon the role of the external actors.

Although events may act as a temporary stimulus, the role of actors, according to Nye, is continuous.(22) Nye cites the favorable impact of external actors upon the early efforts at regional integration in Central America. Moreover, the policies of the major powers may have both intended and unintended effects upon the on-going process of regional integration.(23) At a more general level, interest groups and elites may become more disposed toward regional integration as in-creased benefits are perceived as a result of a stronger international position vis-a-vis external actors through increased cooperative ac-tion.(24) This new process mechanism, Nye concludes, has a strong perceptual content. He notes:

> The way that regional decision makers perceive the nature of the external situation and their response to it is an important condition determining agreement on further integration. There are a variety of relevant perceptions, such as a sense of external threat from a giant neighbor, loss of status felt by the Europeans and Latin Americans as a result of bipolarity, and simple demonstration effects ("everybody's doing it").

And, furthermore, "Agreement on the nature of the external situation and on what the regional organization should do to deal (or not deal) with it is the favorable condition that makes an integrative response to the process mechanisms more probable."(25)

With this extensive process of shaping, rethinking, and adjusting of variables, why did Haas proclaim that, in 1975, neofunctionalism was obsolete, especially in Western Europe,(26) when it was initially con-ceived as the theory especially applicable to the European milieu?(27) Although not addressed by Haas, one reason seems to lie with the nature of the beast. If anything, neofunctionalism has become theory's equivalent to the many-headed Hydra of Greek mythology. The complex sets of variables proposed by Haas and Schmitter and Nye,(28) lead one further from predictive validity, rather than closer to it. The situation is analogous to the construction of regression equations in statistics through the additive process of multiple variable inclusion. It would seem that the more variables one adds to the equation, the greater the predictive power of the total equation (the amount of unexplained variance will decrease). In reality, the addition of more variables, after a certain point is reached, will only marginally increase the over-all strength of the equation, while decreasing the predictive ability of the individual variables themselves. In an effort to construct a more powerful theory, neofunctionalists passed the point of diminishing returns in theory construction. Theoretical elegance and parsimony were thrown to the winds.

Having added this large number of variables to their theory, neofunctionalists have also shown an unwillingness to decide upon, operationally define, and test the primary or crucial variables. Aside from a fundamental belief in incrementalism, neofunctionalists have not reached any sort of agreement on the relative importance each individual variable plays in the process of regional integration. A case in point is that of the role of external actors and/or events. Originally perceived to be peripheral (at best), they came to be considered, nearly a generation later, as one of the more crucial factors in fostering both the genesis and continued development of regional integration schemes. Moreover, there has been little continuity in the neofunctionalist perception of who the main actors are. Early theory emphasized the primacy of interest and pressure groups, elites, and supranational technocrats, and their interaction within the regional setting. Little attention was paid to the balance of decision making capabilities within regional institutions between the supranational organs and the inter-governmental organs. It was felt that the supranational organs, due to spill-over, would eventually supersede the role of governmental representatives. Only later was attention focused on the notions of authority and legitimacy, of both the state and the regional institutions.(29) As Haas notes, authority and legitimacy were perceived to go hand in hand, with the former breeding the latter and vice-versa. In reality, although the vitality of the European Community authority is largely unquestioned on certain matters, legitimacy remains low in comparison to the nation state.(30)

This, of course, leads to the central critique of neofunctionalism: the implied or explicit presumption of the pluralistic democracy model of the integrating region. Although addressing the concept of theory in international relations as a whole, Hoffman's criticism appears to be especially applicable to neofunctionalism:

> Many of the mistakes of modern theoretical attempts in international relations and in international law come from the systematic misapplication of the model of the integrated Rechstaat to the decentralized international milieu — either as a norm for analysis, or as a goal.(31)

Erring on the side of simplicity and fashion (pluralist democracy was the vogue in American political science at the time), theorists adopted this model readily. In so doing, they fell short, as Hansen notes, on three accounts:

> ...first, a failure to relate the process of regional integration closely enough to relevant international systems factors; second, a tendency to deny rather than to investigate the discontinuity between high and welfare politics proclaimed by traditionalists; and, third, a failure to recognize that sizeable (and equitably distributed) economic gains would result from a common market coordinated by sovereign states rather than managed by ceaselessly expanding supranational organizations.(32)

Even though the efforts of revision and self-criticism which characterized later neofunctionalist thought attempted to correct these earlier flaws, the results led to further theoretical difficulties. The over-emphasis on process, as characterized by Lindberg and Scheingold's adaptation of structural-functional analysis(33), led to the abandonment of the key notions of beginning and ending. Little attention was paid to the questions of why regional integration efforts were undertaken, and what would be the final or ultimate shape of institutional arrangements. End-points were seen to be merely temporary way stations on the journey of supranationalism. The concentration upon process seemed to free the neofunctionalist from the necessity of facing up to the fact that the theory, as posited and revised, may not square with the facts of integrative efforts in the real world. In Haas' terminology, the drive for the identification of independent variables had led to the neglect of the all-important dependent variables. It may be correct to assert, then, that neofunctionalism, in both its present and past formulations, is obsolete in terms of scientific theory.

COMMUNICATIONS AND COMMUNITY BUILDING

While regional integration efforts in the real world prospered and declined, and neofunctionalism endured the agonizing throes of retrenchment and reevaluation, a third major theory of regional integration bloomed – the communications approach. Just as neofunctionalism had sprung, essentially, from the head of Ernst Haas, communications theory owes its greatest debt to Karl Deutsch. This approach reflects Deutsch's concern with societal perceptions, values, and sentiments, and the transmission of these concepts within a cybernetic framework of government.

An early work of Deutsch and several collaborators furnished a basis from which to build. Political Community in the North Atlantic Area,(34) an extensive historical study of integration efforts, provided several key foundations. Primarily, the essential element of integration or community building was the development of a "sense of community," which Deutsch defined in much broader terms than the economic focus of functionalism or neofunctionalism. He notes that: "By sense of community we mean a belief on the part of the individuals in a group that they have come to agreement on at least this one point: that common social problems must and can be resolved by process of 'peaceful change.' "(35)

Secondly, and perhaps more importantly, Deutsch and his collaborators described four heuristic end-points of a more definite nature than neofunctionalist thought. Possibilities are delineated along two dimensions: an integratoin threshold and an amalgamation threshold. Thus, four outcomes are predicted: nonamalgamated/nonintegrated (not amalgamated, not security community); amalgamated/nonintegrated (amalgamated but not security community); nonamalgamated/integrated (pluralistic security community); and, amalgamated/integrated (amalgamated security community).(36) The central focus of the study deals with the background conditions which may foster the development of the two most interesting models, the pluralistic and the amalgamated security community. For it is in those two alone that a sense of community has been fostered.

Later, the cybernetic approach to government advocated by Deutsch(37) was successfully operationalized for use in the regional milieu, and the chief indicator of integration was identified as the Index of Relative Acceptance, or RA factor. According to this view, both the rate and the quantitative scope of integration could be measured through various measures of border-crossing communications (i.e., mail flows, electronic communication, student travel, tourism, and relative levels of intraregional trade). These measures, compared to what could be expected among nations (given levels of population, education, industrialization, and GNP), would provide empirical evidence of integration as a social process. The RA factor had the side benefit of the ability to employ repeated measures of the integration process over time, thus allowing an empirical observation of the progress of regional integration programs. Working along these lines, Deutsch and his associates concluded that integration in Europe was on the rise through 1954, when it peaked. Integration maintained this plateau through 1958 and, from then on, began a slow decline.(38)

As a process-oriented theory of regional integration, the communications approach shares a problem similar to that of neofunctionalism – the lack of a causal basis for its assumptions. As Cantori and Spiegel note: "The transactionalists. . .have never been able to set out a causal theory, so it has never been clear whether the transactions being measured are cause or effect of the integration process."(39) And, like their neofunctionalist colleagues, there has never been any clear determination (beyond Deutsch's early work) of an end-point or "goal" of the integration process. Attention has been paid to getting there, rather than where they are going. In fact, the communications approach fails to come to grips with the three elements of causality: determinism, time ordering, and the elimination of spurious relationships.(40)

The validity of the communications approach was uniquely examined by Fisher.(41) Arguing that this approach "is based upon the hypothesis that social assimilation causes political development and, therefore, that social assimilation must exist before political development can occur,"(42) he examined the operation of the paradigm which the communications theorists posit concerning the growth of integration in Western Europe. Fisher concludes that the Deutsch "sociocausal" paradigm exhibits weakness on two points: the failure to relate the key variables of social interaction and political integration and the exclusion of both internal and external variables which other bodies of theory (read neofunctionalism) have explored.(43) More importantly, his study of the paradigm leads him to conclusions which sharply contradict the earlier assertion by Deutsch that integration in Western Europe was declining. To the contrary, Fisher finds a "seven-fold increase between 1953 and 1964."(44)

Finally, the discussion of the communications approach brings to the fore the controversy of traditionalism versus empiricism in international politics. In other words, is measurement alone of sufficient value to explain and predict as the theory intended? Morse notes that the communications approach actually represents theoretical poverty and, that as a theory, "it is illusory because it prevents one from analyzing the qualitative nature of international transactions."(45)

INTEGRATION AND INTERDEPENDENCE

A concept which has been closely allied with the study of regional integration is that of interdependence; a notion which implies the importance of social and economic relationships, especially among advanced industrial economies. The essential rationale of functionalism was based upon the assumption of global interdependence of national societies and the inability of individual governments to confront the resulting problems. However, the study of interdependence has suffered from the same problem as regional integration theory: How does one define it?

Rosecrance and Stein note that there are at least three definitions of interdependence:

> In its most general sense, interdependence suggests a relationship of interests such that if one nation's position changes, other states will be affected by that change. A second meaning, derived from economics, suggests that interdependence is present when there is an increased national "sensitivity" to external economic developments....The most stringent definition...argues that interdependence entails a relationship that would be costly to break.(46)

Moreover, Rosecrance and his colleagues suggest that there are two dimensions of interdependence: horizontal, which "charts the flow of money, men, goods, and so on" (which strongly suggests that the communications approach is actually measuring interdependence rather than integration); and vertical interdependence, which "shows the economic response of one economy to another, in terms of factor prices."(47) None of these explanations of interdependence, however, captures the perceptual qualities of interdependencies. Both horizontal and vertical relationships can be broken, no matter how costly. Similarly, national "sensitivity" can be cushioned by the development of national sources and industries or alternatives. What is important is the perception by the population of a state that their fate, as well as their economy and society, is somehow intertwined with that of a neighboring state, and that this knot cannot be extricated without extremely harmful consequences.

The matter at hand, however, is not the nature of interdependence, but its relationship to regional integration theory. Early functionalist thought, of course, viewed integration as the natural response to problems of an interdependent global or regional society. Hence, interdependence can be perceived as a causal factor for regional integration planning. William Wallace notes that the European experience can be viewed as: "...part of the general response of the governments of industrialized countries to the problems of an interdependent international economy, as part of an overall trend towards the management of interdependence...."(48) Similarly, Haas has noted that the perceptions of interdependence are important in the formation of issue linkages among integrative actors.(49)

On the other hand, others argue that interdependence is an effect or result, rather than a cause of regional integration. In other words, interdependence is a conscious goal to be met through the establishment of agencies of regional decision making. Morse, for instance, views the central role of the EEC as generating "interdependence internally and independence externally."(50) A similar goal was harbored by the planners of LAFTA who saw regional integration as a means to foster regional interdependence and import substitution as a defense against further dependencies upon the advanced industrial states of North America and Western Europe.

WHERE DO WE GO FROM HERE?

The study of regional integration theory seems to be a maze from which there is little hope of escape. There is little real agreement as to the nature of the phenomenon under study, let alone how to study it. The various theories are, in Rosenau's terminology, pretheories in that they exhibit little theoretical power of explanation and prediction. Moreover, there is little agreement as to the relationship between integration and interdependence. It seems that the two are somehow interrelated, but the nature of the relationship is open to discussion.

One possible resolution of this dilemma presents itself in the form of macrotheory synthesis. Rather than taking the pretheories as individual explanations, it may be fruitful to deal with them simply as elements of a larger, more comprehensive conceptual view of the mechanics of regional integration, a variation on the theme of the unified field. By-passing the question of causality for the moment, it is easy to see how such a theoretic "integration" may work, in light of three arenas of integrative activity: policy integration, social integration, and institutional integration.

Neofunctionalism, with its emphasis on the political activities of interest groups and elites, may accurately portray the process of forming common policies by a regional institution. These policies would reflect the extensive bargaining and logrolling which dominates the neofunctional model of decision making. Similarly, the communications approach may, within this framework of macrotheory, provide not only a model but, additionally, a measurement of social integration within a region, a process which coexists temporally with policy integration. Moreover, such a macrotheoretical arrangement would reflect the interaction of policy and social integration in a theoretically recursive model.

Finally, both functionalism and federalism (two of the earliest pretheories of regional integration) may provide the framework of institutional integration within which function the neofunctional and communications processes. Functionalism, with its web of specific organizations within a region, may provide the institutional setting in which the bargaining of neofunctionalism occurs. Secondly, the administrative activities of supranational technocrats within these organizations may provide the forum for increased social learning and facilitate increased transnational communication. Alternatively, the federalist hypothesis may provide the heuristic model of an end-state. Increasing policy and social integration may provide the necessary amount of transnational behavior modification to move from the organizations of functionalism to the institutional constitutional arrangements of federalism.

Pleasant as this alternative may seem, two fundamental weaknesses remain: an agreed definition of what is regional integration, satisfactory to all the various fields; and the all-important question of causality. Although both these problems could, in principle, be overcome, neither the parts nor the sum of the parts, as presently constituted, help to establish causality.

A NATIONAL INTEREST MODEL OF INTEGRATION

Another and perhaps more intriguing alternative lies in the construction of a pretheoretical causal model, based upon the national interests of the chief actor in the integrative process, the nation state.(51) Regional integration (from its lowest form, a free trade area, to its highest form, political union) is seen from the perspective of nation state foreign policy goals. These goals determine the scope and level of integration and define the parameters of the regional institutions to be created. In some regional contexts, such as Western Europe, these institutions have been given a relatively high degree of independence; in other regions, for example Latin-America, their decision making latitude is mostly very limited. Indeed, so far, in all regional arrangements the member states exhibit ultimate control of decision making power and delimit the role of the regional civil service. Thus, the nation states, as central actors in the integration process, are able to pace both the scope and level of regional integration. Four operational concepts give substance to this model.

The first operational definition is, by necessity, that of the concept of "region." In defining what a region is, certain requirements appear to be central to its delineation. Normally, there is a sense of geographical contiguity, which implies spatial proximity and common frontiers. Moreover, the region itself must have a spatial definition for people living within it. In other words, people must think of themselves as being Western European or Latin American as well as being German or Brazilian. Secondly, there should be an historical pattern of political interaction, of conflict and conflict resolution within the borders of the region. This is important for two reasons: first, it defines the region perceptually for decision makers both within and without the region; and, secondly, it provides a perspective in which policy planners of member states can set foreign policy objectives. Each state within the region must be a part of the "historical baggage"(52) of every other element of the region. Following from the second, there must also be a set of social norms which pervades the region. This may entail common political ideals, religion, moral values, class structure, or any of a number of elements of societal interaction. In a sense, then, there must be a "common soil" within which social communication and trans-national learning (social integration) may flourish. Thus, the concept of region leads directly to the concept of integration.(53)

With this definition of region in mind, the operational definition of integration posited by this model is distinctly similar to Haas' second definition. However, regional integration is more than a means of conflict resolution within a regional context. It becomes a means through which nation states seek to maximize benefits, on a long-range basis, in terms of their national interests. Moreover, this definition pertains to a subform of regional integrative activity, the formation of regional institutions with defined decision making capabilities. The process of regional integration, then, is defined by the inputs of national actors. Scope and level of authority is not within the calculus of technocrats, but within the negotiated agreement of the member states. Succinctly stated, integration is:

> the means through which various states within a region, in a peaceful and noncoercive manner, collectively seek to resolve conflicts in either a preemptive or reactive response. Moreover, it is a vehicle through which member states maximize or, attempt to maximize, their national interests on a long-range basis through the creation of supranational institutions and the evolution of regional policies.

Such an orientation to the political motives of states is not outside the realm of discussion in previous theories, but its implications as an important dependent variable have never been fully explored.

A third operational concept which must be understood refers to the chief actors in regional integration: the nation states. Whether defined in terms of sovereignty or gemeinschaft and gesellschaft, it is the national government, rather than elites and interest groups, which is the dominating element in the development of regional integration. This assumes that governmental decision making is rational and coherent in the sense that it serves to further the national interest and the survival of the regime, both domestically and internationally. Coherence refers to the "maturity" of the regime norms, and their ability to shape decisions. Decisions should be formulated within the context of the "structural characteristics" of the state which, according to Wilkenfeld and his colleagues, are "The more stable attributes...providing the static context within which...decisions are made."(54) Or, in Hoffman's framework, there must be a developed national consciousness, a defined national situation, and an acknowledged and respected sense of nationalism.(55) To make a rather broad analogy, a state must exhibit adult rather than child-like decision making.(56) In other words, decision making should work toward meeting long-term goals within a coherent framework of national interest instead of disjointed and fragmented decisions based upon simplistic and impressionistic views of immediate concerns.

A fourth concept of this model which requires definition is that of the national interest. Although the central concern of this format is the pursuit of foreign policy objectives of states which lead to regional development, domestic policies and considerations greatly influence the evolution of integrative planning and the degree of national participation. For the national interest is based not only on the achievement of international power and prestige, but must also consider the continued social and economic health of the state. Thus, domestic policy objectives, as well as foreign policy objectives, lead to rational decision making which encompasses the use of regional institutions.

Intervening Variables

Intervening variables, which either influence the development or shape the nature of decisions to form regional institutions, operate on three levels of analysis: internal, systemic, and macrosystemic.

Internally, it is assumed that the decision making apparatus of the state exhibits mature behavior in terms of the national interest. Not only is this behavior adult-like, it is also coherent in that it serves to further national interests both domestically and internationally within the context of national norms. Moreover, decision makers calculate in terms of high and low political saliency of issue content; in other words, decisions are couched in terms of the high politics/low politics dichotomy. As Nye indicates:

"High" politics is symbol-laden, emotive, and based on attitudes characterized by greater intensity and duration than "low" politics which is consequently more susceptible to the rational calculation of benefits associated with economic problems.(57)

Such a dichotomy, however, is unnecessarily static and fixed for general descriptive or explanatory purposes. As Hansen states, what may have low political saliency for decision makers in advanced industrial economies may have an extremely high saliency, as in the case of heavy industry, for less developed and developing countries.(58) When dealing with the attitudes of decision makers and their perceptions of the national interest, the dichotomy must be more flexible. Kaiser captures the perceptual flavor of the latter concept when he notes that:

A matter that can be expressed in material and quantitative terms can become a topic of high diplomacy where prestige is at stake and the particular circumstances are conducive to such a development.

Moreover, an issue may not occupy the same place on the spectrum between "low" and "high" politics for different countries.(59)

What matters, then, is not simply the political importance of the issue which may serve as the juncture for initiating an integration network, but how the decision makers of each potential member state consciously or subconsciously impose a set of priorities to foreign or domestic policy objectives. It is these priorities which are the result of high and low political salience perceptions of the apparatus of the state.

A second intervening variable is systemic in that it deals with the parameters of international politics within the region. The hypothesis which provides the underpinnings of this variable is that regions, as distinct settings within the international milieu, exhibit various parameter values and "rules of the game" for the conduct of intraregional international politics. Nation states or, rather, the foreign policy elites of nation states perceive and understand the implied nature of the system and system transformation, and foreign policy is executed in terms of the format of the system.

Borrowing from Kaplan,(60) the politics of a region may be a balance-of-power system(61) in which a number of states vie for power within the region and, out of this struggle, an integration plan emerges to formalize the balance. Similarly, one or two states may be dominant(62) within the region and, in order to maintain this position, undertake an integration scheme. Lastly, all states within a region may have attained a level of parity(63) within the region and may undertake regional integration as a means of preemptive conflict resolution, the alternative being regional chaos.

The final intervening variable concerns the relationship of the regional system to the more inclusive global system. Following from Young's concept of discontinuous systems of international politics,(64) no regional system is completely "closed" and, therefore, the impact of external actors and/or events must be weighed in the decision to integrate. Moreover, the potential member states may have ties with the politics of other regions. Therefore, a development in one area of a state's foreign policy field may have consequences on the perception of the entire set of policy objectives. As adjustments in policy are made, repercussions may be felt in the regionally-centered foreign policy which will, in turn, affect that nation's attitude toward regional integration. An event or change in extraregional relationships may make integration either more or less attractive as an alternative for maximizing benefits or political position regionally.

Of equal importance is the role of external actors or events, especially as outlined by Kaiser and Schmitter. Kaiser notes that external superpower involvement may either help or hinder the development of regional integration.(65) Their activity may bring about regional integration as a response to a threat or, on the other hand, they may play an active role as catalyst, in much the same way a chemical catalyst enhances the formation of a chemical compound. In line with this concept of open regions and regional integration, Kaiser also indicates that regional systems may affect the development of integration plans in other subsystems, an emulation effect.(66)

Much of the same conclusion is drawn by Schmitter, although his focus is upon integration in progress rather than integration at its inception. Instead of being a catalyst at genesis, he notes that external events and actors play a role in determining the flow of the scope and level of existing plans. According to Schmitter, members of a regional integration network, due to the effect of external powers and events, ". . .adopt common policies vis-a-vis nonparticipant third parties. Members will be forced to hammer out a collectively external position (and in the process are likely to have to rely increasingly on the new central institutions to do it)."(67)

This model, then, deals with the causal factors which stimulate or lead to regional integration. Rather than address the nature of the process of regional integration after the threshold has been crossed, it attempts to predict the variables which lead up to the threshold. Thus, model or paradigm is an apt description. However, it also presents a framework in which process could be conceptualized. That is, just as a confluence of variables stimulates the initial development of an integrative plan, a similar confluence, with the additional impact of acquired learning, could stimulate growth of further integrative networks within a region. On the other hand, this model may well lead to an exploration of the causes of regional disintegration. The crucial question, however, remains causality and an examination of the European experience, with a focus upon the European Coal and Steel Community (ECSC) will illustrate the intricacies of the model.

Europe: Coal, Steel, and Beyond

When the Schuman Plan was announced on May 9, 1950, it appeared that a radical breakthrough in the pattern of European politics had been accomplished. France and Germany, the major continental powers, appeared to renounce their political enmities to work together in the integration and reconstruction of their heavy industries. During the negotiations, when four other states entered into the process, it appeared that the foundations for a United States of Europe were being built. The background to the Schuman Plan, however, indicates the political strategies which led to the traversal of the integration threshold, especially the political aims of the two major members: France and Germany. The ECSC was less a conscious move toward supranational integration as an end in itself than a means of achieving foreign policy objectives.

The German state of affairs following the end of World War II is well known: dismemberment, occupation, and political subservience. The initial aims of the budding federal institutions under Adenaur were obvious: restoration of legal sovereignty, recovery of the bases of national power, and international recognition, both as an accepted member of the family of nations and as a political power in Western Europe.(68)

The alternatives open to Germany were few. Active rebuilding and rearmament were out of the question due to the critical condition of the industrial base and the occupation. Neutrality, even if guaranteed by the Western powers, was not a policy actively under consideration, especially with the Soviet Union close at hand in the Eastern zone of occupation. Moreover, such a policy would not lead to the goals set by Adenaur. Thus, regional integration became a logical alternative for the new Federal Republic.

Although the plan to pool the coal and steel resources of the "Six" met with heavy domestic opposition, this was overcome by Adenaur and the foreign policy planners because, "ECSC appeared to promise the liberation of the German Federal Republic from the 'fetters' imposed by the victorious allies and its elevation to at least equal status with one of the 'Big Three' western powers – France."(69)

Indeed, the ECSC accomplished several foreign policy objectives for Germany. Generally, it acknowledged Germany's presence as a minimally sovereign state within the European system, with the power to negotiate and conclude treaties. Additionally, the ECSC gave Germany the opportunity to participate, as an equal to France and a superior to other Western European states, within regional cooperative institutions. Thus, two major goals of German foreign policy were met.

In particular, however, ECSC afforded three significant advances. First, with the establishment of ECSC institutions, the controls upon the German economy were lifted, especially the International Authority of the Ruhr(70) which, under the direction of the French, had limited the resurgence of that vital industrial region. Secondly, the ECSC solution took the Saar, which France had claimed as war reparations, out of complete French administration and into the hands of the supranational authority, where Germany would have a degree of input concerning administration and eventual repatriation. Lastly, ECSC provided domestic benefits clearly in the national interest. As Haas notes, the ECSC marked an end to export controls on her redeveloping steel industry and an end to tariff barriers against the export of German coal – two major sources of revenue.(71)

France, on the other hand, viewed regional integration as a means of foreign policy of a different nature. Morgenthau, in his analysis of the European Communities, views the process as a mechanism by which France could either control or dominate a "naturally superior" Germany.(72) In other words, France was attuned to the change in the regional system occasioned by World War II, which had left it as the dominant continental state within the regional balance of power system. Moreover, French foreign policy planners were also cognizant of the fact that Germany could not be kept under Allied control for any extended period of time. This seemed especially true in the heavy industry sector, where the Korean War placed an emphasis on the renewed production of European steel.(73)

In fact, security planning dominated the French decision to propose the Schuman Plan. The genesis of the plan came from the foreign policy planning of Jean Monnet, Etienne Hirsch, Pierre Uri, and Paul Reuter, who, in April, 1950, presented a memo to Prime Minister Bidault which outlined the ECSC as a means of controlling German revitalization and eliminating the possibility of renewed Franco-German hostilities on a long-range basis.(74) As Bok notes, the ECSC presented France with the solution to a serious security dilemma:

> . . .without an expanding industry, and with the growing demand for steel production occasioned by the Korean War, France could not expect the controls upon German production to be continued indefinitely. At the same time, however, the French were fearful of an unbridled development of the Ruhr into a powerful arsenal which might once more become linked with the aggressive policies of a German government. Under these circumstances, the Schuman Plan was conceived by France as a compromise whereby she would give up a part of her sovereign power to secure a degree of international control over German coal and steel.(75)

In overviewing the genesis of the ECSC, then, all facets of the model can be viewed. Clearly, the political motivations of the states involved are illustrated. For France, it meant securing an overriding goal: control, of a sort, over the German warmaking capacity, and the prevention of the recurring nightmare of German invasion. For Germany, the ECSC was a low risk/high payoff proposition. Outside of the possibility of Soviet military intervention, which was highly improbable, Germany would gain not only international recognition but a measure of sovereignty as well. Additionally, the avenues to domestic economic rehabilitation were opened. The other states involved in ECSC, Italy and the Benelux countries, perceived similar national and international benefits. Thus, major political factors coincided.

The interplay of the intervening variables is also displayed. The ECSC presented the solution of "high" political problems: the balance of systemic power in terms of French security and German sovereignty. In terms of a perceived "low" political context, it brought the integration of two prime industrial sectors. Systemically, the ECSC represented an awareness of and institutionalization of the balance-of-power system within the region. Despite its incapacitation by war, Germany continued to be perceived as one of the two dominant powers in the European system. Through the use of supranational institutions, France achieved her balancing agent. Great Britain, the only regional state to stay out of the ECSC, displayed her traditional reluctance to enmesh herself in the affairs of European politics.

CONCLUSION   ·

The question of where regional integration theory is heading remains open. This chapter has attempted to show the development of regional integration theory, and where it has gone astray in its predictive aspects. Additionally, we have begun development of a different perspective on the process of regional integration, centered upon the importance of foreign and domestic policies of member states or potential member states. Implicitly, this model relies upon Haas' notions of disjointed incrementalism and fragmented issue-linkage to portray a process of community development. The central concern of this model, however, deals with the nature of causality. The answer to the question of what starts an integration process appears to rest with inputs from extraregional actors and events and the impact of decision makers' perceptions of the parameters of regional systemic politics, as well as the dynamics of the national interest of countries located within the region. This model, however, remains only preliminary in nature, in that both on-going processes and terminal conditions have been only marginally explored.

In an illustration of the aspects of this model, we have examined the development of the ECSC and touched on more recent events within the European Community. This sketch is designed to be more heuristic than descriptive since a complete exploration would go beyond the scope of this chapter. It could be argued that the model and its application are too narrow in scope, that the case of Western Europe is somehow different from other attempts at regional integration. Possibly, both its explicit political character and its advanced industrial backdrop make it unique in a manner which may lead to erroneous theory construction. But evidence suggests that the same pattern of national interest, systemic politics, political perceptions, and external actors and events influenced both the rise and fall of regional integration efforts in Central and Latin America.(76)

One thing which this model, and this chapter as a whole, does illustrate is that regional integration, either as a real-world phenomenon or as a subject of theoretical inquiry, is not obsolete. The model provides a possible forum for the synthesis of more concrete policy-oriented studies with the more abstract notions of theory. Moreover, it provides a starting point where political economists and foreign policy specialists may find a common ground in the explanation of international politics. Whither regional integration theory? To paraphrase the late Samuel Clemens, reports of its demise are greatly exaggerated.

NOTES

(1) Ernst Haas, The Obsolescence of Regional Integration Theory (Berkeley: Institute of International Studies, University of California, 1975), p. 1.

(2) Ibid.

(3) Ibid., p. 5.

(4) Ibid., p. 9-11.

(5) Ibid., p. 25.

(6) Ibid., p. 26.

(7) Ibid., p. 31.

(8) Stanley Hoffman, "Obstinate or Obsolete? The Fate of the Nation-State and the Case of Western Europe," Daedelus 95 (Summer 1966): 863.

(9) Ernst B. Haas, The Uniting of Europe: Political, Economic, and Social Forces, 1950-1957 (Stanford, Calif.: Stanford University Press, 2nd ed., 1968), p. 16, italics omitted.

(10) Ernst B. Haas, "The Study of Regional Integration: Reflections on the Joy and Anguish of Pretheorizing," International Organization 24 (Autumn 1970): 610.

(11) Karl Deutsch et al., Political Community in the North Atlantic Area (Princeton, N.J.: Princeton University Press, 1957), p. 5.

(12) Amitai Etzioni, Political Unification: A Comparative Study of Leaders and Forces (New York: Holt, Rinehart & Winston, 1965), p. 34.

(13) Attributed to Raymond Aron in Leon N. Lindberg and Stuart A. Scheingold, Europe's Would-be Polity: Patterns of Change in the European Community (Englewood Cliffs, N.J.: Prentice Hall, 1970), p. 16.

(14) David Mitrany, A Working Peace System (London: Royal Institute of International Affairs, 1946), pp. 9-14.

(15) Stanley Hoffman, "Discord in Community: The North Atlantic Area as a Partial International System," International Organization 17 (Summer 1963).

(16) Although the term "spill-over" is not specifically developed in functionalist thought, the concept is referred to through such euphamistic phrases as "ever-widening circles." It appears that neofunctionalists owe a large theoretical debt to their predecessors for the use of this concept.

(17) Haas, The Uniting of Europe.

(18) Charles Pentland, International Theory and European Integration (New York: Free Press, 1973), p. 182.

(19) Lindberg and Scheingold, Europe's Would-Be Polity, Chap. 4.

(20) Philippe C. Schmitter, "A Revised Theory of Regional Integration," International Organization 24 (Autumn 1970): 840-42.

(21) J.S. Nye, Peace in Parts: Integration and Conflict in Regional Organizations (Boston: Little, Brown, 1971).

(22) Ibid., p. 64.

(23) Ibid., p. 190.

(24) Ibid., pp. 89-90.

(25) Ibid., pp. 84, 85.

(26) Haas, Obsolescence, p. 1.

(27) Haas, Uniting of Europe, p. xxxv.

(28) Cf. Ernst B. Haas and Philippe C. Schmitter, "Economics and Differential Patterns of Political Organization: Projections About Unity in Latin America," International Organization 18 (Autumn 1964); and J.S. Nye, "Patterns and Catalysts in Regional Integration," International Organization 19 (Autumn 1965).

(29) See particularly Ronn D. Kaiser, "Toward the Copernican Phase of Regional Integration Theory," Journal of Common Market Studies 10 (March 1972): 207-32.

(30) Haas, Obsolescence, p. 31.

(31) Stanley Hoffman, "International Relations: The Long Road to Theory," World Politics 21 (October 1968): 84.

(32) Roger D. Hansen, "Regional Integration: Reflections on a Decade of Theoretical Efforts," World Politics 21 (January 1969), p. 256.

(33) Lindberg and Scheingold, Europe's Would-Be Polity.

(34) Deutsch et al., Political Community.

(35) Ibid., p. 5.

(36) Ibid., p. 7.

(37) Karl Deutsch, The Nerves of Government (New York: Free Press, 1966).

(38) Karl Deutsch et al., France, Germany, and the Western Alliance: A Study of Elite Attitudes on European Integration and World Politics (New York: Charles Scribner's Sons, 1967), p. 218.

(39) Louis J. Cantori and Steven L. Spiegel, "The Analysis of Regional Integration Politics: The Integration versus the Empirical Systems Approach," International Organization 27 (Autumn 1973): 479.

(40) See Hubert M. Blalock, Causal Inferences in Nonexperimental Research (New York: Norton, 1972), chap. I.

(41) William E. Fisher, "An Analysis of the Deutsch Sociocausal Paradigm of Political Organization," International Organization 23 (Spring 1969).

(42) Ibid., p. 258.

(43) Ibid., p. 288.

(44) Ibid., p. 285.

(45) Edward L. Morse, "The Politics of Interdependence," International Organization 23 (Spring 1969): 318.

(46) Richard Rosecrance and Arthur Stein, "Interdependence: Myth or Reality?" World Politics 26 (October 1973): 2.

(47) Richard Rosecrance et al., "Whither Interdependence?" International Organization 31 (Summer 1977): 429.

(48) William Wallace, "Walking Backward Towards Unity," in Policy-Making in the European Communities, edited by Helen Wallace, William

Wallace, and Carole Webb (New York: John Wiley, 1977), p. 315. See also Haas, Obsolescence, p. 31.

(49) Haas, Obsolescence, p. 31.

(50) Morse, "The Politics of Interdependence," p. 324.

(51) A prototype of this model was developed in Charles A. Duffy, Regional Integration in the Realist Tradition: A Rational Actor Model (New Orleans, La.: Unpublished Master's Thesis, University of New Orleans, 1979).

(52) Hoffman describes historical baggage as a ". . .composite of objective data (inside: social structure and political system; outside: geography, formal commitments) and subjective factors (inside: values, prejudices, opinions, reflexes; outside: one's own traditions and assessments of others, and the other's attitudes and approaches toward oneself);" "Obstinate or Obsolete?" p. 868.

(53) Note, for example, Peter Busch and Donald Puchala, "Interests, Influence, and Integration; Political Structure in the European Communities," Comparative Political Studies 9 (October 1976): 237.

(54) Jonathan Wilkenfeld et al., "Profiling States for Foreign Policy Analysis," Comparative Political Studies 11 (April 1978): p. 11.

(55) Hoffman, "Obstinate or Obsolete?" pp. 867-68.

(56) A case of incoherent, irrational decision making would be the policy of Idi Amin Dada to forcibly expel the Asian population of Uganda, which constituted the backbone of the middle class of that state. For a discussion of adult v. child-like decision making, see Deutsch, Nerves of Government, chap. 10.

(57) Nye, "Patterns and Catalysts," p. 871.

(58) Hansen, "Regional Integration," p. 260.

(59) Karl Kaiser, "The U.S. and the EEC in the Atlantic System: The Problem of Theory," Journal of Common Market Studies 5 (June 1967): 393, 394.

(60) Morton A. Kaplan, System and Process in International Affairs (New York: John Wiley, 1964).

(61) Ibid., p. 22.

(62) Ibid., p. 21: "bipolar" and "hierarchical" systems.

(63) Ibid., p. 50.

(64) Young, "Political Discontinuities."

(65) Karl Kaiser, "The Interaction of Regional Subsystems: Some Preliminary Thoughts on Recurring Patterns and the Role of Super-powers," World Politics 21 (October 1968): 84-85.

(66) Ibid., p. 85.

(67) Philippe C. Schmitter, "Three Neofunctional Hypotheses About Regional Integration," International Organization 23 (Winter 1969): 165.

(68) Deutsch et al., France, Germany, and the Western Alliance, p. 156.

(69) Ibid., p. 157.

(70) F. Roy Willis, France, Germany, and the New Europe 1945-1967 (New York: Oxford University Press, 1968), p. 105.

(71) Haas, Uniting of Europe, p. 129.

(72) Hans Morgenthau, Politics Among Nations: The Struggle for Power and Peace (New York: Knopf, 1978), p. 522.

(73) Derek C. Bok, The First Three Years of the Schuman Plan (Princeton, N.J.: International Finance Section; Department of Economics and Sociology, 1955), p. 3; and Richard Mayne, The Recovery of Europe (New York: Harper & Row, 1970), pp. 91-94.

(74) Mayne, The Recovery of Europe, pp. 177-78. Zurcher notes that the threat of German rearmament and invasion was foremost in the minds of the French governments throughout the immediate postwar decade. The Struggle to Unite Europe 1940-1958 (New York: New York University Press, 1958), p. 60.

(75) Bok, The First Three Years of the Schuman Plan, p. 3.

(76) See Constantine v. Vaitsos, "Crisis in Regional Economic Cooperation (Integration) Among Developing Countries," World Development 6 (June 1978).

Index

About the Contributors

WERNER J. FELD – Professor, Political Science Department, University of New Orleans, Louisiana, USA; author, International Relations: a Transnational Approach (1979), Domestic Political Realities and European Unification (with John K. Wildgen) (1976), The European Community in World Affairs (1976), Nongovernmental Forces and World Politics (1972), and Transnational Business Collaboration among Common Market Countries (1970).

GAVIN BOYD – Professor, Political Science Department, Saint Mary's University, Halifax, Nova Scotia, Canada; editor, with Charles Pentland, Issues in Global Politics (1980); editor, with James N. Rosenau and Kenneth W. Thompson, World Politics (1976); editor, with Wayne Wilcox and Leo Rose, Asia and the International System (1972); author, Communist China's Foreign Policy (1962).

DANIEL DRUCKMAN – Senior Research Analyst, Mathematics, Inc., Bethesda, Maryland; Consultant to US delegation, Vienna talks on Mutual and Balanced Force Reductions; editor, Negotiations: Social-Psychological Perspectives (1977); author, Boundary Role Conflict: Negotiation as Dual Responsiveness (1978); The Person, Role and Situation in International Negotiations (1977), and Cultural Differences in Bargaining Behavior: India, Argentina, and the United States (1976).

CHARLES A. DUFFY – graduate student in political science, University of Indiana, Bloomington, Indiana.

YALE H. FERGUSON – Professor, Political Science Department, Rutgers University, Newark; co-author, The Web of World Politics: Nonstate Actors in the Global System (1976); co-editor, Continuing Issues in International Politics (1973); editor, Contemporary Inter-American Relations (1972), and contributing editor, Handbook of Latin American Studies, forthcoming.

HAROLD K. JACOBSON – Professor of Political Science and Program Director, Center for Political Studies, Institute for Social Research,

University of Michigan; member, Board of Editors, International Organization; author, Networks of Interdependence: International Organizations and the Global Political System (1979).

JAMES A. KUHLMAN – Professor and Chairman, Department of Government and International Studies, University of South Carolina, Columbia, South Carolina; Executive Director, International Studies Association; editor, The Foreign Policies of Eastern Europe: Domestic and International Determinants (1978) and co-editor, Innovation in Communist Systems (1978).

SATISH KUMAR – Associate Professor and Head, Diplomatic Studies Division, Jawaharlal Nehru University, New Delhi, India; author, The New Pakistan (1978), Documents on India's Foreign Policy (1975, 1976, 1977), and Rana Polity in Nepal (1967).

DONALD E. LAMPERT – Assistant Professor, Political Science Department, Arizona State University, Tempe, Arizona; co-author, The Web of World Politics: Nonstate Actors in the Global System (1976) and Beyond the National Interest (1979).

DAVID LEYTON-BROWN – Professor, Political Science Department, York University, Toronto, Ontario, Canada; author of several chapters and articles dealing with Canadian Foreign Policy, Canadian-US relations, and the Politics of Multinational Corporations.

JAMES P. PISCATORI – Assistant Professor, Department of Government and Foreign Affairs, University of Virginia, Charlottesville, Virginia; author of numerous chapters and articles on Middle East politics.

R.K. RAMAZANI – Edward Stettinus Professor and Chairman, Department of Government and Foreign Affairs, University of Virginia; author, The Foreign Policy of Iran, 1500-1941 (1966), Iran's Foreign Policy, 1941-1973 (1975), and Beyond the Arab-Israeli Settlement: New Directions for US policy in the Middle East and The Persian Gulf and the Strait of Hormuz (forthcoming).

LEO E. ROSE – Lecturer, Political Science Department, University of California, Berkeley; editor, Asian Survey; author, The Politics of Bhutan (1977); co-editor, Asia and the International System (1972); author, Nepal, Strategy for Survival (1971); co-author, The Politics of Nepal: Persistence and Change in an Asian Monarchy (1970), Sikkim as a Factor in Himalayan Area Politics (1969), and The Northeast Frontier Agency of India (with Margaret W. Fisher) (1967).

TIMOTHY M. SHAW – Associate Professor, Political Science Department, Dalhousie University, Halifax, Nova Scotia, Canada; co-author, The Politics of Africa (1979); coeditor, Canada, Scandinavia and Southern Africa (1978), Conflict and Change in Southern Africa (1976), and coauthor, Zambia's Foreign Policy (1978).

DUSAN SIDJANSKI – Professor of Political Science, University of Geneva, Switzerland; editor, Political Decision-Making Processes (1973).